Law of Employment

Law of Employment

Eighth edition

Norman Selwyn
LLM, Dip Econ (Oxon), Barrister at Law

Butterworths
London, Dublin, Edinburgh
1993

United Kingdom	Butterworth & Co (Publishers) Ltd, Halsbury House, 35 Chancery Lane, LONDON WC2A 1EL and 4 Hill Street, EDINBURGH EH2 3JZ
Australia	Butterworths, SYDNEY, MELBOURNE, BRISBANE, ADELAIDE, PERTH, CANBERRA and HOBART
Canada	Butterworths Canada Ltd, TORONTO and VANCOUVER
Ireland	Butterworths (Ireland) Ltd, DUBLIN
Malaysia	Malayan Law Journal Sdn Bhd, KUALA LUMPUR
New Zealand	Butterworths of New Zealand Ltd, WELLINGTON and AUCKLAND
Puerto Rico	Butterworth of Puerto Rico, Inc, SAN JUAN
Singapore	Butterworths Asia, SINGAPORE
South Africa	Butterworth Publishers (Pty) Ltd, DURBAN
USA	Butterworth Legal Publishers, CARLSBAD, California; SALEM, New Hampshire

Reprinted 1994

A CIP Catalogue record for this book is available from the British Library.

ISBN 0 406 02437 5

Printed By Antony Rowe Ltd, Chippenham, Wiltshire

Preface

The aim of this book is to state the modern law of employment in a manner which is readable, accurate and up-to-date, for the benefit of employers and employees generally, and, in particular, for lawyers, students, managers, personnel specialists and others who have to advise on the subject.

There are two major legislative changes which have come into effect since the last edition. First, the Trade Union and Labour Relations (Consolidation) Act 1992 has consolidated all the relevant trade union law from the Conspiracy and Protection of Property Act 1875 onwards, although it must be stressed that the Act has not made any changes in the law. Where legal decisions are referred to in this book which were decided under the "old' provisions, the statutory references have been transposed to the new Act, for the sake of convenience and simplicity. Second, the Trade Union Reform and Employment Rights Act 1993 has made considerable changes to the 1992 Act (thus making further consolidation desirable?) and to the Employment Protection (Consolidation) Act 1978 (which now also requires consolidation!) The new provisions in the 1993 Act on maternity leave, maternity suspension and unfair dismissal on grounds of maternity will come into force before 19 October 1994, as required by the EC Directive. The extension of EP(C)A to the armed forces will come into effect on a date to be announced by the Secretary of State for Defence. All other relevant provisions of the new Act will take effect either from 30 August 1993 (except that the new requirements of s 1 EP(C)A do not apply to employees whose employment commenced before 30 November 1993), or, in respect of itemised pay statements and the changes in the constitution and jurisdiction of industrial tribunals etc, at the end of November 1993.

Also included in this edition are the usual significant legal decisions which have been made since the last edition. There has been a rearrangement of the material relating to individual and collective trade union rights, and other sections of the book have been expanded.

A Scottish reviewer has (fairly) criticised previous editions for failing to take into account various differences which exist in that country's jurisdiction. I have tried to remedy this, and hope that in so doing I have not exposed my ignorance still further. As a general principle, the law is the same in both countries, but where Scottish cases are cited, I have transposed certain terminology into the English equivalent, for the sake of simplicity and understanding. I trust that this will not cause any offence north of the border. Also, unless the contrary intention is indicated, the use of the male noun/pronoun includes a reference to the female.

Regular readers may welcome the reintroduction in Appendix I of the various codes of practice issued by ACAS, CRE, EOC and Secretary of State (although the Code on Trade Union Ballots is likely to be revised shortly). Not all these documents are as easily obtainable by interested parties as they should be, and I am grateful to HMSO for permission to reproduce them.*

It may be of some consolation to employers, practitioners, etc, that it is my understanding that the present Government has no plans to make any further major changes in the law of employment, although there will doubtless be the usual knee-jerk reaction to legal decisions (especially those of the European Court) and EC Directives in the fullness of time. Once the latest changes have been digested, a period of calm reflection should follow.

My thanks are due to the various members of staff at Butterworths, who have shepherded this edition through its various stages with a minimum of fuss and a maximum of efficiency.

Norman Selwyn
Solihull, West Midlands
July 1993

* The Improvement and Prohibition notices in Appendix E, the advisory handbook in Appendix G and the codes of practice reproduced in Appendix I are Crown copyright

Contents

Preface v
Table of statutes ix
Table of rules and regulations xvii
Table of cases xix

1 The institutions of employment law 1

2 The nature of a contract of employment 29

3 The formation of a contract of employment 58

4 Legal constraints on terms and conditions of employment 93

5 Employment protection 157

6 Performance of the contract of employment 198

7 Disciplinary powers of management 236

8 Dismissal 265

9 Practice and procedure 343

10 Redundancy 377

11 Duties of ex-employees 395

12 Health and safety at work 410

13 Individual trade union rights 436

14 The law relating to trade unions 464

15 Law relating to industrial relations 490

Appendix A Penalties under the Health and Safety at Work Act 531

Appendix B Redundancy Pay Calculation Table 535

Appendix C Enforcement of Statutory Rights 537

Appendix D Industrial Tribunal Forms 544

Appendix E Improvement and Prohibition Notices 550

Appendix F Names and Addresses 554

Appendix G Discipline at Work (ACAS Advisory Handbook) 556

Appendix H Main Legislative Provisions: 1980-1993 588

Appendix I Codes of Practice 593

(a) ACAS Code of Practice 1 Disciplinary Practice and Procedures in Employment 593

(b) ACAS Code of Practice 2 Disclosure of information to Trade Unions for Collective Bargaining Purposes 599

(c) ACAS Code of Practice 3 Time off for Trade Union Duties and Activities 605

(d) EOC Code of Practice For the elimination of sex and marriage discrimination 613

(e) Code of Practice Race Relations 626

(f) Code of Practice Picketing 648

Index 663

Table of statutes

References to *Statutes* are to Halsbury's Statutes of England (Fourth Edition) showing the volume and page at which the annotated text of the Act may be found.

References in the right-hand column are to paragraph numbers.

PARA

Access to Medical Reports Act 1988 .... 5.71
Arbitration Act 1950 (2 *Statutes* 571) 1.12
Children and Young Persons Act 1933 (6 *Statutes* 18) ... 4.4
Children and Young Persons Act 1969 (6 *Statutes* 136) . 4.4
Civil Evidence Act 1968 (17 *Statutes* 155)
s 11 .... 12.23
Companies Act 1967 (19 *Statutes* 68)
s 26(1) 2.7
Companies Act 1985 (8 *Statutes* 104)
s 235 .... 12.52
Congenital Disabilities (Civil Liability) Act 1976 (45 *Statutes* 654) 6.28
Consumer Protection Act 1987
Sch 3 .... 12.4
Continental Shelf Act 1964 (29 *Statutes* 435) 8.18, 12.2A
Contracts of Employment Act 1963 .... 8.1
Copyright, Designs and Patents Act 1988 (11 *Statutes* 337)
s 11 .... 6.69
Disabled Persons (Employment) Act 1944 (16 *Statutes* 34) 4.126
Disabled Persons (Employment) Act 1958 (16 *Statutes* 55) 4.126

PARA

Dock Work Act 1989 (16 *Statutes* 609) 2.20
Education Act 1918 (15 *Statutes* 110)
s 14 .... 4.4
Education Reform Act 1988 (15 *Statutes* 421)
s 203 .... 2.20
Education (Work Experience) Act 1973 (15 *Statutes* 249)
s 1 .... 4.4A
Employers' Liability Act 1880 . 4.2
Employers' Liability (Compulsory Insurance) Act 1969 (16 *Statutes* 70) 6.19A, 6.35
Employers' Liability (Defective Equipment) Act 1969 (16 *Statutes* 69) 6.35
Employment Act 1980 (16 *Statutes* 432) 1.21, 8.2
Employment Act 1982 (16 *Statutes* 479) 15.39, 15.77
Employment Act 1988 (16 *Statutes* 568) 1.28
Employment Act 1989 (16 *Statutes* 621) 9.14
s 1 .... 4.150
4 .... 4.149
9 .... 4.148
10 .... 4.151
11 .... 8.173
Sch 1 .... 4.149
Sch 3 .... 4.151
Employment Act 1990 .... 1.21, 8.2
Employment Agencies Act 1973 (16 *Statutes* 89) 2.25

PARA

Employment of Children Act 1973 .... 4.4
Employment of Women, Young Persons and Children Act 1920 (16 *Statutes* 25)
s 1–3 .... 4.4
Employment Protection Act 1975 (16 *Statutes* 165) . 1.1, 1.6, 1.16, 1.21, 8.2
s 116 .... 12.2A, 12.28
118(1) 15.20
Sch 15 .... 12.2A
Employment Protection (Consolidation) Act 1978 (16 *Statutes* 232) .. 1.21, 4.131, 5.1, 5.13, 5.106, 5.123, 6.15, 8.2, 8.18, 9.11B, 9.35A, 10.2, 13.1, 14.1
s 1 .... 1.21, 2.17, 2.44, 2.60, 3.27, 3.27A, 3.45, 3.60, 3.62, 3.66, 3.71, 8.33
2 .... 2.60
(2) 8.61
3 .... 2.60
4 .... 2.56, 2.60
8 .... 1.21, 3.69
9, 10 .... 3.69
11 .... 1.21
12 .... 5.2, 5.87
13, 14 .... 5.2
15 .... 5.2, 5.4
16 .... 5.2
17 .... 5.2
(1) 1.21
18 .... 5.2
19 .... 5.7, 5.87
20 .... 5.7
(3) 5.7B
21 .... 5.7
22 .... 5.7
(1) 1.21
22A 1.21, 12.34A, 12.34B
27 .... 5.87
29 .... 5.55, 5.56, 5.57, 5.58
(6) 1.21
31 .... 5.59, 5.87
(6) 1.21
31A 5.61, 5.87
(6) 1.21
33 .... 5.9, 5.13
34 .... 5.35
35, 36 .... 5.35
37 .... 5.35

PARA

Employment Protection (Consolidation) Act 1978—*contd*
s 37(1) 5.19
38 .... 5.35
39 .... 5.17, 5.18, 5.30, 5.35
40–44 .... 5.35
45 .... 5.9
46 .... 1.21
47 .... 1.21, 5.9, 5.87, 8.79
49 .... 2.60, 5.88, 8.189
(1) 8.12
(2) 8.13
50, 51 .... 2.60, 5.88
53 .... 2.14, 8.207, 8.208, 8.210, 8.211, 8.212, 9.8
(2) 8.214
(4) 1.21
54 .... 8.15, 9.11C
55 .... 8.15, 8.47
(2) 8.85
(4) 9.5, 9.7
(5) 8.11, 8.18, 9.7, 9.8
(6) 8.76
56 .... 5.24, 5.25, 8.15, 8.79
56A 8.15
57 .... 8.15, 8.97
(3) 4.6, 8.98, 8.114, 8.168, 8.169, 8.185, 10.32
57A 12.34C
58 .... 8.15
(1) 13.61
59 .... 8.15, 8.167, 8.168A, 13.80
59A 8.167
60 .... 5.30, 5.31, 5.32, 8.15, 8.164B, 8.167
60A 8.187, 8.189, 8.192
61 .... 2.48, 8.15
(1) 8.180
(2) 5.8, 8.180
62 .... 8.15
(3) 9.1
62A 8.15
63 .... 8.15, 13.78
64 .... 8.15, 9.8
(2) 5.7C
(3) 13.62
64A 8.15
65 .... 8.15, 14.16
67(1) 1.21
(2) 9.8
(4) 9.5A
69 .... 8.160, 9.33
71(1A) 9.33, 9.36

PARA

Employment Protection (Consolidation) Act 1978—*contd*
s 72 .... 9.36
72A 9.36, 9.48
73 .... 9.36, 13.80
(3) 9.8
(4A) 9.38
(7B) 9.25, 9.39
(7C) 9.39
74 .... 9.36, 13.80
(1) 9.46A
75–76 .... 9.36
76A 13.79
77 .... 1.21, 12.34E
78 .... 2.56, 12.34E
78A 1.21
79 .... 1.21, 12.34E
81 .... 15.24
82 .... 10.21
(2) 10.39, 10.40
(5), (6) 9.37
83 .... 10.5
(2) 10.16
84 .... 9.37, 10.32
87 .... 6.15, 10.35
88 .... 10.38
91 .... 10.10
(1) 1.21
(2) 10.19
92 .... 10.39, 10.40
93 .... 10.5
96, 100 .... 10.41
101(1), (2) 9.1
108(1) 1.21
112 .... 1.21
122 .... 5.88
(1) 1.21
123 .... 5.88
124 .... 1.21, 5.88
125–127 .... 5.88
128(6) 2.65
130 .... 1.21
131 .... 1.21, 1.24, 1.24A, 9.11D
133 .... 1.9, 13.17
(1) 9.11D
134(1) 9.11D
135, 136 .... 1.18
137 .... 2.62B
138(4) 2.64, 8.206
138A 2.14
139, 139A 2.14
140(1) 8.95, 8.95A
140(2) 1.9

PARA

Employment Protection (Consolidation) Act 1978—*contd*
s 140(3) 1.9, 9.11D
141(5) 8.18
142(2) 10.41
146A 2.65
151 .... 8.21
153 .... 2.4
(1) 2.56
(4) 8.38, 8.39
Sch 1 .... 5.7, 5.7B
Sch 3 .... 8.12
Sch 9 .... 2.65
Sch 11 .... 2.58
Sch 12 .... 5.92
Sch 13 .... 5.70, 8.20, 8.22, 8.23, 8.24, 8.25, 8.26, 8.27, 8.28, 8.29, 8.31, 8.31A, 8.32, 8.34, 8.38, 8.41, 13.63
Sch 14 .... 3.35, 5.9, 9.8
Equal Pay Act 1970 (16 *Statutes* 76) .. 1.44, 1.56, 2.62, 2.62B, 4.17, 4.23, 4.66, 4.68, 4.69, 4.80, 4.82, 4.96
s 1(2) 4.82
(3) 4.82, 4.84, 4.85, 4.88, 4.92A, 4.93
(4) 4.72
(5) 4.78
(6) 4.70B
(8) 2.14
2 .... 1.21, 4.95
(1) 4.83
(4), (5) 4.97
5 .... 1.17
6(1A) 4.69A
7 .... 1.17
European Communities Act 1972 (17 *Statutes* 34) . 1.50, 4.96
European Communities (Amendment) Act 1986 (17 *Statutes* 73) 1.70
Factories Act 1961 (19 *Statutes* 449) 3.23, 4.75, 12.1, 12.50, 12.53D
s 1 .... 12.15
13 .... 12.12
Sch 5 .... 4.149, 5.15
Finance Act 1979 .... 2.41
Health and Safety at Work etc Act 1974 (19 *Statutes* 620): 1.23, 1.46, 2.43, 2.57, 4.53B, 5.9, 5.30, 6.65, 12.1

PARA

Health and Safety at Work etc Act 1974—*contd*
s 2 .... 12.23, 12.25, 12.51, 12.54, 14.16
(3) 12.27
(4) 12.28
(5) 12.28
(6) 12.28, 12.30
(7) 12.28
3 .... 12.23, 12.35, 12.51, 12.54
4 .... 12.23, 12.36, 12.42, 12.51, 12.54
5 ..... 12.23, 12.37, 12.51, 12.54
6 ..... 12.4, 12.23, 12.38, 12.44, 12.51, 12.54
(7) 12.45
7 .... 12.23, 12.47, 12.51, 12.54
8 .... 12.23, 12.48, 12.51
9 .... 12.23, 12.49, 12.51
15 .... 12.50
16 .... 5.7, 12.54
21 .... 12.7
22 .... 12.8
24 .... 1.21, 12.10
25 .... 12.18
26 .... 12.21
28(8) 12.22
33 .... 12.57
36 .... 12.59
37 .... 12.57
42 .... 12.19
47 .... 12.23
50 .... 12.51
53 .... 12.45
Sch 1 .... 12.50
Sch 3 .... 12.50, 12.52
Highways Act 1959 .... 15.105
Hours of Employment (Conventions) Act 1936 (16 *Statutes* 30) 4.152
Income and Corporation Taxes Act 1988 (44 *Statutes* 1)
s 134 .... 2.47
Industrial Relations Act 1971 . 1.14, 6.3, 8.2, 13.18, 14.3, 14.7, 15.37
Industrial Training Act 1964 .. 1.20
s 12 .... 1.21
Industrial Training Act 1982 (16 *Statutes* 450) 1.40

PARA

Insolvency Act 1986 (4 *Statutes* 717) 1.63
Sch 6 .... 5.87
Interpretation Act 1978 (41 *Statutes* 899)
s 6 .... 8.38
Judgments Act 1838 (22 *Statutes* 302)
s 17 .... 9.56A
Juries Act 1974 (22 *Statutes* 481) 5.63
Law Reform (Contributory Negligence) Act 1945 (31 *Statutes* 185) 6.48
Limitation Act 1980 (24 *Statutes* 648) 6.49
Local Government Act 1988 (25 *Statutes* 924)
s 17 .... 4.155
18(2) 4.156, 4.157
Mines and Quarries Act 1954 (29 *Statutes* 168) 4.152
s 124 .... 4.4
National Health Service and Community Care Act 1990 .... 2.16
s 60 .... 12.17
Offices, Shops and Railway Premises Act 1963 (19 *Statutes* 570) 12.1, 12.50, 12.53D
Partnership Act 1890 (32 *Statutes* 636)
s 3 .... 2.10
Patents Act 1977 (33 *Statutes* 127) 6.66, 6.69
s 39 .... 6.66
Public Health Act 1936 (35 *Statutes* 140)
s 205 .... 4.149, 5.15
Public Order Act 1986 (12 *Statutes* 1030)
s 1–5 .... 15.122
Race Relations Act 1976 (6 *Statutes* 828) .. 1.45, 2.58, 2.62, 2.62B, 4.98
s 1(1) 4.100, 4.103
(2) 4.101
2 .... 4.104
3 .... 4.105
(1) 4.107
4(1), (2) 4.110
5 .... 4.111

PARA

Race Relations Act 1976—
contd
s 7 .... 4.112
8, 9 .... 4.113
12 .... 14.19
16 .... 2.18
28 .... 4.114
29 .... 4.115
30 .... 4.116
31 .... 4.117
32 .... 4.119
41 .... 4.124B
54 .... 1.21, 4.122
55 .... 1.9
58 .... 4.125
59, 63, 64 .... 1.21
68(7) 4.122
71 .... 4.153, 4.156
72(2) 2.14
75(5) 4.110
Redundancy Payments Act 1965 .... 6.15, 10.1
Rehabilitation of Offenders Act 1974 (12 *Statutes* 632) 4.130
s 4(3) 4.131
Reserve Forces (Safeguard of Employment) Act 1985 .... 5.65
Restrictive Trade Practices Act 1956 .... 11.8
Road Traffic Act 1988 .... 6.19
Road Traffic Act 1974 (38 *Statutes* 332)
s 84 .... 8.172
Sale of Goods Act 1979 (39 *Statutes* 106) 12.46
Sex Discrimination Act 1975 (6 *Statutes* 753) 1.44, 1.57, 2.3, 2.58, 2.62, 2.62B, 4.8, 4.34, 4.35C, 4.41, 4.68, 4.98, 4.111
s 1(1) 4.10, 4.11A, 4.12, 4.13, 4.37
3(1) 4.10A, 4.11A, 4.12, 4.13
4(1) 4.17
5(3) 4.11A, 4.35
6(1) 4.19, 4.23, 4.25
(2) 4.27, 4.28, 4.33, 4.37, 4.38, 4.62A
(4) 4.43, 4.45, 4.53A
7 .... 4.54
(4) 4.55, 4.56

PARA

Sex Discrimination Act 1975—
contd
s 10 .... 4.56A
12 .... 14.19
17 .... 2.18
38 .... 4.57, 4.60, 4.63
39, 40 .... 4.59, 4.60, 4.63
41 .... 4.61
42 .... 4.59
47 .... 4.27
48 .... 4.56
51(1) 4.53B
52 .... 2.65
57–61 .... 4.65
63 .... 1.21, 4.62, 4.62A
64 .... 1.9, 4.62A
65 .... 4.62A
67 .... 4.66
68 .... 1.21, 4.66
69–71 .... 4.66
72 .... 4.60, 4.63
(3) 1.21
73 .... 1.21, 4.63
76(2) 4.62A
82(1A) 4.28
85(2) 2.14
Sex Discrimination Act 1986 (6 *Statutes* 949) 1.57, 2.58, 4.8, 8.18
s 6 .... 1.21, 4.94
(4A) 4.94A
7 .... 4.150
Shops (Early Closing Days) Act 1965 (19 *Statutes* 613) 4.152
Social Security Act 1975
s 56A 14.16
Social Security Act 1989 (40 *Statutes* 429) 1.61
s 23 .... 4.45
Sch 5 .... 4.45, 5.18
Social Security Contributions and Benefits Act 1992 (40 *Statutes* 492) 2.38
s 151–163 .... 5.76
164–171 .... 5.35
State Immunity Act 1978 (10 *Statutes* 641) 8.18
Statutory Sick Pay Act 1991 (40 *Statutes* 482) 5.76
Trade Disputes Act 1906 .... 15.77
Trade Union Act 1871 .... 14.21

PARA

Trade Union and Labour Relations Act 1974 (16 *Statutes* 127) 1.6, 1.16, 8.2
s 14 .... 15.77

Trade Union and Labour Relations (Consolidation) Act 1992 .... 2.14, 2.62B, 4.137, 8.189, 13.1, 13.73, 14.1, 14.40, 15.37, 15.53
s 1 .... 13.25, 14.2
2 .... 1.16, 14.7
3, 4 .... 1.19
5 .... 1.19, 14.9
(a), (b) 14.14
6 .... 1.16, 1.19, 14.9
9 .... 1.19
10 .... 14.3, 14.4
11 .... 14.21
15 .... 14.48
(3) 1.28A
16 .... 1.28A, 14.50
18 .... 3.38, 15.97
20 .... 15.56, 15.77, 15.90
(3) 15.62
(4) 15.79
(6) 15.90
21 .... 15.80
22 .... 15.84
24 .... 14.17, 14.19
24A 14.18, 14.19
25 .... 14.19
26 .... 1.28A, 14.19
27 .... 14.23C
28 .... 14.42
29 .... 5.107, 14.44
30 .... 14.44, 14.45
31 .... 1.28A, 14.44, 14.46
32 .... 14.42
32A 14.43
33–37 .... 14.42
37B 14.47
38–42 .... 14.42
45–45B 14.47
46 .... 14.24
47 .... 14.29
48 .... 14.30, 14.31
49 .... 14.32
51A 14.35
52 .... 14.37
(4) 14.37
54 .... 14.23B, 14.39
56 .... 1.28A
57A(1) 9.53

PARA

Trade Union and Labour Relations (Consolidation) Act 1992—*contd*
s 59A, 60 .... 13.77
62 .... 1.28A, 13.23, 13.26
(7) 13.26
(8) 13.25
63 .... 13.21
64 ...... 1.21, 13.8, 13.11, 13.12
65 .... 13.2, 13.8
66 .... 13.12
67 .... 1.19
68 .... 1.21, 5.136, 13.42, 13.56, 13.60
(9) 13.57
69 .... 13.18
71 .... 1.28A, 14.52
72 .... 14.52
73–75 .... 14.52
77 .... 14.53
78(4) 14.38
79, 80 .... 14.59
81 .... 1.28A, 14.59
87 .... 2.14, 13.60
88 .... 13.60
90 .... 1.9
94 .... 5.123
95 .... 1.19
97–100 .... 14.62
100A 14.32
100E(6) 14.38
101, 102 .... 14.62
103 .... 1.19, 14.61, 14.62
104 .... 1.19, 14.62
105 .... 14.62
110 .... 1.31
115 .... 14.16, 14.40
116 .... 14.41A
117 .... 14.3
122 .... 14.5
123 .... 14.8A
137 .... 1.21, 4.137, 13.29, 13.34, 13.35
(3) 13.32
(4) 13.33
138 .... 1.21, 13.34
(3) 13.34
139–142 .... 13.37
144 .... 15.111, 15.113
146 ... 13.39, 13.41, 13.44, 14.16
(3), (4) 13.44
(5) 1.21, 13.44
150 .... 13.46

PARA

Trade Union and Labour Relations (Consolidation) Act 1992—*contd*

s 152 ..... 14.16
(1) 8.167
153 ..... 8.167
157 ..... 9.53
160 ..... 13.88
161 ... 1.21, 12.34E, 13.82, 14.16
(1) 1.21
162 ..... 12.34E, 13.82
(3) 13.88
163, 164 ..... 12.34E, 13.82
165, 166 ..... 1.21, 12.34E, 13.82
168 ..... 13.49, 13.53, 14.16
(1) 1.21
170 ..... 13.54, 14.16
(4) 1.21
174 ..... 1.21, 13.2, 13.4, 13.9, 13.11, 13.19, 14.20A
175 ..... 13.20
176 ..... 1.19, 13.20
177 ..... 13.3, 13.19
178 ..... 15.95
179 ..... 15.95, 15.96
180 ..... 3.38, 15.98
181 ..... 14.16, 15.1
183 ..... 1.17
184 ..... 2.14
186 ..... 15.76, 15.114, 15.116
187 ..... 15.115, 15.116
188 ..... 1.58, 2.14, 14.16, 15.6, 15.28
(4) 15.11
(6) 15.12
189 ..... 1.58, 2.14, 5.87, 15.6
(1) 1.21
190, 191 ..... 1.58, 2.14, 15.6
192 ..... 1.58, 2.14, 15.6
(1) 1.21
193 ..... 1.58, 2.14, 10.47
(7) 10.47, 15.15
194 ..... 1.58, 2.14
(1) 10.64
195 ..... 15.24
199 ..... 1.14
201, 202 ..... 1.15A
203 ..... 1.42
207 ..... 1.14
209 ..... 1.1
210 ..... 1.5
211 ..... 1.7
212 ..... 1.12

PARA

Trade Union and Labour Relations (Consolidation) Act 1992—*contd*

s 213 ..... 1.4
214 ..... 1.13
218 ..... 1.6
219 ..... 2.15, 15.49, 15.54, 15.55, 15.68, 15.69, 15.71, 15.73, 15.76, 15.77, 15.83, 15.85, 15.107, 15.110, 15.113, 15.116, 15.121
(1) 15.49
(2) 15.51
220 ..... 15.75, 15.100, 15.104, 15.108
(4) 15.75, 15.101
221 ..... 15.88
(2) 15.89
222 ..... 15.69
(3) 15.113
223 ..... 15.70
224 ..... 15.71
(2) 15.72
225 ..... 15.76, 15.116
226 ..... 15.55, 15.93
226B 14.32
226C 14.33
228 ..... 15.67
229(1A) 15.59
(2) 15.58
(4) 15.60
230(2) 15.61
231A 15.63
232 ..... 15.66
233 ..... 15.64
234 ..... 15.65
234A 15.68
235A 15.93
235B 1.35
236 ..... 6.6, 15.91
237 ..... 13.74
(1A) 13.77
238 ..... 13.70
(1) 13.63, 13.64
(2) 13.64
(2A) 13.77
240 ..... 15.118
241 ..... 15.118, 15.119, 15.120
(1) 15.106, 15.120
244 ..... 1.6, 13.50, 15.38
(1) 13.49
(4) 15.42

PARA

Trade Union and Labour Relations (Consolidation) Act 1992—*contd*
s 247, 248 .... 1.1
251A 1.2
254–256 .... 1.16
257 .... 1.16, 14.7
258 .... 1.16
266 .... 1.28
275 .... 2.64
277 .... 2.14
287 .... 2.62B
296 .... 2.3
Sch 9, 13 .... 5.123
Trade Union Reform and Employment Rights Act 1993 .... 5.13, 8.2, 13.1, 14.1
s 29(5) 15.28
Transport Act 1968 (36 *Statutes* 398) 4.152

PARA

Truck Act 1831 .... 5.127
Truck Act 1896 .... 5.128
Unfair Contract Terms Act 1977 (11 *Statutes* 220) 6.47
s 2 .... 3.13, 6.47
Wages Act 1986 (16 *Statutes* 523) .. 1.21, 1.24A, 2.62B, 5.127, 5.134, 6.17, 7.38, 8.189
s 1 .... 5.129, 5.138, 5.141
(1) 5.133
(5) 5.136
2 ...... 5.137, 5.138, 5.140, 7.38
(4) 5.140
5 .... 1.21, 5.141, 7.39, 13.42, 13.60
6(1) 5.143
7 .... 5.131
8 .... 2.3
Young Persons (Employment) Act 1938
s 9 .... 4.4

Table of rules and regulations

References in the right-hand column are to paragraph numbers.

	PARA
British Transport (Compensation to Employees) Regulations 1970, SI 1970/187	1.21
Companies (Directors' Report) (Employment of Disabled Persons) Regulations 1980, SI 1980/1160	4.126
Conduct of Employment Agencies and Employment Business Regulations 1976, SI 1976/715	2.25, 2.47
Construction (Health and Welfare) Regulations 1966, SI 1966/95	2.34
Control of Lead at Work Regulations 1980, SI 1980/1248	5.7B
Employers' Health and Safety Policy Statements (Exceptions) Regulations 1975, SI 1975/1584	12.27
Employment Protection (Offshore Employment) Order 1976, SI 1976/766	8.18
Equal Pay (Amendment) Regulations 1983, SI 1983/1194:	1.56, 4.68, 4.80
Food Hygiene (General) Regulations 1970, SI 1970/1172	8.173
Funds for Trade Union Ballots Regulations 1984, SI 1984/1654	14.40
Funds for Trade Union Ballots (Amendment) Regulations 1988, SI 1988/1123	14.40
Funds for Trade Union Ballots (Amendment) Regulations 1990, SI 1990/2379	14.40
Funds for Trade Union Ballots Regulations (Revocation) Regulations 1993, SI 1993/233	14.41
Health and Safety (Display Screen Equipment) Regulations 1992, SI 1992/2792	12.53D
Health and Safety (Training for Employment) Regulations 1990, SI 1990/1380	2.57, 12.2
Industrial Tribunals (England and Wales) Regulations 1965, SI 1965/1101	1.20
Industrial Tribunals (Improvement and Prohibition Notices Appeals) Regulations 1974, SI 1974/1925	
reg 13	1.23
Industrial Tribunals (Interest) Order 1990, SI 1990/479	1.26B, 9.56A
Industrial Tribunals (Rules of Procedure) Regulations 1985, SI 1985/16	1.22, 9.13, 9.31
reg 4	9.15A
12	9.29
Industrial Tribunals (Scotland) Regulations 1965, SI 1965/1157	1.20
Insolvency of Employer (Excluded Classes) Regulations 1983, SI 1983/624	5.89

PARA

Ionising Radiations Regulations 1985, SI 1985/1333: 5.9
Local Government (Compensation) Regulations 1974, SI 1974/463 .... 1.21
Management of Health and Safety at Work Regulations 1992, SI 1992/2051 ...... 12.30, 12.53D
Manual Handling of Loads Regulations 1992, SI 1992/2793 .... 12.53D
Occupational Pension Scheme (Certification of Employments Regulations 1975, SI 1975/1927 .... 1.21
Occupational Pension Schemes (Disclosure of Information) Regulations 1986, SI 1986/1046 .... 3.75
Occupational Pension Schemes (Equal Access to Membership) Regulations 1976, SI 1976/142 .... 1.21
Personal Protective Equipment at Work Regulations 1992, SI 1992/2966: 12.49, 12.53D
Provision and Use of Work Equipment Regulations 1992, SI 1992/2932 ..... 12.53D
Race Relations (Prescribed Public Bodies) Regulations 1984, SI 1984/218 .... 4.110
Redundancy Payments (Local Government) (Modification) Order 1983, SI 1983/1160 .... 8.42
Redundancy Payments Pensions Regulations 1965, SI 1965/1932 .... 10.41
Rehabilitation of Offenders Act 1974 (Exceptions) Order 1975, SI 1975/1023 .... 4.136

PARA

Rehabilitation of Offenders Act 1974 (Exceptions) (Amendment) Order 1986, SI 1986/1249 .... 4.136
Rules of the Supreme Court 1965, SI 1965/1776
- Ord 14A 6.5A
- Ord 53 .... 2.69
- Ord 113 .... 15.109

Safety Representatives and Safety Committees Regulations 1977, SI 1977/500 . 1.21, 12.29
Sex Discrimination (Amendment) Order 1988, SI 1988/249 .... 2.65
Trade Union Ballots and Elections (Independent Scrutineers Qualifications) Order 1988, SI 1988/2117 .... 14.32
Transfer of Undertakings (Protection of Employment) Regulations 1981, SI 1981/1974 .... 1.21, 1.59, 2.62A, 5.101, 5.105, 5.123, 6.2, 8.43, 8.185, 10.28, 11.24, 14.16, 15.25
- reg 2(1) 5.106
- 5 .... 5.115, 5.117, 5.122
  - (1) 5.112, 5.119A
  - (2) 5.119
  - (3) 5.114
  - (4) 5.121
- 7 .... 5.121
- 8(1) 5.116, 5.117, 5.118, 8.185
  - (2) 8.185, 8.186, 10.29

Workplace (Health, Safety and Welfare) Regulations 1992, SI 1992/3004 ..... 12.53D

Table of cases

PARA

AB v South West Water Services Ltd [1993] 1 All ER 609, [1993] 2 WLR 507, CA ... 4.122C
AEI Cables v McLay [1980] IRLR 84 ... 8.141
Aberdeen Steak Houses Group plc v Ibrahim [1988] ICR 550, [1988] IRLR 420 ... 9.15, 9.22
Adams v Charles Zub Associates Ltd [1978] IRLR 551 ... 866
Addison v Babcock FATA Ltd [1988] QB 280, [1987] 2 All ER 784, [1987] IRLR 173, CA ... 9.43
Adlam v Salisbury and Wells Theological College [1985] ICR 786, EAT: 13.47
Advocate, Lord v De Rosa [1974] 2 All ER 849, [1974] ICR 480, [1974] IRLR 215, HL ... 10.44
Advocate, Lord v Scotsman Publications Ltd [1990] 1 AC 812, [1989] 2 All ER 852, HL ... 6.17A
Age Concern Scotland v Hines [1983] IRLR 477 ... 8.2, 8.18
Ahmed v National Car Parks Ltd IDS Brief 149 ... 8.18
Ahmet v Trusthouse Forte Catering Ltd IDS Brief 250 ... 2.35
Ainsworth v Glass Tubes and Components [1977] ICR 347, [1977] IRLR 74 ... 4.95
Air Canada v Lee [1978] ICR 1202, [1978] IRLR 392, 13 ITR 574 ... 10.33
Airfix Footwear Ltd v Cope [1978] ICR 1210, [1978] IRLR 396 ... 2.30
Albion Shipping Agency v Arnold [1982] ICR 22, [1981] IRLR 525 ... 4.91
Alexander v Home Office [1988] 2 All ER 118, [1988] ICR 685, CA ... 4.122C
Alexander v Standard Telephones and Cables plc [1990] ICR 291, [1990] IRLR 55 ... 3.25A, 3.27A, 6.2
Ali v London Borough of Southwark [1988] ICR 567, [1988] IRLR 100 .. 7.16A
Allen v Flood [1898] AC 1, [1895–9] All ER Rep 52, HL ... 4.67, 4.131
Allwood v William Hill Ltd [1974] IRLR 258 ... 8.157
AUEW v Cooper Plastics 1976 IDS Brief 90 ... 10.52, 15.14
AUEW v Sefton Engineering Co Ltd [1976] IRLR 318 ... 10.54, 15.7
American Cyanamid Co v Ethicon Ltd [1975] AC 396, [1975] 1 All ER 504, HL ... 6.5A, 11.24B
Anandarajah v Lord Chancellor's Department [1984] IRLR 131 ... 8.101, 9.27
Anderson v Dalkeith Engineering Ltd [1985] ICR 66, [1984] IRLR 429: 8.186
Angel (Morris) & Son Ltd v Hollande [1993] ICR 71, CA ... 5.119A, 11.24D

PARA

Apex Leisure Hire v Barratt [1984] 3 All ER 795, [1984] ICR 452 .. 5.114, 5.115
Appleyard v Smith (Hull) Ltd [1972] IRLR 19 .... 8.172
Argent v Minister of Social Security [1968] 3 All ER 208, [1968] 1 WLR 1749 .... 2.30
Armour v Skeen [1977] IRLR 310, 1977 SLT 71 .... 12.58
Armstrong Whitworth Rolls Ltd v Mustard [1971] 1 All ER 598, 6 ITR 79 .... 3.57
Artisan Press Ltd v Srawley and Parker [1986] ICR 328, [1986] IRLR 126 .... 9.53
Ashford v Association of Scientific, Technical and Managerial Staffs [1973] ICR 296 .... 13.18
Associated British Ports v Palmer [1993] ICR 101, [1993] IRLR 63; revsd. sub nom. Palmer v Associated British Ports [1993] IRLR 336, CA 13.44
Associated British Ports v T & GWU [1989] 3 All ER 822, [1989] 1 WLR 939, [1989] ICR 557, HL 15.53
Associated Dairies Ltd v Hartley [1979] IRLR 171 .... 12.14
Associated Newspapers Ltd v Wilson [1992] ICR 681, [1992] IRLR 440; revsd. sub nom. Wilson v Associated Newspapers Ltd [1993] IRLR 336, CA 13.44
Association of HSD (Hatfield) Employees v Certification Officer [1978] ICR 21, [1977] IRLR 261 .... 14.14
APAC v Kirvin Ltd [1978] IRLR 318, 13 ITR 446 .... 10.52, 15.14
ASTMS v Hawker Siddeley Aviation [1977] IRLR 418 .... 10.58, 15.20
Atkin v Enfield Group Hospital Management Committee [1975] IRLR 217, CA 8.147
Atkinson (Octavius) & Sons Ltd v Morris [1989] ICR 431, [1989] IRLR 158, CA 8.10, 8.166
Attwood v Lamount [1920] 3 KB 571, [1920] All ER Rep 55, CA 11.15
Avon County Council v Haywood-Hicks [1978] ICR 646, [1978] IRLR 118 .... 9.3
Avon County Council v Howlett [1983] 1 All ER 1073, [1983] IRLR 171: 5.136, 6.16
Avonmouth Construction Co Ltd v Shipway [1979] IRLR 14 .... 8.157
Aziz v Trinity Street Taxis Ltd [1986] IRLR 435; affd. [1989] QB 463, [1988] ICR 534, [1988] IRLR 204, CA 4.104

Baker v Cornwall County Council [1990] ICR 452, [1990] IRLR 194, CA: 4.124
Baker v Superite Tools Ltd [1986] ICR 189 .... 1.19A
Balgobin v Tower Hamlets London Borough Council [1987] ICR 829, [1987] IRLR 401 .... 4.38, 4.61
Barber v Guardian Royal Exchange Assurance Group: C-262/88 [1991] 1 QB 344, [1990] 2 All ER 660, [1990] ICR 616, ECJ 1.61, 1.68, 4.45, 4.47, 4.53A, 4.69A
Barclays Bank plc v Kapur [1991] 1 All ER 646, [1991] ICR 208, HL 4.122, 4.122B, 9.1A
Barcock v Brighton Corpn [1949] 1 KB 339, [1949] 1 All ER 251 .... 6.37
Barley v Amey Roadstone Corpn Ltd [1977] ICR 546, [1977] IRLR 299: 8.161
Barnes v BPC (Business Forms) Ltd [1976] 1 All ER 237, [1975] ICR 390, [1975] IRLR 313 .... 9.15
Barratt Developments (Bradford) Ltd v UCATT [1978] ICR 319, [1977] IRLR 403, 12 ITR 478 .... 10.48, 15.8

PARA

Barrel Plating and Phosphating Co Ltd v Danks [1976] 3 All ER 652, [1976] ICR 503, [1976] IRLR 262 .... 9.41
Barretts and Baird (Wholesale) Ltd v IPCS [1987] IRLR 3 .... 15.53
Barthorpe v Exeter Diocesan Board of Finance [1979] ICR 900 .... 2.11
Batisha v Say [1977] IRLIB 4.10, 4.25
Baumann v Hulton Press Ltd [1952] 2 All ER 1121 .... 6.12
Beanstalk Shelving Ltd v Horn [1980] ICR 273 .... 9.4
Beaverbrook Newspapers Ltd v Keys [1978] ICR 582, [1978] IRLR 34, CA 15.47
Bell v Lever Bros Ltd [1932] AC 161, 101 LJKB 129, HL 6.72
Beloff v Pressdram Ltd [1973] 1 All ER 241, [1973] RPC 765 .... 2.26
Bendall v Paine and Betteridge [1973] IRLR 44 .... 7.54
Bengey v North Devon District Council [1977] ICR 15, 11 ITR 211 .... 9.4
Bentley Engineering Co Ltd v Crown [1976] ICR 225, [1976] IRLR 146, 11 TLR 50 .... 8.28, 8.41
Bentley Engineering Co Ltd v Mistry [1979] ICR 47, [1978] IRLR 437 .... 7.19
Benton v Sanderson Kayser Ltd [1989] ICR 136, [1989] IRLR 19, CA 10.34
Bents Brewery Co Ltd v Hogan [1945] 2 All ER 570 .... 15.45
Berkeley Garage (Southampton) Ltd v Edmunds [1975] ICR 228, [1975] IRLR 125, 10 ITR 228 .... 9.59
Berriman v Delabole Slate Ltd [1985] ICR 546, [1985] IRLR 305, CA 8.185, 10.29
Berrisford v Woodard Schools (Midlands Division) Ltd [1991] ICR 564, [1991] IRLR 247 .... 4.35D
Berry v Stone Manganese Marine Ltd (1971) 12 KIR 13, [1972] 1 Lloyd's Rep 182 .... 6.40
Berwick Salmon Fisheries Co Ltd v Rutherford [1991] IRLR 203 .... 8.30A
Bex v Securicor Transport Ltd [1972] IRLR 68 .... 3.56
Bick v Royal West of England Residential School for the Deaf [1976] IRLR 326 .... 4.33
Bigham v GKN Kwikform Ltd [1992] ICR 113, [1992] IRLR 4 .... 13.68
Bika-Kaufhaus GmbH v Weber von Hartz: 170/84 [1987] ICR 110, [1986] IRLR 317, ECJ 2.52A, 4.13A
Birch v University of Liverpool [1985] ICR 470, [1985] IRLR 165, CA: 8.94, 10.6
Bird v British Celanese Ltd [1945] KB 336, [1945] 1 All ER 488, CA 7.41
Birds Eye Walls Ltd v Harrison [1985] ICR 278, [1985] IRLR 47 .... 9.17
Birmingham City District Council v Beyer [1978] 1 All ER 910, [1977] IRLR 211, 12 ITR 409 .... 4.140, 13.31, 13.61
Blackman v Post Office [1974] ICR 151, [1974] IRLR 46 .... 8.130
Blake v Berkel Auto Scale Co Ltd [1974] IRLR 294 .... 3.43
Bliss v South Thames Regional Health Authority [1987] ICR 700, [1985] IRLR 308, CA 6.9
Blockleys plc v Miller [1992] ICR 749 .... 9.69
Blower v Central Electricity Generating Board IDS Supp 25 .... 13.52
Blue Circle Staff Association v Certification Officer [1977] 2 All ER 145, [1977] ICR 224 .... 14.13
Blyth v Scottish Liberal Club [1983] IRLR 245, 1983 SLT 260, Ct of Sess: 8.4
Bonner v H Gilbert Ltd [1989] IRLR 475 .... 10.39
Bonsor v Musicians' Union [1956] AC 104, [1955] 3 All ER 518, HL 14.22E
Boots Co plc v Lees Collier [1986] ICR 728, [1986] IRLR 485 .... 9.34
Borders Regional Council v Maule [1993] IRLR 199 .... 5.58
Bork (P) International A/S (in liquidation) v Foreningen af Arbejdsledere i Danmark: 101/87 [1988] ECR 3057, [1989] IRLR 41, ECJ 5.116

PARA

Boston Deep-Sea Fishing and Ice Co v Ansell (1888) 39 Ch D 339, [1886–90] All ER Rep 65, CA 6.62
Bouchaala v Trust House Forte Ltd [1980] ICR 721, [1980] IRLR 382 ... 8.184
Boulting v ACTAT [1963] 2 QB 606, [1963] 1 All ER 716, CA 13.4, 14.20
Bowater Containers Ltd v McCormack [1980] IRLR 50 .... 3.54
Bowater plc v Charlwood [1991] ICR 798, [1991] IRLR 340 .... 1.26
Bowler v Lovegrove [1921] 1 Ch 642, 90 LJ Ch 356 .... 11.15
Boxfoldia Ltd v National Graphical Association (1982) [1988] ICR 752, [1988] IRLR 383 .... 15.56, 15.85
Boychuk v H J Symons Holdings Ltd [1977] IRLR 395 .... 8.147
Boyd Lind Ltd v Pitts [1986] ICR 244 .... 2.66
Bracebridge Engineering Ltd v Darby [1990] IRLR 3 .... 4.38
Bradford (Earl) v Jowett [1978] IRLR 16, sub nom. Jowett v Earl of Bradford (No. 2) [1978] ICR 431, 13 ITR 141 .... 9.27
Bradford v Robinson Rentals Ltd [1967] 1 All ER 267, [1967] 1 WLR 337: 6.34
Bradford Metropolitan City Council v Arora [1991] 3 All ER 545, [1991] ICR 226, CA 4.122C
Bradley v NALGO [1991] ICR 359, [1991] IRLR 159 .... 13.16
Bradley v Opperman Gears Ltd [1975] IRLR 13 .... 6.10
Bradshaw v Rugby Portland Cement Co Ltd [1972] IRLR 46 .... 8.149
Braithwaite v EETU [1969] 2 All ER 859, 6 KIR 169, CA 14.22B
Brassington v Cauldon Wholesale Ltd [1978] ICR 405, [1977] IRLR 479: 13.48
Braund (Walter) (London) Ltd v Murray [1991] ICR 327, [1991] IRLR 100 .... 9.44
Breach v Epsylon Industries Ltd [1976] ICR 316, [1976] IRLR 180 ..... 6.12
Brennan v Dewhurst Ltd [1984] ICR 52, [1983] IRLR 357, EAT 4.20
Brennan and Ging v Ellward (Lancs) Ltd [1976] IRLR 378 .... 13.39
Brewer & Son v Dunston IDS Supp 145 .... 12.12
Bridgen v Lancashire County Council [1987] IRLR 58, CA 8.65
Briggs v ICI (1968) 5 KIR 492, DC 3.45
Briggs v North Eastern Education and Library Board [1990] IRLR 181, NI CA 4.13A
Briggs v Oates [1990] ICR 473, [1990] IRLR 472 .... 11.24C
Brindley v Tayside Health Board [1976] IRLR 364 .... 4.19
British Aircraft Corpn v Austin [1978] IRLR 332 .... 8.67
British Broadcasting Corpn v Becket [1983] IRLR 43 .... 7.58, 8.74
British Broadcasting Corpn v Hearn [1978] 1 All ER 111, [1977] 1 WLR 1004, CA 15.43
British Broadcasting Corpn v Ioannou [1975] QB 781, [1975] ICR 267, CA 8.60
British Coal Corpn v Cheesbrough [1990] 2 AC 256, [1990] 1 All ER 641, [1990] ICR 317, HL 10.45
British Gas plc v McCarrick [1991] IRLR 305, CA 8.139A
British Gas plc v Sharma [1991] ICR 19, [1991] IRLR 101 .... 4.124
British Home Stores v Burchell [1980] ICR 303n, [1978] IRLR 379 .. 7.19, 7.23, 8.138
British Labour Pump Co Ltd v Byrne [1979] ICR 347, [1979] IRLR 94: 7.5, 8.160
British Leyland (UK) Ltd v Ashraf [1978] ICR 979, [1978] IRLR 330, 13 ITR 500 .... 8.95
British Leyland (UK) Ltd v Swift [1981] IRLR 91, CA 8.102
British Newspaper Printing Corpn (North) Ltd v Kelly [1989] IRLR 222, CA 9.9

PARA
British Railways Board v NUR [1989] ICR 678, [1989] IRLR 349, CA ... 15.57
British Railways Board v Paul [1988] IRLR 20 ... 4.97
BSM (1257) Ltd v Secretary of State for Social Services [1978] ICR 894: 2.35
British Telecommunications plc v Sheridan [1990] IRLR 27, CA ... 9.64
British Telecommunications plc v Ticehurst [1992] ICR 383, [1992] IRLR 219, CA ... 6.60A
British United Shoe Machinery Co Ltd v Clarke [1978] ICR 70, [1977] IRLR 297, 12 ITR 473 ... 8.158, 9.40
Broadbent v Crisp [1974] 1 All ER 1052, [1974] ICR 248 ... 2.3
Broaders v Kalkare Property Maintenance Ltd [1990] IRLR 421 ... 3.1C
Bromley v H & J Quick Ltd [1988] ICR 47, [1987] IRLR 456; revsd. [1988] ICR 623, [1988] IRLR 249, CA ... 4.79
Bromsgrove Casting and Machining Ltd v Martin [1977] 3 All ER 487, [1977] ICR 417 ... 2.9
Brook v London Borough of Haringey [1992] IRLR 478 ... 8.162
Brooks v British Telecommunications plc [1992] ICR 414, [1992] IRLR 66, CA ... 8.18
Brooks v Ladbroke Lucky Seven Entertainment [1977] IRLIB ... 4.133
Brooks & Son v Skinner [1984] IRLR 379 ... 7.24
Broome v DPP [1974] AC 587, [1974] 1 All ER 314, [1974] ICR 84, HL .. 15.105
Brophy v Bradfield & Co [1955] 3 All ER 286, [1955] 1 WLR 1148, CA .. 6.45
Brown v Rolls-Royce Ltd [1960] 1 All ER 577, [1960] 1 WLR 210, CA ... 6.43
Brown v Southall and Knight [1980] ICR 617, [1980] IRLR 130 ... 8.18
Brown v Stockton-on-Tees Borough Council [1987] IRLR 230, CA; revsd. [1989] AC 20, [1988] ICR 410, HL ... 8.164B
Brown v Stuart Scott & Co [1981] ICR 166 ... 8.208
Brown (S C) Communications Ltd v Walker ... 7.14
Browning v Crumlin Valley Collieries [1926] 1 KB 522, [1926] All ER Rep 132 ... 6.14
Brownson v Hire Service Shops Ltd [1978] ICR 517, [1978] IRLR 73: 9.38, 9.41
Brush Electrical Machines v Guest [1977] IRLIB ... 8.113
Buckley v NUGMW [1967] 3 All ER 767, 4 KIR 277 ... 14.23
Budgen & Co v Thomas [1976] ICR 344, [1976] IRLR 174 ... 7.14, 7.20
Bullock v Alice Ottley School [1991] ICR 838, [1991] IRLR 324; revsd [1993] ICR 138, [1992] IRLR 564, CA ... 4.11A, 4.43
Burgess v O'Brien (1966) 1 KIR 99, 1 ITR 164 ... 10.4
Burns and Davies v Ideal Timber Products Ltd [1975] IRLR 19, 10 ITR 14 ... 8.144
Burrows v Ace Caravan Co (Hull) [1972] IRLR 4 ... 6.10
Burton v Boneham and Turner Ltd IDS Supp 15 ... 8.121
Burton, Allton & Johnson Ltd v Peck [1975] ICR 193, [1975] IRLR 87: 8.94, 10.6
Business Seating (Renovations) Ltd v Broad [1989] ICR 729 ... 11.24A
Byrne v Birmingham City District Council [1987] ICR 519, [1987] IRLR 191, CA ... 8.28
Byrne v BOC Ltd [1992] IRLR 505 ... 7.22
Byrne v Kinematograph Renters Society Ltd [1958] 2 All ER 579, [1958] 1 WLR 762 ... 13.41

Cadbury Ltd v Doddington [1977] ICR 982 ... 9.40
Cadoux v Central Regional Council [1986] IRLR 131, 1986 SLT 117, Ct of Sess ... 3.7, 3.29, 3.42

PARA
Cairns v Burnside Shoe Repairs Ltd (1966) 2 KIR 23, 2 ITR 75 .... 10.39
Calder v James Finlay Corpn Ltd (1982) [1989] IRLR 55, [1989] ICR 157n, EAT 4.62A
Caledonian Mining Co Ltd v Bassett and Steel [1987] ICR 425, [1987] IRLR 165 .... 8.51
Cambridge and District Co-operative Society Ltd v Ruse [1993] IRLR 156 .... 10.23
Camden Exhibition and Display Ltd v Lynott [1966] 1 QB 555, [1965] 3 All ER 28, CA 3.27
Campbell v Dunoon and Cowal Housing Association Ltd [1992] IRLR 528, 1992 SLT 1136n, Ct of Sess 9.70
Campey (H) & Sons Ltd v Bellwood [1987] ICR 311 .... 8.191, 13.63
Canadian Pacific Rly v Lockhart [1942] AC 591, [1942] 2 All ER 464, PC: 6.76
Cannon v Barnsley Metropolitan Borough Council [1992] ICR 698, [1992] IRLR 474 .... 1.68, 4.97
Cantor Fitzgerald (UK) Ltd v Wallace [1992] IRLR 215 .... 11.16A
Capper Pass Ltd v Lawton [1977] QB 852, [1977] ICR 83, [1976] IRLR 366 .... 4.72
Carnie (Peter) & Son Ltd v Paton [1979] IRLR 260 .... 8.74
Carr v Alexander Russell Ltd [1976] IRLR 220, 11 ITR 39 .... 8.134
Carrington v Helix Lighting Ltd [1990] ICR 125, [1990] IRLR 6 .. 4.124A, 9.15
Carrington v Therm-A-Stor Ltd [1983] 1 All ER 796, [1983] ICR 208, CA 8.186, 13.62
Carry All Motors Ltd v Pennington [1980] ICR 806, [1980] IRLR 455 ... 10.15
Carter v Credit Change Ltd [1980] 1 All ER 252, [1979] IRLR 309, CA .. 1.26
Cartwright v G Clancey Ltd [1983] ICR 552, [1983] IRLR 355 .... 5.4
Cassell & Co Ltd v Broome [1972] AC 1027, [1972] 1 All ER 801, HL 4.122C
Cassidy v Dunlop Rubber Co Ltd (1972) 13 KIR 255, CA 6.25
Cassidy v Ministry of Health [1951] 2 KB 343, [1951] 1 All ER 574, [1951] 1 TLR 539 .... 2.42
Castledine v Rothwell Engineering Ltd [1973] IRLR 99 .... 6.22, 8.98
Century Insurance Co Ltd v Northern Ireland Road Transport Board [1942] AC 509, [1942] 1 All ER 491, HL 6.76
Chakki v United Yeast Co Ltd [1982] 2 All ER 446, [1982] ICR 140 ..... 8.93
Challinor v Taylor [1972] ICR 129, 7 ITR 104 .... 2.22, 10.4
Chant v Aquaboats Ltd [1978] 3 All ER 102, [1978] ICR 643 .... 13.61
Chaplin v Leslie Frewin (Publishers) Ltd [1966] 1 Ch 71, [1965] 3 All ER 764, CA 4.3
Chapman v Goonvean and Rostowrack China Clay Co Ltd [1973] 2 All ER 1063, [1973] ICR 310, CA 9.9, 10.15
Chapman and Elkin v CPS Computer Group plc [1987] IRLR 462, CA .. 5.119B
Chappell v Times Newspapers Ltd [1975] 2 All ER 233, [1975] ICR 145, [1975] IRLR 90, CA 6.2
Chapple v ETU [1961] 3 All ER 612, [1961] 1 WLR 1290 .... 14.22B
Charlton v Forrest Printing Ink Co [1980] IRLR 331, CA 6.37
Chattopadhyay v Headmaster of Holloway School [1982] ICR 132, [1981] IRLR 487 .... 4.123
Cheall v Vauxhall Motors Ltd [1979] IRLR 253 .... 13.48
Chelsea Football Club and Athletic Co Ltd v Heath [1981] ICR 323, [1981] IRLR 73 .... 9.44
Chesham Shipping Ltd v Rowe [1977] IRLR 391 .... 8.56
Chiltern House Ltd v Chambers [1990] IRLR 88 .... 5.136
Chubb Fire Security Ltd v Harper [1983] IRLR 311 .... 3.55

PARA

City and Hackney Health Authority v National Union of Public Employees [1985] IRLR 252, CA 15.109
Clark v Civil Aviation Authority [1991] IRLR 412 . . . . . 7.12A, 8.103
Clark v NATSOPA (SOGAT '82) [1986] ICR 12, [1985] IRLR 494 . . . . . 13.6
Clarke v Eley (IMI) Kynoch Ltd [1983] ICR 165, [1982] IRLR 482 . . . . . 8.162
Clarke v Hampshire Electro-Plating Co Ltd [1992] ICR 312, [1991] IRLR 490 . . . . . 4.122A, 9.1A
Clarks of Hove Ltd v Bakers' Union [1979] 1 All ER 152, [1978] ICR 1976, CA 10.48, 10.52, 15.8, 15.14
Clarkson v Brown, Muff & Co Ltd [1974] IRLR 66 . . . . . 7.32
Clay Cross (Quarry Services) v Fletcher [1979] 1 All ER 474, [1979] ICR 1 . . . . . 4.84, 4.90
Clayton (Herbert) and Jack Waller Ltd v Oliver [1930] AC 209, [1930] All ER Rep 44 . . . . . 6.12
Clements v London and North-Western Rly Co [1894] 2 QB 482, 63 LJQB 837 . . . . . 4.2
Cleveland County Council v Springett [1985] IRLR 131 . . . . . 12.28
Clift v West Riding County Council (1964) Times, 10 April 3.36
Close v Steel Co of Wales [1962] AC 367, [1962] 2 All ER 953, HL 6.34
Clyde Pipeworks v Foster [1978] IRLR 313 . . . . . 8.164
Coales v John Wood & Co [1986] ICR 71, [1986] IRLR 129 . . . . . 3.70
Coddington v International Harvester Co of Great Britain Ltd (1969) 6 KIR 146 . . . . . 6.41
Cold Drawn Tubes Ltd v Middleton [1992] ICR 318, [1992] IRLR 160 . . . 9.35A
Cole v Fred Stacey Ltd [1974] IRLR 73, 9 ITR 11 . . . . . 3.1B
Cole v Midland Display Ltd [1973] IRLR 62 . . . . . 3.9
Coleman v Magnet Joinery Ltd [1975] ICR 46, [1974] IRLR 343, CA 9.35A
Collier v Sunday Referee Publishing Co Ltd [1940] 2 KB 647, [1940] 4 All ER 234 . . . . . 6.12
Comerford v Swel Foods Ltd [1972] IRLR 17 . . . . . 6.61
Commercial Plastics Ltd v Vincent [1965] 1 QB 623, [1964] 3 All ER 546, CA 11.20, 11.23
Commission for the European Communities v United Kingdom: 61/81 [1982] ICR 578, [1982] IRLR 333, ECJ 1.67, 4.80
Commission for the European Communities v United Kingdom: 165/82 [1984] 1 All ER 353, [1984] IRLR 29, ECJ 1.67, 4.41
Commission for Racial Equality v Amari Plastics Ltd [1982] QB 1194, [1982] ICR 304, CA 4.125A
Commission for Racial Equality v Dutton [1989] QB 783, [1989] 1 All ER 306, CA 4.108
Company's Application, A, Re [1989] Ch 477, [1989] 2 All ER 248, [1989] ICR 449 . . . . . 11.8A
Connor v Halfords Ltd [1972] IRLR 109 . . . . . 6.59
CITB v Labour Force Ltd [1970] 3 All ER 220, 9 KIR 269 . . . . . 2.39, 2.47
CITB v Leighton [1978] 2 All ER 723, [1978] IRLR 60 . . . . . 3.66
Converform (Darwen) Ltd v Bell [1981] IRLR 195 . . . . . 8.118
Conway v George Wimpey Ltd [1951] 2 KB 266, [1951] 1 All ER 363, CA: 6.75
Conway v Matthew, Wright & Nephew Ltd [1977] IRLR 80 . . . . . 7.23A, 8.142
Conway v Wade [1909] AC 506, [1908–10] All ER Rep 344, HL 15.46
Cook v Thomas Linnell & Sons Ltd [1977] ICR 770, [1977] IRLR 132, 12 ITR 330 . . . . . 8.113
Cook (Donald) & Son Ltd v Carter [1977] IRLR 88 . . . . . 7.50
Cooper v Weatherwise (Roofing and Walling) Ltd [1993] ICR 81 . . . . . 9.22

PARA

Coral Leisure Group Ltd v Barnett [1981] ICR 503, [1981] IRLR 204 ... 3.3
Coral Squash Clubs Ltd v Matthews [1979] ICR 607, [1979] IRLR 390 .. 9.23
Corner v Buckinghamshire County Council [1978] ICR 836, [1978] IRLR 320, 77 LGR 268 ... 5.56
Cort (Robert) & Son Ltd v Charman [1981] ICR 816, [1981] IRLR 437: 8.2, 9.7
Cory Lighterage Ltd v T & GWU [1973] 2 All ER 558, [1973] ICR 339, [1973] IRLR 152 ... 3.7, 8.1, 15.41
Costain Civil Engineering Ltd v Draycott [1977] ICR 335, [1977] IRLR 17 ... 10.41
Coulson v Felixstowe Dock and Rly Co Ltd [1975] IRLR 11 ... 8.117
Council of Civil Service Unions v Minister for the Civil Service [1985] AC 374, [1984] 3 All ER 935, HL ... 2.64, 2.68, 2.70, 8.206
Council of Engineering Institutions v Maddison [1977] ICR 30, [1976] IRLR 389, 11 ITR 272 ... 9.11
Courage Take Home Trade Ltd v Keys [1986] ICR 874, [1986] IRLR 427: 1.8
Courtaulds Northern Spinning Ltd v Sibson [1987] ICR 329 ... 8.64
Courtaulds Northern Textiles Ltd v Andrew [1979] IRLR 84 ... 2.5, 8.67
Coward v John Menzies (Holdings) Ltd [1977] IRLR 428 ... 8.111
Cowell v Quilter Goodison Co Ltd and QG Management Services Ltd [1989] IRLR 392, CA ... 5.106
Cox v Wildt Mellor Bromley Ltd [1978] ICR 736, [1978] IRLR 157 ... 9.21
Cox (W E) Toner (International) Ltd v Crook [1981] ICR 823, [1981] IRLR 443 ... 8.75
Crawford v Swinton Insurance Brokers Ltd [1990] ICR 85, [1990] IRLR 42 ... 10.29
Cresswell v Board of Inland Revenue [1984] 2 All ER 713, [1984] ICR 508, [1984] IRLR 190 ... 3.18
Crofter Hand Woven Harris Tweed Co Ltd v Veitch [1942] AC 435, [1942] 1 All ER 142, HL ... 15.33
Cross v BISKTA [1968] 1 All ER 250, [1968] 1 WLR 494, CA ... 14.23
Cross International Ltd v Reid [1985] IRLR 387, CA ... 8.169
Crosville Motor Services Ltd v Ashfield [1986] IRLR 475 ... 8.185, 13.61
Crosville Wales Ltd v Tracey [1993] IRLR 60 ... 13.72
Crown Suppliers (Property Services Agency) v Dawkins [1991] ICR 583, [1991] IRLR 327; affd (1993) Times, 4 February, CA ... 4.109
Crump v Chubb & Sons Lock and Safe Co Ltd [1975] IRLR 293 ... 8.162

Da Costa v Optolis [1976] IRLR 178 ... 8.140
Daley v A E Dorsett (Almar Dolls Ltd) [1982] ICR 1, [1981] IRLR 385 ... 9.42
Daley v Allied Suppliers Ltd [1983] ICR 90, [1983] IRLR 14 ... 2.56
Dalgleish v Kew House Farm Ltd [1982] IRLR 251 ... 2.55
Dalgleish v Lothian and Borders Police Board [1991] IRLR 422, 1992 SLT 721, Ct of Sess ... 6.17A
Dalton v Burton's Gold Medal Biscuit Co Ltd [1974] IRLR 45 ... 6.55, 7.27
Daniels v Whetstone Entertainments Ltd (1961) 106 Sol Jo 284, [1962] 2 Lloyd's Rep 1, CA ... 6.78
Darby v GKN Screws and Fasteners Ltd [1986] ICR 1 ... 6.27
Davidson v John Calder (Publishers) Ltd [1985] ICR 143, [1985] IRLR 97 ... 9.62
Davidson v Pillay [1979] IRLR 275 ... 3.4
Davie v New Merton Board Mills [1959] AC 604, [1959] 1 All ER 346, HL ... 6.35

PARA
Davies v Anglo Great Lakes Corpn Ltd [1973] IRLR 133 .... 7.44
Davies v GKN Birwelco (Uskside) Ltd [1976] IRLR 82 .... 7.17
Davies v Presbyterian Church of Wales [1986] 1 All ER 705, [1986] ICR 280, HL 2.36
Davies v Richard Johnson & Nephew (1934) 51 TLR 115 .... 3.21
Davis v New England College of Arundel [1977] ICR 6, 11 ITR 278 ... 2.32, 2.35
Davison v Kent Meters Ltd [1975] IRLR 145 .... 8.107
Davy v Collins (Builders) Ltd [1974] IRLR 324 .... 8.55
Dean v Polytechnic of North London [1973] ICR 490, 8 ITR 526 .... 2.48
Deane v Ealing London Borough Council [1993] ICR 329 .... 4.122C
Deary v Mansion Hide Upholstery Ltd [1983] ICR 610, [1983] IRLR 195 .... 12.16
Debaughn v Star Cinemas (London) Ltd 8.183
De Brito v Standard Chartered Bank Ltd [1978] ICR 650 .... 4.88
Deeley v British Rail Engineering Ltd [1980] IRLR 147, CA 3.11
De Francesco v Barnum (1890) 45 Ch D 430, [1886–90] All ER Rep 414, 60 LJ Ch 63 .... 4.2
Defrenne v Sabena: 43/75 [1976] ICR 547, [1976] ECR 455, [1976] 2 CMLR 98, ECJ 1.52
De Grasse v Stockwell Tools Ltd [1992] IRLR 269 .... 8.159A
Dekker v Stichting Vormingscentrum voor Jong Volwassenen (VJV-Centrum) Plus: C-177/88 [1992] ICR 325, [1991] IRLR 27, ECJ 1.54, 4.35B, 4.35C, 4.35D
Del Monte Foods Ltd v Mundon [1980] ICR 694, [1980] IRLR 224 ...... 5.32
Delaney v Staples (t/a De Montfort Recruitment) [1991] 1 All ER 609, [1991] IRLR 112, CA; affd [1992] 1 AC 687, [1992] ICR 483, HL 5.135
Denco Ltd v Joinson [1992] 1 All ER 463, [1991] ICR 172 .... 8.147
Denmark Productions Ltd v Boscobel Productions Ltd [1969] 1 QB 699, [1968] 3 All ER 513, [1968] 1 WLR 841, CA 4.3
Depledge v Pye Telecommunications Ltd [1981] ICR 82, [1980] IRLR 390 .... 13.55
Derby City Council v Marshall [1979] ICR 731, [1979] IRLR 261 .... 8.78
Deria v General Council of British Shipping [1986] ICR 172, [1986] IRLR 108, CA 4.113
De Souza v Automobile Association [1986] ICR 514, [1986] IRLR 103, CA 4.110
Devis (W) & Sons Ltd v Atkins [1977] AC 931, [1977] ICR 662, [1977] IRLR 314, HL 9.25, 9.49
Devonald v Rosser & Sons [1906] 2 KB 728, [1904–7] All ER Rep 988, 75 LJKB 688, CA 6.12, 6.14
Dhaliwal v British Airways Board [1985] ICR 513 .... 7.18
Discount Tobacco and Confectionery Ltd v Armitage [1990] IRLR 15 ... 13.61
Discount Tobacco and Confectionery Ltd v Williamson [1993] ICR 371: 5.129, 5.138
Dixon v British Broadcasting Corpn [1979] 2 All ER 112, [1979] ICR 281, CA 8.60
Dixon v Stenor Ltd [1973] ICR 157, [1973] IRLR 28, 8 ITR 141 .... 9.5A
Dixon and Shaw v West Ella Developments Ltd [1978] ICR 856, [1978] IRLR 151, 13 ITR 235 .... 13.43
Doble v Firestone Tyre and Rubber Co Ltd [1981] IRLR 300 .... 8.49
Docherty v Reddy [1977] ICR 365 .... 7.17, 9.24
Donn v Greater London Council IDS Brief 65 .... 2.53, 9.26
Donnelly v Kelvin International Services [1992] IRLR 496 .... 8.27

PARA
Donoghue v Stevenson [1932] AC 562, [1932] All ER Rep 1, 101 LJPC 119, HL 6.35
Donovan v Invicta Airways Ltd [1970] 1 Lloyd's Rep 486, CA 6.8
Doughty v Rolls-Royce plc [1992] IRLR 126, CA 1.53
Dowden and Pook Ltd v Pook [1904] 1 KB 45, 73 LJKB 38, 89 LT 688, CA 11.15
Down v Dudley Coles Long Ltd (1969) unreported 6.25
Doyle v Northumbria Probation Committee [1991] 4 All ER 294, [1992] ICR 121 .... 2.71
Drakard (P J) & Sons Ltd v Wilton [1977] ICR 642, 12 ITR 170 .... 9.59, 9.60
Drew v St Edmundsbury Borough Council [1980] ICR 513, [1980] IRLR 459 .... 8.198, 13.73
Dryden v Greater Glasgow Health Board [1992] IRLR 469 .... 3.42, 8.67A
Duffy v Northampton Area Health Authority IDS Brief 162 .... 7.10B
Dugdale v Kraft Foods Ltd [1977] 1 All ER 454, [1977] ICR 48, [1976] IRLR 368 .... 4.75
Duke v Prospect Training Services Ltd [1988] ICR 521, [1989] IRLR 196 .... 9.63
Duncan v GEC Telecommunications Ltd [1976] IRLR 3 .... 7.51
Dunk v George Waller & Son Ltd [1970] 2 QB 163, [1970] 2 All ER 630, CA 4.5
Dunning (A J) & Sons (Shopfitters) Ltd v Jacomb [1973] ICR 448, [1973] IRLR 206, 15 KIR 9 .... 7.55, 8.108
Duport Steels Ltd v Sirs [1980] 1 All ER 529, [1980] ICR 161, HL 15.71
Dutton v Hawker Siddeley Aviation Ltd [1978] ICR 1057, [1978] IRLR 390 .... 5.60
Dutton & Clark Ltd v Daly [1985] ICR 780, [1985] IRLR 363 .... 8.67
Dwyer v Superguard Ltd [1977] IRLIB 3.52

Eagland v British Telecommunications plc [1990] IRLR 328, [1990] ICR 248, EAT; affd [1992] IRLR 323, CA 3.67
Ealing London Borough Council v Race Relations Board [1972] AC 342, [1972] 1 All ER 105, HL 4.105
Earl v Slater and Wheeler (Airlyne) Ltd [1973] 1 All ER 145, [1972] ICR 508, [1972] IRLR 115 .... 7.4
Early (Charles) and Mariott (Witney) Ltd v Smith and Ball [1978] QB 11, [1977] ICR 700, [1977] IRLR 123 .... 4.87
East Berkshire Health Authority v Matadeen [1992] ICR 723, [1992] IRLR 336 .... 7.23D, 9.64A
East Hertfordshire District Council v Boyten [1977] IRLR 347 .... 7.3
East Lindsey District Council v Daubney [1977] ICR 566, [1977] IRLR 181, 12 ITR 359 .... 8.115
East Sussex County Council v Walker (1972) 7 ITR 280 .... 8.50
Eaton Ltd v Nuttall [1977] 3 All ER 1131, [1977] ICR 272, [1977] IRLR 71 .... 4.77, 4.78
Eclipse Blinds Ltd v Wright [1992] IRLR 133, Ct of Sess 4.128, 8.115A, 9.64B
Edinburgh City v Stephens IDS Handbook 12 .... 8.141
Edwards v Cardiff City Council [1979] IRLR 303 .... 8.193, 13.66
Edwards v West Herts Group Hospital Management Committee [1957] 1 All ER 541, [1957] 1 WLR 415, 121 JP 212, CA 3.23

PARA

Egg Stores (Stamford Hill) Ltd v Leibovici [1977] ICR 260, [1976] IRLR 376, 11 ITR 289 ... 8.90, 8.115
EEPTU v Times Newspaper [1980] QB 585, [1980] 1 All ER 1097 ... 14.4
Electrolux Ltd v Hutchinson [1977] ICR 252, [1976] IRLR 410, 12 ITR 40 ... 4.74
Elliot v Richard Stump Ltd [1987] ICR 579, [1987] IRLR 215 ... 10.34
Elliott v Waldair (Construction) Ltd [1975] IRLR 104 ... 8.48
Elliott Bros (London) Ltd v Colverd [1979] IRLR 92 ... 7.28
Elliott Turbomachinery v Bates [1981] ICR 218 ... 10.20
Emmerson v IRC [1977] IRLR 458 ... 5.56
Enessy Co SA v Minoprio [1978] IRLR 489 ... 9.35A
Equal Opportunities Commission v Robertson [1980] IRLR 44 ... 4.58
Etam plc v Rowan [1989] IRLR 150 ... 4.55
Etherson v Strathclyde Regional Council [1992] ICR 579, [1992] IRLR 392 ... 4.97
Evans v Elemeta Holdings Ltd [1982] IRLR 143 ... 8.176
Evans v Metropolitan Police Comr [1993] ICR 151, [1992] IRLR 570, CA ... 9.29
Evans v National Union of Bookbinding and Printing Workers [1938] 4 All ER 51 ... 14.22A
Evening Standard Ltd v Henderson [1987] ICR 588, [1987] IRLR 64, CA ... 11.8C
Examite Ltd v Whittaker [1977] IRLR 312, CA ... 15.44
Express and Star Ltd v Bunday [1987] ICR 58, [1986] IRLR 477; revsd. [1988] ICR 379, [1987] IRLR 422, CA ... 8.191, 13.63
Express and Star Ltd v NGA [1986] ICR 589, [1986] IRLR 222, CA ... 15.83
Express Newspapers Ltd v Keys [1980] IRLR 247 ... 15.43

Faccenda Chicken Ltd v Fowler [1987] Ch 117, [1986] ICR 297, CA .. 11.2, 11.4
Falconer v ASLEF and NUR [1986] IRLR 331 ... 15.30
Famatina Development Corpn, Re [1914] 2 Ch 271, 84 LJ Ch 48, 30 TLR 969, CA ... 6.19
Faramus v Film Artistes' Association [1964] AC 925, [1964] 1 All ER 25, HL ... 13.4, 14.20
Farnborough v Governors of Edinburgh College of Art [1974] IRLR 245 ... 7.55
Farr v Hoveringham Gravels Ltd [1972] IRLR 104 ... 8.174
Fellowes & Son v Fisher [1976] QB 122, [1975] 2 All ER 829, CA ... 11.23
Fentiman v Fluid Engineering Products Ltd [1991] ICR 570, [1991] IRLR 150 ... 9.43A
Ferguson v John Dawson & Partners (Contractors) Ltd [1976] 3 All ER 817, [1976] 1 WLR 1213, CA ... 2.33, 2.40
Ferguson v Prestwick Circuits Ltd [1992] IRLR 266 ... 8.159A
Ferodo Ltd v Barnes [1976] ICR 439, [1976] IRLR 302, 10 ITR 177 ... 7.17, 9.26
Finch v Betabake (Anglia) Ltd [1977] IRLR 470 ... 4.6, 8.129
Finch v Telegraph Construction and Maintenance Co Ltd [1949] 1 All ER 452, 65 TLR 153 ... 6.38
First Castle Electronics Ltd v West [1989] ICR 72 ... 1.26
Fitch v Dewes [1921] 2 AC 158, [1921] All ER Rep 13, HL ... 11.22
Fitzgerald v Hall, Russell & Co Ltd [1970] AC 984, [1969] 3 All ER 1140, HL ... 8.28

PARA

Fitzpatrick v British Railways Board [1992] ICR 221, [1991] IRLR 376, CA 13.31, 13.61
Folami v Nigerline (UK) Ltd [1978] ICR 277 ..... 2.7
Foot v Eastern Counties Timber Co Ltd [1972] IRLR 83 ..... 8.174
Ford v Warwickshire County Council [1983] 2 AC 71, [1983] ICR 273, HL 8.29
Ford v R Weston (Chemists) Ltd (1977) 12 ITR 369 ..... 4.89
Ford Motor Co Ltd v Hudson [1978] 3 All ER 23, [1978] ICR 482, [1978] IRLR 66 ..... 13.78
Forex Neptune (Overseas) Ltd v Miller [1987] ICR 170 ..... 4.87
Forman Construction Ltd v Kelly [1977] IRLR 468 ..... 8.159, 15.23
Forster & Sons Ltd v Suggett (1918) 35 TLR 87 ..... 11.12
Forsyth v Fry's Metals Ltd [1977] IRLR 243 ..... 13.87
Foster v British Gas plc: C-188/89 [1991] 1 QB 405, [1991] ICR 84, ECJ; apld [1991] 2 AC 306, [1991] ICR 463, HL 1.21, 1.53
Foster v Scaffolding (GB) Ltd (342/73) IDS Brief 13 ..... 6.64
Fougère v Phoenix Motor Co Ltd [1977] 1 All ER 237, [1976] ICR 495, [1976] IRLR 259 ..... 9.42, 9.66
Fowler v Cammell Laird (Shipbuilders) Ltd [1973] IRLR 72 ..... 7.13
Fox Maintenance Ltd v Jackson [1978] ICR 110, [1977] IRLR 306, 12 ITR 593 ..... 8.11, 8.18
Frame v McKean and Graham Ltd [1974] IRLR 179 ..... 6.70, 7.30
Frames Snooker Centre v Boyce [1992] IRLR 472 ..... 8.179
Francovich v Italian Republic: C-6/90 [1992] IRLR 84, ECJ 1.54
Freeman v Sovereign Chicken Ltd [1991] ICR 853, [1991] IRLR 408 ..... 9.11A
Freud v Bentalls Ltd [1982] IRLR 443, EAT 8.161
Fuller v Lloyds Bank plc [1991] IRLR 336 ..... 7.14
Fuller v Stephanie Bowman (Sales) Ltd [1977] IRLR 87 ..... 10.24
FTATU v Lawrence Cabinet IDS Brief 96 ..... 10.52, 15.14
Futty v D and D Brekkes Ltd [1974] IRLR 130 ..... 8.53
Fyfe v Scientific Furnishings Ltd [1989] ICR 648, [1989] IRLR 331 ..... 9.44

GEC Machines Ltd v Gilford [1982] ICR 725 ..... 8.169
GMB v Rankin and Harrison [1992] IRLR 514 ..... 15.15
Gadhok v Commonwealth Secretariat (1977) 12 ITR 440, CA 8.18
Gale (B G) Ltd v Gilbert [1978] ICR 1149, [1978] IRLR 453, 13 ITR 547: 8.81
Gallagher v Post Office [1970] 3 All ER 712, 114 Sol Jo 736 ..... 3.37
Gallear v J F Watson & Son Ltd [1979] IRLR 306 ..... 6.20
Galloway v Export Packing Services Ltd [1975] IRLR 306 ..... 10.46
Galt v Philp [1984] IRLR 156 ..... 15.120
Gardiner v Newport County Borough Council [1974] IRLR 262 ..... 7.32, 8.149
Gardner (F C) Ltd v Beresford [1978] IRLR 63 ..... 3.19, 8.70
Garland v British Rail Engineering Ltd [1983] 2 AC 751, [1982] ICR 420, HL 1.52
Garner v Grange Furnishings Ltd [1977] IRLR 206 ..... 8.78
Garrard v Southey & Co and Standard Telephones and Cables Ltd [1952] 2 QB 174, [1952] 1 All ER 597 ..... 2.46
Garricks (Caterers) Ltd v Nolan [1980] IRLR 259 ..... 8.123
Garvey v J and J Maybank (Oldham) Ltd [1979] IRLR 408 ..... 5.3
Gascol Conversions Ltd v Mercer [1974] ICR 420, [1974] IRLR 155, 9 ITR 282, CA 3.36, 3.39, 10.45
Gateway Hotels Ltd v Stewart [1988] IRLR 287 ..... 8.186

PARA

Gemmell v Darngavil Brickworks Ltd (1967) 2 ITR 20 .... 10.12
General Aviation Services (UK) Ltd v T & GWU (1976) [1985] ICR 615, [1976] IRLR 224, HL 15.31
General Billposting Co Ltd v Atkinson [1909] AC 118, [1908–10] All ER Rep 619, HL 11.24C
General Cleaning Contractors Ltd v Christmas [1953] AC 180, [1952] 2 All ER 1110, HL 12.26
General Engineering Services Ltd v Kingston and St Andrew Corpn [1988] 3 All ER 867, [1989] ICR 88, PC 6.76A
GMWU v Certification Officer [1977] 1 All ER 771, [1977] ICR 183 ..... 14.10
GMWU v Wailes Dove Bitumastic Ltd [1977] IRLR 45 .... 10.53, 15.16
George v Beecham Group Ltd [1977] IRLR 43 .... 9.52
Gibb v Unite Steel Companies Ltd [1957] 2 All ER 110, [1957] 1 WLR 668 .... 2.26
Gibson v National Union of Dyers, Bleachers and Textile Workers (1972) 13 KIR 143, 7 ITR 324 .... 6.70
Gilbert v I Goldstone Ltd [1977] 1 All ER 423, [1977] ICR 36, [1976] IRLR 257 .... 3.21
Gilbert v Kembridge Fibres [1984] ICR 188, [1984] IRLR 52 .... 1.10, 9.11
Gill v Cape Contracts Ltd [1985] IRLR 499 .... 3.6
Gill v Wall's Meat Co Ltd HSIB 22 .... 8.173
Glasgow v Independent Printing Co [1901] 2 IR 278 .... 2.10
Gledhow Autoparts Ltd v Delaney [1965] 3 All ER 288, [1965] 1 WLR 1366, CA 11.16
Glitz v Watford Electrical Co Ltd [1979] IRLR 89 .... 3.50
Global Plant Ltd v Secretary of State for Social Services [1972] 1 QB 139, [1971] 3 All ER 385 .... 2.35
Gorfin v Distressed Gentlefolk's Aid Association [1973] IRLR 290 ...... 8.180
Gorictree Ltd v Jenkinson [1984] IRLR 391 .... 8.185, 10.29
Goring v British Actors Equity Association [1987] IRLR 122 .... 14.21
Goult v Reay Electrical [1977] IRLIB 4.32
Gouriet v Union of Post Office Workers [1978] AC 435, [1977] 3 All ER 70 .... 15.117
Government Communications Staff Federation v Certification Officer [1993] ICR 163 .... 14.15A
Gozdzik v Chlidema Carpet Co IDS Brief 163 .... 8.111
Graham v ABF Ltd [1986] IRLR 90 .... 8.159A, 8.163
Graham v Co-operative Wholesale Society [1957] 1 All ER 654, [1957] 1 WLR 511, 101 Sol Jo 267 .... 6.44
Graham (Maurice) Ltd v Brunswick (1974) 16 KIR 158 .... 2.34
Grandmet International Services v Graham IDS Brief 151 .... 8.18
Gray v C and P Pembroke Ltd (1350/72) IDS Brief 10 .... 6.70, 8.151
Grazebrook (M and W) Ltd v Wallens [1973] 2 All ER 868, [1973] ICR 256, [1973] IRLR 139 .... 9.10
Green v Roberts [1992] IRLR 499 .... 8.23
Greenall Whitley plc v Carr [1985] ICR 451, [1985] IRLR 289 ...... 7.15, 8.103
Greer v Sketchley Ltd [1979] IRLR 445 .... 11.23
Gregory v Ford [1951] 1 All ER 121 .... 6.19
Grieg v Community Industry [1979] IRLR 158 .... 4.11
Grimaldi v Fonds des Maladies Professionnelles: C-322/88 [1989] ECR 4407, [1990] IRLR 400, ECJ 1.65
Grix v Munford Ltd [1977] IRLIB 3.54

PARA

Grundy Teddington Ltd v Willis [1976] ICR 323, [1976] IRLR 118, 11 ITR 26 .... 8.100, 8.165
Gubala v Crompton Parkinson Ltd [1977] IRLR 10 .... 4.31
Guinness (Arthur) Son & Co (Great Britain) Ltd v Green [1989] ICR 241, [1989] IRLR 288 .... 9.30
Gunton v London Borough of Richmond upon Thames [1981] Ch 448, [1980] ICR 755, [1980] IRLR 321, CA 2.67, 3.48, 7.9
Guy v Delanair (Car Heater) Ltd [1975] IRLR 73 .... 8.162
Gwynedd County Council v Jones [1986] ICR 833 .... 4.109

Habib v Elkington & Co Ltd [1981] ICR 435, [1981] IRLR 344 .... 1.21
Hadjioannou v Coral Casinos Ltd [1981] IRLR 352 .... 7.29, 8.141
Haigh (Catherine) Harlequin Hair Design v Seed [1990] IRLR 175 .... 8.212
Hairsine v Kingston upon Hull City Council [1992] ICR 212, [1992] IRLR 211 .... 13.52
Halford v Sharples [1992] 3 All ER 624, [1992] ICR 583, CA 9.16A
Hall v Lodge IRRR (LIB) 76 .... 7.57
Hall (Inspector of Taxes) v Lorimer [1992] 1 WLR 939, [1992] ICR 739 .... 2.36
Hamblin v London Borough of Ealing [1975] IRLR 354 .... 2.53
Hamerton v Tyne and Clyde Warehouses Ltd [1978] ICR 661 .... 2.35
Hamilton v Argyll and Clyde Health Board [1993] IRLR 99 .... 8.143A
Hamilton v Futura Floors Ltd [1990] IRLR 478, Ct of Sess 3.32A
Hampson v Department of Education and Science [1991] 1 AC 171, [1990] 2 All ER 513, [1990] ICR 511, HL 4.124B
Hancill v Marcon Engineering Ltd [1990] ICR 103, [1990] IRLR 51 .... 8.39
Hancock v Middleton [1982] ICR 416 .... 9.59
Handels-og Kontorfunktionaerernes Forbund i Danmark v Dansk Arbejdsgiverforening (acting for Danfoss): 109/88 [1991] ICR 74, [1989] IRLR 532, ECJ 4.70A
Handley v Mono Ltd [1979] ICR 147, [1978] IRLR 534 .... 4.89
Hanks v Ace High Productions Ltd [1978] ICR 1155, [1979] IRLR 32, 13 ITR 524 .... 9.30
Hanley v Pease & Partners Ltd [1915] 1 KB 698, [1914–15] All ER Rep 984 .... 7.43
Hannan v TNT-IPEC (UK) Ltd [1986] IRLR 165 .... 9.12
Hanson v Fashion Industries (Hartlepool) Ltd [1981] ICR 35, [1980] IRLR 393 .... 8.32
Hardwick v Leeds Area Health Authority [1975] IRLR 319 .... 3.39
Harris & Russell Ltd v Slingsby [1973] 3 All ER 31, [1973] ICR 454, [1973] IRLR 221 .... 8.57
Harris (Bevan) Ltd v Gair [1981] IRLR 520 .... 7.57, 8.109
Harris (Ipswich) Ltd v Harrison [1978] ICR 1256, [1978] IRLR 382 .... 7.19
Harris and Shepherd v Courage (Eastern) Ltd [1982] IRLR 509, CA 7.19
Harrison v George Wimpey & Co Ltd (1972) 7 ITR 188, NIRC 8.86
Harrison (Newcastle-under-Lyme) Ltd v Ramsey [1976] IRLR 135 .... 12.15
Hart v A R Marshall & Sons (Bulwell) Ltd [1978] 2 All ER 413, [1977] ICR 539, [1977] IRLR 51 .... 8.91, 8.115
Harvard Securities plc v Younghusband [1990] IRLR 17 .... 8.209
Harvey v Yankee Traveller Restaurant [1976] IRLR 35 .... 8.49
Haseltine Lake & Co v Dowler [1981] ICR 222, [1981] IRLR 25 .... 8.69
Haspell v Rostron and Johnson Ltd [1976] IRLR 50 .... 6.22
Haughton v Olau Line (UK) Ltd [1986] 2 All ER 47, [1986] ICR 357, CA: 4.56A

PARA
Hawkins v Ian Ross (Castings) Ltd [1970] 1 All ER 180 ... 6.31
Hayes v Malleable Working Men's Club and Institute [1985] ICR 703, [1985] IRLR 367 ... 4.35
Hayward v Cammell Laird Shipbuilders Ltd [1987] 1 All ER 503, [1986] ICR 862; on appeal [1988] QB 12, [1987] ICR 682, CA; revsd. [1988] AC 894, [1988] 2 All ER 257, HL ... 4.82
Hazell v Barvis Ltd ... 8.170
Hazells Offset Ltd v Luckett [1977] IRLR 430, 12 ITR 298 ... 8.202, 13.78
Heasmans v Clarity Cleaning Co Ltd [1987] IRLR 286, [1987] BTLC 174, CA ... 6.80
Heath v J F Longman (Meat Salesmen) Ltd [1973] 2 All ER 1228, [1973] ICR 407, [1973] IRLR 214 ... 8.196, 13.70
Heaton's Transport (St Helen's) Ltd v T & GWU [1973] AC 15, [1972] 3 All ER 101, [1972] ICR 308, HL ... 3.39, 15.31
Hedger v Davy & Co Ltd [1974] IRLR 138 ... 8.182
Hedley Byrne & Co Ltd v Heller & Partners Ltd [1964] AC 465, [1963] 2 All ER 575, HL ... 6.21
Hellyer Bros Ltd v McLeod [1987] 1 WLR 728, [1987] ICR 526, CA ... 2.66
Help the Aged Housing Association (Scotland Ltd v Vidler [1977] IRLR 104 ... 9.59
Hempell v W H Smith & Sons Ltd [1986] ICR 365, [1986] IRLR 95 ... 10.32
Hendry v Scottish Liberal Club [1977] IRLR 5 ... 4.131
Hennessy v Craigmyle & Co Ltd [1986] ICR 461, [1986] IRLR 300, CA ... 1.11
Henry v Ellerman City Lines Ltd [1984] IRLR 408 ... 8.168
Hepworths Ltd v Comerford ... 9.44
Hewcastle Catering Ltd v Ahmed [1992] ICR 626, [1991] IRLR 473, CA: 3.1D
High v British Railways Board [1979] IRLR 52 ... 7.59, 8.74
Higham v International Stores [1977] IRLIB ... 7.34
Highland Fabricators Ltd v McLaughlin [1984] IRLR 482 ... 8.195, 13.69
Hill v Archbold [1968] 1 QB 686, [1967] 3 All ER 110, CA ... 14.23A
Hill v C A Parsons & Co Ltd [1972] Ch 305, [1971] 3 All ER 1345, CA .. 6.3, 6.4, 6.11, 8.12
Hill (R F) Ltd v Mooney [1981] IRLR 258 ... 8.64
Hillier v Martintrux IRRR (LIB) 108 ... 8.18
Hillyer v St. Bartholomew's Hospital (Governors) [1909] 2 KB 820, 78 LJKB 958, CA ... 2.42
Hilton v Thomas Burton (Rhodes) Ltd [1961] 1 All ER 74, [1961] 1 WLR 705 ... 6.50, 6.81
Hilton International Hotels (UK) Ltd v Protopapa [1990] IRLR 316, EAT ... 8.67
Hindle v Percival Boats Ltd [1969] 1 All ER 836, 4 ITR 86, 6 KIR 462, CA ... 10.17
Hindle Gears Ltd v McGinty [1984] IRLR 477 ... 8.197, 13.71
Hitchcock v Post Office [1980] ICR 100 ... 2.27
Hivac Ltd v Park Royal Scientific Instruments Ltd [1946] Ch 169, [1946] 1 All ER 350, CA ... 6.71, 8.151
Hobson v GEC Telecommunications Ltd [1985] ICR 777 ... 4.128
Holden v Bradville Ltd [1985] IRLR 483 ... 8.159
Holliday v National Telephone Co [1899] 2 QB 392, [1895–9] All ER Rep 359, CA ... 6.74
Hollier v Plysu Ltd [1983] IRLR 260, CA ... 9.50
Hollister v NFU [1979] ICR 542, [1979] IRLR 238, CA ... 3.55, 8.183
Holt v Markham [1923] 1 KB 504, 92 LJKB 406, CA ... 5.136

PARA
Home Office v Ayres [1992] ICR 175, [1992] IRLR 59 .... 5.136
Home Office v Holmes [1984] 3 All ER 549, [1984] ICR 678 .... 4.12A
Home Office v Robinson [1982] ICR 31, [1981] IRLR 524 .... 2.17
Honeywell Ltd v Scott IDS Handbook 14 .... 4.86, 4.88
Hooper v British Railways Board [1988] IRLR 517, CA 3.1, 3.8B
Hopkins v National Union of Seamen [1985] ICR 268, [1985] IRLR 157: 14.23B
Horcal Ltd v Gatland [1983] IRLR 459 .... 6.62
Horizon Holidays Ltd v Grassi [1987] ICR 851, [1987] IRLR 371 .... 9.43
Horne v Lec Refrigeration Ltd [1965] 2 All ER 898 .... 6.45
Horsey v Dyfed County Council [1982] ICR 755, [1982] IRLR 395 .... 4.13
Horsley Smith and Sherry Ltd v Dutton [1977] ICR 594, [1977] IRLR 172, 12 ITR 351 .... 8.208
Hough v Leyland DAF Ltd [1991] ICR 696, [1991] IRLR 194 .... 15.9
Housman v Bishop of Ely 2.3
Howard v Department of National Savings [1981] 1 All ER 674, [1981] ICR 208, [1981] IRLR 40 .... 8.18
Howe v Gloucester and Severnside Co-operative Society [1975] IRLR 17 .... 8.8
Howgate v Fane Acoustics Ltd [1981] IRLR 161 .... 7.10C
Hudson v GMB [1990] IRLR 67 .... 14.22D
Hudson v Ridge Manufacturing Co Ltd [1957] 2 QB 348, [1957] 2 All ER 229 .... 6.41
Hughes v Gwynedd Area Health Authority [1978] ICR 161, [1977] IRLR 346 .... 5.20
Hulme v Ferranti Ltd [1918] 2 KB 426, 87 LJKB 938, 118 LT 719 .... 6.15
Hunt v British Railways Board [1979] IRLR 379 .... 8.75
Huntley v Thornton [1957] 1 All ER 234, [1957] 1 WLR 321 .... 15.46
Hurley v Mustoe [1981] ICR 490, [1981] IRLR 208 .... 4.13
Hutchins v British Railways Board [1974] IRLR 303 .... 7.14
Hutchinson v Enfield Rolling Mills Ltd [1981] IRLR 318 .... 8.127
Hutchinson v London and North Eastern Rly Co [1942] 1 KB 481, [1942] 1 All ER 330 .... 6.23
Hyland v J H Barker (North West) Ltd [1985] ICR 861, [1985] IRLR 403: 3.2

ITT Components (Europe) Ltd v Kolah [1977] ICR 740, [1977] IRLR 53: 2.51, 8.22
Iceland Frozen Foods Ltd v Jones [1982] IRLR 439 .... 8.100
Igbo v Johnson Matthey Chemicals Ltd [1986] ICR 505, [1986] IRLR 215, CA 8.95, 8.95A
Independent Research Services Ltd v Catterall [1993] ICR 1 .... 9.16A
Industrial Rubber Products v Gillon [1977] IRLR 389, 13 ITR 100 .... 8.64
Initial Services Ltd v Putterill [1968] 1 QB 396, [1967] 3 All ER 145, CA: 11.8
ILEA v Gravett [1988] IRLR 497 .... 9.35A
ILEA v Lloyd [1981] IRLR 394 .... 2.53
IMI Yorkshire Imperial Ltd v Olender [1982] ICR 69n 1.19A
Institute of Journalists v Daily Telegraph IDS Supp 22 .... 15.2
International Aviation Services (UK) Ltd t/a IAS Cargo Airlines v Jones [1979] ICR 371, [1979] IRLR 155 .... 9.67
International Computers Ltd v Kennedy [1981] IRLR 28 .... 10.7
International Computers v Whitley [1978] IRLR 318, 13 ITR 339 .... 9.15
International Paint Co Ltd v Cameron [1979] ICR 429, [1979] IRLR 62: 8.162
International Sports Co Ltd v Thomson [1980] IRLR 340 .... 8.126

PARA

Irani v Southampton and South West Hampshire Health Authority [1985] ICR 590, [1985] IRLR 203 ... 6.4, 8.2
Ironmonger v Movefield Ltd [1988] IRLR 461 ... 2.25, 8.96
Irvine v Prestcold Ltd [1981] IRLR 281 ... 4.62
Irving and Irving v Post Office [1987] IRLR 289, CA ... 4.40, 4.61, 4.120, 6.75

James v Eastleigh Borough Council [1990] 2 AC 751, [1990] 2 All ER 607, [1990] ICR 554, HL ... 4.9
James v Hepworth and Grandage Ltd [1968] 1 QB 94, [1967] 2 All ER 829, CA ... 6.31
Janata Bank v Ahmed [1981] ICR 791, [1981] IRLR 457, CA ... 6.61
Jarmain v E Pollard & Co Ltd (1967) 2 ITR 406 ... 10.39
Jeffries v BP Tanker Co Ltd [1974] IRLR 260 ... 3.43
Jenkins v Kingsgate (Clothing, Productions) Ltd [1980] IRLR 6, [1980] 1 CMLR 81 ... 1.67, 2.52A
Jenkins v Kingsgate (Clothing, Productions) Ltd (No 2) [1981] ICR 715, [1981] IRLR 388 ... 4.89
Jennings v Westwood Engineering Ltd [1975] IRLR 245 ... 2.38
Jeremiah v Ministry of Defence [1979] IRLR 436, CA ... 4.27, 4.30
Jewell v Neptune Concrete Ltd [1975] IRLR 147 ... 3.26, 6.15
Johnson v Cross [1977] ICR 872 ... 10.37
Johnson v Nottinghamshire Combined Police Authority [1974] 1 All ER 1082, [1974] ICR 170, [1974] IRLR 20, CA ... 10.15
Johnson v Tesco Stores Ltd [1976] IRLR 103 ... 8.183
Johnson v Timber Tailors (Midlands) Ltd [1978] IRLR 146 ... 4.110, 4.123
Johnson Matthey Metals v Harding [1978] IRLR 248, 13 ITR 407 ... 7.19
Jones v Associated Tunnelling Co Ltd [1981] IRLR 477 ... 3.21
Jones v British Rail Hovercraft Ltd [1974] IRLR 279 ... 7.23A
Jones v GEC Elliott Automation Ltd [1972] IRLR 111 ... 7.55, 8.111
Jones v Gwent County Council [1992] IRLR 521 ... 2.67, 6.5A
Jones v Lee and Guilding [1980] IRLR 67, CA ... 2.67, 3.48, 7.8
Jones v Lionite Specialities Ltd (1961) 105 Sol Jo 1082 ... 6.45
Jones v London Co-operative Society Ltd [1975] IRLR 110 ... 7.26
Jones v R M Douglas Construction Ltd [1975] IRLR 175 ... 7.61
Jones v University of Manchester. See University of Manchester v Jones
Jowett v Earl of Bradford (No. 2). See Bradford (Earl) v Jowett
Jowett (Angus) & Co v National Union of Tailors and Garment Workers [1985] ICR 646, [1985] IRLR 326 ... 5.119
Jupiter General Insurance Co v Shroff [1937] 3 All ER 67, PC ... 8.4

Kearney & Trecker Marwin Ltd v Varndell [1983] ICR 683, [1983] IRLR 335, CA ... 9.27
Keen v Dymo Ltd [1977] IRLR 118 ... 8.211
Kelly v Liverpool Maritime Terminals Ltd [1988] IRLR 310, CA ... 5.26, 8.96A
Kelly v NATSOPA [1915] 84 LJKB 2236, [1914–15] All ER Rep 576, CA ... 14.22A
Kendrick v Aerduct Productions [1974] IRLR 322 ... 8.53
Kenmir Ltd v Frizzell [1968] 1 All ER 414, [1968] 1 WLR 329 ... 5.111
Kenny v South Manchester College [1993] 265 ... 5.111

PARA
Kent County Council v Gilham [1985] ICR 233, [1985] IRLR 18, CA 8.104, 8.210
Kent Free Press v NGA [1987] IRLR 267 .... 15.83, 15.90
Kent Management Services Ltd v Butterfield [1992] ICR 272, [1992] IRLR 394 .... 5.131B
Kerr v Atkinson's Vehicles Ltd [1974] IRLR 36 .... 4.128
Kerr v Lister & Co Ltd [1977] IRLR 259 .... 4.76, 4.86
Kidd v DRG (UK) Ltd [1985] ICR 405, [1985] IRLR 190 .... 4.14
King v Great Britain-China Centre [1992] ICR 516, [1991] IRLR 513, CA 4.98, 4.123
King v Motorways Tyres and Accessories Ltd [1975] IRLR 51 .... 7.56
King v Webb's Poultry Products (Bradford) Ltd [1975] IRLR 135 .... 8.53
Kirkham v NATSOPA [1981] IRLR 244 .... 13.44
Knight v A-G [1979] ICR 194 .... 2.11
Knox v Down District Council [1981] IRLR 452 .... 3.26
Kolfor Plant Ltd v Wright [1982] IRLR 311 .... 5.25
Kores Manufacturing Co Ltd v Kolok Manufacturing Co Ltd [1959] Ch 108, [1958] 2 All ER 65, CA 11.25
Kowalska v Freie und Hansestadt Hamburg: C-33/89 [1992] ICR 29, [1990] IRLR 447, ECJ 2.52B
Kraft Foods Ltd v Fox [1978] ICR 311, [1977] IRLR 431, 13 ITR 96 ... 7.52, 9.46
Kwik-Fit (GB) Ltd v Lineham [1992] ICR 183, [1992] IRLR 156 .... 8.81A

Ladbroke Racing Ltd v Arnott [1983] IRLR 154, Ct of Sess 7.28, 8.143
Lake v Essex County Council [1979] ICR 577, [1979] IRLR 241, CA .. 2.51, 3.18
Lambeth London Borough v Commission for Racial Equality [1990] ICR 768, [1990] IRLR 231, CA 4.111
Land and Wilson v West Yorkshire Metropolitan County Council [1984] ICR 334, [1981] IRLR 87, CA 3.59
Landsorganisationen i Danmark v Ny Mølle Kro: 287/86 [1989] ICR 330, [1989] IRLR 37, ECJ 5.109
Langston v Chrysler United Kingdom [1974] 1 All ER 980, [1974] ICR 180 .... 6.11, 6.12
Lansing Linde Ltd v Kerr [1991] 1 All ER 418, [1991] 1 WLR 251, [1991] IRLR 80, CA 11.24B
Lanton Leisure Ltd v White and Gibson [1987] IRLR 119 .... 8.18
Larkfield of Chepstow Ltd v Milne [1988] ICR 1 .... 9.60A
Latimer v AEC Ltd [1953] AC 643, [1953] 2 All ER 449, HL 6.43
Laughton and Hawley v Bapp Industrial Supplies Ltd [1986] ICR 634, [1986] IRLR 245 .... 8.7, 11.2
Laurie v Fairburn IDS Brief 109 .... 8.138
Lavery v Plessey Telecommunications Ltd [1983] ICR 534, [1983] IRLR 202, CA 5.25
Lawlor v UPOW [1965] Ch 712, [1965] 1 All ER 353 .... 14.22C
Lazarus v Firestone Tyre and Rubber Co (1963) Times, 2 May 6.24
Lee v GEC Plessey Telecommunications [1993] IRLR 383 .... 3.31
Lee v Lee's Air Farming Ltd [1961] AC 12, [1960] 3 All ER 420, PC 2.6
Lee v Nottinghamshire County Council [1980] IRLR 284, CA 10.16
Lee v Showmen's Guild of Great Britain [1952] 2 QB 329, [1952] 1 All ER 1175, [1952] 1 TLR 1115, CA 14.22A
Lee Ting Sang v Chung Chi-Keung [1990] 2 AC 374, [1990] ICR 409, PC: 2.36

PARA
Lesney Products & Co Ltd v Nolan [1977] ICR 235, [1977] IRLR 77, 12 ITR 6, CA 10.16
Lethaby v Horsman Andrew and Knill Ltd [1975] IRLR 119 .... 7.39
Letts (Charles) & Co Ltd v Howard [1976] IRLR 248, 11 ITR 164 .... 8.108
Leverton v Clwyd County Council [1989] AC 706, [1989] 1 All ER 78, [1989] ICR 33, HL 4.70B, 4.91A
Lewis v Motorworld Garages Ltd [1986] ICR 157, [1985] IRLR 465, CA: 8.73
Lewis v Surrey County Council [1988] AC 323, [1987] ICR 982, HL .. 2.24, 2.52
Lewis Shops Group v Wiggins [1973] ICR 335, [1973] IRLR 205, 14 KIR 528 .... 7.7, 8.148
Leyland Vehicles Ltd v Reston [1981] ICR 403, [1981] IRLR 19 .... 3.35
Lifeguard Assurance Co Ltd v Zadrozny [1977] IRLR 56, 12 ITR 141 ... 8.160
Lignacite Products Ltd v Krollman [1979] IRLR 22 .... 10.39
Lindsay v Fife Forge Co [1976] IRLR 47 .... 7.26
Linfood Cash and Carry Ltd v Thomson [1989] ICR 518, [1989] IRLR 235 .... 7.14, 7.19A
Links (A) & Co Ltd v Rose [1991] IRLR 353, Ct of Sess 8.115A
Lister v Romford Ice and Cold Storage Co Ltd [1957] AC 555, [1957] 1 All ER 125, HL 6.61
Litster v Forth Dry Dock and Engineering Co Ltd [1990] AC 546, [1989] 1 All ER 1134, [1989] ICR 341, HL 5.105, 5.117, 8.186
Litster v M Thom & Sons Ltd [1975] IRLR 47 .... 8.130
Littlewoods Organisation Ltd v Egenti [1976] ICR 516, [1976] IRLR 334 .... 7.3A, 8.108
Littlewoods Organisation Ltd v Harris [1978] 1 All ER 1026, [1977] 1 WLR 1472, CA 11.19
Liverpool City Council v Irwin [1977] AC 239, [1976] 2 All ER 39, HL ... 6.7A
Livingstone v Hepworth Refractories plc [1992] ICR 287, [1992] IRLR 63 .... 9.11B
Lloyd v Brassey [1969] 2 QB 98, [1969] 1 All ER 382, 5 KIR 393, CA 5.111
Lloyd v Grace, Smith & Co [1912] AC 716, [1911–13] All ER Rep 51, HL: 6.79
Lloyds Bank Ltd v Secretary of State for Employment [1979] 2 All ER 573, [1979] ICR 258, [1979] IRLR 41 .... 8.31
Lock International plc v Beswick [1989] 3 All ER 373, [1989] 1 WLR 1268, [1989] IRLR 481 .... 11.6, 11.26
Logan Salton v Durham County Council [1989] IRLR 99 .... 8.95A
London Ambulance Service v Charlton [1992] ICR 773, [1992] IRLR 510 .... 13.50
London International College v Sen [1992] IRLR 292 .... 9.3
London Passenger Transport Board v Moscrop [1942] AC 332, [1942] 1 All ER 97, HL 3.34
London Transport Executive v Clarke [1981] ICR 355, [1981] IRLR 166, CA 3.15, 8.84, 8.87
London Underground Ltd v National Union of Railwaymen [1989] IRLR 341 .... 15.60
Longley v National Union of Journalists [1987] IRLR 109, CA 7.16A
Lotus Cars Ltd v Sutcliffe and Stratton [1982] IRLR 381, CA 10.45
Louies v Coventry Hood and Seating Co Ltd [1990] ICR 54, [1990] IRLR 324 .... 7.14
Lowndes v Specialist Heavy Engineering Ltd [1977] ICR 1, [1976] IRLR 246, 11 ITR 253 .... 6.61, 8.108
Lucas v Norton of London Ltd [1984] IRLR 86 .... 5.29
Lucas (T) & Co Ltd v Mitchell [1974] Ch 129, [1972] 3 All ER 689, CA ... 11.24

PARA

Luce v Bexley London Borough Council [1990] ICR 591, [1990] IRLR 422 ..... 13.54
Lumley v Gye (1853) 2 E & B 216, [1843–60] All ER Rep 208 ..... 15.30
Lynock v Cereal Packaging Ltd [1988] ICR 670, [1988] IRLR 510 ..... 8.124A

M and S Drapers v Reynolds [1956] 3 All ER 814, [1957] 1 WLR 9, CA 11.16
Mabirizi v National Hospital for Nervous Diseases [1990] ICR 281, [1990] IRLR 133 ..... 9.52
McAlwane v Broughton Estates Ltd [1973] 2 All ER 299, [1973] ICR 470 ..... 10.9
McAndrew v Prestwich Circuits Ltd [1990] IRLR 191, 1990 SLT 654, Ct of Sess 9.44
McArdle v Andmac Roofing Co [1967] 1 All ER 583, [1967] 1 WLR 356, CA 2.43
Macarthys Ltd v Smith [1981] QB 180, [1980] ICR 672, CA 1.67, 4.96
McCaffrey v E E Jeavons & Co Ltd (1967) 2 ITR 636 ..... 10.5A
MacCarthy v Daily Mirror Newspapers [1949] 1 All ER 801, 113 JP 229, 65 TLR 501, CA 3.23
McClelland v Northern Ireland General Health Services Board [1957] 2 All ER 129, [1957] 1 WLR 594, HL 2.20
McCormick v Horsepower Ltd [1981] 2 All ER 746, [1981] ICR 535, [1981] IRLR 217, CA 8.193, 13.66
McCree v Tower Hamlets London Borough Council [1992] ICR 99, [1992] IRLR 56 ..... 5.129
Macer v Abafast [1990] ICR 234, [1990] IRLR 137 ..... 8.44
McGhee v Transport and General Workers' Union [1985] ICR 503, [1985] IRLR 198; affd [1985] LS Gaz R 3696, CA 13.19
McGregor v Gibbings Amusements Ltd [1975] ITR 64 ..... 9.59
McKechnie v UBM Building Supplies (Southern) Ltd [1991] ICR 710, [1991] IRLR 283 ..... 4.49
McKellar v Bolton [1979] IRLR 59 ..... 7.4
McKindley v William Hill (Scotland) Ltd [1985] IRLR 492 ..... 10.32
MacLaren v Home Office [1990] IRLR 338, CA 2.70
MacLea v Essex Line Ltd (1933) 45 Ll L Rep 254 ..... 3.30
McLean v Paris Travel Service Ltd [1976] IRLR 202 ..... 4.33
McLory v Post Office [1992] ICR 758 ..... 3.23, 6.12, 7.23C
McLoughlin v Gordons (Stockport) Ltd [1978] ICR 561, [1978] IRLR 127 ..... 4.97A
MacNeilage v Arthur Roye (Turf Accountants) Ltd [1976] IRLR 88 ..... 9.41
McPhail v Gibson [1977] ICR 42, [1974] IRLR 254 ..... 9.47
McPherson v Rathgael Centre for Children and Young People and Northern Ireland Office (Training Schools Branch) [1991] IRLR 206, NI CA 4.92A
MacRae (Kenneth) & Co Ltd v Dawson [1984] IRLR 5 ..... 10.38
MacWilliam v Sir William Arroll Ltd [1962] 1 All ER 623, [1962] 1 WLR 295, HL 6.39
Mailway (Southern) Ltd v Willsher [1978] ICR 511, [1978] IRLR 322 ..... 2.52
Managers (Holborn) Ltd v Hohne [1977] IRLR 230, 12 ITR 379 ..... 10.14
Mandla v Dowell Lee [1983] 2 AC 548, [1983] 1 All ER 1062, HL 4.106
Manifold Industries Ltd v Sims [1991] ICR 504, [1991] IRLR 242 ..... 13.65
Marder v ITT Distributors Ltd [1976] IRLR 105 ..... 8.119

PARA

Maris v Rotherham Corpn [1974] 2 All ER 776, [1974] ICR 435, [1974] IRLR 147 .... 9.49
Market Investigations Ltd v Minister of Social Security [1969] 2 QB 173, [1968] 3 All ER 732 .... 2.30, 2.35
Marleasing SA v La Comercial Internacional de Alimentacion SA: C-106/89 [1990] ECR I-4135, [1992] 1 CMLR 305, ECJ 1.54, 4.35C
Marler (E T) Ltd v Robertson [1974] ICR 72 .... 1.23
Marley v Forward Trust Group Ltd [1986] ICR 891, [1986] IRLR 369, CA: 3.29
Marley Homecare Ltd v Dutton [1981] IRLR 380 .... 7.19
Marley Tile Co Ltd v Shaw [1980] ICR 72, [1980] IRLR 25, CA 13.39, 13.43
Marriott v Oxford and District Co-operative Society Ltd (No 2) [1970] 1 QB 186, [1969] 3 All ER 1126, CA 3.51, 10.5A
Marsden v Fairey Stainless Ltd [1979] IRLR 103 .... 8.192, 13.64
Marsh v Judge International HSIB 15 .... 8.147
Marshall v English Electric Co Ltd [1945] 1 All ER 653, 173 LT 134, 109 JP 145, CA 7.44
Marshall v Gotham Co Ltd [1954] AC 360, [1954] 1 All ER 937, HL 12.24
Marshall v Harland and Wolff Ltd [1972] 2 All ER 715, [1972] ICR 101, [1972] IRLR 90 .... 8.89, 8.122, 10.8
Marshall v Industrial Systems and Control Ltd [1992] IRLR 294 .... 8.7, 11.2
Marshall v Southampton and South West Hampshire Area Health Authority: 152/84 [1986] QB 401, [1986] 2 All ER 584, ECJ 1.53, 4.41, 8.18
Marshall (Thomas) (Exports) Ltd v Guinle [1979] Ch 227, [1978] ICR 905, [1978] IRLR 174 .... 11.7
Martin v MBS Fastenings (Glynwed) Distribution Ltd [1983] ICR 511, [1983] IRLR 198, CA 8.50, 8.83
Martin v Scottish Transport and General Workers' Union [1952] 1 All ER 691, [1952] 1 TLR 677, HL 14.20
Martin v Solus Schall [1979] IRLR 7 .... 3.14
Martin v Yeoman Aggregates Ltd [1983] ICR 314, [1983] IRLR 49 .... 8.57
Mason v Provident Clothing and Supply Co Ltd [1913] AC 274, [1911–13] All ER Rep 400, HL 11.22
Massey v Crown Life Insurance Co [1978] 2 All ER 576, [1978] ICR 590, [1978] IRLR 31, CA 2.33
Mathewson v R B Wilson Dental Laboratory Ltd [1988] IRLR 512 .... 8.150
Mathieson v Noble & Son Ltd [1972] IRLR 76 .... 8.172
Mawson v Leadgate Engineering Ltd [1972] IRLR 105 .... 9.23
Maxwell v Walter Howard Designs Ltd [1975] IRLR 77 .... 8.89
May (Greg) (Carpet Fitters and Contractors) Ltd v Dring [1990] ICR 188, [1990] IRLR 19 .... 5.133
Meade v Haringey London Borough Council [1979] 2 All ER 1016, [1979] ICR 494, CA 15.53
Mears v Safecar Security Ltd [1983] QB 54, [1982] ICR 626, CA 3.17
Meek v City of Birmingham District Council [1987] IRLR 250, CA 9.32
Meer v London Borough of Tower Hamlets [1988] IRLR 399, CA 4.103A
Meikle v McPhail [1983] IRLR 351 .... 8.155, 8.186
Menzies v Smith and McLaurin Ltd [1980] IRLR 180 .... 13.51
Mercury Communications Ltd v Scott-Garner [1984] Ch 37, [1984] 1 All ER 179, CA 15.39
Meridian Ltd v Gomersall [1977] ICR 597, [1977] IRLR 425, 12 ITR 323: 7.27
Mersey Docks and Harbour Board v Coggins and Griffith (Liverpool) Ltd [1947] AC 1, [1946] 2 All ER 345, HL 2.45, 2.46

PARA

Merseyside and North Wales Electricity Board v Taylor [1975] ICR 185, [1975] IRLR 60, 10 ITR 52 ..... 8.120
Messenger Newspapers Group Ltd v NGA [1984] 1 All ER 293, [1984] ICR 345, CA 15.36
Methven v Cow Industrial Polymers Ltd [1980] ICR 463, [1980] IRLR 289, CA 4.87
Michael (John) Design plc v Cooke [1987] 2 All ER 332, [1987] ICR 445, CA 11.17
Middlebrook Mushrooms Ltd v T & GWU (1993) Times, 18 January, CA 15.108
Midland Plastics Ltd v Till [1983] ICR 118, [1983] IRLR 9 ..... 8.196, 8.198, 13.70, 13.73
Mikkelsen v Danmols Inventar A/S: 105/84 [1986] 1 CMLR 316, ECJ 5.106
Miles v Wakefield Metropolitan District Council [1987] AC 539, [1987] ICR 368, HL 2.12, 5.136
Millbrook Furnishing Industries Ltd v McIntosh [1981] IRLR 309 ..... 10.5
Miller v Hamworthy Engineering Ltd [1986] ICR 846, [1986] IRLR 461, CA 3.53, 6.14
Miller v Harry Thornton (Lollies) Ltd [1978] IRLR 430 ..... 2.52
Miller v Shanks and McEwan IDS Handbook 12 ..... 8.75
Milthorn Toleman Ltd v Ford [1978] IRLR 306 ..... 8.78
Mining Supplies (Longwall) Ltd v Baker [1988] IRLR 417, [1988] ICR 676 ..... 8.161
Minter v Wellingborough Foundries Ltd [1981] IDS Brief 202 ..... 8.147
Mirror Group Newspapers Ltd v Gunning [1986] ICR 145, [1986] IRLR 27, CA 4.18
Moncrieff (D G) (Farmers) v MacDonald [1978] IRLR 112, 13 ITR 222 ..... 9.25
Moncur v International Paint Co Ltd [1978] IRLR 223 ..... 9.46
Mont (J A) (UK) Ltd v Mills [1993] IRLR 172, CA 11.8E
Moody v Telefusion Ltd [1978] IRLR 311 ..... 8.180
Moon v Homeworthy Furniture (Northern) Ltd [1977] ICR 117, [1976] IRLR 298, 120 Sol Jo 603 ..... 8.171
Moore v C & A Modes [1981] IRLR 71 ..... 8.150
Moore v Duport Furniture Products Ltd [1982] ICR 84, [1982] IRLR 31, HL 1.10
Mordecai v Jacob Beatus Ltd [1975] IRLR 170 ..... 3.32
Morley's of Brixton Ltd v Minott [1982] ICR 444, [1982] IRLR 270 ..... 7.18, 8.139
Morris v Griffiths [1977] ICR 153 ..... 9.59
Morris v London Iron and Steel Co Ltd [1987] 2 All ER 496, [1987] ICR 855, CA 9.19
Morris v Martin & Sons Ltd [1966] 1 QB 716, [1965] 2 All ER 725, CA 6.79
Morris v Scott and Knowles [1976] IRLR 238 ..... 4.36
Morris v Secretary of State for Employment [1985] ICR 522, [1985] IRLR 297 ..... 5.88
Morris (Herbert) Ltd v Saxelby [1916] 1 AC 688, [1916–17] All ER Rep 305, HL 11.13, 11.22
Morrish v Henlys (Folkestone) Ltd [1973] 2 All ER 137, [1973] ICR 482, [1973] IRLR 61 ..... 6.57
Morton Sundour Fabrics Ltd v Shaw (1966) 2 ITR 84, 2 KIR 1 ..... 10.7
Moyes v Hylton Castle Working Men's Social Club and Institute Ltd [1986] IRLR 482 ..... 7.21
Muffett (S H) Ltd v Head [1987] ICR 1, [1986] IRLR 488 ..... 9.42
Muggridge and Slade v East Anglia Plastics Ltd [1973] IRLR 163 ..... 8.176

PARA

Muir (William) (Bond 9) Ltd v Lamb [1985] IRLR 95 .... 7.14, 9.44
Mullett v Brush Electrical Machines Ltd [1977] ICR 829 .... 9.41
Munro v Allied Suppliers [1977] IRLIB 4.25, 4.29
Murco Petroleum Ltd v Forge [1987] ICR 282, [1987] IRLR 50 .... 8.71
Murphy v Bord Telecom Eirann: 157/86 [1988] ICR 445, [1988] IRLR 267, ECJ 4.83A
Murray v British Rail IDS Handbook 12 .... 7.11
Murray v East Lothian Regional Council IDS Handbook 14 .... 4.86
Murray v Powertech (Scotland) Ltd [1992] IRLR 257 .... 4.62

NAAFI v Varley [1977] 1 All ER 840, [1977] ICR 11, [1976] IRLR 408 .. 4.86
NATFHE v Manchester City Council [1978] ICR 1190 .... 10.47, 15.6
NRG Victory Reinsurance Ltd v Alexander [1992] ICR 675 .... 9.11C
Nagle v Feilden [1966] 2 QB 633, [1966] 1 All ER 689, CA 6.11, 13.4, 13.6, 14.20
Nairne v Highland and Islands Fire Brigade [1989] IRLR 366, 1989 SLT 754, Ct of Sess 9.45
NALGO v Killorn [1991] ICR 1, [1990] IRLR 464 .... 13.9
National Coal Board v Galley [1958] 1 All ER 91, [1958] 1 WLR 16, CA: 3.26
National Coal Board v NUM [1986] ICR 736, [1986] IRLR 439 ... 3.25A, 15.97
National Coal Board v Ridgway [1987] 2 All ER 582, [1987] ICR 641, CA 13.41
National Grid Co plc v Virdee [1992] IRLR 555 .... 9.15A
NUGSAT v Albury Bros Ltd [1979] ICR 84, [1978] IRLR 504, CA ... 10.54, 15.7
NUPE v General Cleaning Contractors [1976] IRLR 362 .... 10.52, 15.14
NUT v Avon County Council [1978] ICR 626, [1978] IRLR 55 ..... 10.49, 15.10
NUTGW v Charles Ingram & Co Ltd [1978] 1 All ER 1271, [1977] ICR 530, [1977] IRLR 147 .... 10.54, 15.7
National Vulcan Engineering Insurance Group Ltd v Wade [1979] QB 132, [1978] ICR 800, [1978] IRLR 225, CA 4.88, 4.93
Natt v Hillingdon Area Health Authority 7.10A
Naylor v Orton & Smith Ltd [1983] ICR 665, [1983] IRLR 233 ..... 8.198, 13.73
Neale v Hereford and Worcester County Council [1986] ICR 471, [1986] IRLR 168, CA 9.64
Nelson v BBC [1977] ICR 649, [1977] IRLR 148, CA 10.11
Nelson v BBC (No 2) [1980] ICR 110, [1979] IRLR 346, CA 9.46
Nelson and Woollett v Post Office [1978] IRLR 548 .... 3.32, 3.59
Nethermere (St. Neots) Ltd v Gardiner [1984] ICR 612, [1984] IRLR 240, CA 2.35
New Victoria Hospital v Ryan [1993] ICR 201 .... 9.16B
Newalls Insulation Co v Blakeman [1976] ICR 543, [1976] IRLR 303 ... 7.49
Newham London Borough v Ward [1985] IRLR 509, CA 9.6
Newham London Borough Council v NALGO [1993] ICR 189, CA 15.64
Newland v Simons and Willer (Hairdressers) Ltd [1981] ICR 521, [1981] IRLR 359 .... 3.4
Newlands v Howard & Co Ltd [1973] IRLR 9 .... 8.8
Newman v Alarmco Ltd [1976] IRLR 45 .... 8.147
News Group Newspapers Ltd v SOGAT '82 [1986] ICR 716, [1986] IRLR 227, CA 15.52, 15.106
Nicoll v Nocorrode Ltd [1981] ICR 348, [1981] IRLR 163 .... 8.21
Nimz v Freie und Hansestadt Hamburg: C-184/89 [1991] IRLR 222, ECJ 4.94A

PARA

Noble v David Gold & Son (Holdings) Ltd [1980] ICR 543, [1980] IRLR 252, CA 4.74
Noel (Auguste) Ltd v Curtis [1990] ICR 604, [1990] IRLR 326 ..... 7.50A
Nokes v Doncaster Amalgamated Collieries Ltd [1940] AC 1014, [1940] 3 All ER 549, 109 LJKB 865, HL 5.100
Nolan v Dental Manufacturing Co [1958] 2 All ER 449, [1958] 1 WLR 936 ..... 6.40
Norbrook Laboratories Ltd v King [1984] IRLR 200, NI CA 15.109
Nordenfelt v Maxim Nordenfelt Guns and Ammunition Co [1894] AC 535, [1891–4] All ER Rep 1, HL 11.21
Norris v Southampton City Council [1982] ICR 177, [1982] IRLR 141 ..... 8.87
North v Pavleigh Ltd [1977] IRLR 461 ..... 5.2
North East Coast Shiprepairers v Secretary of State for Employment [1978] ICR 755, [1978] IRLR 149 ..... 4.7
North Riding Garages Ltd v Butterwick [1967] 2 QB 56, [1967] 1 All ER 644, 1 KIR 782 ..... 10.17
North West Thames Regional Health Authority v Noone [1987] IRLR 357; revsd. [1988] ICR 813, [1988] IRLR 195, CA 4.98, 4.122A
Norwest Holst Group Administration Ltd v Harrison [1985] ICR 668, [1985] IRLR 240, CA 8.77
Notcutt v Universal Equipment Co (London) Ltd [1986] 3 All ER 582, [1986] ICR 414, [1986] IRLR 218, CA 8.12, 8.88
Nothman v London Borough of Barnet [1979] 1 All ER 142, [1979] ICR 111, HL 9.35A
Nova Plastics Ltd v Froggatt [1982] IRLR 146 ..... 8.151

Oakley v Labour Party [1988] ICR 403, [1988] IRLR 34, CA 8.59
O'Brien v Associated Fire Alarms Ltd [1969] 1 All ER 93, 3 ITR 182, 3 KIR 223, CA 10.13
O'Brien v Prudential Assurance Co Ltd [1979] IRLR 140 ..... 8.175
O'Conner v Kontiki Travel IDS Brief 98 ..... 4.55
Office Angels Ltd v Rainer-Thomas [1991] IRLR 214, CA 11.17A, 11.23A
O'Grady v M Saper Ltd [1940] 2 KB 469, [1940] 3 All ER 527, CA 3.5, 3.17
O'Hare and Rutherford v Rotaprint Ltd [1980] ICR 94, [1980] IRLR 47 ..... 10.10, 10.18
O'Keefe v Bristol Channel Ship Repairers Ltd [1977] IRLIB 8.162
O'Keefe v Southampton City Council [1988] ICR 419, [1988] IRLR 424: 9.29A
O'Kelly v Trusthouse Forte plc [1984] QB 90, [1983] 3 All ER 456, [1983] ICR 728, CA 2.36
Oliver v J P Malnick & Co [1983] 3 All ER 795, [1983] ICR 708, [1983] IRLR 456 ..... 2.56
Oliver v Sperry Vickers [1975] IRLR 358 ..... 8.177
102 Social Club and Institute Ltd v Bickerton [1977] ICR 911 ..... 2.11
Open University v Triesman [1978] ICR 524, [1978] IRLR 114 ..... 8.18
Opie v John Gubbins (Insurance Brokers) Ltd [1978] IRLR 540 ..... 8.22
Ord v Maidstone and District Hospital Management Committee [1974] 2 All ER 343, [1974] ICR 369, [1974] IRLR 80 ..... 8.18
O'Reilly v Hotpoint Ltd (1969) 5 ITR 68, 7 KIR 374 ..... 8.122
Osborne v Bill Taylor of Huyton Ltd [1982] ICR 168, [1982] IRLR 17, DC 12.27
Ottoman Bank v Chakarian [1930] AC 277, 99 LJPC 97, 142 LT 465, PC 6.57

PARA

Outlook Supplies Ltd v Parry [1978] 2 All ER 707, [1978] ICR 388, [1978] IRLR 12 .... 4.88
Owen v Crown House Engineering Ltd [1973] 3 All ER 618, [1973] ICR 511, [1973] IRLR 233 .... 9.3
Oxley (Graham) Tool Steels Ltd v Firth [1980] IRLR 135 .... 8.67

P v Nottinghamshire County Council [1992] ICR 706, [1992] IRLR 362, CA 7.18A, 7.59A, 8.139A
Page v Freight Hire (Tank Haulage) Ltd [1981] 1 All ER 394, [1981] ICR 299, [1981] IRLR 13 .... 4.53B, 12.25
Palmanor Ltd t/a Chaplins Nightclub v Cedron [1978] ICR 1008, [1978] IRLR 303, 13 ITR 450 .... 8.67
Palmer v Associated British Ports. See Associated British Ports v Palmer
Palmer v Southend-on-Sea Borough Council [1984] 1 All ER 945, [1984] ICR 372, [1984] IRLR 119, CA 7.10B, 9.2, 9.3
Palmer v Vauxhall Motors Ltd [1977] ICR 24 .... 7.36, 8.147
Panesar v Nestlé & Co Ltd [1980] ICR 144, [1980] IRLR 64, CA 4.103B
Paris v Stepney Borough Council [1951] AC 376, [1951] 1 All ER 42, HL 6.24, 6.30
Parker v Clifford Dunn Ltd [1979] ICR 463, [1979] IRLR 56 .... 8.135
Parker v Orr (1966) 1 ITR 488, 1 KIR 513 .... 10.4
Parker v Westland Helicopters Ltd IDS Supp 15 .... 8.121
Parker Foundry Ltd v Slack [1992] ICR 302, [1992] IRLR 11, CA 9.45A
Parkers Bakeries Ltd v Palmer [1977] IRLR 215, 12 ITR 111 .... 7.17, 8.147
Parr v Whitbread plc (t/a Threshers Wine Merchants) [1990] ICR 427, [1990] IRLR 39 .... 8.178A
Parry v Holst & Co (1968) 3 LTR 317 .... 3.39, 3.58
Parsons v Albert J Parsons & Sons Ltd [1979] ICR 271, [1979] IRLR 117, CA 2.7
Parsons v Fisons Ltd [1977] HSIB 8.129
Parsons v LCC (1893) 9 TLR 619 .... 7.62
Parsons (CA) & Co Ltd v McLoughlin [1978] IRLR 65 .... 8.147
Pascoe v Hallen and Medway [1975] IRLR 116 .... 4.128
Paterson v Barrett Developments (Aberdeen) Ltd [1977] IRLR 214, 12 ITR 295 .... 7.55
Paton Calvert & Co Ltd v Westerside [1979] IRLR 108 .... 10.23
Payne v Spook Erection Ltd [1984] IRLR 219 .... 6.58
Peake v Automotive Products Ltd [1978] QB 223, [1978] 1 All ER 106, CA 3.43, 4.27
Pearce v University of Aston in Birmingham [1991] 2 All ER 461, CA 2.20
Pearson v Kent County Council [1992] ICR 20, [1992] IRLR 110 .... 8.27A
Pel Ltd v Modgill [1980] IRLR 142 .... 4.101
Pengilly v North Devon Farmers Ltd [1973] IRLR 41 .... 6.59, 8.144
Pennington v Minister of Social Security 2.38
Pepper v Webb [1969] 2 All ER 216, [1969] 1 WLR 514, CA 6.56, 8.5
Pepper and Hope v Daish [1980] IRLR 13 .... 3.22, 8.72
Perez v Mercury Display Ltd [1977] IRLIB 10.51, 15.13
Perkins (Dorothy) Ltd v Dance [1977] IRLR 226 .... 4.95
Petrie v MacFisheries Ltd [1940] 1 KB 258, [1939] 4 All ER 281, CA 3.12
Pickstone v Freemans plc [1987] 3 All ER 756, [1987] ICR 867, CA; affd. [1989] AC 66, [1988] 2 All ER 803, HL 4.83

PARA
Piddington v Bates [1960] 3 All ER 660, [1961] 1 WLR 162 .... 15.104
Piggott Bros & Co Ltd v Jackson [1992] ICR 85, [1991] IRLR 309, CA ... 9.64A
Piller (Anton) KG v Manufacturing Processes Ltd [1976] Ch 55, [1976] 1 All ER 779, CA 11.26
Piperdy v UEM Parker Glass IDS Supp 23 .... 4.123
Pirelli General Cable Works Ltd v Murray [1979] IRLR 190 .... 7.14
Pirie and Hunter v Crawford IDS Brief 155 .... 7.43
Pitts v Revertex 7.24
Plowman v Ash [1964] 2 All ER 10, [1964] 1 WLR 568, CA 11.14
Poland v John Parr & Sons [1927] 1 KB 236, [1926] All ER Rep 177, CA 6.77, 6.78
Polentarutti v Autokraft Ltd [1991] ICR 757, [1991] IRLR 457 .... 8.78, 9.49A
Polkey v A E Dayton Services Ltd [1988] AC 344, [1987] 3 All ER 974, [1988] ICR 142, HL 7.5, 8.99, 8.160
Poparm Ltd v Weeks [1984] IRLR 388 .... 8.38
Port of London Authority v Payne [1993] ICR 30, [1992] IRLR 447 ..... 9.35B
Porter v NUJ [1979] IRLR 404, HL 14.22B
Portsea Island Mutual Co-operative Society v Leyland [1978] IRLR 556: 6.82
Post Office v Holder and Mitchel IDS Handbook 12 .... 2.52
Post Office v Moore [1981] ICR 623 .... 9.4
Post Office v Mughal [1977] ICR 763, [1977] IRLR 178, 12 ITR 130 ..... 2.53
Post Office v Roberts [1980] IRLR 347 .... 3.24
Post Office v Union of Communication Workers [1990] 1 WLR 981, [1990] ICR 258, CA 15.58
Potter v Hunt Contracts Ltd [1992] ICR 337, [1992] IRLR 108 .... 5.129
Powell v Brent London Borough Council [1988] ICR 176, [1987] IRLR 466, CA 2.67, 6.5
Power Packing Casemakers v Faust [1983] ICR 292, [1983] IRLR 117, CA 8.198, 13.73
Premier Motors (Medway) Ltd v Total Oil Great Britain Ltd [1984] ICR 58, [1983] IRLR 471 .... 5.109, 10.29
President of the Methodist Conference v Parfitt [1984] ICR 176, [1984] IRLR 141, CA 2.13, 2.38
Presley v Llanelli Borough Council [1979] ICR 419, [1979] IRLR 381 ... 8.76
Prestige Group plc, Re, CRE v Prestige Group plc [1984] 1 WLR 335, [1984] ICR 473, [1984] IRLR 166, HL 4.125
Price v Civil Service Commission [1978] 1 All ER 1228, [1978] ICR 27, [1977] IRLR 291 .... 4.15
Printers and Finishers Ltd v Holloway [1964] 3 All ER 54n, [1965] 1 WLR 1 .... 11.6
Pritchett and Dyjasek v J McIntyre Ltd [1987] ICR 359, [1987] IRLR 18, CA 7.4, 7.14
Procter v British Gypsum Ltd [1992] IRLR 7 .... 8.143A
Property Guards Ltd v Taylor and Kershaw [1982] IRLR 175 .... 4.132
Provident Financial Group plc v Hayward [1989] 3 All ER 298, [1989] ICR 160, CA 6.12, 11.8D, 11.8E
Pruden v Cunard Ellerman Ltd [1993] IRLR 317 .... 9.4C
Pyle v Cleeson Civil Engineering Ltd IDS Handbook 12 .... 8.164

Qualcast (Wolverhampton) Ltd v Haynes [1959] AC 743, [1959] 2 All ER 38, HL 6.40

PARA
Quinn v Leathem [1901] AC 595, [1900–3] All ER Rep 1 .... 15.32
Quinnen v Hovells [1984] ICR 525, [1984] IRLR 227 .... 2.25A, 4.18, 4.70

R v Boal [1992] 1 QB 591, [1992] ICR 495, CA 12.58
R v Certification Officer, ex p EPEA [1990] ICR 682, [1990] IRLR 398, HL 14.40
R v Certification Officer, ex p Royal College of Nursing [1991] IRLR 258, DC 14.40
R v CRE, ex p Westminster City Council [1984] IRLR 230; affd [1985] ICR 827, [1985] IRLR 426, CA 4.102
R v East Berkshire Health Authority, ex p Walsh [1985] QB 152, [1984] 3 All ER 425, [1984] ICR 743, CA 2.69
R v Industrial Tribunal, ex p Cotswold Collotype Co Ltd [1979] ICR 190: 9.28
R v Leicestershire Fire Authority, ex p Thompson (1978) 77 LGR 373, DC 5.136
R v London Borough of Islington, ex p Building Employers' Confederation [1989] IRLR 382, 45 BLR 45, DC 4.158
R v Lord Chancellor's Department, ex p Nangle [1991] ICR 743, [1991] IRLR 343, DC 2.14
R v Secretary of State for the Home Department, ex p Benwell [1985] QB 554, [1984] ICR 723 .... 8.2
R v Secretary of State for Transport, ex p Factortame Ltd (No 2) [1991] 1 AC 603, [1991] 1 All ER 70, [1990] 3 CMLR 375, HL 1.51
R v Swan Hunter Shipbuilders and Telemeter Installations Ltd [1981] ICR 831, [1981] IRLR 403, CA 12.25, 12.35
RS Components v Irwin [1974] 1 All ER 41, [1973] ICR 535 ... 3.46, 8.176, 11.9
Race Relations Board v Applin [1973] 1 QB 815, [1973] 2 All ER 1190, CA 4.100
Rainey v Greater Glasgow Health Board [1987] AC 224, [1987] 1 All ER 65, [1987] ICR 129, HL 4.84, 4.90
Ranger v Brown [1978] 2 All ER 726, [1978] ICR 603 .... 2.58
Rank Xerox (UK) Ltd v Goodchild [1979] IRLR 185 .... 7.14
Rao v Civil Aviation Authority [1992] ICR 503, [1992] IRLR 203 .... 9.35A
Rask and Christensen v ISS Kantineservice A/S: C-209/81 [1993] 133, ECJ 5.111
Rastegarnia v Richmond Design IRRR (LIB 121) 3.1B
Ratcliffe v Dorset County Council [1978] IRLR 191 .... 5.57
Raymond v Sir Lindsay Parkinson & Co Ltd [1974] IRLR 298 .... 7.48
Raynor v Remploy Ltd [1973] IRLR 3 .... 8.98
Rayware Ltd v T&GWU [1989] 3 All ER 583, [1989] ICR 457, CA 15.103
Read (Richard) (Transport) Ltd v National Union of Mineworkers [1985] IRLR 67 .... 15.82
Ready Mixed Concrete (South East) Ltd v Minister of Pensions and National Insurance [1968] 2 QB 497, [1968] 1 All ER 433 .... 2.29, 2.35
Red Bank Manufacturing Co Ltd v Meadows [1992] ICR 204, [1992] IRLR 209 .... 9.47A, 9.68
Redbridge London Borough Council v Fishman [1978] ICR 569, [1978] IRLR 69 .... 3.10
Refund Rentals Ltd v McDermott [1977] IRLR 59 .... 8.142
Reid v Rush & Tompkins Group plc [1989] 3 All ER 228, [1990] 1 WLR 212, [1990] ICR 61, CA 3.23A, 6.19A
Reiss Engineering Co Ltd v Harris [1985] IRLR 232 .... 6.66

PARA
Retarded Children's Aid Society Ltd v Day [1978] ICR 437, [1978] IRLR 128, CA 8.148
Richards v Bulpitt & Sons Ltd [1975] IRLR 134 .... 8.143
Richards v NUM [1981] IRLR 247 .... 14.61
Richardson v Bradford City Metropolitan Council [1975] IRLR 296 .... 8.149
Richmond Precision Engineering Ltd v Pearce [1985] IRLR 179 .... 3.55, 8.178
Rickard v PB Glass Supplies Ltd [1990] ICR 150, CA 5.134
Riddick v Thames Board Mills Ltd [1977] QB 881, [1977] 3 All ER 677, CA 1.25
Ridge v Baldwin [1964] AC 40, [1963] 2 All ER 66, HL 2.19, 8.1
Rigby v Ferodo Ltd [1988] ICR 29, [1987] IRLR 516, HL 3.53, 3.55
Rigden-Murphy v Securicor Ltd [1976] IRLR 106 .... 7.25
Rinner-Kühn v FWW Spezial-Gebäudereinigung GmbH & Co KG: 171/88 [1989] IRLR 493, ECJ 2.52A
Road Transport Industry Training Board v Readers Garage Ltd (1969) 4 ITR 195, 6 KIR 137 .... 2.8
Roadburg v Lothian Regional Council [1976] IRLR 283 .... 4.25
Robb v Green [1895] 2 QB 315, [1895–9] All ER Rep 1053, CA 11.5
Robb v Leon Motor Services Ltd [1978] ICR 506, [1978] IRLR 26 .... 13.40
Robertson v British Gas Corpn [1983] ICR 351, [1983] IRLR 302, CA 3.28
Robertson v Securicor Transport Ltd [1972] IRLR 70 .... 8.50
Robinson v Crompton Parkinson Ltd [1978] ICR 401, [1978] IRLR 61: 3.19, 8.67
Robinson v Flitwick Frames Ltd [1975] IRLR 261 .... 6.60
Robinson v George Sorby Ltd (1966) 2 ITR 148, 2 KIR 189 .... 2.6, 10.4
Robinson v Ulster Carpet Mills Ltd [1991] IRLR 348, NI CA 8.164A
Robson v Brian Mills [1977] IRLIB 8.150
Rogers v Vosper Thornycroft (UK) Ltd [1989] ICR 384, [1989] IRLR 82, CA 8.168A
Rolls-Royce Ltd v Walpole [1980] IRLR 343 .... 8.123
Rookes v Barnard [1964] AC 1129, [1964] 1 All ER 367, HL .. 3.38, 15.34, 15.50
Rose v Plenty [1976] 1 All ER 97, [1976] 1 WLR 141, CA 6.75
Rosenthal v Louis Butler Ltd [1972] IRLR 39 .... 7.54
Ross v Aquascutum Ltd [1973] IRLR 107 .... 8.5
Rothwell v APEX [1976] ICR 211, [1975] IRLR 375 .... 13.5
Rowe v Radio Rentals Ltd [1982] IRLR 177 .... 7.16
Roy v Kensington and Chelsea and Westminster Family Practitioner Committee [1992] 1 All ER 705, [1992] IRLR 233, HL 2.71
Royal Ordnance plc v Pilkington [1989] ICR 737, [1989] IRLR 489, CA: 10.41
Royal Society for the Prevention of Cruelty to Animals v Cruden [1986] ICR 205, [1986] IRLR 83 .... 9.40
Royal Society for the Protection of Birds v Croucher [1984] ICR 604, [1984] IRLR 425 .... 7.19
Ruddiman & Co v Smith (1889) 60 LT 708, 53 JP 518, 37 WR 528 .... 6.77
Rushton v Harcros Timber and Building Supplies Ltd [1993] ICR 230, [1993] IRLR 254 .... 9.43
Russell v Elmdon Freight Terminal Ltd [1989] ICR 629 .... 9.67
Ryan v Shipboard Maintenance Ltd [1980] ICR 88, [1980] IRLR 16 .... 8.96

S and U Stores Ltd v Wilkes [1974] 3 All ER 401, [1974] ICR 645, [1974] IRLR 283 .... 10.45
Sagar v H Ridehalgh & Son Ltd [1931] 1 Ch 310, [1930] All ER Rep 288, CA 3.39

PARA

Sainsbury (J) Ltd v Savage [1981] ICR 1, [1980] IRLR 109, CA 7.10A
St Anne's Board Mill Co Ltd v Brien [1973] ICR 444, [1973] IRLR 309, 8 ITR 463 .... 9.26
St Basil's Centre v McCrossan [1992] ICR 140, [1991] IRLR 455 .... 9.4B
St John of God (Care Services) Ltd v Brooks [1992] ICR 715 .... 8.174A
Salvation Army v Dewsbury [1984] ICR 498, [1984] IRLR 222 .... 8.18, 8.20
Samways v Swan Hunter Shipbuilders Ltd [1975] IRLR 190 .... 3.40
Sanders v Ernest A Neale Ltd [1974] 3 All ER 327, [1974] ICR 565, [1974] IRLR 236 .... 10.10
Santokh Singh v Guru Nanak Gurdwara [1990] ICR 309, CA 2.13
Sartor v P and O European Ferries (Felixstowe) Ltd [1992] IRLR 271, CA 7.15A
Saunders v Bakers Food and Allied Workers' Union [1986] ICR 28, [1986] IRLR 16 .... 13.46
Saunders v Richmond upon Thames Borough Council [1978] ICR 75, [1977] IRLR 362, 12 ITR 488 .... 4.21
Savage v British India Steam Navigation Co Ltd (1930) 46 TLR 294 .... 8.8
Savora v Chiltern Herb Farms Ltd [1982] IRLR 166, CA 8.78
Scala Ballroom (Wolverhampton) Ltd v Ratcliffe [1958] 3 All ER 220, [1958] 1 WLR 1057, CA 15.33
Scally v Southern Health and Social Services Board [1992] 1 AC 294, [1991] ICR 771, HL 3.17A, 6.7A
Scarr v Goodyear & Sons Ltd [1975] IRLR 166 .... 8.89
Scheiddegger (Willy) Swiss Typewriting School Ltd v Ministry of Social Security (1968) 5 KIR 65 .... 2.35
Science Research Council v Nassé [1980] AC 1028, [1979] ICR 921, HL: 9.16
Scott v Pattison [1923] 2 KB 723, 92 LJKB 886 .... 3.41
Scott (Thomas) & Sons (Bakers) Ltd v Allen [1983] IRLR 329, CA 13.53
Scott, Brownrigg and Turner v Dance [1977] IRLR 141 .... 8.18
Scott Packaging and Warehousing Co Ltd v Paterson [1978] IRLR 166: 8.183
Scottish and Newcastle Breweries plc v Halliday [1986] ICR 577, [1986] IRLR 291 .... 9.44
Scottish Co-operative Wholesale Society v Lloyd [1973] ICR 137, [1973] IRLR 93, 8 ITR 178 .... 9.44
Scottish Special Housing Association v Cooke [1979] IRLR 264 .... 8.135
Secretary of State for Employment v ASLEF [1972] 2 QB 455, [1972] 2 All ER 949, [1972] ICR 19, CA 3.42, 6.53, 8.198, 13.73
Secretary of State for Employment v Banks [1983] ICR 48 .... 9.4
Secretary of State for Employment v Newbold [1981] IRLR 305 .... 8.38
Secretary of State for Employment v Spence [1987] QB 179, [1986] 3 All ER 616, CA 5.115, 5.116, 5.118, 10.30
Secretary of State for Employment v Wilson [1978] 3 All ER 137, [1978] ICR 200, [1977] IRLR 483 .... 5.88
Secretary of State for Scotland v Campbell [1992] IRLR 263 .... 7.18A
Secretary of State for Scotland v Meikle [1986] IRLR 208 .... 8.18
Secretary of State for Scotland and Greater Glasgow Health Board v Wright and Hannah [1991] IRLR 187 .... 1.21
Securicor Ltd v Smith [1989] IRLR 356, CA 7.29A
Seide v Gillette Industries Ltd [1980] IRLR 427 .... 4.108
Selby v Plessey Co Ltd [1972] IRLR 36 .... 8.162
Seligman and Latz Ltd v McHugh [1979] IRLR 130 .... 3.49
Seligman (Robert) Corpn v Baker [1983] ICR 770 .... 5.111
Seymour v British Airways Board [1983] ICR 148, [1983] IRLR 55 .... 4.128

PARA
Sharifi v Strathclyde Regional Council [1992] IRLR 259 .... 4.122C
Sharma v West Yorkshire Passenger Transport Executive [1977] IRLIB 7.14
Sheffield v Oxford Controls Company Ltd [1979] IRLR 133 .... 8.81, 9.11
Sheffield Metropolitan District Council v Siberry [1989] ICR 208 ...... 4.81
Shell UK Ltd v Lostock Garage Ltd [1977] 1 All ER 481, [1976] 1 WLR 1187, CA 3.22
Shepherd (F C) & Co Ltd v Jerrom [1987] QB 301, [1986] 3 All ER 589, [1986] ICR 802, CA 8.88, 8.92
Sheppard v National Coal Board (1966) 1 KIR 101, 1 ITR 177 .... 10.22
Shields v E Coomes (Holdings) Ltd [1979] 1 All ER 456, [1978] ICR 1159, CA 4.93
Shipping Co Uniform Inc v International Transport Workers' Federation [1985] ICR 245, [1985] 1 Lloyd's Rep 173 .... 15.74
Shook v London Borough of Ealing [1986] ICR 314, [1986] IRLR 46 .... 8.2
Shortland (W F) Ltd v Chantrill [1975] IRLR 208 .... 4.5
Showboat Entertainment Centre v Owens [1984] 1 All ER 836, [1984] ICR 65 .... 4.100
Sillars v Charrington Fuels Ltd [1989] ICR 475, [1989] IRLR 152, CA .. 8.30
Sillifant v Powell Duffryn Timber Ltd [1983] IRLR 91 .... 8.160
Sim v Rotherham Metropolitan Borough Council [1987] Ch 216, [1986] ICR 897 .... 3.16, 3.22, 5.136, 6.54
Simmonds v Dowty Seals Ltd [1978] IRLR 211 .... 8.66
Simmons v Hoover Ltd [1977] QB 284, [1977] ICR 61, [1976] IRLR 266: 10.40
Simmons v Medway Welding Ltd (1973) 8 ITR 373 .... 9.59
Simper (Peter) & Co Ltd v Cooke [1986] IRLR 19 .... 9.68
Simpson (A) & Son (Motors) v Reid and Findlater [1983] IRLR 401 ..... 8.155
Sinclair v Neighbour [1967] 2 QB 279, [1966] 3 All ER 988, CA 8.5
Singh v British Steel Corpn [1974] IRLR 131 .... 3.33, 3.34, 3.39
Singh v Lyons Maid Ltd [1975] IRLR 328 .... 3.45
Sisley v Britannia Security Systems Ltd [1983] ICR 628, [1983] IRLR 404 .... 4.55
Skillern v Eastwoods Froy Ltd (1966) 2 KIR 183, 2 ITR 112 .... 10.45
Skyrail Oceanic Ltd v Coleman [1981] ICR 864, [1981] IRLR 398, CA: 4.13, 4.34
Slack v Greenham (Plant Hire) Ltd [1983] ICR 617, [1983] IRLR 271 ... 1.10
Slaughter v C Brewer & Sons Ltd [1990] ICR 730, [1990] IRLR 426 ..... 9.46A
Slaven v Thermo Engineers Ltd [1992] ICR 295 .... 5.68
Smith v Austin Lifts Ltd [1959] 1 All ER 81, [1959] 1 WLR 100, HL 6.24
Smith v Baker & Sons [1891] AC 325, [1891–4] All ER Rep 69, HL 6.46
Smith v Du Pont (UK) Ltd [1976] IRLR 107 .... 8.147
Smith v Glasgow City District Council [1987] ICR 796, [1987] IRLR 326, HL 9.20, 9.23
Smith v Royal Alfred Merchant Seamen's Society HSIB 9 .... 8.124
Smith v Stages and Darlington Insulations Co Ltd 6.81A
Snowball v Gardner Merchant Ltd [1987] ICR 719, [1987] IRLR 397 ... 4.39
Snoxell and Davies v Vauxhall Motors Ltd [1978] QB 11, [1977] ICR 700, [1977] IRLR 123 .... 4.85
Solihull Metropolitan Borough v NUT [1985] IRLR 211 .... 15.83
Sonali Bank v Rahman [1989] ICR 314 .... 8.18
Sothern v Franks Charlesly & Co [1981] IRLR 278 .... 8.54, 8.82
Sougrin v Haringey Health Authority [1992] ICR 650, [1992] IRLR 416, CA 4.62B, 4.122B

PARA
South Surbiton Co-operative Society v Wilcox [1975] IRLR 292 .... 12.13A
South West Launderettes Ltd v Laidler [1986] ICR 455, [1986] IRLR 305, CA 8.40
Sovereign Distribution Services Ltd v T&GWU [1990] ICR 31, [1989] IRLR 334 .... 10.57, 15.19
Sovereign House Security Services Ltd v Savage [1989] IRLR 115, CA: 8.82
Spafax Ltd v Harrison [1980] IRLR 442 .... 8.72A, 8.74, 11.9
Spalding v Port of London Authority [1977] HSIB 8.129
Spencer v Paragon Wallpapers Ltd [1977] ICR 301, [1976] IRLR 373, 11 ITR 294 .... 8.119
Spencer and Griffin v Gloucestershire County Council [1985] IRLR 393, CA 10.23
Spencer Jones v Timmens Freeman [1974] IRLR 325 .... 3.39
Spiller v F J Wallis Ltd [1975] IRLR 362 .... 7.75
Spink v Express Foods Group Ltd [1990] IRLR 320 .... 7.6
Spinpress Ltd v Turner [1986] ICR 433 .... 10.36
Spook Erection Ltd v Thackray [1984] IRLR 116 .... 9.64
Spring v Guardian Assurance plc [1993] 2 All ER 273, CA 6.20
Spring v NASDA [1956] 2 All ER 221, [1956] 1 WLR 585 .... 14.22
Squibb United Kingdom Staff Association v Certification Officer [1978] ICR 15, [1977] IRLR 1355; revsd [1979] 2 All ER 452, [1979] ICR 235, CA 14.15
Stacey v Babcock Power Ltd [1986] QB 308, [1986] ICR 221 .... 8.103, 8.166
Stallite Batteries Co Ltd v Appleton (EAT) HSLB 147 .... 5.7B
Stapp v Shaftesbury Society [1982] IRLR 326, CA 8.18
Steel v Union of Post Office Workers and The General Post Office [1978] 2 All ER 504, [1978] ICR 181, [1977] IRLR 288 .... 4.12A
Steere v Morris Bros IDS Handbook 14 .... 4.26
Stephens (G W) & Son v Fish [1989] ICR 324 .... 9.8A
Stern (J & J) v Simpson [1983] IRLR 52 .... 8.56
Stevens v Bexley Health Authority [1989] ICR 224, [1989] IRLR 240 ... 1.68
Stevenson v Tees-side Bridge and Engineering Ltd [1971] 1 All ER 296, 10 KIR 53 .... 3.20
Stevenson, Jordan and Harrison Ltd v MacDonald and Evans [1952] 1 TLR 101, 69 RPC 10, CA 2.28
Stewart (Rex) Jeffries Parker Ginsberg Ltd v Parker [1988] IRLR 483, CA 11.24A, 11.24C
Stoker v Lancashire County Council [1992] IRLR 75, CA 7.14A
Stokes v Guest Keen and Nettlefold (Bolts and Nuts) Ltd [1968] 1 WLR 1776 .... 6.26
Storey v Allied Brewery [1977] IRLIB 8.177
Strange (S W) v Mann [1965] 1 All ER 1069, [1965] 1 WLR 629 .... 11.10
Strathclyde Regional Council v Neil [1984] IRLR 14 .... 11.27
Strathclyde Regional Council v Porcelli [1986] ICR 564, [1986] IRLR 134, Ct of Sess 4.37, 4.61
Suffolk County Council v Secretary of State for the Environment [1984] ICR 882, [1985] IRLR 24, HL 2.63
Sulemany v Habib Bank [1983] ICR 60 .... 13.82
Sun Alliance and London Insurance Ltd v Dudman [1978] ICR 551, [1978] IRLR 169 .... 4.8
Sunderland Polytechnic v Evans (1993) Times, 16 March 5.136
Superlux v Plaidstead (1958) Times, 12 December 6.61
Sutcliffe and Eaton Ltd v Pinney [1977] IRLR 349 .... 8.132, 8.172

PARA
Sutton & Co Ltd v Davies IDS Brief 149 .... 12.12
Sutton and Gates (Luton) Ltd v Boxall [1979] ICR 67, [1978] IRLR 486: 8.108
Swaine v Health and Safety Executive [1986] ICR 498, [1986] IRLR 205: 8.18
Swainston v Hetton Victory Club Ltd [1983] 1 All ER 1179, [1983] ICR 341, [1983] IRLR 164, CA 9.2
Sybron Corpn v Rochem Ltd [1983] 2 All ER 707, [1983] ICR 801, [1983] IRLR 253, CA 6.72
Sycamore v H Myer & Co Ltd [1976] IRLR 84 .... 8.177
System Floors (UK) Ltd v Daniel [1982] ICR 54, [1981] IRLR 475 .... 3.65

Talbot v Hugh M Fulton Ltd [1975] IRLR 52 .... 3.44
Talke Fashions Ltd v ASTWKT [1978] 2 All ER 649, [1977] ICR 833, [1977] IRLR 309 .... 10.57, 15.19
Tanner v D T Kean Ltd [1978] IRLR 100 .... 8.56, 8.81
Taplin v C Shippam Ltd [1978] ICR 1068, [1978] IRLR 450, 13 ITR 532: 13.86
Taylor v Alidair Ltd [1978] IRLR 82, 13 ITR 180, CA 8.8, 8.112, 8.114
Taylor v Conveyancer Ltd [1972] IRLR 37 .... 8.162
Taylor v NUM (Derbyshire Area) [1984] IRLR 440 .... 14.23B
Taylor v NUS [1967] 1 All ER 767, [1967] 1 WLR 532 .... 14.22C
Taylor v Parsons Peebles NEI Bruce Peebles Ltd [1981] IRLR 119 .... 8.141
Taylor v Rover Car Co [1966] 2 All ER 181, [1966] 1 WLR 1491 .... 6.36
Taylor v Triumph Motors, British Leyland (UK) and Secretary of State for Employment [1975] IRLR 369 .... 8.31
Taylorplan Catering (Scotland) Ltd v McInally [1980] IRLR 53 .... 8.116
Tayside Regional Council v McIntosh [1982] IRLR 272 .... 3.11, 8.131
Telephone Information Services Ltd v Wilkinson [1991] IRLR 148 .... 9.11C
Tennants Textile Colours Ltd v Todd [1989] IRLR 3, NI CA 4.81
Terry v East Sussex County Council [1977] 1 All ER 567, [1976] ICR 536, [1976] IRLR 332 .... 8.59
Tesco Group of Companies (Holdings) Ltd v Hill [1977] IRLR 63 .... 7.14, 7.17
Thomas v General Industrial Cleaners Ltd (3964/72) IDS Supp 21 .... 8.52
Thomas v National Union of Mineworkers (South Wales Area) [1985] 2 All ER 1, [1985] ICR 886 .... 15.106
Thomas and Betts Manufacturing Ltd v Harding [1980] IRLR 255, CA: 8.158, 8.167
Thompson v ASDA-MFI Group plc [1988] Ch 241, [1988] 2 All ER 722, [1988] IRLR 340 .... 5.119B
Thompson v Eaton Ltd [1976] 3 All ER 384, [1976] ICR 336, [1976] IRLR 308 .... 8.198, 13.73
Thomson v Alloa Motor Co Ltd [1983] IRLR 403 .... 8.145
Thorn v Meggitt Engineering Ltd [1976] IRLR 241 .... 4.25
Throsby v Imperial College of Science and Technology [1978] QB 438, [1978] ICR 357, [1977] IRLR 337 .... 2.23
Tilgate Pallets v Barras [1983] IRLR 231 .... 8.169
Times Newspapers Ltd v O'Regan [1977] IRLR 101, 11 ITR 259 .... 9.3
Timex Corpn v Hodgson [1982] ICR 63, [1981] IRLR 530 .... 4.55
Tomlinson v Dick Evans "U" Drive Ltd [1978] ICR 639, [1978] IRLR 77: 3.1B
Tomlinson v London Midland and Scottish Rly Co [1944] 1 All ER 537, CA 7.42
Torquay Hotel Co Ltd v Cousins [1969] 2 Ch 106, [1969] 1 All ER 522, CA 15.30

PARA

Tottenham Green Under Fives' Centre v Marshall [1989] ICR 214, [1989] IRLR 147 .... 4.111
Tower Hamlets Health Authority v Anthony [1989] ICR 656, [1989] IRLR 394, CA 7.52
T & GWU v Courtenham Products Ltd [1977] IRLR 8 .... 10.54, 15.7
T & GWU v Dyer [1977] IRLR 93, 12 ITR 113 .... 10.54, 15.7
T & GWU v Howard [1992] ICR 106, [1992] IRLR 170 .... 9.47A
T & GWU v Ledbury Preserves (1928) Ltd [1986] ICR 855, [1986] IRLR 492 .... 10.49, 15.10
T & GWU v Stanhope Engineering IRLR (LIB 121) 10.54, 15.7
T & GWU v Webber [1990] ICR 711, [1990] IRLR 462 .... 13.9
Treganowan v Robert Knee & Co Ltd [1975] ICR 405, [1975] IRLR 247, 10 ITR 121 .... 8.2, 8.11
Trimble v Supertravel Ltd [1982] ICR 440, [1982] IRLR 451 .... 9.61
Trust Houses Forte Hotels Ltd v Murphy [1977] IRLR 186 .... 8.137
Tucker v British Leyland Motor Corpn [1978] IRLR 493 .... 3.71
Turner v Goldsmith [1891] 1 QB 544, [1891–4] All ER Rep 384, CA 6.12
Turner v Labour Party and Labour Party Superannuation Society [1987] IRLR 101, CA 4.16
Turner v Pleasurama Casinos Ltd [1976] IRLR 151 .... 7.33
Turner v Vestric Ltd [1980] ICR 528, [1981] IRLR 23 .... 8.180
Turvey v C W Cheney & Son Ltd [1979] ICR 341, [1979] IRLR 105 .... 10.33
Tye v Mower Scaffolds Ltd [1976] IRLR 91 .... 8.18
Tynan v Balmer [1967] 1 QB 91, [1966] 2 All ER 133 .... 15.104
Tyne and Clyde Warehouses v Hamerton [1978] ICR 661, 13 ITR 661 .... 2.32

Ulsterbus Ltd v Henderson [1989] IRLR 251, NI CA 7.21A
Umar v Pliastar Ltd [1981] ICR 727 .... 8.38
Union Cartage Co Ltd v Blunden [1977] ICR 420, [1977] IRLR 139 .... 9.3
UCATT v Burrage [1978] ICR 314 .... 10.54, 15.7
UCATT v H Rooke & Son Ltd [1978] ICR 818, [1978] IRLR 204 .... 10.57, 15.19
USDAW v Leancut Bacon Ltd [1981] IRLR 295 .... 10.52, 15.14
USDAW v Sketchley Ltd [1981] ICR 644, [1981] IRLR 291 .... 10.54, 15.7
Union Traffic Ltd v T & GWU [1989] ICR 98, [1989] IRLR 127, CA 15.102
United Bank Ltd v Akhtar [1989] IRLR 507, EAT 3.8A, 8.67B, 8.72A
United Distillers v Conlin [1992] IRLR 503 .... 9.64B
United Kingdom Atomic Energy Authority v Claydon [1974] ICR 128, [1974] IRLR 6, 16 KIR 94 .... 6.56, 10.13
United Sterling Corpn Ltd v Felton and Mannion [1974] IRLR 314, [1974] RPC 162, [1973] FSR 409 .... 11.4
Universe Tankships Inc of Monrovia v ITWF [1982] 2 All ER 67, [1982] ICR 262, [1982] IRLR 200, HL 3.7, 15.96
University of Aston v Malik [1984] ICR 492 .... 8.29
University of Manchester v Jones [1992] ICR 52; affd sub nom Jones v University of Manchester (1992) 137 Sol Jo LB 14, CA 4.15A
Unkles v Milanda Bread Co Ltd [1973] IRLR 76 .... 7.45

Valor Newhome Ltd v Hampson [1982] ICR 407 .... 8.168
Van Duyn v Home Office (No 2) [1975] Ch 358, [1975] 3 All ER 190 .... 1.52
Vickers Ltd v Smith [1977] IRLR 11 .... 8.170, 9.27
Vinnyey v Star Paper Mills [1965] 1 All ER 175 .... 6.24, 6.40

PARA
Virdee v ECC Quarries Ltd [1978] IRLR 295 .... 4.123
Vokes Ltd v Bear [1974] ICR 1, [1973] IRLR 363, 15 KIR 302 .... 8.158

WHPT Housing Association Ltd v Secretary of State for Social Services [1981] ICR 737 .... 2.35
Wadcock v London Borough of Brent [1990] IRLR 223 .... 6.2
Waddington v Leicester Council for Voluntary Services [1977] 2 All ER 633, [1977] ICR 266, [1977] IRLR 32 .... 4.86
Wadley v Eager Electrical Ltd [1986] IRLR 93 .... 8.182
Waite v Government Communications Headquarters [1983] 2 AC 714, [1983] 2 All ER 1013, [1983] ICR 653, HL 8.18
Walker v Cotswold Chine Home School (1977) 12 ITR 342 .... 8.14
Walker v Josiah Wedgwood & Sons Ltd [1978] ICR 744, [1978] IRLR 105, 13 ITR 271 .... 8.67
Wall's Meat Co Ltd v Khan [1979] ICR 52, [1978] IRLR 499, CA 9.2
Wall's Meat Co Ltd v Selby [1989] ICR 601, CA 8.159
Walmsley v UDEC Refrigeration Ltd [1972] IRLR 80 .... 6.57
Walters v British Steel Corpn IDS Brief 150 .... 5.55
Walton v TAC Construction Materials Ltd [1981] IRLR 357 .... 8.147
Wandsworth London Borough Council v National Association of School Masters and Union of Women Teachers (1993) Times, 7 April 15.41
Ward v Bradford Corpn (1971) 70 LGR 27, CA 7.16
Warner v Barbers Stores [1978] IRLR 109 .... 3.19
Warner Bros Pictures Inc v Nelson [1937] 1 KB 209, [1936] 3 All ER 160: 6.1
Warren v Henley's Ltd [1948] 2 All ER 935 .... 6.78
Washington Arts Association Ltd v Forster [1983] ICR 346 .... 8.38
Watling (N C) & Co Ltd v Richardson [1978] ICR 1049, [1978] IRLR 255, 13 ITR 333 .... 8.162
Weakley v AUEW (1975) 125 NLJ 621 .... 14.23A
Webb v Anglian Water Authority [1981] ICR 811, [1981] IRLR 494 .... 9.66
Webb v Emo Air Cargo (UK) Ltd [1990] ICR 442, [1990] IRLR 124; affd [1992] 2 All ER 43, [1992] ICR 445, CA; on appeal [1992] 4 All ER 929, [1993] ICR 175, HL 4.35A, 4.35C
Wells v E and A West Ltd [1975] IRLR 269 .... 7.54
Wessex Dairies Ltd v Smith [1935] 2 KB 80, [1935] All ER Rep 75, CA: 11.5
Wessex National Ltd v Long (1978) 13 ITR 413 .... 8.28
West v Kneels Ltd [1987] ICR 146, [1986] IRLR 430 .... 9.7
West v Secretary of State for Scotland [1992] IRLR 399, Ct of Sess 2.71
West Midlands Co-operative Society Ltd v Tipton [1986] AC 536, [1986] 1 All ER 513, HL 7.15
West Midlands Passenger Transport Executive v Singh [1987] ICR 837, [1987] IRLR 351; on appeal [1988] 1 WLR 730, [1988] IRLR 186, CA 4.124A
Western Excavating (ECC) Ltd v Sharp [1978] QB 761, [1978] ICR 221, [1978] IRLR 27, CA 8.63, 8.70, 8.72A
Westminster City Council v Select Managements Ltd [1985] 1 All ER 897, [1985] ICR 353, CA 12.36
Weston v University College, Swansea [1975] IRLR 102, 10 ITR 60 .... 2.54
Westwood v Secretary of State for Employment [1985] AC 20, [1985] ICR 209, HL 5.88
Wheeler v Leicester City Council [1985] AC 1054, [1985] 2 All ER 1106, HL 4.154

PARA

Wheeler v Patel and J Golding Group of Companies [1987] ICR 631, [1987] IRLR 211 .... 8.186
Whitaker v Milk Marketing Board [1973] IRLR 100 .... 8.98
Whitbread & Co plc v Mills [1988] ICR 776, [1988] IRLR 501 .... 7.15A, 8.99
White v Holbrook Precision Castings Ltd [1985] IRLR 215, CA 6.32
White v Kuzych [1951] AC 585, [1951] 2 All ER 435, [1951] 2 TLR 277, PC 13.21
White v Manchester University [1976] ICR 419, [1976] IRLR 218, 11 ITR 143 .... 9.15
White v Pressed Steel Fisher [1980] IRLR 176 .... 12.31
White v Reflecting Roadstuds Ltd [1991] ICR 733, [1991] IRLR 331 .... 8.72A
White (Arthur) (Contractors) Ltd v Tarmac Civil Engineering Ltd [1967] 3 All ER 586, [1967] 1 WLR 1508, HL 2.45, 2.46
Whitlow v Alkanet Construction Ltd [1975] IRLR 321 .... 8.153
Whittaker v Minister of Pensions and National Insurance [1967] 1 QB 156, [1966] 3 All ER 531 .... 2.26, 2.28
Whitwood Chemical Co v Hardman [1891] 2 Ch 416, 60 LJ Ch 428, 64 LT 716, CA 6.1
Wicks v Charles A Smethurst Ltd [1973] IRLR 327 .... 6.57
Wilcox v Humphreys and Glasgow Ltd [1976] ICR 306, [1976] IRLR 222, 11 ITR 43, CA 8.147
Wileman v Minilec Engineering Ltd [1988] ICR 318, [1988] IRLR 144 .. 4.39
Wilkes v Fortes (Sussex) Ltd IRRR 8.128
Wilcox v Hastings [1987] IRLR 298, CA 10.19
Williams v Compair Maxam Ltd [1982] ICR 156, [1982] IRLR 83 .. 8.154, 8.155
Williams v Watsons Luxury Coaches Ltd [1990] ICR 536, [1990] IRLR 164 .... 8.89A, 8.90
Williams v Western Mail and Echo Ltd [1980] ICR 366, [1980] IRLR 222 .... 8.198, 13.73
Wilson v Associated Newspapers Ltd. See Associated Newspapers Ltd v Wilson
Wilson v IDR Construction Ltd [1975] IRLR 260 .... 6.60
Wilson v Maynard Shipbuilding Consultants AB [1978] QB 665, [1978] ICR 376, [1977] IRLR 491, CA 8.18
Wilson v Racher [1974] ICR 428, [1974] IRLR 114, 16 KIR 212, CA 8.4, 8.5
Wilson v TB Steelworks IDS Brief 150 .... 4.100
Wilson v Underhill House School Ltd [1977] IRLR 475, 12 ITR 165 ..... 8.174
Wilson (Joshua) & Bros Ltd v USDAW [1978] 3 All ER 4, [1978] ICR 614, [1978] IRLR 120 .... 10.52, 15.14
Wilsons and Clyde Coal Co Ltd v English [1938] AC 57, [1937] 3 All ER 628, HL 6.29
Wiltshire County Council v NATHFE [1980] ICR 455, [1980] IRLR 198, CA 8.61, 8.96
Wiltshire Police Authority v Wynn [1981] QB 95, [1980] ICR 649, CA: 2.19, 2.56
Wiluszynski v Tower Hamlets London Borough Council [1988] IRLR 154; revsd. [1989] ICR 493, [1989] IRLR 259, CA 5.136, 6.54A
Winterhalter Gastronom Ltd v Webb [1973] ICR 245, [1973] IRLR 120: 8.111
Wishart v National Association of Citizens Advice Bureaux Ltd [1990] IRLR 393, CA 3.1A
Witham v Hills Shopfitters 3.49
Withers v Flackwell Heath Football Supporters' Club [1981] IRLR 307: 2.31
Withers v Perry Chain Co Ltd [1961] 3 All ER 676, [1961] 1 WLR 1314, CA: 6.24

PARA

Wood v Cunard Line [1990] IRLR 281, CA 8.18
Wood v Louis C Edwards Ltd [1972] IRLR 18, 13 KIR 145, 7 ITR 335 .... 8.18
Wood v York City Council [1978] ICR 840, [1978] IRLR 228, CA 8.21
Woods v W M Car Services (Peterborough) Ltd [1982] ICR 693, [1982] IRLR 413, CA 8.78
Woolcocks v Wailes Dove Bitumastic Ltd (1977) 12 ITR 420 .... 8.164
Worringham and Humphreys v Lloyds Bank Ltd [1982] 3 All ER 373, [1982] ICR 299, [1982] IRLR 74, CA 4.69A
Wright v Dunlop Rubber Co (1972) 13 KIR 255, CA 6.25
Wright (Frank) & Co (Holdings) Ltd v Punch [1980] IRLR 217 .... 8.65, 8.72
Writers' Guild of Great Britain v BBC [1974] 1 All ER 574, [1974] ICR 234 .... 2.3

Yeats v Fairey Winches Ltd [1974] IRLR 362 .... 4.126
Yewens v Noakes (1880) 6 QBD 530, 50 LJQB 132, 44 LT 128, CA 2.26
Young v Daniel Thwaites & Co Ltd [1977] ICR 877, 12 ITR 392 .... 5.109
Young and Woods Ltd v West [1980] IRLR 201, CA 2.35
Young, James and Webster v United Kingdom [1981] IRLR 408; refd [1983] IRLR 35, ECt HR 1.69, 8.189
Young's of Gosport Ltd v Kendall [1977] ICR 907, [1977] IRLR 433, 12 ITR 269 .... 9.41

Zarczynska v Levy [1979] 1 All ER 814, [1979] ICR 184, [1978] IRLR 532 .... 4.100

CHAPTER 1

The institutions of employment law

A. Advisory, Conciliation and Arbitration Service

1.1 Although it has been in existence since 1974, the Service (better known as ACAS) was placed on a statutory basis by the Employment Protection Act 1975 and continued by virtue of the Trade Union and Labour Relations (Consolidation) Act 1992 (TULR(C)A s. 247). It is charged with the general duty of promoting the improvement of industrial relations, in particular by exercising its functions in relation to the settlement of trade disputes by conciliation and arbitration (s. 209). Its work is directed by a Council, which consists of a chairman and up to nine other members appointed by the Secretary of State. Three of these are to be appointed after consultations with employers' organisations, and three after consultation with workers' organisations, three 'neutral' (usually academic) appointments are usually made. Additionally up to three deputy chairmen may be appointed. The Secretary of State may appoint two further members of the Council, after consultation with both sides of industry. The appointments will be initially for a period of five years, and may be renewed for a further period (TULR(C)A s. 248).

1.2 ACAS will appoint its own staff, including a secretary, and will also provide staff for the Certification Officer and the Central Arbitration Committee. Although it will perform its functions on behalf of the Crown, it shall not be subject to any directions from any Minister as to the manner in which it is to exercise any of those functions. It is this complete independence from Government control which is a distinguishing feature of

ACAS. It will make an annual report on its activities and those of the Central Arbitration Committee to the Secretary of State, which will be laid before Parliament and published.

Whenever it thinks appropriate to do so, ACAS may charge a fee for its services, and also the Secretary of State may direct ACAS to charge fees, either at a full economic cost or a specified proportion or percentage of the economic cost. However, ACAS must notify the person concerned that a fee may or will be charged (TULR(C)A s. 251A).

1.3 The function of ACAS can be examined under the following headings:

A. Advice

1.4 ACAS may, on request or otherwise, give employers, employers' associations, workers and trade unions such advice as it thinks appropriate on matters connected with or likely to affect industrial relations. General advice on this topic may also be published (TULR(C)A s. 213).

B. Conciliation

1.5 Where a trade dispute exists or is apprehended, ACAS may offer its assistance to the parties, either on its own volition or at the request of any party, with a view to bringing about a settlement. This may be achieved by conciliation or other means, and by the appointment, if necessary, of someone outside ACAS whose assistance may be used. Due regard will be had to the desirability of encouraging the parties to use any appropriate agreed procedures (TULR(C)A s. 210).

1.6 It should be noted that for conciliation purposes, the definition of 'trade dispute' is the old definition (based on the Employment Protection Act 1975), now contained in s. 218 of TULR(C)A, not the more restricted definition (based on the Trade Union and Labour Relations Act 1974) now contained in s. 244 of TULR(C)A. The effect is to give ACAS a wider conciliation brief.

1.7 Conciliation officers will also be appointed for the purpose of settling by conciliation matters which are, or could be, the subject of proceedings before an industrial tribunal under any legislation, whenever passed (TULR(C)A s. 211). When a complaint is presented to an industrial tribunal, a copy will be sent to a conciliation officer, who is an officer of ACAS, and who has a duty to try to promote a settlement without the matter having to be dealt with by the tribunal. He will intervene for this purpose if requested to do so by the complainant or the person against whom the complaint has been made (ie, the respondent), and also in the absence of such request, if he thinks he could act with a reasonable prospect of success. He may also conciliate at the request of either party in respect of a matter which could be the subject of tribunal proceedings, but before a complaint has been presented. In practice, well over 60% of all claims made to industrial tribunals are disposed of as a result of the intervention of the conciliation officer. The majority of these will be settled on the basis of the employer making some financial payment to the applicant, and the rest will be withdrawn or a private settlement reached.

1.8 There is a continuing obligation on ACAS to act until all questions of liability and remedies have been determined by an industrial tribunal (*Courage Take Home Trade Ltd v Keys*).

1.9 Anything communicated to the conciliation officer in connection with the performance of his functions shall not be admissible in evidence in any proceedings before the tribunal without the consent of the party who communicated it. So far as dismissals are concerned, he shall try to promote the re-engagement or reinstatement of the complainant by the employer or by a successor or associated employer on terms appearing to him to be equitable or, if this is not possible, try to promote a settlement on the sum to be paid by way of compensation. Apart from compromise agreements (see EPCA s. 140(3), para 9.11D), it is not possible for a person to contract out of his statutory rights, and any agreement to this effect is generally void, but this rule does not apply to any agreement reached through the intervention of the conciliation officer, and any such settlement agreed between the parties will be legally binding (EPCA s. 140(2)). However, although a conciliation officer may try to effect a settlement in respect of claims brought before an industrial tribunal under *any* legislation, he can only draw up a legally binding settlement in respect of those claims specified in s. 133 of EP(C)A, s. 90 of TULR(C)A, s. 64 of the Sex Discrimination Act, and s. 55 of the Race Relations Act. There are, therefore, some disputes on which he can conciliate, but cannot draw up a legally binding settlement.

1.10 There is no obligation on the conciliation officer to advise or inform the employee of his statutory rights. How he performs his functions is a matter for his discretion, and in the absence of bad faith, or adopting unfair methods, an agreement reached under his auspices cannot be set aside (*Slack v Greenham Plant Hire*). However, the conciliation officer must take care not to give the impression that he favours the views of one side to the dispute. Thus, if the parties have reached an agreement, he should not get involved with its merits, but merely record it on the appropriate form and obtain the parties' signatures (*Moore v Duport Furniture Products*). Indeed, an agreement reached orally between the parties under the auspices of the conciliation officer is equally binding (*Gilbert v Kembridge Fibres*).

1.11 In *Hennessy v Craigmyle & Co Ltd* the applicant was told that he would be dismissed summarily but, provided he signed an agreement which had been prepared by the conciliation officer giving up his rights to bring a complaint before an industrial tribunal, he would be treated as having been made redundant, and would be given certain monies. After taking legal advice, he signed the agreement, but subsequently brought a claim for unfair dismissal. He alleged that his consent had been obtained by economic duress, and hence was void. The argument was dismissed by the industrial tribunal, the EAT and the Court of Appeal. Economic duress was a ground for avoiding an agreement only if the applicant's will was so overborne that his consent was vitiated because he had no real alternative. In this case there was such an alternative, for he could have refused to sign the agreement and taken his chance in the industrial tribunal. In any case, whether economic duress exists is a question of fact for the industrial tribunal to determine.

1.11A As a result of a recent change in policy, ACAS have indicated that they will no longer act as a 'rubber stamp' to an agreement, but will only draw up form COT3 when they have 'taken action' with regard to a settlement, in accordance with their statutory powers.

C. Arbitration

1.12 At the request of one or more parties to a dispute, but with the consent of all of them, ACAS may refer any matter to arbitration for settlement, either by a person appointed from outside ACAS, or by the Central Arbitration Committee. However, arbitration is not to be used unless the parties have exhausted agreed procedures for negotiation or the settlement of disputes, unless there is a special reason which justifies arbitration as an alternative to those procedures (TULR(C)A s. 212). With the consent of all the parties, ACAS may decide to publish the award. The Arbitration Act 1950 does not apply to any arbitration under this section, and thus the award is not capable of being legally enforced in a court of law.

D. Enquiries

1.13 ACAS may enquire into industrial relations generally, or in a particular industry, or in a particular undertaking. After taking into account the views of the parties, such findings may be published (TULR(C)A s. 214).

E. Codes of Practice

1.14 ACAS may issue Codes of Practice containing such practical guidance as it thinks fit for the purpose of promoting the improvement of industrial relations (TULR(C)A s. 199). The old Code of Practice issued under the Industrial Relations Act 1971 has been revoked, and three Codes are currently in force, namely:

(a) Disciplinary Practices and Procedures;
(b) Disclosure of Information for Collective Bargaining purposes;
(c) Time off work for trade union duties and activities (see Appendix I (c)).

1.14A In addition, an Advisory Handbook entitled 'Discipline at Work' has been issued (see Appendix G) which contains useful guidance on the handling of disciplinary and dismissal situations.

1.15 The Codes are first prepared and published in draft form, and then ACAS shall consider any representations made about them (and if necessary modify them) before they are finally submitted to the Secretary of State. If he approves, he shall lay them before Parliament. If he does not approve, he will give reasons for withholding his approval. After completing the Parliamentary procedure, the Code will be issued in the form of a draft by ACAS and will come into effect on a day appointed by the Secretary of State. A failure on the part of any person to observe a Code shall not of itself make him liable to any proceedings, but in any proceedings before an industrial tribunal or the Central Arbitration Committee the Code will be admissible in evidence, and any relevant provision shall be taken into account in determining the issue (TULR(C)A s. 207).

1.15A A Code of Practice may be revised or revoked with the approval of the Secretary of State (TULR(C)A ss. 201-202).

B. Certification Officer (TULR(C)A s. 254)

1.16 The post of Certification Officer was originally created to take over certain administrative functions exercised in connection with trade unions, although nowadays he has wide powers of investigation and supervision (see Chapter 14). He is appointed by the Secretary of State, and will make an annual report to him and also to ACAS. Although the staff of the Certification Officer is provided by ACAS, he is completely independent of that organisation.

Since TULRA 1974 (now TULR(C)A s. 2) the Certification Officer has kept a list of organisations which are trade unions and employers associations within the legal definition. Since the Employment Protection Act 1975 (now TULR(C)A s. 6) he has issued certificates of independence to those trade unions which have applied, and meet the necessary criteria (see Chapter 14). He has issued a booklet entitled 'Guidance for trade unions wishing to apply for a certificate of independence'. He has taken custody of all documents held by his predecessors since 1871, and will keep these for public inspection, along with the list of trade unions and records of all applications for certificates of independence (TULR(C)A ss. 255-258). He will also be in charge of the administrative arrangements involved in the provision of public funds for trade union ballots, although this bounty is gradually being abolished (see para 14.40).

C. Central Arbitration Committee

1.17 This body replaced the Industrial Arbitration Board (formerly known as the Industrial Court) and consists of a chairman (and deputy chairman) appointed by the Secretary of State (after consultation with ACAS) and other persons appointed from representatives of employers and workers. The appointments may be for up to five years, and are renewable. CAC will exercise its functions on behalf of the Crown, but will not be subject to directions of any kind from any Ministers as to the manner in which those functions are to be exercised. The only statutory functions now left to CAC are to adjudicate on claims relating to disclosure of information for collective bargaining purposes brought under TULR(C)A s. 183 (see para 15.2) and to hear references under ss. 5 and 7 of the Equal Pay Act 1970. CAC also acts as a voluntary arbitration panel.

D. Employment Appeal Tribunal (EPCA 1978, ss. 135, 136)

1.18 This tribunal consists of judges of the High Court nominated by the Lord Chancellor in England, and the Lord President of the Court of Session in Scotland, plus other members (appointed on the joint recommendations of the Lord Chancellor and the Secretary of State) who have special knowledge or experience of industrial relations as representatives of employers or of workers. The EAT will be a superior court of record, with a central office in London, but it may sit anywhere in the country, and one or more divisions of the EAT may sit at the same time. In practice, appeals are heard either in London or Edinburgh.

A party may appear before the EAT either in person, or be represented by a solicitor or barrister, or a representative of a trade union or employers' association, or any other person whom he desires to represent him. The EAT will generally regulate its own procedure, but costs will not normally be awarded against either party unless the proceedings were unnecessary, improper or vexatious, or there has been unreasonable delay or unreasonable conduct in bringing or conducting the proceedings.

Appeals will be heard by a judge and either two or four members, so that in either case there is an equal number of persons whose knowledge or experience of industrial relations is as a representative of employers and workers respectively. With the consent of the parties, however, an appeal may be heard by a judge and one or three members. If the appeal is from a decision of an industrial tribunal chairman sitting alone (see para 1.21), the appeal may be heard by the judge alone, unless the judge directs that one or more appointed member should sit also. If the appeal involves an issue of national security, it will be heard by the President sitting alone (see para 2.64).

1.19 The jurisdiction of the EAT is as follows:

(a) to hear appeals on points of law from decisions of industrial tribunals (see para 1.21) except decisions relating to improvement and prohibition notices, which are heard by the Divisional Court (see para 12.16A);

(b) to hear appeals on questions of law from the decisions of the Certification Officer given under the provisions of Chapter VI of TULR(C)A (restrictions on the use of trade union funds for political objects) (see s. 95);

(c) to hear appeals on points of law from decisions of the Certification Officer given under s. 103 of TULR(C)A (resolutions approving instruments of amalgamation) (see s. 104);

(d) to hear appeals on points of law and fact from decisions of the Certification Officer given under TULR(C)A ss. 2-6 (entry on the list of trade unions, and applications for certificates of independence) (see s. 9);

(e) to hear original applications for compensation in respect of unreasonable exclusion or expulsion from a trade union (TULR(C)A s. 176) and similar applications in respect of unjustifiable disciplinary action by a trade union (TULR(C)A s. 67).

1.19A An appeal can only be entertained by the EAT if there is a genuine dispute between the parties (*IMI Yorkshire Imperial Ltd v Olender*) and appeals should not be pursued with other ulterior motives (*Baker v Superite Tools Ltd*). A further appeal will lie on a point of law to the Court of Appeal or, in Scotland, to the Court of Session, and a final appeal will lie to the House of Lords. At any time, however, a tribunal or court can refer a case to the European Court of Justice in Luxembourg, if a question arises as to the application of European law (see para 1.51).

E. Industrial tribunals

1.20 The constitutional basis for industrial tribunals can be found in the Industrial Tribunals (England and Wales) Regulations 1965 and the Industrial Tribunals (Scotland) Regulations 1965, both made under the Industrial Training Act 1964. A Central Office of Industrial Tribunals (COIT) has been set up in Bury St Edmunds and Glasgow, with 11 regional offices in England and Wales, and three offices in Scotland. Industrial tribunals may also sit at other locations.

1.21 An industrial tribunal consists of a legal chairman and two lay members. The chairman can be either a barrister or solicitor, and may be full-time or part-time. The lay members, who are all part-time, are selected from a panel drawn up after consultation with representatives of employers' organisations and trade unions. At an actual hearing, there will always be a representative from each side of industry, although a chairman can sit with one lay member only if both parties to the dispute agree. Each member of the industrial tribunal has an equal vote, and although decisions can be reached by a majority vote, in practice it appears that, despite the somewhat diverse backgrounds, 96% of all decisions reached are unanimous. In the remaining cases, the 'wingmen' are just as likely to unite in outvoting the legal chairman as the latter is likely to have the support of one or the other member. In cases of sex discrimination, it is desirable to have one member of either sex, and in race discrimination cases, a member who has special experience of race relations, but there is no absolute legal requirement that an industrial tribunal should be so composed (*Habib v Elkington & Co Ltd*).

Although, generally speaking, an industrial tribunal will consist of a chairman and two members, in the following circumstances a chairman may sit alone. These are:

(a) applications for interim relief (EPCA ss. 77, 78A, 79 TULR(C)A ss. 161, 165, 166);
(b) employee's rights on employer's insolvency (EPCA s. 124);
(c) unauthorised deductions from wages (Wages Act 1986 s. 5);
(d) damages for breach of contract of employment (EPCA s. 131);
(e) proceedings in which the parties have given their written consent to be heard by the chairman alone;
(f) where the person bringing the proceedings has given written notice withdrawing the case;
(g) proceedings in which the person against whom the proceedings were brought does not contest the case.

However, in any of the above circumstances, the chairman may at any stage decide to have the case heard by a full tribunal

(a) where there is a likelihood of a dispute arising from the facts,
(b) where there is a likelihood of an issue of law arising,
(c) having taken into account the views of any of the parties,
(d) where there are other proceedings which might be heard concurrently and which do not come within the above categories which enable a chairman to sit alone.

If the case involves a question of national security, the Secretary of State may direct that it be heard by the President sitting alone.

The jurisdiction of industrial tribunals is as follows:

a. Industrial Training Act 1982 s. 12 - appeals against assessment of industrial training levies;
b. Equal Pay Act 1970 s. 2 - complaints of breach of equality clauses in contracts of employment;
c. Health and Safety at Work etc Act 1974 s. 24 - appeals against improvement and prohibition notices;
d. Safety Representatives and Safety Committees Regulations 1977 - time off work with pay for safety representatives;
e. Occupational Pension Schemes (Certification of Employments) Regulations 1975 - decisions on whether an independent trade union is recognised for collective bargaining purposes, or whether consultations have been carried on;
f. Occupational Pension Schemes (Equal Access to Membership) Regulations 1976 - decisions on equality clauses which permit equal access to occupational pension schemes;
g. Sex Discrimination Act 1975 s. 63 - complaints of discrimination on grounds of sex or martial status; s. 68 - appeals against non-discrimination notices; s. 72(3)(a) - applications by the Equal Opportunities Commission relating to discriminatory advertisements; s. 73 - applications by the Equal Opportunities Commission prior to county court actions;
h. Sex Discrimination Act 1986 s. 6 - complaints of discriminatory collective agreements;
i. Race Relations Act 1976 s. 54 - complaints of race discrimination; s. 59 - appeals against non-discrimination notices; s. 63 - applications by the Commission for Racial Equality relating to discriminatory advertisements; s. 64 - applications by the Commission for Racial Equality prior to county court actions;
j. Employment Protection (Consolidation) Act 1978 s. 11 - failure to give written statements under s. 1 or failure to give itemised statement under s. 8; s. 17(1) - guarantee payments; s 22(1) - medical suspension payments; s. 22A - detriment in health and safety cases; s. 29(6) - time off work for public duties; s. 31(6) - time off work to look for work or to make arrangements for retraining; s. 31A(6) - time off work for ante-natal care; s 46 - suspension from work on maternity ground; s. 47 - failure to pay during suspension; s. 53(4) - failure to give written reasons for dismissal; s. 67(1)

- complaints of unfair dismissal; s. 77 - applications for interim relief; s. 91(1) - applications for redundancy payments; s. 108(1) - certain redundancy references; s. 112 - redundancy payments for civil servants; s. 122(1) - rights on employer's insolvency; s. 130 - appeals formerly heard by referees or board referees under certain statutory provisions;

k. Transfer of Undertakings (Protection of Employment) Regulations 1981 - failure to inform or consult with trade unions; failure to pay compensation;

l. Local Government (Compensation) Regulations 1974, British Transport (Compensation to Employees) Regulations 1970 - compensation payments for loss of office on reorganisation;

m. It would seem that industrial tribunals have jurisdiction to hear claims under the Treaty of Rome, especially Article 48 (free movement of workers) and Article 119 (equal pay for equal work) even though there is no statutory basis for such jurisdiction (*Secretary of State for Scotland v Wright*). There may also be jurisdiction to hear claims under European Directives, certainly when the employer is an organ of the State (see *Foster v British Gas plc*, para 1.53);

n. Wages Act 1986, unauthorised deductions or payments; employer making deductions outside the 12 months' time limit; receiving payment in respect of a cash shortage or stock deficiency without notifying the worker of total liability; making a deduction exceeding 1/10th of gross pay (or receiving a payment);

o. The following complaints, formerly brought under the provisions of the Employment Protection Act 1975 and the Employment Protection (Consolidation) Act 1978 can now be brought under the corresponding provisions of TULR(C)A 1992; s. 146(5) - action short of dismissal on grounds of trade union membership or non-membership; s. 168(1) - time off work for trade union duties; s. 170(4) - time off work for trade union activities; s. 161(1) - applications for interim relief; s. 189(1) - failure to consult with trade unions on redundancies; s. 192(1) - applications for protective award;

p. The following complaints, formerly brought under the provisions of the Employment Acts 1980-1990 are now brought under the corresponding provisions of TULR(C)A 1992; s. 174 - unreasonable exclusion or expulsion from a trade union; s. 64 - right not to be unjustifiably disciplined; ss. 137-138 - refusal of employment on grounds of trade union membership or non-membership; s. 68 - unauthorised check off.

1.22 The procedure before industrial tribunals is governed by the Industrial Tribunals (Rules of Procedure) Regulations 1985, which provide for the making of originating applications, appearance by respondents, discovery of documents, further and better particulars, witness attendance orders, pre-hearing assessments (or pre-hearing review) procedure at the hearing, applications for review, awards of costs, extensions of time, joinder and other miscellaneous matters. Similar regulations have been made in respect of proceedings in Scotland.

1.23 Proceedings are quite informal, for industrial tribunals have the power to conduct them in whatever manner they consider to be most suitable (see Chapter 9). The parties may represent themselves, or be represented by a solicitor or barrister, or a representative of a trade union or employers' association, or any other person whom they desire to represent them. Costs are not normally awarded, unless a party has acted frivolously, vexatiously, or otherwise unreasonably in bringing or conducting proceedings (*Marler v Robertson*). However, under rule 13 of the Industrial Tribunals (Improvement and Prohibition Notices Appeals) Regulations 1974, a tribunal may make an award of costs in cases of appeals from the imposition of an improvement or prohibition notice issued under the Health and Safety at Work etc Act 1974 (see Chapter 12), on the appropriate County Court Scale.

1.24 Section 131 of the Employment Protection (Consolidation) Act 1978 enables the Lord Chancellor (or, in respect of Scotland, the Lord Advocate) at some future date to provide by Order that claims for damages for breach of contracts of employment, claims for a sum due under such a contract, and claims for statutory monies due may be heard in the industrial tribunals. The Order may place a limit on the amount which the industrial tribunal may award. Such additional jurisdiction to hear matters relating to breach of contract will be concurrent with that of any other court which has power to hear the case. This section will mean that industrial tribunals will be able to hear claims which they cannot entertain at the moment, and which must therefore be taken to the County Court. But no claims will be entertained under the section which relates to damages for personal injuries. These must go to the High Court in the normal way.

1.24A It is important to bear in mind that until the jurisdiction of the industrial tribunals is extended to enable them to deal with other matters of contractual dispute, they have no power to entertain claims which fall outside their statutory jurisdiction. Some confusion has arisen out of the Wages Act 1986, relating to the powers of industrial tribunals to deal with deductions and non-payments (see Chapter 5) and clarification by means of an order under s. 131 has been expected for some time. It is odd that the non-payment of certain monies due to an employee, including holiday pay, insufficient notice, etc, may be brought under the Wages Act, but not a claim for pay in lieu of notice (see para 5.135).

1.25 An industrial tribunal has the power to issue attendance orders for the purpose of compelling a witness to attend, they may require a party to disclose documents to the other side, and to give further and better particulars of any claim or defence (see Chapter 9). Documents which are produced in order to comply with an order for discovery may only be used for the purpose of the hearing, and not for any other cause or action. In *Riddick v Thames Board Mills*, an employee of the defendants wrote a confidential memorandum about the manner of the plaintiff's dismissal, which was allegedly defamatory. The plaintiff got to know about the documents as a result of a court order for discovery, made during the course of a legal action brought against the employer. The action was settled, but the plaintiff brought a further action for defamation. It was held that the public interest required that documents which were compulsorily disclosed on discovery should be used only for the purpose of the action in which they were disclosed, and that each party impliedly undertook not to use them for any other ulterior or improper motive.

1.26 If there are High Court proceedings between the employer and employee in which there are issues in common with an application for unfair dismissal, the tribunal chairman has a discretion to order that the latter claim be postponed, pending the outcome of the High Court proceedings (*Carter v Credit Change Ltd*). He should take into account the convenience, expedition and cost when exercising his discretion (*First Castle Electronics v West*). The test to be applied is 'In which court is this action most conveniently and appropriately to be tried, bearing in mind all the surrounding circumstances, including the complexity of the issue, the amount involved, the technicality of the evidence and appropriateness of the procedure?' Thus, where a managing director was alleging a repudiatory breach of contract by the employers which was claimed to be a wrongful and unfair dismissal, the Employment Appeal Tribunal ordered that industrial tribunal proceedings should be adjourned until after the hearing of the High Court action (*Bowater plc v Charlwood*).

1.26A An award made by an industrial tribunal will now attract interest, on a day-to-day basis, at the stipulated rate of interest, after 42 days from the date when the decision has been sent to the parties. Interest is not payable on costs awarded, nor on any part of the award which is subject to the recoupment provisions.

1.26B Interest is still payable if the tribunal's decision is subject to appeal or review, but if the amount of the award is subsequently varied, interest is payable on the amount as varied (Industrial Tribunals (Interest) Order 1990).

1.27 The Minister has power to make regulations designed to restrict publicity in cases heard before an industrial tribunal and the Employment Appeal Tribunal which involve allegations of sexual misconduct or the commission of sexual offences, so as to prevent the identification of any person making or affected by the allegation, and to restrict reporting until after the promulgation of the decision. It will be an offence punishable by a fine not exceeding level 5 on the standard scale to act in contravention of any such restricted reporting order.

F. Commissioner for the Rights of Trade Union Members

1.28 This new post was created by the Employment Act 1988 (see now TULR(C)A s. 266). The Secretary of State will appoint the Commissioner, who will hold office for five years, and be eligible for re-appointment. She will lay an annual report of her activities before Parliament.

1.28A The Commissioner may provide financial assistance to a member of a trade union who is taking (or contemplating) certain types of legal action against his trade union in respect of applications to the court under the following provisions of TULR(C)A:

(a) s. 15(3) — prohibition of the use of trade union funds to indemnify unlawful conduct;

(b) s. 16 – action against trustees for unlawful use of trade union property;
(c) s. 26 – failure to maintain a register of trade union members;
(d) s. 31 – failure to comply with a request for access to the trade union's accounting record;
(e) s. 56 – failure by the trade union to comply with the duty to hold elections for certain positions in the trade union;
(f) s. 62 – failure by the trade union to hold a ballot before calling industrial action;
(g) s. 71 – use by the trade union of funds for political objects other than in accordance with the provisions of the Act;
(h) s. 81 – failure by the trade union to comply with the requirements as to the holding of a ballot on the use of funds for political objects;
(i) actions in the High Court (or Court of Session) in respect of alleged or threatened breaches of the rules of a trade union relating to:
    (i) the appointment of a person to, or removal from, any office;
    (ii) disciplinary proceeding by the trade union (including expulsion);
    (iii) the authorising or endorsing of industrial action;
    (iv) the balloting of members;
    (v) the application of the union's funds or property;
    (vi) the imposition, collection or distribution of any levy for the purposes of industrial action;
    (vii) the constitution of proceedings of any committee, conference of other body.

1.28B However, under the Act, assistance may only be granted for the above High Court actions if the breach of the rules in question affects members of the union other than the applicant, or similar breaches of the rules have been committed in relation to other members of the union.

1.29 Once an application for assistance has been made, the Commissioner will, as soon as is reasonably practicable, consider it, decide whether to grant it, and to what extent. If she decides not to grant the application, she must notify the applicant of her decision and, if she thinks fit, the reasons for it.

1.30 The assistance given by the Commissioner may include the making of arrangements for the bearing of costs in respect of advice or assistance from a solicitor or counsel, representation, and steps preliminary or incidental to proceedings, including arriving at or giving effect to a compromise to avoid or bring to an end those proceedings.

1.31 In determining whether or not to grant the application for assistance, the Commissioner may have regard to:

a. whether the case raises a question of principle;
b. whether it is unreasonable, having regard to the complexity of the case, to expect the applicant to deal with it unaided; and
c. whether the case involves a matter of substantial public interest (TULR(C)A s. 110).

1.32 The recovery of any expenses incurred by the Commissioner shall be a first charge on any costs or expenses which are payable to the applicant (whether by virtue of a court judgment or agreement or otherwise) and on his rights under any compromise or settlement arrived at to avoid or bring to an end any proceedings.

1.33 It should be noted that where a complaint can be made either to the Certification Officer or to a court (i.e. on political funds, ballots and elections to the principal executive committee of a trade union), the Commissioner is not empowered to provide assistance in the making of an application to the Certification Officer. Nor can the Commissioner give assistance in industrial tribunal proceedings or before the EAT.

1.34 The Commissioner has issued a free 'Guide for Trade Union Members' outlining the nature of the assistance provided.

G. Commissioner for the Protection Against Unlawful Industrial Action; s. 235B, Trade Union and Labour Relations (Consolidation) Act 1992

1.35-1.39 If any individual believes that a trade union is proposing to call for industrial action which would be unlawful in tort or which has not been supported by an appropriate ballot, and which may affect the supply of goods or services (whether or not that individual is entitled to such supply), he may bring an application to the High Court or Court of Session (see Chapter 15). In respect of any such application, the individual may seek assistance from the newly created Commissioner for the Protection Against Unlawful Industrial Action. The Commissioner will consider whether it would be unreasonable to expect the applicant to deal with the case unaided, and whether the case involves a matter of substantial public interest or concern. The Commissioner may pay for advice or assistance by a solicitor or counsel, the costs of representation in preliminary steps or in reaching a settlement, and the costs of actual proceedings. Any costs ultimately awarded to the applicant in proceedings shall constitute a first charge for the benefit of the Commissioner.

H. Industrial Training Boards

1.40 The Industrial Training Act 1982 enables the Minister to set up training boards in any industry in order to provide for industrial and commercial training of persons who are over school-leaving age. A Board will consist of a chairman, with an equal number of persons from either side of industry, educational representatives and additional persons appointed by the Secretary of State, although only the employers' representatives may vote on the imposition of a levy. A Board may provide courses for training purposes, or approve courses run by other institutions, and has wide powers relating to the making or recommendations for training, laying down training standards, and to assist persons to find facilities for being trained for industry. It can pay fees, maintenance allowances, and make grants or loans to organisations providing courses or other facilities which are approved by the Board. At the present time, seven such Boards are still in operation.

1.41 To meet its expenses a Board may impose a levy on employers in the industry, which is assessed by reference to a percentage of the payroll. For this purpose a Board may require employers to furnish returns and information, and keep and produce records. An employer who has been assessed for a levy may appeal to an industrial tribunal, which may rescind or reduce or increase it as the tribunal determines.

I. Department of Employment

1.42 This is the Government department which has over-all responsibility for employment questions, including manpower intelligence, regional economic planning, and general policy matters. It performs administrative duties relating to the provision of unemployment pay, and other benefits. The Secretary of State has power to issue Codes of Practice (TULR(C)A s. 203) and Codes have been made on Picketing (see Appendix I) and Trade Union Ballots and Elections. He may also make various regulations modifying the existing law, increase the amounts payable under the various statutory provisions, and generally oversee employment law.

It is of interest to note that whereas Codes of Practice issued by ACAS (see Appendix I) are admissible before industrial tribunals and the Central Arbitration Committee, Codes issued by the Secretary of State are additionally admissible in the courts.

1.43 The Department of Employment (which has now taken over the functions of the Training Commission), operates a number of temporary and permanent special employment and training schemes, designed to increase employment opportunities generally. Some of these schemes have a limited duration, others are more permanent.

J. Equal Opportunities Commission

1.44 The Sex Discrimination Act 1975 established the Equal Opportunities Commission (EOC), consisting of between eight and fifteen members. It will work towards the elimination of discrimination on grounds of sex, generally promote equality of opportunity between men and women, keep the Sex Discrimination Act 1975 and the Equal Pay Act 1970 under review, and, where necessary, draw up and submit proposals for amendments, and review the relevant statutory provisions relating to health and safety at work in so far as they require different treatment for men and women. The Commission also has power to draw up Codes of Practice giving practical guidance on ways to eliminate discrimination and promote equality of opportunity between men and women. Such Codes will have the same standing as those issued by ACAS. A Code entitled 'For the elimination of sex and marriage discrimination, and the promotion of equality of opportunity in employment' has been approved (see Appendix I). The EOC may carry out formal enquiries (see Chapter 4) and can give financial or other support to actual or potential claimants.

K. Commission for Racial Equality

1.45 The Commission for Racial Equality (CRE) was established by the Race Relations Act 1976, and consists of between eight and fifteen members. It will work towards the elimination of racial discrimination, promote equality of opportunity and good relations between persons of different racial groups, and keep under review the workings of the 1976 Act and, where necessary, draw up and submit proposals for its amendment. The CRE has issued a Code of Practice entitled 'For the elimination of racial discrimination and the promotion of equality or opportunity in employment' (see Appendix I). The CRE may give financial or other assistance to any organisation which has for its objects the improvement of community relations, undertake or promote research or educational activities and has like powers of holding enquiries and giving assistance to claimants as the EOC.

L. Health and Safety Commission

1.46 The Health and Safety at Work etc Act 1974 established the Health and Safety Commission to take over the general supervision of the promotion of health and safety at work. The Commission consists of a chairman, three members representing employers' organisations, three members representing trade unions, and three other members appointed after consultation with local authorities and other interested parties. The duty of the Commission is to do such things and make such arrangements as it considers appropriate:

a. to assist and encourage persons concerned with matters relevant to any of the general purposes of Part I of the Health and Safety at Work etc Act 1974 to further those purposes. Since the bulk of the Act is contained in Part I, this is the widest possible duty of the Commission;
b. to make such arrangements as it considers appropriate for the carrying out of research, the publication of results, the provision of training and information in connection therewith, and to encourage research and the provision of training and information by others;
c. to make arrangements for securing that government departments, employers, employees, employers' organisations and trade unions are provided with an information and advisory service;
d. to submit proposals for the making of regulations.

1.47 The Commission must report from time to time to the Secretary of State (who retains over-all responsibility), act in accordance with proposals approved by him, and give effect to any directions made by him.

1.48 The enforcement and day-to-day supervision of the Act is in the hands of the Health and Safety Executive. This consists of three persons; the Director is appointed by the Commission with the approval of the Secretary of State, and two assistant directors appointed by the Commission with the approval of the Secretary of State after consultation with the Director. The powers of the Executive are wide. Generally, it must exercise on behalf of the Commission such of the Commission's functions as the Commission directs, and give effect to any direction given to it by the Commission, but the Commission may not direct the Executive to enforce any statutory provision in any particular case. At the request of any Minister of the Crown, the Executive must provide him with information concerning activities in which he has an interest, and provide him with advice on such matters.

1.49 In particular, the Commission may direct the Executive or authorise any other person to hold an enquiry into any accident, occurrence, situation or other matter, and regulations have been published concerning the conduct of such enquiries or investigation.

The impact of the European Community

1.50 The European Communities Act 1972 signalled the United Kingdom's accession to the European Community, and enacted that the treaties relating thereto shall be given legal effect in the United Kingdom without further enactment. The major treaty is the Treaty of Rome, which has, as one of its objectives, the harmonisation of the laws of the various members of the Community, in particular on matters relating to 'employment, labour law and working conditions, basic and advanced vocational training, social security, protection against occupational accidents and diseases, occupational hygiene, the law of trade unions, and collective bargaining between workers and employers' (Article 118). The impact of European law on British law has already been considerable, and doubtless this will continue in the coming years.

Community law

1.51 For the purpose of this book, Community law consists of (a) Articles of the Treaty of Rome, (b) Directives passed by the Council of Ministers, (c) Recommendations, and (d) Decisions of the European Court of Justice. It must be borne in mind that any common law or statutory rule which is contrary to European law is void, and if there is any conflict between European law and British law, the former is to be applied. Indeed, if, in any preliminary proceedings, it appears that the sole obstacle towards granting interim relief is a rule of national law which is in conflict with European law, that national law has to be set aside (*R v Secretary of State for Transport, ex p Factortame*).

A. Articles of the Treaty

1.52 If an Article of the Treaty of Rome is clear, precise, unconditional, requires no further implementation, and does not give any discretion to Member States, it is directly applicable and becomes an integral part of the law of Member States (*Defrenne v Sabena*). For example, Article 119 of the Treaty of Rome provides 'Each Member State shall ensure and maintain the application of the principle that men and women should receive equal pay for equal work …' This Article has been invoked in a number of cases, and has been held to confer a distinct legal right on an individual, which can be enforced in national courts, in addition to any legal right conferred by national law (*Garland v British Rail Engineering Ltd*). Similarly, Article 48 of the Treaty provides that Member States shall ensure the free movement of workers within the Community without discrimination as regards employment, remuneration and other conditions of work and employment, and this too has a direct legal effect (*Van Duyn v Home Office (No. 2)*). Thus if a national of a Member State wishes to obtain employment in the United Kingdom, he does not need a work permit, and he must be given equal access to social security benefits, holidays, equal pay, etc.

B. Directives

1.53 A Directive, passed by the Council of Ministers, is binding as to the result to be achieved, but the national authorities are given a choice of form and methods. However, as Directives are binding on Member States, it is the duty of those States to implement them, and if the State fails to do so, an individual may seek to enforce the terms of the Directive against a State in its capacity as an employer (*Marshall v Southampton and South West Hampshire Area Health Authority*). For this purpose, 'the State' includes any body which is an emanation of the State (e.g. a nationalised industry) or which provides a public service under the control of the State. In other words, a State cannot take advantage of its own failure to comply with European law (*Foster v British Gas*).

In *Doughty v Rolls Royce plc* the Court of Appeal laid down three criteria to be applied in considering whether or not any particular body is 'an emanation of the State', following principles laid down by the European Court in *Foster v British Gas*. These are:

(a) whether the entity was made responsible, pursuant to a measure adopted by the State, for providing a public service;
(b) whether the service it provided was under the control of the State; and
(c) whether it possessed or claimed to exercise any special powers.

Thus, although Rolls Royce was 100% owned by the State, it was a commercial undertaking rather than a State body for the purpose of enforcing the provisions of a Directive.

1.54 In strict legal theory, a Directive is not enforceable against a non-State body or a private individual. Thus, if there are no national rules on a subject, it is not permissible to rely on the provisions of a Directive as the basis of a claim. However, the European Court of Justice has gone a greater deal further in two recent cases. In *Dekker v Stichting Vormings–centrum voor Jong Volwassenen (VJV-Centrum) Plus* (see para 4.35B), it was held that it is permissible to rely on the provisions of a Directive in order to interpret national law, and in particular those provisions of national law which were designed to implement a Directive. Thus the European Court will interpret national law in the light of the language and aims of the Directive. In *Marleasing SA v La Comercial Internacional de Alimentaction*, the Court went still further. They stated 'It follows from the obligation on Member States to take all measures appropriate to ensure the performance of their obligation to achieve the results provided for in Directives, that in applying national law, whether it was a case of provisions prior to or subsequent to the Directive, the national court called on to interpret it was required to do so as far as possible in the light of the wording and purpose of the Directive in order to achieve the result sought by the Directive.'

Finally, in an historic decision, the European Court has stated that if a Member State fails to take the necessary steps to achieve the results required by a Directive, an individual who suffers damage thereby may sue the State for the loss suffered which results from that failure. In *Francovich v Italian Republic*, the Italian Government had failed to implement EC Directive 80/987 on the protection of employees on an employer's insolvency. In consequence, an employee was unable to recover wages owed to him following his employer's insolvency, and he sued the Italian Government for compensation. It was held that his claim could succeed as long as three conditions were satisfied. These were that: (a) the result required by the Directive includes the conferring of rights for the benefit of individuals, (b) the contents of those rights may be determined by reference to the provisions of the Directive, and (c) there is a causal link between the breach of the obligation of the State and the damage suffered by the person affected.

Since these three conditions were met, the claim succeeded. However, the European Court appeared to suggest that a claim could be made not only when a Member State fails to implement the terms of a Directive, but also when it incorrectly implements a Directive. Further, national courts are the appropriate forum for such claims, without the necessity of seeking a remedy in the European Court.

Thus, although Directives are addressed to Member States, and can be enforced by intended beneficiaries against the State, there now appears to be an interesting remedy against a State which fails to implement or incorrectly implements a Directive by persons who suffer damage thereby.

1.55 Currently, there are a number of Directives in force which have a particular bearing on employment law, and which have been implemented by UK legislation.

1.56 (i) *Directive 75/117/EEC* (the Equal Pay Directive). This states that the principle of equal pay means, for the same work or for work to which equal value has been attributed, the elimination of all discrimination on grounds of sex with regard to all aspects and conditions of remuneration. Member States shall take the necessary measures to ensure that provisions appearing in collective agreements, wage scales, wage agreements or individual contracts of employment which are contrary to the principle of equal pay shall be declared null and void or may be amended. The Equal Pay Act and the Equal Pay (Amendment) Regulations implement this Directive.

1.57 (ii) *Directive 76/207/EEC* (the Equal Treatment Directive). This states that men and women shall be entitled to equal treatment as regards access to employment, including promotion, and also to vocational training and working conditions. There shall be no discrimination on grounds of sex, either directly or indirectly by reference to marital or family status. To comply with this Directive, reference may be made to the Sex Discrimination Acts of 1975 and 1986. However, there are a number of outstanding problems which still remain to be resolved, particularly with reference to pensions and retirement age generally.

1.58 (iii) *Directive 75/129/EEC* (Collective Redundancies Directive). This Directive requires employers to consult with workers' representatives before making collective redundancies, and also requires that prior notification be given to the competent public authorities. The provisions of TULR(C)A ss. 188-194 meet this Directive.

1.59 (iv) *Directive 77/187/EEC* (Acquired Rights Directive). This Directive provides for the safeguarding of the rights of employees when their employment is transferred from one employer to another. The transferor and transferee are also required to consult with employees' representatives about the consequences of the transfer. The Transfer of Undertakings (Protection of Employment) Regulations were passed to implement the Directive.

1.60 (v) *Directive 79/7/EEC* (Equal Treatment in Social Security Matters). This Directive requires that there should be no discrimination on grounds of sex (either directly or indirectly by reference to marital or family status) in the scope of social security schemes (i.e. sickness, invalidity, old age, occupational accidents and diseases, and unemployment benefits), the conditions of access thereto, contributions, the calculation of benefits (including benefits for spouses and dependants) and the duration of benefits. However, excluded from this Directive are benefits which arise from the determination of pensionable age.

At the present time, women are permitted to receive the State pension at 60, whereas men receive it when they are 65, and this is permissible under the Directive. Other Social Security legislation has been passed to conform to its provisions.

1.61 (vi) *Directive 86/613/EEC* (Equal Treatment in Occupational Pension Schemes). This Directive requires that there shall be no discrimination between men and women in access to and benefits from occupational pension schemes. The Social Security Act 1989 was designed to implement the Directive, but further problems have arisen as a result of the decision in *Barber v Guardian Royal Exchange Assurance Group* (see para. 4.45).

1.62 (vii) *Directive 86/613/EEC* (Equal Treatment for Self-employed). This Directive requires that the laws of Member States relating to self-employment shall not contain any discriminatory provisions, that there shall be protection for self-employed persons and their wives during pregnancy and motherhood, and that discrimination does not arise from the establishing of businesses or other self-employed activities.

1.63 (viii) *Directive 80/987/EEC* (Employers' Insolvency). This Directive requires Member States to guarantee the payment of certain outstanding claims due to an employee when his employer becomes insolvent, subject to certain limits. The provisions of the Insolvency Act 1986 meet the terms of this Directive.

1.64 A number of other Directives relating to health and safety at work have also been passed by the Council of Ministers, and these will be referred to in Chapter 12.

C. Recommendations

1.65 A Recommendation made under Community law has no binding effect, and cannot be relied upon to enforce a legal right in a national court. However, in *Grimaldi v Fonds des Maladies Professionnelles*, the European Court of Justice held that national courts are bound to take recommendations into account when determining disputes which are referred to them, in particular when they clarify the interpretation of laws passed to implement them, or when they are designed to supplement binding Community measures.

1.66 Recommendations have been made on such topics as the employment of disabled persons, hours of work and holidays generally, flexible retirement, vocational training for women and sexual harassment.

D. European Court of Justice

1.67 This Court sits in Luxembourg, and consists of judges who are nominated by the various Member States. The Court has jurisdiction under Article 177 of the Treaty of Rome to give rulings concerning the interpretation of the Treaty of Regulations or Directives made by the Council of Ministers. A Member State may be taken to the Court by another State or by the European Commission (see *Commission for the European Communities v United Kingdom*, para 4.41). A British court may, but is not bound to, make a reference to the Court if it is necessary to enable a decision to be made (see *Macarthys Ltd v Smith*, para 4.96). Once the Court has given its opinion, the matter is referred back to the national court for the application of the opinion to the facts of the case (see *Jenkins v Kingsgate (Clothing Productions) Ltd*).

1.68 It should be noted that there are no specified time limits for bringing a claim under European law, as the provisions of the Treaty of Rome came into force upon accession (see *Stevens v Bexley Health Authority*). Time will start to run against a State body from the day the State makes good its failure to comply with the objectives laid down in the Directive (*Cannon v Barnsley Metropolitan Borough Council*). However, the European Court may, when giving a ruling, indicate that this shall only apply to claims lodged at the date of the ruling (*Barber v Guardian Royal Exchange*).

European Court of Human Rights

1.69 The United Kingdom has ratified the European Convention on Human Rights and Fundamental Freedoms, which gives an individual direct access to the European Commission on Human Rights, and, if the claim is admissible, the matter will then go to the European Court of Human Rights at Strasbourg. Of particular relevance is Article 11 of the Convention (see *Young, James and Webster v United Kingdom*).

European Charter for Fundamental Social Rights

1.70 In 1986, the Single European Act was signed in Luxembourg and The Hague, amending certain provisions of the Treaty of Rome. The UK Government accepted these changes by means of the European Communities (Amendment) Act 1986.

1.71 One of the important changes made concerns the introduction of a system of qualified majority voting on certain matters, as opposed to the principle of unanimity. Qualified majority voting (a system whereby each Member State is allocated a certain number of votes, depending on its population size) can be used to pass Community measures dealing with health and safety matters and proposals on the working environment.

1.72 The European Commission has, in consequence, produced a Charter for Fundamental Social Rights, which it hopes will be passed by the qualified majority voting system, although there appears to be some opposition both to the method and contents. It is argued that some of the proposals fall outside the objectives of Community law, and other proposals will adversely affect the competitiveness of some States, and add to the already heavily regulated system.

1.73 The main areas covered by the Social Charter are as follows:

1. the right to freedom of movement between Member States, restricted only on the ground of public order. A worker from one State should have equality of treatment with the nationals of the State in which he is living, with particular reference to taxation and social security;
2. workers should receive fair remuneration, which should be sufficient to enable them to enjoy a decent standard of living. Part-time workers would be given protection, workers should have free access to job placement facilities, and there would be limits placed on deductions from wages;
3. there would be a commitment to upward harmonisation in order to improve living standards and working conditions,

with limits on the weekly working time, improvements in redundancy provisions, minimum annual paid holidays, and a weekly rest period;
4. there shall be adequate social protection, based on length of service, number of hours worked, and the weekly pay;
5. there shall be freedom to join trade unions (or not to join) enter into collective bargaining arrangements, and pursue industrial action;
6. workers shall be entitled to have vocational training, and to re-train throughout their working life;
7. all discrimination between the sexes should be removed, and support provided to prevent a clash between domestic and work responsibilities;
8. workers should be given information, be consulted and encouraged to participate in decisions, in particular in respect of re-structuring, redundancies, the introduction of new technology, mergers, etc;
9. there must be upward harmonisation of provisions relating to health and safety at work;
10. the working hours of young persons should be subject to limits, and they should receive adequate vocational training for the first two years of their working life;
11. adequate pensions should be provided for retired persons, and others should have appropriate medical and social security assistance;
12. disabled persons should have their working life improved by better access facilities, adequate mobility provisions, suitable transport, etc.

1.74 Several draft Directives have already been issued to implement part of the Social Charter, but, as noted, there is some resistance. Thus the Directive on Working Time has been agreed in principle, although it is to be challenged by the UK Government in the European Court on the ground that it is not properly a health and safety matter. Less controversial are the Directives on health and safety, many of which have been implemented into UK law (see Chapter 12).

1.75 Many of the provisions of the Social Charter were adopted in the Social Chapter as an annex to the Maastricht Treaty, which was designed to accelerate the pace towards ultimate European unity. However, the UK Government negotiated an 'opt out' clause from the Social Chapter, and thus the adoption of any of its provisions by other European States will not bind the UK.

CHAPTER 2

The nature of a contract of employment

2.1 The complex form of modern industrial and commercial organisation enables people to work under a variety of legal arrangements which may be entirely satisfactory to all concerned, but which are difficult to rationalise into well-defined categories necessary for the purpose of legal analysis. Legal rights and responsibilities are frequently at the mercy of verbal distinctions, for modern terminology does not assist in the process of drawing precise lines between different economic relationships. The nineteenth century concept of 'master and servant', though somewhat servile by today's standards, at least had the merit of elegant simplicity.

Workers

2.2 Consider the term 'worker'. This can mean 'anyone who works for a living', and would thus include all from a managing director of a large public company to a machine operator in an engineering factory; a bookmaker's clerk on a race track to a surgeon in a hospital. Nowadays it is surely a mistake to use the term with a socio-economic undertone. On the other hand, the term 'workman' has, in the past, been given a more precise legal meaning, though it appears to be falling into legislative disuse as legal rights are given a wider scope.

2.3 Whatever the currently acceptable meaning of these terms may be, the law can place within its ambit anyone it wishes. Thus, TULR(C)A s. 296 and the Sex Discrimination Act 1975 (SDA) define the term 'worker' in similar, but not identical terms. The latest statutory definition is contained in s. 8 of the Wages Act 1986, which states that a worker is an individual who has entered into or works under:

a. a contract of service; or
b. a contract of apprenticeship; or
c. any other contract whereby the individual undertakes to do or perform personally any work or services for another party to the contract whose status is not by virtue of the contract that of client or customer of any profession or business undertaking carried on by the individual, and whether the contract is in writing or oral, expressed or implied.

As we shall see, the term does not include 'office holders', and policemen and other members of the constabulary are also excluded. The point is that a worker is not necessarily an employee. It is a much wider term, though apparently not wide enough to extend to writers who submitted scripts to the BBC (who were 'selling' the right to perform completed dramatic scripts, see *Writers' Guild of Great Britain v BBC*). Nor does the term include a Church of England clergyman, because he is not a person whose rights and duties are defined by contract (*Housman v Bishop of Ely*). Thus all employees are workers, but not all workers are employees (*Broadbent v Crisp*).

2.4 By contrast EPCA s. 153 defines an employee as an individual who has entered into or works under (or, where the employment has ceased, worked under), a contract of employment and it is with this definition that we shall be mainly concerned in this book. The bulk of the legal rights to be discussed will be applicable to employees only, though a few apply also to workers. From one point of view, a worker may be legally classified as an employee, and yet the same person may be a self-employed person from another standpoint. The 'economic man' refuses to be placed in neat legal pigeon-holes.

Employers

2.5 Thus the language of the lawyer, the economist, the politician and the layman tends to become confused in over-lapping situations. In this book we are dealing with the legal rights and duties of the employer and the employee. The employer is usually a readily identifiable entity, and may be defined as any person, partnership, corporate body or unincorporated association who (or which) employs one or more persons under a contract of employment, although this definition is not particularly helpful. In the building industry, for example, an 'employer' is the term used for someone who 'engages' a main contractor, whereas he ought properly to be described as 'the client'. Frequently, the 'acts' of the employer are in reality done by various levels of management, who are themselves employees, yet it is 'the employer' who will be called to account (e.g. *Courtaulds Northern Textiles v Andrew*).

Directors

2.6 A company director who has a service contract with his company is for all intents and purposes an employee of that company, but a non-executive director who has no such contract is not an employee. This can lead to some curious results. In *Lee v Lee's Air Farming Ltd* Lee owned all the shares bar one in a small company. He was killed whilst piloting an aircraft, and his widow was held to be entitled to a workman's compensation under a New Zealand statute in the same way as if her husband had been an employee of the company. Since a limited company, being a separate legal entity, is the employer, anyone who works for it - even a director who is in practice a sole shareholder - is capable of being an employee. Thus there is no reason why the owner of such a 'one man' business should not be able to obtain a redundancy payment if his company goes into liquidation. In *Robinson v George Sorby Ltd* an application on these grounds was refused, but this was because he could not prove the existence of a service contract between himself and the company.

2.7 A service contract between the company and a controlling director can either be an express or implied agreement. In the case of an implied agreement, it will be a question of fact; did he work as a director, and only occasionally step in for workmen who were away from work, or who needed extra help, or did he keep regular hours, and work only for short or significant periods on directors' duties (*Folami v Nigerline (UK) Ltd*)? In *Parsons v Albert Parsons & Sons Ltd* the applicant was a director of the family firm. Following a disagreement with his brothers, he was removed from office, and he claimed that this constituted unfair dismissal. The Court of Appeal held that as he was not an employee, he could not bring a claim. There was no express contract of service, and on the evidence it was not possible to imply one. He was not paid a wage or salary, but received 'fees and emoluments'; there was no record kept, as required by s. 26(1) of the Companies Act 1967, of details of his contract of service; he, and his brothers, paid self-employed national insurance stamps. On the facts therefore, he was clearly a director of the company, not an employee.

2.8 In *Road Transport Industry Training Board v Readers Garage* the question was whether industrial training levy could be assessed on the earnings of a controlling managing director who also worked as an employee, and the court held that if there was a contract of service implied between him and the company, then the tribunal must assess how much of his drawings from the company were in respect of such service, and the levy assessed on that amount. Any sum he drew as a director would not be assessed for levy purposes.

Business consultants

2.9 A person who works in a consultancy or advisory capacity is capable of being an employee, depending on the legal and factual arrangements which are made. In *Bromsgrove Casting and Machining Ltd v Martin*, the applicant was a managing director of a company. He ceased to hold office, but continued to work as a director and consultant. There was no provision as to the number of hours to be worked, and his salary was unchanged. He was then dismissed, and he brought a complaint of unfair dismissal. It was held that in his capacity as a consultant, he was retained, not employed. His employment only came into being when he was actually called upon to give advice. Therefore, the industrial tribunal should have enquired into the number of hours he was normally required to give advice, to see whether or not his contract was for the requisite number of hours per week in order to qualify for protection from unfair dismissal.

Partners

2.10 A partner is a self-employed person in business who is remunerated by taking a share of the profits. Cases can be found where 'salaried partners' are known to exist. This is clearly a contradiction in terms. Architects and dentists frequently engage 'associates', and may make contractual arrangements which suit all concerned, but in law such persons, however designated, are probably employees. However, the contract of engagement may specify to the contrary. A junior partner, however, is a partner with (usually) a lesser share of the profits and/or a smaller say in the conduct of the partnership business. The modern vogue for co-partnership and profit-sharing schemes may well throw up further problems in the future, for although the mere fact of sharing profits is not evidence that a partnership exists (Partnership Act 1890 s. 3), it could together with other relevant circumstances, lead to that conclusion (see *Glasgow v Independent Printing Co*).

Office holders

2.11 A special category of persons exists who are technically known as office holders. They are not employed by virtue of a contract of employment, and therefore have certain privileges attached to their position. A judge, for example, holds office during good behaviour and may only be dismissed on a resolution passed by both Houses of Parliament. A magistrate is also an office holder (*Knight v A-G*). However, some office holders may also have a contract of employment, e.g. a stipendiary reader in the Church of England (*Barthorpe v Exeter Diocesan Board of Finance*). In *102 Social Club and Institute Ltd v Bickerton*, a club secretary was paid an honorarium of £225 per year. The EAT held that the industrial tribunal should consider whether the money was paid by way of a salary for services rendered, or whether it was an honorarium for work done as a member of the club in his capacity as an office holder. In the former case only would he be regarded as being an employee.

2.12 The earnings received by an office holder are more akin to remuneration for work done than by way of honorarium for tenure of office. Thus his claim for the money is closely analogous to a claim for a salary due under a contract of employment. It follows that the office holder must be willing and able to render the services required to him, and that if he refuses to perform his duties (as a form of industrial action) his paymaster is entitled to withhold the relevant part of his remuneration (*Miles v Wakefield Metropolitan District Council*).

Ministers of religion

2.13 Generally speaking, ministers of religion cannot be said to be employed under a contract of employment (*President of the Methodist Conference v Parfitt*). Although, in the past, industrial tribunals have held that rabbis, Granthis and Inmans are employees, it is likely that those decisions are wrong (*Santokh Singh v Guru Nanak Gurdwara*).

Crown employees

2.14 The precise legal nature of the relationship between the Crown and civil servants has long been a moot point, but it now appears that since such arrangements have an intention to create legal relations, a contract of employment exists, enforceable by private law remedies (*R v Lord Chancellor's Department, ex Nangle*). The provisions of the Equal Pay Act (see s. 1(8)), the Race Relations Act (see s. 72(2)) and the Sex Discrimination Act (see s. 85(2)) do apply to the Crown. All the relevant parts of EPCA now apply to Crown employees (i.e. Parts I, II, III, V, VIII and IX and s. 53 in Part IV), the exceptions being cases based on national security and the right to minimum periods of notice. The provisions of TULR(C)A similarly apply, except the power of the court to make an order against an employer in respect of a failure to ensure that a check-off arrangement excludes a payment to the political fund of a trade union (s. 87), failure to comply with a declaration of the Central Arbitration Committee requiring an employer to disclose information for collective bargaining purposes (s. 184), and the procedure for consulting with trade unions on redundancies (ss. 188-194). Again, cases relating to national security are exempted. So far as the armed forces are concerned (including territorial, auxiliary and reserve forces associations), they will eventually be covered by parts of EPCA (see s. 138A), although by Order in Council it may be provided that a particular complaint or reference shall be excluded from an industrial tribunal until the person aggrieved has availed himself of the services procedure for the redress of complaints applicable to him. Members of the staff of the House of Commons have been accorded the same statutory protection in most fields as that enjoyed by Crown employees by virtue of EPCA s. 139, with Mr Speaker being deemed to be the employer. Staff employed by the House of Lords also have a similar full range of protections, except in relation to time off work for public duties connected with political activities and other minor exceptions (see EPCA s. 139A and TULR(C)A s. 277).

2.15 However, where a person holds any office or employment under the Crown which does not constitute a contract of employment, those terms shall be deemed to be such a contract for the purpose of the law relating to the liability in tort of any person who commits an act which induces another to break a contract, or interferes with the performance of any contract (or induces the interference), or consists of a threat that a contract will be broken or its performance interfered with. In other words, Crown servants will be deemed to have contracts of employment for the purpose of tort liability arising out of industrial action, unless the protections of s. 219 of TULR(C)A apply.

Health Service employees

2.16 Employees of the National Health Service have the full range of employment protection rights (now including the right to redundancy payments, see National Health Service and Community Care Act 1990 s. 60).

Police

2.17 A person is employed in the police service if he serves as a member of any constabulary maintained by virtue of an enactment, or in any capacity by virtue of which he has the powers or privileges of a constable. This includes prison officers (*Home Office v Robinson*), special constables, etc. Although he may be employed under a contract of employment, he has no right to claim unfair dismissal, even in respect of conduct which occurs when he was not exercising those privileges or powers (*Home Office v Robinson*). He/she has no right to an itemised pay statement or written reasons for dismissal, no right to return after confinement, nor to guarantee pay, medical suspension pay, trade union rights, time off work or maternity pay. He does have the right to written particulars under EPCA s. 1, minimum periods of notice, and redundancy pay.

2.18 A policeman is deemed to be employed by the Chief Constable or the police authority for the purpose of the Sex Discrimination Act (s. 17) and the Race Relations Act (s. 16) in respect of any act done by him or the authority in relation to discrimination in employment.

2.19 A policeman cannot be dismissed without a proper hearing in accordance with the rules of natural justice (*Ridge v Baldwin*), and, in the event of wrongful dismissal, he has the right to be reinstated. Police cadets are persons training to become policemen, and are not employees (*Wiltshire Police Authority v Wynn*).

Status

2.20 Over the years a number of different groups of employees had additionally acquired a special legal status which overrode the existence of their contracts of employment (see, e.g. *McClelland v Northern Ireland General Health Services Board*), but it now may be truly said that in employment law, 'there is a movement from status to contract'. Thus registered dock workers no longer enjoy the special protection which they had under the dock labour scheme (see Dock Work Act 1989), and tenure for all University staff appointed or promoted after 20th November 1987 has been abolished (Education Reform Act 1988 s. 203). In respect of University academic staff appointed prior to that date, regard must be had to the terms of their appointment. If these state that dismissal is only possible for 'good cause' then it is not possible to dismiss for any other reason, e.g. redundancy (*University of Aston v Pearce*).

2.21 Generally, therefore, the provisions of existing protective legislation will apply to all categories of employees, without creating a special group with particular privileges. Certain public law remedies remain, but these are progressively being restricted in scope (see para. 2.68).

Employees

2.22 An employee, though easy to define, is not so easy to describe, for the relationship between A (the employer) and B (the employee) is complicated by the fact that there is also a relationship between B and the State. It is possible that a person can be an employee for one purpose, but not an employee for another. Thus in *Challinor v Taylor* a taxi driver was the night driver of a cab which was used during the day by the owner. The latter paid for the fuel, insurance and maintenance of the car, and took 65% of the gross takings. He also paid the cost of the employer's contribution towards the driver's national insurance stamp. The driver, however, was assessed for income tax purposes as a self-employed person under Schedule D. The owner sold the taxi and the driver was thus redundant. It was held that he was not an employee, and therefore not entitled to a redundancy payment.

2.23 There is no reason in principle why an employee cannot have more than two employers, and, provided he is within the appropriate protection of the law, pursue his legal remedies against either of them. Indeed, it is possible for an employee to have two contracts of employment with the same employer, so that if he is dismissed from his employment under one contract, he may pursue his remedy whilst still leaving the other contract subsisting (*Throsby v Imperial College of Science and Technology*).

2.24 However, it is not possible to aggregate hours worked under separate contracts with the same employer so as to achieve the relevant period of continuous employment (*Lewis v Surrey County Council*).

Contract of service

2.25 The basic division for our purposes is between those who are employed persons and those who are self-employed, and the distinction between these categories is that the employed person works under a contract of service, whereas the self-employed person works under a contract for services. Again, it is easy to state this distinction, but in practice it has proved difficult to draw it, and over the years the courts have developed a number of tests designed to produce a given result. Also, under the Conduct of Employment Agencies and Employment Businesses Regulations (made under the Employment Agencies Act 1973) if a person is employed otherwise than under a contract of service or apprenticeship, he is deemed to be self-employed. To rebut this presumption, all the terms of the contract must be examined in detail (*Ironmonger v Movefield Ltd*).

2.25A It is possible for Parliament to ignore the distinction altogether; for example, the Sex Discrimination Act defines 'employment' as meaning employment under a contract of service '... or a contract personally to execute any work or labour ...' which definition clearly includes self-employed persons (see *Quinnen v Hovells*, para 4.70). It must thus be clear that the law may categorise workers as it wishes in accordance with the objectives to be achieved.

Control test

2.26 In the nineteenth century the determining factor was stated to be the control which was exercised by the employer over the manner in which the employee could do his work. Thus if the employer could tell the employee not only what to do, but how to do it, then a contract of service existed (*Yewens v Noakes*). In modern conditions the application of such a test is clearly unreal. An employee may be highly skilled and qualified, and employed specifically because he has professional training and competence, so that the employer is frequently unable (as well as being unwilling) to instruct the employee as to how the work is to be done. Despite this difficulty, some modern decisions have added to the control test a refinement which looks for *the right to control* as being the determinant factor (*Gibb v United Steel Companies Ltd*), or even the existence of the right to control, even though this is seldom if ever exercised in practice. It is clear that the greater the degree of control which is exercisable by the employer, the more likely it will be that the contract is one of service (*Whittaker v Minister of Pensions*), but 'the greater the skill required for an employee's work the less significant is control in determining whether the employee is under a contract of service' (*Beloff v Pressdram*).

2.27 But the exercise of a degree of control is not conclusive. In *Hitchcock v Post Office*, the applicant ran a sub-post office as part of a shop he owned. Although the Post Office exercised control over many of its activities, it was held that this was because of the need to ensure financial control and security, rather than being a control over managerial functions. Consequently, the sub-post master was not an employee of the Post Office.

Organisational test

2.28 In *Stevenson, Jordan and Harrison Ltd v MacDonald and Evans*, Denning LJ suggested a more up-to-date test. 'Under a contract of service', he said, 'a man is employed as part of the business and his work is done as an integral part of the business'. This 'organisational' test has certain advantages, particularly in relation to skilled employees who are 'integrated' into an enterprise, e.g. doctors, nurses etc, in respect of whom the control test is inappropriate. In *Whittaker v Minister of Pensions* a trapeze artiste broke her wrist as a result of a fall in her act. It was held that she was an integral part of the circus business and thus an employee for the purpose of claiming industrial injuries benefit.

Multiple test

2.29 But these problems are too complex to be capable of being resolved by the application of any single simple test, and the courts nowadays will look at all the surrounding features, thus applying what is in fact a multiple test. Certainly the power of selection, the payment of wages, national insurance stamps, income tax, holiday monies and pensions, and the power to suspend and dismiss are all relevant features which need to be taken into account. In *Ready Mixed Concrete v Minister of Pensions* a firm dismissed its drivers, sold all the lorries to them and re-employed them under a contract which contained obligations capable of leading to the conclusion that they were both employed and self-employed persons. The drivers had to wear the company's uniforms, place their lorries at the company's disposal for a certain number of hours, only use them for the company's business, obey the orders of the foreman, and sell the lorries back to the company at an agreed current market valuation. On the other hand, the drivers had to maintain the lorries at their own expense and pay all running costs. In addition, they could employ a substitute driver, and could own more than one lorry. They paid their own income tax and national insurance contributions, had no set hours or meal breaks, and made their own decisions as to how to drive the lorries and which routes to take. MacKenna J held that there were three conditions necessary to establish that a contract of service existed. The first was that the employee agreed to provide his own work and skill in the performance of a service for his employer, the second was that there must be some element of control exercisable by the employer, and the third was that the other terms of the contract must not be inconsistent with the existence of a contract of employment. The fact that the drivers could (and did) employ a substitute was clearly crucial in deciding that they were self-employed haulage contractors.

2.30 More recently the entrepreneurial test seems to be the dominating feature. The problem is looked at from a self-employed person's point of view, and the question asked 'Is he in business on his own?' Again, no exhaustive list of considerations can be formulated. Does he provide his own equipment? Hire his own helpers? Is there any degree of financial responsibility for investment or degree of risk? Does he undertake any other sort of commissions, business or employment? Is there any opportunity to profit from sound management? These questions were raised in *Market Investigations Ltd v Minister of Social Security*, where a company employed women on a part-time basis to do market research. They could work as they chose, but according to a set pattern. It was held that the women were employees, and not employed in business 'on their own'. The more unskilled and untrained a person is, the less likely it will be that the industrial tribunal will hold that he is running his own business. In *Airfix Footwear Ltd v Cope* the applicant was a home-worker making heels for shoes manufactured by the respondent company. She was provided with the necessary equipment and material, and worked in accordance with instructions given to her. The EAT upheld a finding that she was an employee. On the other hand, in *Argent v Minister of Social Security* an actor taught drama on a part-time basis at a school. It was held that he was a self-employed lecturer.

2.31 In *Withers v Flackwell Heath Football Supporters' Club*, the EAT stated that difficult cases could be resolved by using industrial, rather than legal, terminology. Hence, the person could be asked a simple question, 'Are you your own boss?'.

2.32 This pragmatic approach was taken even further in *Davis v New England College of Arundel*, where the applicant was engaged as a lecturer on a yearly renewable contract. He specifically asked to be treated as being self-employed as he wished to retain that status for income tax and national insurance purposes. He was not re-engaged, and claimed that he had been unfairly dismissed. It was held that to determine whether or not he was an employee, the matter had to be looked at objectively. His request to be treated as being self-employed, and the fact that the college so regarded him, did not alter the nature of the contractual relationship between him and his employer. In reality, he was an employee of the college, and hence he was entitled to bring a claim. It is the essence of the arrangement, rather than the form, which is the determinant factor (*Tyne and Clyde Warehouses Ltd v Hamerton*).

2.33 The difficulties inherent in such cases can be seen in *Massey v Crown Life Insurance Co*, where the applicant was an employee of the respondents. It was then agreed that he should be treated as being self-employed, and a new agreement to this effect was signed. Although his actual duties were identical, the applicant was taxed under Schedule D, and paid self-employed insurance. He was then dismissed, and claimed unfair dismissal. It was held that he was employed under a contract for services. While the parties cannot alter the nature of their relationship by putting a different label on it, where the situation was in doubt, or was ambiguous, an agreement which stipulated the nature of the relationship affords strong evidence of what it is. In this case, there was a genuine attempt to change the legal situation to that of an independent contractor. There was no attempt to deceive the Inland Revenue. It was a genuine agreement to enable the applicant to be treated as being self-employed. Consequently, he could not claim that his dismissal was unfair. The Court of Appeal distinguished the case of *Ferguson v John Dawson & Partners Ltd* (see para 2.40) on the ground that in the latter case there was little evidence as to what the actual contract was.

2.34 In truth, before a clear and satisfactory answer can be given to the question 'Who is an employee?' we may well need to pose a second one, namely, 'For what purpose is the question being asked?' A part-time lecturer may well be a self-employed person for income tax purposes but an employee in relation to national insurance contributions, and he may well be an employed person (using the 'organisational test') if the issue was raised as to the vicarious liability of his employer for wrongful acts committed by him during the course of his work. The pragmatic approach adopted by the courts is to say that the matter is a question of fact, to be determined by the evidence in each case. For example, in *Maurice Graham Ltd v Brunswick* a company engaged self-employed bricklayers, who paid their own income tax and were responsible for their own national insurance contributions. The company was convicted of breaches of the Construction (Health and Welfare) Regulations 1966, and argued on appeal that those regulations only applied to 'employees', not independent contractors. It was held that though the outward arrangement gave the appearance of a worker being an independent contractor, this was not conclusive. The company controlled and supervised the men, and supplied them with the necessary equipment and materials, and the court refused to disturb the convictions.

2.35 An industrial tribunal should therefore take the following factors into account, and make its determination accordingly:

a. the contractual provisions (*BSM v Secretary of State for Social Services*);
b. the degree of control exercised by the employer (*Global Plant Ltd v Secretary of State for Health and Social Security*);
c. the obligation of the employer to provide work (*Nethermere (St Neots) Ltd v Gardiner*);
d. the obligation on the employee to do the work (*Ahmet v Trusthouse Forte Catering Ltd*);
e. the duty of personal service (*Ready Mixed Concrete Ltd v Ministry of Pensions*);
f. the provision of tools, equipment, instruments, etc (*Willy Scheiddegger Swiss Typewriting School Ltd v Ministry of Social Security*);
g. the arrangements made for tax, national insurance, VAT, statutory sick pay (*Davis v New England College of Arundel*);
h. The opportunity to work for other employers (*WHPT Housing Association Ltd v Secretary of State for Social Services*);
i. other contractual provisions, including holiday pay, sick pay, notice, fees, expenses, etc (*Hamerton v Tyne and Clyde Warehouses Ltd*);
j. the degree of financial risk and the responsibility for investment and management (*Market Investigations Ltd v Minister of Social Security*);
k. whether the relationship of being self-employed is a genuine one, or whether there is an attempt to avoid modern protective legislation (*Young and Woods Ltd v West*).

2.36 No single factor, by itself, is conclusive, and all the relevant circumstances must be considered. As long as the industrial tribunals take these into account, their decision is a question of fact, not law, and their findings (either way) cannot normally be challenged (*O'Kelly v Trusthouse Forte plc* and see *Hall v Lorimer*) unless they took a view on the facts which would not reasonably be sustained (*Lee v Chung*). However, if there is a written contract which determines the relationship between the parties, the interpretation of that contract is a question of law, which can be considered on appeal (*Davies v Presbyterian Church of Wales*).

Distinction between employees and self-employed persons

2.37 There are a number of reasons for stressing the importance of this distinction between a contract of service and a contract for services, although recent decisions are tending to minimise this importance.

2.38 *a*. Under the Social Security Contributions and Benefits Act 1992 an employer must pay secondary Class 1 contributions in respect of employed earners (the primary contribution being made on an earnings related basis by the employed earner - which term includes an office holder). Self-employed earners pay a flat rate Class 2 contribution, and in addition a Class 4 contribution based on the gains or profits derived which are chargeable to income tax under Schedule D. The employer does not need to deduct PAYE income tax under Schedule E in respect of his self-employed independent contractors (who must make their own arrangements under Schedule D), and he need not pay a levy for industrial training purposes. An independent subcontractor may have to charge VAT on services supplied, which would not be so if he were an employee. But it must be stressed that it is the substance of the relationship which will count, not the form. Thus if a person is an employee in the legal sense, the employer's obligations will arise despite any artificial attempt or arrangements made to avoid such duties (*Pennington v Minister of Social Security*). Nor does the fact that a person pays his own insurance stamps and is responsible for his own income tax payments necessarily mean that he is a self-employed person. In *Jennings v Westwood Engineering Ltd* the applicant was offered employment. He was told that he could work at a lower rate of remuneration on PAYE, or at a higher rate, paying his own tax and insurance, and he chose the latter option. It was held that he was employed under a contract of employment nonetheless. Conversely, in *President of the Methodist Conference v Parfitt*, the fact that the applicant paid Class 1 national insurance and was taxed under Schedule E did not *per se* make him an employee.

2.39 One of the more intractable industrial problems which caused concern some years ago was the existence of the 'lump'. i.e. self-employed sub-contractors in the building industry. In *Construction Industry Training Board v Labour Force Ltd* when main contractors required labour they would contact Labour Force Ltd who would supply the men at agreed rates. The main contractor could dismiss the men but never paid them, and merely told Labour Force Ltd the number of hours each had worked. Labour Force Ltd paid the men on this basis, but the men agreed that they were self-employed, and agreed to be responsible for their own income tax, national insurance and holiday pay. it was held that there was no contract of any kind between the main contractors and the men, and further that there was no contract of service between Labour Force Ltd and the men, and consequently Labour Force Ltd were not liable to pay industrial training levy (which would be normally calculated on a percentage of the payroll).

2.40 More recently, however, the Court of Appeal has also indicated that it is concerned with the realities of the situation, rather than the form of the arrangement. In *Ferguson v John Dawson & Partners Ltd*, a builder's labourer agreed to work on the 'lump', or as the court found, as a 'self-employed labour only subcontractor'. He was seriously injured as a result of the employers' failure to provide a guard rail on a roof, and he sued for this breach of statutory duty. He could only succeed if he could show that he was an employee, and, by a majority, the Court upheld this contention. Megaw LJ agreed that the 'lump' arrangement was a mere device, capable of being put to advantage by each side, but which did not affect the strict legal relationship between the parties. Dissenting, Lawton LJ thought that there was no reason in law why a man could not sell his labour without becoming the employee of the other party. Also, he thought that it was contrary to public policy to allow a man to claim that he was self-employed for the purposes of evading taxation, but an employee for the purpose of claiming compensation.

2.41 The alleged problems caused by the 'lump' illustrate the difficulties in trying to squeeze 'the economic man' into tight legal compartments, for in the building industry there are large numbers of 'genuine' self-employed independent contractors who provide invaluable services, and no satisfactory way has been devised whereby the one can be distinguished from the other. Since one of the problems raised by the 'lump' was income tax avoidance, the Finance Act 1979 provides that an employer in the construction industry must deduct at source 25% of the income price (excluding the cost of materials) of subcontractors, which at least ensures that income tax liability is met by such persons. The 'genuine' sub-contractor may apply for a tax exemption certificate, provided he meets certain stringent requirements. But the problems of the industrial training levy, holiday stamps, safety, etc, remain to be resolved.

2.42 *b*. An employer will not normally be vicariously liable for the tortious acts (civil wrongs) committed by independent contractors (though there are certain exemptions to this rule) whereas he would be so liable for torts, committed by his employees in the course of their employment which cause injury or damage to third parties (see Chapter 6). Two contrasting cases will illustrate this point. In *Hillyer v St Bartholomew's Hospital* the plaintiff selected a consultant who negligently performed an operation. It was held that the hospital was not liable, because the consultant was an independent contractor who was merely using the facilities of the hospital. On the other hand, in *Cassidy v Ministry of Health*, a resident surgeon operated negligently on the plaintiff, and it was held that the hospital board, as the employer, was liable.

2.43 *c*. An employer owes a duty at common law to his employees to take reasonable care for their safety, whereas these duties do not normally apply with respect to his independent contractors, although again, there are exceptions. Thus in *McArdle v Andmac Roofing Co* the plaintiff worked for one of several subcontractors who were employed on converting a building at a holiday camp, who were all under the direction of Pontins (Contractors) Ltd. The latter had made no arrangements for safety precautions with the subcontractors, and as a result, the plaintiff suffered severe injuries when he fell off a roof. It was held that the main contractors (Pontins) assumed the responsibility of co-ordinating the work, and were therefore under a duty to ensure that reasonable safety precautions were taken for all those who were working on the job, even though they were not the employers of those who were working. The duties owed by the employer to his employees under the Health and Safety at Work etc Act 1974 are more extensive than those owed to independent contractors (see Chapter 12). In practice this may mean that a self-employed person who is injured whilst at work may be unable to claim any compensation from the employer, and additionally will be unable to claim industrial injuries benefit and/or sick pay.

2.44 *d.* An employee is entitled to receive details of his terms of employment under EPCA s. 1 and to receive certain minimum periods of notice on his dismissal. He has protection against unfair dismissal under EPCA, Part V, can claim redundancy payments in appropriate circumstances, and has various other rights under the Act. None of these benefits apply if the person is a self-employed independent contractor. On the other hand, a court may be able to make an attachment of earnings order whereby an employer is compelled to make certain deductions from the earnings of an employee; this is not possible in respect of a self-employed person.

Secondment of employees

2.45 Occasionally, an employer may second an employee to another employer for a certain purpose or a given period of time, and the question may then arise as to who is the employer of the loaned employee, particularly when the issue involves the responsibilities of the employer to third parties. For example, in *Mersey Docks and Harbour Board v Coggins & Griffith* the Harbour Board loaned a crane and driver to a firm of stevedores, the latter being responsible for the driver's wages. Because of the driver's negligence, there was an accident. It was held that the Harbour Board was the employer for the purpose of being held vicariously liable for the driver's negligence, for they had failed to discharge the burden of showing that the driver was no longer their employee. The courts will not readily accept that an employee has been transferred from one employer to another unless there is some evidence of his consent. But in *Arthur White v Tarmac Civil Engineering*, a crane and a driver were hired out. Under the contract, which was the standard form used in the plant hire industry, the driver was stated to be under the direction and control of the hirer, and for all purposes was to be regarded as the employee of the hirer. It was held that as between the main employer and the hirer, the latter was liable for damages which resulted from an accident due to the driver's negligence. In other words, the two employers had, as between themselves, come to a contractual arrangement as to their respective liabilities, even though this did not necessarily affect the legal relationship which existed between the driver and his own employer.

2.46 But a person who is the temporary employer may incur liabilities in appropriate circumstances. In *Garrard v Southey & Co and Standard Telephones and Cables Ltd* the plaintiff was loaned by his employers (the first defendants) to the second defendants to carry out some electrical work. The foreman of the second defendants not only told the plaintiff what to do but also specifically controlled the way he was to do his work. The plaintiff was injured and sued both employers for common law negligence. It was held that the temporary employers were liable, as they were his employers for the purpose of ensuring his safety at work. The court drew a distinction between those cases where a complicated piece of equipment was loaned together with an employee, and where an unskilled or semi-skilled workman is loaned on his own. In the former case it may be easier to infer that the general employer does not intend to part with the control over a complex and valuable piece of machinery, but if labour only is loaned, it is easier to infer the transfer of the rights of the general employer to the temporary employer. Further, it will be noted that in the *Mersey Docks* case, the issue was the liability of the employer to third parties, and it will be rare that the courts will accept the transference of the employee in the absence of an express agreement to this effect (as in *Arthur White's* case). In *Garrard's* case the temporary employer was the one who could and should have been responsible for the safety of the employee, and a transfer of that burden was not unreasonable.

Agency workers

2.47 Occasionally an employer may turn to an agency to provide him with staff for a specific or indefinite period. Under the Conduct of Employment Agencies and Employment Business Regulations 1976, an employment agency must give to agency-supplied workers a statement of their terms and conditions, but this statement does not have to define the employment status vis-à-vis themselves, the agency and the client. The matter must be tested in accordance with the usual principles. If the worker who is engaged is under a personal obligation to do the work, then it is likely that the contract of employment may come into existence. On the other hand, if the duty of the agency is to provide workers, but there is no obligation to provide a specific person, then this would be a contract whereby the agency agrees to provide services, and the worker in question would not be an employee. Also if the employer pays the agency for the services provided, and the latter pays the employee, then again, no contract of employment exists. Some agencies act as employers by deducting all lawful stoppages (tax, insurance, etc) at source. Others merely act as a placing bureau. The Income and Corporation Taxes Act 1988 s. 134 provides that if a worker is supplied to the client by an agency, and that worker is subject to supervision, direction or control as to the manner in which those services are rendered (or the client has the right to exercise such supervision, etc) then for the purpose of the Income Tax Acts, such services will be treated as if they were provided under a contract of employment, and any payments received by the worker, whether from the client or from the agency, shall be taxable under Schedule E. There are, however, a number of loopholes in this provision. The terms of the contract between the worker and the agency may be relevant in determining the legal relationship which may exist in this tripartite situation (see *Construction Industry Training Board v Labour Force Ltd*).

Temporary employees

2.48 A temporary employee has all the rights of any other employee as long as he has the appropriate length of service and works the necessary hours. An exception here is to be found in EPCA s. 61, which states that if an employee is employed on a temporary basis in order to replace a woman who has been given maternity leave or to replace someone suspended on medical grounds, and the latter returns to work, the temporary employee does not acquire a full range of rights in respect of unfair dismissal. It is essential, however, that the contract specifically points out the temporary nature of the employment. This provision has ceased to have any practical effect since the qualifying period of employment for unfair dismissal has been raised to two years. Also, in *Dean v Polytechnic of North London*, Sir John Donaldson thought that the temporary nature of the employment could well amount to 'some other substantial reason' so as to justify a dismissal, though the industrial tribunal would have to be convinced that the employer had acted reasonably in the circumstances.

Part-time employees

2.49 The fact that a person only devotes part of his week to the employment may have some bearing on the issue of whether or not he is an employee, but since there are a number of possible permutations this factor cannot be conclusive. A person may have more than one employment, or may be partly employed and partly self-employed, or totally self-employed, pursuing a number of businesses.

2.50 But if a contract of employment exists, then any person who is employed for more than 16 hours per week under that contract for more than two years or who has been continuously employed for more than eight hours but less than 16 hours for the previous five years, has in effect a full range of legal protections, and the part-time nature of the employment is irrelevant (see Appendix C).

2.51 If an employee is required to work at home as part of his job, these may be included in the reckonable total. In *Lake v Essex County Council*, a part-time teacher was employed for just over 19 hours per week. Her claim for unfair dismissal was rejected by the industrial tribunal as she did not work for the requisite number of hours each week (21 hours, as the law then was). In the hours she worked, nearly four hours were set aside for marking and preparation, but she argued that this was not enough, and had to do additional work at home. The Court of Appeal upheld the decision of the industrial tribunal. Any work outside school hours which she chose to do was a voluntary act outside her contractual obligations. Since it is only normal working hours which can be computed for statutory purposes, it follows that voluntary overtime work does not come into the calculation (*ITT Components Ltd v Kolah*).

2.52 To qualify for the various rights, the employee need not actually be working for the relevant number of hours. It is sufficient if he is employed under a contract which normally involves employment for more than 16 hours (or between 8-16, as the case may be). If no set hours are laid down by the contract, the custom and practice may be looked to (*Post Office v Holder and Mitchell*). However, it is not permissible to average working hours so as to arrive at a minimum of 16 hours per week (*Mailway (Southern) Ltd v Willsher*) unless the normal working week is contemplated to be 16 hours or more (*Miller v Harry Thornton (Lorries) Ltd*). Nor is it permissible to aggregate hours worked under separate contracts so as to achieve the relevant period of continuous employment (*Lewis v Surrey County Council*).

2.52A However, the position of part-time workers under European law is more complex. It appears to be accepted that more women than men work part-time, and therefore that to treat a part-timer less favourably than a full-time worker can amount to an act of discrimination on grounds of sex. In *Jenkins v Kingsgate (Clothing Productions) Ltd* (see para 4.89), it was held that paying a part-time worker less pay per hour than a full-time worker was discriminatory on grounds of sex contrary to Article 119 of the Treaty of Rome (see para 1.52) unless the differential was capable of being objectively justified on the basis of factors other than sex (e.g. the extra employment costs incurred when employing part-timers, the need to reduce absenteeism and obtain the maximum utilisation of plant etc). In *Rinner-Kuhn v FWW* the European Court held that the fact that national legislation permitted the exclusion from statutory sick pay of employees who worked for less than ten hours per week was also a breach of Article 119, where a greater proportion of women than men were disadvantaged by the provision. And in *Bilka-Kaufhaus v Weber von Hartz* it was held that the exclusion of a part-time worker from a supplementary occupational pension scheme would constitute a breach of Article 119 unless the national court found that the object served by the exclusion was necessary and justifiable.

2.52B Indeed, any national provision which adversely affects part-time workers, and which thus contains an element of sex discrimination, must be set aside, if it is contrary to Article 119 of the Treaty of Rome, or the European Directives. In *Kowalska v Freie und Hansestadt Hamburg*, a collective agreement provided for a severance payment to be made in certain circumstances, but to be eligible, the worker had to work for a minimum of 38 hours per week. The European Court held that the provision was contrary to Article 119, unless it could be shown that it was justified on objective factors unrelated to discrimination on grounds of sex.

2.52C More recently, the European Commission has submitted a draft Directive on part-time workers which requires them to be treated in all respects (as regards remuneration, benefits, etc) as a full-time worker, on a pro-rata basis.

Probationary employees

2.53 The essence of a probationary appointment is that the employer retains the right not to confirm the appointment after a specified period, particularly on the grounds of capability. The majority of the tribunal in *Donn v Greater London Council* thought that the tests which are applied to a probationary employee are not necessarily the same as those which apply to a confirmed appointment, and a decision not to retain a probationer may be justified even though a similar decision made with respect to a fully established employee may not be justified. This view has been followed on a number of occasions (e.g. *Hamblin v London Borough of Ealing*), for a probationary employee must know that he is on trial, and must therefore establish his suitability for the post. The employer, however, must give the employee a proper opportunity to prove himself, and give a warning if the required standards are not being met (*Post Office v Mughal*). A probationary employee is still an employee, and is therefore entitled to have appropriate guidance and advice (*ILEA v Lloyd*).

2.54 Certainly, if the probationary period is less than two years, few problems will arise, but a longer probationary period could create difficulties. In *Weston v University College, Swansea* the applicant was appointed as a lecturer for the probationary period of three years. At the end of this time he was not placed on the permanent staff. It was held that he was entitled to pursue his complaint in respect of his alleged unfair dismissal, for his contract was not for a fixed term. The employer must still show that he acted reasonably in dismissing a probationer, and that the reason was within the statutory requirements, and it is submitted that if a different test is to be applied, the employer must show a valid reason why a probationary period of such a length of time is required in order to establish the suitability of the employee for the post in question.

2.55 If an employee is told that his appointment is subject to a probationary period of a certain length of time, this does not give him a legal right to be employed for that length of time, and the employer may lawfully dismiss him before that period has expired (*Dalgleish v Kew House Farm Ltd)*.

Trainees

2.56 Section 153(1) of EPCA defines a contract of employment as 'a contract of service or apprenticeship, whether express of implied, and (if it is express) whether it is oral or in writing'. It is clear, therefore, that an apprentice is employed under a contract of employment, and this includes, for example, an articled clerk employed by a solicitor (*Oliver v Malnick & Co*). However, not all such trainees are so employed. In *Wilts Police Authority v Wynn*, it was held that police cadets are not employees, but persons who are training to become policemen. During their training, even though they are being paid, they are not employed under a contract of employment. Similarly, in *Daley v Allied Suppliers Ltd* a young black girl was working on a Youth Opportunities scheme operated by the respondents. She alleged that she had been discriminated against on the ground of race, but it was held that the Race Relations Act was not applicable, as she was not a person employed within the meaning of s. 4 and s. 78 of the Act.

2.57 Indeed, the fact that young people on work experience courses are not employees has caused some concern, particularly in relation to their health and safety, for many of the duties owed by an employer are only owed to employees. Consequently the Health and Safety (Training for Employment) Regulations 1990 apply the provisions of the Health and Safety at Work etc Act 1974 to youth trainees as if they were employees.

Domestic servants

2.58 A domestic servant is an employee, and provided she has the requisite periods of continuous employment, may claim appropriate statutory rights. She may claim redundancy payment, for employment in a private household is deemed to be a business like any other. However, this does not apply if she is a close relative of the employer (see para 10.41). Nor do the special rules relating to the transfer of a business apply, except where the head of the household dies, for here there may be a transfer to the new head of the household for redundancy purposes (see EPCA Sch 11 para 21 and *Ranger v Brown*). The Race Relations Act 1976 does not apply to employment for the purpose of a private household, and under the Sex Discrimination Act 1975 (as amended in 1986) the sex of a person may be 'a genuine occupational qualification' (see para 4.54) if the employment is in a private home.

Foreign employees

2.59 A person who is not a national of an EC Member State must obtain a work permit to take up employment in Great Britain (otherwise the employment may be illegal, see para 3.1B), with the exception of certain Commonwealth citizens, citizens of Gibraltar, certain professional persons, representatives of overseas newspapers and broadcasting organisations, and self-employed persons. The Immigration Rules also specify other categories of permit-free employment. The procedures and rules can be obtained from the Overseas Labour section of the Department of Employment (Advice Booklet OW5 and OW21). A foreigner who works in this country has the full range of appropriate rights.

Overseas employment

2.60 The provisions of ss. 1-4 (written particulars of terms of employment) and ss. 49-51 (minimum periods of notice) do not apply to employment during a period when the employee is engaged to work outside Great Britain, unless the employee ordinarily works inside Great Britain, and the overseas employment is for the same employer or unless the law which governs the contract of employment is the law of England and Wales or of Scotland. The right to an itemised pay statement, written reasons for dismissal, the employment protection rights of Parts II, III and V of the Act (guaranteed pay, medical suspension pay, trade union membership and activities, time off work, statutory maternity pay, right to return to work after pregnancy, and unfair dismissal rights) do not apply where the employee ordinarily works outside Great Britain. However, Part VII of the Act (priority of certain debts on the employer's insolvency, payment of unpaid contributions to an occupational pension scheme, and guaranteed debts payable from the Redundancy Fund) is only excluded if the employee works outside the Member States of the European Community.

2.61 Part VI of the Act (redundancy payments) does not apply if, on the relevant date, the employee is outside Great Britain, unless he ordinarily works outside Great Britain. If he ordinarily works outside Great Britain, he will not be entitled to a redundancy payment unless on the relevant date he is in Great Britain in accordance with instructions given to him by his employer.

2.62 The Equal Pay Act, Sex Discrimination Act and the Race Relations Act do not apply in relation to employment at an establishment outside Great Britain.

2.62A The Transfer of Undertakings (Protection of Employment) Regulations 1981 do have a limited applicability to overseas employees. Certain weeks where an employee is abroad may not count for continuity purposes, but do not break continuity, the general rule being (for redundancy purposes) that a week will not count unless the employee remained an employee as regards the payment of national insurance contributions.

Offshore employment

2.62B Offshore employment is defined as employment for the purposes of activities:
(a) in the territorial waters of the United Kingdom; or
(b) connected with the exploration of the seabed or subsoil, or the exploration of their natural resources, in the United Kingdom sector of the continental shelf; or
(c) connected with the exploration or exploitation, in a foreign sector of the continental shelf, of a cross-boundary petroleum field (EPCA s. 137; TULR(C)A s. 287).

Orders have been made extending the provisions of various employment legislation to offshore employment, including the Employment Protection (Consolidation) Act 1978 (except time off work for public duties), Sex Discrimination and Race Relations Acts, Equal Pay Act, Wages Act 1986 and Trade Union and Labour Relations (Consolidation) Act 1992. Employment in the Grigg Gas Field comes within the scope of the various Acts if the employer is a British company, or has a place of business in Great Britain from which the activities are directed.

Retainers

2.63 A person who is retained for employment is not an employee merely because he is 'on call' even though he is paid during that time. Employment involves work or other activity carried out for the employer. In *Suffolk County Council v Secretary of State for the Environment* it was held that a retained fireman, who was permanently on call, was not an employee, for a contractual obligation to remain on call within a prescribed area did not constitute employment. His hours of work only began when he was on duty following a call.

National security

2.64 By virtue of s. 138(4) of EPCA the Secretary of State may exclude certain Crown employments from the scope of the Act by issuing a certificate requiring the employment to be excepted on the ground of national security, which certificate shall be conclusive (but not if the complaint is one of unfair dismissal based on the new law on health and safety and pregnancy-related reasons: Sch 9, para 2(2) of EP(C)A). A similar provision in TULR(C)A s. 275 was invoked to remove the rights of employees at GCHQ Cheltenham to join trade unions (see *CCSU v Minister for the Civil Service*).

2.65 However, the Minister is no longer able to issue such a certificate in relation to claims concerning employment or training under the Sex Discrimination Act 1975 s. 52 (Sex Discrimination (Amendment) Order 1988).

If the Minister thinks that the disclosure of certain information would be contrary to national security (written particulars, health and safety and maternity rights), nothing in the relevant provisions of the Act shall require any person to disclose the information (EPCA s. 146A). Also, if national security issues are involved, the Minister may require a hearing before an industrial tribunal to be heard in private, and may direct that the hearing be before the President alone. Similar provisions apply to the Employment Appeal Tribunal (see s. 128(6) and Sch. 9 of EPCA).

Global contracts

2.66 There are some employees who work on short-term periodic contracts, with various breaks of employment in between.

Attempts have been made to treat such employees as having been employed under one 'global contract', but so far with limited success (see *Boyd Line Ltd v Pitts*). For a global contract to exist, there must be mutual legally binding obligations on both sides, and it cannot be brought into existence merely by counting together a number of individual contracts which have subsisted over a period of time (see *Hellyer Bros Ltd v Mcleod*).

Common law remedies

2.67 Although most of the cases involving employment law are brought in industrial tribunals, there has been a small resurgence in recent years of claims seeking the old common law remedies. Thus actions may still be brought for wrongful dismissal (see para 8.2), and also for damages based on a failure by the employer to follow contractual disciplinary procedures, the measure of damages being the loss suffered by the employee as a result of that failure (*Gunton v London Borough of Richmond upon Thames*). Also, an application may be made for an injunction to restrain an employer from purporting to act in breach of a contractual disciplinary procedure (*Jones v Lee and Guilding*) and, somewhat rare, an action seeking specific performance of the contract (*Powell v London Borough of Brent*). These matters will be explored in Chapter 6 (and see *Jones v Gwent County Council*).

Public law remedies

2.68 An application may be made for judicial review, seeking to ensure that a public body carries out its public duties in a manner consistent with the legal requirements. Generally speaking, there are three grounds on which judicial review may be granted: (1) where the public body has acted illegally, i.e. contrary to the legal rights and duties of the parties; (2) where the public body has acted irrationally, i.e. where the decision arrived at was so outrageous that no sensible body or person acting responsibly could have reached that decision; and (3) where there has been a procedural impropriety, i.e. a failure to act with procedural fairness (*CCSU v Minister for the Civil Service*, per Lord Diplock).

2.69 Attempts have been made by employees in the public sector to establish legal rights based on such principles, but with mixed success. The claim must be brought within the procedure laid down in Order 53 of the Rules of the Supreme Court (judicial review) and the remedy is not generally available if a remedy based on contractual principles would suffice. There must be a further element of a public right or the enforcement of a public duty (*R v East Berkshire Health Authority, ex p Walsh*). The public law remedies sought will be certiorari, prohibition and a declaration.

2.70 In *McLaren v Home Office*, Lord Justice Woolf suggested that there are four general principles which apply when an employee of a public body is proposing to proceed by way of judicial review: (1) in relation to personal claims against an employer, an employee of a public body is in the same situation as other employees; (2) however, if there exists some disciplinary or other body established under the Royal Prerogative or a statute to which disputes can be referred, judicial review may be the appropriate remedy; (3) if an employee of a public body is adversely affected by a decision of general application, judicial review of that decision may be sought (see *R v Secretary of State, ex p CCSU*); (4) if disciplinary procedures are of a domestic nature, judicial review will not be sought.

2.71 However, if a person is seeking to enforce a private right which has a public law element, he can pursue his claim through the normal procedure of issuing a writ, and is not required to seek redress by means of judicial review (*Roy v Kensington and Chelsea and Westminster Family Practitioner Committee*), This is of particular importance if the public law issue is raised after the time for applying for judicial review has lapsed (*Doyle v Northumbria Probation Committee*).

In Scotland, however, for historical reasons, the situation is slightly different. Scots law does not depend on a distinction between public and private law, but the court will accept jurisdiction by way of judicial review to regulate the process by which decisions are taken by a person or body to whom a power has been delegated by statute, agreement or other instrument, in order to ensure that the person or body does not exceed or abuse that power. But there must always be a tripartite relationship between the person or body to whom the power has been delegated, the person or body by whom it has been delegated, and the person for whose benefit the power is to be exercised. Strict contractual rights, such as those which exist between employer and employee, are not amenable to judicial review (*West v Secretary of State for Scotland*).

CHAPTER 3

The formation of a contract of employment

3.1 A contract of employment can be entered into formally or informally. It can emerge as a result of interviews, negotiations, exchange of letters, or a casual conversation at the factory door. It can be made orally or in writing, although apprenticeship deeds and articles for merchant seamen by definition must be written. But essentially it is a contract like any other contract, and in principle subject to the general contractual rules of the common law. The normal cannons of legal construction must be applied (*Hooper v British Railways Board*).

3.1A There must be an offer of employment, and an acceptance of that offer. In *Wishart v National Association of Citizens Advice Bureaux Ltd*, the plaintiff was offered a job 'subject to the receipt of satisfactory references'. The defendants received references from the plaintiff's existing employer which indicated that he had been absent from work through illness for a considerable number of days, and consequently the offer was withdrawn. The plaintiff sought an interlocutory injunction to restrain the defendants from appointing anyone else to the post and requiring them to provide him with the job in question. The injunction was granted by a deputy High Court Judge, but on appeal the decision was reversed by the Court of Appeal. On the facts, there was a conditional offer of employment, and the only obligation on the defendants was to consider the references in good faith. Whether or not the references were satisfactory was a subjective matter. The Court of Appeal suggested that it was possible to make a conditional offer of employment subject to something which could be objectively determined, e.g. the passing of a medical examination, but that did not apply in this case.

3.1B In addition, there must be an intention to create legal relations, consideration (but this doctrine does not apply in Scotland) and the absence of vitiating elements (mistake, misrepresentation, illegality, etc). In *Cole v Fred Stacey Ltd*, the employee was given an additional payment which was not taxed as income. He was subsequently made redundant, but it was held that he was not entitled to a redundancy payment, as the contract was illegal and unenforceable, being a contract to defraud the Revenue (see also *Tomlinson v Dick Evans U Drive Ltd*). In *Rastegarnia v Richmond Design* the applicant (who came from Iran) had been granted a work permit for a specific job. Without obtaining permission from the Department of Employment he changed his job and went to work for the respondents. He was subsequently dismissed, but his claim for unfair dismissal was rejected. His employment was unlawful, and he could not obtain any legal rights thereunder.

3.1C However, a fraud or dishonesty against an employer, whilst it may be grounds for dismissal, does not make the contract inherently illegal so as to make it void ab initio (*Broaders v Kalkare Property Maintenance Ltd*).

3.1D Nor will the contract be unenforceable for illegality if the employee does not receive any benefit from the illegality. In *Hewcastle Catering Ltd v Ahmed* the employers devised a scheme to avoid paying VAT, and gave certain instructions to the employees to facilitate the scheme. The employees did not receive any direct benefit. Following investigations by the Customs and Excise, the employers were prosecuted, and the employees were called as prosecution witnesses. They were subsequently dismissed, and claimed that the dismissals were unfair. The employers argued that the contracts of employment, being tainted with illegality, were unenforceable, but this claim was rejected by the industrial tribunal, the EAT and the Court of Appeal. The employers had involved the employees in the fraud, but the employees did not benefit from it and were not essential parties to it. It would be contrary to public policy to deny the employees compensation when the employers had involved them in the fraud and dismissed them because they gave evidence in criminal proceedings taken against the employers.

3.2 For an employee to have statutory rights, he must be continuously employed under a legal contract of employment, and any period wherein the contract becomes illegal cannot be relied upon in counting towards that continuity. Thus a period of time prior to the illegality, when the contract was legal, is lost, and continuity can only be reckoned from the date when the contract became legal (*Hyland v J H Barker (North West) Ltd*).

3.3 If the alleged illegality lies in the performance of the contract, then a distinction must be drawn between the cases where the contractual obligation is to do an act which is unlawful, and those where the obligations are capable of being performed lawfully, but which were in fact performed by unlawful means. In *Coral Leisure Group Ltd v Barnett*, the applicant was dismissed from his post as a public relations executive. He alleged that part of his duties was to keep rich punters happy by obtaining for them, among other things, the services of prostitutes. It was held that the fact that an immoral or unlawful act was committed during the course of the employment did not render the contract void, unless it was entered into with the object of doing that unlawful or immoral act, or the contract itself (as opposed to the mode of performance) was prohibited by law.

3.4 But the contract will only be void if the party seeking to enforce it was aware of the illegality. If it can be shown that the employee was not a party to the illegality, or did not know about it, he can still rely on the contract as an innocent party (*Davidson v Pillay*). Thus if an employee is paid part of his wages in cash as a tax-free payment, the essential question to ask is, has the employee knowingly been a party to a deception on the Revenue (*Newland v Simons and Willer Ltd*)?

3.5 Within the constraints imposed by the common law and by statute (see Chapter 4), the parties are free to negotiate such terms and conditions as they wish, and once having done so, these will bind them until there is a mutually agreed variation. In *O'Grady v Saper*, MacKinnon LJ said that the contract of employment was 'usually concluded orally by people who rarely think out, and still more rarely express, any terms'. Such an approach nowadays is fraught with problems, and the modern trend is to treat the contract of employment with much more formality. It is of the utmost importance that at its commencement all the relevant terms are agreed and clearly stated or are ascertainable, so that both sides will know the precise nature

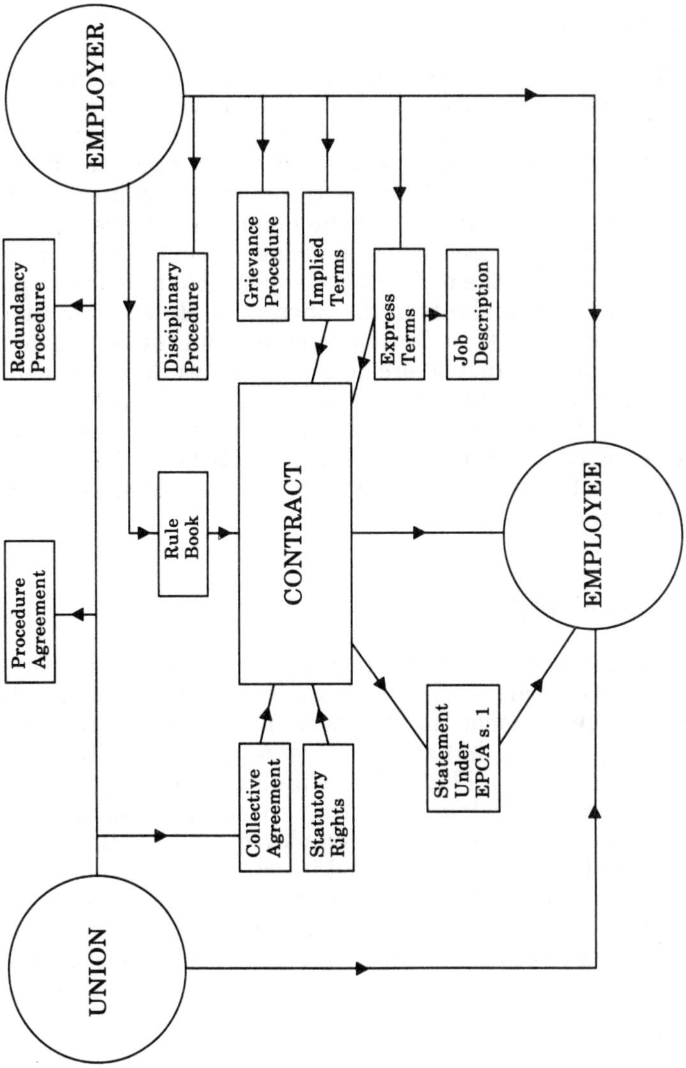

The Contract of Employment

of the legal obligations incurred. A failure to do so may well lead to subsequent legal, as well as practical, difficulties.

Collateral contracts

3.6 At common law, when an employer terminates the contract of employment, the only remedy for the employee is to claim money for the period of notice to which he is entitled (see para 8.12). However, if the employer promises that the contract will subsist for a certain period of time, this may be a collateral contract to the main contract, and the employee may be able to claim damages for a breach of that collateral contract. In *Gill v Cape Contracts Ltd* the plaintiff gave up his job in Belfast to go to work for the defendants in the Shetlands. He was told that the work would last for at least six months, but the defendants repudiated the contract before he could start work. It was held that the plaintiff was entitled to damages for a breach of contract by the defendants, who had made representations which had been acted on by the plaintiff to his detriment. These representations formed a collateral contract to the main contract of employment.

Terms and conditions

3.7 It is usual to speak of the 'terms and conditions of employment' which are part of every contract of employment, although no attempt ever appears to have been made to define or delineate this expression (but see *Cory Lighterage v T & GWU* and *Universe Tankships v ITWF*). It is submitted that the terms of the employment are bilateral, i.e. they are part of the agreement made between the employer and employee, whereas the conditions of employment are unilateral instructions which are laid down by the employer. The result is that a change in the terms can only be made by an express or implied agreement to that effect, whereas a condition can be changed by the employer unilaterally at any time (see *Cadoux v Central Regional Council*) on giving reasonable notice.

3.8 Terms of employment can be found in express or implied agreements, collective agreements, and various statutory provisions; conditions of employment are usually contained in works rules, disciplinary and grievance procedures and job descriptions. Care should be taken not to place a term or condition in the wrong category. For example, it may be a term of a contract that an employee shall be entitled to four weeks holiday per year; it will be a condition that he shall take those holidays at particular times of the year. A term will specify the number of hours he shall work; a condition will instruct him as to when he shall work those hours. A term will specify his employment duties, a condition will lay down how he shall perform those duties. The fact of payment is a term; the mode of payment is a condition.

Interpretation of terms

3.8A Under the modern law of employment, contractual terms must be applied reasonably, not literally. In *United Bank v Akhtar*, the applicant was subject to a clause in his contract which required him to work anywhere in Great Britain. On 5 June he was informed that as from 8th June he would be required to transfer from Leeds to a branch in Birmingham. He requested that the transfer be delayed for three months, because of his wife's illness, and also the impending sale of his house. This request was refused. He then asked if he could take 24 days leave due to him to enable him to sort out his affairs, and he offered to commence work in Birmingham on 10 July, but he received no reply to this request. His pay was then stopped as from 5 June, so he resigned, and claimed he had been constructively dismissed. His claim succeeded. There was an implied term in his contract that the employers would give reasonable notice if they wished to exercise their rights under the mobility clause.

3.8B Similarly, an employer may still be acting fairly even though he dismisses an employee in circumstances which amount to a breach of contract by the employer, for statutory rights and obligations exist concurrent with, but are sometimes different from, those which exist at common law (see *Hooper v British Railways Board*).

Express terms

3.9 At the conclusion of the negotiations the parties may have expressly stated the terms which form the basis of the contract.

These terms may deal with wages, salaries, commissions, bonuses, hours of work, the nature of the duties, holidays, overtime, sick pay, pension schemes and so on. The task of the courts and tribunals is to interpret the meaning of such express terms in a manner consistent with industrial realism. Thus in *Cole v Midland Display Ltd* the employee was a manager employed on a 'staff' basis. He refused to do overtime without pay, and his subsequent dismissal was held to be fair. The essence of being employed as 'staff' meant that he was guaranteed his wages whether there was work or not, and during sickness. In return, 'staff' are apparently required to work reasonable overtime without pay if required to do so.

3.10 On the other hand, in *Redbridge Borough Council v Fishman*, the employee was appointed as a teacher in charge of a resource centre. Gradually, she was asked to teach more and more, and eventually dismissed when she refused. Her dismissal was held to be unfair. A headteacher could require teachers to do work other than that for which they were engaged, provided that such requests were reasonable. In this case, the teaching was ancillary to her main job, which was as a director of the resource centre. Consequently, the headmaster's instructions went beyond the strict contractual obligations of the employee, and were therefore unreasonable.

3.11 Although it may be permissible to refer to statements made in a job advertisement to ascertain the terms of a contract (*Tayside Regional Council v McIntosh*), such statement cannot override the express terms. In *Deeley v British Rail Engineering Ltd*, the employers advertised for a 'Sales Engineer (Export)'. The applicant applied for the job and was appointed, but his contract was for a 'Sales Engineer'. It was held that there were no grounds for implying the word 'Export' into his contract.

3.12 An express term may be used to negate a liability. In *Petrie v MacFisheries Ltd* the employers posted a notice stating that half pay for sickness would be paid as an act of grace by the company to all employees with over six months' service. All the employees knew of the position and the company acted on it consistently. It was held that the company was not bound to make payments when employees were off sick.

3.13 If an employer provides facilities for his employee's property (e.g. car parks, cloakrooms, etc) he cannot restrict his liability for death or personal injury resulting from negligence, and he may only be able to restrict or exclude his liability for damage to the employee's property by a term in the contract which is reasonable in the circumstances (Unfair Contract Terms Act 1977 s. 2).

3.14 If the employee is in breach of a contractual term this will be ground for dismissal. Equally, if the employer is in breach, the employee may accept the breach and bring a claim for constructive dismissal (see Chapter 8). In either event, the fairness or unfairness of the dismissal has to be determined in accordance with established legal principles, though clearly the breach of a contractual term must be regarded with greater seriousness than the breach of a non-contractual term. In *Martin v Solus Schall*, the applicant signed a contract which included a clause stating 'you will be expected to work such overtime as is necessary to ensure continuity of service'. This was held to be a contractual obligation, and on the facts his dismissal for refusing to do overtime was fair.

3.15 At one time it was thought that a breach of contract by an employee amounted to a 'constructive resignation', but this view is now regarded as being incorrect (see *London Transport Executive v Clarke* para 8.84). The legal position is that the employer may 'accept' the breach or not, as he wishes. If he does accept the breach, he dismisses the employee, and the fairness of the dismissal must be justified in accordance with the usual principles (see Chapter 8).

3.16 A strike by an employee is a breach of contract, as is a refusal to perform contractual duties. Either of these events give rise to legal consequences, including the right of the employer to deduct a sum of money from the wages or salary of the employee, calculated on a proportional basis (*Sim v Rotherham Metropolitan Borough Council*).

Implied terms

3.17 Occasionally the courts and tribunals are prepared to imply a term into the contract in circumstances where the parties did not expressly insert a term to meet a particular contingency. The theory adopted was that the term in question was so obvious that the parties did not see the need to state it expressly. Clearly, a certain amount of judicial hindsight is required in order to imply a term after a dispute has arisen, and there is frequent room for disagreement on whether or not the court was correct in making its assumptions. However, in *Mears v Safecar Security Ltd*, the Court of Appeal held that the correct approach was to consider all the facts and circumstances before implying a term into the contract, including the way the parties had carried out the contract since it was formed. There is no presumption either way about an implied term. For example, in *O'Grady v Saper* the employee claimed his wages for a period in which he had been off work through sickness. He had been away sick before, and had not received any wages. Indeed, he never asked for them nor expected them, until he saw an item in a newspaper which led him to believe that he might be able to claim. It was held that there was an implied term that he would not be paid.

3.17A The original justification for the implied term theory was the need to give business efficacy to the contract, but there is now a much wider approach, implying terms which are a necessary incident of a definable category of contractual relationship. In *Scally v Southern Health and Social Security Services Board*, the plaintiff was a doctor, whose terms and conditions of employment were to be found in a statutory scheme. This scheme gave doctors the right to purchase added years of pension entitlement, but this valuable right had to be exercised within certain time limits. The plaintiff was never informed about the scheme, and so he failed to exercise his option to purchase the added years pension. When he did discover the existence of the scheme, he was outside the time limits. He claimed that his employers had broken an implied term of the contract by failing to take reasonable steps to bring to his notice his right to enhance his pension entitlement by the purchase of added years. The House of Lords unanimously upheld his claim. It was noted that the terms of the contract had not been negotiated with the individual employee, but were negotiated with a representative body or otherwise incorporated by reference. The contract thus contained a valuable right for the employee, but this was contingent on him taking action to avail himself of the benefit. He could not be expected to do this unless the term was drawn to his attention. There was an implied term, therefore, that the employer could take reasonable steps to bring the provisions of the pension scheme to the employee's attention, so that he could enjoy its benefits if he so wished.

3.18 It is not possible to imply terms which are too vague or unpredictable to be given efficacy, or to which the parties would not have agreed had the matter been drawn to their attention (*Lake v Essex County Council*, para 2.51). Thus, in *Cresswell v Board of Inland Revenue*, staff employed by the Inland Revenue habitually carried out their tasks be dealing manually with files and records. The Inland Revenue introduced a programme of computerisation, and the plaintiff alleged that in so doing there was a breach of contract, arguing that there was an implied term that he could not be required to perform tasks or carry out functions in a manner other than that which they had habitually used by custom and practice. He sought a declaration that he could not be required to operate computerised systems. It was held that the employers were not in breach of the contract by requiring employees to use computer systems. An employee is expected to adapt himself to new methods and techniques introduced in the course of his employment. It is a question of fact whether the retraining involved the acquisition of such esoteric skills that it would not be reasonable to expect the employee to acquire them. Nowadays, it is not unusual to ask an employee to acquire basic skills such as retrieving information from a computer or feeding information into one. However, the employer must be expected to provide any necessary training for the acquisition of these skills.

3.19 Recent cases have established that there is an implied term that an employer will treat the employee with respect and trust, and will not treat an employee in an arbitrary or vindictive manner. Thus to falsely accuse an employee of theft (*Robinson v Crompton Parkinson Ltd*), unreasonably to deny an employee an increase in remuneration which had been granted to other employees (*Gardner Ltd v Beresford*) and, in the case of a large firm, to refuse to give an employee time off work to deal with a domestic emergency (*Warner v Barbers Stores*), have all been held to amount to conduct by the employer which could constitute a breach of the implied term that the employer should treat an employee fairly and reasonably.

3.20 It may be possible to imply a term by reference to the practices of the industry and/or the national agreements which are in force. For example, in *Stevenson v Tees-side Bridge and Engineering Ltd* a steel erector's employment was governed by the national agreement for the time being in force in the industry. Although there was no express term in his contract stating that he was expected to work away from home, this was clearly envisaged, for the national agreement made provision for lodging allowances, travelling expenses, etc. The court held that there was an implied term in his contract that he could be sent anywhere abroad to work, for it was recognised that in the construction steel industry, where sites are, by their very nature, scattered around the country, employees know that mobility is a feature of their employment.

3.21 There is an implied term that the employer will not prevent the employee from performing his contract of employment, or delay or hinder him so as to prevent him from earning his full remuneration, but the employer is entitled to take steps which may improve that performance, and to see that the work is done in a proper manner, for example, by engaging time and motion experts (*Davies v Richard Johnson & Nephew Ltd*). If an employee is contractually obliged to do overtime without pay, there is an implied term that the requirements of overtime will always be reasonable, and would not be excessive (*Gilbert v Goldstone*). On the other hand, if a contract of employment is silent on the actual place of work, it may be necessary to imply a term to give that contract business efficacy. In *Jones v Associated Tunnelling* it was held that there was an implied term that the employers were entitled to require the employee to work anywhere within a reasonable daily commuting distance from his home.

3.22 The basis for the implied term theory is that it is the court's (or tribunal's) view about a provision that was 'obvious' where the contract was silent. In *Shell UK Ltd v Lostock Garage Ltd*, Lord Denning suggested that if a contract of employment did not define the obligations of the parties, the courts (or tribunals) should ask what would be reasonable in the general run of such cases, and then say what the obligation shall be. This view was followed in *Pepper & Hope v Daish* (see para 8.72) but in view of the importance of the issues involved, a more authoritative ruling is needed. There is a fundamental difference between importing into a contract an implied term which is 'obvious' and one which is 'reasonable'. However, the contracts of employment of professional employees do not always detail the contractual obligations, and these may be defined by reference to the nature of the profession, and the obligations incumbent on those who follow that profession (*Sim v Rotherham Metropolitan District Council*).

3.23 There is no implied term that an employer will look after the employee's property (clothes, car, etc) which are left on the employer's premises (*Edwards v West Herts Group Hospital Management Committee*), though there appears to be an obligation independent of contract under the Factories Act 1961 for the employer to provide adequate and suitable accommodation for clothing which is not worn during working hours (*MacCarthy v Daily Mirror Newspapers*). Nor is there an implied term that an employee will be entitled to work overtime if the employer is not contractually obliged to provide overtime (*McLory v Post Office*).

3.23A There is no implied term that the employer will provide personal accident insurance for the benefit of an employee who is required to work abroad, or that the employer should give specific advice on special risks, and advise the employee to take out personal accident insurance (see *Reid v Rush & Tompkins Group*, para 6.19A). Nor can a duty in tort be imposed to enlarge on contractual duties.

3.24 It is clear that if an employer breaks an express term of the contract, the employee may 'accept' the breach, resign from his employment, and claim that he had been 'constructively' dismissed (see para 8.62). This is equally true in the case of a breach of an implied term, and in particular when the conduct of the employer amounts to a breach of the implied term of mutual trust and confidence which must exist between the parties (*Post Office v Roberts*). These developments will be considered in detail in Chapter 8.

Express incorporation of the terms of a collective agreement

3.25 A collective agreement is an agreement made between an employers' association, or a single employer, on the one hand, and a trade union on the other, which, as well as laying down the procedure which will govern the relationship between the signatories will also provide for the terms and conditions of employment of those covered by the agreement. It is estimated that about nine million employees in this country are governed by a sophisticated network of such agreements. There are, however, a number of different situations to consider. There can be a national or federation agreement, made between an employers' association and a trade union, on the conclusion of which the individual employers who are members of the association will start to apply its provisions to their employees. There is no rule of law which requires this, only the practice of industrial relations. The terms of the agreement will be binding in law on the individual employer and the employee if, and only if, they are expressly or impliedly incorporated into the individual contract of employment. The same rule applies to a local or plant agreement, which is usually made between a single employer and a trade union. Also, there are some employers who, though not members of the employers' association, voluntarily undertake to observe the terms of a negotiated agreement.

3.25A Certain terms contained in a collective agreement govern the relationship between the trade union and the employer. Other terms are designed to benefit individual employees, and this becomes part of the contract of employment (*National Coal Board v National Union of Mineworkers*). These latter terms are said to have a 'normative' effect. In *Alexander v Standard Telephones and Cables plc*, the plaintiff was employed on the basis of the terms contained in a collective agreement. The agreement contained a redundancy procedure, which stated that LIFO would be the basis of selection in the event of compulsory redundancies. The company wished to select on the basis of skills and flexibility, and the plaintiff sought an injunction to prevent this. The application failed, but it was suggested that there was an arguable case that the terms of the collective agreement formed part of his contract of employment. Any remedy for breach of that contract would lie in an action for damages and the case was sent for trial on that basis (see para 3.27A).

3.26 The 'normative' terms of a collective agreement may be incorporated into the individual contract of employment by an express provision to this effect. For example, employment may be undertaken on the basis of 'union rates of pay', or 'union conditions'. It is at least arguable that the former term refers solely to the wages rates clauses in the collective agreement, whilst the latter term may be somewhat wider, and may include other provisions. In *Jewell v Neptune Concrete*, the employee's written particulars stated that his rate of wages was to be based on the national agreement. It was held that this did not, by itself, incorporate the working rule agreement's lay-off provisions into his contract of employment. Employees who work for public bodies are normally engaged on the basis of the appropriate scale laid down by the negotiating bodies (e.g. Burnham Scale for teachers), and the only scope for individual bargaining may be on the precise point of entry into the scale for salary purposes. Thus in *Knox v Down District Council* the Northern Ireland Court of Appeal were prepared to incorporate into the employee's contract of employment a car assisted purchase scheme which had been negotiated by the National Joint Council, the terms of which were expressly incorporated into this contract. In *National Coal Board v Galley*, the defendant was employed on the basis of 'the national agreements for the time being in force'. These agreements required him to do a certain amount of overtime, and when he refused to do a Saturday morning shift it was held that he was in breach of his contract.

3.27 Frequently the terms of a collective agreement will be expressly incorporated into the individual contract by means of the statement given to the employee under EPCA s. 1. In *Camden Exhibition and Display Ltd v Lynott* notices issued to the employees stated that their hours of work, wages, etc, would be in accordance with the working rule laid down by the National Joint Council for the industry. Rule 6 of this agreement stated that 'Overtime required to ensure the due and proper performance of contracts shall not be subject to restriction, but may be worked by mutual agreement and direct arrangement between the employer and operatives concerned.' Workmen who were dissatisfied with a wage award decided to cease overtime working. It was held that rule 6 was a term of the contracts of employment of each employee. However, its effect was obscure. Lord Denning thought that it meant that the workmen would not collectively impose an overtime ban, but Russell LJ thought that the rule did not import into the contract of any individual an agreement not to limit overtime save for a reason special to himself.

3.27A To determine whether or not the terms of a collective agreement can be incorporated into an individual's contract of employment, regard must be had to the contractual intentions of the parties. In *Alexander v Standard Telephones and Cables plc*, the plaintiff was given a statement of written particulars, issued under s. 1 of EPCA. This stated that the basic terms and conditions of employment were in accordance with and subject to the provisions of a plant agreement negotiated by his employers and a trade union. One of the terms of the collective agreement provided that in the event of redundancy, selection will be on the basis of service with the employers. When the company wished to make a number of employees redundant, it was decided to retain employees whose skills and flexibility were best suited to the circumstances. The trade union insisted that selection should be on the basis of length of service. After negotiations broke down, the employers went ahead with their proposals, and the plaintiff was one of those dismissed. He sought an interlocutory injunction to restrain the employers from terminating his employment without applying the principles of collective agreement, but this was refused. He also claimed damages for breach of contract, arguing that he would have continued in his employment until retiring age.

His claim for damages was dismissed. The only relevant document applicable to the plaintiff's employment was the written statement issued under s. 1 of EPCA. This had to be construed in accordance with the relevant contractual principles. The statutory statement did not deal with redundancy matters, and therefore it did not incorporate the terms of the collective agreement into his contract of employment. The collective agreement itself, not being a contract, could be incorporated into the individual contract of employment if there was a cogent indication that this was intended. However, the clauses in question had to be considered in the context of a joint consultation scheme of a procedure agreement, and it was not sufficiently cogently worded to support the inference of incorporation into the individual contract of employment.

3.28 Once the terms of a collective agreement are incorporated into the individual contract of employment, they are part of that contract, and cannot be unilaterally altered. In *Robertson v British Gas Corpn*, the employee was appointed as a gas meter reader/collector, his letter of appointment stating that an incentive bonus scheme would apply. The terms of this scheme were negotiated between the employers and a trade union. Subsequently the employers gave notice to the trade union to terminate the scheme, and no new scheme was negotiated. The employee brought an action for arrears of pay. It was held that the letter of appointment was a binding contract, which gave the right to an incentive bonus scheme. Although the collective agreement had no legal force as between the signatories, it was incorporated into the employee's contract, and the employers could not terminate the scheme unilaterally.

3.29 Indeed, the fact that the collective agreement contains a clause to the effect that its terms are binding in honour only does not affect the legal enforceability of those terms which are expressly or impliedly incorporated into the individual contract (*Marley v Forward Trust Group Ltd*). However, a distinction must always be made between contractual terms, which are bilateral in effect, and rules, which are unilateral. The latter do not have a legally binding effect (*Cadoux v Central Regional Council*).

Implied incorporation of the terms of a collective agreement

3.30 It is equally possible to incorporate the terms of a collective agreement into an individual contract of employment by implication. In certain industries where a closed shop has been accepted as a rule for many years it is clearly obvious that the terms of a collective agreement will be binding. One can hardly imagine a coal-miner being employed nowadays on terms other than those agreed between the union and the National Coal Board, even if his own contract is silent on the subject. In *McLea v Essex Line Ltd*, the plaintiff took a job as a seaman, and the court implied into his contract the contents of an agreement made by the National Maritime Board, which was the negotiating body for the industry.

3.31 If the terms of a collective agreement have been incorporated into the individual contracts of employment, it appears that any change in those terms must be accepted by the individuals concerned. The trade union is not, *per se*, an agent of its members with authority to unilaterally negotiate a variation. Thus, in *Lee v GEC Plessey Telecommunications*, the employers had reached an agreement with trade unions in 1985 which gave enhanced redundancy terms to its employees. In 1990 they purported to withdraw those terms, but, following objections from the unions, negotiations took place on revised terms. An agreement appeared to have been reached which enabled the employers to withdraw the enhanced redundancy payments and substitute less favourable terms, but this was on the basis that there would be no further redundancies in the future. However, redundancies were announced, and individual employees brought an action for a declaration that the attempt to vary the enhanced redundancy terms was ineffective. Their claim succeeded in the High Court. It was not necessary to give fresh consideration every time a new collective agreement was reached, for a continuation by the workforce in their employment was a value attributed to the employer. Although the employers could unilaterally determine the collective agreement, this would not be effective to change the terms contained in the individual contracts of employment. Nor were the trade unions acting as agents for their members when they attempted to negotiate the change. They were acting in a collective manner, not on behalf of each individual.

3.32 Nonetheless, it is submitted that the correct approach is to ascertain if the employee's union representatives have accepted the agreement on his behalf, and therefore incorporated it into his contract by implication. After all, such employees would have no difficulty if they were seeking to obtain a benefit or advantage based on the existence of the agreement. Whether management is entitled to treat a breach of that agreement by the employee as an automatic reason for disciplinary or dismissal proceedings is entirely another matter. Here, it is possible to argue that express notice of the terms must be made known to the employee before management can take any action on it. It is this failure to distinguish between the incorporation of the agreement, and the consequences which may flow from such incorporation, which sometimes leads tribunals astray. The tribunals ought not to look to the conduct of the employee in continuing in employment after having knowledge of the agreement as evidence of his acceptance (see *Mordecai v Jacob Beatus Ltd*) for his acceptance should stem from the implied authority of the trade union to negotiate, not from his own personal acceptance of the terms of the agreement (see *Nelson and Woollett v Post Office*). While such an approach may not conform to the strict contractual theory, it does at least have the merit of industrial realism.

3.32A If the employers are not members of the employers' association, there is little scope for the implied incorporation of the terms of the collective agreement into the individual contract of employment. There would have to be strong evidence to indicate that the agreement had been so incorporated by way of custom and practice (*Hamilton v Futura Floors Ltd*).

Collective agreements and non-unionists

3.33 Just as the terms of a collective agreement may be binding on a non-federated employer who assents to it, so also will those terms apply to a non-unionist if his contract of employment states so expressly. In the absence of such express incorporation, the collective agreement will not apply. In *Singh v British Steel Corpn*, the employee's contract stated that he was to work a 15-shift system over a five-day week. He resigned from his trade union, and instructed his employers to cease paying the union subscription under a check-off agreement. The union then negotiated a new agreement with the employers which provided for a 21-shift system over a seven-day week, but the employee refused to agree to this, and was dismissed. It was held that there was nothing in his contract which permitted a change in the system of working, either by the employers unilaterally or by means of a collective agreement. The tribunal thought that while he was a member of the union he was bound by such agreements because it was his negotiating body, but when he left, he ceased to be bound. The union and the employers had no power to vary the terms of his agreement without his consent.

3.34 There is clearly less scope for the implied incorporation of the terms of a collective agreement into the contracts of employment of non-unionists. In *London Passenger Transport Board v Moscop* a collective agreement provided that on a disciplinary charge, an employee could take with him a trade union official. The plaintiff was a member of another union which had not been a party to the agreement, and he wished to be accompanied by an official of his own union. It was held that the terms of the agreement were not necessarily applicable to employees who were not members of the signatory union. In *Singh v British Steel Corpn* (above) it was equally held that there was no implied term of his contract that as a non-union member he would be bound by union agreements.

3.35 A further problem can arise when the terms of a collective agreement are back-dated. As a general rule, it would seem that there is no implied term in a contract of employment that a wage award can be back-dated, although this may come about by an express agreement to that effect. However, an express agreement cannot override the statutory position. In *Leyland Vehicles Ltd v Reston* the applicant was made redundant in February, and received his redundancy payment calculated on the basis of the wages he was then receiving. In April a new wage agreement was negotiated with the union, and this was backdated to January. The applicant contended that his redundancy pay should be calculated so as to take account of the increase in his wage rate, but his claim was dismissed by the EAT. Schedule 14 of EPCA (which is used to calculate redundancy payments) refers to the amount of pay actually payable at the calculation date. It does not include increases made by agreement concluded after the employment has ended, even though the agreement provided for the back-dating of the increase. The payment of a back-dated wage increase to employees who have left the firm is usually a matter to be considered on an *ex gratia* basis.

Conflicting collective agreements

3.36 A difficulty sometimes arises when there is an overlap between the national agreement and a local agreement which covers the same or similar ground. In *Clift v West Riding County Council* the plaintiff was paid less by virtue of a local agreement than he would have received on the basis of a national agreement. It was held that since the local agreement was later in time, its terms prevailed. But 'the latest agreement prevails' doctrine is not a rule of law, as *Gascol Conversions ltd v Mercer* demonstrates. Here, a national agreement provided that the working week should be 40 hours, and overtime worked as necessary. It also stated that if the national agreement was at variance with any local agreement, the national agreement was to prevail. A subsequent local agreement provided that the working week should be 54 hours. The employee was made redundant, and the question arose as to whether his redundancy payment was to be calculated on the basis of a normal working week of 40 hours or one of 54 hours. The Court of Appeal held that the employee was employed on the basis of the national agreement, and though it was at variance with the local agreement, its terms took precedence.

Which terms are employment terms?

3.37 Another difficulty is to determine which terms of a collective agreement are to be incorporated into the individual contract of employment. Clearly, there are many terms which are capable of such incorporation, such as wage rates, hours, overtime payments, travel allowances, and so on. Equally, there are other terms which govern the relationship which is to exist between the signatories, and have no relevance to the individual contract of employment. Since the law on collective bargaining is still in its infancy, we may well expect further developments in this field in the coming years. For example, in *Gallagher v Post Office*, the defendants recognised two trade unions for negotiating purposes, and informed their employees that they were entitled to join either union. Recognition was then withdrawn from one union, and the plaintiff alleged that this constituted a breach of contract. It was held that there was no term, express or implied, that the Post Office should continue to recognise the union to which the plaintiff belonged. Any statement about recognition was purely informative, and not part of the contract of employment of any individual employee.

3.38 Some difficulty has been experienced in the past with the 'no strike' clause, or the procedural aspects of settling disputes. In *Rookes v Barnard*, this clause was held to have been incorporated into the contracts of employment of the employees, but as the point was conceded rather than argued, the case adds little to our knowledge of the subject. A great deal may well turn on the precise wording of the agreement. Supposing this states 'the union will not call a strike until the procedure for settling the dispute is exhausted'. This is an obligation on the union, and is not part of the contracts of employment of the employees. Supposing the agreement states 'the employees will not go on strike until the procedure for settling the dispute is exhausted'. This term is clearly capable of being so incorporated. However, by TULR(C)A s. 180 the incorporation of such a clause will not be binding unless:

a. the collective agreement is in writing;
b. it expressly states that the terms are to be incorporated into the individual contract;
c. a copy of the collective agreement is reasonably accessible to the employees concerned;
d. the agreement is made by an independent trade union; and
e. the individual contract of employment expressly or impliedly incorporates the terms of the collective agreement.

However, it must be borne in mind that a strike, whether in breach of a collective agreement or not, is always a breach of contract at common law, so that the effect of s. 18 must be minimal.

Custom as a source of employment terms

3.39 It is sometimes argued that terms of employment can be found in those practices which are customary in a particular industry or local area, or even within a single firm. Support for this view can be gleaned from the case of *Sagar v Ridehalgh*, where a deduction from the wages of a cotton weaver for bad workmanship was upheld by virtue of the existence of a long-standing custom of the trade which, apparently, was well known. But a custom, to be upheld, must be long established, reasonable, certain, not contrary to law, and must be strictly proved. In *Hardwick v Leeds Area Health Authority* the applicant was dismissed after exhausting her period of sick pay, which was an entitlement of two months on full pay and two months on half pay. This was in accordance with the normal practice of the Health Service. It was held that such an automatic rule, whereby an employee could be dismissed irrespective of the circumstances, was totally outmoded and unreasonable, and the dismissal was held to be unfair. In *Singh v British Steel Corpn* (para 3.33) the fact that the applicant had considered himself in the past to be bound by trade union agreements was not sufficient evidence to establish a custom to that effect. Moreover, in *Gascol Conversions v Mercer* (para 3.36) the court stated that if the parties had reduced the contract to writing, it is not permissible to say that they intended something else, and thus it would appear that a custom cannot override a written statement of the terms of employment. This point has considerable implications when, as sometimes happens, an appeal is made to 'custom and practice' as a basis of employment terms. It is true that in *Heaton's Transport Ltd v T & GWU* the House of Lords upheld custom and practice as being the basis of the authority of a shop steward to initiate action on behalf of a trade union, but this was a case where the union rule-book was silent on the point. However, it might be easier to argue that 'custom and practice' can override the terms of a collective agreement which has been incorporated into an employment contract (see *Parry v Holst*, para 3.58). It is also arguable that a 'custom' is different from a 'practice'. The former has a legal significance which the latter does not possess. In *Spencer Jones v Timmens Freeman*, it was a 'common practice' in the hairdressing trade for shops to be open on Saturday afternoons, but this did not make it a custom.

3.40 Clear and compelling evidence is required to establish that a custom and practice exists. In *Samways v Swan Hunter Shipbuilders Ltd* the applicant, who was originally employed as a labourer, was appointed as a chargeman over a gang, and was given an additional £4 per week allowance. The company then informed him that owing to a reduction in production, it was necessary to withdraw the allowance, and he was offered employment as a labourer. It was held that this constituted a dismissal for reason of redundancy, as there was a reduction in the requirements of the company for chargemen. An argument by the company that by virtue of custom and practice chargemen's allowances were temporary payments for additional responsibility so long as this lasted was rejected by the tribunal, who thought that the 'allowance' was in fact remuneration. That other men had, in the past, reverted from the job of chargeman to their former positions was not sufficient to establish a custom, for their conduct could be explained on the ground that they wanted to keep their job with the firm, and it did not follow that they were contractually bound to do so.

3.41 It may be possible to claim sick pay if there is a local custom to this effect which can be proven to exist (*Scott v Pattison*).

3.41A It is submitted that with the increasing formalisation of contracts of employment, the scope for custom and practice as a source of employment terms has decreased.

Works/Staff rules

3.42 Some employers issue booklets or post notices containing the rules of the workplace, and the legal significance of these is still being explored. Such rules can either be part of the contractual terms or unilaterally imposed instructions, a distinction which is important, because in the former case, they can only be changed by mutual assent and agreement, whereas in the latter case, the employer may, at any time and on reasonable notice, change them (see *Cadoux v Central Regional Council*) and substitute new instructions or impose new obligations, and a failure by the employee to obey would be a breach of his duty to follow all lawful and reasonable orders.

3.42A The fact that the change bears hard on a particular individual does not justify an inference that the employer has acted in such a way as to repudiate the contract of employment. In *Dryden v Greater Glasgow Health Board*, the applicant was a heavy smoker, and was accustomed to smoking cigarettes in areas of the hospital where she worked set aside for this purpose. The employers decided to ban smoking throughout the hospital and, after extensive consultations, imposed a no-smoking ban. The applicant decided that she could not continue to work without smoking, and resigned her employment. She claimed that she had been constructively dismissed. It was held that 'the right to smoke' was not a customary term nor an implied term of the contract, and the employers had not acted in such a way as to frustrate the employee's ability to perform her contract. In *Secretary of State for Employment v ASLEF*, railwaymen proposed to engage in a work-to-rule campaign. If the rule book, by which they were working, was a part of their contracts of employment, then, by adhering to it, albeit strictly, they could hardly be said to be breaking their contracts. However, one of the rules stated that employees should 'make every effort to facilitate the working of trains and prevent unavoidable delay', which would clearly prohibit any deliberate attempt to interpret the rules in such a way as to achieve disruption of services, and to that extent there was clearly a breach of contract on either view of their legal significance. But Lord Denning held that the rules were 'in no way terms of his (i.e. the individual railwayman's) contract of employment. They were only instructions to a man on how he was to do his work.' It will clearly be an implied term of his contract of employment that he will interpret those rules reasonably.

3.43 In *Peake v Automatic Products* it was held that the contents of a rule book were non-contractual administrative arrangements for running the factory. If this view is correct, then works rules are non-negotiable instructions laid down by the employer. They may deal with all manner of subjects, including the method of performing the work, safety policy, disciplinary matters, concessions and privileges, and so on. A breach of the rules may lead to appropriate penalties. In *Blake v Berkel Auto Scale Ltd* an employee was summarily dismissed for a serious breach of the company's rules, and the dismissal was held to be fair. Indeed, a rule may be enforced even though the employee is in no way blameworthy. In *Jeffries v BP Tanker Co Ltd* the company had a rule that an employee with a history of cardiac disease should not be employed at sea as a radio officer, and an employee who had had two heart attacks was held to have been fairly dismissed, even though he had made an excellent recovery. The rule in this case was more in the nature of company policy.

3.44 But this does not mean that an employer can lay down rules and act on them in an autocratic manner, for the courts and tribunals will use the test of reasonableness to circumscribe management prerogatives. The rules must be clear and unambiguous; their contents must be made known to the employees, and reasonable in the circumstances. Thus in *Talbot v Hugh Fulton Ltd* an employee was dismissed for having long hair, contrary to the works rules. It was held that this would only be reasonable if there was a safety hazard, and if the exact length which was acceptable was made known. Presumably the rule should have applied to female employees as well, otherwise it would have been an act of prejudice against modern styles worn by young persons.

3.45 However, it is submitted that there may be circumstances when some aspects of the works rules can be regarded as contractual terms, despite their unilateral nature. In *Briggs v ICI* the complainant was employed as a process worker at a cyanide plant. The employers decided to pull the plant down and build another one, and consequently he was asked to work elsewhere in the firm as a process worker. He refused and claimed that he was entitled to a redundancy payment. The Divisional Court dismissed his appeal from a tribunal finding that he was not entitled. His terms of employment were governed by the statement given under EPCA s. 1 (see para 3.60), which stated that his pay would vary with the job he was performing, and clearly this contemplated that he could be transferred from one job to another. Also, he had been issued with a booklet containing the works rules of the factory, rule 17 of which stated 'You must accept the right of management to transfer you to another job with a higher or lower rate of pay, whether day work, night work or shift work.' The court held that rule 17 was a term of his employment, but this is probably because there was some implied (if obscure) reference to the works rules in his contract of employment. It would seem to follow that if the contract makes express reference to the works rules as being part of the contract of employment, they will more readily be regarded as part of the contractual terms. In *Singh v Lyons Maid Ltd* it was a requirement of the company that employees should not wear beards; this was in order to maintain the company's high standards of hygiene. The applicant knew of this rule, but none the less grew a beard in accordance with his religious beliefs. The dismissal was held to be fair. He had refused to obey a contractual term which the employers felt to be fundamental and which did not appear to be unreasonable.

3.46 At this stage it can only be said that the legal significance of the rules is a question of fact, to be determined by the circumstances of each case. For example, if the company's rule permits security guards to search employees before they leave the premises, will a refusal to be searched amount to a breach of an express term of the contract, or will it amount to a breach of the duty to obey a lawful (and reasonable) order? If a company does not have such a 'search' policy, but wishes to introduce one, can it be done unilaterally, or must the consent of each individual employee be obtained? Would a refusal to agree to be searched amount to 'some other substantial reason' for dismissal, by analogy with *R S Components v Irwin* (see Chapter 11)? It is clear that there are a number of possibilities in this field which require further exploration.

Disciplinary and grievance procedures

3.47 It is generally a condition of the contract that the employment is subject to the disciplinary and grievance procedures which are in force from time to time. These procedures are unilateral in the sense that it is the employer's responsibility to draw them up, with the co-operation of the employee and/or any relevant trade union if possible, without such assistance if necessary. Some form of incorporation into the individual contract of such conditions is also desirable, especially if these procedures are contained in a collective agreement, for this will then avoid the problems of incorporation so far as non-unionists are concerned.

3.48 But if a disciplinary procedure is incorporated into the contract, it must be adhered to, and a failure may attract the usual legal remedies. In *Jones v Lee and Guilding*, the plaintiff was dismissed from his post as headmaster of a Roman Catholic school after he had divorced his wife and remarried. His conditions of tenure stated that before any decision to dismiss a teacher was taken, the teacher had a right to be heard and to be represented before the local education authority. This procedure had not been followed, and the Court of Appeal granted an injunction restraining the school managers from purporting to dismiss the plaintiff without a hearing being held by the local education authority. In *Gunton v London Borough of Richmond* the plaintiff was given one month's notice of dismissal, though the disciplinary procedure, which was conceded to be part of his contract of employment, had not been fully implemented. The Court of Appeal held that his damages for wrongful dismissal should be limited to the loss he had suffered, which was assessed by reference to a reasonable period it would have taken the employer to implement the disciplinary procedure.

3.49 Disciplinary procedures, discussed in Chapter 7, are designed to ensure that the employee is given every possible opportunity to put right any conduct which is likely to be the subject of critical appraisal; to this extent, the object of the procedure is corrective rather than punitive. Grievance procedures are designed to ensure that the individual employee has a proper outlet for such complaints that he may have, so as to prevent an employee from nursing a grievance. The importance of such procedures can be seen from the case of *Witham v Hills Shopfitters*, where a foreman swore at an employee, using somewhat foul language. The employee resigned, and claimed that this constituted constructive dismissal. It was held that the language used was fairly commonplace on the shop floor, and hence was not conduct which was destructive of the contract of employment. Moreover, the applicant should have gone through the company's grievance procedure before he made the hasty move to resign, for then the foreman could have been made to apologise to him. In other words, it is contrary to good industrial relations for an employee to go running to an industrial tribunal with a claim without first exploring and exhausting such internal procedures as may exist. While there are circumstances where such action may be justified (e.g. if the employer has broken a term of the contract, see *Seligman & Latz Ltd v McHugh*), other grievances should first be resolved if possible within the internal machinery.

Job description

3.50 A modern practice is to draw up and hand to an employee a job description document, detailing the nature of his duties. Again, this should be a unilateral document, and should be specific enough to identify the employee's tasks, yet general enough to enable variations to take place within the context of the contract. The ambit of contractual obligations is not the same as the ambit of the duties which an employee in fact performs. This is especially true in small firms, where greater flexibility is needed, and thus the former may be wider than the latter (*Glitz v Watford Electrical Co Ltd*). An employer may be able to change the job description provided the proposed work is still within the contractual obligations.

Variation of contractual terms

3.51 The terms of the contract of employment may only be varied with the consent of both parties, and there is no power which enables one side to act unilaterally. It follows that a unilateral variation which is not accepted amounts to the repudiation of the contract. Thus if an employee is demoted, this will be repudiatory conduct by the employer, and a consequent resignation by the employee will be an acceptance of the repudiation and hence is, in law, a dismissal by the employer (see *Marriott v Oxford and District Co-operative Society*). But if, subsequent to the variation, the employee stays on with the firm for a considerable length of time, it is likely that he will be regarded as having accepted the change, and the modified contract will be in existence. Where an employee protests about the change, but continues with the employment, it is a question of fact in each case as to whether or not he has accepted it (albeit under protest).

3.52 The employer unilaterally varies the contract if he insists that the employee performs duties other than those contained in the contract, as in *Dwyer v Superguard Ltd*, where the applicant was engaged as a telephonist-typist. Typing work declined, and she was under-employed. She was asked to take on other work, splitting invoices, but she refused and was dismissed. This was held to be unfair, for her contract could only be varied with her consent. However, such a situation could be dealt with in future cases either by stating in the contract an obligation 'to perform such other duties as may be assigned from time to time', or by declaring a redundancy situation and making an offer of alternative employment.

3.53 An employer has no right unilaterally to vary the terms of a contract of employment, e.g. by reducing wages or salaries (*Miller v Hamworthy Engineering Ltd*), and if he does so, the employee is entitled to a common law remedy for the whole of the time the employer is in breach, and not merely for the period of notice which the employer could lawfully give to terminate the contract. In *Rigby v Ferodo Ltd* the plaintiff's wages were £192 per week, and his contract of employment terminable by 12 weeks' notice. As a result of a financial crisis, the employers tried to get the trade unions to agree to wage reductions, but the unions refused to agree. The employers then unilaterally reduced the plaintiff's wages by £30 per week. The plaintiff continued to work at the lower rate, but issued a writ claiming damages for breach of contract. The House of Lords upheld his claim. The employers had unilaterally repudiated the contract, but the employee had not accepted that repudiation, and thus the contract had not been terminated by the reduction in wages. Thus the employee was entitled to damages for the breach of contract for the whole of the period of the breach, and not for the period after 12 weeks when the employers could have lawfully terminated the contract.

3.54 But a contract of employment cannot remain static over the years, and some element of change is inevitable. In strict law, a variation must be mutually agreed by both sides, but if an employee refuses to accept such a change, this does not mean that he can exercise a power of veto over any new proposal. Ultimately, the employer retains an equal right to lawfully terminate the contract. In *Grix v Munford Ltd* the employee was dismissed when she refused to work a new shift system at a service station, which the employers had claimed was necessary on the grounds of efficiency and financial expediency. The industrial tribunal, in holding that the dismissal was fair, gave some guidelines on the approach which employers should adopt in these circumstances. They should consult fully and properly with the employee, and they must give reasonable and due consideration to any objections or alternative suggestions. It is also necessary to prove that the change is necessary, and thus amounts to 'some other substantial reason' should a dismissal prove to be necessary. In *Bowater Containers Ltd v McCormack*, the applicant was a supervisor. After a reorganisation, it was decided that another small section should come under his supervision. He refused to take on these additional duties, as he maintained that he was not contractually obliged to do so. His dismissal was held to be unfair by the industrial tribunal, but the decision was reversed by the EAT. The reason for the dismissal, i.e. consequent on the reorganisation, was some other substantial reason and, in the circumstances, the employers had acted reasonably.

3.55 Thus if the employer wishes to vary the contract, and the employee refuses to accept the variation, the employer must give notice to terminate the contract (*Rigby v Ferodo Ltd*). This will, of course, amount to a dismissal, and would normally give the employee a right to bring a claim for unfair dismissal. In such proceedings, the industrial tribunal may make a finding as to the advantages to the employers of the proposed changes, and whether it was reasonable for them to implement them by terminating the contract and offering a new one. The question then becomes, have the employers acted reasonably in dismissing the employee for his refusal to enter into the new contract (*Chubb Fire Security Ltd v Harper*)? To answer this question, the nature of the new offer, the advantages to the employer, and the method of handling the situation, the incentives offered, etc, all become relevant considerations (*Hollister v NFU*). The dismissal will be fair if the offer is one which a reasonable employer would make in the circumstances (*Richmond Precision Engineering Ltd v Pearce*).

3.56 However, the express terms of the contract may permit substantial variations, and if this is so, the other party is bound to accept, whether he agrees in principle or not. The terms may expressly permit a change in the location of employment, or the duties of the employee, or any other relevant matter. In *Bex v Securicor Transport Ltd* it was a condition of the employee's contract that the nature of his work could be changed by the company. When they appointed him to another position, which he regarded as a demotion, he resigned. It was held that as the employers were expressly entitled to require the employee to serve the company in any capacity, there had been no breach of contract by the employer, and consequently his resignation did not amount to a dismissal. He had the choice of carrying out his contract, or resigning.

3.57 An implied variation, accepted by both sides. may be inferred from the parties' conduct. In *Armstrong Whitworth Rolls v Mustard*, when the employee was engaged, his hours were fixed by a national agreement, and he worked an eight-hour shift for five days per week. One of his workmates left, and he was asked to work twelve-hour shifts for five days per week. This arrangement continued for seven years, and when he was eventually made redundant, it was held that his redundancy payment was to be based on a normal working week of 60 hours. Although there was no express mutual agreement to vary his hours, such agreement could clearly be inferred from the conduct of the parties.

3.58 A contract may also be varied by virtue of the terms of a collective agreement. In *Parry v Holst* the claimant's employment was expressly governed by the terms of the Working Rule Agreement of the Civil Engineering Construction Conciliation Board, Clause XD (f) of which provided that 'At the discretion of the employer, an operative may be transferred at any time during the period of his employment from one job to another'. The employee's work in South Wales came to an end, and his employers asked him to work in Somerset. He refused, and claimed a redundancy payment. It was held that he was not entitled. His employment was subject to the Working Rule Agreement, which provided for travelling and shift allowances, and there was nothing unusual about the employers' request. However, if the proposed transfer had been so unreasonable that it could be said to be outside the contemplation of the parties to the contract, then the literal application of Clause XD (f) would be precluded. Also, it was suggested that the Clause would not apply if there was a custom and practice of a particular company which would have the effect of varying the way the rule operated. None of these considerations applied in this case, and the application for a redundancy payment was rejected.

3.59 Where a variation of an existing contract is based on a change brought about by a revised collective agreement, the change will only be binding on individual employees if it is accepted by them, or if they were collectively represented at the time the change was agreed (*Land and Wilson v West Yorkshire Metropolitan County Council*). Thus employees who are not union members, or who are members of another union, are not necessarily bound by the change. But if the collective agreement is expressly incorporated into the individual's contract, or if the union has authority to negotiate a change, the variation will bind (*Nelson and Woollett v Post Office*).

Written particulars of the contract of employment

3.60 Section 1 of the Employment Protection (Consolidation) Act 1978 provides that no later than two months after the commencement of employment, the employer shall give to the employee a written statement containing the following information:

(1) (a) the names of the employer and employee;
 (b) the date when the employment began;

- (c) the date on which the employee's period of continuous employment began, taking into account any employment with a previous employer which counts towards continuity;

(2) as at a specified date, not more than seven days before the statement is given;

- (a) the scale or rate of remuneration, or the method of calculating remuneration;
- (b) the intervals at which remuneration is paid;
- (c) any terms and conditions relating to hours of work;
- (d) any terms and conditions relating to:
  - (i) entitlement to holidays, including public holidays, and holiday pay (being sufficient to calculate the entitlement, including accrued holiday pay on the termination of employment);
  - (ii) incapacity for work due to sickness or injury, including any provision for sick pay;
  - (iii) pensions and pension schemes;
- (e) the length of notice the employee is obliged to give, and entitled to receive to determine the employment;
- (f) the title of the employee's job;
- (g) if the employment is not intended to be permanent, the period for which it is expected to continue; if it is for a fixed term, the date when it is to end;
- (h) either the place of work or, where the employee is required or permitted to work at various places, an indication of that, and of the address of the employer;
- (j) any collective agreement which directly affects the terms and conditions of employment; where the employer is not a party to the agreement, the persons by whom they are made;
- (k) where the employee is required to work outside the United Kingdom for more than one month:
  - (i) the period for which he is to work outside the United Kingdom;
  - (ii) the currency in which remuneration is to be paid while so working;
  - (iii) any additional remuneration payable to him, and any benefits to be provided by reason of his working abroad; and
  - (iv) any terms and conditions relating to his return to the United Kingdom.

3.61 So far as the above matters are concerned, it should be noted that:

(1) if there are no particulars to be entered under any of these headings, that fact should be stated;
(2) the written statement may refer the employee to the provisions of some other document which he has a reasonable opportunity of reading in the course of his employment, or which is made reasonably accessible to him in some other way, in respect of sick pay and pensions schemes;
(3) all the above particulars shall be given in one document (known as the principle statement) except terms and conditions relating to sickness, pensions, length of temporary or fixed term contracts, collective agreements and details given to employees who are to work outside the United Kingdom. These terms may be contained in a separate document or documents;
(4) the statement shall be given to the employee notwithstanding that his employment has ended before the end of two months from its commencement.

3.62 In addition to the matters required to be given under s. 1, the statement shall include a note:
(a) specifying any disciplinary rules applicable to the employee, or referring him to the provisions of a document which he has reasonable opportunities of reading in the course of his employment, or is made reasonably accessible to him in some other way, and which specifies such rules;
(b) specifying, by description or otherwise a person to whom the employee can apply if he is dissatisfied with any disciplinary decision relating to him, the person to whom he can apply for the purpose of seeking redress of any grievance relating to his employment, and explaining any further steps which may be taken, or referring to a document which the employee has a reasonable opportunity of reading or which is made accessible to him. However, the provisions relating to disciplinary procedures do not apply if, on the date when the employee's employment began, the relevant number of employees was less than 20 (including employees employed by an associated employer). Nor do the provisions relating to rules, disciplinary decisions, grievances or procedures apply if they are related to health and safety at work.

3.63 If there is any change in the matters specified in the written particulars, the employer shall give, within one month of the change, the relevant particulars.

3.64 It is not necessary to give written particulars to an employee is his employment continues for less than one month, or if his contract normally involves working for less than eight hours weekly.

3.65 It must be borne in mind that the statement given by virtue of s. 1 is not necessarily a contract, and is not conclusive evidence of that contract (*System Floors (UK) Ltd v Daniel*). But it certainly helps to establish what those contractual terms were, and a failure by an employer to provide such a statement may well lead an industrial tribunal to draw adverse presumptions against that employer in subsequent litigation, should the terms of the contract be in dispute.

3.66 If an employer does not provide the written statement under s. 1, or if it is incomplete, the employee can require a reference to be made to an industrial tribunal to determine what particulars ought to be included in such a statement. But this power only extends to matters which should be in the statement in accordance with the above statutory requirements. The tribunal has no power to amend or rewrite a contract of employment merely because there is some misunderstanding about its meaning (*CITB v Leighton*).

3.67 An industrial tribunal may only state those terms which have been agreed. They cannot remake the contract and insert terms which should have been agreed. 'Mandatory' terms can be determined by looking at all the evidence, including the express, implied and statutory terms. If there has been no agreement on the 'non-mandatory' terms, the industrial tribunal should record this (*Eagland v British Telecommunications plc*). There is no power to invent terms which have not been agreed, except, perhaps, terms which are necessarily imposed by law, e.g. reasonable notice.

Itemised pay statement (Employment Protection (Consolidation) Act 1978 ss 8-10)

3.69 Provided that he works for eight hours or more per week (or 16 or more if his employer employs less than 20 employees), every employee has the right to be given by his employer an itemised pay statement, giving particulars of the gross amount of wages or salary, the amount of any variable or fixed deductions, and the purposes for which they are made, the net wages or salary payable and, where the net amount is paid in different ways, the amount and method of each part-payment. A pay statement need not contain separate particulars or fixed deductions as long as the aggregate amount of all deductions is stated, and the employer had given to the employee a standing statement of fixed deductions which contains all the relevant details. Such standing statement must be re-issued every 12 months.

3.70 If an employer fails to give an itemised pay statement, the employee may require a reference to be made to an industrial tribunal, to determine what particulars ought to be included in such a statement. But where the tribunal finds that the employer has failed to give an employee any itemised pay statement, or that it does not give the required particulars concerning deductions, the tribunal shall make a declaration to that effect (*Coales v John Wood & Co*) and, if there have been any unnotified deductions from the employee's pay within 13 weeks preceding the date of the application for the reference to the tribunal, then the tribunal may award that the employer shall pay to the employee the aggregate of the deductions made. However, no application for a tribunal reference can be made more than three months after the employment has ceased. The requirement to give an itemised pay statement does not apply to employees who work outside Great Britain, share fishermen or merchant seamen.

Holidays

3.71 There is no general legal requirement that an employer should give holidays to his employees, either annual or Bank or Public holidays. The number of days/weeks of holidays, payment for holidays, accrued holiday pay, basis of holiday entitlement, over-time for working on holidays, days off in lieu of holidays, must all be matters to be resolved by the terms of the contract of employment. Details should be contained in the contract, the written statement given under s. 1 of EPCA, or contained in the works rules/staff handbook etc. It may be possible to resort to an implied term based on custom and usage (*Tucker v British Leyland Motor Corpn*).

3.72 An EC Recommendation suggested that employees should be given four weeks' holiday each year, but, as noted, this has no legal force.

3.73–3.74 An employee who wishes to sue in respect of his employer's failure to pay holiday pay must bring the claim before a County Court, the industrial tribunal having no jurisdiction to deal with such matters.

Occupational pension schemes

3.75 The Occupational Pension Schemes (Disclosure of Information) Regulations 1986 require an employer who runs an occupational pension scheme to disclose automatically certain information to members and beneficiaries, including details of the scheme, rights of leavers, amount of pension payable to a new pensioner, and options available to persons on the death of a member or beneficiary. Other information is to be disclosed on request, including trust deeds and rules, benefit statements, trustees' annual report and the actuarial valuation report.

3.76 The persons entitled to this information include current members and deferred pensioners, prospective members and their spouses, and recognised independent trade unions (except that the latter are not entitled to benefit statements).

3.77 The provision of such information was also recommended by the Code of Practice issued by the National Association of Pension Funds.

CHAPTER 4

Legal constraints on terms and conditions of employment

4.1 In a number of instances the law has intervened to impose on the parties to a contract of employment certain terms and conditions, so as to supplant the free bargaining arrangements which may otherwise operate. The intervention of statutory rules in employment situations is a significant development in recent years, and is a process which will no doubt continue. This is not the place to analyse the cause and effect, which require a consideration of social, political and economic factors, but the totality of the legal constraints have added pressures on general employment policies.

Minors

4.2 A contract of employment entered into by a minor (i.e. a person under the age of 18) is a valid agreement provided that on the whole it is substantially for his benefit. Otherwise, it will be void. Even though the contract contains terms which are onerous or detrimental to his interests, one must look at the effect of the whole agreement. In *De Francesco v Barnum* a 14 year-old girl bound herself by an apprenticeship deed to the plaintiff in order to become a professional dancer. She agreed not to marry during this time, and to perform engagements only with the plaintiff's permission. The plaintiff was under no obligation to provide engagements, but when he did, the pay was somewhat ungenerous. It was held that the deed was void, for it was totally unreasonable, and was not in the interests of the girl. In contrast, we can consider *Clements v London and North-Western Rly Co*, where a boy entered into the defendants' employment on terms which excluded his right to sue under the Employers' Liability Act 1880, in respect of injuries suffered during his employment. Instead, he was covered by the company's own insurance scheme, which had a wider range of protection, though the benefits were somewhat lower than the State scheme. It was held that on the whole the contract was to his advantage and was therefore binding.

4.3 Recent cases on this subject illustrate somewhat graphically the changing social scene. In *Denmark Productions v Boscobel Productions* a contract by four infant members of a pop group to employ a manager was held to be binding, and in *Chaplin v Leslie Frewin (Publishers) Ltd* the son of a famous film star contracted to assign to a firm of publishers a book containing his life story. This too, was held to be binding, as it conferred a financial benefit on him.

Children

4.4 Children are minors below school leaving age (currently age 16). If they are aged 13 or over they may engage in part-time work, provided this does not amount to more than two hours per day on school-days or on Sunday. They may not work during school hours, or before 7 am or after 7 pm on school-days. Local authorities have certain supervisory powers over the employment of children when the provisions of the Employment of Children Act 1973 are fully in force, and they may make byelaws restricting their employment (Children and Young Persons Acts 1933–1969). A child may not be employed in an industrial undertaking or on a sea-going boat, unless the undertaking or boat is one in which only members of the child's family are employed (Employment of Women, Young Persons and Children Act 1920 ss. 1–3). A child may not be employed in a factory (Education Act 1918 s. 14) nor employed underground in a mine, except for the purpose of receiving prescribed instruction (Mines and Quarries Act 1954 s. 124). A child may not be required to lift, carry or move anything so heavy as to be likely to cause injury. There are special provisions relating to the employment of children in the field of entertainment (Young Persons (Employment) Act 1938 s. 9).

4.4A School children may be employed for work experience from the beginning of the school term preceding the start of the school year in which they become entitled to leave school (Education (Work Experience) Act 1973 s. 1, as amended).

Apprentices

4.5 A contract of apprenticeship is an agreement whereby the apprentice binds himself to his employer in order to learn a trade, and the employer on his part agrees to teach and instruct him. The contract must be in writing, signed by the parties, and cannot be terminated by the employer except for grave misconduct (such as theft) or a refusal to attend to his duties. An apprentice who is wrongfully dismissed may claim by way of damages not only his immediate loss, but a sum representing the value of his loss of future prospects as a qualified person (*Dunk v George Waller & Son Ltd*). Also, since an employer is, in one sense, *in loco parentis* to an apprentice, a certain latitude must be shown in respect of minor lapses in conduct. For example, in *Shortland v Chantrill*, an apprentice was criticised by a managing director about his work, and he retorted 'You couldn't have done any fucking better'. For this, he was dismissed. It was held that the dismissal was unfair; one isolated step of impudence did not warrant the termination of an apprenticeship which had only ten months to run.

4.6 But although a contract of apprenticeship is essentially a common law concept, with the old (i.e. pre-1971) remedies still applying, an apprentice is also within the protection of the new laws. This could cause a certain conflict. For example, in *Finch v Betabake (Anglia) Ltd* the applicant was an apprentice motor mechanic. The employers received a report from an ophthalmic surgeon that the apprentice could not continue to work at that job without undue danger to himself and to other employees. Consequently, he was dismissed. It was held that the fairness of the dismissal had to be determined under EPCA s. 57(3) (see Chapter 8). The fact that the employers may have been in breach of the apprenticeship agreement did not mean that the dismissal was unfair. The circumstances which could justify the dismissal of an apprentice were very limited, but in the instant case, the employers acted fairly and reasonably.

4.7 If, on the expiry of an apprenticeship agreement, the apprentice is not re-employed, he has not been dismissed for reason of redundancy (*North East Coast Shiprepairers v Secretary of State for Employment*).

Sex discrimination

4.8 Although it is generally considered that the Sex Discrimination Act 1975 (as amended by the Sex Discrimination Act 1986) was designed to prevent unlawful discrimination against women, the Act makes it equally unlawful to discriminate against men, or against a married person of either sex on the grounds of that person's marital status. But no account is to be taken of special treatment afforded to women because of pregnancy or childbirth. It is permissible, however, to discriminate against (but not in favour of) a single person of either sex. Thus if a firm wishes to offer cheap mortgage facilities to its staff, then if these facilities are made available to married men, they must be equally available to married women (*Sun Alliance and London Insurance Co v Dudman*). But it is permissible to exclude single persons of either sex from the scheme.

What constitutes discrimination?

4.9 The test for determining whether or not an act was discrimination is objective, not subjective. In other words, regard must be had to what was done, not the reasons or motives behind what was done. The question to be asked is 'would the complainant have received the same treatment from the defendant but for his or her sex'? In *James v Eastleigh Borough Council*, Mr and Mrs James were both aged 61. The local authority adopted a policy whereby children under 3 years of age, and members of the public over pensionable age, were permitted free entry into the local swimming pool, whereas everyone else had to pay 75p entrance fee. Mr James complained that he had been discriminated against because of his sex, as he was required to pay an admission fee, whereas his wife was not. The House of Lords upheld his contention. Lord Bridge stated that the purity of the discriminator's subjective motive, intention or reason for discriminating cannot save the criterion applied from the objective taint of discrimination on grounds of sex. Lord Ackner stated that the reason why the local authority adopted its particular policy (i.e. to benefit State pensioners) cannot affect the fact that men were treated less favourably than women.

4.9A So far as discrimination in employment is concerned, there are three types of circumstances to consider:

A. Direct discrimination (s. 1(1)(a))

4.10 This arises when a person of one sex is treated less favourably than a person of another sex, and the sex of that person is the reason for the unfavourable treatment. To refuse to employ a woman because 'it is a man's job' is an example of direct discrimination (*Batisha v Say*).

4.10A Discrimination against a married person of either sex is also covered (s. 3(1)(a)).

4.11 Discrimination can take place even though the act is done with the best of motives, and in the best interests of the person concerned. In *Grieg v Community Industry*, the applicant and another woman were appointed to two jobs, which involved working with men. The other woman failed to turn up for work, and so the applicant was not allowed to start work, as in the past there had been problems with one woman working with an all-male team. It was held that this constituted direct discrimination; the motive of the employers was irrelevant.

4.11A Section 5(3) provides that a comparison of the cases of persons of different sex or marital status under ss. 1(1) and 3(1) must be such that the relevant circumstance in the one case are the same, or not materially different, in the other. Those 'relevant circumstances' must be judged objectively. In *Bullock v Alice Ottley School* the employers decided to establish a common retiring age for all members of their staff irrespective of sex. Teaching, administrative and domestic staff had to retire at 60, and gardeners and maintenance staff at 65. The higher retirement age of the latter group was necessary because of the difficulty in obtaining such personnel, and the need to keep them in employment as long as possible. The applicant was required to retire when she became 60, and she claimed she had been discriminated against on grounds of sex, because all the gardening and maintenance staff, who stayed on until 65, were men. An industrial tribunal dismissed her complaint holding that it was not discriminatory to have differing retiring ages for persons in different groups provided it was applied irrespective of sex. The EAT reversed the decision, holding that the 'like for like' comparison had to be made in respect of all the staff, not separate groups. On a further appeal, the Court of Appeal restored the decision of the industrial tribunal. The conclusion that everyone employed by the same employer had to have the same retiring age was one which could not be accepted. The comparison between the applicant (who was domestic staff) and the maintenance and gardening staff could not be made, since there were special difficulties in recruiting the latter which justified the later retiring age. The 'relevant circumstances' in s. 5(3) had to be those circumstances which were relevant to the comparison.

Further, the claim based on indirect discrimination would also be dismissed. The employers had objectively justified the later retirement age for gardeners and maintenance staff, for reasons which had nothing to do with sex. There was a genuine need for the later retirement age for the latter group of employees, i.e. the difficulty in recruiting them, and the need to retain their services as long as possible.

B. Indirect discrimination (s. 1(1)(b))

4.12 Indirect discrimination arises:

a. when a person applies a condition or requirement to another,
b. but which is such that the proportion of persons from one sex who can comply with that condition or requirement is considerably smaller than the other sex,
c. it cannot be shown that the condition or requirement is justified irrespective of the sex of the person to whom it is applied, and
d. which is to that person's detriment because he/she cannot comply.

Indirect discrimination against a person on the ground of marital status is also covered (s. 3(1)(b)).

4.12A Thus to advertise for a 'Male or female clerk, must have a large beard' would amount to an indirect discrimination, unless the whiskered requirement can be justified. There is a heavy burden of proof on the employer to satisfy the industrial tribunal that the requirement or condition is necessary (*Steel v Union of Post Office Workers*). In *Home Office v Holmes*, it was held that an obligation on an employee to work full-time as opposed to part-time was a requirement or condition, which, on the facts, could not be justified.

4.13 Whether or not the requirement or condition is justified must be assessed objectively, not subjectively. In other words, it matters not if the discriminator genuinely thought the requirement or condition to be justified, if, looking at the matter objectively, it is not. For example, an employer must be careful not to discriminate indirectly by making generalised assumptions based on sex or marital status. In *Hurley v Mustoe* the applicant, who was a married woman with four young children, applied for a job as a waitress. The manager decided to give her a trial, but on the first night at work the proprietor of the restaurant asked her to leave. It was against his policy to employ women with young children, as he thought they were unreliable. The EAT held that the applicant had been directly discriminated against on grounds of sex contrary to s. 1(1)(*a*) and indirectly discriminated against on grounds of marital status contrary to s. 3(1)(*b*). There were other ways of finding out whether or not a potential employee was reliable without imposing a blanket rule which excluded all women with children. Equally, it is wrong to 'assume' that a married woman will leave her job to be and live with her husband in another town (*Horsey v Dyfed County Council*) or that a man will be 'the breadwinner' of the family (*Skyrail Oceanic Ltd v Coleman*).

4.13A However, in *Briggs v North Eastern Education and Library Board*, the Northern Ireland Court of Appeal took the view that a contractual requirement imposed on a teacher that she should assist in the taking of school games outside school hours was a requirement which was justified irrespective of a person's sex or marital status. A balance must be made between the discriminatory effect of the requirement or condition and the reasonable needs of the employer, objectively determined (see also *Bilka-Kaufhaus v Weber von Hartz*).

4.14 Some difficulty has been experienced in trying to ascertain the proper section of the community for the purpose of making the appropriate comparison. In *Kidd v DRG (UK) Ltd* the applicant was a woman who worked part-time. All the other workers in her section, whether part-time or full-time, were also women. When redundancies were announced, it was agreed with the trade union that part-time workers would be discharged first. The applicant complained that this indirectly discriminated against her on grounds of sex and marital status. She argued that women in general, and married women in particular, were, to an appreciably greater extent, unable to comply with the requirement that they should work full-time because of commitments to look after children. Her complaint was dismissed by the industrial tribunal and the EAT. The industrial tribunal refused to assume (in the absence of evidential support) that a considerably greater proportion of married women with young children (or of women than of men) regularly undertake a child-caring role, which precludes the acceptance of full-time employment. Otherwise, as the industrial tribunal pointed out, every advertisement for a full-time employee would automatically constitute indirect discrimination on grounds of sex or marital status. In any case, even if this redundancy scheme was discriminatory, it was capable of being justified irrespective of sex, for there were a number of marginal advantages in retaining the full-time employees.

4.15 The tribunals must consider not merely whether as a matter of theoretical exercise a woman can comply with the condition which has been imposed, but whether, as a matter of reality and practice, it is possible to do so. This was the reasoning of the EAT in *Price v Civil Service Commission*, where employers advertised for executive officers, a requirement being that candidates had to be over the age of 17½, but under the age of 28. The applicant, who was aged 36, contended that this amounted to indirect discrimination, because far fewer women than men could comply with this requirement in practice, as they were out of the labour market having or bringing up children. In theory, there is hardly any difference in the numbers of men and women in those age groups, but the EAT held that it was relevant to take into account the realities of the situation, which suggested that there were indeed fewer women available for employment in this age group. As the applicant could not comply, and as it was to her detriment that she could not comply, the EAT remitted the case to the industrial tribunal for further consideration. The industrial tribunal subsequently held that the respondents had failed to show that the requirement that direct entrants to the Executive Grade of the Civil Service has to be under the age of 28 was justified irrespective of sex. The test of 'justified' was that the requirement or condition should be necessary, not merely convenient. Consideration should be given to whether there is some other non-discriminatory manner of achieving the desired objective without imposing a discriminatory requirement or condition.

4.15A However, an age requirement is not, *per se*, discriminatory, and an applicant cannot select the appropriate 'pool' merely because it is convenient to do so, where, in fact, a non-discriminatory pool exists. Further, the objective balance which can justify discrimination must take into account the reasonable needs of the person applying the age condition against its discriminatory effect, and if the discrimination affects only a small proportion of the total number of eligible persons adversely, the industrial tribunal is not entitled to concentrate on the particular circumstances of the complainant (*University of Manchester v Jones*).

4.16 Whether or not a person 'can comply' with a condition or requirement depends on whether he/she is able to comply, not on whether he/she does not wish to comply. In *Turner v Labour Party* the applicant was a divorcee. She was required to join her employer's occupational pension scheme, which provided, inter alia, for a pension for a surviving spouse. Since she was not likely to have any such survivor, she claimed that the scheme was discriminatory. It was held that although the applicant may not wish to marry, it could not be said that she could not marry. Consequently, she was able to comply with the requirement.

C. Victimisation (s. 4(1))

4.17 It is also unlawful to victimise a person because he/she has:

i. brought proceedings under the Act, or the Equal Pay Act 1970, or
ii. given evidence or information in connection with proceedings under either Act, or
iii. done anything in relation to either Act to the discriminator or any other person, or
iv. has made allegations of a contravention of either Act unless the allegation was false and not made in good faith.

Discrimination in employment

4.18 Part II of the Act prohibits unlawful discrimination in employment, which is defined as 'employment under a contract of service or apprenticeship or a contract personally to execute any work or labour'. This definition is wider than the relationship of employer/employee, and can include self-employed persons (*Quinnen v Hovells*, see para 4.70), but there must be a personal obligation to perform that work or labour, and that performance must be the dominant purpose of the contract (*Mirror Group Newspapers Ltd v Gunning*).

There are five types of unlawful discriminatory acts which may be committed against a person in relation to employment at an establishment in Great Britain.

1. The arrangements a person makes for the purpose of determining who shall be employed (s. 6(1)(a))

4.19 The arrangements must ensure that job opportunities are available to all, irrespective of sex. Although advertising is subject to a separate provision (see para 4.57) it has been held that an individual may complain if he feels that he has been discriminated against, for advertisements are part of the arrangements for determining who shall be employed (*Brindley v Tayside Health Board*).

4.20 Even if an advertisement in itself is non-discriminatory, an unlawful act may be committed if subsequent events disclose an intention to discriminate. In *Brennan v Dewhurst Ltd*, a girl applied for a job as a butcher's assistant. She was interviewed by the branch manager, who made it clear that he had no intention of employing a woman in the job. However, the district manager, who had the responsibility for making the appointment, decided that the vacancy need not be filled. The EAT held that the interview by the branch manager, which was a 'first filter' arrangement, operated so as to discriminate against the girl, even though it was not made for that purpose.

4.21 Questions which are asked at interviews are also part of the employment arrangements, as can be seen from *Saunders v Richmond-upon-Thames Council*, where a woman applied for a job as a professional golfer. She was confronted with questions which were not put to male applicants, and which were concerned with the ability of a woman to do the job in question ('Are there any other woman golf professionals?', 'Are you blazing a trail?', etc). It was held that to put certain questions to women applicants which are not put to men does not necessarily make those questions an indication that the employer intends to discriminate. Clearly, an employer may wish to put certain questions to a woman which may be more pertinent in her case (e.g. 'do you intend to have children?' or 'who will look after the children if they are off school sick?' etc), and which are capable of indicating an intention to discriminate on ground of parenthood rather than sex. Further, although there is no legal requirement that a selection board should comprise of both sexes, such an arrangement may well prove to be advantageous to any employer in pre-empting a possible claim of sex discrimination. In *Saunders'* case, the chairman of the board, who asked the questions complained of, was in fact a woman, and no doubt this assisted the employers in discharging the burden of proof.

4.22 A similar problem may arise at some future date over the use of application forms, for it could be argued that some of the questions which are directed to finding out factual information (e.g. sex, marital status, number of children, etc) are discriminatory in that they have no bearing on the employment situation. On this point there is no direct decision.

2. The terms on which a person offers employment to another (s. 6(1)(b))

4.23 If an employer makes an offer of employment to a woman on terms which are less favourable than those offered to a man, then clearly an act of discrimination has occurred. This does not apply to any provision for the payment of money unless her contract is subject to an equality clause by virtue of the Equal Pay Act 1970 (see below), in which case it is discriminatory. To make an offer of employment to a woman on terms which are different from those offered to a man will be *prima facie* discriminatory. But if the employer can show that the variation was due to a genuine material difference between the two applicants which had nothing to do with their sex, it will not be unlawful. For example, if a woman is offered employment commencing at 9 am because she has to take her children to school, a man must be offered the same facility if he is in a similar situation. A problem may arise if an offer is made which is more favourable than the terms enjoyed by existing employees, for the latter may well decide to make a subsequent complaint.

4.24 It is permissible to discriminate in the terms offered which relate to death or retirement (see para 4.43).

3. Refusing or deliberately omitting to offer employment because of a person's sex (s. 6(1)(c))

4.25 In *Batisha v Say* a woman was turned down for a job as a cave guide because 'it is a man's job', and in *Munro v Allied Suppliers* a man was not taken on as a cook because women employees would not work with him. In both cases it was held that an act of discrimination had occurred. A more difficult situation arises if there is an act of discrimination, but in the final event no one is appointed to the post. Can it thus be argued that the person concerned has been treated less favourably? On this, there are tribunal decisions both ways; in *Roadburg v Lothian Regional Council*, the applicant was told that she was unsuitable because she was a woman. This was held to be unlawful discrimination even though no one was appointed to the post. In *Thorn v Meggitt Engineering*, the tribunal dismissed a claim of sex discrimination on its facts, but added that even if there had been discrimination, the complainant was treated no less favourably than a man, for no one was appointed to the job.

4.26 An employer still retains his prerogative right to choose the person he believes will best do the job, and the fact that a rejected candidate has qualifications or experience which are better than the appointee will not be sufficient to found a claim of discrimination. As long as there is no evidence of discrimination on grounds of sex, the employer may select a candidate on the basis of any criteria he thinks fit. In refuting a claim, an employer may well point to the fact that women have been engaged in such positions before, and indicate that there were other reasons why the candidate was not offered employment. Thus in *Steere v Morris Bros* a woman applied for a job as a heavy goods vehicle driver. When she was rejected, she claimed she had been discriminated against. The employers were able to show that they had employed women drivers in the past, and the reason she was not appointed was because she lived too far away from the place of employment. The reasons for her non-appointment had nothing to do with her sex.

4. In the way a person offers access to opportunities for promotion, transfer or training, or to any other benefits, facilities or services, or by refusing or deliberately omitting to afford her/him access to them (s. 6(2)(a))

4.27 To deny a woman an opportunity for promotion (e.g. by refusing to send her on a development course), or to restrict her training opportunities would be discriminatory, although it may be noted that a crash programme of single sexed training is permissible under s. 47 in order to alter an imbalance of the sexes in a job which has become apparent within the previous 12 months. The words 'benefits, facilities or services' are capable of covering almost any discriminatory practice in employment. For example, in *Peake v Automative Products*, the terms and conditions of employment of men and women were the same. However, it was an established practice of the firm, going back some 30 years, that women and disabled persons were allowed to leave work at 4.25 pm, whereas the men left at 4.30 pm. This arrangement was made for safety reasons, in order to prevent women and handicapped employees from being jostled in the rush to the gate. The male applicant complained that this amounted to an act of unlawful discrimination on grounds of his sex. His claim was rejected by the industrial tribunal, but on appeal, the EAT held that he had been refused access to a benefit (of leaving early) and had been subjected to a detriment (of not being allowed to leave at 4.25 pm) on grounds of his sex. This decision was reversed by the Court of Appeal. Lord Denning held that the Act did not obliterate all the chivalry and courtesy which it was expected that men would give to women. Nor did the Act require that elemental differences of sex must be disregarded in the interpretation of an Act of Parliament. Arrangements which were made in the interests of safety or good administration were not infringements of the law. In the last analysis, Lord Denning was prepared to adopt the rule *de minimis non curat lex* (the law does not concern itself with trifling matters). This decision has been criticised on the ground that the interests of safety and good administration could be met without relying on a scheme which was fundamentally based on sex, and that some other equally efficacious manner of achieving these objects could be devised without perpetuating the myth of 'the weaker sex'. Indeed, the Court of Appeal subsequently held that the only sound reason for the decision in *Peake's* case is the *de minimis* rule, and in so far as the decision rested on chivalry and administrative convenience, it was no longer to be relied upon (*Jeremiah v Ministry of Defence*).

5. By dismissing a person, or subjecting her/him to any other detriment (s. 6(2)(b))

4.28 The term 'dismissal' includes constructive dismissal (see para 8.62) and the non-renewal of a fixed term contract (s. 82(1A)).

4.29 A dismissal on grounds of sex is unlawful even though the employer acts under pressure from other employees. In *Munro v Allied Suppliers*, a man was offered a job as a cook. He was dismissed before he started work, as other women employees indicated that they would not work with him. This was held to violate the Act.

4.30 A detriment may exist even though the employee is compensated for it. In *Jeremiah v Ministry of Defence*, it was the practice of the respondents not to require women to do certain dirty work, as they did not wish to take showers afterwards. When men did the work, they received extra pay. It was held that the fact that the employee was compensated for the dirty work by an additional payment did not mean that he was not subjected to a detriment. An employer cannot buy the right to discriminate.

4.31 The industrial tribunals have met with some difficulties in those cases where a woman has been dismissed, but sex, although relevant, has not been the primary consideration. In *Gubala v Crompton Parkinson*, the choice of a dismissal in a redundancy situation lay between a man and a woman. The woman had longer overall service, but the employers took into account the fact that the man was 58 years old, and had a family to support and a mortgage to keep up. The woman was young, married, with a husband who was working, and she was dismissed. It was held that this amounted to unlawful discrimination; the tribunal refused to accept the 'breadwinner' criterion as a basis of redundancy selection. It is submitted that this conclusion is wrong. Long service, although an important feature of any selection procedure, is not the sole basis for retention. As long as the 'breadwinner' criterion is applied irrespective of the sex of the person, then this ought not to amount to unlawful sex discrimination. After all, there are many who would accept that the 'breadwinner' criteria is a perfectly humane and reasonable method of selecting for redundancy, and as long as the same tests are applied to men as well as women, the sex of the person eventually chosen for redundancy is irrelevant.

4.32 A somewhat different result was reached in *Goult v Reay Electrical*, where the applicant was dismissed when it was discovered that she had married a sales representative who was in the employ of a competitor. The industrial tribunal held that she was not dismissed because of her sex, or her marital status, but because she had formed a relationship between an employee of her employer's principal competitor. The marriage was irrelevant except in so far as it indicated that there was a close relationship between her and her husband!

4.33 Further difficulties have been met in cases where a woman has been dismissed because she has announced an intention to get married. It will be recalled that discrimination on grounds of marital status is dealt with in s. 3 of the Act. In *Bick v School for the Deaf*, it was held that to dismiss a single woman who announced her intention to get married was not discrimination on grounds of her marital status, for she was not yet married! The tribunal did not appear to consider s. 6(2)(b) (dismissal by way of discrimination) as there does not appear to have been any evidence that men were treated in a different manner if they made a similar announcement. On the other hand, in *McLean v Paris Travel*, it was contrary to the company's policy to employ married couples, and the applicant was dismissed when she announced her intention to marry the assistant manager. This was held to be contrary to s. 6(2)(b), and she was awarded £200 for injury to her feelings, as well as compensation for unfair dismissal.

4.34 A case which illustrates some of the difficulties arising from dismissal on grounds of sex and marital status is *Skyrail Oceanic Ltd v Coleman*, where the applicant was employed as a booking clerk in a travel agency. She then became engaged to a man who worked for a rival firm. The two employers discussed the matter, as it appeared that there would be a possibility of leakage of confidential information. It was agreed that the applicant's husband-to-be would be the breadwinner of the marriage. After the marriage had taken place, she was dismissed. An industrial tribunal awarded her £666 compensation for unfair dismissal and £1000 for injury to feelings under the Sex Discrimination Act. The EAT allowed the employer's appeal under the Sex Discrimination Act, but this was reversed by a majority of the Court of Appeal, who held that an assumption that men are more likely to be the breadwinner of the family than women was an assumption based on sex. Therefore, the dismissal of a woman based on that assumption amounted to sex discrimination. However, the Court of Appeal reduced the compensation of £100, as the original award was out of all proportion to the injury proven. In a powerful dissenting judgment,

Shaw LJ thought that the claim was totally unmeritorious and an abuse of the idealistic principles behind the Sex Discrimination Act.

4.35 To dismiss a woman because she is pregnant can be discrimination on grounds of sex (as well as an unfair dismissal *per se*, see para 5.30). Although there is no identical comparison, for a man cannot become pregnant, pregnancy is capable of being matched by analogous circumstances applying to a man, e.g. sickness. Section 5(3) of the Act requires that for the purpose of comparison, the two cases must be the same or not materially different. It is thus possible to make a comparison between the treatment accorded to a pregnant woman and to a man who is sick (*Hayes v Malleable Working Men's Club and Institute*).

4.35A The process of comparing 'like with like' received further support from the EAT in *Webb v Emo Air Cargo (UK) Ltd*, where a female clerk informed her employer that she was pregnant, and would eventually be taking maternity leave of absence. The applicant was taken on as a temporary replacement, it being recognised that she would require several months' training in order to learn how to do the job. A few weeks after commencing her employment, she informed the employer that she too was pregnant. The employers dismissed her, and she therefore claimed that she had been unlawfully discriminated against on grounds of sex. Her claim failed. She was not dismissed because of her sex, or because of her pregnancy. A man who announced that he would be absent for a comparable period would, in the circumstances, have been treated in a like manner. The applicant's dismissal was therefore for a neutral reason.

4.35B However, a completely different approach was taken by the European Court of Justice in *Dekker v Stichting Vormingscetrum voor Jong Wolwassenen (VJV-Centrum) Plus*, where the applicant applied for a job as a training instructor. In fact, all the applicants were women. The applicant told the selection committee that she was pregnant, but although she was the most suitable candidate, she was not offered the job. The reason was that the employers' insurers would not reimburse the employers for the sickness benefit they would have to pay her, because she was pregnant at the time of the application. Mrs Dekker claimed that the refusal to offer her employment was contrary to the Dutch equal treatment law, and also contrary to the Equal Treatment Directive EEC 76/207 (see para 1.57). The European Court upheld her claim. Whether a refusal to employ results in direct discrimination on grounds of sex depends on whether the reason for the refusal was a reason which applied without distinction to persons of both sexes, or whether it applied exclusively to one sex. Since she was refused employment because she was pregnant, and only women can be pregnant, the refusal was because of her sex. Further, the fact that there were no male applicants for the post was irrelevant, for if the reason for the refusal to employ her was a reason which exclusively applied to one sex, the reason is inherently discriminatory.

4.35C The decision in *Webb v Emo Air Cargo (UK) Ltd* (above) was upheld by the Court of Appeal and the House of Lords, but the latter decided to refer the matter to the European Court of Justice for a determination on whether there was a breach of the Equal Treatment Directive and if it was possible to construe the Sex Discrimination Act accordingly. Although the Directive is not enforceable against a non-State employer (see para 1.54), it is the duty of UK courts to construe domestic legislation so as to accord with the interpretation of a Directive given by the European Court, if this can be done without distorting the meaning of domestic legislation. This is so whether the domestic legislation was passed before or after the Directive came into force. But, following *Marleasing SA v La Commercial Internacional de Alimentacion* (see para 1.54) domestic law must be open to an interpretation which is consistent with the Directive, for the latter cannot be used as a direct substitute for the former. Thus a decision of the European Court in *Webb v Emo Air Cargo* should resolve any conflict between that case and *Dekker*.

4.35D But if a woman is dismissed for a reason other than pregnancy, even if that reason flows from the pregnancy, this is not discriminatory. In *Berrisford v Woodard Schools* the applicant was employed as a matron at a Church of England girls boarding school. She informed the headmaster that she was pregnant. Initially, he congratulated her, and made certain proposals regarding married accommodation, but his attitude changed when the applicant informed him that she had no intention of marrying the father of the child. She was subsequently dismissed, and claimed she had been discriminated against on grounds of sex and family status, contrary to the Sex

Discrimination Act and the Equal Treatment Directive. Evidence was given that the school governors expected somewhat high moral standards from their staff, and it was argued that the applicant was dismissed because her pregnancy manifested extra-marital sexual activity. The industrial tribunal dismissed her complaint, holding that the reason for the dismissal was the adverse example to the pupils at the school conveyed by the pregnancy, coupled with the continuing unmarried status. The decision was upheld by the EAT. It was the example given to the pupils at the school which was the objectionable conduct, and a man who displayed continuing evidence of extra-marital sexual activity would have been treated in a similar fashion. *Dekker's* case was distinguished because it concerned a woman who was pregnant, and nothing more, whereas in the present case the dismissal was not because of pregnancy, but because of the adverse effect, by way of example, of the pregnancy on the pupils at the school.

As the school was not an organ of the State, the Equal Treatment Directive could not be enforced directly, but in any event, the EAT were not convinced that the Directive had been infringed, because no discrimination on grounds of sex had been shown.

4.36 To put women only on short-time working is to subject them to a detriment, and hence is unlawful (*Morris v Scott*).

Sexual harassment

4.37 To subject a person to unpleasant treatment of a sexual nature can amount to treating a person less favourably on grounds of sex (s. 1(1)(a)), and may amount to a detriment. In *Strathclyde Regional Council v Porcelli*, Mrs Porcelli was a science laboratory technician at a school. She alleged that two male laboratory technicians were sexually harassing her as part of a campaign to make her leave, by deliberately brushing against her and making suggestive remarks of a sexual nature. Accordingly, she felt obliged to apply for a transfer to another school, and complained that she had been unlawfully discriminated against, and subjected to a detriment contrary to s. 6(2)(b) of the Act. It was held that as she had been subjected to treatment of a sexual nature to which a man would not have been vulnerable, unlawful discrimination had occurred. The Act is concerned with less favourable treatment, not with motive.

4.38 A single incident, provided it is sufficiently serious, can constitute a detriment within the meaning of s. 6(2)(b) (*Bracebridge Engineering Ltd v Darby*). But if the same treatment had been meted out to a man, a woman is not treated less favourably, and therefore there is no detriment to her. In *Balgobin v Tower Hamlets London Borough Council*, the applicants were cleaners at a hostel run by the council. It was alleged that a male cook sexually harassed them, and a complaint was made to management. The cook was suspended pending an investigation, but management were unable to determine the truth of the allegations. The women were then required to continue to work with the man, and they therefore claimed that they had been discriminated against. An industrial tribunal dismissed the claim, and the EAT upheld the decision. Although there may be a risk of sexual harassment, the reason they were exposed to that risk was because of the inconclusive nature of the investigation. Had the victim been a man to whom homosexual advances were made, the matter would have been dealt with in the same way.

4.39 Further, compensation for sexual harassment must reflect the degree of detriment. There must be an assessment of the injury to the woman's feelings, looked at both objectively, i.e. with reference to what any ordinary reasonable female employee would feel, and subjectively, with reference to the particular individual. In *Snowball v Gardner Merchant Ltd* a woman claimed that she had been sexually harassed by her manager. The allegations were denied, and when she gave evidence, she was cross-examined about her sexual attitudes, in an attempt to show that even if there was harassment, she did not suffer any injury to her feelings. Thus, it was alleged that she referred to her bed as a 'play pen', and that she slept between black satin sheets. When she denied these allegations, it was proposed to call evidence to establish the truth. On appeal, it was held that such evidence was admissible. If it could be established that she was unlikely to be upset by a degree of familiarity with a sexual connotation, then it could hardly be said that she had suffered a detriment or hurt feelings. And in *Wileman v Minilec Engineering Ltd* the EAT refused to disturb an award of £50 made for injury to feelings, because the applicant had worn scant and provocative clothing, which made it inevitable that sexually orientated remarks would be made.

4.40 It must also be borne in mind that an allegation of sexual harassment (as with allegations of other acts of sex discrimination) may be met with certain defences, in particular (a) that the act was not done within the course of employment (see *Irving v Post Office*, para 4.120), and that (b) the employer took such steps as were reasonably practicable to prevent an employee from doing the act complained of (see para 4.119).

Amendment of the Act

4.41 As noted, the Sex Discrimination Act 1975 was amended in 1986, to comply with the rulings of the European Court in the cases of *Marshall v Southampton and South West Hampshire Area Health Authority* and *European Commission v United Kingdom*. The latter case had held that the provisions in the 1975 Act which exempted small firms and private households were contrary to the Equal Treatment Directive (76/207). In *Marshall's* case it was held that the Directive was directly enforceable against a State organisation (but not a private employer), so that the exclusion of a woman's right to bring a claim for unfair dismissal after she had reached the age of 60 (whereas a man could bring a claim up to the age of 65) was also discriminatory.

4.42 The 1986 Act was designed to rectify the law so as to enable the United Kingdom to comply with its European obligations, but the results can scarcely be described as being satisfactory.

Exceptions to the Act

4.43 Provisions relating to death or retirement are excluded from the Act (s 6(4)), but this does not permit discrimination against a person in provisions relating to retirement in the field of promotion, training, transfer, demotion or dismissal. But it is permissible to discriminate in relation to retirement in the provision of benefits, facilities or services. Thus, if there is an age at which men retire, or beyond which they cannot be promoted, trained, etc, it is not permissible to have a lower age limit for women (see *Bullock v Alice Ottley School*, above). But occupational pension schemes which take effect on retirement, as well as benefits relating to death are excluded from the Act.

4.44 The age at which the State retirement pension is payable is also permitted to be discriminatory (EC Directive 79/7, Article 7).

4.45 It was the intention of the Government to introduce a measure of equality into occupational pension schemes on a gradual basis, and the Social Security Act 1989 was intended to bring about equality of treatment (see s. 23 and 5th Schedule). The relevant provisions were due to come into force in January 1993, and would coincide with the implementation of the EC Directive on Equal Treatment in occupational pension schemes (86/378/EEC). However, the whole situation has been thrown into some confusion by the decision of the European Court in *Barber v Guardian Royal Exchange Assurance Group*. In this case, the employers operated a non-contributory pension scheme, the normal pensionable age for men and women being 62 and 57 respectively. In the event of redundancy, men who reached the age of 55, and women who were 50 were entitled to an immediate pension. There was also a terminal payment, the calculation of which depended on whether the employee was receiving an immediate pension or not. Mr Barber was dismissed by reason of redundancy when he was 52 years old, and he complained that he had been unlawfully discriminated against on grounds of sex. Had he been a woman aged 52, he would have received an immediate pension. Although his terminal payment would have been lower, the overall value of the benefits would have been less than those paid to a woman. His claim was dismissed by an industrial tribunal and the EAT on the ground that s. 6(4) of the Sex Discrimination Act excludes that Act in relation to any provision which relates to retirement.

4.46 The Court of Appeal referred the complaint to the European Court, posing five questions for the Court's opinion. The European Court held as follows:

1. benefits paid by an employer to a worker in connection with the latter's redundancy fall within Article 119 of the Treaty of Rome (as opposed to the Equal Treatment Directive). It does not matter if the payment is statutory redundancy pay or paid under the contract of employment or on an ex gratia basis;

2. a pension paid under a contracted out private occupational pension scheme also falls within Article 119;
3. it is contrary to Article 119 for a man who was made compulsorily redundant to be entitled to claim only a deferred pension when a woman of the same age would receive an immediate pension;
4. Article 119 may be relied on by any person in the national courts;
5. because of the impact the ruling was likely to have on existing pension schemes, the ruling would only apply to those claims which had been made at the date of the European Court's decision.

The effect of the *Barber* decision

4.47 Although it is recognised that the *Barber* case will have profound effects on pension entitlements, the precise implications of the case are not quite clear, and it may well be that further guidance will be needed. The problem is further compounded by the inequality of State pensionable ages, but to lower the pensionable age of men to 60 would be expensive, and to raise women's pensionable age to 65 would be unpopular. The Government has not yet decided how to deal with this prickly nettle.

4.48 Meanwhile, certain tentative conclusions may be suggested.

4.49 First, it is clear that any form of compensation paid to an employee in connection with his/her retirement from employment must be equalised, whether the payment is statutory, contractual or provided on an ex gratia basis, and whether it is to take effect immediately or in the future. Each constituent part of the package must also be equal. The equalisation of statutory payments has been effective in the UK since 1989, when women became entitled to receive redundancy pay and claim unfair dismissal up to the age of 65. Claims for payments due prior to the change in the law could still be made based on Article 119, if they were made within the appropriate time limits (*McKechnie v UBM Building Supplies*).

4.50 Second, pension benefits must be made available to both sexes at the same age, and if early retirement is offered this must be available on identical terms. Any cut-off based on State pensionable age is unlawful.

4.51 Third, policies which exclude part-timers or ignore part-time service are unlawful, and indeed, it is not impossible to argue that the provisions in UK law which require a person to be working for more than 16 hours per week before s/he can have access to certain statutory benefits may well be held to be unlawful.

4.52 Fourth, because the European Court acknowledged the enormous financial implications of the decision, the ruling will only apply to those workers who made claims or initiated legal proceedings prior to 17th May 1990 (the date the decision was made). It would appear (though the point is not certain) that the ruling will affect all those who start to draw their occupational pension after that date, but with regard to all their pensionable service.

4.53 Finally, it is submitted that commutations, lump sums, survivors' pensions, death benefits and provisions for early or delayed retirement, in contracted out private occupational pension schemes, must apply to both sexes.

4.53A The *Barber* decision has thrown up a number of practical and legal problems, which no doubt will be the subject of future litigation. Certainly, further attention will have to be given to the provisions of s. 6(4) of the Sex Discrimination Act.

Permissible discrimination

(a) Health grounds, s. 51(1)

4.53B Nothing in Part II of the Act (which deals with discrimination in employment) shall render unlawful any act done by a person in relation to a woman if it is necessary to comply with any existing statutory provision concerning the protection of women, or a relevant statutory provision within the meaning of the Health and Safety at Work etc Act 1974, and the act was done for the purpose of the protection of women. Thus it is permissible to discriminate against women in order to protect them against definable health risks, which are specific to women, including risks associated with pregnancy and childbirth (see *Page v Freight Hire (Tank Haulage) Ltd*).

(b) Genuine occupational qualification (s. 7)

4.54 It is permissible to make arrangements which will lead to a person being offered a job, or to refuse another person that post, if the sex of the person is a genuine occupational qualification (GOQ) for the job, and it follows that an employer does not unlawfully discriminate if he does not employ, or if he denies an opportunity for promotion or transfer to, or training for, such employment to a person of the other sex.

4.55 The sex of a person is a genuine occupation qualification for the job in the following circumstances:

a. The essential nature of the job calls for authentic male or female characteristics (excluding physical strength or stamina). Thus it is permissible to advertise for a man to play Hamlet, or for a woman to play Ophelia. It would be interesting to know if it is discriminatory to advertise for a man to play the role of a Dame in a pantomime, or for a woman to take the role of Principal Boy! But if the job merely calls for an ability to haul around 25 kg parcels, it must be open to either sex.
b. The job needs to be held by a person of one sex in order to preserve decency or privacy, because:
   (i) it is likely to involve physical contact with a person in circumstances where that person may reasonably object to it being carried out by a person of the opposite sex. For example, it may be presumed that women would object to men assisting them whilst trying on underwear. In *Etam plc v Rowan* a man applied for a job as a sales assistant in a shop which sold women's and girls' clothing. He was refused employment because the employers considered that a major part of the work involved personal contact with women when they were in a state of undress, and in response to a claim of sex discrimination, pleaded the defence of genuine occupational qualification. However, his claim was upheld by an industrial tribunal and, on appeal, by the EAT. On the facts of the case, a man would have been able to carry out adequately the job of a sales assistant, and such functions as he could not perform could easily have been done by one of the other female sales assistants without causing any inconvenience or difficulty. Further, s. 7(4) (see below), which negates the defence of genuine occupational qualification, was applied. In

Timex Corpn v Hodgson the applicant was a supervisor who was dismissed for reason of redundancy. A female supervisor, who had less service, was retained. The employers sought to justify this on the grounds that all other female supervisors were leaving and they needed to retain one woman supervisor (a) to deal with the private problems of female shop-floor employees, (b) to take women to the first aid room (a man would have to be accompanied), (c) to ensure there was an adequate supply of sanitary towels and pills for period pains kept in the ladies' lavatory, and (d) to take urine samples from women engaged on work involving toxic materials. The EAT held that the male employee had not been discriminated against on grounds of sex. The employers had discriminated by selecting the female supervisor to do a revised job. They had failed to transfer a man to that job, and deliberately refused to offer a man employment in that job. But the sex of the person who was to do the job was relevant, and it amounted to a GOQ;

(ii) persons of one sex might reasonably object to the presence of the opposite sex because they are in a state of undress or using sanitary facilities. This might cover, for example, lavatory attendants, or swimming pool attendants (see *Sisley v Britannia Security Systems Ltd*);

(iii) the job is likely to involve the holder doing his work, or living, in a private home, and needs to be held by a person of one sex because objection might reasonably be taken to allowing a person of the other sex
   (a) the degree of physical or social contract with a person living in the home, or
   (b) the knowledge of intimate details of such a person's life, which would be allowed to, or available to, the holder of the job.

c. The employee is required to live in premises provided by the employer, and those which are available are not equipped with separate sleeping accommodation and sanitary facilities, and it is not reasonable to expect the employer so to equip those premises or to provide such facilities, or to provide other premises. Thus employment on a remote site, or a lighthouse, could be single-sex.

d. Where the job has to be done by a person in a hospital, prison, or other establishment for people who need special care, supervision or attention, and all the inmates thereof are persons of one sex (disregarding the presence of persons of the other sex whose presence is exceptional), and it is reasonable, having regard to the essential characteristics of the establishment that the job should be held by a person of a particular sex. This would cover, for example, a single-sex mental institution.

e. The holder of the job provides individuals with personal services promoting their welfare or education, which can be most effectively provided by one sex. A tough male youth club leader, for example, may be required for a Boys' Club.

f. The job needs to be held by a man because it is likely to involve performance of duties outside the United Kingdom in a country whose laws or customs are such that such duties could not effectively be performed by someone of the opposite sex. There could be difficulties, for example, in sending a woman to negotiate with an Eastern Potentate! In *O'Conner v Kontiki Travel*, a woman was turned down as a coach driver, because it was argued, she would have to drive through Moslem countries, where women drivers are unacceptable. If true, this would have amounted to a GOQ, but it was found that the only Moslem country to which the tour was going was Turkey, and as no evidence had been produced that there would be such objections to women drivers in that country, this amounted to unlawful discrimination.

g. The job is one of two held by a married couple.

4.56 It is not permissible to discriminate in the filling of a vacancy if the employer already has employees of one sex capable of carrying out the above duties (except g. above), whom it would be reasonable to employ on those duties and whose numbers are sufficient to meet the employers' likely requirements in respect of those duties without undue inconvenience (s. 7(4)). Also, s. 48 permits an employer to train members of one sex only for a job which has been previously performed exclusively, or nearly so, by members of the other sex during the preceding twelve months but the anti-discrimination provisions in selection and recruitment still apply. Thus positive action is encouraged, but not positive discrimination. There are special exemption provisions for police, prison officers, and ministers of religion.

Employment outside Great Britain (s. 10)

4.56A The provisions relating to discrimination in employment only apply to employment in an establishment in Great Britain. If the work is to be performed wholly or mainly outside Great Britain, the provisions of the Act do not apply (see *Haughton v Olau Line (UK) Ltd*). This exclusion will not apply to employment on a ship, aircraft or hovercraft registered in Great Britain unless the work is done wholly outside Great Britain. Offshore installations are within the scope of the Act (see para 2.62B).

Employment advertisements (s. 38)

4.57 It is also unlawful to advertise in a manner which might be taken as indicating an intention to discriminate, and the use of job descriptions in advertisements with a sexual connotation, such as 'waiter', 'salesgirl', 'postman', 'stewardess' etc will be assumed to be discriminatory unless the advertisement contains an indication to the contrary. The EOC has issued a document called 'Guidance on Employment Advertising Practice' which contains some useful information and advice on this subject.

4.58 To determine whether an advertisement shows an intention to discriminate unlawfully, it must be read as a whole, according to what an ordinary reasonable person, without any special knowledge, would find to be the natural and ordinary meaning of the words used. In *Equal Opportunities Commission v Robertson*, the respondent placed an advertisement for 'a good bloke (or blokess to satisfy fool legislators)'. It was held that this might reasonably be understood to indicate that the job was not open to women, the word 'blokess' being inserted as a formality. On the other hand, an advertisement for a 'departmental manager' was not discriminatory, as in this context there was no sexist connotation.

Unlawful Acts (ss. 39-40, 42)

4.59 It is unlawful:

a. for a person who has authority over another to instruct that other to do an unlawful act (s. 39);
b. to induce another to do an unlawful act by offering a benefit or threatening a detriment (s. 40); and
c. to aid another person to do an unlawful act (s. 42).

4.60 It should be noted that ss. 38, 39 and 40 may only be enforced by the Equal Opportunities Commission (see s. 72).

Liability of employers (s. 41)

4.61 Anything done by a person in the course of his employment shall be treated as having been done by the employer, whether or not it was done with the employer's approval. Whether or not the act was done 'in the course of employment' is a question of fact. Thus, in *Strathclyde Regional Council v Porcelli* (see para 4.37) the point was conceded, but contested successfully in *Irving v Post Office* (see para 4.120). However, an employer will not be liable for such unlawful acts if the employer can prove that he took such steps as were reasonably practicable to prevent the employee from doing the act. Thus, in *Balgoblin v Tower Hamlets London Borough Council* (see para 4.38) the EAT commented that it was difficult to see what steps could have been taken by the employers in practical terms to prevent harassment from occurring.

Enforcement of the Act (s. 63)

4.62 Any person may complain to the industrial tribunal that another person has committed an act of discrimination. Initially, the conciliation officer will try to promote a settlement, but if this fails, the tribunal, if it finds the complaint well founded, may:

a. make an order declaring the rights of the complainant;
b. order the respondent to pay compensation which may be up to £11,000, and may include an award for injured feelings, which is fundamental to a claim based on discrimination (*Murray v Powertech (Scotland) Ltd*); and/or
c. make a recommendation that the respondent takes action to obviate or reduce the adverse effect on the complainant of any act of discrimination to which the complaint relates.

In the latter case, a failure to comply may lead to an increase in the amount of compensation awarded. However, the industrial tribunal has no power to recommend that a certain wage shall be paid in the future, as this is covered by the provision which enables compensation for the loss suffered to be awarded (*Irvine v Prestcold Ltd*).

4.62A A complaint of discrimination in the field of employment must be laid before the industrial tribunal within three months of the act complained of being done, unless it was not practicable to present it earlier (ss. 63-65). The 'act' of discrimination can be a single act, or a continuing one. In the latter case, the right to bring legal proceedings will continue until three months from the end of the period when the discrimination ceases. In *Calder v James Finlay Corpn Ltd*, the employers operated a mortgage subsidy scheme. In order to be eligible to join the scheme, employees had to be over the age of 25. Shortly after the applicant became 25, she applied for a mortgage subsidy, but this was refused, no reason being given. She continued in her employment for a further six months, she then left, and claimed that she had been discriminated against on grounds of sex. An industrial tribunal concluded that the reason she was refused the mortgage subsidy was because of her sex, but also held that her application was out of time. On appeal, the EAT reversed the decision. Section 6(2)(a) of the Act makes it unlawful to refuse her access to benefits, facilities or services, and thus she was subjected to a continuing discrimination throughout her employment. Also, as long as the employment continued, she was being subjected to a detriment, contrary to s. 6(2)(b). As her claim was brought within three months of her leaving her employment, she was entitled to succeed. Further, the EAT noted that s. 76(2)(b) states that an act extending over a period shall be treated as done at the end of that period.

4.62B However, it is important to distinguish between an act of continuing discrimination and an act of discrimination which has continuing consequences. In the latter case, the time limit of three months will normally apply (see *Sougrin v Haringey Health Authority*, para 4.122B).

4.63 The EOC may itself bring proceedings in respect of alleged violations of certain provisions in the Act (i.e. ss. 38, 39 or 40, see above) and obtain an injunction from a county court or sheriff court to restrain a person from repeating the unlawful act (s. 72). The Commission may also bring a preliminary action in an industrial tribunal on behalf of a person, even though that person has not made a complaint, and the industrial tribunal can make an order of rights or a recommendation that appropriate action be taken to obviate or reduce the adverse effect of the discrimination (s. 73).

4.64 The Commission may give help to persons who feel that they have been discriminated against, in order to assist them in obtaining the necessary information, and questionnaires have been approved which can be sent to the alleged discriminator.

Assistance to an aggrieved person may also be given by means of advice, attempting to procure a settlement by conciliation, arranging for legal advice and assistance, and arranging for and paying for legal representation. It may also undertake or assist in any research or other educational activities.

4.65 The Commission may carry out formal investigations, either on its own initiative or at the request of the Secretary of State, with specific terms of reference, and notice will be given to persons affected. Any person may be required to furnish information, or to attend a hearing and give oral information on specified matters, and to produce any relevant documents. If a person fails or refuses to comply, the Commission may apply to a County Court (or sheriff's court) for an order requiring him to comply, and failure to do so may be punishable in like manner as neglecting a witness summons. To wilfully alter, suppress, conceal or destroy a document, or knowingly or recklessly to make a statement which is false in a material particular is an offence punishable on summary conviction by a fine not exceeding level 5 on the standard scale. In the light of their findings, the Commission may make recommendations with a view to promoting equality of opportunity between men and women (ss. 57-61).

4.66 If, in the course of investigations, the Commission is satisfied that a person is committing an unlawful discriminatory act, or contravening an equality clause under the Equal Pay Act 1970, the Commission may issue a non-discriminatory notice. They must first inform the person of their intention, specifying the grounds, and give him an opportunity to make oral or written representations and take these into account. An appeal may be lodged to the industrial tribunal within six weeks against any requirement, and the tribunal may quash the requirement if it thinks it is unreasonable. A register of non-discrimination notices shall be kept, and if at any time within five years of the notice becoming final it appears to the Commission that the discriminatory act is likely to be repeated, the Commission may apply to a county court for an injunction restraining that person from doing so (ss. 67-71).

4.67 In *Allen v Flood*, Lord Davy said: 'An employer may refuse to employ (a workman) for the most mistaken, capricious, malicious or morally reprehensible motive that can be conceived, but the workman has no right of action against him'. So far as race or sex discrimination is concerned, it is clear that this dictum is no longer good law.

Equal pay

4.68 The Sex Discrimination Act 1975 is concerned with the elimination of discrimination in the recruitment, training, promotion and other aspects of the employment relationship. The Equal Pay Act 1970 is concerned with the establishment, where necessary, of equal terms and conditions of employment. This Act, as amended by the Sex Discrimination Act and by the Equal Pay (Amendment) Regulations 1983, has now been examined by the EAT and higher courts on a number of occasions as well as by the European Court of Justice, and the broad principle has emerged that as it is essentially a reforming statute, it must be interpreted accordingly. The industrial tribunals must therefore apply its provisions in accordance with the statutory objective of eliminating discrimination in terms and conditions of employment which exist solely because of a person's sex.

4.69 It must be stressed that the application of the Equal Pay Act and the Equal Value Regulations (as well as the decisions of the UK courts and tribunals), is subject to the overriding views of the European Court of Justice, applying Article 119 of the Treaty, and the Equal Pay Directive. In the event of a conflict arising, or a disputed interpretation, it is European law which will be applied.

4.69A Article 119 provides that Member States shall maintain the application of the principle that men and women should receive equal pay for equal work. As we have noted (see *Barber v Guardian Royal Exchange*, para 4.46), the term 'pay' is very wide, and means 'the ordinary basic or minimum wage or salary and any other consideration, whether in cash or kind, which a worker receives, directly or indirectly, in respect of his employment from his employer'. In *Worringham v Lloyd's Bank*, female clerical officers under the age of 25 were not required to contribute to a pension scheme. Male clerical officers under the age of 25 were required to contribute 5% of their salary to the scheme, but to compensate them for the difference the men were paid 5% more. The Equal Pay Act (s. 6(1A)(b)) excluded terms relating to death or retirement or any provision made in relation to death or retirement. On a reference to the European

Court of Justice it was held that Article 119 had a direct effect so as to confer an enforceable Community right on all individuals within the EEC. Thus the scheme operated by the Bank was in violation of Article 119, which overrode s. 6(1A)(b) of the Equal Pay Act.

4.70 The Act can apply to self-employed persons as well as employees, for it covers 'employment under a contract of service or apprenticeship, or a contract personally to execute any work or labour'. In *Quinnen v Hovells*, the appellant was a self-employed salesman engaged by the respondent to demonstrate goods for sale in a department store. He complained that two female demonstrators were receiving a higher rate of pay, and the EAT held that he was entitled to have his claim considered on its merits, for the definition of employment in the Act clearly covered self-employed persons.

4.70A Whereas under UK law, the burden of proof lies upon an applicant to show that, on the balance of probabilities, s/he is not receiving equal pay, the decision of the European Court in *Handels v Dansk Arbejdsgiverforening* (the '*Danfoss*' case) indicates that if a pay system manifestly produces inequalities of pay between the sexes, the burden lies upon the employer to show that the criteria used which produces those inequalities are not discriminatory.

4.70B Men and women are entitled to equal pay if they are employed 'in the same employment'. This means that they must be employed at the same establishments at which common terms and conditions of employment are observed (s. 1(6)). In *Leverton v Clwyd County Council*, a nursery nurse was employed by a local authority, and she sought equal pay with male clerical staff employed by the same authority in different establishments. She and her comparators were covered by the same national collective agreement, but they were on different pay scales, with different hours and holiday entitlements. The employers contended that there were no common terms and conditions, and hence that the Act did not apply, but this view was rejected by the House of Lords. The terms and conditions, as laid down in the collective agreement, were applied generally, even though there were differences when applied to individual employees. (NB, the claim failed under the defence of 'genuine material factor' see para 4.91A).

4.71 The Act requires that the contract of employment of all women shall be deemed to include an equality clause. This will operate when a woman is employed either on:

a. like work (i.e. work which is the same or broadly similar), or
b. work which has been rated as being equivalent under a job evaluation scheme, or
c. work which is of equal value to that performed by a man in the same employment.

If any of these three situations exist, then any term in a woman's contract which is less favourable than a man's contract shall be modified so as to be not less favourable, and any benefit in a man's contract shall be included in the woman's contract.

Like work (s. 1(4))

4.72 To determine whether a woman is employed on like work, the Act states that the work must be the same or broadly similar, and any differences between the work done are not of practical importance. In *Capper Pass v Lawton*, a woman worked as a cook in a company directors' dining room, providing lunches for between 10 and 20 persons. She sought equal pay with two assistant chefs who worked in the factory canteen, and who prepared 350 meals each day. Other differences were that she worked 40 hours per week, and had no one supervising her, whereas the men worked 45 hours per week, and were under the supervision of a head chef. The EAT upheld a decision of the industrial tribunal that she was entitled to equal pay. The work did not have to be the same; it was sufficient if it was broadly similar, and the differences were not of practical importance. It would have been wrong to take a too pedantic approach, or to find that there was no like work because of insubstantial differences.

4.73 If there are differences between the work done, the tribunals must ask if these are such that it is reasonable to expect to see them reflected in different wage settlements which contain no element of sex discrimination. Three such differences which may be of practical importance have been identified.

(a) Different duties

4.74 In *Electrolux v Hutchinson* it was held that as well as there being a contractual obligation to perform different duties, those duties must be actually performed to an extent which was significant enough to warrant different pay treatment. In this case, men and women were performing broadly similar work, but the men were graded on a higher rate. The employers argued that the men had different contractual obligations, such as accepting transfer to different work, working compulsory overtime, and working nights. The EAT upheld a decision of the industrial tribunal that the women were entitled to equal pay; the question had to be asked, what happens in practice? If and when the men performed these additional obligations, the situation could be dealt with by paying additional premiums. This, however, should not affect the basic grade which was applicable. In *Noble v David Gold & Son (Holdings) Ltd*, men worked in a warehouse loading and unloading, whereas women did lighter work such as sorting, packing and labelling. The Court of Appeal agreed with the finding of the industrial tribunal that the women were not on like work. Nor was the work broadly similar, for the differences were of practical importance in relation to terms and conditions of employment.

(b) Different hours

4.75 In *Dugdale v Kraft Foods Ltd* men and women worked on broadly similar work, but the men had to work a compulsory night shift, and a voluntary shift on Sunday mornings. It would have been unlawful by virtue of the Factories Act 1961 for women to have worked on these occasions. It was held that the hours at which the work is performed is by itself no bar to equal pay at the basic rate. The men could be compensated for these extra burdens by a night shift payment or premium. The equality clause does not have to produce equal pay if in fact the men were paid for something which the women did not do, e.g. work nights.

4.76 But this reasoning only applies when the difference in hours applies only to men. If in fact *men and women* work different hours to other employees (men and/or women), then because the difference has nothing to do with the sex of the person who is working those different hours, the difference in hours is a genuine material difference other than sex, and hence basic rates can vary between the employees concerned (*Kerr v Lister & Co Ltd*, see para 4.86).

(c) Different responsibilities

4.77 In *Eaton Ltd v Nuttall*, a man and woman worked on like work, but the man received a higher rate of pay because his responsibilities were greater. He handled more expensive products, and consequently a mistake by him would have had far more serious financial consequences. The EAT held that it was proper to take into account the additional responsibilities which the job entailed.

Work rated as being equivalent (s. 1(5))

4.78 A woman's work will be considered to have been rated equivalent to that of a man if it has been given equal value under a properly conducted job evaluation scheme, in terms of the different demands made upon an employee, e.g. effort, skill, decision, etc. In *Eaton Ltd v Nuttall* it was stated that such a scheme must be capable of satisfying the test of being thorough in analysis and impartial in application. Once it is established that it is a genuine scheme, it must be accepted by the parties and the industrial tribunals, for the latter cannot act as an appeal court from a valid job evaluation scheme. In placing an employee in a particular grade, it is then proper to take into account such factors as merit, seniority, etc.

4.78A It is irrelevant that there is a difference between the actual points scored under the job evaluation scheme, if there is no difference in the allocation to a particular salary grade or scale at the end of the evaluation process. In *Springboard Sunderland Trust v Robson*, the applicant was awarded 400 points following a job evaluation, but on appeal this was increased to 410 points. She claimed equal pay with a male comparator who had been awarded 428 points. The relevant salary scales provided were Grade 3 for 360-409 points, and Grade 4 for 410-449 points. Thus, although her job was not rated as being equivalent to the comparator, her claim succeeded, because what mattered was the grade to be allocated to her following the evaluation, rather than the values assigned to her under the evaluation.

4.79 A job evaluation scheme has to be carried out with a view to evaluating jobs in terms of the demands made of a worker under various headings (e.g effort, skill, decision, etc) so as to lead to a fair comparison with the comparator's job. This is the so-called 'analytical' approach, which is to be preferred to the 'felt fair' or 'whole job' approach (*Bromley v H & J Quick Ltd*).

Equal value

4.80 In *Commission for the European Communities v United Kingdom*, the European Court held that the Equal Pay Act did not comply with Article 119 of the Treaty of Rome, for although the Act provided for equal pay when a job evaluation scheme was in existence, there was no way a woman could compel her employer to undertake such a scheme. Consequently, the Equal Pay (Amendment) Regulations 1983 were passed, which are designed to enable a woman to claim equal pay on the ground that her work is of equal value to that of a man.

4.81 A claim for equal value may be made to an industrial tribunal, which will first determine whether or not it can be dealt with under the headings of like work or job evaluation study. In the latter case, the claim may only proceed if it can be shown that the study discriminates on grounds of sex. The industrial tribunal may also dismiss the claim if there are no reasonable grounds for determining that the jobs are of equal value (for example, if a nurse should seek equal pay with a surgeon, see *Sheffield Metropolitan District Council v Siberry*). Otherwise, the industrial tribunal will commission an expert (from a list of such persons held by ACAS) to prepare a job evaluation study, to see whether the jobs are of equal value. However, the report of the expert is not binding on the tribunal, for whether jobs are of equal value is a question of fact for the tribunal to decide (*Tennants Textile Colours Ltd v Todd*). If the industrial tribunal conclude that this is so, they may make an award of equal pay, which may be back-dated two years.

4.82 The first major case under the new Regulations was *Hayward v Cammell Laird Shipbuilders Ltd*, where the applicant joined the company as a catering trainee. During the first three years of her employment, she was paid at the same rate as apprenticed painters, insulation engineers and joiners, but thereafter she was paid at a lower rate than these skilled workers. However, she enjoyed superior sickness benefits, paid meal breaks and extra holidays. Her claim for equal pay based on 'work of equal value' was referred to an independent expert, who evaluated the jobs under the headings of (a) physical demands, (b) environmental considerations, (c) skill and knowledge, (d) planning and decision making, and (e) responsibility. He concluded that the work of the applicant was of equal value with the three selected male comparators who were now earning higher rates. When the case came back to the industrial tribunal, it was held that the terms and conditions of employment *as a whole* must be not less favourable, and not just the actual cash pay received by her. Thus her claim for equal pay was dismissed, and the decision was upheld by the EAT and the Court of Appeal. The argument was based on Article 119 of the Treaty of Rome, which provides that 'pay' means 'the ordinary basic or minimum wage or salary, and any other consideration, whether in cash or in kind, which a worker receives, directly or indirectly, in respect of his employment from his employer'. Thus it was thought that although her cash pay was less than her selected comparators, her other terms and conditions had to be taken into consideration.

However, on a further appeal, the House of Lords reversed the decision and upheld her claim. Lord MacKay, the Lord Chancellor thought that the word 'term' in s. 1(2) of the Act meant a distinct provision or part of the contract, and, in this case, the basic salary of the appellant had to be compared with the basic salary in the men's contracts. Lord Goff stated that a simple question should be asked: is there, in each contract, a term of a similar kind, which makes comparable provision for the same subject matter? If so, then the term in the woman's contract and the men's contract can be compared, and if, on that comparison, the term in the woman's contract proves to be less favourable than the term in the men's, then the term in the woman's contract is to be treated as being modified so as to make it not less favourable. Their Lordships thought that the Equal Pay Act required the courts and industrial tribunals to look at a particular term in a woman's contract which was less favourable, and did not require a holding that terms as a whole should not be less favourable.

Although the decision will inevitably result in a process of leap-frogging on contractual terms and conditions (doubtless the male joiners, insulation engineers and painters will be able to pursue a claim for better sickness benefits, paid meal breaks and extra holidays), the long-term impact of this decision will be to increase the momentum towards greater harmonisation of terms and conditions of employment, not only between the hourly-paid and staff employees, but also between those occupations which are traditionally regarded as being male or female preserves.

It should be noted that in *Hayward's* case the employers did not plead a possible defence they may have had under s. 1(3) of the Act (genuine material factor, see para 4.84)), and it is arguable that the additional perks which the appellant enjoyed could constitute a genuine material factor which would defeat a claim for equal pay.

4.83 An equal value claim may be brought by a woman even though she works with men doing the same work and who are paid the same as she, as long as there is another man with whom she wishes to be compared earning a higher wage. In *Pickstone v Freemans plc* the applicant was a warehouse operative, who worked alongside other male warehouse operatives, and who all received the same pay. She brought an equal value claim, naming as her comparator a male checker warehouse operative who was paid at a higher rate. It was held that she was entitled to succeed under s. 2(1)(c) of the Act. To hold otherwise would enable an unscrupulous employer to defeat equal value claims by ensuring that one man worked alongside women. On the other hand, the House of Lords did not appear to consider the leap-frogging effect of the decision, for undoubtedly the other male warehouse operatives would subsequently be able to claim equal pay with the applicant, once she was given the higher rate.

4.83A The principle of equal pay applies even if it is discovered that the applicant is in fact doing work which is of greater value than the comparator (*Murphy v Bord Telecom Eirann*), as long as she is paid less.

Genuine material factor (s. 1(3))

4.84 Even though a woman can show that she is employed on like work, or work rated as equivalent, or work of equal value, the employer may still be able to resist an equal pay claim on the ground that the variation in pay 'is genuinely due to a material factor which is not the difference of sex'. However, at this stage an important distinction must be made. If the claim is based on like work or work rated as being equivalent under a job evaluation study, the employer has to show that the material factor which causes the difference in pay *must* be a material difference between the woman's case and the man's, whereas in a claim based on equal value, the material factor *may* be such a material difference. The distinction between these two cases is as follows. In a claim based on like work or work rated as the same, any variation in pay can only be based on non-sex factors (e.g. long service, red-circling, etc, see below). Market forces are not such a factor, for this was one of the reasons the Act was passed (*Clay Cross (Quarry Services) Ltd v Fletcher*; but see *Rainey v Greater Glasgow Health Board*, para 4.90). In equal value claims, however, there may be other forces at work which account for the difference in pay. For example, it may be necessary to pay the men more because their skills are in short supply, or because in that area it is necessary to pay the going rate for men in order to attract them, or because their work is more profitable and hence they demand higher pay. In other words, where equal value claims are concerned, since like is not being compared with like, there are a number of material factors at work which *may* (but must not) be a material difference.

4.85 The defence of 'genuine material factor' cannot apply to any difference in the actual work done, for this must be considered when it is decided whether or not there is like work or work rated as being equivalent. Thus if a man is employed lifting heavy weights, this is relevant to the question of whether a woman is employed on like work; it should also be given an appropriate weighting in any job evaluation scheme. Further, once like work or work rated equivalent has been established, there is a burden of proof on those who seek to show that there is a difference in treatment which is 'genuinely due to a material factor' which has nothing to do with the sex of the person concerned. Thus if the underlying reason for a difference in treatment is sex based, even though this is of historical origin, it cannot amount to a material difference. In *Snoxell v Vauxhall Motors Ltd* men and women were doing like work as inspectors. The men were in a 'red circle' group, i.e. their pay was higher because many years ago they were part of a separate male group who received higher wages, but as a result of a revision in pay structure, they were re-graded. By being placed in the 'red circle' (so-called because of the practice of putting a circle in red around the names of the affected employees on the tables of wages) their higher wage rates were protected until the group was phased out. The red circle group was clearly an historical anomaly, but the EAT held that the women inspectors were entitled to equal pay with them, for s. 1(3) could never provide a defence when past discrimination had contributed to the variation.

4.86 Non-sex based factors which could amount to material differences include additional responsibility allowances (*Waddington v Leicester Council for Voluntary Services*), extra pay for academic qualifications (*Murray v East Lothian Regional Council*), long service increments (*Honeywell Ltd v Scott*) and differences in the place where the work is done (*NAAFI v Varley*). As noted above, a difference in hours which is not sex based could be a material difference. In *Kerr v Lister & Co Ltd* men and women doing the same work on the night shift were paid the same rate, but this was higher than that paid to the women who worked on the day shift. Thus the differences in the rate had nothing to do with sex, it was paid in order to attract workers (of either sex) to the night shift. Since the difference was between that of day and night work and not due to a difference of sex, there was a genuine material factor which justified the employers' contention that a woman worker was not entitled to equal pay.

4.87 Similarly, a red circle treatment whereby employees can have their wages protected for reasons other than sex could also amount to a genuine material factor. Thus if an employee on a higher grade is made redundant, and given employment on work which is graded at a lower rate, it is permissible to give him red circle treatment without attracting a successful claim for equal pay on the part of the other employees in the lower grade (*Charles Early & Marriott Ltd v Smith*). This also applies if a man is demoted or downgraded, but is permitted to retain his former (higher) rate of pay (*Forex Neptune Ltd v Miller*). But if a man's wages are protected on a transfer, the industrial tribunal must be satisfied that the reason was not just that he was a man, or that the job to which he was appointed was not one which has been exclusively reserved for men (*Methven v Cow Industrial Polymers*).

4.88 If the defence under s. 1(3) is being raised, the burden is on the employer to prove, on the balance of probabilities, that the differences are due to a genuine material factor other than sex. Thus a grading scheme which operates according to skill, experience or ability can be an integral part of good management. As long as it is applied fairly, irrespective of sex, it is not rendered inoperative by the Act (*National Vulcan Engineering Group Ltd v Wade*). If the differences are due to length of service, the employer must show the terms and conditions relating to service increments, or at least show some evidence as to how the differences have come about. It is not sufficient merely to state the fact, without some attempt to justify any variation (*Honeywell Ltd v Scott*). Similarly, the mere attaching of a label, such as 'red circle' will not, without further evidence, constitute a defence (*Outlook Supplies Ltd v Parry*). However, it is permissible to take into account experience and training (*De Brito v Standard Chartered Bank*).

4.89 The mere fact that a woman carried out the same duties as a man for a short period of time or as a deputy as a temporary measure does not entitle the women to equal pay with that man, for basically their responsibilities are different (*Ford v Weston (Chemists) Ltd*). Also, if a woman works substantially fewer hours than a man, e.g. as a part-timer, and men and women who work full time are paid the same, the part-time nature of the employment is a relevant factor in concluding that the variation in her pay is a genuine material factor (*Handley v Mono Ltd*). However, in *Jenkins v Kingsgate (Clothing Productions) Ltd* the EAT referred to the European Court the question as to whether a woman part-timer could claim the same hourly rate as a full-time man. The Court held that a difference in pay between full-time and part-time workers does not constitute discrimination prohibited by Article 119 of the Treaty of Rome unless it is in reality an indirect way of reducing the pay of part-time workers who were wholly or predominantly women. When the case returned to the EAT it was held that it was not sufficient for an employer to show that he had no intention of discriminating on grounds of sex. Any variation in the pay of part-time women and full-time men had to be justified by reference to some non-discriminatory objective. The case was thus remitted to the industrial tribunal to determine whether the lower rates for part-time workers were reasonably necessary in order to reduce absenteeism and obtain the maximum utilisation of plant.

4.90 In determining whether or not there is a genuine material factor between 'her case and his' in like work and work rated as equivalent claims the industrial tribunal may have regard to the extrinsic forces which led to the man being paid more. In *Rainey v Greater Glasgow Health Board*, a health authority decided to set up its own prosthetic fitting service. The rates of pay for qualified prosthetists was to be on the same scale as medical physics technicians. However, in order to attract a sufficient number of qualified persons to get the service started, it was necessary to make a higher pay offer to those who came from the private sector. The applicant, who came into the service direct from her training, sought equal pay with a man on a higher salary who had come from the private sector. It was held that the difference in pay was due to a genuine material factor which had nothing to do with sex. The reason the man was paid more was because of the need to attract qualified persons (of either sex) from the private sector in order to form the nucleus of the new service. The House of Lords thought that the earlier decision of *Clay Cross (Quarry Services) v Fletcher* was unduly restrictive, for economic grounds, objectively justifiable, were capable of being a genuine material factor.

4.91 Thus, genuine economic considerations, such as a change in the volume of the work reflecting the profitability of the firm, may amount to a genuine material factor (*Albion Shipping Agency v Arnold*).

4.91A A disparity between other terms and conditions may constitute the defence of genuine material factor. In *Leverton v Clwyd County Council* (see para 4.70B) the applicant was required to work 32½ hours per week and had holidays which were conterminous with school holidays, whereas the male comparators worked for 37 hours per week, and only had 20 days annual holidays. Thus the notional hourly rate (taken over the year) did not reveal any significant difference, and the inequality in pay was thus justified by the criteria of reasonable necessity and objective justifiability.

4.92 Also, as has already been noted, market forces may be raised as a genuine material factor which justifies unequal pay if the claim is based on equal value.

4.92A A point on which there has been some judicial observations, but no direct decision, concerns the 'anomalous' comparator. The question arises, must the women compare herself with a representative man, or can she compare her position with any man, even though that man represents an anomaly? In *McPherson v Rathgael Centre for Children etc*, the applicant, a woman, worked alongside five men as an outdoor pursuits instructor. She, and all the men bar one, were on the same pay scale, which was appropriate to them as instructors without a teaching qualification. One man, however, was paid £1500 more. This was because it had previously been assumed that certain qualifications he possessed entitled him to be paid as a qualified teacher. It was then discovered that this was not so, but it was decided to continue to pay him as a qualified teacher. The applicant brought a claim for equal pay with him. The industrial tribunal dismissed her claim, holding that she was not being paid less than the norm, but rather the comparator was being paid more, due to an initial mistake which had never been rectified. There were men being paid the same rate as the applicant, and it was merely fortuitous that the person being paid more was a man. Thus it was held that the employers had established a defence under s. 1(3). On appeal, the Northern Ireland Court of Appeal reversed the decision. It was not sufficient for the employer to show that he did not intend to discriminate on grounds of sex. There must be an objective justification for the variation which exists. An understandable error could not amount to the statutory defence.

However, the court queried whether the applicant was entitled to select the anomalous man as a comparator, rather than the other men who were paid at the same rate as she. Presumably, once the applicant succeeded in her claim, the other men would be entitled to claim equal pay with her, resulting in an escalation of all the salaries. Further, it cannot be right that the sex of the anomalous person gives a right to persons of the opposite sex, although not to a person of the same sex. However, as the matter had not been canvassed before the industrial tribunal, the court reserved their opinion. Perhaps it should have been argued that the 'anomalous man' was a 'red circle' case.

4.93 If the employer seeks to rely on the defence in s. 1(3) (genuine material factor), he can do so with the ordinary civil burden of proof on the balance of probabilities, and the burden is no heavier than this (*National Vulcan Engineering Insurance Group Ltd v Wade*). However, in deciding whether the differences in the work done by the relevant employees were of practical importance in relation to terms and conditions of employment, this can be done by looking at the observed activities of the employees, not their notional paper obligations. In *Shields v E Coomes (Holdings) Ltd* a woman counter clerk in a betting shop sought equal pay with a male clerk doing the same work.

The employers argued that the man was paid more because he was needed to cope with trouble that could arise from customers. In fact, there was no evidence that this need ever arose. Nor was the man specially trained to tackle intruders. Thus the only reason for his higher rate of pay was because of his sex, and hence it was held that she was entitled to equal pay with the male counter-hand.

Pay structures, etc

4.94 Any discrimination based on sex must be eliminated from an employer's pay structure, employment conditions, collective agreements, wage regulation orders, etc. Any term contained in a collective agreement, employers' rules, rules made by a trade union or an employers' association or professional or training body, which is discriminatory, is void. But this is without prejudice to the rights of the person discriminated against in respect of any lawful term of the contract (Sex Discrimination Act 1986, s. 6).

4.94A An individual who considers that the terms of a collective agreement could affect him as being contrary to the principle of equal treatment may present a complaint to an industrial tribunal. This applies to actual and potential employees. If the complaint is well-founded, the tribunal will declare the term to be void (Sex Discrimination Act 1986, s. 6(4A)). Also, a collective agreement which indirectly discriminates against part-time employees (the majority of whom are women) is contrary to Article 119 of the Treaty of Rome, unless the employers can objectively justify the discrimination (*Nimz v Freie und Hansestadt Hamburg*).

Remedies under the Act

4.95 A complaint by an aggrieved party of the contravention of the equality clause, including a claim for arrears of remuneration or damages, may be presented to an industrial tribunal, and a dispute as to its effect may similarly be resolved on an application by the employer (s. 2). On such a complaint, the industrial tribunal should first consider the contract of employment and draw its appropriate conclusions, but if there is no such guide, it is permissible for the tribunal to visit the premises and actually observe the woman at work and the man with whom she wishes to be compared (*Dorothy Perkins v Dance*). Moreover, the applicant may choose the man with whom she wishes to be compared, and the industrial tribunal cannot substitute another man whom it thinks would be more appropriate for the purpose of comparison. Thus if a woman is getting equal pay with some men, she can still seek equal pay with a man who is paid at a higher rate, if his work is the same or broadly similar, etc (*Ainsworth v Glass Tubes and Components*).

4.96 It is also possible to use a former employee as a comparator. In *Macarthys Ltd v Smith* a man was employed as a stockroom manager, and was paid £60 per week. He left the job, and four months later the woman applicant was appointed as stockroom manageress, and was paid £50 per week. She subsequently brought a claim for equal pay. This was upheld by the industrial tribunal and EAT, but the Court of Appeal doubted that she could succeed under the Equal Pay Act. However, the matter was referred to the European Court to consider the effect of Article 119 of the Treaty of Rome. This Court held that the principle that men and women should receive equal pay for equal work applied also to the situation where a woman received less pay than a male predecessor, provided they were both doing the same or broadly similar work. Since, under the European Communities Act 1972, the provisions of EEC law take precedence whenever there is a conflict with British law, the interpretation of Article 119 had to be applied in British courts, and the Court of Appeal subsequently upheld her claim.

4.97 A claim cannot be referred to an industrial tribunal if the applicant has not been employed in the employment within the six months preceding the date of the reference (s. 2(4)). The decision in *British Railways Board v Paul*, which appears to suggest that this does not apply to a 'claim' made by a complainant is generally thought to be incorrect and was disapproved in *Etherson v Strathclyde Regional Council*. In any case, if the claim (or reference) is upheld, the industrial tribunal may award payment for arrears of remuneration or damages, but not in respect of any employment earlier than two years prior to the date on which the proceedings were instituted (s. 2(5)). However, if a claim is made based on the failure by the State to implement the terms of an EC Directive, time will only start to run against a claimant from the date when the State made good its obligations (*Cannon v Barnsley Metropolitan Borough Council*).

4.97A Once a claim for equal pay has been dismissed, a further claim based on the same facts will be defeated by the doctrine of *re judicata* (*McLoughlin v Gordons (Stockport) Ltd*).

Racial discrimination

4.98 The Race Relations Act 1976 is the third legislative provision on racial discrimination to be introduced in recent years, and is bound to be a powerful influence in the fight to eliminate discrimination on racial grounds. The Act is modelled closely on the Sex Discrimination Act 1975, and doubtless the decisions on the latter legislation will be looked to for guidance. Direct evidence of race discrimination is likely to consist of inferences raised from primary facts (*King v Great Britain-China Centre*), If these lead to a provisional conclusion that there has been discrimination, the employer will be required to give an explanation. If this is not forthcoming, or if it is unsatisfactory, the complaint will succeed (*North West Thames Regional Health Authority v Noone*).

4.99 Generally speaking, it is unlawful to discriminate against a person on grounds of race, and this could arise in any of three ways.

A. Direct discrimination (s. 1(1)(a))

4.100 This occurs if on racial grounds a person treats another person less favourably than he would treat someone else. Thus if the grounds for the discrimination are racial, the race of the person discriminated against is irrelevant, for it is possible for A to discriminate against B on grounds of C's colour or race (*Race Relations Board v Applin*). In *Zarczynska v Levy* a barmaid alleged she was dismissed for refusing to obey an order not to serve coloured persons in a pub. The EAT held that even though she had not been personally discriminated against on grounds of her race, she had been treated less favourably on racial grounds, and was entitled to pursue a claim. (The case was remitted to the industrial tribunal, which found that no such unlawful instruction had been given; see also *Showboat Entertainment Centre v Owens*.) In *Wilson v TB Steelworks* a white woman was on the point of being offered a job, but when she disclosed that her husband was black, the offer was withdrawn. It was held that this amounted to unlawful discrimination.

4.101 The Act specifically states (s. 1(2)) that the segregation of a person on racial grounds is to be regarded as treating him less favourably, but this does not mean that congregation is unlawful. Thus to provide separate (but equal) toilet facilities for Asians and non-Asians would be discriminatory, and hence unlawful, but to allow an Asian night shift to develop in a factory because this is the wish of all concerned does not amount to unlawful conduct. The employer, however, would be acting unlawfully is he insisted that Asians went on the night shift (*Pel Ltd v Modgill*).

4.102 There can be unlawful discrimination under the Act even though it was done for a worthy notice. In *R v CRE, ex p Westminster City Council*, a black person applied for a job as a refuse collector. He was given a temporary appointment, but this was later withdrawn, as it was feared that other workers would take industrial action. The High Court held that the CRE were entitled to issue a non-discrimination notice. For an employer to give in to such threats would frustrate the purpose of the Act.

B. Indirect discrimination (s. 1(1)(b))

4.103 This occurs when:

a. a person applies a requirement or condition,
b. which is such that the proportion of persons from the same racial group who can comply is considerably smaller than persons who are not of that racial group, and
c. it cannot be shown that the condition is justified irrespective of the racial origins of the person concerned, and
d. it is to that person's detriment that he cannot comply.

4.103A The requirement or condition has to be one which the applicant 'must' comply with. If it is a factor which 'may' be taken into account, there is no indirect discrimination. In *Meer v London Borough of Tower Hamlets*, the respondents advertised a vacancy for a head of their legal department. There were 23 applicants, 12 of whom were put on a 'long list'. The council applied 10 criteria for drawing up the 'long list' one of which was experience with Tower Hamlets. Of those on the 'long list' four had such experience. The applicant, who was not placed on the long list, complained that he had been indirectly discriminated against on ground of race, arguing that the proportion of this racial group who could comply with the requirement was smaller than other groups. His claim was dismissed. The requirement was not one with which the successful applicants 'must' comply; it was a factor which the local authority were entitled to take into account.

4.103B Even though there is indirect discrimination, a complaint will not succeed if it can be shown that the requirement or condition is justified irrespective of race. In *Panesaar v Nestlé & Co Ltd* a factory rule prohibited beards and long hair. This was indirect discrimination against the applicant, who was a Sikh, but the Court of Appeal held that the condition was justified in the interests of hygiene and safety.

C. Victimisation (s. 2)

4.104 It is unlawful to treat a person less favourably because he has:

i. brought proceedings under the Act;
ii. given evidence or information connected with proceedings brought by another person;
iii. done anything under the Act in relation to the discriminator; or
iv. made allegations that a person has committed an unlawful act of racial discrimination.

However, it is not unlawful victimisation if a person is accorded less favourable treatment as a result of an allegation which is untrue and not made in good faith (*Aziz v Trinity Street Taxis*).

Racial grounds (s. 3)

4.105 The Act defines racial grounds as meaning colour, race, nationality or ethnic or national origins. This definition may give rise to a number of problems. The term 'nationality' was included to overrule the decision of the House of Lords in *Ealing Borough Council v Race Relations Board*, where it was held that 'national origins' meant race rather than citizenship. Now, both meanings are included. Thus, it is now unlawful to discriminate against, e.g. nationals of EEC countries. In a case which aroused considerable publicity, it was noted that it was unlawful to advertise for a 'Scots cook', and the right way to proceed in this situation would be to advertise for a person skilled in Scottish cooking. In truth, whether the Scots are a separate national grouping either as a racial or ethnic group or citizens of a national state is at least arguable, and the point may be taken further with other separatist groups. There appears to be no reason why it is lawful to state 'No Yorkshiremen need apply' and yet unlawful to discriminate against another which has pretensions to nationhood.

4.106 In *Mandla v Dowell Lee*, the House of Lords held that the term 'ethnic' was appreciably wider than 'race'. For a group to constitute an ethnic group for the purpose of the Act, it must regard itself as a distinct community by virtue of certain characteristics. These include:

1. a long shared history, of which the group is conscious as distinguishing it from other groups, and the memory of which keeps it alive, and
2. a cultural tradition, including social customs and manner.

In addition, some of the following factors may be relevant:

1. a common geographical origin or descent from common ancestors;
2. a common language (but not necessarily peculiar to the group);
3. a common literature;
4. a common religion different from that of neighbouring groups;
5. being a minority or being an oppressed or a dominant group within a large community.

With these factors in mind, the House of Lords had no hesitation in holding that Sikhs were a racial group within the meaning of the Act.

4.107 The Act does not appear to cover religion as such, but this may be covered under the concepts of race, ethnic or national origins. And since reference to a person's racial group includes reference to any racial group into which a person falls (s. 3(1)), converts are clearly within the definition. But if it is unlawful to advertise 'No Jews need apply', then why should it not be equally unlawful to state 'No Catholics need apply'? (In Northern Ireland, such discrimination is specifically declared to be unlawful.) Are all Muslims of the same racial, ethnic or national origins? If the legislation wished to include discrimination on religious grounds, it is submitted that a clear and specific statement to this effect would have been a simple matter.

4.108 In *CRE v Dutton*, the Court of Appeal held that gypsies were a racial group within the meaning of the Act, defined by reference to their racial origins. In *Seide v Gillette Industries* the EAT held that although religion is not within the provisions of the Act, the term 'Jewish' can mean membership of a race or of an ethnic group as well as being a follower of a particular religious faith. If what happens to a person is for the former reason, not the latter, this can amount to racial discrimination.

4.109 An ability to speak a particular language is not, *per se* an essential factor in the definition of a racial group, and a requirement of such an ability may be justified irrespective of racial origins. Thus in *Gwynedd County Council v Jones*, it was accepted that Welshmen were a distinct ethnic group, but the EAT held that there was no distinction between Welsh-speaking Welsh and English-speaking Welsh. However, a requirement that applicants for a post should be able to speak Welsh was held, in the particular circumstances, to be justifiable. Rastafarians are a religious, not an ethnic, group. Consequently, to refuse employment to a man because he wore his hair in 'dreadlocks' is not discrimination on grounds of race (*Crown Suppliers (PSA) v Dorkins*).

Racial discrimination in employment (s. 4)

4.110 It is unlawful to discriminate against a person on racial grounds:

a. in the arrangements for determining who shall be offered employment;
b. in the terms on which employment is offered;
c. by refusing or deliberately omitting to offer him employment (s. 4(1); *Johnson v Timber Tailors (Midlands) Ltd*).

Once a person is employed, it is unlawful to discriminate against him on racial grounds:

a. in the terms of employment which are afforded to him;
b. in the way he is afforded access to opportunities for promotion, transfer or training, or any other benefit, facilities or services, or to refuse or omit to afford him access to them;

c. by dismissing him, or subjecting him to any other detriment (s. 4(2)). In *De Souza v Automobile Association* it was held that a racial insult, by itself, was capable of constituting a detriment.

The above provisions do not apply to employment for the purpose of a private household, although the provisions relating to victimisation do so apply. Also s. 75(5) allows discrimination on grounds of birth, nationality, descent or residence for Civil Service Posts and employment with certain public bodies (see Race Relations (Prescribed Public Bodies) Regulations 1984).

Genuine occupational qualifications (s. 5)

4.111 It is permissible to discriminate where being a member of a particular racial group is a genuine occupational qualification for the job. There are four racial GOQs, and hence the provisions are more restrictive than the corresponding provisions in the Sex Discrimination Act 1975. Racial GOQs are as follows:

a. the job involves participation in a dramatic performance or other entertainment in a capacity for which a person of that racial group is required for reasons of authenticity;
b. the job involves participation as an artist's or photographic model in the production of a work of art or of visual images, for which a person of that racial group is required for reasons of authenticity;
c. the job involves working in a place where food and drink is provided to, and consumed by, members of the public in a particular setting (e.g. a Chinese restaurant), for which a person of that racial group is required for reasons of authenticity;
d. the holder of the job provides persons of that racial group with personal services promoting their welfare, and those services can be most effectively provided by persons of that racial group.

In *Tottenham Green Under Fives Centre v Marshall*, the EAT thought that the phrase 'promoting their welfare' was a wide expression, and the view was expressed that it was unnecessary to seek to limit the scope of the words. But in *Lambeth London Borough v CRE*, the Court of Appeal refused to uphold the decision of a local authority to confine applications for vacant posts in their housing benefits department to applicants from Afro-Caribbean or Asian communities, because the jobs were essentially managerial in nature, and did not involve the provision of personal services promoting the welfare of a particular racial group.

Contract workers (s. 7)

4.112 As well as giving protection to job applicants and employees, the Act also covers contract workers, and thus preempts any attempt to circumvent the anti-discrimination provisions. It is unlawful for a principal to discriminate against a person, even though the latter is employed by a third party (e.g. an employment agency). It is also unlawful for the principal to discriminate against a contract worker

a. in the terms on which he is allowed to do the work
b. by not allowing him to do it
c. in the way he affords him access to benefits, facilities or services
d. by subjecting him to any other detriment.

Application of the Act

4.113 The Act only applies to employment at an establishment in Great Britain (*Deria v General Council of British Shipping*). There are some special provisions relating to seamen (see ss. 8-9).

Other unlawful acts

1. Discriminatory practices (s. 28)

4.114 It is unlawful to apply a discriminatory practice, i.e. conduct which, while not amounting to discrimination, in fact is designed to produce unlawful discrimination. For example, if it is well known that blacks need not even bother to apply for a job at a certain factory, because they stand no chance of being appointed, this can amount to a discriminatory practice even though no one applies and is discriminated against.

2. Discriminatory advertisements (s. 29)

4.115 Other than the permitted exceptions (i.e. where race is a GOQ) it is unlawful to publish an advertisement which indicates an intention by a person to do an act of discrimination.

3. Instructions to discriminate (s. 30)

4.116 It is unlawful for a person who has authority over another to instruct him to do an unlawful act, or to procure the doing by him of an unlawful act.

4. Pressure to discriminate (s. 31)

4.117 It is unlawful to induce or attempt to induce a person to do any act which is unlawful. Thus to call (or threaten to call) a strike over the appointment of a black supervisor would be unlawful.

4.118 Proceedings in respect of the above four unlawful acts may only be brought by the Commission for Racial Equality.

4.119 Any act done by an employee in the course of his employment shall be treated as having been done by the employer as well, whether or not it was done with the employer's knowledge or approval. However, it is a defence for the employer to show that he took such steps as are reasonably practicable to prevent the employee from doing the act in question (s. 32).

4.120 Moreover, an employer is not liable for an act of race discrimination committed by an employee who was not acting in the course of his employment. In *Irving v Post Office*, Irving was a black Jamaican. He lived next door to Edwards, but they did not get on too well. Edwards was a postman, whose duties included writing on letters to ensure they were properly dealt with. While sorting some mail, Edwards came across a letter addressed to Irving, and he wrote an offensive message and cartoon on the back of the envelope. When the Post Office discovered that Edwards was the culprit, he was disciplined. However, Irving brought an action against the Post Office for a declaration that they had unlawfully discriminated against him, and for an injunction to prevent a repetition of such acts. He also sought damages. It was held that as Edwards was not acting in the course of his employment, the Post Office was not vicariously liable for his actions. His act of writing on the envelope was an act of personal malevolence. The fact that his employment gave him the opportunity for misconduct did not mean that the misconduct formed part of his duties.

4.121 Whether or not a person is acting in the course of his employment is a question of fact.

Enforcement by individuals (s. 54)

4.122 Any claim in respect of discrimination in employment must be submitted to an industrial tribunal within three months from the date of the alleged act, unless it is just and equitable to extend the time limit. However, by virtue of s. 68(7)(b), any act extending over the period shall be treated as having been done at the end of that period. Thus where there is a continuing act of discrimination, the three months time limit does not run until the discrimination ceases (*Barclays Bank plc v Kapur*).

4.122A In determining the time limits, a distinction has to be drawn between an act of continuing discrimination and an act of discrimination which has continuing consequences. In *Clarke v Hampshire Electro-Plating Co Ltd* the applicant, who was black, saw an advertisement for a supervisory job with his present employers. On 25 April he saw his employer about the vacancy, but was told that he would not be considered. On 4 September a white man was appointed to the job, and the applicant then submitted a complaint, alleging he had been discriminated against on grounds of race. The industrial tribunal held that his complaint was out of time, because the discrimination (if this was so) dated from 25 April, but on appeal the decision was reversed by the EAT. Time will start to run from the date the cause of action crystalised, not from when the applicant feels he has been discriminated against. In this case, the applicant's cause of action had not crystallized when his application for promotion was rejected, but from the date a white man was appointed, because this provided the comparison which enabled him to believe that he had been discriminated against.

4.122B A somewhat different approach was taken by the Court of Appeal in *Sougrin v Haringey Health Authority*, where the applicant, a black nurse, appealed internally against her employer's decision to place her in a certain salary grade. Her appeal was unsuccessful, although an appeal by a white colleague succeeded. Six months later she submitted her application to an industrial tribunal, arguing that she had been discriminated against on grounds of race, and that the discrimination was a continuing act. The industrial tribunal held that the claim had not been submitted within the statutory time limits, a decision which was upheld by the EAT and the Court of Appeal. The regrading decision was a one-off act with the continuing consequence that she was being paid less than a white colleague. There was no suggestion that the employers had a policy to pay black nurses less than white nurses; had there been such a policy, it is arguable that there was a continuing act of discrimination (*Barclays Bank v Kapur*).

4.122C A copy of the complaint will be sent to a conciliation officer, but if he fails to promote a settlement, the matter will go to an industrial tribunal for hearing. If it is decided that the complaint is well-founded, the tribunal may make one of the following orders:

a. a declaration of the rights of the complainant,
b. an order that the respondent shall pay compensation up to a pecuniary maximum of £11,000. If the act of discrimination has caused pecuniary loss, such as a refusal to offer employment, or dismissal from employment, the amount of damages is readily quantifiable. However, damages may also be awarded for injury to feelings, humiliation and insult. The award for these should not be minimal, but should be restrained. Injury to feelings will normally be of a relatively short duration, and the award should reflect this (*Sharifi v Strathclyde Regional Council*). Although it has been stated that aggravated damages may be awarded if a defendant has behaved in a manner which is oppressive or malicious, in accordance with the principles laid down in *Cassell & Co Ltd v Broome* (see *Alexander v Home Office*), and exemplary damages were awarded for outrageous conduct in *Bradford Metropolitan City Council v Arora*, these awards have recently been doubted (see *AB v South West Water Services Ltd*), and the EAT has refused to make such awards on the ground that the earlier decisions were incorrect (*Deane v Ealing Borough Council*),
c. a recommendation that the respondent shall take, within a specified period, such action as appears to the tribunal to be practicable for the purpose of obviating or reducing the adverse effect on the complainant of any act complained of (*Noone v North West Thames Regional Health Authority*). If the respondent fails to comply with any such recommendation, the tribunal may increase the compensation award, or make such an award if they have not already done so.

4.123 The burden of proof is on the applicant to show that an act of racial discrimination took place. It would be unusual to find direct evidence of such, and thus the industrial tribunal is entitled to draw inferences from primary facts (*King v Great Britain-China Centre*). The fact that the employer already employs people of different racial groups is not conclusive (*Johnson v Timber Tailors (Midlands) Ltd*), but it is a relevant consideration of evidential value (*Piperdy v UEM Parker Glass*). If an employer's replies to a questionnaire sent by the CRE are evasive, it could lead to an inference that discrimination took place (*Virdee v EEC Quarries*). Evidence of events which took place subsequent to the alleged act of discrimination is admissible where it is logically probative of a relevant fact (*Chattopadhyay v Holloway School*).

4.124 If discrimination takes place in circumstances which are consistent with the treatment being meted out because of a person's race, an industrial tribunal should be prepared to draw the inference that it was unlawful discrimination, unless the alleged discriminator can satisfy them that there was some other innocent explanation (*Baker v Cornwall County Council*). Otherwise, the general burden of proving the case lies upon the applicant. If, after hearing all the evidence, the industrial tribunal find primary facts which, in the absence of explanation, point to unlawful discrimination, and no such acceptable explanation is offered, then the tribunal may find, by inference, that discrimination existed (*British Gas v Sharma*).

4.124A A complainant may be able to obtain the discovery of existing statistics, showing the number of persons from the different racial groups who have applied for posts, been engaged, or promoted, for such evidence may have some probative value, from which inferences may be drawn that the employer has adopted racially discriminatory practice or policies (*West Midlands Passenger Transport Executive v Singh*). But an industrial tribunal has no power to order a respondent to produce details of the ethnic or racial composition of the workforce, where such evidence does not exist, for this is not 'discovery' of documents, and not 'particulars' of the grounds on which the respondents seek to rely. Nor is there power to order interrogatories (*Carrington v Helix Lighting Ltd*).

Statutory immunity (s. 41)

4.124B A discriminatory act shall not be unlawful if it is done in pursuance of any enactment, or any instrument made under any enactment, or in order to comply with any condition or requirement imposed by a Minister by virtue of any enactment. However, in *Hampson v Department of Education and Science*, the House of Lords gave a very restricted meaning to this immunity, holding that a decision given on a matter where the statute gives a discretion was not within the section.

Enforcement by the Commission (s. 58)

4.125 The Commission for Racial Equality has the power to carry out a formal investigation into any practice carried on by an individual or an organisation, either on its own volition or at the request of the Secretary of State, and has wide powers to obtain any necessary information. If the investigation is confined to the activities of named persons, an opportunity must be given for them to make oral or written representations (*Re Prestige Group plc*). A report may then be issued, with or without recommendations. If, in the course of such investigations, the Commission conclude that a person is committing an unlawful act, the Commission may serve a non-discriminatory notice on him requiring him not to commit any further such acts, to inform the Commission on what changes (if any) have been made in such practices, and to notify the other party concerned. Before issuing the notice, the Commission must inform the person, specifying the grounds, and offer him an opportunity of making oral or written representations.

4.125A If there is any repetition of the discriminatory act or practice within the five years following the issuing of a non-discriminatory notice, the Commission may obtain an injunction in the County Court against that person, restraining him from committing further discriminatory practices. An appeal may be made against a non-discriminatory notice within six weeks to an industrial tribunal, who may quash any requirement contained therein, or, if they so wish, substitute their own directions. On such an appeal, it is open to the person against whom the order has been made to challenge the findings of fact on which the order was made (*CRE v Amari Plastics*). A public register will be maintained of all non-discriminatory notices.

Disabled persons

4.126 By the Disabled Persons (Employment) Acts 1944 and 1958 firms employing more than 20 employees must ensure that 3% of their workforce consists of registered disabled persons. Special jobs, such as car park and lift attendants, are designated as being suitable for disabled persons and they must be employed in preference to able-bodied persons. There are, however, certain exceptions with reference to special industries, where the employment of a disabled person might be hazardous. It is also possible to apply for a special permit if the full quota of disabled cannot be fulfilled because the work is unsuitable or because no suitable disabled candidate has come forward. It is an offence to break the provisions of the Act, but proceedings cannot be brought unless a special advisory committee so decides, after hearing representations from the employer. In practice extremely few prosecutions have been brought, for the problem is one which must be solved by persuasion, rather than compulsion. Indeed, in *Yeats v Fairey Winches Ltd* a tribunal thought that compensation for future loss of earnings for a disabled person was to be calculated on the basis that he was more likely to obtain employment than an able-bodied person, because there are special facilities and extra efforts made on his behalf. By the Companies (Directors' Report) (Employment of Disabled Persons) Regulations 1980, in respect of companies which employ (on average throughout the year) more than 250 employees, the annual directors' report shall include a statement describing such policy as the company has applied during the preceding year as to the employment, training, career development and promotion of disabled persons.

4.127 Formerly, if an employer wished to pay a disabled person below the rate established by a Wages Council, he had to obtain a special permit. Wages Councils have now been abolished, so that there is now no special protection in respect of the wages of a disabled person.

4.128 An employer cannot expect the normal standard of work or output from a disabled person (*Kerr v Atkinson's Vehicles Ltd*) but if it is below that which could reasonably be expected, a dismissal may be fair, for the employer is entitled to say 'I cannot employ this Green Card holder any longer' (*Pascoe v Hallen & Medway*). But the employer's conduct in dismissing a disabled person must always be judged by the standards of reasonableness (*Seymour v British Airways Board*), after considering the employee's personal circumstances (*Hobson v GEC Telecommunications Ltd*). As always, consultation with the employee beforehand is to be expected in the normal case, although it has to be recognised that there are exceptional circumstances when this is neither necessary nor desirable (*Eclipse Blinds Ltd v Wright*).

4.129 Several years ago the Manpower Commission produced a 'Code of Good Practice on the Employment of Disabled People', which, although purely voluntary, sets out the aims and objectives of a desirable policy on the employment and training of disabled persons.

Rehabilitated persons

4.130 The Rehabilitation of Offenders Act 1974 seeks to ensure that if a person has made a genuine effort to rehabilitate into society after conviction for a serious criminal offence, he may be spared the indignity and embarrassment of subsequently having to disclose his unsavoury past. Provided he does not commit a serious offence within the rehabilitation period, he may, at the end of that time, be regarded as a rehabilitated person, and his conviction will be treated as having been 'wiped off the slate'. The Act is somewhat complex, but the general rule is that the length of the rehabilitation period will depend on the age of the offender at the time of conviction, and the sentence given for the offence. Thus the period will vary from six months in the case when an absolute discharge was granted up to ten years in respect of a sentence of imprisonment of thirty months. A sentence of imprisonment of more than thirty months will never become 'spent'. Once a person has become 'rehabilitated' evidence of his previous conviction is not generally admissible, and he may not be asked about it or, if he is asked, he need not tell the truth, and may deny his previous conviction. The rehabilitation period runs from the date of the conviction, not from the expiry of the sentence.

4.131 So far as the law of employment is concerned, s. 4(3)(b) of the Act provides that (subject to certain exceptions) a 'spent' conviction, or failure to disclose such, shall not be grounds for dismissing or excluding a person from any office, profession, occupation or employment, or for prejudicing him in any way in any occupation or employment. However, the limits of the section need to be noted. At common law, an employer has the right to please himself whether or not to employ someone (see *Allen v Flood* (para 4.67) and although to refuse to employ a rehabilitated person may be to 'exclude' him, the section provides no remedy for a person who may feel that he has been discriminated against. Equally, a refusal to promote a rehabilitated person may amount to prejudicing him in that employment, but again no remedy is provided. On the other hand, if an employee who was a rehabilitated person was dismissed, and the sole ground was the discovery of his past convictions, this would undoubtedly amount to an unfair dismissal if he was otherwise within the protection of EPCA, Part V (see Chapter 8). In *Hendry v Scottish Liberal Club*, one of the reasons why the applicant was dismissed was connected with the discovery that he had been convicted many years ago of possessing cannabis. This conviction was 'spent' within the meaning of the Act, and hence it was not a statutory reason for dismissal.

4.132 In *Property Guards Ltd v Taylor and Kershaw* the two applicants were employed as security guards. On commencing their employment they signed a statement to the effect that they had never been guilty of a criminal offence. When the employers discovered that they had both been convicted of minor offences of dishonesty, they were dismissed. The EAT upheld the finding of the industrial tribunal that the dismissals were unfair. In both cases the convictions were 'spent' within the meaning of the Act. They were entitled not to disclose their previous convictions.

4.133 If an employer subsequently discovers that the employee has had a previous conviction, he must make all necessary enquiries to ascertain whether or not the conviction is spent before he starts taking action. In *Brooks v Ladbroke Lucky Seven Entertainment*, the applicant was dismissed when it was discovered that he had had a prior conviction. It was argued on behalf of the employer that the dismissal was necessary in view of the nature of their business (as a gambling club), and as they did not know that the conviction was spent, they were not acting unreasonably. It was held that the employer should have sought further information about the nature of the offence and the penalty imposed, and a failure to do so rendered the dismissal unfair.

4.134 The main rehabilitation periods are as follows:

Sentence	*Rehabilitation period*
Imprisonment or youth custody of more than 6 months and up to 2½ years	10 years
Imprisonment or youth custody of 6 months or less	7 years
Fine or community service order	5 years
Probation order, conditional discharge, bind over, care order, or supervision order.	One year, or until the order expires, which ever is the longer
Absolute discharge	6 months

4.135 Other sentences which come within the Act include orders for custody in a remand home, an approved school, an attendance order, and a hospital order. There are certain reductions in the period of rehabilitation in the case of a person under 17 at the time of conviction. In the case of imprisonment, it is the period of sentence imposed by the court which counts (including a suspended sentence) not the actual time spent in prison. The rehabilitation period runs from the date of the conviction. A prison sentence (or youth custody sentence) of more than 2½ years is never 'spent'.

4.136 The Act does not apply to questions which are asked of a person in order to assess the suitability of a person for admission to the professions of medical practitioner, barrister, accountant, solicitor, dentist, dental hygienist or auxiliary, veterinary surgeon, nurse, midwife, ophthalmic or dispensing optician, pharmaceutical chemist, or a Scottish registered teacher. Such people must still tell the truth about their previous convictions. Nor can a person tell a lie if the questions are asked for the purpose of assessing his suitability for the following employments, namely, certain legal appointments and offices, certain employment connected with the punishment of offenders, constables, traffic wardens, probation officers, further education teachers, proprietors of independent schools, certain local government social workers, hospital workers, persons who work for building societies or who provide financial services, youth club leaders and employment with cadet forces. Certain other occupations are also excluded from the provisions of the Act (see the Rehabilitation of Offenders Act 1974 (Exceptions) Orders 1975 and 1986).

Unfair recruitment (TULR(C)A s. 137)

4.137-4.147 There are provisions in the Trade Union and Labour Relations (Consolidation) Act 1992 which protect a person from being refused employment on grounds of trade union membership or non-membership. These matters will be considered in Chapter 13.

Employment of women

4.148 Most of the statutory provisions passed for the protection of female employees have been repealed in so far as they enabled different treatment to be accorded to women. Thus women may now clean parts of machinery while in motion, they may work underground in mines, and perform a number of other tasks which were previously not open to them (see Employment Act 1989 s. 9). This is in accordance with the Equal Treatment Directive (see para 1.57) and the desire of the Government to reduce the legislative and administrative burdens on industry.

4.149 However, a number of statutory provisions relating to the health and safety of women have been retained, particularly dealing with those risks associated with pregnancy, childbirth and other risks specifically affecting women. Thus a woman may not work in a factory within four weeks of childbirth, (Factories Act 1961 Sch 5, Public Health Act 1936 s. 205), they are prohibited from working in certain processes and activities involving lead products (including lead paint), there are limits on exposure to ionising radiations, and on working in an aircraft or at sea while pregnant (Employment Act 1989 s. 4 and Sch 1). Indeed, it is lawful to discriminate against a woman in so far as it is necessary to comply with the above restrictions (see para 4.53B).

4.150 Restrictions on hours of work (including overtime and night work) for women were abolished in the Sex Discrimination Act 1986 (s. 7) but the position is now governed by the Employment Act 1989 (s. 1) which effectively nullifies any statutory provision which produces a discrimination as regards access to employment and working conditions (see para 4.54).

Employment of young persons

4.151 All legislative provisions which dealt with the hours of work and holidays of young persons (defined as persons over school-leaving age) have been repealed (Employment Act 1989 s. 10 and Sch 3). The provisions relating to health and safety are unchanged.

Adult workers

4.152 The sole remaining legislation imposing restrictions on the hours of work of adult workers are (1) Mines and Quarries Act 1954 (underground miners), (2) Hours of Employment (Conventions) Act 1936 (sheet glass workers), (3) Shops (Early Closing Days) Act 1965 (shop assistants), and (4) Transport Act 1968 (vehicle drivers).

Duty of local authorities

4.153 Section 71 of the Race Relations Act provides that it shall be the duty of every local authority to make appropriate arrangements with a view to securing that their various functions are carried out with due regard to the need:

a. to eliminate unlawful discrimination, and
b. to promote equality of opportunity and good relations between persons of different racial groups.

4.154 A local authority cannot use the powers conferred by this section to punish a person who has done no wrongful act (*Wheeler v Leicester City Council*).

Contract compliance

4.155 Section 17 of the Local Government Act 1988 provides that in exercising any function dealing with public supply or works contracts, a public authority must not take account of non-commercial considerations. These include such matters as a contractor's terms and conditions of employment, the composition of his workforce, arrangements for promotion, transfer or training of the workforce, or the country of origin of supplies to contractors, the location in any country of the business activities of contractors, etc.

4.156 Clearly, since race relations matters are non-commercial considerations, the 1988 Act imposes a limit on the operation of s. 71 of the 1976 Act. However, s. 18(2) of the 1988 Act permits a local authority to ask approved questions, in writing, seeking information or undertakings relating to workforce matters, and considering the responses to them, and may also include in draft contracts terms or provisions relating to workforce matters, if the information, the undertaking or the inclusion of the terms are reasonably necessary to secure compliance with s. 71. A local authority may also request evidence in support of any answer given.

4.157 The Secretary of State will specify the approved questions and description of evidence which may be requested for the purpose of s. 18(2).

4.158 Somewhat curiously, there are no corresponding statutory provisions relating to sex discrimination (*R v London Borough of Islington, ex p Building Employers' Confederation*).

CHAPTER 5

Employment protection

5.1 In this chapter we will consider a number of miscellaneous legal rights given to employees in the Employment Protection (Consolidation) Act and other legislation. These are minimum standards which can be exceeded by agreement or negotiation, but they cannot be denied to an employee.

Guarantee payments (ss. 12-18)

5.2 Provided an employee has been continuously employed for at least one month, and is not employed under a fixed term contract of three months or less, the employer is bound to pay him a guarantee payment in respect of any whole day in which the employee is not provided with work because

a. there is a diminution in the requirements of the employer's business for work of the kind which the employee is employed to do, or
b. any other occurrence affecting the normal working of the employer's business in relation to work of that kind.

In *North v Pavleigh Ltd* the owner of a company closed his factory for Jewish holidays. The industrial tribunal held that no guarantee payment could be claimed. Section 12 only applies to a diminution of work, or an 'occurrence', such as a power failure or national disaster. It was not intended to cover the religious habits of the proprietor.

5.3 However, if the contract of employment is expected to last no more than three months, there is no right to a guarantee payment, i.e. seasonal workers are excluded. A guarantee payment is not payable if the workless day occurs in consequence of a trade dispute involving any employee of the employer or of any associated employer. In *Garvey v Maybank (Oldham) Ltd* there was a national lorry drivers' strike, and pickets at the employer's entrance refused to let the firm's own lorries in or out. The employer ordered the firm's drivers (who were not involved in the strike) to cross picket lines, but they refused. As a result, there were insufficient supplies coming into the firm, and the applicant was laid off. It was held that he was not entitled to guarantee pay. The refusal of the drivers to cross the picket lines meant that the lay off occurred in consequence of a trade dispute. Nor is the employee entitled to the payment if the employer offers to provide alternative work which is suitable in all the circumstances (whether or not it is within the employee's contract) and he unreasonably refuses that offer. The employee must also comply with reasonable requirements imposed by the employer with a view to ensuring that his services are available.

5.4 The employee is entitled to be paid at the guaranteed hourly rate (which is one week's pay divided by the number of normal working hours) for the number of normal working hours in respect of any whole day he is laid off. He is entitled to be paid for five working days in any period of three months, at a rate of a maximum of (currently) £14.10 per day (EPCA s. 15, as amended). In other words, the present position is that an employee will be entitled to no more than £14.10 per day for a maximum of 20 days in each year. If the employee already has a contractual right to remuneration in respect of a workless day (e.g. by means of a collective agreement, etc) then any payment made under that agreement will go towards discharging the employer's liability to make the statutory guarantee payment, and equally, the latter will go towards discharging the contractual liability. If there is a guaranteed week agreement in existence, then the contractual remuneration shall be apportioned rateably between the workless days, and the statutory minimum will be used to 'top up' as appropriate. However, workless days when a contractual payment is made are taken into account when calculating the number of days guarantee pay is payable in any period of three months (*Cartwright v G Clancey Ltd*). It should be noted that if a contractual or statutory guarantee payment is being made, the employee is not entitled to apply for unemployment benefit.

5.5 If an employer fails or refuses to pay the whole or part of the guarantee payment, the employee may complain within three months to an industrial tribunal. If they find the complaint well founded, they will order the employer to pay to the complainant the amount due to him.

5.6 If there is a collective agreement in force which already relates to guarantee payments, then all the parties thereto may apply to the appropriate Minister for an exemption order. This will be granted if he is satisfied that the statutory provisions should not apply to those employees, but the collective agreement must contain provisions for an aggrieved employee to take a dispute about non-payment of the guarantee payment either to arbitration (or other procedure) or to an industrial tribunal. A number of such exemption orders have been granted.

Suspension on medical grounds (ss. 19-22)

5.7 Provided an employee has been continuously employed for more than one month, and is not employed under a fixed term contract of three months or less, or a contract to perform a specific task which will last less than three months, he will be entitled to be paid remuneration if he is suspended from work in consequence of a requirement imposed by certain statutory provisions or a recommendation made under a Code of Practice issued or approved under s. 16 of the Health and Safety at Work etc Act 1974 (see Chapter 12). The statutory provisions in question are regulations listed in Schedule 1 of the Employment Protection (Consolidation) Act 1978, dealing generally with lead, radioactive substances and the COSHH Regulations. If a health risk occurs within the scope of these provisions, certain processes must be suspended, and the result now is that in these circumstances the affected employees will be entitled to be paid for a period of up to six months from the day when the suspension period begins. An employee is not entitled to be paid during the suspension period is he is incapable of work because of illness or injury, or if he unreasonably refuses alternative work offered to him by the employer (whether within the terms of his contract or not) or if he does not make himself available for work.

5.7A An employee who is thus suspended on medical grounds is entitled to a week's pay in respect of each week the suspension lasts, and though the contractual right to remuneration is unaffected, the contractual and statutory remuneration can be set off against each other as appropriate. If the employer fails to pay the whole or any part of the employee's remuneration, the latter may present a complaint to the industrial tribunal within three months, and if it finds the complaint well-founded, it shall order the employer to pay to the employee the amount due to him.

5.7B It must be stressed that a medical suspension payment can only be claimed if the employee is fit for work. In *Stallite Batteries Co Ltd v Appleton*, the applicant became ill after falling into a skip containing lead paste. In consequence, his blood lead level exceeded the limit laid down in the Control of Lead at Work Regulations 1980 (see Schedule 1, Employment Protection (Consolidation) Act), but no medical suspension certificate was issued by the employment medical adviser. Nonetheless, the applicant's own doctor considered that he was not fit for work. The EAT held that he was not entitled to a medical suspension payment. He was not available for work due to sickness, and his claim was excluded by s. 20(3) of the Act.

5.7C If an employee is dismissed for a reason which would otherwise amount to a medical suspension, he is only required to have been employed for one month (instead of the usual two years) in order to present a claim for unfair dismissal (s. 64(2)).

5.8 If the employer wishes to engage a temporary employee to take the place of the suspended employee, then, as long as he has informed the temporary employee in writing that the employment will be terminated when the suspension has ended, a dismissal of the temporary employee in order to allow the suspended employee to return to work will amount to 'some other substantial reason' for the dismissal (see Chapter 8), although the employer will still have to show that he acted reasonably (EPCA s. 61(2)). In practice, this provision is otiose.

Suspension from work on maternity grounds (s. 45)

5.9 A woman is suspended from work on maternity grounds if she is suspended by her employer because she is pregnant, or has recently given birth to a child, or is breastfeeding a child, and the suspension is due:

(a) to any statutory requirement (e.g. Ionising Radiations Regulations 1985); or

(b) to any recommendation contained in a Code of Practice issued under the Health and Safety at Work etc Act 1974 (see Chapter 12).

5.10 If an employer has available suitable alternative work for her, she has a right to be offered such work before being suspended on maternity grounds. The alternative work must be of a kind which is suitable in relation to her and appropriate in the circumstances. If the terms and conditions differ from her normal contract of employment, they must not be substantially less favourable. A failure to make such an offer may result in the woman bringing a complaint to an industrial tribunal, which may make an award of compensation as the tribunal considers just and equitable in all the circumstances.

Maternity suspension pay (s. 47, EPCA)

5.11 A woman who is suspended from work on maternity grounds is entitled to be paid a week's pay in respect of each week of suspension, reduced proportionately if the suspension is for less than a week. There is no statutory maximum figure for the week's pay, which is to be calculated in accordance with Schedule 14.

5.12 A failure by the employer to pay the whole or any part of the remuneration due will enable the employee to bring a complaint to an industrial tribunal, which, if it finds the complaint well-founded, shall order the employer to pay the amount of remuneration due to her.

General right to maternity leave (EPCA s. 33 (as amended))

5.13 The Trade Union Reform and Employment Rights Act 1993 has made a number of changes in the maternity provisions formerly contained in the Employment Protection (Consolidation) Act 1978, mainly to ensure compliance with the new EC Directive on the Protection of Pregnant Women at Work. The new provisions will come into force some time before 19 October 1994.

5.14 Every woman has the right to a maternity leave period of 14 weeks, irrespective of the length of her period of continuous employment. During that period, she will be entitled to the benefit of the terms and conditions of employment which would have been applicable to her if she had not been absent. However, this does not entitle her to any remuneration, unless her contract of employment so provides, because she may take advantage of statutory or contractual rights, whichever are the more favourable. She must notify her employer of the date her maternity leave period is to commence not less than 21 days before the commencement or, if that it not reasonably practicable, as soon as is reasonably practicable. If she is absent from work wholly or partly because of pregnancy or childbirth before the notified leave date or before she has notified the employer of the date, she must notify the employer as soon as is reasonably practicable that she is absent for that reason. If the childbirth occurs before the notified leave date or before she has notified the employer of the date, she must notify the employer that she has given birth as soon as is reasonably practicable after the birth. Any notification she is required to give shall, if the employer so requests, be given in writing.

5.15 If she is prohibited by law from returning to work within a certain period from childbirth (Public Health Act 1936 s. 205; Factories Act 1961 Sch. 5), the maternity leave period is extended until the end of the later period. However, if she is dismissed after the commencement of the maternity leave period, but before it ends, the period will end at the date of dismissal.

5.16 At least 21 days before the maternity leave period commences (or as soon as is reasonably practicable) she shall inform her employer in writing (a) that she is pregnant, and (b) the expected week of childbirth. If requested, she shall produce for inspection a certificate from a registered medical practitioner or registered midwife stating the expected week of confinement.

5.17 There is no provision in the Act which specifically states that a woman has the right to return to work after her maternity leave period, but since it will be an unfair dismissal to dismiss when her maternity leave period comes to an end and the reason for the dismissal is because she gave birth to a child, (see para. 5.30), the right to return is implicit in the legislation even if she lacks the qualifying period of employment to return to work under the provisions of s. 39. After all, she is 'on leave' from her work for the statutory period. Also, she retains the benefits of her contract of employment (other than remuneration) as if she had not been absent. Thus there is no doubt that she will have an automatic right to return to work after her maternity leave period has expired. However, where, during her maternity leave period, it is not practicable by reason of redundancy to continue to employ her under her existing contract of employment, she shall be entitled, where there is a suitable available vacancy, to be offered alternative employment with her employer (or his successor or associated employer), under a new contract which takes effect immediately her old contract expires. The new contract must be such that the work to be done is of a kind which is suitable for her and appropriate for her to do in the circumstances, and its provisions as to capacity and place, and other terms and conditions of employment, should not be substantially less favourable than the previous contract.

A woman who wishes to return to work earlier than the end of her maternity leave period must give seven days' notice of the date on which she intends to return.

Right to return to work (s. 39)

5.18 In addition to the maternity leave period, a woman has a right to return to work any time up to 29 weeks from the end of her maternity leave period. To qualify for this right, she must have been continuously employed for not less than two years (or, if she works between 8-16 hours per week, for a continuous period of five years) at the week beginning with the eleventh week before the expected week of confinement. She is entitled to return to work with her former employer (or his successor where appropriate) in the job in which she was formerly employed, on terms and conditions as to remuneration not less favourable than those which would have applied had she not been absent from work, and with her seniority, pension rights, etc as they would have been if the period between the end of her maternity leave and her return to work were continuous (with certain credits being given for periods of absences, see Social Security Act 1989 Sch 5 para 5). Other terms and conditions should be no less favourable than those which would have been applicable to her had she not been absent after the end of the maternity leave period.

5.19 To exercise the right to return to work, she must provide the information specified in s. 37(1)(above), i.e. inform the employer in writing (21 days before her maternity leave period is to commence) that she is pregnant, and the expected week of confinement (or, if the childbirth has occurred, the date on which it occurred). She must also notify the employer that she intends to return to work. Any time after three weeks before the end of the maternity leave period, the employer may request her to give a written confirmation that she intends to exercise the right to return to work, and she shall give that confirmation within two weeks of receiving the request (or, if that is not reasonably practicable, as soon as is reasonably practicable). The employer's request for confirmation shall be in writing, and shall be accompanied by a statement that she will lose her right to return to work unless she does reconfirm her intention to do so.

5.20 In *Hughes v Gwynned Area Health Authority*, the EAT gave some guidelines on the approach to be adopted if a woman changes her mind about her intention to return to work. If a woman resigns, so that her resignation takes effect prior to the eleventh week prior to her confinement, and she states that she does not intend to return to work, then her resignation is effective, and she has no legal right to change her mind. If she states that she does not intend to return to work, but does not leave until after the eleventh week prior to her confinement, then the statutory provisions come into effect, and as long as she gives the requisite notice three weeks prior to her leaving, then she is entitled to change her mind and exercise her statutory option. A mere statement by a pregnant woman that she does not intend to return to work after her pregnancy, without any leaving date being fixed, is not a resignation, and hence she may always change her mind in the appropriate circumstances.

5.21 If it is not practicable by reason of redundancy for the employer to permit her to return to work, she shall be entitled, where there is a suitable available vacancy, to be offered alternative employment with her employer, his successor, or an associated employer, under a new contract of employment. The work to be done under the new contract must be suitable in relation to the employee and appropriate for her to do in the circumstances. The terms as to the capacity and place of her employment, and other terms and conditions should not be substantially less favourable than if she had returned to work pursuant to her right to return.

5.22 The employee will exercise her right to return by giving written notice to her employer (or successor) at least 21 days before the notified day of return. The employer may postpone her return for a period of four weeks after the notified day of return. The employee may herself extend the period in which

Right to Return After Childbirth

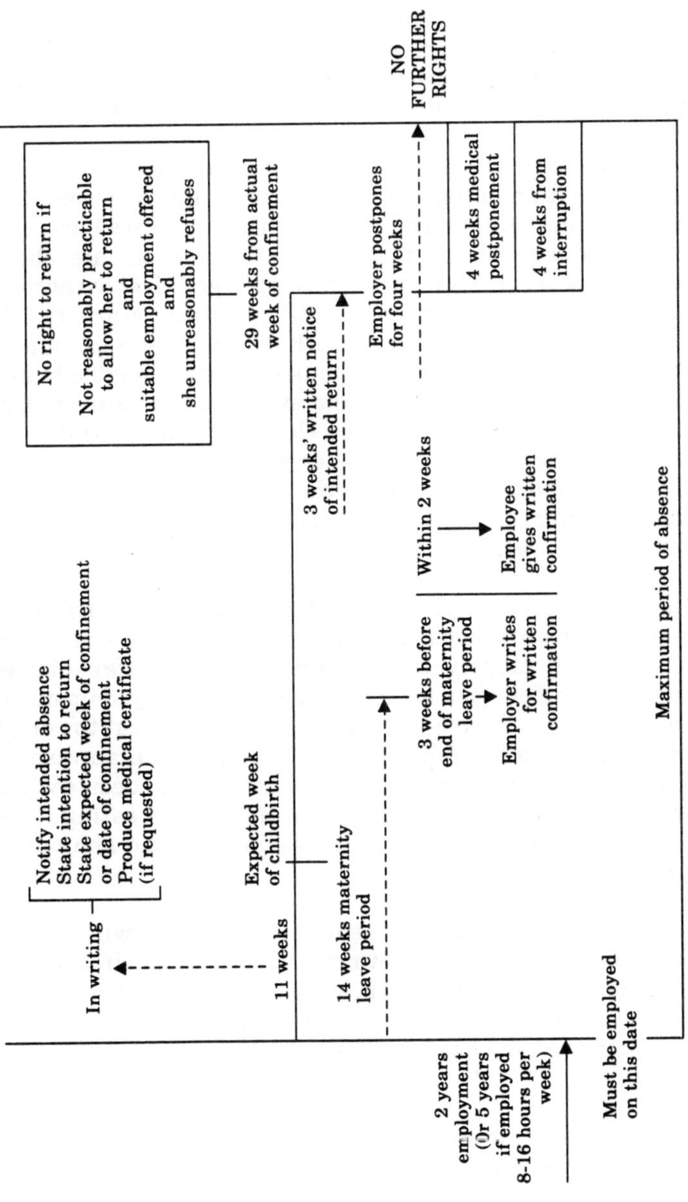

she can exercise her right to return beyond the 29th week from the week of the childbirth for a further four weeks if she provides a medical certificate stating that by reason of disease or bodily or mental disablement she is incapable of work at the end of that period. However, once having exercised the right of postponement, she will not be entitled to do so again.

5.23 If the employee has notified a date of return, but she is prevented from doing so by reason of an interruption of work (whether due to industrial action or other reason) which renders it unreasonable for her to return on the notified date, she may return to work as soon as is reasonably practicable thereafter. Similarly, if there has been no notified date of return, but there has been an interruption of work (whether due to industrial action or other reason) which makes it unreasonable to expect her to return to work before the expiry of the 29th week from childbirth, and in consequence she fails to notify a day of return, then she may exercise her right to return at any time before the end of 28 days from the end of the interruption, notwithstanding that this results in a return to work outside the period of 29 weeks from the week of the childbirth.

5.24 Where an employee is not permitted to return to work under these provisions, then she will be treated as having been continuously employed for redundancy and unfair dismissal purposes as if she had been continuously employed up until the notified date to return to work. She may now treat the employer's refusal to allow her to return as a case of unfair dismissal, under EPCA s. 56, and the tribunal will have to decide whether or not the employer has acted reasonably in treating the reason as sufficient reason for dismissing her had she not been absent from work.

5.25 On the other hand, if she fails to comply with the strict procedures laid down, e.g. by not giving the requisite notice that she intends to return to work, she will lose her rights altogether (*Lavery v Plessey Telecommunications Ltd*), for she cannot then complain that she has been dismissed by virtue of s. 56 (*Kolfor Plant Ltd v Wright*).

5.26 Further, if she fails to return after the end of the 29 weeks, or she is not permitted to return because the 29-week period, together with any four-week extension which may have been added because of her illness, has expired, then the contract has come to an end, but as she has not been dismissed, she will have no further statutory rights (*Kelly v Liverpool Maritime Terminals Ltd*).

5.27 The actual right to return may be exercised by the woman against her employer or a successor of his. The offer of suitable alternative employment etc may be made by the employer or an associated employer.

5.28 If the employer has engaged a temporary replacement to do the work of the absent pregnant employee, then, if he has informed him/her in writing that the employment will be terminated on the return to work of the latter, and the employer then dismisses the temporary employee to give work to the returning employee, the dismissal shall be regarded as having been for a substantial reason of a kind to justify the dismissal, but the employer must still show that he acted reasonably in treating that reason as a sufficient ground for dismissal (see Chapter 8). With the raising of the qualifying period of employment to two years, this provision ceases to have any practical effect.

5.29 Finally, we must consider the situation where the woman does not rely on her statutory rights, e.g. if she fails to give the initial notice that she intends to return to work. If her contract of employment subsists during the period she is absent from work (i.e. if she has permission to be absent) then the employer, having waived the obligation of service, is obliged to take her back on reasonable notice. If he fails to do this, she is dismissed in law, and is entitled to pursue her claim for unfair dismissal in the usual way (*Lucas v Norton of London Ltd*).

Dismissal on the ground of pregnancy or childbirth (s. 60, EPCA)

5.30 Generally speaking, a dismissal on the ground of pregnancy or childbirth is an inadmissible reason, and hence no period of continuous employment is required to bring a claim for unfair dismissal. Any such dismissal will be unfair if the reason (or, if there was more than one, the principal reason) is:

(a) that she is pregnant or any other reason connected with her pregnancy;
(b) that she has given birth to a child or any other reason connected with her having given birth to a child, with the re-

sult that her maternity leave period is ended by the dismissal;

(c) where her contract of employment was terminated after the end of her maternity leave period, and she was dismissed because she took, or availed herself of the benefits of, maternity leave;

(d) if, before the end of her maternity leave period, she gave her employer a certificate from a doctor stating that she would be incapable of work at the end of that period, and her contract was terminated within four weeks from the end of her maternity leave, and the certificate remains current, then it will be an unfair dismissal if her contract was terminated because she gave birth to a child or for any other reason connected with the birth of the child;

(e) she was dismissed because she is prevented from doing the work in question because of a statutory restriction or recommendation in a Code of Practice issued under the Health and Safety at Work etc Act 1974 (see para 12.54);

(f) she has been made redundant, during the maternity leave period, and she has not been offered alternative employment under s. 39 (above, para 5.18).

5.31 A woman who is dismissed because she has been selected for redundancy, and the reason for her selection was one of any of these set out in s. 60(a)-(e) (above), will be able to claim that her dismissal was for an inadmissible reason, and consequently automatically unfair. So far as s. 60(f) is concerned, a breach does not amount to an inadmissible reason, but no period of qualifying employment is required. Presumably, therefore, the reasonableness of the decision not to offer alternative employment must be tested in the usual way.

5.32 Of course, if an employer does not know that a woman is pregnant, and dismisses her for a reason not connected with her pregnancy, she will not be able to claim that her dismissal was contrary to s. 60 (*Del Monte Foods Ltd v Mundon*).

5.33 Finally, a woman who is dismissed at any time while she is pregnant or after childbirth when the maternity leave period ends by reason of the dismissal is entitled to have written reasons for her dismissal, without any request being made (see para 8.214).

5.34 For the purposes of the Act, childbirth is defined as the birth of a living child or the birth of a child whether living or dead after 24 weeks of pregnancy.

Statutory Maternity Pay (SMP): Social Security Contributions and Benefits Act 1992 ss. 164-171

5.35 From April 1987 the maternity pay scheme (EPCA ss. 34-44), administered by the Department of Employment, has been abolished, and the Maternity Fund wound up. This has been replaced by Statutory Maternity Pay, which is payable by employers, and recouped by them from the national insurance contributions they pay to the Inland Revenue. SMP is payable for a maximum of 18 weeks: of these, six may attract the higher rate of SMP (corresponding to the old maternity pay) and 12 weeks (or, in some cases, all 18 weeks) will attract SMP at the lower rate.

5.36 The first qualification for SMP is that the woman must be an 'employed earner', i.e. whose earnings attract a liability for employer's Class 1 national insurance contributions. This is somewhat different from the definition of 'employee' generally used in employment law (see Chapter 2). The result could well be that a woman is regarded as being self-employed for employment protection purposes, and hence unable to benefit from the legal right to return to work after pregnancy (see para 5.18), yet still be entitled to SMP.

5.37 Second, she must have been continuously employed for the requisite period of continuous employment up to the qualifying week, which is the week immediately prior to the 14th week prior to the expected week of confinement. If her continuous employment up to the qualifying week has been more than two years (or, if she works between 8 and 16 hours per week, more than five years) she will be entitled to higher and lower rate of SMP. If she has worked for less than six months up to the qualifying week, she will not be entitled to SMP, but will be entitled to receive maternity allowance from the Department of Social Security.

5.38 Third, her normal weekly earnings in the last eight weeks ending with the qualifying week must not be less than the lower

Statutory Maternity Pay (SMP)

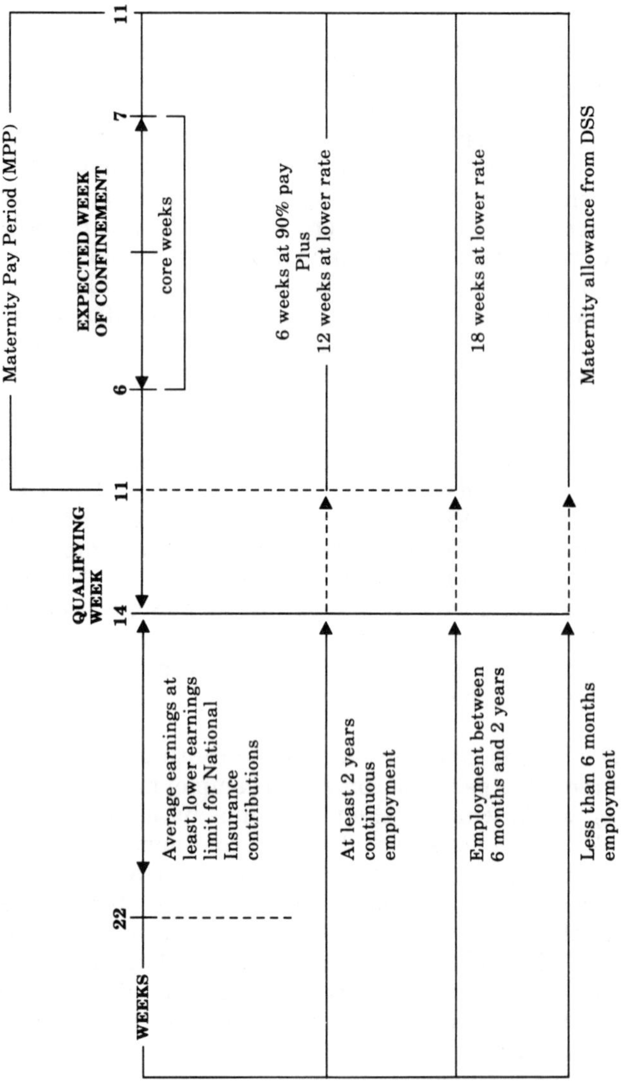
Maternity Pay Period (MPP)
EXPECTED WEEK OF CONFINEMENT
QUALIFYING WEEK
WEEKS
22
14
11
6
7
11
core weeks
Average earnings at least lower earnings limit for National Insurance contributions
At least 2 years continuous employment
6 weeks at 90% pay
Plus
12 weeks at lower rate
Employment between 6 months and 2 years
18 weeks at lower rate
Less than 6 months employment
Maternity allowance from DSS

earnings limit for the payment of national insurance contributions.

5.39 Fourth, she must produce a medical certificate stating the expected week of confinement (which cannot be given earlier than the 14th week prior to the expected week of confinement), and she must inform her employer 21 days before her absence from work is due to begin, or as soon as is reasonably practicable, that she intends to stop work because of her pregnancy.

5.40 Fifth, she can only receive SMP for weeks in which she does not work.

5.41 The Maternity Pay Period begins on the 11th week prior to the expected week of confinement, and ends on the 11th week following the expected week of confinement. Within this period, for a woman who is entitled to the higher rate (see above), there is a certain flexibility. There is a 'core period' of 13 weeks, starting within the 6th week before the expected week of confinement, and the higher rate may be paid before the expected week of confinement, depending on when she finishes work. The remaining weeks will be paid at the lower rate. For women who are only entitled to the lower rate, the Maternity Pay Period runs for 18 weeks from the 11th week prior to the expected week of confinement.

5.42 SMP is not payable if, during the Maternity Pay Period, she becomes disqualified, i.e. from the commencement of a week when she is outside the European Community, or is in legal custody, or dies. There are a number of other provisions which deal with various situations which may arise, and which may thus affect entitlement to SMP, including when she is dismissed because of pregnancy, when the business is transferred from one employer to another, when the baby is born earlier than the expected week of confinement, and so on.

5.43 If the employer refuses to pay SMP, a woman is entitled to a written statement of the reasons, and she can apply to an adjudication officer of the DSS for a formal decision, with a right of appeal to the Social Security Appeal Tribunal.

5.44 Finally, it will be noted that a woman who does not qualify for SMP because she lacks the relevant period of continuous employment can apply to the DSS for a maternity allowance.

5.45-5.54 The amount of SMP payable is as follows: the higher rate is payable for six weeks, and is 90% of her average earnings. The lower rate is payable for 12 to 18 weeks (as appropriate) and is currently £47.95.

Time off for public duties (EPCA s. 29)

5.55 An employer shall permit an employee to have time off for the purpose of performing his duties as a

a. justice of the peace
b. member of a local authority
c. member of a Broads Authority
d. member of a statutory tribunal
e. member of a Regional Health Authority, Area Health Authority, District Health Authority, Family Practitioners Committee or Health Board
f. member of the managing or governing body of an educational establishment maintained by a local authority, or (in Scotland) a school or college council, or governing body of a central institution or a college of education
g. member of a governing body of a grant-maintained school
h. member of the governing body of a higher education corporation or the board of management of a college of further education
i. member of the National Rivers Authority or a river purification board
j. member of a Board of Visitors for Prisons, remand centres and young offenders institutions.

The permission is to be given in order to enable the employee to attend meetings of the body, or its committees or sub-committees, or to do anything approved by the body for the purpose of discharging its functions. The amount of time off permitted for these purposes, the occasions on which and the conditions subject to which time off may be taken are those that are reasonable in all the circumstances, having regard in particular to

a. how much time off is required for the performance of the duties,
b. how much time off the employee has had already in respect of trade union duties and activities, and
c. the circumstances of the employer's business and the effect of the employee's absence on the running of that business.

In *Walters v British Steel Corpn* the applicant was transferred to an essential job, and it was difficult to release him for public duties. When he took the job, he had agreed that his public duties would take second place. Consideration of safety required certain minimum manning levels, and his colleagues refused to cover for him. It was held that he was not entitled to time off work for public duties, as the circumstances of the employer's business had to be taken into account.

5.56 In considering the amount of time off to be given under s. 29, the needs of the employee to perform his public duties adequately must be balanced carefully with the requirements of the employer to have the work done. In *Emmerson v IRC* the applicant was the leader of the opposition party on Portsmouth Council. He had been given 18 days' leave (paid) each year to perform his duties, but this was insufficient. His application for further unpaid leave of absence was refused by his employers, as it was argued that he could not be spared from his job. The industrial tribunal thought that the problem could be overcome by appointing a deputy to give him some assistance, for in other areas there was more than one person doing the same job as the applicant, who should not be put at a disadvantage because he was extra-efficient. Since the applicant was prepared to use some of his own holidays for public duties, the tribunal thought that he should be given a further 12 days' leave of absence without pay. However, in *Corner v Bucks County Council*, the EAT held that the industrial tribunal has no power to make any recommendations of this nature, or to impose conditions.

5.57 Section 29 requires the employer to give time off work to the employee. Re-arranging hours of work, and swapping duties so that the same number of hours are worked is not giving time off (*Ratcliffe v Dorset County Council*).

5.58 It should be noted that there is no legal requirement that the employee be paid for time off work under s. 29. But if he is refused time off, he may present a complaint to an industrial tribunal within the usual period of three months from the date of refusal. The industrial tribunal must take account of all the relevant considerations (*Borders Regional Council v Maule*), and if the complaint is upheld, the tribunal shall make a declaration, and may award compensation of such amount as it considers just and equitable, having regard to the employer's default and any loss sustained by the employee.

Time off to look for work (EPCA s. 31)

5.59 An employee who is dismissed for reason of redundancy shall be entitled, before the expiration of his notice, to be given reasonable time off during his working hours to look for new employment or to make arrangements for retraining. This right, however, only applies to employees who have been continuously employed for more than two years. The redundant employee is entitled to be paid at his appropriate hourly rate, and if the employer unreasonably refuses to allow him to have the time off, or fails to pay him for it, a complaint may be presented to an industrial tribunal within three months. An award of up to two-fifths of a week's pay may then be made.

5.60 It is not a pre-requisite for time off that the employee should provide the employer with details of interviews or appointments he has made, as he is entitled to go to look for a job without having made any such arrangements. But if an employer thinks that the request for time off is not bona fide, it may be that he does not unreasonably refuse to permit it (*Dutton v Hawker Siddeley Aviation Ltd*).

Time off for ante-natal care (EPCA s. 31A)

5.61 An employee who is pregnant and who, on the advice of a registered medical practitioner, midwife or health visitor, has made an appointment to attend any place for the purpose of receiving ante-natal care shall have the right not to be unreasonably refused time off during her working hours to enable her to keep the appointment. If requested to do so, she must produce a certificate stating that she is pregnant, and some documentary evidence of the appointment (but not for the first appointment). She is entitled to be paid for the period of absence at the appropriate hourly rate. A complaint may be made to an industrial tribunal (within three months or such further period as the tribunal considers reasonable) that her employer has unreasonably refused to permit her to have time off, or has failed to pay her the whole or part of the amount to which she is entitled. The tribunal shall award her an amount equal to the remuneration to which she would have been entitled.

Other employment rights

5.62 There are a number of further provisions giving employment protection rights which are contained in the Employment Protection (Consolidation) Act and the Trade Union and Labour Relations (Consolidation) Act. These will be considered under the following headings:

(a) the right not to suffer a detriment or dismissal in health and safety cases (see Chapter 12);
(b) the right not to suffer a detriment or dismissal because of trade union membership or non-membership (see Chapter 13);
(c) the right to have time off work for trade union duties and activities (see Chapter 13);
(d) time off work for safety representatives (see Chapter 12);
(e) interim relief for dismissed trade unionists and non-unionists (see Chapter 13);
(f) interim relief in health and safety cases (see Chapter 12);
(g) the right not to be unfairly dismissed for asserting a statutory right (see Chapter 8).

Jury service (Juries Act 1974)

5.63 An employee who is summoned to attend for jury service must be given time off work for that purpose, unless he is within one of the excused categories, or unless he has been excused service on application to the appropriate authority or the court. Failure to attend without reasonable cause may result in a fine being imposed of up to £200. A juror is entitled to claim travel and subsistence allowances, and payment for financial loss at prescribed rates.

Other time off work

5.64 An employee who wishes to take time off work for other purposes (e.g. Territorial Army, extended holidays, etc) may only do so with the agreement of the employer. An employee who persists in taking unauthorised time off may find that his subsequent dismissal is fair.

Armed Forces Reserves

5.65 Reservists who are called up to serve in the Armed Forces (including those who volunteer for such service) have their civil employment rights protected by the Reserve Force (Safeguard of Employment) Act 1985. When the military service comes to an end, an employer must re-employ the employee

a. in the occupation in which he was last employed before the full-time service, on terms and conditions not less favourable than those which would have been applicable had he not undertaken full time service, or
b. if reinstatement is not reasonable and practicable, the employee must be offered the most favourable occupation, and on the most favourable terms and conditions which are reasonable and practicable in his case.

5.66 The employee must apply for reinstatement in writing, before the end of the third Monday after the full-time service has ceased, unless he was prevented from making it within that time by illness or other reasonable cause. The employer must be notified of a date (not more than three weeks) when the employee will be available for employment.

5.67 If the employer has already filled the vacancy, he cannot claim that it was not reasonably practicable to reinstate the reservist because he would have to dismiss that other person, and in practice it should be made clear to the replacement that the appointment may be for a temporary period.

5.68 A person who claims that his rights under the Act have been infringed may make an application to a Reinstatement Committee (see *Slaven v Thermo Engineers Ltd*). They may order the employer to reinstate the employee, or make an award of compensation of between 13 and 52 weeks' pay, depending on his length of service prior to being called up. A further appeal will lie to an umpire. It is a criminal offence to fail comply with an order of the Reinstatement Committee or the umpire.

5.69 If an employee is dismissed before the commencement of military service, and the reason is the call-up, then, in addition to a claim being made for unfair dismissal, the employer again faces the prospect of being prosecuted for a criminal offence.

5.70 Once the employee returns to his employment, his employment will be deemed to be continuous. The period of absence will not count towards continuity, but will not break it. However, if the employee received permission from the employer to go, he will be absent from work by arrangement or agreement, and the period of absence will count under the provisions of Sch 13, para 9(1)(c) of EPCA (see para. 8.31).

Access to medical reports

5.71 The Access to Medical Reports Act 1988 gives an employee the right to refuse permission to his employer who is seeking a medical report on the employee, the right to see any such report before it is supplied to the employer, and the right to correct any errors contained in the report.

5.72 A medical report is defined as being a report relating to the physical or mental health of an individual which has been prepared by the medical practitioner who is responsible for the clinical care of the individual. This would normally be the employee's own doctor or specialist consultant. Thus the Act does not apply to examinations and reports made by a company's own medical advisers, or a specialist report made on an ad hoc basis.

5.73 If an employer wishes to obtain a medical report from the employee's own doctor (or specialist), he must inform the employee, in writing, that he intends to make such an application, inform the employee of his rights under the Act, and obtain the employee's consent. If the employee refuses to give his consent, that is the end of the matter, and the employer may take any other steps he deems necessary, having regard to the refusal. Alternatively, the employee may agree to the application being made, but may insist on seeing the report before it is sent to the employer. He may then refuse consent to it being sent to the employer, or request the doctor to make amendments to the report which the employee considers to be incorrect or misleading. If the doctor refuses to do this, the employee may request the doctor to attach to the report a written statement from the employee, setting out his views in respect of any part of the report which the doctor declines to amend.

5.74 A doctor is not obliged to show to an employee any part of a medical report if he is of the opinion that the disclosure would cause serious harm to the employee's physical or mental health, or would indicate the doctor's intentions with regard to another person. Also, the doctor would not give access to any part of a medical report if this would reveal information about another person (unless that person consents).

5.75 An employee is entitled to access to a medical report which has been supplied for employment purposes any time within the preceding six months.

Statutory Sick Pay (SSP)

5.76 Under the provisions of the Social Security Contributions and Benefits Act 1992 ss. 151-163, employers will be responsible for paying to their employees statutory sick pay in respect of the first 28 weeks of absence through sickness. The Statutory Sick Pay Act 1991 provides that employers will be able to recover 80% of the amount thus paid from the national insurance contributions due to be paid over or, if this is insufficient, from the monthly tax return. There is a Small Employer Relief (SER) which provides for 100% recoupment once an employee has been receiving SSP for more than six weeks in a period of incapacity. A 'small employer', for the purpose of this legislation, means an employer who has paid (or is liable to pay) £16,000 (currently) or less gross national insurance contributions (i.e. employers' and employees' shares) in the qualifying tax year. Details of how the scheme works can be obtained from the Department of Social Security. In practice, the scheme shifts the administrative burden of paying sick pay from the State to the employer.

5.77 To understand the scheme, certain expressions must be defined

1. *A day of incapacity for work*
   This is any day when an employee is incapable, by reasons of some specific disease or mental or bodily disablement, of doing work of a kind he might reasonably be expected to do.
2. *A period of incapacity for work*
   This means any period of four or more consecutive days, each of which is a day of incapacity for work in relation to the employee's contract of employment.
3. *A period of entitlement*
   This period starts with the first day of incapacity for work, and ends when either
   a. the period of incapacity has ended, or
   b. the entitlement to SSP has been used up, or
   c. the contract of employment is terminated, or
   d. a woman who is pregnant becomes disqualified under the provisions of the Act.
4. *Qualifying days*
   These are days on which the employee is required by his contract of employment to be available for work.

5.78 To qualify for SSP, three conditions must be satisfied, namely

1. the employee's day of incapacity for work must form part of the period of incapacity for work (i.e. four or more consecutive days)
2. the day must be within the period of entitlement
3. the day must be a qualifying day.

If there are two periods of incapacity (for the same or different reasons) separated by not more than two weeks, they will be treated as a single period of incapacity. This means that an employee will not have to re-qualify with another three 'waiting days'. Moreover, if an employee leaves his job and starts another one, his period of incapacity with his previous employer counts with his new one.

5.79 The entitlement to SSP is a flat rate payment for a maximum period of 28 weeks in any one period of entitlement, or in any one tax year. Thereafter, the employee will be able to claim State Sickness Benefit. The amount of SSP will depend on the employee's earning level, and will be reviewed each year. The proposed payments from April 1993 are as follows:

Earnings	*SSP*
Between £56-£195	Lower rate, £46.95
More than £195	Higher rate £52.50

5.80 The above provisions apply to part-time employees (provided they earn the requisite amounts) and there is no minimum service qualification. SSP will be deemed remuneration, and therefore subject to deductions in respect of tax and national insurance contributions. Married women and widows who pay reduced national insurance contributions will qualify for SSP even though they do not qualify for State sickness benefit.

Exclusions from entitlement

5.81 The following employees are excluded from entitlement:

a. employees who are incapacitated from work for less than four days;
b. employees who are over pensionable age (however, State Sickness Benefit may be payable);
c. employees who are employees under contracts of employment for 12 weeks or less (State Sickness Benefit may be payable);

d. employees who earn less than the current specified amount (at present, this is £56 per week);
e. pregnant women whose first day of sickness is within the disqualifying period (i.e. 18 weeks beginning with the 11th week prior to the expected week of confinement);
f. employees who would be workless on the day when the period of entitlement would begin because of trade dispute, unless they can prove that they did not take part in the strike or did not have a direct interest in it;
g. employees who are sick on the day they are due to start a new employment (State Sickness Benefit may be payable);
h. employees whose first day of sickness is within 57 days of a claim in respect of one of the following State benefits: State sickness benefit, invalidity pension, maternity allowance, or unemployment benefit if there has been a previous entitlement to invalidity benefit.

Leaver's statement

5.82 When an employee leaves his employment his employer must give him a 'Leaver's Statement' if the employee has a period of incapacity for work which is separated from the date the contract ends by 56 calendar days, and SSP was payable for one week or more. The new employer will take account of the weeks of SSP shown, which may reduce his maximum liability towards the new employee in his period of incapacity for work, by the amount shown on the statement.

Industrial injuries claims

5.83 One of the consequences of the new scheme is that Industrial injuries benefit claims have been abolished, and an employee who is thus injured will be entitled to SSP followed, where necessary, by invalidity benefit.

Enforcement

5.84 If an employee has not been paid SSP, he may refer the matter to the local insurance officer. There is a right of appeal to the Social Security Appeal Tribunal, with a further appeal to a Social Security Commissioner. A decision made in the employee's favour can be enforced in the County Court, should this be necessary. Certain questions may be referred directly to the Secretary of State for Social Services for a decision, namely

a. whether a person is, or was, the employee or employer of another person
b. whether an employer is entitled to deduct SSP from his contribution payments
c. whether two or more contracts of employment, or two or more employers, shall be treated as one for SSP purposes.

5.85 Any agreement which purports to exclude, limit or modify an employee's entitlement to SSP shall be void, but this does not prevent an employer from operating a sick pay scheme which is more favourable than the statutory scheme.

Self certification of illness

5.86 Since June 1982, doctors are no longer required to issue sick notes until after seven days of absence from work (instead of three days). Employees now have to obtain Sickness Benefit Claims Forms, which are widely distributed to trade unions, employers, doctors' surgeries, or is obtainable from the DSS. This must be completed and signed by the employee, which amounts to a self-certification of absence through illness. If the illness lasts for a period longer than seven days, a continuation claim form can be obtained from the doctor. The result will be that there will be a decline in some of the more dubious sick notes which hitherto have been difficult for an employer to challenge. It is generally felt that self-certification enables an employer to set up more efficient control procedures to monitor persistent absenteeism, and thus take effective action to deal with the problem.

Rights in insolvency (Insolvency Act 1986, Sch 6)

5.87 If an employer becomes insolvent (through bankruptcy or liquidation) certain debts are paid in priority to others. These include

a. up to four months' wages, up to £800 (Insolvency Act 1986 Sch 6),
b. accrued holiday pay,

c. any guarantee pay due under s. 12 of EPCA,
d. remuneration payable on medical suspension under s. 19 of EPCA or remuneration payable or suspension on maternity grounds under s. 47 of EPCA,
e. any payment due for time off work for trade union duties (s. 27) time off to look for work (s. 31) and time off for ante-natal care (s. 31A of EPCA),
f. remuneration due under a protective award (s. 189, TULR(C)A),
g. holiday pay, contractual sick pay and statutory sick pay.

Payments from the National Insurance Fund (EPCA ss. 122-127)

5.88 Certain monies due to an employee as a result of the employer's insolvency may be paid by the Secretary of State out of the National Insurance Fund. He must be satisfied that the employer is insolvent, that the employee was entitled to be paid the whole or part of the monies due, and that the employee has not received payment as a preferred creditor. The debts are:
a. any arrears of pay for a period not exceeding eight weeks. This also includes any guarantee pay, remuneration or suspension on medical grounds and maternity grounds, payment for time off work for trade union duties, time off to look for work, and time off for ante-natal care;
b. any minimum period of notice as computed by EPCA ss. 49-51 (see Chapter 8). The rights of the employee to claim against the Secretary of State are no greater than those he has against the employer. In *Secretary of State for Employment v Wilson* the employee was dismissed without notice, but he obtained employment immediately. His former employers went into liquidation, and he claimed four weeks' notice from the Secretary of State. It was held that he was not entitled. He was under a duty as against his former employers to mitigate against his loss, and having done so, he would have had no claim against them. Consequently, he had no claim against the Minister. But the employee is not obliged to bring into account any social security benefits received (*Westwood v Secretary of State for Employment*);
c. any holiday pay due in the preceding 12 months (but not exceeding six weeks' pay);
d. any basic award for compensation for unfair dismissal (but not a compensatory or higher award);

e. any reasonable sum by way of reimbursement of the whole or part of a premium paid by an apprentice or articled clerk;
f. any of the priority debts mentioned above (para 5.87) which have not been satisfied as preferential debts in bankruptcy or liquidation, for a period not exceeding in the aggregate eight weeks.

There is a maximum liability on the National Insurance Fund of £205 per week in respect of any debt which is referable to a period of time (with a proportionate reduction for periods of less than a week). The Secretary of State is entitled to deduct tax and national insurance contributions (*Morris v Secretary of State for Employment*). The person who is in charge of the winding up must provide the Secretary of State with a statement of the amount of the debt which is owed to the employee, although this is not essential if more than six months have elapsed since an application by the employee was made, and there appears to be a further delay, in which case the Secretary of State has a discretion to make the payment. The Act also provides that the Secretary of State may make payment out of the Fund in respect of any unpaid contributions which an insolvent employer has failed to make to an occupational pension scheme.

5.89 By the Insolvency of Employer (Excluded Classes) Regulations 1983, the right to claim payments on insolvency is extended to employees who, under their contracts of employment, ordinarily work in a Member State of the European Community.

5.90 If the Secretary of State fails to make any of these payments, a complaint may be made to an industrial tribunal within three months from his refusal (or within such further time as is reasonable). If the tribunal thinks that the payment ought to be made, it shall make a declaration to that effect, and state the amounts which the Secretary of State ought to pay.

5.91 On making the payment, the Secretary of State becomes subrogated to the rights of the employee (or pension fund) as a preferential creditor in the insolvency.

Death of the employer or employee

5.92-5.99 Schedule 12 to the Employment Protection (Consolidation) Act 1978 deals with the situation where the employer or the employee has died. Tribunal proceedings under any relevant provision may be instituted, continued or defended by the personal representatives of the parties or in the case of a deceased employee, by a person appointed by the tribunal for that purpose. The personal representatives will have to perform all the obligations of the deceased, and any rights which accrue after death shall continue to devolve, and any liability which has not so accrued prior to death shall be treated as if it was a liability of the deceased employer immediately before death. For example, if an employer dies before or during a tribunal hearing, at the time of the death, no liability has been incurred; once the tribunal makes an award, the liability shall be treated as if it had occurred prior to the death. If, on a claim of unfair dismissal, the employee dies, the reinstatement or re-engagement provisions obviously cannot apply, but the tribunal can nonetheless consider the question of compensation.

Transfer of undertakings

5.100 At common law, a contract of employment was a personal contract between the employer and the employee; when that relationship ceased, the contract of employment came to an end. Thus if a business was sold, the purchaser had the right to choose whom to employ, and the employee had the right to choose who he would work for. Indeed, '... the right to choose for himself whom he would serve ... constituted the main difference between a servant and a serf' (*Nokes v Doncaster Amalgamated Collieries*). Thus the sale or transfer of any business resulted in the termination of any existing contract of employment.

5.101-5.103 The position has been altered by the Transfer of Undertakings (Protection of Employment) Regulations 1981, which generally tries to put the transferee employer in the same position as the transferor, so that the rights and obligations contained in the contract of employment between the employee and the transferor are passed to the transferee.

Origin of the Regulations

5.104 In 1977 the Acquired Rights Directive (77/187/EEC) was passed (see para 1.59). Briefly, its aims are:

a. to ensure that when an employer transfers his business (or part of it) to another employer, the transferor and the transferee shall inform the representatives of the employees who are affected by the transfer, and consult with them;

b. to ensure that when the transfer takes place, the contracts of employment of the employees of the transferor are transferred to the transferee;
c. that the terms and conditions laid down in any collective agreement made by the transferor with the representatives of the employees shall be observed by the transferee for at least one year;
d. that the transfer, by itself, shall not constitute a ground for dismissal by the transferor or transferee, although this does not prevent dismissals brought about by economic, technical or organisational reasons;
e. if, as a result of the transfer, the employee suffers a substantial change in his working conditions to his detriment, this may constitute a dismissal.

5.105 Following the passing of the Directive, the Transfer of Undertakings (Protection of Employment) Regulations were passed. They were considered by the House of Lords in *Litster v Forth Dry Dock and Engineering Co Ltd*, and it was decided that they must be given a 'purposive' construction, so as to achieve the objectives intended by the Directive.

When do the Regulations apply?

5.106 The Regulations apply to an employee, defined as 'any individual who works for another person, whether under a contract of service or apprenticeship or otherwise' (reg 2(1)). This definition is somewhat wider than the one used in the Employment Protection (Consolidation) Act, and may, for example, include agency supplied workers, casual workers, and so on. In *Mikkelsen v Danmols Inventar A/S*, the European Court of Justice held that the meaning of the term 'employee' was a matter for the national courts to decide. However, the definition does not include persons who work under a contract for services (see *Cowell v Quilter Goodison Co Ltd*).

5.107 The Regulations apply on the transfer of an 'undertaking', which is defined as including any trade or business. Originally the Regulations did not apply to non-commercial undertakings, but this exception has now been removed (TULR(C)A s. 29)

5.108 The Regulations will apply where part of an undertaking is transferred, as long as that which is transferred is a separate and self-contained part of the original business, and the employee is actually employed in the part of the undertaking which is being transferred.

What is a transfer?

5.109 A relevant transfer can take place by sale or other disposition or by operation of law. There is no transfer if there is a sale or transfer of shares, because the corporate personality of the company does not change. But as long as there is a change in the identity of the employer, it does not matter if there is no formal legal transfer (*Landsorganisationen i Denmark v Ny Molle Kro*). Thus a transfer can take place on a grant, or the surrender and re-granting of a lease (*Premier Motors (Medway) Ltd v Total Oil GB Ltd*). In *Young v Daniel Thwaites & Co Ltd*, it was held that there was a relevant transfer when a change took place in the tenancy of a public house.

5.110 A transfer may be affected by two or more transactions, and it is irrelevant whether or not any property passes from the transferor to the transferee. Thus a concession, a permit to operate a licence, etc, now come within the scope of the Regulations.

5.111 However, there must be the transfer of a business, not a mere transfer of the assets of a business (*Lloyd v Brassey*). The European Court has held that it is for the national court to consider all the factual circumstances and assess whether they are characteristic of a transfer of an undertaking within the meaning of the Directive. The decisive factor is whether the business retains its identity, but it is also necessary to take into account the type of undertaking concerned, whether tangible assets were transferred, the value of intangible assets at the time of the transfer, whether or not the majority of employees were taken on by the new owner, whether customers were transferred, the degree of similarity between the activities carried on before and after the transfer, and the period, if any, for which those activities were suspended (*Rask and Christensen v ISS Kantineservice A/S*). Thus if the essential business activity is carried on by the new owner, it is likely that there has been a transfer within the meaning of the regulations (*Kenny v South Manchester College*). The transfer of goodwill (as opposed to physical assets) has been used as a criteria in a number of cases (e.g. *Kenmir Ltd v Frizzell*), and the fact that there was no transfer of goodwill has been used to hold that a transfer was outside the scope of the Regulations (*Robert Seligman Corpn v Baker*).

The effect of the transfer

5.112 Regulation 5(1) provides that a relevant transfer shall not operate so as to terminate the contract of employment of any person employed by the transferor in the undertaking transferred, but any such contract shall have effect after the transfer as if originally made between the employee concerned and the transferee.

5.113 This provision is the nub of the Regulations, and constitutes a form of statutory novation of the contract of employment. The transferee 'steps into the shoes' of the transferor, from the date the employment originally commenced. But a transfer will not operate to transfer an employee's contract of employment, and the rights, powers, duties and liabilities under it, if the employee informs the transferor employer that he objects to becoming employed by the transferee. In such circumstances, the transfer shall terminate the contract of employment with the transferor, but the employee shall not be treated for any purpose as having been dismissed by the transferor.

5.114 However, reg 5(3) provides that any reference to a person employed in an undertaking transferred by a relevant transfer is a reference to a person employed 'immediately before the transfer'. The meaning of this latter phrase has given rise to some difficulties. In *Apex Leisure Hire v Barratt*, an employee was made redundant on a Friday, and the business was transferred on the following Monday. Was the employee employed 'immediately before the transfer'? The EAT held that the gap between his dismissal and the transfer was so small that he was employed immediately before the transfer, and he could therefore claim that he had been unfairly dismissed by the transferee. Although this decision was followed in a number of cases, doubts were also expressed.

5.115 The matter was taken further by the Court of Appeal in *Secretary of State for Employment v Spence*. In this case, employees were dismissed at 11 am and the business was sold at 2 pm the same day. The workforce were re-engaged by the transferee, but the employees sought a redundancy payment from the Secretary of State, as the transferor had gone into liquidation. They argued that they were not employed 'immediately before the transfer'. The Court of Appeal upheld their claims. Regulation 5 only operates to transfer the contracts of employment of those employees who were still in the employment of the transferor at the moment of the transfer. There was no room for a gap in time, and *Apex Leisure Hire* and other similar cases were overruled.

5.116 However, the saga continued! In *Bork International A/S v Foreningen*, the European Court of Justice agreed that the Directive only applies to workers who were employed at the time of the transfer (as was held in *Spence*). However, the Court held further that in construing the Directive, regard must be had to Article 4(1) (which has been enacted by reg 8(1) of the Regulations). This prohibits a dismissal because of a transfer, except where there are 'economic, technical or organisational reasons'. Thus, if the worker was dismissed before the transfer, at the behest of the transferee, then, if this was in breach of Article 4(1), the worker is to be regarded as being employed at the time of the transfer.

5.117 The matter was finally resolved so far as the Regulations are concerned by the House of Lords in *Litster v Forth Dry Dock and Engineering Co Ltd*. In this case, the employee was dismissed an hour before the transfer. He claimed that he had been unfairly dismissed by the transferor, but this claim was ineffective, because the transferor had gone out of business. Nonetheless, the House of Lords held that he could proceed against the transferee. It is true that there was a gap in time between his dismissal and the transfer, but reg 5 had to be read in the light of reg 8(1). The result was that reg. 5 has to be construed as if after the words '... immediately before the transfer ...' there were inserted the words '... or would have been so employed if he had not been dismissed in the circumstances described in regulation 8(1)'.

5.118 The House of Lords were satisfied that the decision in *Spence* was correct, because the reason for the dismissal in that case was economic circumstances, and therefore the dismissal would not have been unfair within reg 8(1). But if a dismissal takes place before the transfer, which is unconnected with the transfer, then since this would be unfair by virtue of reg 8(1), the employee will be regarded as being employed 'immediately before the transfer'. On the other hand, a dismissal before the transfer which is brought about by economic, technical or organisational reasons will have the effect of depriving the employee of a remedy against the transferee.

What obligations are transferred?

5.119 Regulation 5(2) provides for the transfer to the transferee of all the transferor's rights, powers, duties and liabilities under or in connection with the contract of employment. It is thus clear that statutory rights, such as equal pay, maternity rights, etc, are transferred, but not apparently an employer's liability for a protective award, because this does not arise in connection with the contract of employment, but stems from the failure of the employer to consult with a recognised trade union (*Angus Jowett & Co Ltd v National Union of Tailors and Garment Workers*). Restrictive covenants made by the employee with the transferor are transferred, but clearly these need to be looked at in the light of the new situation.

5.119A For example, in *Morris Angel & Son Ltd v Hollande*, the defendant was the managing director of a company called Altolight Ltd. His service agreement provided that within one year after leaving his employment he would not seek business from any person with whom the company had done business within one year of the end of his employment. The company was then sold to the plaintiffs, who sought to enforce the restrictive covenant. The question was whether, in the light of reg 5(1), the covenant was transferred to the plaintiffs in respect of their business or whether it remained enforceable only against the business of Altolight Ltd. It was held that the effect of reg 5(1) was to put the plaintiffs in the place of the transferor company (Altolight Ltd), and thus the covenant could be enforced to prevent the defendant from seeking business with anyone who had done business with that company within the year. It did not refer to the business activities of the plaintiffs. Any other construction would impose a much wider obligation on the defendant, because at the time he entered into the covenant there was no possibility of him contemplating accepting a restraint in respect of the plaintiff's business activities.

5.119B Share option and profit sharing schemes are transferred (*Thompson v ASDA MFI Group plc*), although these might not always be capable of surviving the transfer (*Chapman and Elkin v CPS Computer Group plc*).

5.120 The liability of the transferor for tortious acts committed against his employees will be transferred, but it is not certain if the transferor's vicarious liability to third persons is transferred, because it does not arise under or in connection with the contract of employment.

5.121 The transferor's liability to be prosecuted, convicted and punished for a criminal offence is not transferred (reg 5(4)), and occupational pension schemes are also excluded (reg 7).

5.122 Once reg 5 has operated so as to give effect to the consequences of the transfer, the transferred employee cannot pursue a successful claim against the transferor in respect of any matter transferred by the Regulations.

The Regulations and EPCA

5.123-5.125 The Transfer of Undertakings Regulations sat uneasily alongside certain provisions of the Employment Protection (Consolidation) Act, especially s. 94 and Sch 13, because basically they sought to achieve different objectives, and there were a number of practical differences. However, s. 94 has now been repealed (TULR(C)A Sch 9) and all transfers must now be considered under the provisions of the Regulations.

5.126 For the effect of the Regulations on the unfair dismissal provisions, see para 8.185, on redundancy, see para 10.28, and on consultations with trade unions, see para 15.25.

Cashless pay

5.127 Under the provisions of the Truck Act 1831 the wages of manual workers had to be paid in current coin of the realm. That Act (together with a number of similar legislative provisions) has been repealed by the Wages Act 1986, and now cashless pay is perfectly lawful for all employees. The actual mode of payment of wages is a matter for agreement between the employer and employee.

5.128 Also repealed were the provisions of the Truck Act 1896 relating to fines and deductions, and the new Act provides a complex set of rules which must be observed.

General restrictions on deductions (Wages Act s. 1)

5.129 An employer must not make any deductions from the wages of any worker employed by him, or receive any payments from him, unless:

a. the deduction is required to be made or is authorised by a statutory provision (e.g. PAYE, national insurance); or
b. the deduction is authorised by a relevant provision in a worker's contract (e.g. contributions to an occupational pension scheme); or
c. the worker has signified his agreement to the deduction in writing in advance (e.g. to repay a loan made to purchase a season travel ticket). Further, the agreement should indicate with sufficient clarity the source from which deductions are to be made, i.e. the employee's wages, and that the employee authorised the deduction from that source. Otherwise, all that may exist is an agreement to repay a loan, not an agreement which authorises a deduction from wages (*Potter v Hunt Contracts Ltd*). However, the authority for the making of the deduction must not relate to anything which happened before that agreement was signified (see *Discount Tobacco and Confectionery Ltd v Williamson*).

Thus, if there is no statutory authority, no provision in the worker's contract, or no express agreement, a deduction is unlawful (*McCree v Tower Hamlets London Borough Council*) unless one of the exceptions mentioned below apply.

5.130 Subject to certain exceptions (below) a deduction which does not fall into one of the above categories is made in breach of the Act, and a worker may apply to an industrial tribunal for an appropriate remedy.

What are 'wages'? (s. 7)

5.131 The term 'wages' is defined as any sums payable to the worker by his employer in connection with his employment, including any fee, bonus, commission, holiday pay or other emoluments referable to his employment, whether payable under his contract or otherwise.

5.131A Also included in the definition are
a. any sum payable pursuant to an order for reinstatement or re-engagement
b. any sum payable pursuant to an order for interim relief
c. certain payments due to an employee on the employer's insolvency
d. statutory sick pay
e. statutory maternity pay.

5.131B In *Kent Management Services Ltd v Butterfield*, the employee was told that in addition to his salary, he would be able to participate in commission and bonus schemes, although these would be discretionary and *ex gratia*. When he was dismissed, he was paid all salaries due to him, but was told that the company would not be exercising their discretion in his favour in respect of outstanding commission. He claimed that this constituted an unlawful deduction from his wages. It was held that although the commission was expressed to be discretionary and non-contractual, it was '... a commission ... referable to his employment, whether payable under his contract or otherwise ..., and was thus a sum payable to him by his employer in connection with his employment. Thus he was entitled to receive the commission which he had already earned. The EAT suggested that if the payment of commissions and/or bonuses were to be non-contractual and discretionary, depending on satisfactory performance or other compliance with the contract of employment, simple words to that effect would have been included in the contract.

5.132 Loans, expenses, pensions, benefits in kind, redundancy payments, pay in lieu of notice, and compensation for loss of office are not within the definition.

5.133 A non-payment of any of the above monies is a deduction within the meaning of the Act, even though the employer claims he has a 'set-off' against the employee, and even though the employer disputes the amount which is claimed. For example, in *Greg May (Carpet Fitters and Contractors) Ltd v Dring*, the employee's contract stated that on the termination of his employment he would be entitled to accrued holiday pay. However, this would not be paid if he was dismissed through gross misconduct. The employers dismissed the employee for what they claimed to be gross misconduct, and refused to pay him the accrued holiday pay. The employee complained to an industrial tribunal that the employers had made an unlawful deduction, contrary to s 1(1) of the Act. It was held that whether or not the sum 'was properly payable' was for the industrial tribunal to investigate. On the facts, the employee had not been guilty of 'gross misconduct', and hence the accrued holiday pay was properly payable.

5.134 If there is a non-payment of wages, it appears that the ordinary courts have a concurrent jurisdiction with the industrial tribunals (*Rickard v PB Glass Supplies Ltd*). It would seem that a highly paid employee could bring a claim in an industrial tribunal, and obtain an award which is substantially in excess of the statutory limits which normally apply, for there is no limit to the amount which can be awarded under the Wages Act.

5.135 However, if an employee is wrongfully dismissed, and is not given pay in lieu of notice, he cannot claim under the Act. His claim is not for a sum 'referable to his employment' but is for damages for breach of contract consequent on the termination of his employment. This claim must go to the county court in the usual way (*Delaney v Staples*).

Exceptions (s. 1(5))

5.136 If one of the following exceptions apply, a worker does not have the right to complain to an industrial tribunal. However, he would still have his normal remedy in the county court, arguing that the employer has acted in breach of the contract. The exceptions are as follows:

(a) A deduction by the employer which is designed to reimburse the employer for an overpayment of wages or expenses paid to the worker. Thus if the worker disputes that there has been an overpayment, the matter must be resolved in the county court on the basis of the usual principles relating to a mistake of law and/or fact. If the overpayment was made under an error of law, it is not generally recoverable, unless the worker was aware of the error, and it would be inequitable in the circumstances to permit him to retain the money (*Holt v Markham*). If the overpayment was due to a mistake of fact, it is generally recoverable, unless the worker was led to believe that he was entitled to the money, he changed his position in consequence, and the overpayment was not primarily the fault of the worker (*Avon County Council v Howlett*, see para 6.16).

(b) A deduction or payment made in consequence of disciplinary proceedings held under a statutory provision (e.g. in respect of the police or fire services (see *Chiltern House Ltd v Chambers*). Such proceedings, however, may be the subject of judicial review (*R v Leicestershire Fire Authority, ex p Thompson*).

(c) A deduction authorised by statute (e.g. an attachment of earnings order).

(d) A payment made to a third party on behalf of the worker in accordance with a relevant provision in his contract to which the worker has signified his consent in writing (e.g. a union check-off agreement). However, if the worker subsequently informs the employer that he has ceased to be a member of the trade union, the employer shall no longer deduct the union subscription. An action may be brought by the employee in the county court to prevent future deductions, but the action to recover past deductions wrongfully made must be brought in the industrial tribunal (TULR(C)A s. 68).

(e) A deduction made (or repayment required) because the worker has taken part in a strike or other industrial action (*Sim v Rotherham Metropolitan Borough Council*). Thus if the employee is not performing any of his duties, the employer may deduct an amount which represents a fair proportion of his salary (*Miles v Wakefield Metropolitan District Council*). If the employer deducts more than a fair proportion, the employee's remedy lies in the county court, not in the industrial tribunal. In *Sunderland Polytechnic v Evans* an employee took part in a half-day strike. The employer deducted a full day's salary from her monthly pay, and she complained of an unlawful deduction within the meaning of the Wages Act. Although s. 1(5)(e) permits the employer to make a deduction in respect of strike action, it was argued on behalf of the employee that this only applied to a 'lawful' deduction. The industrial tribunal held that they had jurisdiction to decide whether the deductions were lawful, but the decision was reversed by the EAT. In an unusual move, the EAT decided to look at *Hansard*, and it was noted that in both the House of Commons and the House of Lords, Government ministers were clear that if a worker believed that a deduction was not contractually authorised, the remedy would lie in an action in the county court, not the industrial tribunals. Thus it would appear that if an employer is entitled to make a deduction, then if the amount of that deduction is in dispute, this must be settled in the county court, not the industrial tribunal. A decision of the EAT to the contrary (*Home Office v Ayres*) was disapproved. More difficult is the situation where the employee works the full hours, but only performs part of his duties during those hours. In this case there is likely to be a substantial performance of the contract, and the employer will be entitled to deduct part of the wages, i.e. based on the time when the employee is not working properly (*Wiluszynski v Tower Hamlets London Borough Council*).

(f) A deduction made with the prior agreement of the worker to satisfy an order made by a court or tribunal requiring the payment of any amount to the employer.

Deductions and payments in retail employment (s. 2)

5.137 Special rules apply for the protection of persons who are engaged in retail employment, which is defined as:

a. the carrying out of retail transactions, i.e. the sale or supply of goods or services (including financial services); or
b. the collection by the worker of amounts payable in connection with retail transactions carried out by other persons, or other individuals in their personal capacities.

Thus the definition covers a wide range of activities, including shop assistants, bus drivers, bank cashiers, insurance agents, petrol pump attendants, etc.

5.138 Under s. 2 of the Act, it is permissible to make a deduction (or require a payment) in respect of cash shortages or stock deficiencies, subject to two conditions. First, the requirements of s. 1 (above) must be met, i.e. there must be a contractual agreement enabling the deductions (or payments) to be made. The contractual arrangement must have been agreed to before the happening of the event which was the cause of the disputed deduction, because the Act is designed to prevent pressure being put on the employee to agree to the deduction (*Discount Tobacco and Confectionery Ltd v Williamson*). Second, the deduction (or demand for payment) must not exceed 10 per cent of the gross wages payable on the day in question. If the shortage or deficiency is greater than the sum deducted or demanded, the employer may continue to deduct or demand the balance on subsequent pay days, provided that on each occasion the deduction or demand does not exceed 10 per cent of the gross wages payable.

5.139 Generally, the deductions or demand must be made within 12 months from the date when the employer discovered the cash shortage or stock deficiency, except:

a. if the deduction is one of a series of deductions in respect of the same shortage or deficiency, in which case the 12-month period applies from the first deduction or demand of the series; or
b. if the employer ought reasonably to have discovered the cash shortage or stock deficiency earlier, the 12-month period will run from the date when he ought to have discovered it, not from when he actually did so.

However, when the employment comes to an end, there is no limit on the amount which the employer may deduct or demand.

5.140 An employer cannot evade the provisions of the Act by defining wages by reference to cash shortages or stock deficiencies, for in such circumstances the gross wages are to be treated as being the amount they would have been but for the shortage or deficiency. Further, an employer cannot evade the provisions of s. 2 by claiming that the worker's conduct amounted to a breach of contract (e.g. dishonesty or negligence) see s. 2(4).

Complaints to an industrial tribunal (s. 5)

5.141 A worker may make a complaint to an industrial tribunal that his employer has:

a. made a deduction or demanded a payment in contravention of s. 1;
b. made a deduction which is outside the 12-month time limit;
c. received a payment in respect of a cash shortage or stock deficiency without notifying the worker in writing of his total liability, or without making the demand in the prescribed manner;
d. made a deduction or received a payment in excess of the limit of 10% of the gross pay on a particular day.

5.142 The complaint must be made within three months from when the deduction was made or payment received by the employer, with the usual extension of time if the industrial tribunal is satisfied that it was not reasonably practicable to present it earlier. If they find the complaint well-founded, the industrial tribunal shall make a declaration to that effect, and order the employer to reimburse the worker the amount of any unauthorised deductions made or payment received.

5.143 It should be noted that the only remedy for a breach of the Wages Act is by way of a complaint to an industrial tribunal (s. 6(1)), and the former jurisdiction of the county court in respect of these specific matters has been abolished. However, there are still some odd situations which may arise when the old county court jurisdiction is still available (see para 5.136) and, it is submitted, an unauthorised deduction may still amount to a breach of contract so as to give rise to a claim of constructive dismissal (see para 8.75).

Scope of the Act

5.144 The Act applies to 'workers', which is a term wider than employees, and includes self-employed persons who work under a contract for personal service (other than professional persons or persons who are operating their own business). Employees who ordinarily work outside Great Britain are excluded, as is employment under a crew agreement under the Merchant Shipping Act. The Act applies to the Crown other than the Armed Forces.

CHAPTER 6

Performance of the contract of employment

Personal nature of the contract

6.1 A contract of employment is essentially one of personal service, which gives rise to duties and obligations on both sides, but the courts will not compel either side to carry out that contract by means of an order for specific performance or an injunction. In *Warner Bros v Nelson* a film actress agreed to work for the plaintiffs, and not to work for any other film company. It was held that an injunction would be granted restraining her from breaking the negative stipulation, for while she could not work for a rival film company, there were presumably other ways in which she could earn her living. However, the injunction would not be granted if its effect would be to compel the performance of the contract. In *Whitwood Chemical Co v Hardman* a manager agreed to devote the whole of his time to the company's business. He intended to work part-time for a rival company, and his employers sued for specific performance. It was held that the agreement was not enforceable, for while they could have obtained an injunction to restrain him from working for a competitor, the court would not compel him to work for the plaintiffs.

6.2 By the same rule, the courts will not normally order an employer to continue to employ an employee, though there are cases where this had been done (see para 6.5) and in recent years the courts have been more willing to do so than hitherto (see the cases cited in *Wadcock v London Borough of Brent*). There are also pressures on employers to offer reinstatement or re-engagement following industrial tribunal proceedings (see

Chapter 9) and a contract of employment may transfer from one employer to another when the Transfer of Undertakings (Protection of Employment) Regulations apply (see para 5.100). But the rule generally remains. In *Chappell v Times Newspapers*, members of a trade union were carrying on a disruptive campaign in support of a wage demand. The employers' association sent a telegram to the union stating that unless the campaign was called off, the members would be regarded as having broken their contracts of employment and thereby terminated their engagements. Several employees brought an action for an injunction to restrain their employers from terminating their contracts. It was held that, even on the assumption that the employers were acting in breach of contract, an injunction would not be granted, for to do so would be to compel specific performance by the employers. In particular, an injunction will not be granted if damages would be an adequate remedy for the alleged breach of contract (*Alexander v Standard Telephones and Cables plc)*.

6.3 An exceptional case was *Hill v Parsons*, where, following the making of a closed shop agreement with a trade union, the employers wrote to the plaintiff giving him one month's notice of dismissal because of his failure to join the union. The court thought that the plaintiff, who was a senior engineer, was entitled to at least six months' notice, and granted an injunction restraining the employers from treating the notice as having terminated the contract. (The effect of this was to delay the dismissal until after the coming into effect of the Industrial Relations Act 1971, which would have protected the plaintiff from dismissal from non-membership of the union.) But the court conceded that there were special circumstances in the case which enabled them to grant the injunction. There was no loss of confidence between the employers and the plaintiff, for the employers were acting under union pressure, and therefore there was no difficulty in enforcing the continuance of the contract.

6.4 *Hill v Parsons* was followed in *Irani v Southampton and South West Hampshire Health Authority*, where the plaintiff was employed by the defendants as a part-time ophthalmologist. The plaintiff quarrelled with the consultant in charge of the clinic, and he was thus dismissed, although the defendants failed to operate the disputes procedure laid down in the Whitley Council Conditions of Service. The plaintiff was granted an injunction preventing the defendants from implementing the decision without invoking the disputes procedure. The court advanced three reasons. First, there was no lack of confidence in the plaintiff, for his professional competence was not in issue. Second, the plaintiff was seeking the protection of the disputes procedure which was incorporated into his contract. Third, damages would not be an adequate remedy. The balance of convenience lay in the granting of the injunction.

6.5 Whether the employee retains the confidence of the employer must be judged on the circumstances of the case, including the nature of the work, the people with whom the work is to be done, and the effect on the employer's operations if the injunction is granted. In *Powell v London Borough of Brent*, the plaintiff was told that she had been selected for promotion. It was then thought that the selection may have been in breach of the council's equal opportunity code, and her promotion was rescinded and the post re-advertised. The plaintiff brought an action for an injunction to restrain the council from treating her other than as being promoted. By the time the case came to court, she was able to show that she had worked in the senior post without any complaints about her work and there were no problems in her working relationships. It was held that the injunction would be granted. A bare assertion by her employers that there was a lack of confidence was not sufficient.

6.5A The normal remedy in such cases is for the employee who is being threatened with dismissal to seek an interlocutory injunction restraining the proposed dismissal until the trial of action. The court must then consider whether the balance of convenience requires such a course of action (see *American Cyanamid Co v Ethicon Ltd*), leaving the substantial merits of the case to be argued subsequently at a full hearing. However, in *Jones v Gwent County Council*, the court held that under the new Order 14A of the Rules of the Supreme Court a judge can give a final ruling on any question of law or construction of document without a full trial of action, and such ruling can finally determine the matter, subject to an appeal. In this case, the plaintiff had been subjected to two disciplinary hearings which ended in her favour. Nonetheless the council brought further disciplinary proceedings on the ground that her return to work would cause an irrevocable breakdown in relationships between management and staff. It was decided that she should be dismissed. It was held that a declaration could be made that her dismissal was not valid, and a permanent injunction was granted, restraining the council from dismissing her other than in accordance with the proper procedure as laid down in her terms of appointment, and unless proper grounds existed.

6.6 TULR(C)A s. 236 provides that no court shall compel an employee to work or attend at a place of work through the making of an order for specific performance, or an injunction. Thus an order cannot be granted, for example, to call off a strike.

Implied duties of the employer

6.7 We have seen (in Chapter 3) that there are a number of different ways by which the terms of a contract of employment may come into existence. We must now consider a number of duties and obligations which are imposed by law on both parties during the continuance of the performance of the contract. Some of these arise by virtue of the common law, but others arise out of the implications of legislative policy.

6.7A The distinction between those duties which are imposed by law and those which operate as an implied term of the contract is not at all clear. In more recent years, the courts have veered away from construing tortious liabilities in circumstances where contractual relationships exist. Prior to the massive explosion in employment law, which began about 30 years ago, there were few legal authorities on the contractual aspect of the employment relationship, and hence tort obligations emerged. More recently there is no dearth of legal authority arising from the contractual aspect, and rights have developed accordingly. The problem was explored by the House of Lords in *Scally v Southern Health and Social Services Board* (see para 3.17A). But since the implied term theory is no longer limited by the 'business efficacy' test, but can also be extended to include terms which can be implied as a necessary incident of a definable category of contractual relationship (see *Liverpool City Council v Irwin*), it is possible to see the employers' duties as arising out of implied terms of the contract, rather than obligations imposed by law. The obligations once identified thus become implied terms of the contract.

A. Implied duty of mutual respect

6.8 Now that the age when management could 'hire and fire' at will has gone, it is possible to assert that the employer has a legal duty to treat his employees with due respect and consideration, mindful of their needs and problems, sympathetic to their difficulties. It is no longer possible to treat an employee as an expendable chattel, or as an object without feelings and emotions. This duty is implicit in a number of cases which will be considered in due course when dismissal or disciplinary policies are discussed, but it is particularly evident where the employer is alleged to have been carrying out provocative conduct. In *Donovan v Invicta Airways Ltd* the employee resigned after what he considered to be a number of incidents where he thought the employer was being unfair, and claimed damages for breach of contract. In the circumstances it was held that such conduct, though irritating, was not substantial enough to amount to a breach, but it was stated that there was an implied duty that each of the parties to a contract of employment should treat the other with such a degree of consideration and courtesy as would enable the contract to be carried on.

6.9 However, if there is a breach of contract, damages are to be assessed on the basis of the actual loss suffered, and it is not permissible to make an award of general damages for frustration, mental distress, injured feelings or annoyance caused by the breach (*Bliss v South East Thames Regional Health Authority*).

6.10 This duty arises at the outset of the employment, and continues during its performance right up to its termination. Employers will have to examine very closely their personnel and recruitment policies, for a mistake in selection or a failure to handle a problem in a proper manner could lead to an expensive action being brought in the future. For if an employer selects someone for a particular job, and that person does not have the necessary experience or capability for doing it, it is likely that the employer must accept some of the blame (*Bradley v Opperman Gears Ltd*). As a result, many employers are now commencing employees on the basis of a probationary period in order to assess properly their capabilities. The employer also has an obligation to ensure that the employee is provided with an adequate job description, with objectives clearly mapped out, is provided with adequate facilities and support staff, and is properly trained and supervised where necessary. A failure by the employer to attend to these and allied matters may well mean that any shortcomings on the employee's part may not be entirely his own fault, and it could well be unfair to dismiss him in these circumstances (*Burrows v Ace Caravan Co (Hull) Ltd*).

B. Duty to provide work

6.11 The whole question of 'the right to work' is a confused one, principally because of the different meanings which may be given to the phrase. It may mean the right to work without a trade union membership card, as in *Hill v Parsons*, or the right not to be unreasonably discriminated against, as in *Nagle v Feilden*, where the plaintiff argued that she had a right to obtain a licence to train horses despite the existence of an unwritten rule of the Jockey Club not to grant such licences to women. It can even mean the right to call on the State to provide jobs. In *Langston v Chrysler United Kingdom* the plaintiff objected to being compelled to join a trade union. The other employees threatened a strike, and so Chrysler suspended him. In the Court of Appeal it was suggested that the courts would protect a man's right to work in appropriate circumstances, particularly if he was being denied job satisfaction. However, when the case was remitted to the National Industrial Relations Court, it was held that such documents as the Universal Declaration of Human Rights, paragraph 9 of the Code of Practice, and other poetic allusions were considerations of public policy, rather than statements of contractual rights, and it was the contract which is the determining factor.

6.12 As a general rule, the employer is not under an obligation to provide work for his employee. As Asquith J said in *Collier v Sunday Referee Publishing Co*, 'Provided I pay my cook her wages regularly, she cannot complain if I choose to take any or all of my meals out'. Indeed, there are many circumstances when the employer may find himself unable to provide work for his employees, for example, as a result of reorganisation, shortage of materials, lack of orders, due to a strike, etc, where the employer may prefer to keep his workforce together and pay them for doing nothing. However, there are certain special circumstances where the failure to provide work may result in the breach of a legal duty.

a. If the failure to provide work can lead to a loss of reputation or publicity. In *Herbert Clayton & Jack Waller Ltd v Oliver*, an actor was given a leading role in a musical comedy. He was subsequently offered a lesser role, but at the same salary. It was held that the employer was in breach of contract, because the nature of the work was as important as the salary to be paid.
b. If the failure to provide work leads to a reduction in the employee's actual or potential earnings. Thus an employee

is entitled to be given an opportunity to earn his commission (*Turner v Goldsmith*) or to earn a reasonable sum if he is on piecework (*Devonald v Rosser & Sons*). In *Baumann v Hulton Press* it was held that the employers 'were bound to give the plaintiff a reasonable amount of work to enable him to earn that which the parties must be taken to have contemplated'. It was the lack of opportunity to earn premium payments for hours worked on night-shift and overtime which constituted the breach of contract by the employers in *Langston's* case (above).

c. There are dicta in *Langston's* case which suggest that if an employee needs practice in order to maintain or develop his skills in employment, the employer is under a duty to provide a reasonable amount of work for this purpose. This view has received further support from the 'garden leave' cases (see *Provident Financial Group v Hayward*, para 11.8D).
d. Recent decisions seem to lean to the view that a failure to provide work may constitute a repudiation of the contract by the employer if it is possible to imply a term into the contract that the employer shall provide suitable work. This appears to be particularly true when the employee is appointed to a specific office. In *Breach v Epsylon Industries Ltd*, the EAT thought that some of the earlier decisions on this subject were somewhat out of date and perhaps old fashioned in their approach. Consequently, in modern cases there may be facts which more readily lead to the conclusion that there is an implied term to the effect that there is an obligation to provide work.
e. If the contract of employment provides for suspension with pay pending the outcome of disciplinary enquiries, or criminal proceedings, there is no obligation on the employer to provide the employee with work or an opportunity to work overtime (*McLory v Post Office*).

C. Duty to pay wages or other remuneration when there is no work

6.13 The express terms of the contract will normally determine the amount of remuneration to be paid to the employee, but we must consider the situation where, because there is no work to do, the employee cannot earn his money. The question is, to what extent, if at all, does the employer undertake to pay the employee wages if the employer cannot provide work for the employee to do? To seek the answer, we must state the general rule, and then seek any modification which may exist by virtue of any express or implied terms of the contract of employment.

6.14 The general rule at common law is that an employer must pay the wages of all employees if they are available for work but none is provided by the employer. Clearly, this is the position in respect of salaried staff (who are paid weekly or monthly see *Miller v Hamworthy Engineering Ltd*, para 3.53), and there is no legal distinction between them and hourly-paid workers or piece-workers. An hourly-paid worker is entitled to be paid for the number of hours he makes himself available for work, not the number of hours the employers permit him to work, and a piece-worker, though paid for the work actually done, is entitled to expect that the employer will give him an opportunity to earn his wages. Because of this general common law rule, it was a comparatively simple matter to imply into the contract of an employee a term that he would be paid if there was no work. In *Devonald v Rosser & Sons* the plaintiff was a piece-worker. His employers closed down the factory, and gave him one month's notice. It was held that there was an implied term in his contract that the employer would find him work to do, and he recovered damages based on his prior average earnings. An argument by the employers that there was a trade custom to the contrary was rejected by the court, because a custom has to be reasonable, certain and notorious. But if the failure to provide work was due to circumstances outside the control of the employer, different considerations could apply. In *Browning v Crumlin Valley Collieries* a colliery had to close down because it was in a dangerous condition, through no fault of the employers. It was held that there was an implied term that the employers were not obliged to pay wages in these circumstances.

6.15 The common law rule, however, can be varied by an express or implied term to the contrary. Thus if the contract states that there shall be no payment during a lay-off or in respect of short-time working, the employers will incur no obligation to pay. In *Hulme v Ferranti Ltd* the plaintiff was employed on terms that if there was no work, he would not be paid. He was laid off as a result of a strike involving other workers in the plant, and it was held that he was not entitled to be paid during that time. But the modern practice of concluding guarantee payment agreements lends greater credence to the view that the present law is that in respect of hourly or piece-workers, there is an implied term that they will not be paid during a lay-off or short-time working. For example, if an employer agrees to pay a minimum guarantee week to employees who have been employed by him for a certain period, those who do not qualify can scarcely be in a better position. The very existence of the guarantee payments rights in the Employment Protection (Consolidation) Act 1978 (see Chapter 5) supports this view, for such rights would virtually be unnecessary if the common law rule was of general application. Nonetheless, a lay-off without pay is either a temporary suspension or a dismissal with the prospect of re-engagement, and the employer may only treat it as a suspension if there is an expressed or implied term in the contract giving him that right (*Jewell v Neptune Concrete*). In the absence of such a term the employee is entitled to treat the suspension as repudiatory conduct by the employer, and hence a dismissal. In appropriate circumstances (see Chapter 10) he may claim redundancy pay. Indeed, since there must be few contracts of employment which made provision for such eventuality, the Redundancy Payments Act 1965 was apparently based on the assumption that there is a general existence of an implied term that employees who are laid off or who are on short time are not entitled to be paid (see now EPCA s. 87).

6.16 If an employer inadvertently overpays the employee, this is a mistake of fact, not law. Consequently, the employer can recover the amount overpaid. However, the employer will be estopped from claiming restitution if:

a. he made a representation of fact which led the employee to believe that he was entitled to treat the money overpaid as his own;
b. the employee, bona fide and without notice of the mistake, consequently changed his position (e.g. by spending the money);
c. the overpayment was not caused by the fault of the employee (*Avon County Council v Howlett*). However, if it would be inequitable to allow an employee to plead estoppel, the court would refuse to permit the plea.

6.17 It will be recalled that over-payments of wages can be recovered without an employer being in breach of the Wages Act 1986 (see para 5.136).

D. Duty of confidentiality

6.17A Just as there is a duty on employees not to disclose confidential information about the employer's business (see para 11.2) so there is a similar duty on an employer not to disclose to third persons confidential information about the employee. This duty does not depend on any express or implied term of the contract (*Lord Advocate v Scotsman Publications Ltd* per Lord Couldsfield). In *Dalgleish v Lothian and Borders Police Board*, the employers held the names and addresses of all their employees. They were asked to provide this information to a local authority, for the purpose of discovering the identity of persons who had not paid the poll tax. The plaintiffs sought an interim injunction restraining the employers from disclosing this information, which was granted. The information was not in the public domain, and was given by the employees to the employers for the purpose of the employment relationship, and for no other purpose. Hence it retained a characteristic of being confidential information, which could not be disclosed without the consent of the employees.

E. Duty to indemnify

6.18 Any expenses reasonably incurred by the employee in the performance of his contract ought properly to be met by the employer. Normally, one would expect express agreement to this effect, for example, travelling or lodging allowances, but circumstances do arise when an employee spends his own money in pursuance of his employer's business, and it is submitted that he is entitled to be reimbursed. More difficult is the situation which arises when the employee commits a wrongful act. If this was done for the employer's business, and was authorised, or if the employee was acting under his employer's orders, then the employee is entitled to be indemnified for any personal loss he suffers.

6.19 For example, if an employer requires an employee to take out the firm's van, which has a defective tyre, and the employee is consequently fined, then it is reasonable to expect the employer to reimburse the amount, even though he may be prosecuted in addition. But if the work can be done in a lawful or unlawful manner, and the employee choose the latter option, the employer would not be required to reimburse such expenditure. For example, if the employee, in order to deliver some goods, parks illegally, then unless he was told to perform his work in this manner, he must bear any subsequent fine himself. In *Gregory v Ford*, the plaintiff was injured due to the negligent driving of the defendant, whose employer did not have a valid third-party insurance policy as required by the Road Traffic Act 1988. It was held that there was an implied term of the contract that the employer would not require the employee to do an unlawful act, and therefore the employer should indemnify the employee in respect of the damages which were awarded to the plaintiff. In *Re Famatina Development Corpn*, a consulting engineer employed by the company was asked to prepare to report on the conduct of the managing director. The latter brought an action for an alleged libel, which the engineer defended. It was held that he was entitled to be indemnified by the company for his costs in defending the action, for he had been requested by his directors to make the report, which was therefore in the course of his duties as an employee.

F. Duty to insure

6.19A In respect of work activities taking place within the United Kingdom, an employer is obliged to take out compulsory employers' liability insurance, for the benefit of his employees (Employers' Liability (Compulsory Insurance) Act 1969). However, an employer owes no duty in tort to any employee who is working abroad to take out appropriate insurance cover against special risks, or to advise the employee to take out his own cover. In *Reid v Rush & Tompkins Group*, the plaintiff worked for the defendants in Ethiopia. He received severe injuries in a road accident, which was the fault of the other driver, for whom the defendants were not responsible. The plaintiff was unable to obtain compensation from the other driver, as there is no third-party insurance in Ethiopia, and so he claimed damages from his employers. His statement of claim was struck out. An employer does not owe a duty to inform or advise on the potential danger of suffering economic loss in the form of uncompensated injuries.

G. References

6.20 An employer is under no legal duty to provide an employee or an ex-employee with a reference (*Gallear v Watson & Co Ltd*), and indeed, this may well prove to be a hazardous operation. A derogatory reference may expose him to an action for defamation. This may be defended on the grounds that the statement made was true, or, if untrue, it was made on an occasion when the law confers qualified privilege, and the statement was made without malice, in the sense of an improper motive. But the only action against a person who allegedly gives a false or misleading reference lies in the tort of defamation. There is no liability for negligent misstatement (*Spring v Guardian Assurance plc*). Thus if, as a result of an unsatisfactory reference being given, a person loses the prospect of employment, he cannot recover against the referee, if the reference was accurate, or if it was made honestly, and without any improper motive.

6.21 On the other hand, to give a commendatory reference about a prospective employee which is untrue, and which is relied upon by a subsequent employer to his detriment, may well lead to an action based on deceit or negligent misstatement, unless the reference is qualified by a disclaimer of responsibility (*Hedley Bryne & Co Ltd v Heller & Partners Ltd*).

6.22 A further problem associated with the provision of a reference can arise in dismissal cases. In *Castledine v Rothwell Engineering Ltd*, one of the reasons given by the employer for dismissing the firm's buyer was that he was incapable of performing his job adequately. The tribunal found this difficult to reconcile with the reference given by the employer, which stated that the employee 'had carried out his duties satisfactorily, often under difficult conditions'. Not surprisingly, the tribunal found that the employee had been unfairly dismissed! And in *Haspell v Rostron & Johnson Ltd* the respondents gave a reference which was laudatory of the applicant. It was held that they were estopped from relying on criticisms of her performance as a reason for her dismissal. Faced with these problems, a prudent employer may well prefer to refuse to give a reference in doubtful cases.

H. Duty to ensure employee's safety

6.23 Undoubtedly the most important aspect of the employer's duty which is implied by law is the duty to take reasonable care to ensure the safety of his employees. There are a number of common law rules which determine the extent of that duty, and in addition there are certain statutory provisions designed to ensure the employee's safety which, if broken or not observed by the employer, may lead to an action for damages by an injured employee based on a breach of statutory duties. Frequently, the two actions are run together, so that an employee may succeed for breach of the common law duty and/or a breach of the statutory duty, though, of course, only one set of damages will be awarded. The purpose of the common law rules is to compensate for injuries incurred as a result of the employer's negligence; the object of the statute will be accident prevention enforced by criminal penalties, but with a potential liability for compensation as well. But as Goddard LJ said in *Hutchinson v London and North Eastern Rly Co*, 'The real incentive for the observance by employers of their statutory duties ... is not their liability to substantial fines, but the possibility of heavy claims for damages'. The whole question of compensation for injuries at work was reviewed by the Royal Commission on Civil Liability (the Pearson Commission, see para 6.51), but no significant changes were recommended in its report.

6.24 The duty of the employer to take care is one aspect of the law of negligence which requires everyone to ensure that his activities do not cause injury or damage to another through an act of negligence. The standard of care which an employer must observe is, as Lord Oaksey pointed out in *Paris v Stepney Borough Council*, 'The care which an ordinary prudent employer would take in all the circumstances'. The employer does *not* guarantee that an employee will not be injured; he only undertakes to take reasonable care, and he will only be liable if there is some lack of care on his part in failing to prevent something which was reasonably foreseeable. The employee, on his part, must be prepared to look after himself, and not expect to be able to blame the employer for every incident which takes place. In *Vinnyey v Star Paper Mills*, the plaintiff was instructed by the foreman to clear and clean a floor area which had been made slippery by a viscous fluid. The foreman provided proper equipment and gave clear instructions. The plaintiff was injured when he slipped on the floor, and it was held that the employer was not liable, for there was no reasonably foreseeable risk in the performance of such a simple task. So too, in *Lazarus v Firestone Tyre and Rubber Co Ltd*, where the plaintiff was knocked down in the general rush to get to the canteen. The court held that this was not the sort of behaviour which grown persons could be protected against. Such cases are in line with a number of judicial statements made in recent years deprecating 'any tendency to treat the relationship between employer and skilled workman as equivalent to that of nurse and imbecile child' (per Lord Simmons in *Smith v Austin Lifts*), or that of 'schoolmaster and pupil' (per Devlin LJ in *Withers v Perry Chain*).

6.25 Equally, if an employer does not know of the danger, and could not be expected to know in the light of current knowledge, or did not foresee the danger and could not be expected to foresee it, he will not be liable. In *Down v Dudley, Coles Long Ltd* an employee was partially deafened by the noise from a cartridge-assisted hammer gun. At the then state of medical knowledge (i.e. in 1964), a reasonable employer would not have known of the potential danger of using this particular piece of equipment without providing safety precautions, and hence the employer was not liable for the injury. But once the danger is discovered, he must take all reasonable steps to protect his employees from the consequences of risks which have hitherto been unforeseeable. In *Wright and Cassidy v Dunlop Ltd*, the employers used an anti-oxidant known as Nonox S from 1940 onwards. The manufacturers then discovered that the substance was capable of causing bladder cancer, and informed the defendants that all employees who had been exposed to it should be screened and tested. This was not done for some time, and thus the employers, as well as the manufacturers, were held liable to the plaintiffs.

6.26 The matter was summarised by Swanwick J in *Stokes v GKN Ltd*.

a. The employer must take positive steps to ensure the safety of his employees in the light of the knowledge which he has or ought to have.
b. The employer is entitled to follow current recognised practice unless in the light of common sense or new knowledge this is clearly unsound.
c. Where there is developing knowledge, he must keep reasonably abreast with it, and not be too slow in applying it.
d. If he has greater than average knowledge of the risk, he must take more than average precautions.
e. He must weigh up the risk (in terms of the likelihood of injury and possible consequences) against the effectiveness of the precautions needed to meet the risk, and the cost and inconvenience.

6.27 Applying these tests, if the employer falls below the standards of a reasonable and prudent employer, he will be negligent. On the other hand, if the employer takes all such steps as are reasonably practicable, he will not be liable at common law (*Darby v GKN Screws and Fasteners Ltd*).

Duty to unborn children

6.28 Under the Congenital Disabilities (Civil Liability) Act 1976, an employer may be liable to a child of an employee who is born disabled as a result of any breach of legal duty, whether imposed by statute or by common law, to the child's parent. The child may thus sue in respect of a pre-natal injury suffered, whether or not the parent suffered any injury, and whether or not the employer knew of the existence of the foetus. The Act was intended to be a stop-gap measure until the passing of legislation consequent on the Pearson Report (para 6.51). The right of the child to sue is contingent on the existence of a right for the parent to sue; in other words, the claim is as good as, but no better than, the claim of the parent. Any contributory negligence on the part of the parent may reduce the child's damages.

Personal nature of the duty

6.29 The duty of the employer is a personal one, in the sense that he cannot absolve himself by delegating the duty to someone else. In *Wilsons and Clyde Coal Co v English*, the employer was compelled by law to employ a colliery agent who was responsible for mine safety; nonetheless, it was held that the employer was liable for an unsafe system of work in the mine. Thus it can never be a defence to argue that the employer has assigned the task of securing and maintaining safety precautions to a safety officer or other person.

6.30 Equally, the duty is owed to each employee as an individual, not to them all collectively. This means that one must take greater precautions when dealing, for example, with inexperienced employees, or with new and untrained employees or with young persons, etc, than one might do with more responsible staff. In *Paris v Stepney Borough Council* the plaintiff worked chipping away at rust and other superfluous rubbish which had accumulated underneath buses. Goggles were not provided for this work, for it was not customary to do so. The plaintiff only had one eye, and he was totally blinded when a splinter entered his good eye. It was held that the employers were liable. They should have foreseen that there was a risk of greater injury to the employee, and provided goggles for him, even though they may not have been under such a duty with respect to other employees.

6.31 Clearly, a higher standard of care must be shown to employees who lack a sufficient or adequate command of the English language, to ensure that they are properly trained and clearly instructed, so as not to cause injuries to themselves and to others. In *James v Hepworth & Grandage Ltd* the employers put up large notices informing employees that they should wear spats for their personal protection. Unknown to them, the plaintiff could not read, and when he was injured he claimed damages from his employers. His claim failed. He had observed other workmen wearing spats, and the court concluded that his failure to make enquiries meant that even if he had been informed about the notice, he would not have worn them. But with the growth of foreign labour in our factories, the problem is likely to cause growing concern, particularly as such labour tends to concentrate in the initial stages in those industries which have serious safety hazards. The responsibility of the safety officer, as the 'agent' of the employer, to ensure that the work can be done in safety is likely to be very onerous in practice (see *Hawkins v Ian Ross (Castings) Ltd*).

6.32 An employer has a duty to warn an employee of risks to his health and safety where those risks are not common knowledge and cannot be guarded against by the taking of sensible precautions, and where that knowledge would affect the employee's decision to accept the work. But the employer does not guarantee absolutely the safety of the employee. In *White v Holbrook Precision Castings Ltd* the plaintiff was employed as a grinder. He developed Reynaud's Disease (vibration white finger) and sued for damages. His claim was dismissed. The plaintiff knew of the risk when he accepted the employment, and the employers were merely aware that the disease could cause minor discomfort. No precautions had ever been suggested or were viable. The plaintiff would still have taken the employment had he been specifically told of the risk.

The three-fold nature of the duty

6.33 Although recent cases have stressed that there is only one single duty to take care, it is convenient to examine the nature of that duty under three sub-headings.

A. Safe plant and appliances

6.34 This means that all the equipment, tools, machinery, plant, etc, where the employee works shall be reasonably safe for work. In *Bradford v Robinson Rentals*, a driver was required to drive an unheated van on a 400-mile journey during a bitterly cold spell of weather. It was held that the employer was liable when the driver suffered frost-bite as a consequence. In *Close v Steel Co of Wales*, it was suggested by Lord Goddard that if an employer knows that a machine has a tendency to throw out flying parts so as to constitute a danger to the operative, this could well amount to common law negligence on the part of the employer if he fails to take reasonable precautions.

6.35 However, if an employer purchased tools or equipment from a reputable supplier, and has no knowledge of any defect in them, he will have performed his duty to take care, and will not be liable for negligence (see *Davie v New Merton Board Mills*). This would not be so if the equipment was bought second-hand from, say, a scrap yard. If a remedy existed in *Davie's* case, it would be for the injured employee to sue the person responsible for the defect under the general law of negligence as propounded in the leading case of *Donoghue v Stevenson*, but frequently this might prove to be difficult or impossible in practice. The employee might not be in a position to prove just who was negligent. It might be a firm of stevedores at the docks, a foreign manufacturer, and so on. In view of these problems, the law was changed with the passing of the Employers' Liability (Defective Equipment) Act 1969. This provides that if an employee suffers a personal injury in the course of his employment in consequence of a defect in equipment provided by his employers for the purpose of the employers' business, and the defect is attributable to the fault of a third party, the injury shall be deemed to be attributable to the negligence of the employer. Thus, should facts similar to *Davie's* case arise again, the employee would be able to sue his employer for the 'deemed' negligence, and the employer, for his part, would be able to recover the amount of damages paid from the third party whose fault it really was. At the same time, the Employers' Liability (Compulsory Insurance) Act 1969 was passed, to ensure that all employers had valid insurance cover to meet personal injuries claims from their employees.

6.36 If an employer is aware that there are defects in tools or equipment he has bought then he should withdraw them from circulation if he wishes to avoid liability. In T*aylor v Rover Car Co* a batch of chisels had been badly hardened by the manufacturers. One had, in fact, shattered, without causing any injury, but the batch was still in use when another chisel shattered, injuring the plaintiff in his eye. The employers were held liable.

B. Safe system of work

6.37 Here we must consider all the factors which concern the manner in which the work is to be done. The layout, the systems laid down, the training and supervision, the provision of warnings, protective clothing, special instructions, and so forth, are all relevant. In *Barcock v Brighton Corpn*, the plaintiff was employed at an electricity sub-station. A certain method of testing was in operation, which was unsafe, and in consequence the plaintiff was injured. The employers were held liable. But if the employer gives proper instructions which the employee fails to observe, the employer will not be liable for a subsequent injury. In *Charlton v Forrest Printing Ink Co Ltd* a senior employee was required to collect the firm's wages of £1,500 each Friday from the bank. Because, several years earlier, there had been a wage snatch of the firm's payroll, the managing director had given instructions that the collection arrangements should be varied each week, for example, by using taxis instead of private cars, by going at different times and by different routes. Contrary to these instructions, in the course of time, a collecting pattern set in, and the employee suffered severe injuries when he was robbed in an attack. In the High Court, the judge found for the plaintiff arguing that the employers had been negligent in not employing a professional security firm, but this decision was reversed on appeal. The vast majority of firms of that size in that area made their own payroll collection, and hence the employers could not be said to be negligent in carrying on with that practice. Although there was a risk, they had taken reasonable steps to minimise or eliminate it. The Court of Appeal thought that the plaintiff's remedy would be through an application to the Criminal Injuries Compensation Board, which has funds for such contingencies.

6.38 If there are safety precautions laid down, the employee must be told what they are; if safety equipment is provided, it must be available for use. In *Finch v Telegraph Construction and Maintenance Co* the plaintiff was employed as a grinder. Goggles had been provided, but he was not told where they were. The employers were held to be liable when he was injured by a flying piece of metal whilst doing his work.

6.39 But if the employer, though not providing the safety precautions, can show that even if he had provided them the employee would not have used them, he may escape liability. In *MacWilliam v Sir William Arroll Ltd*, a steel erector fell from a scaffolding and was killed. The employer had provided safety belts in the past, but these had not been used, and they had been taken away to be used on another site. It was held that even though the employer was negligent in not providing the safety belts, it was unlikely that the employee would have used them had they been available. Accordingly, the employer's negligence was not the cause of the death, since this would have occurred anyway.

6.40 The more dangerous the process, the greater the need for safety precautions. On the other hand, the employer cannot be expected to be held liable in respect of accidents which occur in simple situations, as *Vinnyey's* case (para 6.24 above) illustrates. A situation which gives rise to some legal difficulties is where the employer provides the safety precautions, but the employees fail or refuse to use them. Is the duty of the employer a merely passive one, to provide and do no more? Or is it an active one, to exhort, propagandise, instruct or even compel their use? It is submitted that the answer to these questions can be given in four propositions.

a. If the risk is an obvious one, and the injury resulting from the failure to use the precautions is not likely to be serious, then the employer's duty is a passive one of merely providing the precautions, informing the employees and leaving it to them to decide for themselves whether or not to use them. In *Qualcast (Wolverhampton) Ltd v Haynes*, an experienced workman was splashed by molten metal on his legs. Spats were available, but the employers did nothing to ensure that they were worn. The injury, though doubtless painful, was not of a serious nature, and the employers were held not liable.

b. If the risk is that of a serious injury, then the duty of the employer is a higher one of doing all he can to ensure that the workmen will use the safety precautions which are provided. In *Nolan v Dental Manufacturing Co* a toolsetter was injured when a chip flew off a grinding wheel. Because of the seriousness of the injury should such occur, it was held that the employer should have insisted that protective goggles were worn.

c. If the risk is an insidious one, or one the seriousness of which the employee would not readily appreciate, then again, it is the duty of the employer to do all he can by way of propaganda, constant reminders, exhortations, etc, to try to get the employees to use the precautions. In *Berry v Stone Manganese*, the plaintiff was working in an environment where the noise levels were dangerously high. Ear muffs had been provided, but no effort was made to ensure their use. It was held that as the workmen would not readily appreciate the dangers of injury to their hearing if they did not use the ear muffs, the employers were liable, as they had failed to take steps to impress on them the need to use the protective equipment.

d. When the employer has done all he can do, when he has not only provided the protection, but instructed on its use, advised on how to use it properly, pointed out the risks involved in a failure to use, and given constant reminders about its use, then he can do no more, and from that time he will be absolved from liability. Admittedly, this does not solve the problem, which is how to ensure that employees do their work safely. It is possible to make the use of safety equipment part of the contract of employment, or a provision in the works rules, and, it is submitted, a failure to observe these terms or instructions may, after due warning, enable the employer to fairly dismiss the employee. There appears to be no legal duty to do so in order to protect the employee from the physical consequences of his own folly.

C. Reasonably competent fellow employees

6.41 If an employer engages an incompetent person, whose actions injure another employee, the employer will be liable for failing to take reasonable care. In *Hudson v Ridge Manufactur-*

ing Co an employee who was known to be prone to committing practical jokes, carried one of his pranks too far, and injured a fellow employee. The employer was liable. The answer in these circumstances, is, after due warning, to dispense firmly with the services of such a person, for he is a menace to himself and to others. On the other hand, in *Coddington v International Harvester Co of Great Britain Ltd*, for a joke, an employee, M, kicked a tin of burning thinners close to X, and another employee, Y, was scorched by the flames, and in the agony of the moment, kicked the tin away so that it enveloped the plaintiff in flames, causing him severe injuries. It was held that the defendants were not liable. There was nothing in M's previous conduct which suggested that he might endanger others, and his act was completely outside the scope of his employment.

Defences to an action based on common law negligence

6.42 Since the duty of the employer is to take reasonable care, and not an absolute duty to prevent accidents, it follows that there are certain defences available.

A. Denial of negligence

6.43 The employer may deny that he failed to take reasonable care, or claim that he did all that a reasonable employer would have done in the circumstances. In *Latimer v AEC Ltd* a factory floor was made slippery owing to the interaction of water from an unprecedented rainfall with the oily surface of the floor. The management ordered sand and sawdust to be spread around, but there was not enough to cover the whole factory. The employee slipped on an untreated part and was injured. It was held that the employer had done all that a reasonable employer could have done, having regard to the nature of the risk. The only other alternative would have been to close down the factory, which would have been unreasonable in the circumstances. In *Brown v Rolls Royce Ltd* the plaintiff contracted dermatitis owing to the use of an industrial oil. The employers did not provide a barrier cream on the advice of their chief medical officer, who doubted its efficiency. It was again held that the employers were not liable, for they were entitled to rely on the skilled judgment of a competent adviser, and no more could be expected. Indeed, the medical officer had instituted his own preventative methods, as a result of which the incidence of dermatitis in the factory had decreased.

6.44 The duty of the non-specialist employer in these circumstances is somewhat different. After all, not every firm can be expected to employ their own medical officer. Nonetheless, they must pay attention to the current literature which is available to them, either through their employers' associations or other sources. In *Graham v CWS* the plaintiff worked in a furniture workshop where an electric sanding machine gave off a quantity of fine wood dust. This settled on his skin and caused dermatitis. No general precautions were taken against this, although the manager had received all the information which was commonly circulated in the trade. It was held that the employers had not been negligent. They did not know of the danger, nor ought they to have known. The had fulfilled their duty to take reasonable steps to keep their knowledge up to date.

B. The injury was the sole fault of the employee

6.45 If it can be shown that the accident or injury was solely due to the fault of the employee, the employer will not be liable. In *Jones v Lionite Specialities Ltd* a foreman was addicted to a chemical vapour from a tank. One weekend he was found dead, having fallen into the tank. The employers were not liable. In *Brophy v Bradfield* a lorry driver was found dead inside a boiler house, having been overcome by the fumes. He had no reason to be there, and his employers had no reason to suspect his presence. Again, the employers were not liable. And in *Horne v Lec Refrigerations*, a tool-setter had been trained to operate a machine, but was killed because of his failure to operate a safety drill. The employers were not liable, even though they were in breach of their statutory duty to ensure secure fencing.

6.46 It is sometimes inferred that this defence is one of *volenti non fit injuria*, i.e. that a person consents to the risk of being injured. But *volenti* rarely succeeds in employment cases. The fact that an employee knows that he runs the risk of being injured does not mean that he consents to that risk because of the employer's negligence (*Smith v Baker*). The payment of 'danger money' to specialised employees (e.g. stunt artistes) may indicate that there is a special risk which cannot be guarded against, and to that extent *volenti* may be raised; but even so, the real question to be asked is: was the employer negligent in the circumstances.

6.47 Moreover, the Unfair Contract Terms Act 1977 applies to those employment situations where the employer seeks to exclude his liability for injury to the employee by means of a prominently displayed notice or even a contract term. Section 2 of the Act states that a person cannot by reference to a contract term or to a notice exclude or restrict his liability for death or personal injury resulting from negligence. Thus an employer cannot escape his legal responsibility if he has been negligent.

C. Contributory negligence

6.48 This defence is based on the Law Reform (Contributory Negligence) Act 1945, which provides that if a person is injured, partly because of his own fault and partly due to the fault of another, damages shall be reduced to the extent the court thinks fit, having regard to the claimant's share in the responsibility for the damage. The defence is successfully raised in a number of cases. The employer will argue that even though he was negligent, so too was the injured employee, and a reduction in the amount of damages awarded will be the result. The actual percentage reduction made is scarcely based on scientific principles, and appeal courts may take a different view of the share of the blame to be apportioned.

Limitation of actions (Limitation Act 1980)

6.49 Any action in respect of negligence, nuisance or breach of statutory duty which has resulted in personal injury must be brought within three years from the date when the cause of action accrued, or from the date when the plaintiff had knowledge of the injury. 'Knowledge' in this connection, means when the injured person had knowledge that

a. the injury was significant
b. the injury was attributable wholly or partly to the act or omission which gave rise to the legal liability
c. the defendant was responsible
d. any other fact supporting the bringing of an action against the defendant.

A person's knowledge includes knowledge which he might reasonably be expected to acquire from facts which are observable by him, or from facts ascertainable by him with the help of medical or other expert advice which it is reasonable for him to seek. The Act does not apply in Scotland.

The Royal Commission on Civil Liability

6.50 For a number of years, voices have been raised against the whole system of tort liability, and in particular against the unfair manner in which it appears to operate. The function of the law seems to be directed to apportioning blame and awarding compensation, rather than in acting as a catalyst to eliminate fault, and the requirements of the rules of evidence have all been joined together to produce a system which has been castigated as being capricious in operation and unjust in its results. Two employees may be injured; the one who can point the finger of blame successfully at his employer will be compensated, the other may be unable to do so and will get nothing. But their needs are probably just the same. Because all employers are now obliged to have appropriate insurance cover, it may well be a matter of indifference to them whether or not they are legally liable, and indeed, it is not unknown for an employer to lean over backwards in order to make himself liable (see *Hilton v Thomas Burton (Rhodes) Ltd*).

6.51 In 1973 the Royal Commission on Civil Liability and Compensation for Personal Injuries (the Pearson Commission) was appointed, to consider 'to what extent, in what circumstances, and by what means compensation should be payable in respect of death or personal injuries (including ante-natal injuries) suffered by any person (a) in the course of employment ... having regard to the cost and other implications of the arrangements for the recovery of compensation, whether by way of compulsory insurance or otherwise'.

6.52 In its report, the Commission thought that the present system of compensating employees for injuries received at work was fundamentally sound, and no substantial changes were recommended. It concluded that the industrial injuries scheme constituted a substantial 'no fault system of liability', which could be extended and improved, but did not require radical alteration. The common law action for damages on tort liability could not be improved on a scale which warranted abolition and only minor changes were proposed.

Implied obligations of the employee

A. Duty of faithful service

6.53 Since the relationship between the employer and employee is one of trust and confidence the law implies into the contract of employment the term that every employee shall serve his employer faithfully. This is a fundamental obligation, and any serious or persistent course of conduct which is inconsistent with that obligation may well amount to a breach of contract. Examples which readily spring to mind include persistent lateness, incompetence, wilful neglect and theft of the employer's property. A strike, a go-slow, a work-to-rule, a sit-in, being contrary to the fundamental nature of the contract - which is to work in return for a reward - are also within this category, and an employee may be dismissed for them (see Chapter 8). The employee undertakes to perform his duties carefully and competently, with due regard for the interests of the employer. In *Secretary of State for Employment v ASLEF* (see para 6.42A) Roskill LJ thought that it was an implied term that each employee would not, in obeying lawful instructions, seek to carry them out in a manner which had the effect of disrupting the employer's business. Whether the 'implied term' theory can stand up to analysis is another matter; all members of the Court of Appeal were prepared to import some form of obligation of fidelity arising from the very nature of the contract of employment.

6.54 In *Sim v Rotherham Metropolitan Borough Council* (para 6.22) it was held that the contractual obligations of a person employed in a professional capacity were those defined by the nature of his profession and the obligations incumbent on those who follow that profession.

6.54A If an employee fails to perform part of his duties, but indicates that he is prepared to perform the remainder, the employer may make it clear that he is not prepared to accept such partial performance, and may lawfully refuse to pay the employee the whole of the remuneration due (*Wiluszynski v London Borough of Tower Hamlets*).

6.55 A wrongful act which does not necessarily benefit the employee may still be a breach of fidelity if it is harmful to the employer's business. In *Dalton v Burton's Gold Medal Biscuit*

Co Ltd the employee was dismissed for falsifying the clock-card of a fellow employee, and this was held to be a fair dismissal. A more difficult situation arises if there is a conflict between the duty of fidelity on the one hand, and an obligation the employee owes by virtue of his membership of a professional organisation on the other. It is submitted that there is an implied term that the employer will not require an employee to act in a manner contrary to professional ethics, and that this would override the duty to the employer.

B. Duty to obey lawful and reasonable orders

6.56 The employee undertakes to obey all lawful and reasonable orders. In *United Kingdom Atomic Energy Authority v Claydon*, the employee's contract required him to work anywhere in the United Kingdom. He refused to transfer to another base, and was dismissed. The order was clearly lawful and reasonable, for it was within the express terms of the contract. In *Pepper v Webb*, a gardener used some choice expletives accompanied by words which indicted that he had no intention of obeying this employer's instructions, and it was this refusal, rather than the language which accompanied it, which was held to be the breach of contract.

6.57 But if the employee can show that the order was unlawful, he need not obey it. In *Morrish v Henlys (Folkestone) Ltd* the employee refused to falsify some records, and was dismissed. It was held that he was entitled to refuse to obey an unlawful order, and the dismissal was unfair. Whether an order is unreasonable may well be a question of fact in each case. In *Walmsley v UDEC Refrigeration* the applicant was dismissed after refusing to work in Wexford in Eire on the grounds that it was a hotbed of IRA activity. He could not substantiate these allegations, and it was held that he had refused to obey a reasonable order. Had he been told to go to Belfast, a refusal may well have been justified, for this might involve a serious risk which was not contemplated at the time of the formation of the contract (*Wicks v Smethurst Ltd*). An employee need not obey an order which would expose him to the risk of danger to life or liberty (*Ottoman Bank v Chakarian*).

6.58 To determine whether or not an order is reasonable, principles of good industrial relations may be taken into account. Thus in *Payne v Spook Erection Ltd*, a foreman was instructed to compile a merit table each week, listing the performance of 25 employees, and to send warning letters to those whose name appeared at the bottom of the list. As he did not see all the employees each week, he refused to operate the system, as he thought that it would be based largely on guesswork. He was told that unless he operated the system he would be dismissed, but he refused to comply. An industrial tribunal, although they had little sympathy with the system, held the dismissal to be fair, but the decision was reversed by the EAT. In considering whether or not a decision of an industrial tribunal was perverse, matters of good industrial relations could be considered. The weekly merit rating system was clearly unfair, and to dismiss the foreman for refusing to operate an unreasonable order was also unfair.

6.59 Difficulty is frequently caused by loose contractual expressions relating to overtime. If this is stated to be voluntary, then the employee is entitled to refuse. If it is stated to be worked by arrangement, then again, it becomes a matter for negotiation. But if it is clear that some overtime is to be worked, and the negotiations are merely about the details, the refusal may well be unreasonable, particularly if this is designed to bring improper pressure to bear on the employer (*Pengilly v North Devon Farmers Ltd*). As we have seen (in Chapter 3) a refusal to accept a demotion or a change in contractual terms is not necessarily unreasonable, but refusal to obey instructions which are within the contract may be unreasonable. In *Connor v Halfords Ltd* the employee was obliged to 'obey all orders and instructions received from the directors'. He was dismissed because he refused to go on a training course, and the dismissal was held to be fair.

6.60 However, it does not follow that an employee who refuses to obey a lawful order may automatically be dismissed, any more than it can be said that an employee cannot be dismissed if he refuses to obey an order which is outside his contractual obligations, for the strict legal rights are only relevant in considering the 'lawfulness' of the dismissal, but not its fairness. Two recent tribunal decisions will illustrate this point. In *Wilson v IDR Construction Ltd* the applicant was contractually bound to move from site to site in accordance with management instructions. He was asked to move to a new site, but refused, as his wife was ill, and he was having difficulty with his car. Although his refusal to obey a lawful and reasonable order would have entitled the employers to dismiss him at common law, the tribunal held that this was not an invariable rule so far as unfair dismissal law was concerned. The employers should have given him a chance to explain his refusal, taken into account the genuineness of the reason, the fact that he had never refused to change sites before, and that his refusal related only to that one day. In the circumstances, the dismissal was held to be unfair. On the other hand, in *Robinson v Flitwick Frames Ltd* the applicant was dismissed following his refusal to work overtime, although he was not contractually bound to do so. All the other employees in his section worked the necessary overtime, and the applicant gave no satisfactory explanation for his refusal. The tribunal held that his dismissal was for 'some other substantial reason' and that the employers had acted reasonably in the circumstances, for it would have caused considerable problems if the applicant had to be employed on terms different from the other employees.

6.60A If the employees are not prepared to give an undertaking that they will desist from future disruptive conduct, an employer may suspend them from work until they do so, and the employees, though willing to work, will not be entitled to remuneration for the period of suspension (*British Telecommunications plc v Ticehurst*).

C. Duty to use skill and care

6.61 The employee undertakes to perform his work competently, using reasonable skill and care. This, of course, must be combined with the employer's duty to provide all necessary assistance, etc (see above), but if the employer has done all he can, then a dismissal for incompetence will usually be fair. Also, the employee undertakes to take proper care of the employer's property. In *Superlux v Plaidstead* the employee negligently allowed some of his employer's property to be stolen from a van, for which he was held responsible. More recently, however, a tribunal has held that an employee who negligently lost the company cat should receive some disciplinary action short of a dismissal! For a dismissal to be warranted, the act of negligence must be a serious one (*Comerford v Swel Foods Ltd*) or a series of minor acts of neglect (*Lowndes v Specialist Heavy Engineering Ltd*, para 8.108). It is an implied term of the contract of employment that an employee will exercise skill and care in the performance of his duties, and a breach of that term entitles the employer to claim damages in respect of the negligent performance of the contract. In *Janata Bank v Ahmed*, the employee worked as a bank manager. It was alleged that he had been negligent in the way he carried out his duties, and after his dismissal, the bank issued a writ claiming £34,640 damages. The Court of Appeal upheld the claim. He had failed to exercise proper skill and care, as implied by his contract. It is irrelevant that the cause of action arises in contract or in tort (see *Lister v Romford Ice and Cold Storage Co Ltd*).

D. Secret bribes and commissions

6.62 The employee undertakes not to accept any secret bribes or commissions or gifts, or any reward in respect of his work other than from his employer. This rule applies even though the employee is in no way influenced by the favours he has received, for there is always the possibility that there will be a suspicion that his conduct has been influenced, or that it might be affected in the future. Tips, however, are a recognised method of being paid, and do not constitute a bribe which must be disclosed. An employee can only serve one employer, and it will inconsistent with his obligation of faithful service to accept anything from another person in respect of things done within the performance of his work. In *Boston Deep-Sea Fishing and Ice Co v Ansell* the defendant was a managing director of the plaintiff company. He placed orders for supplies with other companies, from whom he received a commission. It was held that his dismissal was justified. It is a violation of the duty of honest and faithful service for an employee to have an interest in a firm which is transacting business with his employer without disclosing that interest, and on discovering the facts, the employer is entitled to dismiss the employee summarily (*Horcal Ltd v Gatland*).

6.63 The rule is easy to state, but in practice it may be hard to apply, for there is no simple line between acts which are part of social or business intercourse and bribery. No one is going to quibble if a salesman offers a cigarette to the firm's buyer, or if two people go for a working lunch at a modest cafeteria. A hundred cigarettes or a slap-up lunch at an expensive restaurant may fall into a different category. Some firms may anticipate this problem by laying down the standards of conduct expected from those in a position of authority who may be affected by the rule. Employees may be warned not to accept gifts from suppliers, not to accept hospitality which might have a significant value, or to allow others to pay travel or hotel bills on their behalf.

E. Confidential information

6.64 The employee must not disclose any confidential information about the employer's business to an unauthorised person. Such information may be as to its profitability, new designs or models, mode of operation, or anything relating to the business. In *Foster v Scaffolding (GB) Ltd* the employee gave confidential information to a rival company which was to the disadvantage of the employer, and he was held to have been fairly dismissed. The obligations of an employee who leaves (or is about to leave) his employment will be considered in Chapter 11.

6.65 The rule will not apply if the employee is obliged by law to disclose information. For example, an employee is under a legal duty to give any necessary information to an inspector carrying out an examination or investigation under the Health and Safety at Work etc Act 1974 (see Chapter 12), and to produce any necessary books or documents.

F. Patents, inventions and copyright

6.66 The law relating to inventions made and patents taken out by employees has been altered drastically as a result of the Patents Act 1977, which came into force in 1978. According to s. 39, an invention made by an employee shall belong to the employer if (a) it was made during the employee's normal duties, or if such duties were specifically assigned to him and in either case the circumstances were such that an invention might reasonably be expected to result from those duties, or (b) because of the employee's particular responsibilities, he has a special obligation to further the interests of the employer's undertaking. Any other invention made by an employee shall belong to him, notwithstanding any term to the contrary in the contract of employment (see *Reiss Engineering Co Ltd v Harris*). Even if the invention belongs to the employer, the employee may apply to the Comptroller General of Patents (or Patents Court) for an award of compensation, which may be awarded if the patent is of outstanding benefit to the employer (having regard to the size and nature of the employer's undertaking) and it is just that compensation should be awarded. The amount of compensation should be a fair share of the benefit which the employer has derived, taking into account a number of factors, including (a) the nature of the employee's duties, his remuneration, etc, (b) the effort and skill provided by others, including any advice and assistance received from other employees, (c) the contribution made by the employer, whether by way of assisting in the manufacture, marketing, or other contribution.

6.67 If the invention belongs to the employee, he is free to dispose of it as he wishes. If he assigns his interest to his employer (whether by way of an assignment in the right to a patent, or a licensing arrangement, etc), then he is still entitled to apply for an award of statutory compensation, if he can show that the financial return he has received is inadequate in relation to the benefit derived from the patent by the employer, and it is just that compensation should be paid in addition to the benefit received from the relevant contractual arrangement between the parties. Such compensation will amount to a fair share of the benefit which the employer has derived from the assignment or licence, taking into account, *inter alia*: (a) any condition granted in respect of the licence or the patent, (b) the extent to which the invention was made jointly by the employee and any other person, and (c) the contribution made by the employer in the making, developing, manufacturing and marketing of the invention.

6.68 However, an award of compensation cannot be made if there is in force a relevant collective agreement which provides for payment of compensation for inventions made by employees. The collective agreement is only relevant if it is made by a trade union to which the employee belongs and by the employer, or an employers' association to which the employer belongs, which is in force at the time of the making of the invention. Nonunionists, therefore, may apply for compensation under the Act.

6.69 By the Copyright, Designs and Patents Act 1988, if the maker of a written work is employed under a contract of employment, the employer becomes the first owner of the copyright (s. 11). This rule extends to literary, dramatic, musical or artistic works, but it is subject to any agreement to the contrary. There are no provisions in this Act for employee compensation on the lines of the Patents Act 1977.

G. 'Moonlighting'

6.70 The employee is obliged not to act in any manner which is inconsistent with his duty of fidelity. In *Gibson v National Union of Dyers, Bleachers and Textile Workers* a full-time trade union official worked in a mill during his holidays. There was clearly a conflict of interests between his union position and his spare-time employment, and his dismissal was only held to be unfair because of the manner in which it was done. Indeed, the modern practice of 'moonlighting' whereby an employee undertakes spare-time work outside his employment hours can raise problems, particularly if the work is in competition with the employer's business. In *Gray v C & P Pembroke Ltd* the employee agreed not to be engaged in any other business without the written consent of his employer. Contrary to this agreement, he took a part-time job with a rival employer. As well as being in breach of an express term of his contract, it was also a breach of fidelity, and his dismissal was held to be fair. On the other hand in *Frame v McKean & Graham Ltd* the National Working Agreement for the Building Industry provided that no operative should undertake any jobbing work on his own account. This had never been enforced or referred to by the employer, and there was no mention of it in his contract of employment. The tribunal held that his dismissal for doing some work for a former customer of the firm was unfair, but the decision seems to rely heavily on the fact that the employer had, in the past, condoned his employees doing spare-time work, and even allowed them to purchase materials for this purpose.

6.71 In the absence of any contractual term, it appears that the employee may not work for a competitor in his spare time. In *Hivac v Park Royal Scientific Instruments Co* an injunction was granted against the competitor restraining him from employing the plaintiff's employees who were making valves for him in their spare time. On the other hand, an employee cannot be restrained from working in a different business in his spare time which does not compete with his employer's business, provided, of course, that this does not interfere with his normal work.

H. Duty of disclosure

6.72 An employee is under no duty to disclose facts which are inimical to the employer (except in response to a direct question), nor to disclose his own misconduct (*Bell v Lever Bros Ltd*). However, he is under a duty to disclose the misconduct of his subordinates even if, by doing so, he incriminates himself. In *Sybron Corpn v Rochem Ltd*, a man called Roques was the European manager for Gamblem Chemical Co (UK) Ltd. During his employment, payments were made on his behalf by the company into a pension scheme, and on his retirement he received a lump sum payment. It was then discovered that Roques, together with several subordinates, had been conspiring to set up in direct competition with Gamblem, and the company sought restitution of the pension payments, claiming that under the rules of the pension scheme, Roques could have been dismissed for gross misconduct, and the payments would not have been made. The Court of Appeal held that the company was entitled to have the money repaid. As a senior executive, Roques was under a duty to report the continuing misconduct of his subordinates, and for this breach of duty he could have been dismissed summarily. The money was therefore paid under a mistake of fact, since, had Gamblem known about the breach, they could have invoked the rules of the pension fund.

Employers' vicarious liability

6.73 If an employee commits a wrongful (i.e. tortious) act in the course of his employment which causes injury or damage to a third party, the employee will, of course, be personally liable. In addition, however, the employer may be vicariously liable to compensate that third party. Two reasons are usually adduced for this principle. The first is that the employer, having initiated or created the situation where the employee has been in a position to cause the harm, should properly bear the loss; the second is the more practical reason that the employee will usually be unable to meet any substantial claim for damages, whereas the employer will normally have the financial resources to do so, or, at least, will be insured against such contingencies.

6.74 There are also a number of exceptional circumstances where an employer will be liable for the tortious acts of his independent contractors; for example, if he authorises the wrongful act, or where he has a responsibility to take care which cannot be delegated by employing someone else to do the work, e.g. if there is a hazardous task to be undertaken (see *Holliday v*

National Telephone Co). It is also true that in recent years the courts appear to be gradually extending this principle of legal liability, and to that extent the distinction between an independent contractor and an employee (discussed in Chapter 2) is becoming possibly less important than before. But the general rule remains as stated.

6.75 The major problem is to determine which acts are committed by the employee 'in the course of his employment', and there are a number of marginal situations which cause difficulty (see *Irving v Post Office*, para 4.120). It is clear that if the employer expressly authorises the wrongful act, he will be liable. Equally the employer will be liable if he authorises the act, and the employee performs it in a wrongful manner, for this is the very essence of the legal principle under discussion. If the employer expressly forbids the act, he may still be vicariously liable if it can be shown that nonetheless the act was done in the scope of the employment, or for the purposes of the employer's business. In *Conway v George Wimpey Ltd* the employers issued instructions to their drivers that no person other than a fellow employee was permitted to ride as a passenger in their lorries. In breach of these instructions, a driver gave a lift to a non-employee, and the passenger was injured as a result of an accident. It was held that the employers were not liable, for the express prohibition had taken the act (of giving lifts) outside the scope of the employment. But in *Rose v Plenty* the employers had made it clear that children were not allowed to travel on milk floats. In breach of this instruction, a milkman engaged a young boy to help him deliver and collect milk bottles, and as a result of negligent driving the boy was injured. The Court of Appeal held that the employers were nonetheless liable vicariously. The Court distinguished cases like *Conway v George Wimpey Ltd* on the ground that in the latter case, employees who disregarded instructions by giving lifts to unauthorised persons were acting outside the scope of their employment, because what they did was not for the purpose of the employers' business. In *Rose v Plenty*, the act (of giving a lift to an unauthorised person), although prohibited, was done for the purpose of the employers' business and hence was within the scope of the employment.

6.76 If the employers permit the act, they cannot escape liability by prohibiting it from being done in a wrongful manner. In *Canadian Pacific Rly v Lockhart*, the employers issued instructions that staff should not drive uninsured cars while on company business. One of their employees disregarded this prohibition, and through negligent driving, injured the plaintiff. The employers were held to be vicariously liable. It was not the driving which was prohibited, and the prohibition merely limited the way in which the employee was to do his work. The same principle applies if the employee negligently performs his duties. In *Century Insurance Co Ltd v Northern Ireland Road Transport Board*, a driver of a petrol lorry, whilst transferring petrol from his lorry to an underground storage tank at a garage, struck a match in order to light a cigarette. He then threw the match on the floor, and an explosion ensued. It was held that the employers were liable. He was doing that which he was employed to do namely, deliver petrol, although he was negligent in the manner in which he was performing his work.

6.76A If employees are acting in a manner which clearly indicates that they are in breach of their contracts of employment, they cannot be said to be acting in the course of their employment. In *General Engineering Services v Kingston and St Andrew Corpn* firemen adopted a 'go slow' policy. They were called out to deal with a fire at the plaintiff's premises, but travelled there slowly, frequently stopping, with the result that the plaintiff's building and its contents were destroyed. Had they responded with normal speed, little damage would have resulted. The plaintiff's claim for damages failed. The firemen were acting in a wrongful manner, which was not authorised, and were not acting in the course of their employment.

6.77 The course of the employment can be extended to acts which are outside the employee's working hours, and need not be on the employers' premises, provided the act is done for the purpose of the employers' business. In *Ruddiman & Co v Smith* a clerk used a washroom provided by his employers after he had finished work, and left a tap running. His employers were held liable for the ensuing flooding of the adjoining premises, even though the employee had finished his work, for the wrongful act was consequential to that work. In *Poland v Parr,* while an employee was travelling home for his lunch, he saw a boy trying to steal some sugar from a lorry belonging to his employer. The employee struck him a blow which caused serious injury. The employer was held liable, for the employee was acting in what he believed to be the interests of his employer by protecting the employer's property, even if his methods were somewhat over-enthusiastic.

6.78 However, if an employee uses excessive zeal or violence, this may take the act outside the scope of his employment. In *Warren v Henley's Ltd* a garage attendant had a violent altercation with the plaintiff, who was a customer, and committed an assault on him. It was held such acts were no part of his duties as an employee, and the employer was not liable for what was, in fact, the pursuit of a personal vendetta. A case which illustrates the distinction between *Poland v Parr* and *Warren v Henley's Ltd* is *Daniels v Whetstone Entertainments Ltd*, where a steward at a dance hall assaulted the plaintiff. After being ordered to return to his duties, he committed a second assault on the plaintiff. The first assault was within the course of his employment, for he was doing work which he was employed to do, namely keep order at the dance hall, even though this method was unauthorised. The second assault was outside his employment, for it was in pursuance of his own personal grievance.

6.79 The fact that the employee is seeking to obtain a personal gain will not necessarily take his acts outside the course of his employment. In *Lloyd v Grace, Smith & Co* a managing clerk of a firm of solicitors induced the plaintiff, a client of the firm, to sign some documents, which transferred the plaintiff's properties to him. The firm was held liable, even though they stood to obtain no personal gain from the wrongful act. The clerk was merely performing the class of duties for which he was employed. This principle was taken further in *Morris v Martin & Sons Ltd* where the plaintiff took a fur to a furrier for cleaning. This was stolen by an employee whose duty it was to do the work, and the employers were held liable.

6.80 A more restrictive view was taken in *Heasmans v Clarity Cleaning Co Ltd*, where the defendants entered into a contract for the regular cleaning of the plaintiff's telephones. The defendants employed an employee to do this work, and the employee, while on the plaintiff's premises, made £1,400 worth of overseas telephone calls. The Court of Appeal held that the defendants were not liable. The fact that the employee had an opportunity to commit a crime or a tort was not sufficient. For the employer to be vicariously liable there had to be some nexus other than mere opportunity established between the wrongful act and the circumstances of the employment.

6.81 On the other hand, an employer will not be liable for an incident which does not arise from the employment, and is not for his benefit. In *Hilton v Thomas Burton (Rhodes) Ltd* a gang of demolition workers were driven in the firm's van to the site. After working for a short time, they made several journeys to a public house, which was some miles away. The plaintiff's husband was killed due to the negligent driving of the van driver, as they were returning from the pub. Despite valiant efforts by the employer to make himself liable, the court could not accept that the men, while driving to and from the pub, were acting in the course of their employment. Older cases have established that if an employee makes a detour, it is a question of degree whether or not he is still acting in the course of his employment, or acting 'on a frolic of his own'. And even more difficult are those cases where, having made a detour, the employee purports to resume his employment duties.

6.81A If an employee is travelling to or from work, whether or not he is acting in the course of his employment at the material time will depend on whether he was going about his employer's business. A distinction must be drawn between travelling to work, and being on duty while travelling to work. In *Smith v Stages and Darlington Insulations Co Ltd*, Lord Lowry laid down a number of propositions which would generally apply to hourly paid workers, though not necessarily to salaried employees. The reality in these cases is that they are usually fought between two insurance companies, one holding the employers' liability policy, the other holding the third party motor insurance policy.

6.82 It is also possible for an employer to be held liable under criminal law for an act committed by his employee. The main relevance of this rule today lies in the numerous statutory duties which create absolute offences, and thus the act of the employee is regarded as being the act of the employer. Each statute must be construed with reference to its objects, for there may be certain defences available in appropriate cases. Thus in *Portsea Island Mutual Co-op v Leyland* the appellants employed a milk roundsman who, contrary to instructions, took a ten-year-old boy with him to assist him delivering milk and collecting empties. A conviction for employing the boy contrary to a local bye-law was quashed. Neither the employer nor his agent (e.g. a personnel manager) had taken on the boy, and as the milkman had no authority to take on staff, the employer had committed no offence.

CHAPTER 7

Disciplinary powers of management

7.1 During the performance of the employment contract the employer may find it necessary, through his appropriate manager, foreman, supervisor or committee charged with the necessary responsibility, to exercise some form of disciplinary authority over the employee, which may take one of a number of forms. It will be recalled (Chapter 3) that the employer must give a note to each employee specifying any disciplinary rules which are applicable to him (or referring him to a reasonably accessible document which contains those rules) and any appeal procedure.

7.2 Further guidance can be found in the Code of Practice on Disciplinary Practices and Procedures in Employment and in the ACAS Advisory Handbook (set out at Appendix G), which should be studied in detail by all levels of management. Basically, we are concerned with the procedures required for the exercise of disciplinary powers, the matters which will give rise to those procedures being implemented, and the exercise of the actual disciplinary powers.

A. Disciplinary procedures

7.3 The responsibility for drawing up a disciplinary procedure is on the employer. Clearly, if he can obtain the co-operation and assistance of any relevant trade union, or of his employees, so much the better, but in the absence of such co-operation, the employer must draw up a procedure. The advantages of having trade union involvement either in the drawing up stages or having the unions accepting the procedures which have been laid down, are numerous. For example, in *East Hertfordshire District Council v Boyton*, the applicant was dismissed for fighting in the street with another employee. He appealed through the internal machinery, which had been accepted by all the unions in the industry. The procedure permitted either side to call witnesses and have them cross-examined, but none was called at the appeal hearing, and the dismissal was confirmed. The industrial tribunal thought that the appeal committee should, on its own volition, have called as witnesses the other employee involved in the fight as well as other employees who witnessed the incident. On appeal, the EAT held that the employer, by acting in accordance with the disciplinary machinery which had been drawn up with the approval of the unions could not be said to have act unreasonably. It was not for the industrial tribunals to re-write that machinery.

7.3A There is a distinction between disciplinary proceedings which are brought for misconduct, and those which are used in cases of capability, and indeed, the two things should ideally be dealt with under different procedures altogether. It has been held that misconduct procedures should be strictly construed, and hence pursued with all due formality, whereas the same strictness is not essential if the matter concerns the capability of the employee (*Littlewoods Organisation Ltd v Egenti*). Indeed, disciplinary procedures should only be used for matters which are truly issues of discipline.

7.4 On the other hand, the absence of a disciplinary procedure (except in very small establishments, see *McKellar v Bolton*), or the existence of an unfair procedure, makes it very difficult for an employer to argue that he has acted fairly. This also applies to the unfair operation of a fair procedure, unless it can be shown nonetheless that the employer acted reasonably in the circumstances (*Earl v Slater & Wheeler (Airlyne) Ltd*). For example, in *Pritchett and Dyjasek v J McIntyre Ltd*, the employers received confidential information which implicated the appellants in a series of thefts. It was not possible to disclose to the employees the source of the information, and so they were dismissed without being given a chance to say anything in their defence. In the special circumstances of the case, the dismissals were held to be fair. The employers had acted on a genuine belief that the employees were guilty of theft, that belief was held on reasonable grounds, and there had been a full investigation into the whole matter. Had the employees been invited to comment on the allegations, there would have been merely a series of general denials. Thus a disciplinary hearing would have been a meaningless formality.

7.5 If the employer did not follow a fair procedure, it was long thought that the industrial tribunal could engage in a hypothetical exercise and ask themselves whether, if a fair procedure had been followed, the employee would have been fairly dismissed. If this was so, it was argued, then the unfair procedure did not make any difference to the end result (*British Labour Pump Ltd v Byrne*). However, the House of Lords have recently confirmed that this view is incorrect. Whether or not a dismissal is fair is to be judged by what the employer did, not on what he might have done. In *Polkey v A E Dayton Services Ltd*, the appellant was one of four van drivers. It was decided to reorganise the work, and the four van drivers were to be replaced by two van salesmen and one representative. Only one of the four drivers was considered suitable for the new reorganised system, and hence the other three were made redundant. The appellant was called into the manager's office and was told that he was being made redundant with immediate effect. An industrial tribunal held that there had been a complete disregard for the provisions of the Code of Practice in not consulting with or warning the appellant, but also held that had there been such consultation and warning, the result (i.e. the dismissal) would have been the same, and therefore the dismissal was fair. This finding was upheld by the EAT and the Court of Appeal, but the House of Lords reversed the decision, and remitted the case to another industrial tribunal. If an employer could reasonably conclude in the light of circumstances known to him at the time that consultation and/or warnings would be utterly useless, then he might well act reasonably even if he did not observe the provisions of the Code of Practice. But an industrial tribunal was not entitled to consider whether, if the employer had acted differently, he might have dismissed fairly. In other words, it is necessary to concentrate on what the employer did, not upon what he might have done. Thus, unless the employer has reasonable grounds for believing that consultation would be useless, the lack of a fair procedure will inevitably lead to a finding of unfair dismissal. The line of cases conveniently known as the *British Labour Pump* principle was consequently overruled.

7.6 However, it will still be necessary to look at the effect of the failure to follow a fair procedural for the purpose of assessing the amount of compensation to be awarded, for this is awarded on the basis of it being just and equitable to do so. Thus, if a dismissal is unfair because of a procedural defect, compensation may be reduced by a percentage, representing the chance that the employee would still have lost his employment (*Spink v Express Foods Group Ltd*).

7.7 A failure to follow the Code of Practice does not mean automatically that a dismissal will be unfair (*Lewis Shops Group v Wiggins*), but employers will ignore the Code at their peril. Further, if a disciplinary procedure is incorporated into the contract of employment, a failure to follow that procedure may constitute a breach of contract by the employer.

7.8 In some circumstances, an employee may be able to obtain an injunction to restrain the employer from taking disciplinary action in breach of the agreed procedure (see *Jones v Lee and Guilding*, para 3.48). Alternatively, an employee may be able to resign and claim that he was 'constructively dismissed' (see Chapter 8), although the employer would still be able to argue that the 'dismissal' was fair in the circumstances.

7.9 Further, the employee may also be entitled to bring a claim for damages at common law, based on the additional length of time he would have been employed had the procedure been followed (*Gunton v London Borough of Richmond upon Thames*).

7.10 If an employee is dismissed, but is given a right to make an appeal in accordance with the company's disciplinary procedure, what is his legal position up to the time the appeal is heard? There are two possibilities.

7.10A First, if he is dismissed (with or without notice) the dismissal takes effect from the effective date of termination, and the fact that an appeal is pending does not alter that date. In *J Sainsbury Ltd v Savage* the applicant was dismissed for gross misconduct. On the effective date of termination he did not have the requisite period of continuous employment (26 weeks, as the law then was), but by the time the appeal was heard, more than 28 weeks had elapsed since the commencement of his employment. It was held that he could not pursue a claim for unfair dismissal. Thus using domestic appeal machinery merely suspends the dismissal; if the appeal is rejected, the original decision is confirmed (*Natt v Hillingdon Area Health Authority*).

7.10B Second, if he is dismissed, and placed on full pay pending an internal appeal, there is a suspension which does not terminate the contract, and hence he is still an employee up to the time of the appeal hearing (*Duffy v Northampton Area Health Authority*). But if an employee is qualified to bring a claim for unfair dismissal, and delays in presenting it to an industrial tribunal because an internal appeal is pending so that he is outside the normal time limits, he would not normally be able to argue that it was not reasonably practicable to present his claim earlier, and is unlikely to be able to benefit from the escape clause (*Palmer v Southend-on-Sea Borough Council*).

7.10C On the other hand, if a person is dismissed, and then his appeal against dismissal is allowed, his period of employment is to be regarded as being continuous, for it is implicit in the contract that the period between the dismissal and appeal is one of suspension, and the result of the ultimate decision of the appeal process relates back to the date of the purported dismissal (*Howgate v Fane Acoustics*).

7.11 The composition of any disciplinary body will doubtless be determined by each employer in accordance with the size of the firm and the circumstances of each case. The procedure will lay down who can exercise authority, the extent of the authority, and the circumstances when it is exercised. For example, informal warnings may be given at a certain level by supervisors, formal warnings should be given in writing, and signed by someone who has power to issue and act on them, and so on. If an appeal may be made to a disciplinary board, its composition should be specified, with due regard to providing substitutes as appropriate. Once a fair procedure has been laid down, an employee must follow it through even though he has little confidence in it (*Murray v British Rail*), for it will form part of his conditions of employment.

7.12 The actual operation of the procedure should be flexible enough to deal with all the likely occurrences. Thus, in a serious case, it should be possible to by-pass the early stages of procedure and go right to the final stage; if an employee committed an act of serious neglect or gross misconduct, it would be idiotic if this had to be dealt with by an informal warning, on the ground that this is the first stage!

7.12A In *Clarke v Civil Aviation Authority*, the EAT gave some broad guidance on how disciplinary proceedings should be conducted. The purpose of the meeting should be explained, those present identified, representation should be arranged, the employee should be informed of the allegations being made, the evidence should be presented in statement form or through witnesses, the employee or his representative should be permitted to ask questions, the employee should be permitted to call witnesses, he or his representative will then explain or argue his case, both sides can then argue on the allegations and any possible consequences, including mitigation, and the employee will finally be asked if there is any further evidence or enquiry which will help his case. The decision will then be reduced to writing (whether or not an earlier oral decision has been given).

7.13 Particular care should be taken when it is proposed to take disciplinary action against shop stewards, and the Code of Practice recommends that it is advisable to discuss the circumstances of the case with a full-time official of the union concerned. However, being a shop steward is not a passport to disciplinary immunity (*Fowler v Cammell Laird Ltd*).

7.14 A disciplinary hearing must be conducted fairly. To achieve this, a number of rules should be observed.

a. The employee is entitled to know the nature of the charge against him, in sufficient detail to enable him to prepare his case (*Hutchins v British Railways Board*). It is no bad thing to put this in writing, particularly if the employee's command of English is weak, so that he can get someone else to explain to him the nature of the allegations he has to meet (*Sharma v West Yorkshire Passenger Transport Executive*). Witness statements should be shown to him (*Louies v Coventry Hood and Seating Co Ltd*) although it is acknowledged that there may be occasions when it is necessary to preserve anonymity (*Linfood Cash and Carry v Thomson*, see para 7.19A). But in *Fuller v Lloyds Bank* an employee of the respondents was in a public house on Christmas Eve, and received severe facial injuries from a glass which the applicant held in his hand. The employers took statements from a number of witnesses, but these were not disclosed to the applicant, as a matter of policy. Following a disciplinary hearing, he was dismissed, and claimed his dismissal was unfair. An industrial tribunal dismissed his claim, arguing that the applicant knew the nature of the allegations. An appeal to the EAT failed. The procedure adopted was not so defective as to make the overall result unfair.

b. An employee should always be given an opportunity to state his case (*Tesco v Hill*) no matter what the circumstances are. He is entitled to plead that he did not do the alleged act, or that he did not intend the construction which has been put on it, or that mitigating circumstances relating to his case should be taken into consideration (*Budgen v Thomas*, below). However, it is not essential that he should be present in person throughout the hearing, when all the evidence is being given, if his representative is there (*Pirelli General Cable Works v Murray*). There would have to be the most exceptional circumstances when a hearing would not produce any worthwhile information, and when the failure to provide for a hearing would not, by itself, render a dismissal unfair (*Pritchett and Dyjasek v J McIntyre Ltd*, para 7.4).

c. He should be permitted the right to have a trade union representative to speak on his behalf, or another employee who is willing to do so. A failure to permit representation as provided by the procedure may well render a dismissal unfair (*Rank Xerox v Goodchild*).

d. He should be informed of his right to appeal to a higher level of management, who have not previously been involved in the decision (*S C Brown Communications Ltd v Walker*), or to an independent arbitrator. If he fails or refuses to exercise that right, then he does not contribute to the unfair dismissal, nor does he fail to mitigate his loss (*William Muir (Bond9) Ltd v Lamb*).

7.14A If a disciplinary procedure has been incorporated into the employee's contract of employment, it must be strictly complied with, for, no matter how 'fair' has been the employee's treatment with regard to a hearing, a reasonable employer is expected to comply with the full requirements of the appeal machinery laid down (*Stoker v Lancashire County Council*). Thus, if the procedure is cumbersome, it must be followed unless the employee agrees to a variation. The proper way to proceed is to alter the procedure subsequently to avoid future problems, rather than to depart from it when a problem first presents itself.

7.15 If the initial procedure is flawed in some way a refusal by the employer to permit an employee to exercise the right of appeal to which he is contractually entitled will render a dismissal unfair (*West Midlands Co-operative Society v Tipton*). If an employer's decision to dismiss would be fair at the time when the appeal machinery is exhausted, that decision does not become unfair because further information comes to light after the appeal has been dismissed (*Greenall Whitley plc v Carr*).

7.15A Whether an appeal hearing should be a rehearing of all the evidence *de novo*, or a review of all the evidence with an opportunity to make further representations, is a matter of style. However, if there is a substantial unfairness at the original hearing, this is unlikely to be corrected on review, and the appeal should then be a rehearing, when the unfairness can be rectified (*Whitbread & Co plc v Mills* and *Sartor v P and O European Ferries (Felixstowe) Ltd*).

7.16 However, it is very important that internal appeals procedures operated by commercial concerns should not be cramped by legal requirements which impose impossible burdens on the way they conduct their affairs. In *Rowe v Radio Rentals* the applicant was alleged to have been guilty of gross misconduct, and was dismissed by the Area Manager. An appeal was made to the Regional Manager and at the hearing the Area Manager outlined the facts of the case and remained present throughout the hearing. It was held that the appeals procedure was perfectly fair, even though it may appear to have offended against the rules of natural justice. It was inevitable that those who take the original decision to dismiss must be in daily contract with their superiors who would be hearing the appeal. Rules about lack of contact cannot be applied in the majority of cases. The EAT quoted with approval Lord Denning in *Ward v Bradford Corpn*, 'We must not force these disciplinary bodies to become entrammelled in the nets of legal procedure. So long as they act fairly and justly, their decision should be supported'.

7.16A Attempts to treat disciplinary and investigatory hearings with the same standards of strict legal proceedings have been resisted in a number of cases (e.g. *Longley v National Union of Journalists*), and the courts have insisted that they will only interfere in the most exceptional circumstances. Thus in *Ali v London Borough of Southwark*, a local authority received allegations of mistreatment at an old persons' home, and set up an independent panel to investigate. The report of the panel contained detailed allegations of mistreatment by named members of staff, but the source of allegations was not disclosed, as the persons concerned had been promised confidentiality. The local authority then set up a disciplinary hearing, and the only evidence produced was the report. The plaintiff sought an injunction restraining the local authority from hearing the disciplinary charges without adducing evidence from witnesses to support the allegations, as required by the disciplinary procedure. The application was refused. A domestic tribunal would not be restrained unless it was acting improperly, or proposing to do so. The local authority could not substantiate the charges by direct evidence (indeed, they did not know the names of the witnesses who gave evidence before the panel of enquiry), but it was open to them to consider the report, and to weigh the evidence, along with all other matters. Further, although the report of the panel of enquiry was hearsay evidence which might not be admissible in a court of law, it was properly admissible before a domestic disciplinary hearing.

Investigations by the employer

7.17 There are certain limits to the extent an employer may properly make enquiries into an incident, particularly if the charge is a serious one, such as theft, for there may well be an improper interference with the processes of justice (*Tesco v Hill*). The important thing is that the employer does not have to prove that an offence took place, or even satisfy himself beyond all reasonable doubt that the employee committed the act in question. The function of the employer is to act reasonably in coming to a decision. Thus in *Ferodo Ltd v Barnes*, an employee was dismissed for vandalism. The industrial tribunal was not satisfied that the employee was guilty, and therefore held that the dismissal was unfair. This finding was reversed by the EAT. The question was not whether or not the industrial tribunal was satisfied that the employee was guilty, but whether they were satisfied that the employer had reasonable grounds for believing that the employee had committed the offence, and had acted reasonably in dismissing for that offence. The employer is not concerned to apply standards of proof which may be relevant in a criminal court. In *Docherty v Reddy*, the employee was dismissed for stealing 50p from the till. The employers took into account that they had suspected him of stealing similar sums on previous occasions, and it was held that they were entitled to have regard to their past suspicions. Clearly, a suspicion of previous theft is hardly evidence which would be admitted in a criminal court, but the issues are different. The employer is having to decide whether or not he wishes to retain the employee, not whether or not he was guilty of a particular offence. Thus the test is, what would a reasonable employer have done on the facts which he knew, taking into account the Code of Practice and current industrial relations practice (*Parkers Bakeries Ltd v Palmer*). The industrial tribunal must not act as a court of appeal, nor retry a case, and the fact that in subsequent criminal proceedings an employee is acquitted of a charge against him is irrelevant to the issue of whether or not the employer has acted reasonably (*Davies v GKN Birwelco (Uskside) Ltd*).

7.18 Evidence which is not admissible in criminal proceedings may fairly be considered by an employer in disciplinary proceedings (*Dhaliwal v British Airways Board)* and a confession which would be inadmissible in a criminal court is also properly admissible before a disciplinary board (*Morley's of Brixton Ltd v Minott*).

7.18A If an employee pleaded guilty to a criminal offence in a court of law, or has been found guilty by the court, it is reasonable for an employer to believe that the offence has been committed by the employee. Any other conclusion 'would be ridiculous' (*P v Nottinghamshire County Council*). The fact of conviction might well form an adequate basis for dismissal, although the nature of the offence would be a relevant factor. Thus to dismiss for a trivial offence would not be reasonable (*Secretary of State for Scotland v Campbell*).

7.19 The employer is not obliged to hold a full scale trial, but there must be a careful examination of all the relevant matters. An investigation should not be conducted with such haste that important evidence is overlooked (*Johnson Matthey Metals v Harding*), neither should it be delayed so long that issues become stale and hazy in the minds of witnesses (*Marley Homecare v Dutton*). There is no particular form of procedure to be adopted, as long as the employee is given a fair hearing (*Bentley Engineering Co v Mistry*). If it is necessary to consider disciplinary action in advance of criminal proceedings, it is still possible to discuss the matter without prejudicing a fair trial (*Harris (Ips-*

wich) Ltd v Harrison), and a decision may be made on the basis of known facts, even though the employee has been advised to remain silent. If the evidence produced is sufficiently indicative of guilt (in the absence of any explanation) the employer is entitled to take some action. If, however, there are doubts, fairness may require the employer to wait until the criminal proceedings have been concluded (*Harris and Shepherd v Courage (Eastern) Ltd*). The object in holding a full investigation is to confirm suspicions or clear up doubts as to whether or not a particular act of misconduct has occurred (see *British Home Stores v Burchell*). If an employee admits the offence, there is no need for a full investigation, unless some useful information could come to light (*Royal Society for the Protection of Birds v Croucher*).

7.19A When an allegation of an employee's misconduct has been made by an informant, a balance must be maintained between the need to protect the informant and respect his anonymity, and providing a fair hearing to the accused employee. In *Linfood Cash and Carry Ltd v Thomson*, the EAT laid down the following guidelines which could usefully be followed:

1. the information should be reduced into writing, although it may be necessary to 'doctor' the statement in order to prevent identification,
2. the statement should contain all the relevant facts, including dates, times, places, etc, the opportunity of the informant to observe clearly and with accuracy, circumstantial evidence, and whether the informant had any reason to fabricate the evidence, whether from a personal grudge or any other reason,
3. further investigation should then take place to confirm, corroborate or challenge the information,
4. tactful enquiries should be made about the background of the informant, and to find any other information which would add to or detract from the value of the information given,
5. if the informant is not prepared to attend the disciplinary hearing, a decision will have to be taken on whether to continue or not,
6. if it is decided to continue, the person responsible for conducting the hearing should interview the informant, and assess the weight to be given to the information,
7. the written statement of the informant should be made available to the employee and his representatives,

8. if there are matters to be put to the informant, the person conducting the hearing should adjourn to make further enquiries,
9. full and careful notes of the disciplinary hearing should be taken,
10. evidence from the investigation officer should be prepared in a written form.

7.20 A distinction must be drawn between the investigatory function and the disciplinary function. If the same person undertakes both, there is usually no problem, but when they are separate and distinct, there is an obligation to give an employee a hearing at both stages. In *Budgen v Thomas*, an employee was dismissed after she had signed a written confession that she had stolen a small sum of money. The matter had been investigated by the security officer, and on the basis of his report, which was sent to the company's head office, the decision to dismiss was taken. This was held to be unfair. She was an 18-year-old girl, diabetic, and subsequently claimed that she was confused at the time she signed the confession, and that it was not true. It could not be said that in view of her personal circumstances the management would have dismissed her had she been given the opportunity to present her case; the person who took the decision to dismiss should at least have given her a hearing.

7.21 A person who is a witness in disciplinary proceedings should not act as a judge in those proceedings, otherwise this could be regarded as a breach of the principles of natural justice. However, there may be occasions when the person who has to take the decision to dismiss is also the person who witnessed the incident, and while this can be acceptable (and indeed inevitable) it is preferable for this dual role to be avoided (*Moyes v Hylton Castle Working Mens' Social Club*).

7.21A In those cases where witnesses are not part of the employer's organisation, it is not necessary for the employer to carry out a quasi-judicial hearing, with a confrontation and cross-examination of those witnesses (*Ulsterbus Ltd v Henderson*).

7.22 A person who is involved in the investigatory stage should not, if possible, be involved in the appeal stage, as this would put him in a situation of being a judge in his own cause, and justice would not be done, as well as not appear to be done (*Byrne* *v BOC Ltd*). However, in the case of small employers, this counsel of perfection may not be possible.

7.23 At the end of the day, the employer must satisfy the threefold test laid down in *British Home Stores v Burchell*. First, the employer must show that he genuinely believes the employee to be guilty of the misconduct in question; second, he must have reasonable grounds upon which to establish that belief; third, he must have carried out such investigation into the matter as was reasonable in all the circumstances.

Precautionary suspension

7.23A If an employee is suspended as a precautionary measure, and not for disciplinary purposes, the position is somewhat different. In *Jones v British Rail Hovercraft Ltd* the employee was suspended from duty without pay pending the outcome of investigations and proceedings against him which were brought by the police. He claimed that this amounted to a dismissal, but this argument was rejected. The rule book, which was part of his employment conditions, mentioned the distinction between precautionary and punitive suspension, and it was reasonable for the employer to take precautionary steps to protect his interest and his property. That the suspension was without pay could be dealt with by making up his back pay if the proceedings ended in his favour.

7.23B The Code of Practice states that precautionary suspension pending investigation should be with full pay, and this is probably correct in the absence of any contrary term in the contract. This could give rise to difficulties if the investigation is outside the control of management, for this could possibly go on for weeks or months. It is submitted therefore that precautionary suspension should be with pay if there is to be an internal investigation, but this may not be the rule in the case of external investigations. If this were not so, then the only alternatives available to the employer would be to retain an employee on full pay, or to dismiss him, and it is submitted that suspension without pay may turn out to be a better practice in some cases. In *Conway v Matthew, Wright & Nephew*, the applicant was a nightwatchman, and he was charged by the police with maliciously causing damage to the company's property. The company investigated the matter, and dismissed him. Subsequently, all criminal charges against him were dropped. It was argued that the company should have suspended him pending the outcome of criminal proceedings, but it was held that there was no legal obligation to do so, as it could have been many months before such charges were disposed of. The employers were under no obligation to refrain from dismissing him until the guilty conduct was established beyond reasonable doubt in a criminal court.

7.23C If there is an express contractual right to suspend with or without pay pending an investigation, this is subject to an implied term that the imposition of the suspension and its continuance would be on reasonable grounds. In *McLory v Post Office* three postmen were involved in a fight with employees from another office, and they were arrested and charged by the police with various offences. The Post Office suspended them on full pay, but without any payment for overtime which they would otherwise have worked. After making various enquiries, they were permitted to return to work some seven months later, and subsequently were acquitted of all the criminal charges. They brought an action for a declaration that their suspension had been in breach of their contracts of employment and they also sought damages for loss of overtime pay which they would have earned but for the suspension.

It was held that there was no breach of the employment contract. There was no duty on an employer to give reasons for the suspension or to give the employee an opportunity to be heard before it was imposed. The court refused to import the rules of natural justice into what is essentially a contractual arrangement between employer and employee. There was an implied term that the employer would exercise the express contractual right to suspend and to continue to suspend, only on reasonable grounds. To hold otherwise would enable an employer to suspend indefinitely. On the facts of the case, the employer had acted reasonably, and that aspect of the claim was dismissed.

The court also dismissed the claim for loss of overtime pay. The employees could not show that they had a right to overtime pay, only an obligation to work overtime when required. There was no duty on the employer to provide overtime on a regular basis, and thus the loss of a chance to work extra hours could not constitute the basis of a legal claim.

7.23D There is no legal requirement to suspend an employee prior to the undertaking of a full investigation, and a failure to do so does not weaken an allegation of gross misconduct. As a general rule, it is unwise to draw any conclusion from the act of or absence of suspension (*East Berkshire Health Authority v Matadeen*).

B. Disciplinary rules

7.24 The actual rules which an employee is expected to observe can be found either in the disciplinary procedure itself, or in the works or staff rules (see Chapter 3) or even a combination of both. At one time it was customary to write them on a prominently displayed notice posted somewhere in the works, but this is not particularly satisfactory nowadays. The important thing is that they must be brought to the employee's attention, whether on an induction course, or in a specially prepared handbook or other suitable method. In *Pitts v Revertex* the employer posted a notice near the canteen on a notice board stating that any employee who absented himself without authority would be guilty of gross misconduct. The applicant was found to be absent, and was dismissed. It was held that if a rule was so important, posting a notice was not sufficient. It should have been communicated individually to each employee. The need to communicate the relevant rules to the employees concerned was stressed once again in *Brooks & Son v Skinner*, where the employers agreed with a trade union that employees who over-indulged themselves at a Christmas party so that they were unable to attend work would be instantly dismissed. This agreement was not communicated to the employees. The applicant was dismissed for failing to turn up for work on the nightshift after a Christmas party, and his dismissal was held to be unfair. He would not have realised that this conduct would attract instant dismissal, and his lack of knowledge of the rule meant that the employers had acted unreasonably.

7.25 The rules should be clear and readily understandable by all affected employers, and should not be confused with extraneous matters. In *Rigden-Murphy v Securior*, the applicant was dismissed after being seen to be breaking a company rule concerning the transfer of money from a bank to his vehicle. The rule in question was contained in a manual, which had 'Ten golden rules'. At the end, there was a statement that a failure to comply may lead to instant dismissal. Some of the 'rules' were in fact mere exhortations, such as 'Beware of complacency. Build up the habit of self-discipline'. Other rules had in the past been dealt with by a warning. It was held that the dismissal was unfair. The rules were somewhat ambiguous, in that they contained matters which were unconnected with discipline, and there was no clear line between those rules which attracted dismissal as a punishment, and those which were dealt with (if at all) with lesser severity.

7.26 Industrial tribunals have been most inconsistent in dealing with rules which contain automatic as opposed to discretionary sanctions. For example, in *Jones v London CWS* the staff code in a departmental store stated that an incorrect recording of a customer's purchase was a serious offence, 'and the employee *will be* summarily dismissed'. It was held that such a rule was too rigid, for it failed to distinguish between a genuine error and a calculated act. On the other, in *Lindsay v Fife Forge*, the works rules states that employees who left the premises without permission '*may be* subject to instant dismissal' and the industrial tribunal held that this did not amount to a clear and specific warning!

7.27 The problems caused by such sophistry can be illustrated by comparing *Dalton v Burton's Gold Medal Biscuits Ltd* and *Meridan Ltd v Gomersall*. In the former case, a man of 22 years' service was dismissed for a clocking offence, the works rules stating that such action 'will result in instant dismissal'. The National Industrial Relations Court held the dismissal to be fair. In the latter case, it was stated in the works rules that anyone guilty of a clocking offence 'will render themselves liable to instant dismissal'. The EAT upheld a tribunal decision that a dismissal was unfair, because the employee might take the view that to be caught once, even suspected of doing it previously, would not necessarily lead to an instant dismissal!

7.28 The question, in reality, is not the mandatory nature of the sanction, but whether the employer acts reasonably in imposing that sanction, or whether some other equally efficacious sanction could be imposed. It must be wrong to dismiss an employee for minor misconduct no matter how strongly worded is the rule, for the mandatory nature of a disciplinary rule does not exclude the jurisdiction of the industrial tribunal to decide whether or not the employer has acted reasonably *(Ladbroke Racing Ltd v Arnott)*. On the other hand, automatic penalties fail to permit an employer to take account of mitigating circumstances, the employee's record, general conduct and so forth. The employer should be able to tailor the punishment to the offence, and then to the offender. He should be consistent in his procedures, but can be flexible in his punishments. In *Elliott Bros Ltd v Colverd* the EAT resolved doubts by stating that there is no legal requirement that a rule must indicate that a breach would inevitably lead to a dismissal, and a rule book did not need to indicate a distinction between the possibility and inevitability of dismissal. However the rule is worded, the employer is entitled to look at all the circumstances.

7.29 An employer must be prepared to justify any alleged disparity of treatment between different employees. In *Hadjioannou v Coral Casinos Ltd* the applicant was dismissed for breaking a rule which forbade socialising with members or guests at a gambling club. He argued that in the past other employees had broken the rule and had not been dismissed. In upholding a decision of the industrial tribunal that the dismissal was fair, the EAT commented that action taken by the employers in previous cases was only relevant in three circumstances (a) to show that there may be certain categories of misconduct which may be overlooked (or at least not dealt with by the sanction of dismissal), (b) if it leads to the conclusion that the purported reason for the dismissal was not the real or genuine reason, and (c) to show that some lesser penalty would have been more appropriate. The EAT went on to comment that it was of the highest importance that flexibility should be retained, and employers should not be encouraged to think that there was a 'tariff' approach to industrial misconduct.

7.29A Disparity of treatment is acceptable if culpability is not the same. In *Securicor Ltd v Smith*, the applicant and another employee were security guards, collecting and delivering cash. The employers had strict rules about the way they did their work. Following an incident when the rules were breached, the employers held a disciplinary hearing, and both employees were dismissed. An appeal was made to the area manager, who affirmed the dismissals. Both employees then lodged a further appeal to a special panel set up by the company, and at this level it was decided that as the other employee was less blameworthy, he would not be dismissed, but the dismissal of the applicant was confirmed. An industrial tribunal held that his dismissal was unfair. They held that the original decision to dismiss both men was reasonable, but the final appeal body acted unreasonably in dismissing one employee but not the other on the ground that the other employee was less blameworthy. The decision was confirmed by the EAT. However, the Court of Appeal reversed the decision. The real question was whether the final appeal panel's decision was so unreasonable that no reasonable employer would have accepted it. Indeed, had the employers refused to accept the decision of the appeal panel not to dismiss the other employee, he would have had an unanswerable case for unfair dismissal in an industrial tribunal. The appeal panel, having thoroughly investigated the matter, had distinguished the culpability of the two employees, and their decision was not unreasonable.

7.30 Once an employer lays down a particular rule, a failure to enforce it consistently may weaken any subsequent attempt to do so. In *Frame v McKean*, the applicant was dismissed for doing work on his own account contrary to the Working Rules for the industry. His dismissal was held to be unfair. The rule had never been enforced in the past, and indeed, such conduct had been condoned. Moreover, he had not taken any work away from the employer, for the customer for whom he worked had severed the relationship with the employer.

7.31 Rules may be of a general nature, e.g. defining conduct which, by the generality of the law of employment, cannot be tolerated; they may be specific, defining the sort of conduct which *this* employer will not tolerate, and they may be special, dealing with instant circumstances which have not arisen hitherto.

A. General rules

7.32 These are rules which govern conduct which is such that by common consent, disciplinary sanctions will be imposed. Examples which readily spring to mind include theft of the employer's property, theft from fellow employees, serious neglect, wilful damage, dangerous practices, and so on. It is not generally advisable to list all the matters which come under the heading of gross misconduct, for this could mean that an employee would be safest from dismissal who committed an act which was so outrageous that no-one thought it would ever happen (*Gardiner v Newport County Borough Council*). In *Clarkson v Brown*, 'gross misconduct' was defined as being 'dishonesty, arson, violence, obscenity, neglect and insubordination'. It was held that this definition did not cover an employee who had been telling lies. Some firms make it clear that the definitions of gross misconduct contained in their rules are examples only, and any list of misdeeds is not intended to be exhaustive!

B. Specific rules

7.33 These rules cover the sort of misconduct which *this employer* will not tolerate under any circumstances. Thus each employer must judge for himself the standards which are to apply, based on his own circumstances. Thus fighting, swearing, lateness, absenteeism, drunkenness, trading, betting, and so forth, may all amount to industrial misconduct which, in the individual case, attracts disciplinary sanctions. Such rules must be fair and reasonable. In *Turner v Pleasurama*, the applicant was an inspector who was employed to observe gaming tables, to ensure that there was no dishonesty by croupiers. He was dismissed for 'neglect of duty' after a complaint that a croupier and a member of the public had been cheating under his nose. The allegation was denied by him, but after a full and proper investigation, the employer found against him. It was held that the dismissal was fair; the gaming world is a hard world, and even the smallest of mistakes could not be tolerated.

7.34 Provided such rules meet the standards of reasonableness, they can generally be enforced. In *Higham v International Stores*, the applicant was given to wearing sandals and clogs, and other casual clothes. He was told that he must comply with the company's requirement to wear proper shoes and socks, and to wear a tie and overall when serving customers. After failing to heed due warnings, he was dismissed for not complying with the rules. It was held that an employer is entitled to insist on a reasonable standard of dress. What was reasonable is always a question of fact, to be determined in each case by all the circumstances. Different standards apply in Bond Street and in Petticoat Lane. In this case, the shop had a middle class clientele in a conventional town, and the dismissal was thus fair.

C. Special rules

7.35 Since the rules cannot conceivably cover every possible situation, an employer must be free to lay down a rule specifically to deal with a matter which has not hitherto arisen. In

Spiller v Wallis Ltd a company rule stated that employees should not have deep emotional relationships with other members of the staff which might impair their marital status. This rule had been promulgated after an incident where the spouse of an employee had come on to the premises and created an unpleasant scene. The applicant was in fact having a love affair with a senior employee, and she refused to discontinue the relationship. Her dismissal was held to be fair. She was told of the rule, but choose not to comply.

7.36 Finally, the interpretation of the rules, and their reasonableness, is a matter for the industrial tribunal to determine. In *Palmer v Vauxhall Motors*, the applicant was dismissed for spending 15 minutes in the club bar after her lunch break. It was alleged that this constituted gross misconduct in accordance with the works rules. It was held that even though the rules were somewhat ambiguous, the industrial tribunal was entitled to find that the dismissal was fair. The EAT would only reverse that finding if it could be said that no person instructed in the relevant law could have come to that decision.

C. Disciplinary powers

7.37 The exercise of disciplinary powers is a corrective function, not punitive. The object is to improve an employee's performance, so that he can remain a valued and useful employee, not to give vent to management frustrations. The choice of the disciplinary sanction must therefore reflect this objective, and should, so far as is possible, be tailored to the individual case, bearing in mind the need to show some form of consistency in like cases. The Code of Practice should be borne in mind at all times.

Fines and deductions

7.38 It is possible to impose a fine or make a deduction for bad or negligent work, but the new principles laid down in the Wages Act 1986 (see para 5.127) must be observed. There must be a specific contractual power, and in respect of persons employed in retail employment the restrictions in s. 2 of the Act must be observed. Deductions or payments made in consequence of disciplinary proceedings held under a statutory provision are excluded from the Act (e.g. police and fire service).

7.39 The Act specifically states that the only remedy for a breach is by way of a complaint to an industrial tribunal under s. 5, but it is submitted that an unauthorised deduction or payment may still give rise to a complaint of constructive dismissal. Thus, in *Lethaby v Horsman Andrew & Knill Ltd* the employer made a deduction from the employee's wages to cover the loss of the firm's property. This was done in the absence of any contractual authority to make such a deduction, and the employee, who refused to agree to it, resigned. It was held that this constituted repudiatory conduct by the employer of the contract, and as such constituted a dismissal (see Chapter 8). It is submitted that this decision is unaffected by the Wages Act.

7.40 The employer's power to fine or make deductions must be contained in the express terms of the contract, and it is now no longer possible to rely on an implied term, or (more likely) a customary term to this effect. This makes a number of current employment practices of dubious validity. For example, some firms make a practice of deducting 15 minutes from the pay of an hourly worker when he is a few minutes late (known as quartering); it is doubtful if the unilateral imposition of such a practice would be upheld in law.

Suspension without pay for misconduct

7.41 If there is an express term in the contract which permits the employer to suspend an employee for a specific reason, such as misconduct, the courts will uphold such a term provided the suspension is carried out in strict conformity with the laid down procedure. Sometimes the grounds for suspension, and the procedure to be adopted, will be laid down in the works rules, and the extent to which those rules will form part of the individual contract of employment will be a question of fact in each case. Even so, if an employee is, or ought to be, aware of the practice of a firm, or if there is a custom in the trade or industry or locality, then he will be bound by it. In *Bird v British Celanese Ltd* an employee was suspended for two days in accordance with the firm's practice, and this was held to be a valid exercise of disciplinary power by the employer.

7.42 Alternatively, the grounds for suspension and procedure to be adopted may be contained in a collective agreement, in which case there may be an express or implied incorporation of those terms into the individual contract of employment. In *Tomlinson v LMS Railway* a trade union negotiated with the defendant company an agreement which, *inter alia*, laid down the procedure for dealing with breaches of discipline, and this was held to have been incorporated into an employee's contract of employment.

7.43 It is clear that the right of suspensory lay-off must be based on a contractual power, which will be either expressed, or implied, or based on custom and practice. The courts and tribunals are quite willing to discover such a power when minor disciplinary matters are concerned, though they appear to require strict proof if there is a major disciplinary matter which can lead to a dismissal. Recently, the EAT held that it may not be difficult to draw an inference that a contract contains an implied power to suspend as a disciplinary matter, or to enable an investigation to take place (*Pirie & Hunter v Crawford*). But in the total absence of such a power, it is clear that the employer may not purport to exercise it, for this would virtually enable him to assess unilaterally the damages for an employee's misconduct. It further follows that if an employee is wrongfully suspended without pay, he may recover any lost pay by way of damages. In *Hanley v Pease & Partners*, an employee was suspended for one day without pay, and it was held that he was entitled to the money which had been withheld.

7.44 If an employer lawfully suspends an employee, the legal position at common law appears to be that the employment has been temporarily put in abeyance, with a right for the employee to apply for reinstatement at the end of the suspension period (*Marshall v English Electric Co Ltd*). Presumably there is no break in continuity of employment in these circumstances. If the suspension is wrongful, the employee will be entitled to treat this breach as repudiatory conduct by the employer, and he will be entitled to resign and sue for wrongful or unfair dismissal. In *Davies v Anglo Great Lakes Corpn* an employee was suspended without pay after allowing his trade union membership to lapse, and this was held to be repudiatory conduct by the employer.

7.45-7.47 But if an employee decides to resign as a result of wrongful suspension he may find the tribunal somewhat unsympathetic, for he would have to argue that he was entitled to resign by reason of the employer's (wrongful) conduct, which the tribunal may not accept as a valid reason, particularly if the employer had reasonable cause to suspend, and the employee's conduct would otherwise have to be dealt with by a dismissal which would have been fair. It can hardly be right for an employer to be saddled with the burden of compensation if he exercises a lesser disciplinary power than he might have done. Another view which may be taken is that the employee's conduct was such that it 'contributed' to the repudiation by the employer, and hence reduced compensation may be awarded. Thus if the employee's conduct is such as to warrant a dismissal, but the employer suspends him without having the contractual power to do so, an action for unfair dismissal would probably fail because the constructive dismissal would be justified because of the misconduct, while an action for wrongful dismissal is unlikely to meet with any greater success. There have been a number of cases where the tribunals have held that an employee should not have been dismissed for misconduct, but the offence warranted some lesser disciplinary measure, such as suspension, even though the employer had no contractual right to do so. Thus in *Unkles v Milanda Bread Co Ltd* an employee was dismissed for smoking in breach of the company's rules. The tribunal thought that an appropriate penalty might have been a suspension for one month without pay, but there is no evidence in the report to suggest that the employer had the power to do this by virtue of the contract of employment. In seeking to encourage employers to exercise this lesser power, it would be inconsistent for the tribunals to penalise them for doing so.

Warnings

7.48 An employer does not need contractual power to issue warnings, but frequently this will be the subject of a disciplinary code or part of the works rules. These may state the procedural steps (for example, first oral warning, first written warning, final written warning), before further disciplinary action is taken. Strict adherence to these steps is necessary and a failure by the employer to observe them may lead to difficulties in unfair dismissal proceedings. Thus a failure to give a warning in writing as required by the agreed procedure resulted in a dismissal being held to be unfair in *Raymond v Sir Lindsay Parkinson Ltd.*

7.49 Nonetheless, the warning system must be operated sensibly, not merely as a form of mechanical procedure. It is possible to give an employee a final warning for a serious misdemeanour without having first to go through the processes of informal warning, first written warning, etc; equally, the fact that an employee has received a final warning does not mean that the next occasion on which he commits an 'offence' will be visited with an automatic sanction. Either course could lead to ludicrous results. There is no substitute for a full and fair investigation of all the facts. In *Newalls Insulation v Blakeman*, the applicant was dismissed for being absent on two occasions within fourteen days, following a final warning for absenteeism. Prior to this, he had had two verbal warnings. The EAT held that the industrial tribunal should look at all the circumstances of the case, and not simply whether it was reasonable to dismiss for two days' absence after the final warning. The issues were, what happened before the final warning was given, how many absences were there, why was he absent, and how did the absences fit in as part of the general picture?

7.50 A warning can deal with specific conduct which is the subject of complaint, and it should also deal with general matters, so that the totality of the employee's conduct can eventually be taken into account. This solves the problem, sometimes raised by management, as to whether or not, having given three warnings for one type of misconduct, it is necessary to give a further three warnings in respect of a different series of offences! Thus in *Donald Cook v Carter*, the applicant received a number of warnings; one for using bad language, and a year later, another one for the same offence. Two months later he was given a final warning for inefficiency, with a threat to demote or dismiss. Three months later, he was given another final warning for leaving work before the normal finishing time and he was suspended for five days. He was then guilty of inefficiency, and was dismissed. The industrial tribunal held that the dismissal was unfair, in that he should have been given a further final warning, but this was reversed by the EAT. As long as the matter leading to the dismissal was properly investigated and the proper procedure followed, it was not open to the industrial tribunal to find that fairness required a further warning being given, or that the employers should have suspended the employee, as they had done so previously.

7.50A This approach was recently confirmed by the EAT in *Auguste Noel Ltd v Curtis*, where an employee was dismissed for mishandling company property. He had previously received two final written warnings for different offences. An industrial tribunal held that the previous warnings were not relevant, but the decision was reversed on appeal. The existence of previous warnings, the dates, numbers, and substance of the complaints were all relevant matters which an employer was entitled to take into account.

7.51 The warning should refer to the past conduct which is the subject of complaint, and to future conduct. It should, where possible, state the remedial action to be taken, and should specify the period of time in which such action should be taken. Frequently, a disciplinary procedure will specify the length of time the warning will last, but perhaps a better approach is for the warning itself to state the operative period, for mechanical and automatic approaches to disciplinary problems are not sound policy. A warning can also be suspensive, when it will stay on the employee's record until such time as it is removed, or can be ignored, or resolutive, which will lapse on compliance. The latter can therefore be ignored when its objective has been achieved. In *Duncan v GEC Telecommunications Ltd* an employee failed to send in a medical certificate as required by the company's rules. After being warned, she sent in an appropriate certificate. A few months later she again failed to send in a medical certificate. It was held that the earlier warning had lapsed on her compliance, and therefore her dismissal was unfair.

7.52 A warning may lapse after a certain period of time, but an employer is not to be criticised because he is over-generous and extends the warning period, instead of acting on it. Being over-generous is not the same as being unreasonable (*Kraft Foods Ltd v Fox*). Further, a warning which is itself the subject of a pending appeal may be taken into account by an employer when considering dismissal for subsequent misconduct (*Tower Hamlets Health Authority v Anthony*).

7.53 Tribunals have frequently stressed the need to issue warnings before the power of dismissal is exercised. The warnings should be given by a person in authority, should be clear, incisive and firm. They should make clear the nature of the conduct which will not be tolerated, and spell out in no uncertain terms that the consequence of a failure to heed the warning will be a dismissal. Formal warnings should be given in writing and this is of particular importance when there are language or communication problems.

7.54 Failure to follow these rules may lead to the tribunal making a finding adverse to the employer. In *Wells v West Ltd* the employers gave a warning to an employee that his 'employment might be in jeopardy'. In holding that this was not a sufficient warning, the tribunal held that those who use circumlocutions will have to bear the burden which they subsequently impose. In *Bendall v Paine and Betteridge* the employee was given a verbal warning that smoking would not be tolerated on the premises. It was held that a failure to give a written, final warning meant that the dismissal was unfair. And in *Rosenthal v Louis Butler Ltd* the employee used some offensive language to her manager. It was held that she ought to have been warned about future conduct, and been given an opportunity to apologise before dismissal was warranted.

7.55 It must be stressed that there is no rule of law which requires warnings to be given in all cases; it is merely a rule of good industrial relations practice. Warnings are matters of substance, not procedure (*Paterson v Barrett Developments (Aberdeen) Ltd*). Whether a warning should have been given will depend on all the circumstances of the case, including its effectiveness, and the alternative course which may have been available or adopted. If a tribunal considers that had a clear warning been given, a dismissal would not have been necessary, then it will conclude that a dismissal without such a warning will be unfair (*Jones v GEC Elliott Automation Ltd*). Conversely, if a warning would have had no effect, then a failure to give one will not by itself render a dismissal unfair (*Dunning & Sons Ltd v Jacomb*). There should be no need to give a warning to a highly paid and qualified employee that he will be dismissed if there is dissatisfaction with his work, for he should know this. Nor is there a need to give an educated person in a responsible position a warning that he must co-operate with his head of Department (*Farnborough v Edinburgh College of Art*). Each case must be determined on its own merits.

Reprimand

7.56 The same is probably true about a reprimand, which is mark of displeasure about past conduct and a warning about the future. Tribunals have held that misconduct which is not 'gross' should in some circumstances be punished by a reprimand rather than a dismissal, though to what extent a reprimand constitutes a punishment is somewhat difficult to see. Further, employers could be forgiven for thinking that this area of tribunal law is full of hazardous speculation, for when 'misconduct' becomes 'gross' is a somewhat subjective concept. In *King v Motorway Tyres and Accessories Ltd* a manager told his superior to 'fuck off' in the course of an argument. It was held that this did not amount to gross misconduct sufficient to warrant dismissal, and that in view of his long service and satisfactory record, he should have been 'severely' reprimanded! The precise distinction between a reprimand and a severe reprimand, and whether the latter is equivalent to a final warning, has yet to be decided. It is submitted that a reprimand is an appropriate sanction to be used when taking disciplinary action against management, or staff employees.

Demotion

7.57 An employee whose conduct is such that the employer has lost all confidence in his ability to do the job in question may be demoted, with or without review, and at a lower earning rate if this is appropriate. If there is an express power to do this in the contract or rules, then provided the sanction has been fairly exercised, there should not be any legal problem. In the absence of such a power, it could be a breach of contract by the employer, and hence amount to constructive dismissal (see Chapter 8). But if the employer has acted fairly, and with the interests of the employee at heart, such dismissal will be fair. In *Hall v Lodge*, the applicant was promoted from a supervisory post to manage a shop. Following serious stock deficiencies, her appointment was terminated, and she was offered re-engagement as a supervisor at another branch, at a lower salary. This offer was refused. It was held that her dismissal was fair. The company had made a mistake in promoting her too soon to a job which was too big for her. Having realised this, they then acted fairly by considering the alternatives which were available, by offering her a post which was within her competence. However, there is no legal requirement that an employer should demote a person who is incompetent (*Bevan Harris Ltd v Gair*).

7.58 But if a demotion on disciplinary grounds is out of all proportion to the offence, the employee may regard the employer as having repudiated the contract, and claim constructive dismissal. In *BBC v Beckett*, the applicant was employed for 14 years as a scenic carpenter. He was negligent in his work on one occasion, and was demoted to the position of building maintenance carpenter, at a lower salary. He resigned and claimed constructive dismissal, a claim which was upheld by the industrial tribunal and by the EAT. The punishment was out of all proportion to the offence, given his long period of satisfactory service.

Transfer

7.59 Similar considerations apply to the transfer of an employee from one department to another, or one job to another. This power, however, would be used in different circumstances. Merely to transfer an incompetent employee from one department to another is to export one's problems from one manager to another. Transfer is best used as a means of overcoming personality clashes, so as to minimise the likelihood of future problems arising, or to place an employee in a job which he can do, rather than leaving him doing work which is beyond his competence. In *High v British Railways Board*, it was held that a disciplinary transfer which resulted in the employee suffering a drop in his earnings did not give rise to a claim for constructive dismissal.

Alternative employment

7.59A In appropriate cases, it may be unfair to dismiss an employee without considering whether there was any alternative work he could do, notwithstanding that he cannot be permitted to continue in his old job. However, there is no requirement that this should be investigated before the decision to dismiss is taken, as opposed to after the decision has been taken but before the expiry of any period of notice which may be given. To hold otherwise would mean that an employee would be unfairly dismissed notwithstanding that during his notice period alternative employment was found for him and the notice never took effect (*P v Nottinghamshire County Council*).

Other sanctions

7.60 There are a number of other disciplinary powers which may be used on appropriate occasions, and provided these are exercised in accordance with the relevant rules and procedures, these should cause few problems. For example, it may be possible to withdraw privileges for a certain period of time so as to deny to an employee certain non-contractual benefits, or to provide for the loss of so many year's seniority for certain purposes (but this does not affect the operation of the legal rules relating to continuity of employment). An employee who is persistently late in starting work may have flexi-time withdrawn, as an alternative to, or a pre-condition of, the implementation of other disciplinary action.

Non-employment situations

7.61 The above instances of disciplinary powers can only apply to acts of employees committed in the course of employment. An employer has no inherent power to discipline for acts which have occurred outside the employment, though if such acts adversely affect the employer's business, he may be justified in dismissing the employee (see Chapter 8). But if an employee is convicted of an offence outside his employment which may have an effect on his job, the employer should consider the employee's long and blameless record, and consider, for example, if some other means of dealing with the situation can be found. In *Jones v R M Douglas Construction Ltd* the employee, who was a plant engineer, was dismissed after being convicted of handling a stolen engine. The tribunal thought that the employer should have given some consideration to demoting him to his original trade of mechanic/fitter. Clearly, such a power cannot be found in the contract of employment, and amounts to a unilateral assessment by the employer of the necessary steps to be taken to protect his interests. A demotion is, as we have seen, equivalent to a dismissal, and one can only assume that if such steps are taken in serious disciplinary cases, the exercise of a lesser disciplinary power short of dismissal will, in cases of grave misconduct outside the employment, also be looked upon more favourably by the tribunals.

7.62 If the employee is convicted of an offence in connection with matters outside his employment, he is still entitled to present his side of the story to his employers, and the latter should not treat the fact of conviction *per se* as being conclusive without at least giving a chance to the employee to state his version (*Parsons v LCC*).

CHAPTER 8

Dismissal

8.1 Under the law which existed prior to 1971 an employer was entitled to dismiss an employee for any reason or for no reason at all; the only issues involved were whether or nor the employee was entitled to a certain period of notice, or whether his conduct was such as to warrant instant (summary) dismissal without notice. The Contracts of Employment Act 1963 (repealed and subsequently re-enacted) did lay down certain minimum periods of notice which had to be given in respect of a lawful dismissal, but such notice could be increased either because there was an express provision to this effect in the individual contract of employment or because the position of the employee was such that a period in excess of the statutory minimum could be implied into that contract, and the decisions of the court in the latter cases ranged from one week to one year, depending on the facts of each case. It will be recalled that there were those special cases where the right not to be dismissed was enshrined into an employee's contract by virtue of a special 'status' (see para 2.20) and there were other cases when a dismissal could not be carried out unless the rules of 'natural justice' were observed (see *Ridge v Baldwin*), or because the approval of some other person or body had to be obtained (see *Cory Lighterage v T & GWU*). These matters were dealt with in Chapter 2.

8.2 In 1971 the Industrial Relations Act created a right for many employees not to be unfairly dismissed, and though that Act was repealed, the law was substantially re-enacted (with some minor amendments) in the Trade Union and Labour Relations Act 1974, and further amendments were made by the Employment Protection Act 1975. All the relevant law was brought together in the Employment Protection (Consolidation) Act 1978, and there were a number of additional amendments to be found in the Employment Acts 1980-1990 and the Trade Union Reform and Employment Rights Act 1993. But although this new legal right has largely subsumed the old learning, it is still necessary to examine the old law relating to summary, lawful and wrongful dismissal, because there may be situations when the common law remedy is more advantageous, or indeed, the only remedy available. In particular, we may note the following circumstances:

a. the maximum compensatory award for unfair dismissal is currently £11,000, plus an appropriate basic award. A highly paid employee who is entitled to a long period of notice may be able to obtain substantially higher damages at common law;
b. an employee who lacks a sufficient period of continuous employment to qualify for unfair dismissal rights may nonetheless sue for wrongful dismissal, and may also be able to sue for the loss of his right to bring a claim for unfair dismissal (see *Robert Cort & Son Ltd v Charman*);
c. an employee who is past the normal retiring age or over the age of 65 may be able to bring a claim for breach of contract based on wrongful dismissal (*Age Concern Scotland v Hines*);
d. a fair dismissal may nonetheless be a wrongful dismissal (*Treganowan v Robert Knee & Co Ltd*);
e. an application for unfair dismissal is likely to be time-barred after three months from the effective date of termination, whereas a claim for wrongful dismissal may be brought within six years of the breach;
f. the dispute may have a public law element, and not be concerned with contractual rights (*R v Secretary of State for the Home Department, ex p Benwell*);
g. a dismissal which is in breach of a contractual or statutory dismissal procedure may enable an employee to bring an action for breach of contract (*Shook v London Borough of Ealing*) or to seek an injunction to restrain the breach (*Irani v Southampton and South West Hampshire Health Authority*, see para 6.4).

8.3 Since the jurisdiction of industrial tribunals is concurrent with that possessed by the ordinary courts, an employee will thus opt for whichever remedy will produce the most advantageous results (see para 1.26).

Summary dismissal

8.4 In *Jupiter General Insurance Co v Shroff* the Privy Council stated that summary dismissal was a strong measure, to be justified only in the most exceptional circumstances. Despite this implicit warning, a report published in 1970 estimated that there were about 300,000 cases of summary dismissal each year, and one may assume that it was the inadequacy of legal procedures in failing to provide a cheap and simple method for dealing with such disputes which restrained many of those dismissed from testing or enforcing their legal rights. Nonetheless, there are a number of well-recognised grounds on which an employer may dismiss an employee summarily; these include gross misconduct, wilful refusal to obey a lawful and reasonable order, gross neglect, dishonesty, and so forth (see, e.g. *Blyth v Scottish Liberal Club*). Whether the conduct in question is serious enough to warrant dismissal is always a question of fact in each case, and the standards to be applied are those of the current *mores*, not those which may have become somewhat outdated. In *Wilson v Racher*, Edmund-Davies LJ said 'Many of the decisions which are customarily cited in these cases date from the last century and may be wholly out of accord with current social conditions. What would today be regarded as almost an attitude of Czar-serf, which is to be found in some of the older cases where a dismissed employee failed to recover damages, would, I venture to think, be decided differently today. We have by now come to realise that a contract of service imposes upon the parties a duty of mutual respect'. It is thus clear that many of the older decisions on this subject lack authority today, and must be treated with reserve, if not disdain.

8.5 But certain principles remain constant. In *Sinclair v Neighbour* a manager took £15 from a till and left an IOU in its place. He intended to replace the money a few days later. His conduct was regarded as being dishonest and his summary dismissal was upheld. In *Ross v Aquascutum Ltd* the employee was a nightwatchman. He was observed to be absent from the building he was guarding for two hours of each night, and it was held that his conduct constituted a breach of contract so serious as to justify summary dismissal. When considering conduct which results from the interaction of human personalities, it is necessary to apply the standards of ordinary people, not those of the angels. In *Pepper v Webb* a gardener was asked to do certain work, but he refused to do so in language which was somewhat vulgar. His summary dismissal was held to be justified, for by refusing to obey a lawful and reasonable order he had broken his contract. Indeed, his conduct had been such as to give rise to a history of complaints for insolence, and the incident which gave rise to his dismissal was merely the last straw. On the other hand, in *Wilson v Racher* a gardener swore at his employer using some even choicer obscenities. Although this could have amounted to gross misconduct, the court held that '... it requires very special circumstances to entitle a servant who expresses his feelings in such a grossly improper way to succeed in an action for wrongful dismissal'. On the facts of the case, the special circumstance existed, and these lay in the employer's own conduct which had provoked the outburst.

8.6 The breach of an express term of the contract or of a provision in the works rules may justify summary dismissal, provided it has been brought expressly to the attention of the employee that there is certain conduct which the employer will on no account tolerate. Certain airlines, for example, have a rule that any pilot who takes drugs (other than on medical prescription) or is discovered drunk whether on or off duty will be instantly dismissed. Other employers may specify other conduct which is detrimental to the business and which may warrant summary dismissal. For example, smoking in prohibited areas, unhygienic practices in food premises, breach of safety rules which may lead to hazards or risk of injury to others, all constitute conduct which may, in the special circumstances, warrant dismissal. The importance of having a consistent and well-defined policy on this subject will be stressed when the cases dealing with unfair dismissal are discussed.

8.7 An employee is not in breach of his contract of employment merely because he indicates his intention to open a business in competition with his employer. In *Laughton and Hawley v Bapp Industrial Supplies Ltd* the two applicants, who were employed by the respondents, wrote to the company's suppliers stating that they intended to commence trading in the near future, and asked for product lists, prices and terms. When the employers discovered this, the employees were dismissed instantly without notice. The dismissals were held to be unfair. There was no abuse of their positions as employees, no breach of any covenant in restraint of trade, and no disclosure of trade secrets or confidential information. The employees had not failed to devote their efforts to their employer's business during working hours, and thus their activities did not constitute gross misconduct. But where a managing director formed a new business entity, sought to persuade his employer's major client to transfer business to it, and induced two senior employees to join him in the new venture which was in direct competition with the employer, it was held that this amounted to gross misconduct warranting summary dismissal (*Marshall v Industrial Systems and Control Ltd*).

8.8 A more difficult problem arises if conduct of the employee is in the nature of neglect, which causes damage to the employer. Should one consider the act itself, which may be of a minor or major nature, or should one consider the consequences, which may be insignificant or serious? In *Savage v British India Steam Navigation Co* it was stated that it was the nature of the act, not the consequences, which was relevant. A failure to observe instructions which resulted in damage was held to be of sufficient seriousness to warrant summary dismissal in *Howe v Gloucester and Severnside Co-operative Society*, but excessive zeal which caused damage did not warrant such drastic measures in *Newlands v Howard & Co Ltd*. Neglect by senior employees who hold responsible positions appears to amount to a greater dereliction of duty than junior staff, and hence more likely to attract instant dismissal. As a general rule, for an employee to be summarily dismissed on the grounds of neglect, the neglect should be something approaching habitual conduct, but a single act of neglect could justify instant dismissal if its consequences are likely to be serious enough (*Taylor v Alidair Ltd*).

8.9 A strike is a breach of contract by the employee, and is thus an act of such a nature as to justify summary dismissal. So too is any other conduct designed to disrupt the employer's business, such as go-slow tactics, work-to-rule, etc. Persistent lateness, drunkenness, fighting, swearing, immorality, skylarking, are all examples of conduct which could attract summary dismissal in particular circumstances. But it must be stressed that although dismissal would not be wrongful at common law, in most cases, the test of 'fairness' will have to be considered additionally, and this will be explored later in this chapter.

8.10 A summary dismissal takes affect immediately. Any rights an employee may have, e.g. for pay in lieu of notice, expenses, etc may be claimed by an action for damages for breach of contract in the ordinary courts (*Octavious Atkinson & Sons Ltd v Morris*).

Lawful dismissal

8.11 In those cases where an employer has a legal right to dismiss, though not summarily, the employee will be entitled to a period of notice specified by or implied into his contract of employment. This will include those dismissals which are 'fair' under EPCA, or lawful at common law. In *Treganowan v Robert Knee & Co Ltd* a summary dismissal was held to be fair, but the tribunal thought that it was wrongful at common law, in that the employee ought to have received the appropriate notice. If the employer so chooses, he may dispense with the services of the employee and pay him wages or salary in lieu of notice, but he cannot 'short notice' the employee and thus prevent the latter from obtaining a statutory benefit. Thus if an employee has been employed for one year and 51 weeks, and is dismissed without notice, his effective date of termination of employment is at the time he leaves, and not having the requisite period of two years employment, he cannot claim in respect of unfair dismissal. The Employment Protection (Consolidation) Act 1978 s. 55(5) states that the effective date of termination will be the date on which his statutory notice expires. In other words, he is entitled to add to his period of employment the weeks' notice to which he is entitled by statute. On the other hand, the dismissal operates for computation purposes from the date when the statutory notice expires, not from when the entitlement to contractual notice expires. Thus, if an employee has been employed for one year and 50 weeks, and is entitled to four week's notice, and he is dismissed immediately with his wages in lieu of notice, then his period of employment is only for one year and 51 weeks. The employee is entitled to add to his period of employment the statutory minimum notice but not a potentially longer contractual period (*Fox Maintenance Ltd v Jackson*).

8.12 If the contract of employment expressly states the period of notice which the employee is entitled to receive, then at least that period must be given. If the contract is silent on the point, then reasonable notice must be given, and this will depend on the position held by the employee. It will be recalled that in *Hill v C A Parsons & Co Ltd* the Court of Appeal thought that a senior engineer was entitled to more than one month's notice, and reasonable notice in such a case could have been anything from six months to one year. But whatever the contract of employment states, there are certain minimum periods of notice which must be given to all employees, which are determined by their length of service. These periods can now be found in EPCA s. 49(1), and are as follows: after one month's employment, the employee will be entitled to one week's notice, and this will apply until he has been employed for up to two years. Thereafter he will be entitled to one week's notice in respect of each year's employment, i.e. two weeks' notice after two years, up to a maximum of twelve weeks' notice in respect of employment which has continued for twelve years or more. During the period of his notice, the employee is entitled to be paid his average wages for any period where no work is provided by the employer, or where the employee is absent through sickness or injury, or absent because of agreed holidays (see EPCA Sch 3). But he is not entitled to be so paid if he takes part in strike action after notice has been given. Nor is he entitled to be paid during his notice period if the effect of the sickness absence is to frustrate the contract, for the contract is ended by frustration, not dismissal (*Notcutt v Universal Equipment Co (London) Ltd*).

8.13 Section 49(2) of EPCA provides that an employee must give a minimum of one week's notice if he wishes to leave his employment, though of course the individual contract could lay down a longer period. In strict legal theory an employee who failed or refused to work out his period of notice could be sued for breach of contract, but this is scarcely a practical proposition for an employer, and the most that a recalcitrant employee stands to lose is his reputation, if any, as a responsible employee.

8.14 If an employee is dismissed with notice, and is asked to work until the expiry of the notice, then the dismissal does not take effect until the notice expires. Consequently, if he leaves before the notice has expired, he terminates his own employment, and is not dismissed (*Walker v Cotswold Chine Home School*) unless he leaves his employment early with his employer's agreement.

Unfair dismissal

8.15 The basic structure of the law on unfair dismissal is comparatively easy to state, and is contained in ss. 54-65 of EPCA. The interpretation of that law by the courts and tribunals has led to hundreds of reported decisions which have laid down guidelines varying from legal ingenuity, through sound common sense, and ending up, on occasions, with cabalistic mystery! But many decisions can only be explained on their own special facts and on a consideration of the actual evidence presented to the tribunal, and it must be borne in mind that industrial tribunal decisions are not, in themselves, binding precedents. Sometimes the successful applicant will be awarded a reduced compensation because of his own contributory conduct, and there have been cases where a dismissal though unfair, has resulted in a nil award.

8.16 Nonetheless, the decisions of the reported cases repay detailed study. In the first place, they give guidance to a generalised stream of thought which is rapidly becoming dominant thinking in employment law; guidance on how an employer should act so as to be regarded as being reasonable and fair, guidance on how disciplinary procedures should be operated, and on when an employer may adopt standards which are less than those expected by a perfectionist. Secondly, the decided cases point out the pitfalls into which other employers have fallen, and thus enable a conscientious personnel manager to so direct his policies as to avoid those very traps. Finally, they provide interpretation of the legislative provisions which have a persuasive effect until a higher court has had an opportunity to pronounce on their validity.

8.17 Every employee to whom the Act applies has the right not to be unfairly dismissed, and the remedy for the infringement of that right is by way of a complaint to the industrial tribunal, and not otherwise. This means that unfair dismissal cases must go to the industrial tribunals, whereas a person who wishes to sue in respect of *wrongful dismissal* must bring the action in the ordinary courts in the normal way.

Exclusions

8.18 The following categories of employees are not protected by the provisions of EPCA:

a. any employment as a master or member of the crew of a fishing vessel where the employee is remunerated by a share of the profits.
b. any contract of employment where the employee ordinarily works outside Great Britain. If an employee works for most of his time outside Great Britain, or even for a majority of his time, then he can be said ordinarily to work outside Great Britain (*Tye v Mower Scaffolds*). In *Wilson v*

Maynard Shipbuilding Consultants AB, it was stated that the proper criterion was to look at the terms of the contract (express and/or implied) in order to ascertain where the employee's base was to be. In the absence of special factors leading to a contrary conclusion, the country where the base was to be would be the place where he was to be treated as ordinarily working under his contract. Where this was in practice would depend on an examination of all the relevant contractual terms. For example, in *Hillier v Martintrux*, the applicant was an HGV driver who spent about 90% of his time driving on the continent. He was paid in sterling, was subject to British income tax, and his home was in England. The industrial tribunal held that it had jurisdiction to hear the case. His base was clearly in this country, and the foreign travel did not mean that he ordinarily worked abroad.

Clearly, much will depend on the facts of each case. In *Scott, Brownrigg & Turner v Dance*, the EAT held that although an employee was working abroad, he was not ordinarily working there. The period spent abroad needs to be related to the total length of the employment, the contract, and what was reasonably contemplated. The industrial tribunal had found that the applicant's period abroad was an interlude during his working life, and the EAT refused to disturb a finding that the tribunal had jurisdiction to hear a claim for unfair dismissal. In *Grandmet International Services v Graham* the applicant was employed to work anywhere in the world. Applying the 'base' test, it was held that London was his base, and the industrial tribunal had jurisdiction to hear his claim.

Although a reference to the contract of employment is useful, it is not, *per se*, conclusive. In *Sonali Bank v Rahman* the employers had a contractual right to transfer the employee to any branch of the Bank, whether in or outside of Bangladesh. In practice, he only worked in Great Britain. On a preliminary point of jurisdiction, the employers argued that since they had a contractual right to transfer him to Bangladesh, he could not be said to be ordinarily working in Great Britain. The argument was dismissed by the industrial tribunal and the EAT. An essential factor to take into account is what happens in practice.

Merchant seamen may pursue claims for unfair dismissal provided they are employed to work on ships registered in Great Britain (i.e. excluding Northern Ireland, the Isle of Man and the Channel Islands) unless their employment is wholly outside Great Britain, or they are not ordinarily resident in Great Britain (s. 141(5)). In *Wood v Cunard Line Ltd*, the applicant was engaged in Southampton, and then joined a ship which cruised around the Caribbean. It was held that his employment was wholly outside Great Britain.

Under the Employment Protection (Offshore Employment) Order 1976, employees who work in oil rigs and offshore installations in British territorial waters or areas designated under the Continental Shelf Act 1964 are not excluded from the provisions of the Employment Protection (Consolidation) Act 1978.

c. any employment where the employee has been continuously employed for less than two years. The period of continuous employment begins with the day on which he is due to start work under the contract (*Salvation Army v Dewsbury*). An employee who had been employed for one week less than the qualifying period of two years, and is dismissed, is entitled to add to his computation the week's statutory notice to which he is entitled (s. 55(5)), but not his contractual notice (see *Fox Maintenance Ltd v Jackson*, para 8.11). But if he is dismissed without notice for gross misconduct, he cannot rely on s. 55(5) 'To pull him past the post' (*Ahmed v National Car Parks Ltd*)!

The fact that the reason for the dismissal is designated as 'gross misconduct' does not preclude the operation of s. 55(5), for the industrial tribunal can enquire into the facts on their merits, and decide whether in the circumstances the employer was entitled to terminate the contract without notice. If they decide that the employer was not so entitled, s. 55(5) comes into operation (*Lanton Leisure Ltd v White and Gibson*).

If there is no adequate reason which would justify the summary dismissal, and if the consequence is to deprive an employee of his right to bring a claim for unfair dismissal by depriving him of the relevant period of continuous employment, the employee may have a remedy at common law for damages for unfair dismissal. The measure of damages will include the loss of his right to claim unfair dismissal (*Stapp v Shaftesbury Society*).

As a general rule, a dismissal will not operate until it has been received by the employee. Thus if it is sent by post, it will be effective from the time when the employee has actually read the letter, or had a reasonable opportunity to do so. In *Brown v Southall and Knight* the employers sent a letter of dismissal to the applicant who, on that date, did not have the requisite period of continuous employment. He was away on holiday when the letter arrived, and thus did not read it until he returned a week later, by which time he had the necessary qualifying period. It was held that he was entitled to pursue his claim for unfair dismissal. Of course, if he deliberately did not open the letter, or went away in order to avoid reading it, he would have been debarred from saying that the notification of dismissal was not given to him.

d. an employee who has reached the normal retiring age as laid down in his contract of employment (*Howard v Department of National Savings*).

The normal retiring age is not the same thing as the normal pensionable age, for the latter may merely be the age at which the employee is entitled to retire on a pension, without being obliged to do so. Thus to retire someone compulsorily short of the normal retiring age may be unfair, even though he has passed the pensionable age (*Ord v Maidstone and District Hospital Management Committee*). In *Wood v Louis Edwards Ltd* a tribunal went even further, and awarded compensation to a 62-year-old manager on the basis that he would not have retired until he was 70, for although the exclusion prevents a person over 65 from claiming, it does not apparently prevent compensation being based on the assumption that a person below that age may continue to work after 65.

The starting point for the normal retiring age is the contractual retiring age. However, this may be displaced by evidence that the contractual retiring age is departed from in practice, or that there is some other age at which employees of that description in the relevant group can reasonably expect to be compelled to retire (*Age Concern Scotland v Hines*). Where there is a contractual retiring age applicable to all, or nearly all, of the relevant employees, there is a presumption that the contractual retiring age is the normal retiring age. But that presumption can be rebutted by evidence that there is in practice some higher age which those employees have reasonably come to regard as their normal retiring age (*Secretary of State for Scotland v Meikle*). If the contractual retiring age has been abandoned, so that employees retire at a variety of ages (e.g. between the ages of 60 to 63, see *Swaine v Health and Safety Executive*), then there is no normal retiring age (*Waite v Government Communications Headquarters*), and the exclusion at the age of 65 operates. If an employer wishes to introduce a new retirement age which will then constitute the normal retirement age then, so long as there is no breach of the employee's contract, and there is no suggestion that it is a sham policy, and it has been properly communicated to the employee, it will take immediate effect, even though it destroys a previous expectation of being retained in employment until a higher age (*Brooks v British Telecommunications plc*).

e. if there is no normal retiring age, or if the contractual retiring age discriminated between men and women, the age limit of 65 applies to all employees. Formerly women over the age of 60 could not bring claims for unfair dismissal, but as a result of the decision of the European Court in *Marshall v Southampton Area Health Authority*, the law was changed by the Sex Discrimination Act 1986 to equalise the position of men and women.

f. a fixed term contract of one year or more where the dismissal consists of a failure to renew, if, before that term has expired, the employee agrees in writing to exclude a claim in respect of his dismissal. This is one of the very few instances in the modern protective legislation where an employee can voluntarily surrender his legal rights to bring a claim. In so far as successive fixed term contracts are concerned, it is the length of the final contract which matters. If this is for less than one year, an exclusion clause cannot operate (*Open University v Triesman*).

g. any employment covered by a dismissals procedure agreement which has been designated and approved by the Secretary of State. This enables an employer and an independent trade union to create their own dismissals procedure which, provided it conforms with the laid down criteria, may be approved by the Minister, and those employees covered by it are excluded from the provisions of the Act. Very little use has been made of this procedure (see Dismissals Procedure Agreement made between the Electrical Contractors Association and the EEPTU).

h. employees who work for foreign governments and other international organisations which enjoy diplomatic immunity (e.g. see *Gadhok v Commonwealth Secretariat*) can only bring appropriate claims if that diplomatic immunity is waived; otherwise the industrial tribunals have no jurisdiction. However, by the State Immunity Act 1978, a State is not immune in respect of proceedings relating to a contract of employment if (a) the contract was made in the United Kingdom, or (b) the work is to be wholly or partly performed in the United Kingdom. The Act does not apply if at the time of the claim the applicant was a national of the State concerned, or at the time when the contract was made he was neither a national of the United Kingdom nor habitually resident here, or if the parties have agreed to exclude the provisions of the Act.

8.19 In respect of the above exclusions, it should be noted that c. (two years qualifying employment), d. (retiring age) and e. (age 65) are not excluded if the reason for the dismissal was the employee's membership of an independent trade union (or his intention to join), his taking part in the activities of that union, or his refusal to join or remain a member of a union, or if the dismissal was on maternity grounds (see para 5.30) or a health and safety case (see para 12.34C) or because of the assertion of a statutory right (see para 8.187).

Continuous employment

8.20 Before an employee can qualify for the majority of employment rights (see Appendix C), he must have the appropriate period of continuous employment, now calculated in terms of years or months, beginning with the day on which the employee starts work under the contract. If the starting date is a non-working day (e.g. a holiday) employment will be continuous from that date, even though he does not start work until the following day (*Salvation Army v Dewsbury*). The rules relating to the computation of continuity are among the most abtruse and complex to be found in employment law generally and are to be found in Sch. 13 of EPCA. We will analyse these rules under three headings, (a) computing continuity, (b) preserving continuity despite breaks, and (c) continuity when there is a change of employer.

Computing continuous employment

8.21 The first rule to note is that there is a legal presumption that continuity exists; thus once an employee can show the date on which employment commenced, it is presumed to be continuous until the employer proves to the contrary (EPCA s. 151, see *Nicholl v Nocorrode Ltd*). An employee may change his place of work, his terms of employment, or even his contract of employment, without his continuity being affected, provided he is employed by the same employer (*Wood v York City Council*). The employer, on the other hand, may show that there are weeks which do not count towards continuity, or he may show that continuity was in fact broken.

8.22 Secondly, a week counts for continuity purposes if the employer is employed for 16 hours or more per week. This refers to normal contractual hours, not, for example, any overtime which may be worked (*ITT Components Ltd v Kolah*). Thus if an employee goes away on holiday, continuity is preserved, for he is employed under a contract which normally involves him working the minimum hours required to preserve continuity (Sch 13, para 3). 'Normal working hours' does not mean average working hours (*Opie v John Gibbons Ltd*).

8.23 Thirdly, an employee may show that he has a contract which normally involves employment for 16 or more hours, in which case weeks will count even though he does not necessarily work for 16 hours in any particular week (para 4). If the contract is silent on the number of hours to be worked, regard must be had to what actually happened in practice. Thus if the contract is for the employee to work such number of hours as the employer may reasonably require, it will still fall within para 4 of Sch 13 and, if the evidence shows that the employee in fact has worked the necessary number of hours, over the requisite period, continuity can be computed within the provisions of the Schedule (*Green v Roberts*).

8.24 Fourthly, if the employee changes from working 16 hours to a contract which requires him to work less than 16 hours, then, provided he works for more than 8 hours per week, he is entitled to count up to 26 weeks towards continuity (Sch 13 para 6).

8.25 Fifthly, if an employee works between 8 and 16 hours per week, and has done so for more than five years, then for all purposes he will be deemed to have continuous employment (Sch 13 para 6).

Preserving continuity (Sch 13 paras 9-18)

8.26 If a week does not count under the above headings, then normally the continuity is broken, and the employee must start counting again. However, there are a number of rules which preserve continuity, and it is thus possible to join together periods of employment for continuity purposes even though there may be breaks between those periods.

8.27 Firstly, if an employee is absent from work through sickness or injury, then, in addition to any contractual sick leave, he is entitled to add the first 26 weeks of his absence towards continuity, and thus there is no break in his continuity (para 9(1)(a)). This rule has been applied not only when the employee is absent through sickness or injury, but also when he leaves his employment through sickness and is subsequently re-engaged. In *Donnelly v Kelvin International Services*, the employee resigned from his employment with the respondents because his doctor advised him to obtain lighter work. He obtained employment with another employer, but five weeks later, was re-employed by the respondents. He was subsequently dismissed, and his claim for unfair dismissal could only proceed if he could link the two periods of employment. An industrial tribunal dismissed his claim, holding that although he had resigned his employment because of sickness, he was not incapable of work because of sickness, because he had demonstrated his fitness for work by working for another employer. The EAT allowed the employee's appeal, and remitted the claim for reconsideration by a different tribunal. The phrase 'incapable of work' did not mean incapable of work of any kind. It referred to the work the employee was doing prior to the period which interrupted the continuity of employment, and the fact that the employee has taken up employment during the period of interruption did not mean that he had ceased to be incapable of work by reason of sickness within the meaning of para 9(1)(a). The proper approach was to look at what happened in the intervening period between the two employments in question. If, for example, the employee took employment of light work, in the hope that he might be able to return to his previous employment in time, this may not interrupt the continuity of employment. But if the intervening employment was undertaken as full-time permanent employment, then it is possible to conclude that his absence from the first employment was not because of incapacity for work.

8.27A A different conclusion appears to have been reached in *Pearson v Kent County Council*, where the employee decided to resign his employment on 31 May on health grounds. He was offered, and accepted, a less demanding job with his employers, and commenced his new position on 11 June. Four years later he was made redundant, and sought to link the two periods of employment for the purpose of obtaining a redundancy payment in respect of his overall period of employment. His claim failed. There was no medical reason why he could not have commenced his new job immediately after he left his old job. Hence he was not absent from work because of sickness or injury, and the two periods of employment could not be linked to form one period of continuous employment.

8.28 Secondly, weeks count where an employee is absent from work (without a contract) on account of a temporary cessation of work, due to any cause other than the employee going on strike (Sch 13 para 9(1)(b)). This provision is designed to deal with those industries where there may be temporary lay-offs, e.g. the construction industry, but the practical effect has been much wider (see *Fitzgerald v Hall, Russell & Co Ltd*). A period of two years absence for reason of redundancy was held to be a 'temporary absence' in *Bentley Engineering v Crown*, for the test to be applied is one of hindsight, not foresight! But if an employee resigns, or is dismissed, e.g. for misconduct, and is subsequently re-employed by the employer (or an associated employer - see Sch 13 para 18), he is not absent from work on account of temporary cessation (*Wessex National Ltd v Long*). Also, the 'cessation of work' means that the quantum of work no longer exists, and was therefore no longer available to the employee. If the work is available, but given to someone else, there is no cessation of work within the meaning of para 9(1)(b) (see *Byrne v Birmingham City District Council*).

8.29 A person is absent from work for the purpose of para 9(1)(b) if there is an interruption in the availability of work which, but for that interruption, would have to be performed by the employee. In *Ford v Warwickshire County Council*, the applicant was a teacher employed on a sessional basis. Each year she taught for three terms, and when the July term ended, her contract came to an end, although it was renewed in September. This arrangement continued for eight years, when she was not re-engaged at the commencement of a new session, she sought compensation for unfair dismissal and redundancy. The

House of Lords held that the word 'temporary' was used in the sense of being 'transient', so that the absence was only for a relatively short time. Whether a particular absence was temporary in this sense was a question of fact for the industrial tribunal to determine. Successive periods of employment with the same employer will be continuous under para 9(1)(b) if the length of time between those periods is short compared with the length of time the employment has lasted, so that the intervals in between can truly be regarded as being temporary. The reason why there is a temporary cessation of work is irrelevant (*University of Aston v Malik*).

8.30 A number of cases have revealed that there are employees who are employed on 'intermittent contracts', each of varying lengths, and separated by varying periods of non-employment. The correct approach is to consider all the relevant circumstances, and in particular to consider the length of the periods of absence from work in the context of the period of employment as a whole (*Sillars v Charrington Fuels Ltd*). On occasions, attempts have been made to circumvent this enquiry by finding a 'global contract', but with mixed success (see para 2.66).

8.30A So far as seasonal workers are concerned, if a greater time is spent out of employment than in, the period of unemployment cannot be regarded as being absence on account of a temporary cessation of work (*Berwick Salmon Fisheries Co Ltd v Rutherford*).

8.31 Thirdly, any period when an employee is absent from work where by arrangement or custom he is regarded as continuing in his employment (Sch 13 para 9(1)(c)). This would cover, for example, an employee who had been seconded from one employer to another, or who has been given leave of absence for personal reasons (*Taylor v Triumph Motors Ltd*). But there must be an arrangement or custom whereby the employee is regarded as having continuity for all or any purposes. In *Lloyds Bank Ltd v Secretary of State for Employment* an employee worked one week on and one week off for five years. She became pregnant, the employers paid her statutory maternity pay, and sought to recover the amount from the Maternity Fund. It was held that her employment was continuous for five years, her absence was by arrangement and having rightfully paid her the money, they were entitled to the rebate from the fund.

8.31A Fourthly, if a woman is absent from work because of pregnancy or confinement, continuity is preserved for the statutory period of 26 weeks (para 9(1)(d)). But if she returns to work in accordance with her statutory rights, the whole of her period of absence counts towards continuity (para 10).

8.32 Fifthly, if an employee goes on strike or is locked-out, the total number of days (including non-working days e.g. Saturday and Sunday) between the last working day before the strike or lock-out and the day of resumption of work will not count towards continuity, but the strike or lock-out will not break continuity. The start of the employee's period of employment is advanced by the number of days lost. Thus, if an employee starts work on 1st January, and subsequently goes on strike for seven days, his employment will be deemed to have started on 8th January. However, the days will not be disallowed if the employee is unable to work because of a strike by someone else. If an employee is dismissed during the strike, and then re-engaged, his continuity is preserved even though the period on strike does not count (Sch 13 para 15; *Hanson v Fashion Industries (Hartlepool) Ltd*).

Change of employer

8.33 Continuity is preserved in some circumstances if there is a change of employer, provided certain appropriate legal requirements are met. The changes may come about through economic forces, e.g. a take-over bid, or through technical considerations, e.g. where there is a change in a partnership, or on the death of an individual employer, and so on. There can always be such continuity if the respective employers agree to this, and any new statement given under s. 1 of the Employment Protection (Consolidation) Act 1978 should contain a statement indicating any previous employment with the old employer which counts for continuity purposes. In addition to such contractual agreements, there are certain legal rules which may bring about such continuity.

8.34 Firstly, if a trade or business or undertaking is transferred from one person to another, the period with the first employer will count as a period of employment with the second employer (Sch 13 para 17). The business must have been transferred as a going concern, and not merely as a collection of assets, so that the transferee can carry on the activities without interruption.

8.35-8.36 Secondly, if the respective employers expressly refute any intention to transfer the business as a going concern, this may be sufficient to refute continuity. This may be done if the first employer deliberately ends the employment contracts of his employees, and then the new employer expressly re-engages them under a new contract. It is then for the industrial tribunal to find, on the facts of the case, if there has been a transfer of the business as a going concern or not.

8.37 Thirdly, a part of a business may be transferred, for the employee to gain continuity, provided that that part is a separate identifiable entity. The transfer must result in the same business being under new ownership.

8.38 Fourthly, if an employee is transferred from an employer to an associated employer, the transfer does not break continuity (Sch 13 para 18). However, the two employers must be 'associated' in the legal sense, in accordance with the definition contained in s. 153(4) of EPCA. This states that any two employers are to be treated as being associated if one is a company of which the other (directly or indirectly) has control, or if both companies are controlled by a third person. 'Control' is a legal, not a factual concept (*Washington Arts Association Ltd v Forster*), to be determined by the number of votes attached to shares which can exercise control of a company in general meeting (*Secretary of State for Employment v Newbold*). Further, by the Interpretation Act 1978, s. 6, the singular includes the plural; thus, if one or more people own 51% or more of the shares of X Company, and the same person(s) hold a simple majority of the shares in Z Company, the two companies will be associated, since they are both controlled by a third person (*Unmar v Pliastar Ltd*). But if the 'third person' who has control of the two companies is in fact two or more persons, they must be the same individuals with respect to both companies. Thus, if a man and his wife control X Company, and he and his sister control Z Company, the two companies are not associated (*Poparm Ltd v Weeks*).

8.39 The word 'company' in s. 153(4) is not confined to companies incorporated under British law. In *Hancill v Marcon En-*

gineering Ltd, the applicant was employed by a company incorporated under American law. He then returned to the United Kingdom and worked for a British company. Both companies were wholly owned subsidiaries of a Dutch company. It was held that he could combine his service with the American and British companies for the purposes of computing his period of continuous employment.

8.40 The definition of control does not extend to 'negative' control, so as to mean that a person who has exactly 50% of the shareholding of a company has control, merely because he can thwart the wishes of those who hold the remaining 50% (*South West Launderettes v Ladilet*).

8.41 A combination of paras 9 and 18 produces an unusual result. In *Bentley Engineering v Crown* the applicant was employed by George Blackburn Ltd until 1963, when he was made redundant. He obtained other employment, but two years later, he was taken on by Bentley Engineering Ltd, which was an associated company of Blackburn's. He was made redundant again in 1974, and it was held that the whole period of employment with the two companies was continuous. His absence from Blackburn's was a 'temporary cessation' (para 9), he was then employed by an associated employer (para 18), and both together combined to preserve his continuity.

8.42 Fifthly, by the Redundancy Payments (Local Government) (Modification) Order 1983, successive employment in different local government organisations or various other public bodies will be deemed to be continuous for redundancy payment purposes as if they were associated employers.

8.43 Finally, continuity is preserved when there has been a relevant transfer within the meaning of the Transfer of Undertakings (Protection of Employment) Regulations 1981. When an undertaking is sold or is otherwise disposed of (other than by a sale of shares, which does not affect the legal corporate entity) this will not operate to terminate the contract of employment of any person employed by the transferor, but will have the effect as if the contract was made between the employee and the transferee (see para 5.112).

8.44 In particular it should be noted that artificial breaks in employment consequent on a transfer are not to be favoured, and the Regulations are to be given a broad interpretation so as to preserve continuity where possible (*Macer v Abafast Ltd*).

8.45 For the effect of the Regulations on the unfair dismissal provisions, see para 8.185, and on redundancy, see para 10.28.

The effect of the continuity rules

8.46 The purpose of establishing continuity is to enable an employee to qualify, by virtue of his length of employment, for certain statutory rights. In particular, however, additional years of employment which can be saved by the continuity rules are of great value to an employee whose employment ultimately comes to an end for reason of redundancy, for he can then obtain a larger redundancy payment. Thus when there is a transfer of the business from one employer to another, if there is no continuity, he can obtain his redundancy payment, and then start afresh with the new employer; on the other hand, if there is to be continuity, the new employer takes over the financial obligation of an ultimate redundancy payment should this prove to be necessary in the future.

What is dismissal? (EPCA, s. 55)

8.47 There are four ways in which a dismissal may take place.

A. Employer termination

8.48 Where the contract of employment is terminated by the employer, with or without notice. It follows that (subject to the doctrine of constructive dismissal, discussed below) if an employee resigns of his own volition, there is no dismissal. In *Elliot v Waldair (Construction) Ltd* the applicant was engaged as a driver, and mainly drove a heavy lorry. It was decided that this work was too hard for him, and he was instructed to drive a smaller van. This he refused to do because it would reduce his opportunity of overtime earnings, and he resigned. It was held that the order to drive a different vehicle at the same hourly rate but with less opportunity to earn overtime could not be said to constitute a dismissal by the employer.

8.49 Equally, a mutually agreed termination does not amount to a dismissal. In *Harvey v Yankee Traveller Restaurant*, the applicant became pregnant, and although her employer made various arrangements to accommodate her, these were not satisfactory. After a discussion with her employer, she agreed to resign. It was held that this could not amount to a dismissal. A warning that a dismissal is being contemplated in the future (e.g. for reason of impending redundancy etc) is not a dismissal (*Doble v Firestone Tyre and Rubber Co Ltd*).

8.50 The fact that the employer invited the employee to resign may, however, constitute a dismissal, for the alternative may be expressed or implicit in the request. in *Robertson v Securior Transport Ltd* the applicant had broken a company rule by signing for a container which had not been received. When this was discovered, he was given the alternative of resigning or being dismissed, and he chose the respectable course. It was held that he had been dismissed nonetheless. But although a resignation under duress may be a dismissal (*East Sussex County Council v Walker*), an invitation to resign as an alternative to facing a disciplinary hearing which may result in a dismissal is not, by itself, a dismissal (*Martin v Glynwed Distribution Ltd*). If the choice is put to the employee 'perform your contract or resign' this is not a dismissal, for the employee is making a decision not to carry out the terms of the contract which the employer is legally entitled to expect.

8.51 To falsely inveigle an employee to resign may also amount to a dismissal (*Caledonian Mining Co Ltd v Bassett and Steel*).

8.52 A dismissal can take place even though the employee invites this course of action. In *Thomas v General Industrial Cleaners Ltd* the applicant was in poor health, but did not wish to resign because of fears that he might lose certain benefits. He left the decision to the employers, who accepted the initiative and terminated his employment. The tribunal held that there was a dismissal by the employers.

8.53 Traditionally, the words used by the employer to denote that a dismissal has taken place are usually quite clear and explicit, but the niceties of social intercourse are not always observed in real life. In *Kendrick v Aerduct Productions*, the employer told an employee to 'fuck off'! Could this be construed as being equivalent to 'you're fired'? Or was it an expression of abuse with no other ulterior implication? If the words used are ambiguous, the industrial tribunal must ask themselves, what would a reasonable man understand by the expression in the context of the industry and the surrounding circumstances. In *Futty v Brekkes Ltd* the employee was a fish filleter. During an altercation with the foreman he was told 'if you do not like the job, you can fuck off'. He took this as a dismissal, found another job and claimed compensation. It was held that in the context of the particular trade, the words meant no more than 'if you do not like the work you are doing, you can clock off'. Indeed, had the applicant not received a promise of another job, he would have gone back to work the following day, and hence he had resigned, and had not been dismissed. But there is little doubt that there can be circumstances where telling an employee to 'fuck off' will amount to a dismissal (*a fortiori*, telling him to 'fuck off and piss off', see *King v Webb's Poultry Products Ltd*).

8.54 Equally, if the words used are unambiguous, the industrial tribunal must give them their natural and ordinary meaning (*Sothern v Franks Charlesly & Co*).

8.55 A further refinement on this theme was pursued in *Davy v Collins (Builders) Ltd*. During an argument, the employer said to the employee 'if you are not satisfied, you can fuck off'. The employee left and brought a claim for unfair dismissal, which failed. With dialectic ingenuity the tribunal drew a distinction between an employer saying 'I am not satisfied, so you can fuck off', and 'if you are not satisfied, you can fuck off'. In the former case there is likely to be a dismissal; in the latter case, the employer is saying to the employee, 'If you don't like it, you can lump it' and the applicant, not liking it, lumped it!

8.56 It is thus not the actual words which are used which are significant, but the intention behind them, and this must be ascertained from all the surrounding circumstances and the accompanying words as well as the industry, the relationships between the parties, and so on (*J & J Stern v Simpson*). If an employer or his manager, speaking in anger, behaves in a way which he might not do ordinarily, and utters abusive words, the industrial tribunal should consider very carefully whether the words amount to a dismissal, or whether they were little more than abuse (*Chesham Shipping Ltd v Rowe*). Events which followed the utterance of the offensive words and preceding the departure of the employee may be taken into account in so far as they throw light on the employer's intentions (*Tanner v Kean*).

8.57 Once a dismissal (or resignation) has taken place, it cannot be withdrawn unilaterally (*Harris & Russell Ltd v Slingsby*), but words used in the heat of the moment, and withdrawn almost immediately may be ignored, for it is vital to good industrial relations that either the employer or the employee should be given the opportunity to recant (*Martin v Yeoman Aggregates Ltd*).

B. Fixed term contract expires

8.58 Where the employee is employed for a fixed term, a dismissal takes place if that term expires without being renewed under the same contract. The exclusion of certain fixed term contracts has already been noted above, and it follows that a contract not within those exclusions will result in a dismissal if it is not renewed.

8.59 But a dismissal which takes place in this manner must still be tested for fairness in terms of the reasonableness of the employer's action in not renewing the contract. Thus if there is a genuine need for an employee to have a fixed term contract (e.g. of a temporary nature, or for a specific purpose, etc) then it may be reasonable not to renew this after expiry. It is important that employees should not be deprived of their statutory rights by dressing up an ordinary job as a fixed term contract (*Terry v East Sussex County Council*). Further, when a fixed term contract expires, an employer may be acting unreasonably if he fails genuinely to consider the employee for employment in some other suitable post (*Oakley v Labour Party*).

8.60 A fixed term contract was defined in *BBC v Ioannou* as a contract which must run for a fixed period, and one which cannot thus be terminated earlier except for a gross breach by either party. Some difficulty has arisen with what might be described as 'apparent fixed term contracts', i.e. contracts which are for a period of time (e.g. two years) but which contain a clause that either side may terminate the contract by giving (say) one month's notice. Since such a contract is not bound to run for the whole period, it cannot be a fixed term contract. As such, if it does run the whole period, and expires without being renewed, this cannot amount to a dismissal, for the rule only applies to fixed term contracts. In a number of cases, the industrial tribunals followed the principle in *BBC v Ioannou*, even though this exposed an obvious loophole in the law, but in *Dixon* *v BBC*, the Court of Appeal held that a fixed term contract existed if it was for a specific term, even though it was terminable by notice on either side during that term.

8.61 However, s. 2(2) of EPCA requires that in respect of fixed term contracts, the statement given under s. 1 of the Act shall state the date when the contract will expire. It follows therefore, that a contract to perform a specific task, e.g. to complete a sea voyage, or a contract terminable on some future event, e.g. at the end of the present Parliament, cannot be fixed term contracts, as they are of uncertain duration (*Wilts CC v NATHFE and Guy*).

C. Constructive dismissal

8.62 Where the employee himself terminates the contract, with or without notice, in circumstances that he is entitled to terminate it without notice by reason of the employer's conduct. This is sometimes referred to as 'constructive dismissal', for although the employee resigns, it is the employer's conduct which constitutes a repudiation of the contract, and the employee accepts that repudiation by resigning.

8.63 The doctrine of constructive dismissal has had a somewhat chequered history. The real problem was to determine the nature of the conduct of the employer which entitles the employee to resign. Did such conduct have to amount to an actual breach of contract by the employer, or could any unreasonable conduct by the employer be sufficient to entitle an employee to resign? For a long time the latter theory held sway, leading to some of the most bizarre and eccentric decisions in the whole of employment law. This view was firmly disposed of by the Court of Appeal in *Western Excavating Ltd v Sharp*, and all previous decisions must be read subject to this case. The facts were that the employee was dismissed for taking unauthorised time off work. He appealed to the internal disciplinary board, which substituted a penalty of five days' suspension without pay. This he accepted, but being short of money, he asked his employers if he could have an advance on his accrued holiday pay. This was refused. He then asked if he could have a loan of £40, but this too was refused. Consequently he resigned (in order to get his holiday pay) and brought a claim for unfair dismissal, alleging that he was forced to resign by virtue of the employer's conduct. His claim was upheld by the industrial tribunal;

the conduct of the employers was so unreasonable that the employee could not fairly be expected to put up with it, and justified him leaving. On appeal, the EAT was not sure that they would have come to the same decision had they heard the case, but held that the industrial tribunal were entitled to come to that decision. This was reversed by the Court of Appeal. The test for constructive dismissal was to be determined by the contract test, i.e. did the employer's conduct amount to a breach of contract which entitled the employee to resign. The 'unreasonable conduct' theory was dismissed as leading to a finding of constructive dismissal on the most whimsical grounds. Since there had been no breach of contract by the employers in *Sharp's* case (for the employers were under no contractual obligation to make the payments which were requested) there was no dismissal, constructive or otherwise.

8.64 It follows, therefore, that only those cases where the employer's conduct amounts to a significant breach, going to the root of the contract, can now be regarded as being authoritative. Thus, if the employer tries to impose a unilateral change in employment terms, such as a change in the job, a lowering in earnings (*Hill Ltd v Mooney*), a significant change in the location of employment (*Courtaulds Northern Spinning Ltd v Sibson*), a demotion, then provided there is no contractual right to do so, such conduct will entitle an employee to resign. However, it must be borne in mind that although this may amount to a dismissal in law, whether the dismissal is fair or unfair has still to be determined by the facts of the case, and whether or not the employer has acted reasonably (*Industrial Rubber v Gillon*).

8.65 If there is a genuine dispute concerning the nature of the parties' contractual obligations, this does not indicate an intention on the part of the employer to break the contract, and hence this will not be grounds for claiming constructive dismissal. In *Frank Wright & Co Ltd v Punch* the applicant claimed that he was entitled to receive cost of living increases in his salary. The employers disputed that they were contractually obliged to pay, and so he resigned, claiming constructive dismissal. The EAT held that where there was a genuine dispute as to the construction of a contract, or a genuine mistake as to fact or law, the courts would be unwilling to hold that an expression of intent by a party to carry out the contract in accordance with his (possibly erroneous) interpretation amounts to a repudiation of that contract. In *Bridgen v Lancashire County Council* the Master of the Rolls (Sir John Donaldson) expressed the view that the mere fact that a party to the contract takes a view of construction which is ultimately shown to be wrong does not, of itself, constitute repudiatory conduct. It has to be shown that he did not intend to be bound by the contract as properly construed. If the reasoning in these two decisions is correct, a number of previous decisions on constructive dismissal must be regarded as being of doubtful authority.

8.66 It finally remains to be resolved what sort of breach of which sort of terms will entitle an employee to resign. There is little problem if the breach is of an express term, or not within the scope of the contract at all. In *Simmonds v Dowty Seals Ltd* the applicant was a night worker. He was threatened with disciplinary action if he refused to work on day shift, and it was held that in attempting unilaterally to change his contract, the employers had repudiated it, entitling him to resign. But a failure to pay salary on the due date was held not to have been so serious a breach in *Adams v Charles Zub Associates*. The employer's action did not show an intention not to be bound by the contract.

8.67 More difficult are those cases where the employee claims he is entitled to resign because the employer has broken an implied term of the contract (see para 3.17) because the nature of these terms may sometimes be a matter for speculation and conjecture. In *British Aircraft Corpn v Austin* a failure to investigate a complaint about the inadequacy of protective spectacles was held to be a breach of the employer's implied duty to take reasonable care for the employee's safety, and in *Graham Oxley Tool Steels Ltd v Firth* it was held that there was an implied term that the employer will provide a proper working environment. If no reasonable employer would have expected the employee to work in those conditions, then there is a fundamental breach of the contract of employment (*Dutton & Clark Ltd v Daly*). It will be recalled (para 6.8) that there is an implied duty of mutual respect, and therefore any action by or on behalf of the employer which runs contrary to that duty may amount to constructive dismissal. This could be the use of foul and abusive language (*Palmanor Ltd v Cedron*), making unjustifiable complaints or giving unjustified warnings (*Walker v Josiah Wedgwood*), making statements which destroy or seriously damage the relationship of trust and confidence which must exist between the parties (*Courtaulds Northern Textiles Ltd v Andrew*), such as ill-founded allegations of theft (*Robinson v Crompton Parkinson*), offensive and insensitive conduct by a supervisor (*Hilton International Hotels Ltd v Protopapa*), and so on.

8.67A There is no implied term in a contract which entitles an employee to facilities for smoking, and if an employer introduces a general rule which has the effect of banning smoking on the premises, this does not operate so as to frustrate the employee's attempt to perform the contract because he cannot comply with the rule. Such a rule has a legitimate purpose, and the fact that it bears hard on a particular individual does not warrant an inference that the employer had repudiated the contract so as to enable the employee to claim he has been constructively dismissed (*Dryden v Greater Glasgow Health Board*, see para 3.42A).

8.67B Even if there is an express term in the contract enabling an employer to transfer the employee to another location, there is an implied term that the employer will give reasonable notice of the transfer and, where appropriate, relocation and other allowances will be made, so as to make it feasible for the employee to comply with the contractual obligation to transfer (*United Bank Ltd v Akhtar*).

8.68 A further problem arises when the employer makes life as difficult or as uncomfortable as possible, in the hope (or expectation) that the hint will be taken, and the employee will resign. No doubt a great deal will depend on the extent of the evidence which shows whether or not the employer is in breach of an express or implied term of the contract. Situations do occur when the parties wish to part company, but the employer is scared to take the initiative for fear of having a claim being brought against him, and the employee is reluctant to resign without at least having an opportunity to collect some financial reward which is available under modern legislative provisions. It is here that the vagaries of the doctrine of constructive dismissal present the greatest menace, for the uncertainties are enormous.

8.69 In *Haseltine Lake & Co v Dowler* the applicant was told that there was no future with the firm for him and that he should seek another job elsewhere. Eventually he found another job, resigned his employment and claimed he had been constructively dismissed. The EAT rejected his claim. No date had been fixed by the employers for his resignation, and before a contract of employment can terminate, there must be an ascertainable date on which it came to an end. This was not a case of 'resign or you will be dismissed', and therefore there was no repudiation of the contract by the employers.

8.70 There is a serious danger that the breach of an implied term theory will replace the 'unreasonable conduct' test and become just as capricious and whimsical in its results. Already the EAT has given its blessing. In *Gardner v Beresford* an employee resigned because she had not had a pay increase for two years, whereas other employees had. It was held that although there was no express term of the contract relating to pay increases, in most cases it was possible to imply a term that an employer would not treat an employee capriciously, arbitrary or inequitably in matters of remuneration. The EAT remitted the case to the industrial tribunal to ascertain whether or not in fact the employer had thus treated the employee, and if so, there would be a good claim for constructive dismissal under the new test in *Western Excavating v Sharp*.

8.71 But this does not mean that a failure to give an annual pay rise to an employee is a breach of contract, for it is impossible to say that there is an implied term to that effect. The test is whether such failure is arbitrary and capricious. Thus, if the employer can show a good reason, such as inadequate performance by the employee, there is no breach of the duty of mutual trust and confidence (*Murco Petroleum Ltd v Forge*).

8.72 Even more disturbing was the re-appearance of the 'unreasonable conduct' test in a new disguise. It will be recalled that in constructive dismissal cases, one must look for the breach of contract. There is generally no difficulty in ascertaining the express terms, but the implied terms are discovered by looking at what was 'obvious', so obvious in fact that the parties omitted to insert them (para 3.22). However, in *Pepper & Hope v Daish* the EAT took the view that it was possible to imply a term into a contract if it was 'reasonable' to do so! In this case the applicant negotiated a personal hourly wage rate for himself in December 1978. In January 1979 there was a general increase for all hourly workers of 5%, but this was not given to the applicant. He resigned and claimed constructive dismissal.

It was held that he could succeed, on the basis that it was reasonable to imply a term into his contract that he would also be given general wage increases. It will be noted that the reasoning in this case is inconsistent with the later decision in *Frank Wright & Co Ltd v Punch* (para 8.65) for there appeared to be a genuine dispute as to the interpretation of the contract.

8.72A However, the EAT changed direction again in the recent case of *White v Reflecting Roadstuds Ltd.* Here, the employee was working in the employer's despatch department but, as his own request, he was transferred to the mixing department, which involved higher pay, but also harder work. After about a year, he requested a move to lighter work, which was not then possible. From then on, his attendance deteriorated, and, after being given a formal warning, he was transferred to the pressing department, which involved a considerable drop in his pay. He then resigned, claiming that the decision to move him to another department constituted a fundamental breach of his contract of employment. In their defence, the company pointed to a flexibility clause in the contract which gave them the right to transfer employees to alternative work if the requirements of operational efficiency so dictate, and also that a willingness of employees to do so was a condition of the contract. An industrial tribunal held that the express right to transfer from one department to another was subject to two implied terms, namely (a) that it would be exercised in a reasonable manner, and (b) that the transfer would not result in a unilateral reduction in the employee's pay. On appeal, the EAT reversed the decision on both grounds. On the first point, the EAT stated that to imply a term that a flexibility or mobility clause should be handled reasonably would be to introduce the 'reasonableness' test into constructive dismissal cases by the back door and would fly in the face of the authority of *Western Excavating (ECC) Ltd v Sharp*. Although a 'capricious' decision would not come within the express authority (*United Bank v Akhtar*), if there are reasonable and sufficient grounds for operating the clause, the employers are entitled to reach such decisions. On the second point, it was held that if an employer acts within the contract, the fact that the change results in a unilateral reduction in the employee's pay does not constitute a fundamental breach of the contract (see *Spafax Ltd v Harrison*).

8.73 Also, if the employer is in breach, but the employee does not resign, and subsequently alleges a further breach, the industrial tribunal should take into account the whole of the employer's conduct, and not merely the latest incident which led to the resignation (*Lewis v Motorworld Garages Ltd*).

8.74 Lawful conduct by an employer is not capable of constituting a repudiation (*Spafax Ltd v Harrison*). Thus a disciplinary transfer, carried out in accordance with a proper procedure, which results in an employee suffering a drop in his earnings, is not a constructive dismissal (*High v British Railways Board*). Nor can an employee claim constructive dismissal merely because he is moved away from that part of his job which he enjoys the most on to less interesting work, if he is contractually obliged to do that work (*Peter Carnie & Son v Paton*). However, a disciplinary sanction which is disproportionate to the offence, even though carried out in accordance with the terms of the contract, can be a constructive dismissal (*BBC v Beckett*, para 7.58).

8.75 Since the employee is claiming that the employer has broken the contract, he must resign as a result of that breach. If he continues to report to work, he may be deemed to have waived the breach, and can hardly bring a claim subsequently based on the employer's repudiation, for 'the law does not allow him to have his cake and eat it' (*Hunt v British Railways Board*). But if he protests about the breach, but stays on until he finds himself another job, he may not necessarily be deemed to have accepted the employer's breach (*Miller v Shanks & McEwan*) provided that he acts reasonably expeditiously (*Cox Toner (International) Ltd v Crook*). But a distinction must be drawn between the waiver of a breach and the non-waiver of a continuing breach.

8.76 If the employee resigns with notice, he may present his claim before that notice has expired (*Presley v Llanelli Borough Council*), but if he resigns without notice, he can rely on the provisions of s. 55(6) to 'pull him past the post' if he lacks the necessary period of continuous employment.

8.77 If the employer announces an intention to break the contract at a future date, and the employee does not accept the breach, it is open to the employer to inform the employee that the contract will be performed. The employee will thus lose the right to claim constructive dismissal (*Norwest Holst Group Administration Ltd v Harrison*).

8.78 It must be stressed again that the fact that there is constructive dismissal does not necessarily mean that the dismissal is unfair (*Milthorn Toleman Ltd v Ford*), and there have been a number of cases where a constructive dismissal has been held to be a fair dismissal (e.g. *Savoia v Chiltern Herb Farms Ltd*). Even if it is unfair, compensation may still be reduced for contributory conduct. An employer faced with a constructive dismissal claim should be prepared to fight it on two fronts: (a) he may argue that there was no dismissal, and (b) in the alternative, if there was a dismissal, it was fair because ... etc. A failure to adopt this course may result in a finding that there was a (constructive) dismissal, and, if no reason for the dismissal is advanced, it must automatically be unfair (*Derby City Council v Marshall*). Whether an employer's conduct amounts to a constructive dismissal is a question of fact for the industrial tribunal to determine (*Woods v W M Car Services (Peterborough) Ltd*).

D. Deemed dismissal

8.79 If a woman is entitled to return to work after confinement, and has purported to exercise her rights in accordance with s. 47, but is not permitted to return to work, then for the purpose of the unfair dismissal provisions, she shall be treated as being employed until the notified date of return, as having been continuously employed until that date, and as having been dismissed for the reason she was not permitted to return to work (s. 56).

Termination of the contract

8.80 There are a number of ways in which a contract may come to an end, but which do not amount to a dismissal in law.

A. Resignation

8.81 If an employee resigns, then (unless it is a constructive dismissal) he has not been dismissed. If the words used by the employee are clear and unambiguous (e.g. 'I am leaving, I want my cards') then there are no grounds for the industrial tribunal to find that the words have a significance other than their plain meaning (*Gale Ltd v Gilbert*). If the words are ambiguous, then the test is, what would a reasonable employer have understood by those words in that context (*Tanner v Kean Ltd*)? If an employee is threatened that if he does not resign he will be dismissed, a consequent resignation will amount to a dismissal, but if his resignation is brought about by other factors, such as an offer of a financial inducement, this is not a dismissal (*Sheffield v Oxford Controls*).

8.81A Words spoken or action taken by an employee in the heat of the moment or under extreme pressure should not necessarily be taken at face value. The employer should allow a reasonable time to elapse before accepting such an apparent resignation to see whether this was what was really intended. If the employer fails to make a proper investigation, he runs the risk that an industrial tribunal may hold that there are special circumstances where the apparent resignation was not really intended by the employee (*Kwik-Fit (GB) Ltd v Lineham*).

8.82 For a resignation to be effective to terminate the contract there must be an ascertainable date (express or implied) on which it will take effect. To say 'I am resigning at some future point in time' is a statement of intention, not a resignation, but to say 'I am resigning' is not ambiguous, for it indicates a present intention (*Sothern v Frank Charlesly & Co*). An industrial tribunal is entitled to conclude on the evidence that the words of apparent resignation used by the employee 'in the heat of the moment' should not be accepted at their face value (*Sovereign House Security Services Ltd v Savage*).

8.83 Whether an employee has resigned or was dismissed is a question of fact for the industrial tribunal to determine, and their findings cannot be challenged unless their conclusions were such that no reasonable industrial tribunal could have reached them (*Martin v Glynwed Distribution Ltd*).

B. Constructive resignation

8.84 If a breach of contract by the employer entitles the employee to resign and claim constructive dismissal, then why should not a breach of contract by the employee entitle the employer to claim that the contract has been terminated by 'constructive resignation'? This view was supported by a number of decisions by the EAT and industrial tribunals, but must now be discounted in the light of the decision of the Court of Appeal in *London Transport Executive v Clarke*, and all earlier decisions must be read in the light of this case. The facts were that Clarke wanted to go to Jamaica on extended unpaid leave, but permission was refused by the employers as he had already exhausted his entitlement under the rules. When he asked what would happen if he went without permission he was told that his name would be removed from the books. Nonetheless he went to Jamaica, stayed for seven weeks, and on his return he submitted a medical note, which the industrial tribunal viewed 'with some surprise'. While he was away, the employers wrote to his home address, stating that if no reply was received within 14 days, it would be assumed that he did not wish to continue his employment, and eventually his name was removed from the books. When he returned from Jamaica, he applied for his job back, and when this was refused, he claimed he had been unfairly dismissed. For the employers, it was argued that the applicant had 'resigned' but this view was rejected. It is trite law that if a person breaks a contract, the other party has two options; he can either accept the breach, and treat the contract as being at an end, or refuse to do so, and treat the contract as still subsisting. If he accepts the breach, he terminates the contract. Thus Clarke had been dismissed, and had not resigned. However, the Court of Appeal then went on to find that the dismissal, in the circumstances, was fair.

8.85 There is no doubt that this analysis is correct. The reason for the doctrine of constructive dismissal is because there is a statutory provision for it (EPCA, s. 55(2)(c)). There is no statutory doctrine of constructive resignation. Thus if an employee walks out of his job, or commits any other breach of contract, but nonetheless claims that he is entitled to resume his work, the employer must expressly or impliedly accept the repudiation, and this will constitute a dismissal. He must then satisfy the industrial tribunal that in the circumstances, having regard to the equity and substantial merits of the case, he acted reasonably in treating the repudiatory conduct as sufficient reason for dismissing the employee.

C. Implied resignation

8.86 However, it is submitted that there may be circumstances of implied resignation or resignation by conduct. Thus, if an employee disappears, and does not respond to the employer's communications, or if it is discovered that the employee is working for another employer, it may not be difficult to infer that he has resigned his employment. The point was made by Sir John Donaldson in *Harrison v George Wimpey Ltd*. 'Where an employee so conducts himself as to lead a reasonable employer to believe that the employee has terminated the contract, the contract is then terminated'.

D. Frustration of the contract

8.87 If the performance of the contract of employment is rendered impossible by some intervening event, then it will be terminated by frustration, not by dismissal. Frustration can only arise where there is no fault by either party, e.g. where accident or illness prevents the employee (or employer) from performing the contract. Where there is fault by one party, this is repudiatory conduct, not frustration. It is thus up to the other party to accept the repudiation and terminate the contract, or keep the contract open, as he chooses (*London Transport Executive v Clarke*, above). Clearly, if the repudiatory conduct was serious (e.g. being sent to prison) it would be rare for the dismissal to be categorised as being unfair (*Norris v Southampton City Council*).

8.88 There are two situations which commonly occur, and which may give rise to the doctrine of frustration. The first is long-term absence through accident or illness (*Notcutt v Universal Equipment Ltd*), the second is imprisonment (*FC Shepherd v Jerrom*).

8.89 To decide whether or not a contract will terminate by frustration, regard must be had to the length of time the employee is likely to be away from his work, and thus be unable to perform his contract, the need for the employer to obtain a replacement, the length of time he has been employed, his position, and so forth. In cases where the employee is absent for a long time through sickness, all these factors are relevant, and in addition the employer must consider the nature of the illness (or injury), how long it has continued and the prospects for recovery, as well as the terms of the contract, including the provision of sick pay (see *Marshall v Harland & Wolff Ltd*). The mere absence from work, even for a long time, will not automatically constitute frustration. Thus in *Maxwell v Walter Howard Designs Ltd* the applicant was away sick for nearly two years, during which time he sent in regular sick notes. His job, as a cabinet maker, was one which did not need to be filled by a permanent replacement, and so, despite the passage of time, it was held that the contract had not been frustrated.

8.89A But if it is clear that on the medical evidence, the employee is unlikely to return to work for a considerable time, then there must come a point at which the employer is entitled to decide that the employee will not be returning to work, and consequently treat the contract as being frustrated. The problem is, when, exactly, does that point in time come about, and to this question there is no easy answer (see *Scarr v Goodyear & Sons Ltd*). In employment cases, the courts and tribunals must guard against too easy an application of the doctrine of frustration, especially when redundancy occurs, or where the true reason for the dismissal is disability (*Williams v Watsons Luxury Coaches Ltd*).

8.90 In *Egg Stores v Leibovici*, the EAT stated that there may be a long process before it can be said that illness has brought about a frustration of the contract. But if the time arrives when one can say that matters have gone on for so long, and the prospects for future employment are so poor, that it is no longer practical to consider the contract as still subsisting, then frustration will occur. Among the matters to be taken into account to reach this conclusion are (1) the length of the employment (2) how long it would have been expected to continue (3) the nature of the job (4) the nature, length and effect of the illness (5) the need to appoint a permanent replacement (6) the risk to the employer of acquiring further obligations in respect of redundancy payments or unfair dismissals (7) whether wages are still being paid (8) the acts and statements of the employer in relation to the employee, including his failure to dismiss, and (9) whether in all the circumstances a reasonable employer could be expected to wait for the employee any longer. To this we may add (a) the terms of the contract as to sick pay, and (b) a consideration of the prospects of recovery (*Williams v Watsons Luxury Coaches Ltd*).

8.91 That none of these tests, by themselves, can be conclusive can be seen from the decision in *Hart v Marshall (Bulwell) Ltd* where the applicant became sick in April 1974. In August of that year, the employers engaged a permanent replacement but the applicant continued to send in sick notes. In January 1976 the applicant presented himself for work, but was told there was no job for him, and he was given his cards. He claimed that this constituted unfair dismissal, but the EAT upheld a tribunal finding that the contract had been frustrated. The failure by the employers to act on the absence by dismissing the applicant was not, by itself, evidence that they will continue to regard him as an employee. Otherwise an employer would be in a difficult situation with regard to a sick employee; if he dismissed him prematurely, this might be unfair, if he engaged a temporary replacement, he might have to pay compensation at the end of that contract in order to permit the sick employee to return to work. Nor was the fact that the employee continued to send in sick notes indicative of anything other than the employee was keeping in touch in case there was a prospect of future employment. The crucial factor appears to be the finding that the applicant occupied a key position, which had to be filled, and thus the contract was frustrated.

8.92 Imprisonment, though self-induced, is not strictly speaking repudiatory conduct, for it does not amount to a breach of the contract of employment. But there is an inherent contradiction, because the doctrine of frustration arises when an event occurs without the fault of either party, and a person who had been given a custodial sentence will invariably be at fault. The answer appears to be that the person asserting the frustration (i.e. the employer) must show that there was no fault on his part, and the person against whom frustration is being asserted (i.e. the employee) cannot rely on his own misconduct by way of an answer (*FC Shepherd v Jerrom*).

8.93 Frustration arises by operation of law, not a conscious decision by the parties, and whilst it is not necessary to be able to point to the exact moment in time when the relationship between the parties is dissolved, the burden of proving that the contract has been frustrated lies on the employer. Thus, if an employee is sent to prison, this can be an instantaneously frustrating event or a potentially frustrating event. Accordingly, regard has to be paid to:

a. when it was commercially necessary for the employer to make a decision about the employee's future;
b. what a reasonable employer would consider to be the likely length of the employee's absence; and
c. whether it was reasonable to engage a permanent rather than a temporary replacement (*Chakki v United Yeast Co Ltd*).

E. Consensual termination

8.94 A consensual termination arises when the employment is terminated by mutual agreement, and the reason for that agreement is generally irrelevant (*Birch v Liverpool University*). Since there is no dismissal, no statutory rights ensure. However, a person who volunteers for redundancy has volunteered to be dismissed, and is entitled to a redundancy payment (*Burton Allton & Johnson Ltd v Peck*).

8.95 A mutual agreement whereby the employment will come to an end on the happening of a future event is not a consensual termination. In *Igbo v Johnson Matthey Chemicals Ltd* the applicant wished to take extended leave. She signed a document which stated that she agreed to return to work by a certain date, and that if she failed to do so the contract of employment would automatically terminate. She failed to return to work on the due date, and her employers treated the contract as being at an end. She claimed that she had been unfairly dismissed. The Court of Appeal applied s. 140(1) of EPCA which stipulates that any provision in an agreement shall be void in so far as it purports to limit the operation of any provision in the Act. The document she signed purported to take away her right to claim that she was unfairly dismissed, and it was therefore void. The Court of Appeal overruled earlier authorities on this topic (including the case of *British Leyland v Ashraf*) and remitted the case to the industrial tribunal to determine whether her dismissal was fair or unfair.

8.95A However, a mutual agreement to bring a contract of employment to an end, made for good consideration, after the employee had received proper advice, and made without duress, is effective. In *Logan Salton v Durham County Council*, the applicant was due to attend a disciplinary hearing which was to consider a recommendation that he be dismissed. An agreement was then reached whereby, on terms, his employment would come to an end by mutual agreement. He subsequently claimed he had been unfairly dismissed, but his claim failed. The agreement was not void by virtue of s. 140(1) of EPCA, because it was not a contract of employment, or the variation of a contract of employment. The EAT distinguished this type of situation from that which occurred in *Igbo v Johnson Matthey Chemicals* (above).

F. Project termination

8.96 If a person is employed for a specific project, then on its completion, the employment will come to an end, and there is no dismissal (*Ironmonger v Movefield Ltd*). The contract is discharged by performance. For example, a contract to build a house, or to complete a sea voyage, will terminate when the object has been achieved (*Wilts CC v NATHFE and Guy*). In *Ryan v Shipboard Maintenance Ltd* the applicant worked for the employers on 31 jobs over a five-year period. Each job varied in time from one to eleven weeks, and at the end of each job, he would draw unemployment benefit until the next lot of work was available. After waiting eight weeks for a job, he decided to make a claim for a redundancy payment. It was held that his employment was on a job-to-job basis, at the end of which there was a discharge by performance. Thus he had not been dismissed.

G. Failure to return to work

8.96A A woman who fails to return to work after her maternity leave (together with any extension of time because of illness) has expired has not been dismissed, but the contract is 'terminated' (*Kelly v Liverpool Maritime Terminals Ltd*).

Fair and unfair dismissal (EPCA s. 57)

8.97 Once it has been established that a dismissal has taken place, it must then be determined whether or not the dismissal was unfair. Section 57 of the Employment Protection (Consolidation) Act 1978 lays down five grounds on which a dismissal is capable of being fair, as follows:

a. a reason relating to the capability or qualifications of the employee for performing the work of the kind which he was employed by the employer to do. 'Capability' includes any assessment by reference to skill, aptitude, health or other physical or mental quality, and 'qualifications' means any degree, diploma or other academic, technical or professional qualification relevant to the position which the employee holds;
b. a reason which relates to the conduct of the employee;
c. the redundancy of the employee;

d. because the employee could not continue to work in the position which he held without contravention (either on his part or on the part of the employer) of a restriction or a duty imposed by or under a statute;
e. some other substantial reason such as to justify the dismissal of an employee holding the position which he held.

8.98 Whether a particular dismissal based on one or more of these five reasons will be fair or unfair will depend on whether in the circumstances of the case (including the size and administrative resources of the employer's undertaking) the employer acted reasonably or unreasonably in treating the reason as a sufficient reason for dismissing the employee, and the question will be determined in accordance with equity and the substantial merits of the case (EPCA s. 57(3)). Further, whereas it is for the employee to prove that he was dismissed, it is for the employer to show the reason for the dismissal, and that it was one of the above five reasons. It will then be for the industrial tribunal to find, on the basis of the evidence presented, whether or not the employer had acted reasonably in treating that reason as a sufficient ground for dismissal. Thus if he fails to show the reason, or fails to show a reason which is one of the above five, the dismissal is automatically unfair. In *Raynor v Remploy Ltd* a group general manager was dismissed for alleged lack of business judgment and general inefficiency. He had been employed for five years, and the tribunal rejected the company's allegations as spurious. Since there was no evidence of incapability, the dismissal was unfair. In *Castledine v Rothwell Engineering Ltd* (see para 6.22) the tribunal refused to accept the general allegations of incompetence, pointing to the favourable reference given to an employee subsequent to his dismissal. The employer cannot expect to win his case if he fails to give or call evidence on which the tribunal can reach its conclusion on the reason for the dismissal or its reasonableness, and general allegations without such evidence will normally be insufficient. In *Whitaker v Milk Marketing Board*, an artificial inseminator was dismissed for incompetence and misconduct. Although the Board mentioned various farmers who were supposed to be dissatisfied with the service they had received, none was called to give evidence, and the dismissal was held unfair.

8.99 Broadly speaking, there are two stages in the process of determining whether or not a dismissal was fair. The first is the means whereby the decision is reached. This involves going through proper procedures (see Chapter 7) bearing in mind especially the provisions of the Code of Practice, so that there is a full investigation, a proper hearing, a right to appeal, etc. If the employer fails to follow a fair procedure, he must show that nonetheless he acted reasonably on the basis of the information at his disposal (*Polkey v A E Dayton Services Ltd*, see para 7.5), otherwise the unfair procedure will result in a dismissal being unfair, with compensation being reduced, if necessary (*Whitbread & Co plc v Mills*). The second stage is the actual decision taken, bearing in mind the reason for the dismissal, the need to consider mitigating circumstances, consistency and/or flexibility as appropriate, the terms of the contract, the size and nature of the employer's undertaking, and so on. No single factor, by itself, can be conclusive, and each case will turn on its own peculiar facts.

8.100 Further, the test is 'did the employer act reasonably?' not 'did the industrial tribunal agree with what the employer did?' (*Grundy (Teddington) Ltd v Willis*). A decision on whether the employer acted reasonably is a question of fact for the industrial tribunal to decide (*Iceland Frozen Foods Ltd v Jones*), which can only be challenged if the decision was perverse or based on an incorrect perception of the law.

8.101 In *Anandarajah v Lord Chancellor's Department*, the President of the EAT, Mr Justice Waite, made a major policy statement about the use of precedents in industrial tribunal hearings. Although these are of great practical assistance, they must not be relied upon as being of binding authority, but rather treated as guidelines. He continued:

> 'Sometimes the judgment in a particular case will be found to express, in helpful and concise language, some concept which is regularly found in this field of enquiry and it becomes of great illustrative value. But reference to such a case can never be a substitute for taking the explicit directions of the statute as a guiding principle.'

8.102 To determine whether or not the employer has acted reasonably in dismissing the employee, the current test is 'What would a reasonable employer have done'? There is a band of reasonableness within which one employer might decide to dismiss, whilst another might decide not to do so. If the circumstances of the case are such that a reasonable employer might dismiss, the dismissal will be fair even though not all the employers would take that view (*British Leyland (UK) Ltd v Swift*).

8.103 The point in time at which the reasonableness of the employer's decision to dismiss is to be tested is when the employment comes to an end, not when the decision is taken, nor when the notice to terminate is given (*Stacey v Babcock Power Ltd*). Thus if an initial decision to dismiss was unfair because of a defect in the disciplinary proceedings, it may be cured if an appeal hearing is properly conducted (see *Clark v Civil Aviation Authority*, para 7.12A). Matters which come to light after the employment has ended are generally irrelevant (*Greenall Whitley plc v Carr*).

8.104 In *Kent County Council v Gilham* the Court of Appeal stressed once again that whether or not an employer acts reasonably is a question of fact for the industrial tribunal. That two industrial tribunals, considering the same broad issues, had reached opposite conclusions did not indicate that either had misdirected themselves in law. It is endemic in the system that different answers will be given to broadly similar situations, and the decision cannot be challenged just for that reason.

Reasons for the dismissal

8.105 Although the Act lays down five potentially fair reasons for dismissal, it will be convenient to make further sub-divisions, so that in practice ten reasons for fair dismissal appear. This enables a more practical analysis to be made. Bearing this in mind, we can examine the general approach of the courts and tribunals to the problems of dismissals.

1. Inherent inability

8.106 To dismiss an employee who is not capable of performing his job properly will be fair provided the employer acts reasonably in the circumstances. Thus, faced with the problem of an incompetent worker, what does the reasonable employer do? He enquires into the matter, to find out why the employee cannot do the job adequately. Has he been trained properly, so that he knows how the job should be done? Has he been properly supervised, been given an adequate job description? Does he have proper equipment, sufficient support staff and facilities? In other words, the employer's first task is to find out the reason for the alleged incompetence, and so far as it is possible, do something about it from the employer's point of view.

8.107 For example, in *Davison v Kent Meters Ltd* the applicant was dismissed for assembling nearly 500 components in the wrong sequence. She claimed that she had followed the pattern of work in accordance with the instructions received from her chargehand, but the latter denied having shown her how to assemble the parts, and maintained that she was entirely to blame for the errors. The industrial tribunal thought that if the chargehand had not shown her what to do, he should have done so, and the mistakes were therefore hardly her fault! Further, he should have checked on her performance, and supervised her properly. Not surprisingly, the dismissal was held to be unfair.

8.108 A warning should not be given merely for the sake of conforming with a laid down procedure, for this is to treat it as a mechanical system with no real significance. A warning is designated to do a job of work; it should have as its purpose the object of bringing an employee away from the brink of dismissal. It follows, therefore, that if the employee is suffering from an irredeemable incompetence, no amount of warnings will make any difference, and therefore there cannot be a need to issue them (*Sutton & Gates Ltd v Boxall*). In *Littlewoods Organisation Ltd v Egenti* the EAT pointed out that there is a distinction between disciplinary procedures and capability procedures. The former should be applied strictly, whereas this does not need to be so with regard to the latter. To give a warning in capability cases is not a matter of procedure; it is a matter of substance (*Dunning (Shopfitters) Ltd v Jacomb*). In other words, the question is, would a warning have done any good? Would it have rendered this dismissal unnecessary? If the answer is yes, then the warning should have been given. If the answer is no, then, since no amount of warnings would make any difference, there is no need to give them. Thus in *Lowndes v Specialist Heavy Engineering Ltd* the applicant was dismissed after five serious and costly errors. No written warnings were given, and he was not allowed an opportunity to state his case. The dismissal was held to be fair; it would have made no difference had a different procedure been adopted. But if the industrial tribunal finds that a fair procedure might have rendered the dismissal unnecessary, then a failure to follow that procedure would make the dismissal unfair (*Charles Letts & Co Ltd v Howard*).

8.109 Finally, the reasonable employer will consider alternatives before he dismisses the employee. Is there some other work which can be offered within the level of competence of the employee? Would he accept it if it was offered? Would he make a success of it? Clearly, much will depend on the circumstances of the case. In *Bevan Harris Ltd v Gair*, the applicant, who had been employed as a foreman, was dismissed after 11 years' service for poor performance, about which he had been warned on four occasions. The industrial tribunal held the dismissal to be unfair, because a reasonable employer would have demoted him rather than resort to dismissal. The decision was reversed by the EAT. The employer had given serious consideration to offering the applicant another job, but had decided against it. The small scale of the business, and the loss of confidence in the employee's abilities, meant that the decision to dismiss fell within the band of reasonableness, and in the circumstances, the dismissal was fair.

2. Neglectful incompetence

8.110 Here we must consider the employee who could do the job, but is not achieving his potential. The object of the exercise is to bring him up to the standards which he is capable of reaching, and for this purpose, the disciplinary procedure should be invoked, in accordance with the gravity of the matter.

8.111 If an employee is not working as well as he could, then a warning is appropriate; if he is refusing to obey instructions or is being generally unco-operative, then he should be told, firmly and by someone in authority, of the consequences which are likely to ensue. If the tribunal considers that had a clear warning been given a dismissal would not have been necessary (*Winterhalter Gastronom Ltd v Webb*), then it will conclude that a dismissal without such warning being given will be unfair (*Jones v GEC Elliott Automation Ltd*). An employee with long service is entitled to more consideration, if only because the employers can hardly be heard to say that it took them many years to discover his incompetence, but the fact that the employer has tolerated poor performance in the past is not conclusive, if the employee fails to respond to proper warnings (*Gozdzik v Chlidema Carpet Co*). A newly appointed employee should be given a chance to prove himself, and not judged on short-term results. Senior staff should have a greater appreciation of what is expected from them, whereas employees not in the managerial range should have greater attention paid to their requirements. If possible, the employer may consider giving the employee further training, should suitable facilities be available, assuming, that is, that the employee would be likely to benefit from such training. If the employee refuses to take advantage of this offer, at least the employer has acted in a reasonable manner, and a consequent dismissal may well be fair (*Coward v John Menzies (Holdings) Ltd*).

8.112 If there is a minor act of neglect, a warning is appropriate, to be followed, as necessary, with a further or final warning. A serious act of neglect might lead to an immediate final warning. But there are some acts of neglect which dare not be repeated, and hence dismissal is not inappropriate. In *Taylor v Alidair Ltd*, an airline pilot landed his aeroplane in a manner which caused some concern among the passengers and crew. After a proper investigation, it was decided that he had been negligent, and was dismissed. This was held to be fair: there are some activities where the degree of skill required is so high, or where the potential consequences of a departure from the highest standards are so serious, that one failure is sufficient to justify dismissal. A warning in such cases is totally inappropriate.

8.113 The law which prevents unfair dismissal must not be used to impede the efficient management of business by compelling employers to retain incompetent employees (*Cook v Thomas Linnell Ltd*), and once an employer has lost confidence in the employee's ability to do the job, then it is reasonable to dismiss and offer other employment should this be available. But the employer is not bound to create a vacancy if none exists; he should at least consider the possibility, and consider if the employee would make a success of it (*Brush Electrical Machines v Guest*).

8.114 If an employee is dismissed because of his incapability, the correct test to apply is whether the employer honestly and reasonably held the belief that the employee was not competent, and whether there are reasonable grounds for that belief. It is not necessary for the employer to *prove* that the employee was incompetent (*Taylor v Alidair Ltd*). In other words, the test under s. 57(3) is a subjective one. The industrial tribunal must consider the employer's state of mind as well as his reasons. But it is sufficient if the employer honestly believes on reasonable grounds that the employee is incompetent.

3. Long-term sickness

8.115 An employee who is absent from work for a long time because of sickness or ill-health is entitled to sympathetic consideration by the employer, but the employer can only be expected to act within sensible limits. The questions to be asked are (a) how long has the employment lasted (b) how long had it been expected the employment would continue (c) what is the nature of the job (d) what was the nature, effect and length of the illness (e) what is the need of the employer for the work to be done, and to engage a replacement to do it (f) are wages continuing to be paid (h) why had the employer dismissed (or failed to do so) and (i) in all the circumstances, could a reasonable employer have been expected to wait any longer (*Egg Stores v Leibovici*)? In other words, the employer is entitled to consider his business needs, as well as the employee's situation. An important point to consider is 'has the time arrived when the employer can no longer reasonably be expected to keep the absent employee's post open for him?' (*Hart v Marshall & Sons Ltd*). Thus if an employee is away for a long time, the employer should not dismiss as an automatic matter, but consider whether it is necessary to dismiss. The employer should make all necessary enquiries, from the employee, from his doctor, and if possible obtain an opinion from the firm's medical advisers (*East Lindsey District Council v Daubney*).

8.115A In all cases where dismissal on the grounds of ill-health is being considered, there is a need for enquiry, consultation, warnings, a search for alternatives etc, before the decision is taken (*A Links & Co Ltd v Rose*). But while in the normal case consultation is necessary, in wholly exceptional circumstances the absence of consultation does not render a dismissal unfair (*Eclipse Blinds Ltd v Wright* (para 4.128)).

8.116 The purpose of consulting with the employee about his health is to weigh up the situation, balancing the need of the employer to get the work done against the employee's need for time in order to recover his health. Without such consultation, the employer may act precipitously, with unfair consequences. But consultation is not demanded by law; if it is clear that the consultation would not have made any difference to the result, a failure to consult does not make a dismissal unfair (*Taylorplan Catering v McInally*).

8.117 Earlier cases had stated that an employer should warn an employee that unless he returns to work he will be dismissed, but this view is erroneous, for an employee cannot be warned that he has got to be in good health. However, the employer should make all proper and necessary enquiries from the employee, and not act in a precipitous manner. Perhaps the best way to express the employer's obligation is to say that he should treat the employee with sympathetic consideration, and that he should hold the job open for as long as is possible. In *Coulson v Felixstowe Dock and Rly Co Ltd* the applicant was away from work due to ill-health for considerable periods of time. He could no longer perform his duties, and was put on light clerical work. He was told that if he could not return to his old job, he would be regraded, and was given six months in which to prove his fitness. However, he fell ill again and was dismissed. It was held that the employer had treated the employee with every consideration, but there must come a time when the employer cannot be expected to keep someone on who is not doing his work. The tribunal had to consider fairness to the business as well as to the employee.

8.118 On the other hand, in *Converform (Darwen) Ltd v Bell*, the applicant was a works director who was off work because of a heart attack. He recovered, but the employers refused to permit him to return to work, as they thought there was the risk of another attack. His subsequent dismissal was held to be unfair. A risk of future illness cannot be used as a ground for fair dismissal unless the nature of the employment is such that the risk made it unsafe for the employee to continue in the job.

8.119 A good employer will try to fix a date by which time he must know when the employee expects to be able to give information about the likely date of return to work (*Marder v ITT Distributors Ltd*), but once having explained and discussed the situation with the employee, the employer is entitled to make a decision in the light of the information available (*Spencer v Paragon Wallpapers Ltd*).

8.120 In *Merseyside and North Wales Electricity Board v Taylor* the Divisional Court held that there is no rule of law which requires the employer to create a special job for an employee who is off sick. Nor is there a rule that an employer is obliged to find alternative employment for an employee plagued by ill-health. Each case must be judged on its own facts in the light of the employer's circumstances. It may be that the employer has some light work available of the kind which is within the employee's capacity to do, and the employee should be encouraged to take such a post, even at reduced rates of pay, before dismissal is considered.

8.121 In larger firms it may be possible for the company to place a sick employee in some form of holding department, so that he can recommence employment when fit, but there are certain legal problems about such a course which require further consideration. In *Burton v Boneham & Turner Ltd*, the management placed an employee in such a holding department after several spells of absence through illness. It was held that such conduct amounted in law to a dismissal, although in the circumstances, it was held to be fair. On the other hand, in *Parker v Westland Helicopters Ltd* a sick employee was transferred from the department concerned with sick employees to a holding department, where she had to wait for a suitable vacancy before being employed again. As this was done with her agreement, on the facts it was held that no dismissal had taken place.

8.122 The legal significance of placing employees in a holding department has yet to be fully explored. In *Marshall v Harland & Wolff Ltd* the NIRC held that such a transfer meant that the employee ceased to be employed in a legal sense, but the employers merely undertook some obligation to provide work if and when possible. If this is so, then the act of placing in the holding department amounts to a dismissal. On the other hand, it has been suggested (*O'Reilly v Hotpoint Ltd*) that such transfer suspends the contract of employment. If this view is correct, then continuity will doubtless be preserved for redundancy and other purposes, and presumably there is a legal (as opposed to moral) obligation to find an employee work when he recovers. It is clear that the matter should be subject of a defined policy which can be stated in the works/staff rules, so that the legal situation will be determined by the contractual obligations which can be laid down by the parties in accordance with the objective which they seek.

8.123 Employers cannot be expected to go to unreasonable lengths in seeking to accommodate a sick employee, and what is reasonable is largely a question of fact and degree in each case (*Garricks (Caterers) Ltd v Nolan*). In the last analysis, the employer must act within the range of reasonable responses, depending on the circumstances (*Rolls Royce Ltd v Walpole*).

4. Persistent absenteeism

8.124 The employee who is persistently away from work ill (or other reasons) for short periods at a time presents a different problem. This employee can be cautioned about his absences; he can be confronted with his record, told that it must improve, and be given a period of time in which an improvement can be monitored. Indeed, the employer should not ignore the powerful medicinal effect of a final warning, and a failure to give one may mean that the employee is unaware that the situation is causing the employer great concern. The effect of such a warning might be to stimulate the employee into seeking proper medical advice in case there is an underlying cause of the continuous minor ailments, it may deter the employee from taking time off when not truly warranted, and it may even lead the employee to look for other work where such absences could be tolerated (*Smith v Royal Alfred Merchant Seamen's Society*).

8.124A The employer should approach the situation with 'sympathy, understanding and compassion'. Factors to be taken into account include: (a) the nature of the illness, (b) the likelihood of it recurring, (c) the length of the various absences and the spells of good health in between, (d) the need of the employer to have that work done by that employee, (e) the impact of the absences on other employees, (f) the adoption and carrying out of the policy, (g) a personal assessment of the ultimate decision, and (h) the fact that the employee is fully aware that his employment will be terminated unless there is an improvement (*Lynock v Cereal Packaging Ltd*).

8.125 At the same time, the employer can hold out a helping hand; he can enquire from the employee the nature of all these minor ailments, offer such medical help as the firm can provide, provide counselling, etc, in those case where the employment is itself a major contributing factor to the illness, and so on.

8.126 In *International Sports Ltd v Thomson* the applicant was away from work for about 25% of the time, with a variety of complaints (all of which were covered by medical certificates) including dizzy spells, anxiety and nerves, bronchitis, virus infection, cystitis, althrugia of the left knee, dyspepsia and flatulence. She was given a series of warnings, including a final warning, and before deciding to dismiss her, the company consulted their medical adviser. He saw no useful purpose in examining her, as none of the previous illnesses could be verified, there was no common link between them and she was not suffering from any chronic illness. She was then dismissed, and the EAT held that the dismissal was fair. The company had undertaken a fair review of her attendance record, she had been duly warned and given the opportunity to make representations. A further medical investigation would have produced no worthwhile results. There must come a point in time when a reasonable employer is entitled to say 'Enough is enough'.

8.127 It is normal for many firms to have contractual entitlement to a certain amount of sick leave, some of which may be regarded as 'certified' or covered by sick notes. Certainly, an employee should keep his employer informed by the proper means, and a failure to do so may mean that the employee contributes to his own dismissal and receives a reduced compensation. But sick notes, by themselves, can never be conclusive, for there are serious doubts about their factual validity. Thus, if an employer believes that a sick note is phoney, or may not be accurate, then he is entitled to disregard it (*Hutchinson v Enfield Rolling Mills Ltd*).

8.128 In *Wilkes v Fortes (Sussex) Ltd* the EAT placed particular emphasis on a consideration of the size of the firm in determining whether or not it would be fair to dismiss an employee who is off work intermittently for sickness reasons. In a large firm, the disruption caused by such illnesses may be minimal; it is easy to have a float of overmanning to cover for absent employees. But in a small business, such absences may be extremely serious or even disastrous.

8.129 If a person's health if such that continued employment may well constitute a hazard, either to himself, to other employees, or is likely to cause damage to property, then provided the employer undertakes full consultation with the employee, and obtains expert medical opinion, this is capable of being a fair dismissal (*Spalding v Port of London Authority*), and it is not necessary for the employer to wait until an accident occurs before taking steps to dismiss (*Parsons v Fisons Ltd*). In *Finch v Betabake (Anglia) Ltd* the applicant was an apprentice motor mechanic. The employers received a report from an ophthalmic surgeon that the boy could not continue to work without undue danger to himself and to others. He was therefore dismissed. It was held that the circumstances in which an apprentice could be dismissed were limited, but in the circumstances, the dismissal was fair.

8.129A If the persistent absenteeism is due to factors other than ill-health, then warnings, as appropriate, should be given.

5. Lack of qualifications

8.130 There have been very few cases concerning the lack of qualifications for the job as a reason for dismissal. In *Blackman v Post Office* a telegraph officer was required to pass an aptitude test, but he failed after a maximum number of attempts. It was held that his dismissal was fair on the ground of lack of qualifications. But there must be a contractual obligation (express or implied) to hold the relevant qualification. In *Litster v Thom & Sons Ltd* the applicant was employed as a foreman fitter/driver. Government regulations required that special driving licences had to be obtained for drivers of heavy goods vehicles, and the applicant failed the necessary test. Nonetheless he was continued in employment as a fitter. His contract of employment contained no reference to the necessity of having an HGV licence. Following a dispute, he was told that unless he obtained such a licence, he would be dismissed. It was held that since his contract did not require him to hold that particular licence, a dismissal based on his lack of qualifications would be unfair.

8.131 However, it may be permissible to go outside the formal requirements of the contract. In *Tayside Regional Council v McIntosh*, the employers advertised for a vehicle mechanic, an essential requirement being that the successful applicant should have a driving licence. The applicant was appointed to the job, but his contract of employment made no mention of the need to hold a driving licence. He was subsequently disqualified from driving, and as there was no other suitable employment for him, he was dismissed. The EAT held that he had been fairly dismissed. The nature of the job clearly required the holding of a valid driving licence.

8.132 But even though it can be shown that the employee lacks the necessary qualification for the job, the employer must still act reasonably in treating that reason as a sufficient ground for dismissal. Thus in *Sutcliffe & Eaton v Pinney* the applicant was dismissed from his job as a trainee hearing aid dispenser after he failed to pass the necessary examinations. It was held that the employers should have applied for an extension of his training period so that he could take the examination again. In other words, as always, the reasonable employer will look around for alternatives to dismissal.

6. Conduct inside the employment

8.133 Under this heading we can consider all those acts of the employee which occur during the performance of the contract, and which are alleged to have an adverse effect on that contract. Such acts may be sub-divided in accordance with their gravity, i.e. acts of trivial nature (minor misconduct), serious matters (major misconduct) and extremely serious matters (gross misconduct). The importance of such a classification lies in the methods which are required to be adopted to solve the problem in question. For acts of minor misconduct, these can usually be dealt with by a warning (informal, then perhaps formal), but it would be wrong to utilise the full weight of a disciplinary sanction in order to deal with a trivial matter. Thus to give an employee a final warning 'if you come in late again you will be dismissed' is bound to lead to trouble at some later stage, for the sanction is out of all proportion to the offence. Such a person could be dealt with, for example, by a short period of suspension. Further, for some acts a single repetition would suffice to warrant dismissal (e.g. theft) and hence the warning would spell this out. But other acts may have to be monitored over a period of time, (e.g. lateness, absenteeism), and hence the warning will indicate the period, spell out the improvement required, and state the ultimate sanction. An act of major misconduct could be handled by an immediate final warning, without the need to go through stages in a procedure (i.e. informal warning, first written warning, etc), for the seriousness of the matter is sufficient to leap over other stages. And acts of gross misconduct, once proven, can lead to instant dismissal without notice, for this amounts to a breach by the employee which in effect repudiates the contract.

8.134 For all acts of misconduct, the employer must show that he gave the matter a prompt and thorough investigation, that he gave the employee an opportunity to state his case, interviewed witnesses and collected evidence so far as it was possible to do so, but there are limits to the power to an employer to investigate, and indeed, it may well be improper for him to do so on occasions. This is particularly true when the matter is to be the subject of criminal charges or investigation by the police. Thus in *Carr v Alexander Russell*, the applicant was dismissed when it was learned that the police had found some company property in his possession, and that he was to be charged with theft. It was held that the employers had no duty to carry out any detailed form of enquiry, for it would have been improper of them to do so, and a subsequent trial might have been seriously prejudiced.

8.135 There is no absolute prescription that an employee must be given an opportunity to explain his conduct before he is missed, though this course is clearly desirable. In *Parker v Clifford Dunn Ltd* the employers received information from the police that the applicant had admitted stealing from the company. He was therefore dismissed in accordance with the works rules. He did not appeal through the procedure, and made no protestation of innocence. His dismissal was held to be fair: it was reasonable for the employers to rely on the police investigations rather than carry out their own. But the mere fact that the police intend to charge an employee with theft is not conclusive, as they may decide not to proceed with the charge, or the evidence may be too weak to secure a conviction, and so on. Some enquiry may therefore be necessary (*Scottish Special Housing Association v Cooke*).

8.136 The acts which can constitute misconduct inside the employment are too numerous to categorise. Fighting, swearing, trading, drunkenness, betting, horseplay, incompetence, theft, neglect, dangerous or obstructive conduct, clocking offences, breach of safety rules, immorality, refusal to obey orders, breach of hygiene rules, insubordination, unauthorised absenteeism, disloyalty, breach of confidence, taking unlawful drugs, sleeping while on duty, computer hacking or seeking unauthorised access to a computer program, telling lies, unsuitable clothing, dishonesty, taking property without authorisation and lateness, have all, in their turn, been the subject of industrial tribunal proceedings. To deal with such conduct, the employer must consider the gravity of the offence, its effect on the employment generally, and the previous history of the employee. In other words, the employer, it is submitted, must take into account the offence, and the offender.

8.137 It is not the function of the industrial tribunal to substitute its views and opinions for those of management, but merely to decide if management has acted reasonably. For example, if an employee has committed an act of theft, it is for management to decide what should be done in the circumstances of the case, and provided a fair procedure is adopted, the eventual decision is that of management. In *Trust Houses Forte Hotels Ltd v Murphy*, the applicant was a night porter. He kept a small supply of liquor for hotel guests, but when his stock was checked, there was a deficiency of £10. He admitted taking some of this for his own use, and was dismissed. The industrial tribunal found this to be unfair, but the decision was reversed on appeal by the EAT. It would place an unreasonable burden on employers if they could not fairly dismiss employees who had stolen property which had been entrusted to their care. Although management might have been influenced by compassionate grounds, and might have decided not to dismiss an employee who had stolen a small amount of property, a reasonable management may have taken either view. Hence it was not possible to argue that this employer had acted unreasonably.

8.138 Nor need the employers prove that an offence has been committed beyond reasonable doubt, for this would impose on them a higher commitment than would ever be possible to fulfil, and impose a duty which rightfully belongs to a court of trial. The employers must genuinely believe that the employee has been guilty of the misconduct in question, they must have reasonable grounds for that belief, and they must have carried out such investigation into the matter as is reasonable in the circumstances (*British Home Stores v Burchell*). In *Laurie v Fairburn* the applicant was dismissed because the employers believed that she was stealing from them. The industrial tribunal was not convinced that this was so, and held the dismissal to be unfair. This was reversed on appeal; the question is not whether or not the employee was guilty, or would have been found guilty if tried, but whether it was reasonable for the employers to dismiss her, taking into account all the circumstances and facts known to the employers at the time of the dismissal.

8.139 If an employee makes a confession, this is a fact which the employer is entitled to take into consideration when forming his views, and the rules about the non-admissibility of confessions made involuntarily (the Judge's Rules) have no application in such circumstances (*Morley's of Brixton Ltd v Minott*).

8.139A Where an employee has pleaded guilty to a criminal offence, or been found guilty by the decision of a court or the verdict of a jury, it is reasonable for an employer to believe that the employee committed the offence. Any other conclusion would be ridiculous (*P v Nottinghamshire County Council*). This is so even if the employee alleges that he pleaded guilty on the advice of his lawyers, in order to avoid a prison sentence (*British Gas v McCarrick*).

8.140 The fact that an employee faces criminal charges subsequently, and is acquitted on those charges, is also irrelevant to the issue of the fairness of the dismissal. In *Da Costa v Optolis* the applicant was dismissed from his job as a book-keeper for not keeping proper accounts, and he subsequently faced criminal charges, though these ended in his favour. It was held that the fact the Crown Court had acquitted him did not preclude a finding by the industrial tribunal that the dismissal was fair. The issues involved were different. In the Crown Court, it has to be decided whether he was guilty of the charge beyond reasonable doubt, whereas in the industrial tribunal, it had to be shown whether the employer had reasonable grounds for dismissing him.

8.141 It must surely be sound policy for the employer to be consistent in his procedure, flexible in his decisions. Thus an employer may take into account the fact that the employee has had a long record of exemplary conduct (*City of Edinburgh v Stephens*), but the importance of such mitigating factors is a matter for the employer's discretion (*AEI Cables v McLay*). In *Taylor v Parsons Peebles Ltd* the applicant, who had been employed for 20 years without complaint, was dismissed for fighting. The EAT held the dismissal to be unfair. The company's policy had to be considered in the light of a reasonable employer's reaction to the incident. Given that the applicant had 20 years' good conduct, a reasonable employer would not have applied a rigid sanction of automatic dismissal. In failing to take account of mitigating circumstances, the employers had acted unreasonably. In *Hadjioannou v Coral Casinos Ltd* (see para

7.29) it will be recalled that the EAT stressed the need for flexibility in dealing with industrial misconduct, saying that a tariff approach was not correct.

8.142 If the conduct in question amounts to gross misconduct, then this should be acted upon immediately by management, for a delay may lead the industrial tribunal to conclude that the conduct was not so wrongful as to warrant the drastic punishment of instant dismissal, although in rare cases it is proper to dismiss summarily a long time after the event (*Refund Rentals v McDermott*). Normally, it would be reasonable to suspend pending an investigation, but again, this counsel of perfection cannot always be followed (*Conway v Matthew Wright & Nephew*).

8.143 If the conduct falls under the heading of breach of works rules (e.g. smoking in prohibited areas, fighting, failing to observe safety precautions, etc) then provided the rule is a reasonable one, has been duly promulgated and brought to the attention of the employees, then the tribunals will usually uphold management action (*Richards v Bulpitt & Sons Ltd*). But a minor breach should not be treated as an excuse for dismissal, no matter how strongly worded the rule may be (*Ladbroke Racing Ltd v Arnott*).

8.143A Before dismissing for gross misconduct, the employer should consider any alternative course of action, for it is not inconsistent with a finding of gross misconduct to offer the employee alternative employment in a different capacity (*Hamilton v Argyll and Clyde Health Board*). Each case must be considered on its merits, taking into account the special facts and mitigating circumstances. If, in the past, an employee has not been dismissed for a similar offence, management should enquire into those circumstances. The dangers of a tariff or consistent approach in cases where there is no true comparability should be avoided (*Procter v British Gypsum Ltd*).

8.144 Equally difficult is conduct by the employee which is strictly within his contractual rights, but which is obstructive in nature. In *Pengilly v North Devon Farmers Ltd* it was held that a refusal to work overtime, even though not compulsory within the terms of the employee's contract, warranted a dismissal, as the refusal was contrary to the normal practice, and the employee was trying to put improper pressure on the employer. But in *Burns v Ideal Timber Products* it was held that a refusal to work overtime in order to get the employer to improve working conditions did not amount to improper pressure.

8.145 The conduct of the employee must in some way reflect on the employment relationship. In *Thomson v Alloa Motor Co Ltd*, the applicant was employed as a petrol pump attendant. One day she finished work, and drove off in her car, but collided with a petrol pump, causing substantial damage. She was summarily dismissed, because of the seriousness of the damage and the fact that her employers would have to sue her for compensation. The dismissal was held to be unfair. The accident had no bearing on her ability to do her work, it was an incident unlikely to be repeated, and her employers were undoubtedly covered by insurance.

8.146 Whilst it may not generally be possible to dismiss an employee who is acting within the terms of the contract, it should be possible to call for a variation of that contract, or to terminate it and offer a new one (see Chapter 3). Provided the proper procedure is adopted, a subsequent dismissal may well be for 'some other substantial reason' (see below).

8.147 Other types of conduct which have been held to warrant dismissal include a refusal to wear the appropriate clothing required for the job (*Atkin v Enfield Hospital Management Committee*), wearing provocative badges contrary to instructions and warnings (*Boychuk v Symons Holdings Ltd*), carrying on sexual relations during business hours (*Newman v Alarmco*), passing on information to a former employee of the firm who is working for a competitor (*Smith v Du Pont (UK) Ltd*), refusing to cut exceptionally long hair after being warned of a safety hazard (*Marsh v Judge International*), breach of works rules (*Palmer v Vauxhall Motors Ltd*), suspected dishonesty (*Parkes Bakeries Ltd v Palmer*), breach of safety instructions (*Wilcox v Humphreys & Glasgow*), fighting (*Parsons v McLoughlin*), being a drug addict (*Walton v TAC Construction Materials Ltd*), refusal to go on a training course (*Minter v Wellingborough Foundries Ltd*), unauthorised access to a computer (*Denco Ltd v Joinson*), and so on.

8.148 Every employer is strongly urged to observe the provisions of the Code of Practice on Disciplinary Practice and Procedures, and although a breach of the Code will not automatically make a dismissal unfair (*Lewis Shops Group v Wiggins*), in practice it can be said that the provisions of the Code matter most when the decision to dismiss is at its weakest. Thus it is still possible to dismiss summarily for gross misconduct (*Retarded Children's Aid Society v Day*), but procedural fairness should always be observed, and a failure to follow the Code's recommendations may lead to a finding that the dismissal was unfair, even though the compensation may be reduced because of the employee's contributory conduct.

7. Conduct outside the employment

8.149 The problem which arises here is, what has it got to do with the employer what an employee does outside his working hours? The answer may well depend on a number of factors, including the nature of the employment, the position held by the employee, the nature of the incident and its effect on the employer, on customers, on fellow employees, and so on. If it can be said that the conduct in question has an adverse effect on the employer's business, then a dismissal may be fair. For example, the conduct may be a conviction by a court of law for a criminal offence unconnected with the employment. In *Richardson v City of Bradford Metropolitan Council* the applicant was a senior meat inspector, who was convicted of theft of money from his local rugby club on several occasions. When his employers were informed, he was suspended, but as there were no other suitable vacancies which could be offered to him, he was dismissed. This was held to be fair. The integrity of a public servant who was in a position of trust was of prime importance. In *Bradshaw v Rugby Portland Cement Co Ltd* the applicant was dismissed following a conviction for incest with his own daughter, for which he was placed on probation by the Crown Court. The dismissal was held to be unfair. The offence had no bearing on his work as a quarryman, the firm's customers would not have objected to his continued employment, and his relationship with his fellow-employees had not deteriorated to the extent that they objected to working with him. There must have been strong mitigating circumstances for the court to deal with the matter so leniently, and the tribunal did not see any reason to impose a further punishment. Clearly, different considerations would have applied had the applicant been (say) a schoolmaster. In *Gardiner v Newport County Borough Council* the applicant was a lecturer at an Art College, in charge of a foundation course on which were pupils who were between the ages of 16-18. He was convicted of gross indecency with another man in a public lavatory, and his dismissal by the College was held to be fair. The tribunal held that *Bradshaw*'s case was no authority for saying that a person who receives a moderate punishment from the court is immune from dismissal, for the courts are frequently being reminded in mitigation that whatever punishment they impose is only part of the misfortune which will befall the accused. The employers could not be expected to waive the consequences which the courts had anticipated and possibly allowed for in fixing the penalty. Nor is it relevant that the employer never told the employee of the kind of conduct outside his employment which would warrant dismissal, for an employer cannot possibly specify or anticipate all the possible circumstances which may lead to a dismissal. To hold otherwise would mean that an employee would be safest from dismissal if he committed some act which was more outrageous than anyone ever envisaged.

8.150 Thus an employer is entitled to make a judgment based on the criminal conduct of the employee, as to whether or not the conviction has impaired the employee's ability to do the job, and whether there has been a loss of confidence in the employee (*Robson v Brian Mills*). In *Moore v C & A Modes* the applicant was a section leader in a store, where she had been employed for 20 years. It was alleged that she had been caught shoplifting at another store. Her consequent dismissal was held to be fair. No-one should be more alive to the damage caused by shoplifters than such an employee, and it was unreal to expect an employer in the retail trade not to dismiss an employee whom he believed to be stealing from another store. In *Mathewson v R B Wilson Dental Laboratory Ltd*, the appellant was arrested during his lunch break for purchasing a small amount of cannabis. His subsequent dismissal was held to be within the range of reasonable responses which a reasonable employer might take.

8.151 'Moonlighting', i.e. the taking of additional employment outside normal working hours, may be grounds for dismissal if this has an adverse effect on the employer's business (see para 6.70). It will be recalled (para 6.71) that in *Hivac Ltd v Park Royal Scientific Instruments Ltd* the employees were in breach of their contracts for which they could have been dismissed, although this was prevented at the time by the operation of the Essential Works Order. The Court stated that it would be reluctant to impose on the employees a restriction which would hamper their ability to increase their earnings in their spare time, but on the facts they were inflicting great harm on the employer's business. In *Gray v C & P Pembroke Ltd* the applicant agreed to not engage in any other business without the written consent of the employer. Contrary to this agreement he took a part-time job with a rival company, and this was held to be a breach of faith for which he could be fairly dismissed. However, in *Nova Plastics v Froggatt* the applicant was employed as an odd-job man. He was dismissed when it was discovered that he was working for a rival firm. The dismissal was held to be unfair. Having regard to the nature of his work as an odd-job man, he could hardly be contributing very seriously to the competition from the rival firm, and in the circumstances there was no breach of duty towards his own employer merely because he worked for a competitor in his spare time.

8.152 In some circumstances, it may be relevant to consider whether or not the outside activity is compatible with the dignity of the employee holding a particular post; in other circumstances an employer may be entitled to forbid an employee engaging in certain leisure pursuits or additional employment if the result is that the employee is too exhausted to follow his normal occupation. If an employee wishes to stand at a parliamentary or local election, this is of concern to the employer only if the activity spills over into the employment scene. For example, supposing a supervisor, who controls a labour force made up largely of coloured immigrant workers, announces his intention of standing for election as a National Front candidate. It could be argued that the potential disruption likely to be caused to a contented workforce may well justify an employer dismissing the employee concerned.

8.153 The conduct in question must be such as to cause a loss of confidence in the employee. Thus in *Whitlow v Alkanet Construction Ltd* the applicant was asked by the company's executive to do some work on the latter's house. There he met the executive's wife, and love play took place between them in the house, and they had sexual intercourse elsewhere. Although the tribunal recognised that the applicant had been subjected to a temptation which few men would have resisted, his dismissal was held to be fair.

8. Redundancy

8.154 Although a redundancy situation may be grounds for dismissal, in respect of which the employee may be able to obtain a redundancy payment (see Chapter 10), it does not follow that such a dismissal will automatically be fair, or that the employer acts reasonably in treating that reason as a sufficient ground for dismissal. In *Williams v Compair Maxam Ltd* the EAT laid down five principles for good current industrial relations practice which should be adopted in appropriate circumstances:

1. the employer will give as much warning as possible of impending redundancies so as to enable trade unions and employees to consider alternative solutions and seek alternative employment;
2. the employer will consult with the unions as to the best means by which the desired object can be achieved with as little hardship as possible. In particular, the criterion for selection should be agreed, and the actual selection should be made in accordance with that criterion;
3. the criterion for selection should not depend solely on the opinion of the person making the selection, but should be one which can be objectively checked;
4. the employer must ensure that the selection is made in accordance with that criterion, and will consider any representations made;
5. the employer will ascertain whether there is any alternative employment which can be offered.

8.155 However, the principles laid down in *Williams v Compair Maxam* are guidelines, not rules of law. They refer primarily to the situation found in large companies when a significant number of redundancies are being contemplated. They should be applied with caution in small firms (*Meikle v McPhail*) or where there is no trade union involved. The principles should not be regarded as a shopping list with a finding of unfairness if one or more points have not been followed (*Simpson & Son (Motors) v Reid*).

8.156 Bearing this in mind, there are three ways in which redundancies should be handled.

8.157 a) *Consideration of alternatives.* Faced with a redundancy situation, the reasonable employer considers whether it is necessary to act on it, or whether there is some other way of dealing with the problem. For example, it may be possible to restrict recruitment, cut down on overtime, introduce work-sharing, introduce short-time working. In *Allwood v William Hill Ltd* the employers closed down 12 betting shops and declared the managers redundant. No warning was given and no alternative employment within the company was offered. It was held that merely because a redundancy situation existed, it did not follow that the employees had to be made redundant. There was a high wastage in the industry, and more effort should have been made to transfer them to other establishments, even on a temporary basis. The employers should also have considered retraining the employees until vacancies arose through wastage or expansion. It may be possible to offer a redundant employee another job which amounts to a demotion, and leave it to him to decide whether or not to accept (*Avonmouth Construction Ltd v Shipway*).

8.158 The reasonable employer also takes steps to see if the employee can be absorbed elsewhere in the concern, or with associated companies (*Vokes Ltd v Bear*), but the employer need only take such reasonable steps as are available for this purpose, and though an industrial tribunal must scrutinize critically a complaint of unfair redundancy, it should also guard against adopting a standard which is unrealistic, and it should not find a dismissal unfair merely as a means of topping up an inadequate redundancy payment (*British United Shoe Machinery Co Ltd v Clarke*). If an employer merely states that he decided not to offer a redundant employee alternative work, without advancing any reasons for the decision, he does not discharge the burden of showing that he has acted reasonably (*Thomas and Betts Manufacturing Ltd v Harding*). If the employer has failed to act reasonably in searching round for alternative employment, the industrial tribunal must consider whether in fact any loss has accrued to the employee as a result of that failure, or whether in fact it made no difference. In the latter case, there could be a finding that the dismissal was consequently not unfair, or that even if it was unfair, no loss was suffered by the employee, and therefore he is not entitled to any compensation.

8.159 b) *Lack of consultation*. To dismiss without warning or proper consultations, or without considering the recommendations of the Code of Practice relating to redundancies, may also result in a finding that a dismissal is unfair. But a failure to consult with the unions as provided by s. 188 of TULR(C)A (see Chapter 15) does not by itself mean that a dismissal is unfair (*Forman Construction Ltd v Kelly*). At the same time, consultation with trade unions does not preclude consultation with individuals (*Walls Meat Co Ltd v Selby*). If the employer fails to consult with the affected individuals, he must supply a cogent reason why it was not possible to do so (*Holden v Bradville Ltd*).

8.159A The fact that the employer has established a policy not to consult in the event of redundancies being imminent, based on previous experience and the wishes of the workforce in the past, is not, *per se*, sufficient reason not to consult (*Ferguson v Prestwick Circuits Ltd*), particularly when the criteria for selection is vague and subjective (*Graham v ABF*). Even a small company is expected to act reasonably. Thus, if redundancy is being proposed, the size of the undertaking may affect the nature or formality of the consultation process, but it does not excuse the lack of consultation (*De Grasse v Stockwell Tools Ltd*).

8.160 The effect of a failure by the employer to consult or warn an employee of an impending redundancy was examined by the House of Lords in *Polkey v A E Dayton Services Ltd* (see para 7.5). The test of fairness is to be judged by what the employer did, and not by what he might have done. Thus if, on the basis of information which he has available at the time of the dismissal, or circumstances which are known to him, he can be said to have acted reasonably despite the absence of a warning or consultation, then the dismissal may still be fair even though the provisions of the Code of Practice were not followed. However, if he acted unreasonably (even though the decision would have been fair had he followed the correct procedure) the dismissal must be regarded as being unfair. It does not follow that in these circumstances the employee will receive additional compensation on top of his statutory redundancy pay (*Lifeguard Assurance v Zadrozny*), for the consequence of the unfairness can be reflected by reducing the amount of the compensatory award by a percentage reflecting the chance that the employee would still have lost his employment (*Sillifant v Powell Duffryn Timber Ltd*). Further, if the dismissal is thus held to be unfair, an industrial tribunal may exercise the option of awarding reinstatement or re-engagement under s. 69 EPCA, should there be altered circumstances which justify this course (per Lord

Bridges in *Polkey v A E Dayton Services Ltd*). In thus overruling the line of cases which supported to so-called *British Labour Pump* principle, the House of Lords re-emphasised the importance for employers of following fair procedures before taking a decision to dismiss, on whatever ground the decision is taken.

8.161 But the applicant must still show that a loss has resulted from the unfairness, and the industrial tribunal must not speculate, guess, or indulge in conjecture. The applicant must show a sensible and coherent suggestion as to what was the result of the failure to consult or warn, and what would have happened had there been no such failure. The employer must then refute such suggestions (*Barley v Amey Roadstone Corpn Ltd*). The industrial tribunal may then decide that the failure made little or no difference, and reduce compensation to an amount they deem appropriate, to reflect the additional period of time by which the employee's employment would have been extended had consultations taken place (*Mining Supplies (Longwall) Ltd v Baker*).

8.162 c) *Proper selection procedures*. It is the duty of the industrial tribunal to examine the employer's procedures for selecting redundancies to ensure that these are fair. Even a selection system which is based on custom and practice in the industry can be challenged if it is unreasonable (*Watling & Co v Richardson*). The tribunal is entitled to know (a) who made the decision to select (b) what information was taken into account and (c) upon what criteria the information was assessed (*O'Keefe v Bristol Channel Ship Repairers Ltd*). Otherwise unfair selection for redundancy may also amount to an unfair dismissal. Faced with the decision of choosing which employee(s) shall be made redundant, the employer must engage in a genuine exercise in reaching his choice. If there is an established procedure in existence, he should follow it; in the absence of such pre-arranged procedure, the general rule in industry for redundancy selection is based on the principle of Last in, First out (LIFO), and this principle should always be considered as an important feature of any redundancy agreement (*Brook v London Borough of Haringey*). LIFO is always subject to any reasonable and proper modification, particularly if this has been considered by shop-stewards and management acting in concert (*Crump v Chubb & Sons Lock and Safe Co Ltd*). In *International Paint Co v Cameron* it was held that the customary arrangements of LIFO, without further specification, had to be based on continuous service, not cumulative service, so that an employee with longer continuous service ought to be retained in preference to an employee with a longer overall service, but less continuous service. If there is no agreed procedure or customary arrangement, the employer may take into account long services, superior abilities and experience, and the respective hardship caused. In *Selby v Plessey Co Ltd*, it was held that a selection based on an effective evaluation system, which was customary in the company, was fair. Adherence to a redundancy agreement made with a trade union is generally sufficient evidence to rebut fairness (*Taylor v Conveyancer Ltd*) though a failure to consult that union as provided by the agreement may be unfair. Also, if the redundancy agreement is discriminatory on grounds of sex and race, it would be unfair to follow it (*Clarke v Eley (IMI) Kynoch Ltd*). However, if the decision has to be made in a hurry for sound reasons, and consultations with the union or employees would result in serious delay, the employer does not act unfairly in failing to consult (*Guy v Delanair Ltd*).

8.163 Although the actual selection criteria is for management to determine, it is sound practice to agree this in advance with trade unions. The more vague and subjective the criteria, the greater is the need to consult with affected employees (*Graham v ABF Ltd*).

8.164 In *Clyde Pipeworks v Foster*, selection for redundancy was based on a points system, which took into account bad time keeping, workmanship, absenteeism, and merit on conduct. This procedure had been agreed with the unions, but they were not consulted about its implementation. It was held that there was no need to involve the unions in the detailed arrangements for selection for redundancy, provided the method was fair in general terms. But if management were to take into account improper factors (such as a disciplinary warning which should have been expunged from his record) there could be an unfair selection (*Pyle v Cleeson Civil Engineering Ltd*). If jobs are inter-changeable between departments, then the basis for selection is between employees of the same description within the whole concern, not on a departmental basis (*Woolcocks v Wailes Dove Bitumastic*).

8.164A If a dismissal for redundancy is generally fair in terms of the procedure adopted and the selection criteria, it does not become unfair because of a failure by the employer to give the affected employees a right of appeal against their dismissal, even though an employee dismissed for gross misconduct would have that right. There is no suggestion in the Code of Practice that there should be a right of appeal against a dismissal for redundancy (*Robinson v Ulster Carpet Mills Ltd*).

8.164B To select a woman for dismissal because she is pregnant, or on maternity leave of absence, would be unfair under s. 60 (see para 5.31), but if a woman is made redundant because of the operation of a fair selection procedure (e.g. based on LIFO), then the fact that she is or was pregnant is coincidental, and has nothing to do with her selection., Her dismissal would be fair in accordance with the usual criteria (*Brown v Stockton-on-Tees Borough Council*).

8.165 But in the last analysis, the test is not whether the industrial tribunal agrees with the actual selection made by the employer, but whether the employer acted reasonably. Thus it is not the duty of the industrial tribunal to decide who they would have made redundant had they had to make the choice, but to ensure that management acts from genuine motives. In *Grundy Teddington Ltd v Willis*, the choice for making an employee redundant lay between two persons. Management chose one, but the industrial tribunal held that this was unfair, in that the other should have been chosen. The EAT reversed this finding; the ultimate decision must remain with management, provided it acts fairly.

8.166 If an employee is given notice of dismissal, for reason of redundancy, and during that notice period new work becomes available, it may be unfair not to rescind the notice and offer further employment to him (*Stacey v Babcock Power Ltd*). However, if the alternative employment becomes available after the employee's contract of employment has ended, an employer does not act unreasonably in failing to offer that employment to him (*Octavius Atkinson & Sons Ltd v Morris*).

8.167 In four cases, selection for redundancy will automatically be unfair under the provisions of EPCA ss. 59 and 59A. If it can be shown that other employees in the undertaking who held similar positions to the person made redundant were not dismissed, and the reason that person was selected was

(a) because of his union membership/activities/non-membership (TULR(C)A ss. 152(1)-153), or
(b) contrary to an agreed procedure or customary arrangement and there were no special reasons which justified a departure from that agreement or arrangement (*Thomas and Betts Manufacturing Ltd v Harding*), or
(c) he exercised his functions in health and safety cases (see para 12.34C), or
(d) an inadmissible reason on pregnancy or childbirth grounds (s. 60(a)-(e), see para 5.30)

then the dismissal will be unfair.

8.168 Selection for redundancy on grounds of trade union membership or non-membership would, of course, be manifestly unfair. So far as selection is in accordance with an agreed procedure (whether express or implied, see *Henry v Ellerman City Lines Ltd*) or a customary arrangement, provided the employers have adhered to the agreement or arrangement, it would be difficult to envisage that the dismissal is unfair under s. 57(3), unless the procedure or arrangement is manifestly unfair (*Valor Newhome Ltd v Hampson*).

8.168A But the customary arrangement which is alleged to have been ignored must be a part of the selection procedure, not a preliminary shifting process of those who might be considered for selection. In *Rogers v Vosper Thornycroft (UK) Ltd* it was the company's practice to call for volunteers when making employees redundant. Following the cancellation of a large order, it became necessary to make 304 employees redundant, and the company decided to make their selection on the need to retain a viable workforce. The applicant argued that his eventual selection for redundancy dismissal was automatically unfair under s. 59, because the company had acted contrary to the customary arrangement of calling for volunteers, but his claim was dismissed. Section 59 is directed to the actual selection arrangements. The practice of calling for volunteers was not part of the customary arrangements, but a preliminary sifting process which preceded the selection procedure.

8.169 However, if the employer departs from the agreement or arrangement, he must show that there were special reasons for doing so, usually by the introduction of some objective criteria (*Tilgate Pallets v Barras*). The industrial tribunal will then consider whether the dismissal is fair under s. 57(3) (*GEC Machines Ltd v Gilford*). Whether there are special reasons justifying a departure from the agreed procedure is a decision which has to be made by the industrial tribunal, acting as an industrial jury (*Cross International Ltd v Reid*).

8.170 In *Hazell v Barvis Ltd* the industrial tribunal upheld a decision to dismiss the applicant, even though there were three other employees with shorter service than him, and the normal basis for selection was LIFO. The employers were able to justify their departure from the customary procedure on a number of grounds. And in *Vickers v Smith* the applicant was made redundant even though another employee, with longer service had volunteered to take his place. It was held that nonetheless the final decision was that of management, and the EAT would only interfere if the decision of management was so wrong that no reasonable or sensible management could have come to that decision.

8.171 Finally, it should be noted that the industrial tribunal has no right to go into an investigation as to the reasons which have brought about the redundancies, or to require the employers to justify them on economic grounds. In *Moon v Homeworthy Furniture*, a factory was closed down after a series of labour disputes. It was held that TULRA had taken away any right of the courts or tribunals to interfere in industrial relations matters, and the tribunals refused to entertain an argument that the closure was unnecessary.

9. Statutory restriction

8.172 An employer cannot be expected to continue to employ an employee if such employment would be contrary to the law. For example, if an employee is employed as a driver, and it is a term (express or implied) of his contract that he should hold a valid driving licence, then clearly, if he loses that licence, the employee is barred from pursuing that occupation by statute (Road Traffic Act 1974 s. 84). Additionally, the employer may be guilty of an offence if he permits a disqualified driver to drive. But this does not mean that a dismissal will always be fair in such circumstances. The test is, as always, the reasonableness of the employer's action (*Sutcliffe & Eaton Ltd v Pinney*). He must consider the length of the disqualification, the needs of the business, whether the employee can do his job without driving a motor vehicle, whether alternative arrangements can be made, whether the employee could be given some other work to do until his licence is restored, and so on. In *Mathieson v Noble & Son Ltd* the applicant was a salesman who was disqualified from driving. He made arrangements to engage a chauffeuse at his own expense to drive him around during the period of disqualification, but his employers decided to dismiss him. It was held that the employers had acted unreasonably in not giving him a chance to see if the new arrangements were satisfactory. This may be contrasted with *Appleyard v Smith (Hull) Ltd* where it was an essential requirement for the mechanics that they should hold valid driving licences so that they could test vehicles which they had repaired. When the applicant lost his licence, the company had given some thought to placing him elsewhere in the business, but this was not practicable in such a small firm, and his dismissal was held to be fair.

8.173 There are a number of other legal restrictions on the employment of certain employees in special circumstances. For example, under the Power Press Regulations, it is necessary to have a certificate of competence in order to inspect power presses, and it could be fair to dismiss an employee who had his certificate revoked. In *Gills v Walls Meat Co Ltd* the applicant, who was a Sikh, was involved with dealing with open meat. When he commenced employment he was clean shaven, and did not observe his religion by growing a beard, but after a while he was 'converted back to the paths of righteousness' and grew a beard. To have continued to employ him in this capacity would have involved a breach of the Food Regulations 1970, and so the employers, after offering him alternative employment which he refused, dismissed him. This was held to be fair. (It may be noted that a refusal by a Sikh to wear a safety helmet on a construction site as required by Regulations made under the Health and Safety at Work etc Act does not entitle an employer to dismiss him as long as he is wearing his turban, see Employment Act 1989 s. 11).

10. Some other substantial reason

8.174 It was never intended that the above nine reasons for fair dismissal could constitute an exhaustive catalogue of the circumstances in which the employer would be justified in terminating the services of an employee, and there have been a number of cases where 'some other substantial reason' for the dismissal has been held to be fair. In *Wilson v Underhill House School Ltd* the applicant was a schoolteacher in a school which was in financial difficulties, and which could not pay in full a pay award. All the other teachers except her agreed to take less, but she refused and was dismissed. Her dismissal was held to be fair for some other substantial reason. In *Foot v Eastern Counties Timber Co Ltd* the applicant, who was a valued employee, was dismissed when it was discovered that her husband had started a business which was in competition with the employers. It was held that the company had acted reasonably in dismissing an employee who had access to confidential information at a time when her husband was running a rival business. In *Farr v Hoveringham Gravels Ltd* the company had a rule that employees must live within reasonable travelling distance of the firm, and they dismissed a manager who had moved to live 44 miles away. A person in his position may have to be called out in an emergency, and this would prove to be difficult in view of the distance involved. Hence the dismissal was fair.

8.174A It has to be recognised that frequently the legitimate interests of the employer in making a change in employment terms are irreconcilable with the equally legitimate interests of the employee. Thus a sound good business reason for a particular reorganisation has to be looked at in that context (*St John of God (Care Services) Ltd v Brooks*).

8.175 An employer need not wait until a problem arises before he takes action to protect his commercial interests. In *O'Brien v Prudential Assurance Co*, the applicant applied for a job as a district insurance inspector, but deliberately concealed that he had a history of mental illness. When this came to light, the company obtained further medical reports, on the basis of which he was dismissed. Again, this was to be for some other substantial reason, and in the circumstances fair. As an inspector, he would have to go into people's homes, and the company could not risk the possibility that an unsavoury incident might occur.

8.176 Although an employee is not legally obliged to accept a variation in the terms of his contract, a refusal to do so may amount to a substantial reason for dismissal if it is in the commercial interests of the firm that a variation should be made, and it is a reasonable request to make in the circumstances. In *Muggridge v East Anglia Plastics Ltd* the employers found it necessary to change the working hours, and fairly dismissed two ladies who refused to accept the change, and in *RS Components v Irwin* (see para 11.9) the company fairly dismissed a salesman who refused to sign a restrictive covenant. However, a dismissal for refusing new contractual terms may be unfair if there is no immediate need for the variation (*Evans v Elemeta Holdings*).

8.177 A change in employment terms may well be necessary even though these are to the detriment of the employee, if commercial necessity so dictates, for a contract of employment cannot remain static throughout the whole of its existence. In *Sycamore v H Myer & Co Ltd* the applicant refused to accept a new payment system which would have resulted in his wages being reduced from £130 per week to about £90 per week. The new system was negotiated with the trade union because the old method of payment was clearly defective. All the other employees accepted the change, and it was held that the applicant's dismissal was for some other substantial reason, and fair in the circumstances. The new terms were not ungenerous, and had been negotiated with the trade union concerned. In *Storey v Allied Brewery*, the respondents introduced a rota system of working due to the changing pattern of their trade. The applicant refused to work on Sundays, as she wished to go to church. Her dismissal was held to be fair. The change was necessary in the interests of economy, and to balance and share the workload with all the relevant employees. In *Oliver v Sperry Vickers*, the applicant was dismissed for refusing to accept a change in his job title and job content following a reorganisation of the supervisory structure. He was the only one of 22 employees affected who refused. Although this involved minor additions in his duties, he would have received a higher rate of pay. The dismissal was held to be for some substantial reason, and in the circumstances, fair, for he had no reasonable objection to the change.

8.178 The test in these cases is whether the offer of new terms is within the range of offers which a reasonable employer would make in the circumstances. The task of weighing the advantages to the employer against the disadvantages to the employee is merely one factor to be taken into account (*Richmond Precision Engineering Ltd v Pearce*).

8.178A A difficult situation arises when an employer knows that a disciplinary offence (e.g. theft) has been committed, but is unable to identify the actual person responsible. Can he then dismiss all the suspects? In *Parr v Whitbread plc* the applicant was a branch manager of an off licence. There were three other employees working in the shop. It was discovered that the sum of £4,600 was missing, but the circumstances were such that each of the four employees had an equal opportunity of committing the theft. After carrying out a thorough investigation, all four were dismissed. An industrial tribunal held that the dismissal was for some other substantial reason, and fair in the circumstances, and the decision was upheld by the EAT. The following guidance was offered: (1) the act must be one which would justify dismissal if committed by an individual; (2) the employer must carry out a reasonable and thorough investigation; (3) as a result of the investigation, the employer must reasonably believe that one of the employees committed the act; (4) the employers must have acted reasonably indentifying the group of employees one of whom could have committed the act; and (5) as between the members of that group, the employer could not reasonably have identified the actual perpetrator.

8.179 But the employer does not have to dismiss all of the group, if he can show solid and sensible grounds for differentiating between members of the group. In *Frames Snooker Centre v Boyce*, three managers had access to a safe in the employers' premises. After several burglaries had occurred, the police formed the view that each burglary was an inside job. There was no evidence against any of the managers, but the employer decided to dismiss two of them. He did not dismiss the third, because she was his daughter, and he had faith in her honesty and integrity. An industrial tribunal held that the dismissal of the two managers was unfair because of the failure to dismiss all the suspects, but the decision was reversed on appeal. There is no 'all or none' principle in dismissing a group when it is not possible to identify the culprit.

8.180-8.181 To dismiss one of two incompatible employees in order to restore harmony among the workforce (*Gorfin v Distressed Gentlefolk's Aid Association*) may be fair provided that steps are taken to investigate the conflict and attempts are made to see whether or not an improvement in the relationship can be effected (*Turner v Vestric Ltd*). Equally, to dismiss an employee who is unable to obtain a fidelity bond (*Moody v Telefusion Ltd*), can be a substantial reason for dismissal. If an appointment is expressed to be of a temporary nature, pending the return to work of an absent employee, this could also constitute grounds which a tribunal may feel justified a dismissal. In particular, the Employment Protection (Consolidation) Act 1978 provides that in two specific instances the dismissal of a temporary employee will be regarded as a substantial reason. These are where a temporary replacement is taken in because there has been a suspension on medical grounds (s. 61(2)), or a temporary appointment has been made to replace a woman who is absent on maternity leave (s. 61(1)). In both these cases the replacement must be informed in writing of the temporary nature of the appointment, and that he/she may be dismissed when the absent employee returns to work. However, although such dismissal amounts to a substantial reason, it will be without prejudice to the application of the rule that the tribunal must find that the employer has acted reasonably in treating the reason as sufficient ground for dismissal.

8.182 An industrial tribunal will not accept any reason advanced by the employer as coming within the definition of another substantial reason. In *Hedger v Davy & Co Ltd* the employer received a request from an employment agency for a reference in respect of the applicant. This was held not to be another substantial reason for the dismissal. And in *Wadley v Eager Electrical Ltd* the applicant was a valued worker who had been employed for 17 years. His wife, who worked at the same firm, was summarily dismissed for theft, and the employers felt that they has lost confidence and trust in the applicant. They also felt that his continued employment would have an adverse effect on customers. His dismissal was held not to be for some other substantial reason. It was unfair to dismiss an employee because some other person in the household was fairly dismissed.

8.183 It must be remembered that even though a reason is capable of being another substantial reason for the dismissal, the employer must still act reasonably in treating that reason as a sufficient reason for dismissal. To do this, he should have a full investigation of the problem, and explore any alternatives which may be available (*Scott Packaging and Warehousing Co v Paterson*). There is no absolute requirement that consultation with the employee should take place, but this is one of the factors to be taken into account in determining if the employer has acted reasonably (*Hollister v National Farmers' Union*). In *Johnson v Tesco Stores Ltd* the applicant made a false statement on his job application form. He was subsequently employed for 18 months before the falsity came to light, during which time he was perfectly satisfactory. Nonetheless he was dismissed, and this was held to be unfair. In *Debaughn v Star Cinemas (London) Ltd* it was contrary to the company's policy to employ people who had had previous criminal convictions, particularly for violence, and they dismissed a doorman who had been employed satisfactorily for 12 months when it was discovered that he had failed to disclose a previous conviction for assault. This was held to be fair. The distinction between these cases lies in the fact that in the former case, there was no real need to act on the information which had come to light, whereas in the latter case the firm's policy could not admit of exceptions for very sound reasons.

8.184 It is frequently useful for an employer to plead or argue 'some other substantial reason' in addition to another reason advanced, for this enables him to have two bites at the cherry! Thus, to dismiss an employee who has been sent to prison may be regarded as conduct or frustration or some other substantial reason. But whatever the 'label', the employer must always be prepared to show that he had acted reasonably in treating the reason as a sufficient reason for dismissing the employee (*Bouchaala v Trust House Forte plc*).

Dismissal on transfers

8.185 The general principles of the Transfer of Undertakings (Protection of Employment) Regulations have already been discussed (see para 5.106). Regulation 8(1) provides that where, either before or after the transfer, an employee of the transferor or transferee is dismissed, this will amount to an automatically unfair dismissal, if the principle reason for the dismissal was the transfer, or a reason connected with it. However, reg 8(2) provides that if the employee was dismissed for an economic, technical or organisational reason which entailed a change in the workforce, the dismissal will be for a substantial reason of the kind such as to justify the dismissal of the employee holding the position which that employee held. However, the employer must still be able to show that he acted reasonably in treating that reason as a sufficient reason for the dismissal. If he does, the dismissal will be fair under s. 57(3), and the employee will be able to claim a redundancy payment, for redundancy is the commonest of the economic, technical or organisational reasons (*Gorictree Ltd v Jenkinson*). However, the decision must be one made on the need to entail changes in the workforce. If something else is sought to be changed (e.g. the pay of the employees who are transferred) the resultant dismissal does not come within reg 8(2), and the dismissal will be unfair (*Berriman v Delabole Slate Ltd).*

8.186 Potentially, 'economic, technical or organisational reasons' is a wide phrase, but it has been given a restricted meaning. In *Wheeler v Patel*, the EAT held that an economic reason entailing a change in the workforce must relate to the conduct of the business concerned, so that the transferor's attempts to obtain a higher price for the sale by acceding to the demands of the transferee to dismiss the workforce did not constitute an economic reason. An earlier decision to the contrary (*Anderson v Dalkeith Engineering Ltd*) has been disapproved (see *Gateway Hotels Ltd v Stewart*). But if the transferee does not need the transferor's workforce, so that a redundancy situation is produced, this is within reg 8(2) (*Meikle v McPhail*). And if, on the transfer of the business, employees are dismissed for reason of redundancy without the transferor being contractually required to do so, this will be evidence of the unfairness of the dismissals (*Litster v Forth Dry Dock and Engineering Co Ltd*).

Dismissal for asserting a statutory right (s. 60A)

8.187 It will be unfair to dismiss an employee because:
(a) he has brought proceedings against an employer to enforce a relevant statutory right; or
(b) he has alleged that the employer has infringed a right of his which is a relevant statutory right.

8.188 It is immaterial whether or not the employee in fact has the right, or whether or not it has been infringed, as long as the employee makes the claim in good faith. Nor need the employee specify the right, as long as it is made reasonably clear to the employer what the right claimed to have been infringed was.

8.189 The relevant statutory rights for the purposes of s. 60A are as follows:
(a) all the rights contained in EPCA for which the remedy for infringement is to make a complaint or reference to an industrial tribunal;
(b) a claim for miniumum periods of notice under s. 49 of EPCA;

(c) complaints made under the Wages Act 1986;
(d) the following rights made under TULR(C)A — the right not to have the deduction of unauthorised or excessive trade union subscriptions, or unauthorised payment to the union's political fund, right not to have action taken short of dismissal on the ground of union membership or non-membership, right to have time off work for trade union duties or activities.

8.190 It will also be unfair to select a person for redundancy on any of the above grounds.

8.191 The right will apply irrespective of the employee's length of service, because no qualifying period of continuous employment is required.

8.192 The interesting thing about this new right is that the 'dismissal' referred to in s. 60A must inevitably include a constructive dismissal. Hence, if an employee feels that he is being deprived of his statutory rights, he can resign and make a claim accordingly.

Other dismissals

8.193-8.205 For dismissals on grounds of trade union membership or non-membership, in closed shop situations, lockouts, strikes, and industrial pressure, see Chapter 13. Dismissal on grounds of sex or race are dealt with in Chapter 4, maternity dismissals in Chapter 5, and dismissals in health and safety cases in Chapter 12.

National security

8.206 As already noted (see para 2.64), a Minister of the Crown may issue a certificate that specified employment or a specified person be excluded from the protection of the legislation for the purpose of safeguarding national security (EPCA s. 138(4) and see *CCSU v Minister for the Civil Service*).

Written reasons for dismissal (EPCA s. 53)

8.207 Where an employee is dismissed, either with or without notice, or by the expiry of a fixed-term contract, he is entitled to receive, on request, a written statement of the reasons for his dismissal within 14 days. This statement shall be admissible in any proceedings before a tribunal or a court. He will not be so entitled unless he has been continuously employed for two years. A complaint may be presented to an industrial tribunal by an employee that the employer has unreasonably failed to provide a written statement, or that the statement which has been given is inadequate or untrue. If the tribunal finds the complaint well founded, it may make a declaration as to what it finds were the employer's reasons, and shall make an award of two weeks' pay.

8.208 To be adequate under s. 53, the written statement must be such that anyone reading it can know the essential reasons for the dismissal. No particular technicalities are involved, and no particular form is required (*Horsley Smith & Sherry Ltd v Dutton*). If the employer denies that the employee has been dismissed, the industrial tribunal must make a finding on that issue before it can consider whether or not there was an unreasonable refusal to provide a written reason. But if the employer reasonably and conscientiously believes that there was no dismissal, the industrial tribunal is unlikely to find that there was an unreasonable refusal to give a reason for a dismissal which the employer genuinely believed did not occur (*Brown v Stuart Scott & Co*).

8.209 The reason given by the employer must be the true reason for the dismissal, but it does not have to be an adequate reason. That is a matter for subsequent investigation should the employee pursue his claim for unfair dismissal (*Harvard Securities plc v Younghusband*).

8.210 It is not sufficient compliance to refer to other documents, for to be adequate, the written reasons should make it quite clear to anyone reading them why the applicant was dismissed. But if, in reply to a request for written reasons, the employer *sends* a copy of an earlier document which contains those reasons, this is sufficient compliance with s. 53 (*Kent County Council v Gilham*).

8.211 But s. 53 has to be strictly construed; in *Keen v Dymo Ltd* the employers sent written reasons by second class post, so that it arrived a day outside the 14-day period; this was held to be an unreasonable refusal to supply written reasons. The written reasons must be in a distinct document. Filling in a reply on Form IT3 (respondent's reply to an application to an industrial tribunal) is not a sufficient compliance with s. 53.

8.212 If an employee does not make a request for written reasons, he cannot complain that the reasons which were given were untrue, and an industrial tribunal has no power to make an award under s. 53 in the absence of any such request (*Catherine Haigh Harlequin Hair Design v Seed*).

8.213 It should be noted that the industrial tribunal has a discretion whether or not to make a declaration as to the reasons, whereas the award of two weeks' pay is mandatory. This award is *not* subject to the statutory maximum limit of £205 per week.

Dismissal on maternity grounds; s. 53(2)

8.214 A woman is entitled to written reasons for her dismissal if she is dismissed at any time while she is pregnant, or after her childbirth in circumstances in which her maternity leave period ends by reason of her dismissal. She does not need to have the requisite period of continuous employment, and she must be given the written statement irrespective of whether or not she makes a request for it.

CHAPTER 9

Practice and procedure

9.1 An employee who wishes to seek the enforcement of a statutory right, or to obtain a remedy for a breach of that right, must present his claim within the appropriate time limit. If he is dismissed for redundancy, he must apply for a redundancy payment within six months from the dismissal (EPCA s. 101(1)), though the tribunal have a discretion to extend the period for a further six months if they think it would be just and equitable to do so (EPCA s. 101(2)). A claim for unreasonable exclusion or expulsion from a trade union must be brought within six months of the act complained of, as may a claim based on a failure to re-engage after being dismissed for taking part in strike action (contrary to s. 62(3)).

9.1A All other individual claims must be presented within three months of the act complained of, unless it was not reasonably practicable to present the claim earlier, or, so far as claims based on race or sex discrimination are concerned, the industrial tribunal consider that it is just and equitable to extend the time limit. If the act complained of is a continuing act (e.g. race or sex discrimination) which extends over a period, time will run from the end of the period (*Barclays Bank plc v Kapur*). The date on which the cause of the action crystalised will depend on the facts of each case (see *Clarke v Hampshire Electro-plating Co Ltd*, para 4.122A).

9.2 In deciding whether or not to allow an application which is out of time, the industrial tribunal must first enquire into the circumstances as to why it was not reasonably practicable to present it before the end of the relevant period. 'Practicable', in this connection, means 'feasible', and it is a question of fact for the industrial tribunal to determine as to whether it was reasonably feasible to present the claim in time (*Palmer v Southend-on-Sea Borough Council*). Thus if the time limit expires on a non-working day (e.g. Sunday), an application will be out of time if it is presented on the following day (*Swainston v Hetton Victory Club Ltd*). However, the industrial tribunal will consider whether to exercise their discretion to allow the complaint to be presented out of time, but this will only be permitted in exceptional circumstances (*Walls Meat Co v Khan*).

9.3 If an employee or his representatives (e.g. trade union official or solicitor) are at fault in not presenting the claim in time, then it is likely that the industrial tribunal will refuse jurisdiction (*Times Newspapers v O'Regan*), but if an employee is blameless, it may be easier to infer that it was not reasonably practicable to present the claim in time (*Union Cartage Co Ltd v Blunden*). The fact that an internal appeal was being pursued by the applicant is not a ground on which he may claim that it was not reasonably practicable to present the claim earlier (*Palmer v Southend-on-Sea Borough Council*), but if the employer expressly requests that the application be delayed so that negotiations can take place with a view to reaching an amicable settlement, then it may not be practicable to present the claim within the time limit (*Owen v Crown House Engineering Ltd*). Ignorance of one's legal rights is not an excuse for not presenting the claim within the three-month period (*Avon County Council v Haywood Hicks*), but mistaken advice given by a member of the staff of the industrial tribunal may be a ground for extending the time limit (*London International College v Sen*).

9.4 All complaints must actually be received (*Secretary of State for Employment v Banks*) by the Central Office of Industrial Tribunals within the appropriate time limits (before midnight, see *Post Office v Moore*), although an application received by a Regional Office will be valid if presented in time (*Bengey v North Devon District Council*). If the application does not arrive in time because of an abnormal delay in the post, the applicant will have to rely on the escape clause (*Beanstalk Shelving Ltd v Horn*).

9.4A If an application is posted, then delivery in the ordinary course of the post may be expected:

(a) in the case of first class mail, on the second working day after posting;

(b) in the case of second class mail, on the fourth working day after posting.

Working days are Monday to Friday, excluding Bank Holidays.

9.4B Thus if an application is posted, but arrives one day after the time limits have expired, it is open to the industrial tribunal to decide if the applicant could have reasonably expected the application to be delivered in the ordinary course of the post. This is a question of fact for the industrial tribunal to determine on the evidence (*St Basil's Centre v McCrossan*).

9.4C If an employee is dismissed on the 14th of the month, his claim must be presented on or before the 13th day of the third month following. If the month in question has no corresponding date (i.e. because it is a shorter month) the three-month period will expire at the end of the relevant month. Thus if an employee is dismissed on 30 November, his claim must be presented by 28 February (or 29th, if it is a Leap Year); see *Pruden v Cunard Ellerman Ltd*.

Effective date of termination (s. 55(4))

9.5 So far as unfair dismissals are concerned, the claim must be presented within three months from the effective date of termination of employment. This date can be

a. if the employment is terminated with notice, the date on which that notice expires, or
b. if the employment is terminated without notice, the date on which the termination takes effect, or
c. in the case of a fixed term contract, the date on which the term expires.

9.5A Certain problems have arisen out of this. In *Dixon v Stenor Ltd* Sir John Donaldson pointed out that there were four situations commonly met. The first is where the employee is given notice, and works to the end of that notice. The second is where there is a summary dismissal, and the third is where the employee is given money in lieu of notice. These cases are fairly straightforward, but the fourth situation presented a problem. This was where the employee is dismissed with notice, but is not required to work the period of that notice. In effect, he is on paid leave, and his employment does not effectively terminate until the notice expires, even though he may not be working during that time. If he were to submit an application during this period, in effect it would be premature. However, EPCA s. 67(4) provides that if a dismissal is with notice, a tribunal may consider a complaint notwithstanding that it is presented before the effective date of termination of the employment. In other words, an employee may bring a complaint as soon as he receives his notice, or within three months from the effective date of termination of his employment.

9.6 The fact that the employer retains the employee's P45 is irrelevant to the effective date of termination (*Newham London Borough v Ward*).

9.7 If an employer dismisses an employee without notice, but gives him a payment in lieu of notice, the effective date of termination is the date of dismissal (EPCA s.55(4)). Consequently, if on that date the employee does not have the requisite length of continuous employment, he cannot pursue his claim for unfair dismissal, unless, of course, he can add on his statutory notice 'to pull him past the post' (EPCA s. 55(5), see para 8.18). However, a dismissal without notice is a breach of contract at common law, and in *Robert Cort & Son Ltd v Charman* it was suggested that the damages to be claimed may include not only the relevant period of lawful notice, but also the loss of the right to bring a claim for unfair dismissal which he would have had if he had been given notice of termination. Further, if notice of termination is given orally, the period of notice commences the day after it has been given, and the effective date of termination is calculated accordingly (*West v Kneels Ltd*).

9.8 It should be noted that s. 55(5) will extend the effective date of termination by the requisite statutory notice for the purposes of s. 53 (right to have written reasons for dismissal), s. 64 (unfair dismissal), s. 73(3) (calculation of the Basic Award) and Sch 14 para 8(3) (increases the maximum allowable week's pay), but not for the purpose of computing the time limit within which a claim must be brought under s. 67(2).

9.8A If an employee's claim is based on a constructive dismissal, the effective date of termination is the date when the employee accepts the alleged breach of contract by the employer (*G W Stephens & Son v Fish*).

Submitting a complaint

9.9 There is no requirement that an applicant shall complete Form IT1 (see Appendix D) although this is commonly used. A complaint merely has to be in writing, specifying the name and address of the complainant and respondent, and contain a statement of the grounds on which relief is sought and particulars thereof. In other words, it is not sufficient merely to allege 'I was unfairly dismissed'; the applicant must state why he thinks the dismissal was unfair. In his reply, the employer must set out sufficient particulars to show the grounds on which he intends to resist the claim. Tribunals will use their wide powers to allow amendments in order to ensure that justice is done, for the actual relief may be a technical matter to be decided by the tribunal, and applicants may not have the necessary legal knowledge (see *Chapman v Goonvean and Rostowrack China Clay Co Ltd*). In allowing amendments, the industrial tribunal should consider whether there would be any hardship or injustice to the parties if the amendment was permitted (*British Newspaper Printing Corpn Ltd v Kelly*).

9.9A Once the complaint has been made, copies will be sent to the respondent (the employer) and to the conciliation officer. The latter is under a statutory duty, either at the request of the parties or on his own initiative if he thinks he can be successful, to endeavour to promote a settlement without the matter going to a tribunal hearing, either by getting the parties to agree on reinstatement or re-engagement of the applicant, or securing agreement on the amount of compensation to be paid, or to get the applicant to withdraw his claim because it has little prospect of success. The conciliation officer may also be approached to use his good offices in those cases where a complaint has not yet been made, but which could be made.

9.10 From the available figures, it would appear that more than half of the complaints are settled without a tribunal hearing, though the confidential nature of the work of the conciliation officer is such that we have little knowledge of the terms or circumstances. About 70% of the cases referred to conciliation officers are settled on the basis of some form of monetary payment by the employer. The bulk of the remaining cases are settled because the applicant withdraws the claim, and in a few cases, there will be an agreement for reinstatement or re-engagement. Any communication to the conciliation officer is not admissible in evidence without the consent of the party who communicated it. In *Grazebrook v Wallens* certain documents, which had been prepared by the personnel manager after the applicant had been dismissed, were shown to the conciliation officer. It was held that the documents were not covered by the privilege, for to find otherwise would enable a party to prevent disclosure of evidence by deliberately communicating it to the conciliation officer. On the other hand, if the documents had been specially prepared for the purpose of showing them to the conciliation officer then no disclosure can be ordered.

9.11 Any settlement made under the auspices of the conciliation officer made in writing or orally (*Gilbert v Kembridge Fibres Ltd*) is binding on the parties, and can be enforced in the same way as an award made by the tribunal. Conversely, any settlement made privately between the parties, even one purporting to be in full and final settlement of all outstanding matters, cannot prevent an employee from presenting a claim to the industrial tribunal, for an employee cannot opt out of his statutory rights. The two exceptions to this rule are (a) an agreement in writing by an employee who has a fixed term contract of one year or more that he will forgo his statutory rights in respect of unfair dismissal and/or redundancy payments if his contract is not renewed, and (b) a compromise agreement (see para 9.11D). Thus in *Council of Engineering Institutions v Maddison* the employee accepted £1,600 in consideration that he would forgo any claim against his former employers. This was held to be void. The object of the legislation is to prevent hasty and imprudent agreements being entered into by the employee. On the other hand, such an agreement, whilst void, can be taken account of by the industrial tribunal, and if it provides for compensation at a level not less than that which would have been awarded by the tribunal, then the employee will not have suffered any loss, and no further award will be made. Further, it will be recalled (para 8.81) that an agreement for a financial settlement as a price for a resignation is not void under the Act (*Sheffield v Oxford Controls*). In practice, if an agreed settlement is reached, it is sound policy to call in the conciliation officer, thus turning the agreement into a binding one, although whether they will take action in such circumstances is a matter for conjecture (see para 1.11A).

9.11A Where a counsel, solicitor, CAB adviser or member of a law centre, who has been named as a representative, holds himself out as having authority to negotiate and reach a settlement on behalf of a claimant, then, in the absence of any notice to the contrary, the other party is entitled to assume that the adviser has such authority. Thus an agreement reached between the adviser and the conciliation officer will be binding on the applicant whether or not the adviser has actual authority to enter into it. Thus the ostensible authority of the adviser extends beyond the pleadings and presentation of the case, but includes all the actual and potential issues which are known to the parties (*Freeman v Sovereign Chicken Ltd*).

9.11B But a COT3 agreement will only apply to the matters contained therein. Thus if a settlement is made to an unfair dismissal claim made under EPCA 1978, this will not bar a subsequent claim under other legislation, e.g. Sex Discrimination Act etc unless such claims have been specifically excluded (*Livingston v Hepworth Refractories plc*).

9.11C A claim under s. 54 of EPCA has two objects. First, the claimant will be seeking a finding that he has been unfairly dismissed and, second, he will be seeking compensation. Both those matters are heard before the industrial tribunal. Thus, if the employers offer to pay the maximum compensation which would be payable, this does not prevent the claimant from proceeding with his claim in order to obtain a finding that the dismissal is unfair, where the employers are unwilling to concede this (*Telephone Information Services Ltd v Wilkinson*). It will be recalled that an agreement reached whereby the employee agreed to waive his statutory rights is void unless made under the auspices of a conciliation officer, and hence the fact that the employee has accepted a sum in settlement (even though this may be in excess of the statutory compensation limits) does not preclude an industrial tribunal from hearing the claim (*NRG Victory Reinsurance Ltd v Alexander*), and it is not vexatious or frivolous to pursue such a claim.

Compromise agreements (EPCA s. 140(3))

9.11D We have seen that any agreement by an employee which has the effect of nullifying his statutory rights is generally void (see para 9.11). However, provided certain conditions are satisfied, an agreement for instituting or continuing any proceedings before an industrial tribunal will be binding. The conditions are:

(a) the agreement must be in writing;
(b) it must relate to a particular complaint;
(c) the employee must have received independent legal advice from a qualified lawyer (solicitor, barrister or advocate) as to the terms of the proposed agreement and its effect;
(d) the adviser must have a professional indemnity insurance policy;
(e) the agreement must identify the adviser; and
(f) the agreement must state that the conditions regulating the compromise agreement under the Act are satisfied.

Compromise agreements may be made in respect of all claims specified in ss. 133(1) and 134(1) of EPCA (except claims for breach of contract which may arise if and when s. 131 is activated), which includes most of the claims which may be made under that Act, and also the Wages Act, TULR(C)A (except a failure to consult with trade unions on redundancies), Sex Discrimination Act, Equal Pay Act and Race Relations Act.

Employer's reply

9.12 A copy of Form IT1 will be sent to the employer, who should reply on Form IT3 (see Appendix D) within 14 days, although it is permissible to apply for an extension of time. The response should state sufficient particulars to indicate the grounds upon which the application will be resisted. The 'label' attached to those grounds is generally irrelevant, for this is a matter which may well be determined on consideration of the factual evidence. Thus, if an employer submits that the reason for the dismissal was 'redundancy', and the facts are fully investigated by the industrial tribunal, it is open to them to find that the reason was for 'some other substantial reason' (*Hannan v TNT-IPEC (UK) Ltd*).

Pre-hearing assessments

9.13 In order to try to eliminate those cases which appear to be hopeless in terms of their merits, or frivolous, either party may apply for a pre-hearing assessment (PHA) to take place, and the industrial tribunal may arrange for one on its own volition (Industrial Tribunals (Rules of Procedure) Regulations 1985). An informal hearing will then take place, without witnesses, at which the parties will be invited to outline their positions. If the industrial tribunal form the opinion that the claim or defence is without merit, it will issue a warning to the party concerned to the effect that if he proceeds with his claim (or defence), and at a subsequent hearing he loses, the second tribunal may award costs against him. The warning does not debar the party concerned from pursuing or defending his claim, but he does so with full knowledge of the likely consequences.

Pre-hearing review

9.14 The Employment Act 1989 empowered the Secretary of State to make regulations which would enable an industrial tribunal to carry out a pre-hearing review. If it is then thought that the proceedings are unnecessary, the tribunal may order a party to pay a deposit of up to £150, as a pre-requisite of the case going further. The general idea is to discourage unmeritorious complaints.

9.14A The pre-hearing assessment procedure has only had a limited success as a 'sifting' device. Costs could only be awarded after the expense had been incurred, and the amount of costs awarded generally bore little relationship to the actual expenses. Whether the pre-hearing review, with its refundable deposit system, will work any better, is a matter for the future.

9.14B At the time of writing, no regulations implementing the pre-hearing review have been made. It is expected that the pre-hearing review will replace the pre-hearing assessment procedure.

Industrial tribunal procedure

9.15 The tribunal will generally regulate their own procedure, and can issue directions to the parties as to how the case is to proceed (see generally, the cases cited in *Aberdeen Steak Houses Group v Ibrahim)*. If a party is dissatisfied with the way the proceedings have been conducted by the chairman, he can only succeed on an appeal if it can be shown that he had been prejudiced thereby (*Barnes v BPC (Business Forms) Ltd*). The tribunal also have powers, at the request of one party or on their own volition, to order the other party to deliver further and better particulars of their case (*International Computers v Whitley*), and to disclose for inspection documents or other relevant evidence and to allow the other party to make any copies. However, in keeping with the non-legalistic approach of the tribunals, such orders are not made as a matter of routine procedure, but only if the party requiring the information can show that he will be prejudiced without such information (*White v University of Manchester*). An industrial tribunal cannot order a part to produce 'evidence', or to create documentary evidence which was not in existence. An order for discovery is limited to those documents which are in being (*Carrington v Helix Lighting Ltd*). Attendance orders, compelling witnesses to attend, may also be granted in appropriate circumstances.

9.15A If an order for further particulars or discovery of documents is not complied with, the industrial tribunal has the power to strike out the whole or part of the claim or defence, as appropriate (Industrial Tribunal (Rules of Procedure) Regulations, reg. 4), but this punitive power should only be exercised if a fair trial is not possible due to the failure to comply. If there is a last-minute compliance, due to an acceptable explanation, it is not appropriate to strike out the claim or defence (*National Grid Co v Virdee*).

9.16 If one party is seeking the disclosure of documents which the other side regards as being of a confidential nature, such as references, confidential assessments on the applicant or other employees, and so forth, the chairman of the industrial tribunal should himself inspect the document to satisfy himself that discovery is essential in order to dispose fairly of the proceedings. If he does decide that they should be disclosed, the interests of third parties can be protected by 'covering up', substituting names, and, in rare cases, hearing the proceedings in camera (*Science Research Council v Nassé*).

9.16A If privilege is claimed from disclosure, a balance must be held between the public interest in non-disclosure and that of justice in the production of the documents (*Halford v Sharples*). Communications between parties headed 'without prejudice' should be excluded from the evidence submitted, unless the material was such that without them a dishonest case was being presented (*Independent Research Services v Catterall*).

9.16B Privilege from the discovery of documents only applies to communications between clients and professional legal advisers, such as solicitors and barristers (*New Victoria Hospital v Ryan*).

9.17 There is no general duty on a party to disclose any documents in his possession or power, in the absence of any formal order to that effect. However, if he voluntarily discloses documents, there is a duty not to be selective in that disclosure, and he must not withhold other documents if there is a risk that the non-disclosure might convey a false or misleading impression as to the nature of any document disclosed (*Birds Eye Walls Ltd v Harrison*).

9.18 If there is no prior settlement or withdrawal, the industrial tribunal will hear the case. A date, time and place for the hearing will be notified to the parties, although applications for adjournments will be considered on appropriate grounds. At the hearing, as a general rule, the burden of proof is on the applicant, and he should therefore give evidence first in order to support his allegations. This is true of race or sex discrimination claims, employment protection rights, claims made out of time, allegations by the respondent that the applicant was not an employee, or that he was not dismissed, etc.

9.19 If an industrial tribunal is unable to come to a conclusion on a question of fact, they may apply the burden of proof. Thus in *Morris v London Iron and Steel Co Ltd* the tribunal could not decide whether an employee had been dismissed or resigned, and they held that he had not discharged the burden of proof which was on him to show that he was dismissed.

9.20 In unfair dismissal cases, if the dismissal is admitted, the employer will be required to give evidence first, and he must establish:

a. the reason for the dismissal (or, if there is more than one reason, the principal reason, see *Smith v Glasgow City District Council*), and
b. that it was a statutory reason.

He should then seek to show that he acted reasonably in the circumstances.

9.21 From a practical point of view, the employer should recognise that there are a number of matters within his knowledge about which the tribunal may wish to learn, and therefore should be prepared to give evidence on these matters. Thus it is not sufficient to show a reason for dismissal; the reasonableness of acting on that reason must also be shown. For example, if an employee was dismissed because of redundancy, an employer should at least be prepared to show that (a) he had explored alternatives to the dismissal (b) that he looked around to see if there was an alternative employment he could offer to the employee, and so on (*Cox v Wildt Mellor Bromley Ltd*). If the dismissal is for incompetence, the employer would need to show all those matters which a reasonable employer should have done before taking the decision to dismiss (see Chapter 8).

9.22 If one party is taken by surprise by the evidence of the other side, it will normally be possible to apply to introduce rebutting evidence, even if it is necessary to apply for an adjournment in order to produce the necessary evidence and/or witnesses. However, unreasonable applications for adjournments may be visited by an award of costs against the offending party although costs cannot be awarded as a pre-condition for resuming a hearing (*Cooper v Weatherwise (Roofing and Walling) Ltd*). An industrial tribunal may permit a witness to be recalled for further examination, but should then give the other party an opportunity to make a further rebuttal (*Aberdeen Steak House Group v Ibrahim*).

9.23 The standard of proof, i.e. the quantum of evidence which must be given in support of any particular allegation, must be sufficient to establish the balance of probabilities in that party's favour. The informality of tribunal procedure can sometimes mislead the parties into thinking that they can escape with a standard of proof which is in fact unacceptable. If the employer, for example, fails to prove the reason or the principal reason for the dismissal (*Smith v Glasgow City District Council*) or fails to show any reason, or gives a reason which the tribunal does not believe, then he will have failed to discharge the burden of proof which is placed on him, and the dismissal will be unfair. Although the tribunals will admit hearsay evidence in the proceedings, the weight which is given to such evidence is a matter for them to decide (*Coral Squash Clubs v Matthews*) and they will seldom base a decision in favour of an employer on such evidence, particularly if it is controverted by the direct evidence (or denials) of the applicant (*Mawson v Leadgate Engineering Ltd*). The tribunals will give such assistance as they can to a person who is not legally qualified or represented, but it is the duty of the parties to present all the relevant evidence before the tribunals, and applications of adjournments may be made if a party considers it necessary to call someone whose attendance was not thought necessary.

9.24 The evidential requirements in the industrial tribunals are not the same as other courts. For example, in *Docherty v Reddy*, the applicant was dismissed for suspected theft. The tribunal permitted the employer to introduce evidence that the applicant had stolen on previous occasions. Such evidence would scarcely have been admissible in the criminal courts, as its probative value would have been exceeded by its prejudicial value, but the EAT held that the evidence was rightly admitted. The issues in the industrial tribunals and the criminal courts are different; in this case, the tribunal had to decide if the employer had reasonable grounds for dismissing, and the applicant's previous conduct was a relevant factor to be taken into account.

9.25 Equally, whether a dismissal was fair or unfair can only be determined on the basis of the facts which were known to the employer at the time he dismissed the employee, and subsequent information which comes to light is only relevant if it confirms that reason. Such information cannot be admissible to show a separate and additional reason for dismissal, because when the employer dismissed the employee, he did not know of those facts. This can be illustrated by *Devis & Sons Ltd v Atkins*, where the company dismissed a manager for failing to follow company directives. After he had left, it was alleged that facts were discovered which indicated that he had been guilty of gross misconduct, in that he had been taking secret commissions from customers, for which he could have been dismissed summarily. The industrial tribunal refused to allow such evidence to be called on the issue of the fairness of the dismissal, and this was upheld on appeal to the House of Lords. It was permissible to adduce evidence which was discovered after the dismissal to prove the fairness of that reason, but not for the purpose of showing that the employers had discovered subsequently another reason which would have enabled them to dismiss fairly. However, if the dismissal is found to be unfair, the subsequent evidence can then be admitted for the purpose of determining the remedies which would be considered by the tribunal, whether by way of a refusal to make an order for reinstatement or re-engagement, a reduction in the amount of compensation to be paid, or an award of nil compensation (*Moncreiff v MacDonald*) or a reduction of the basic award (EPCA s. 73(7B)).

9.26 After considering all the facts, hearing the witnesses, and studying any evidence tendered, the industrial tribunal must determine the issue on the basis of the relevant legal requirement. Thus if the issue is whether or not the employer has acted reasonably, this does not mean that the tribunal must agree with the employer's decision, for in many cases more than one course of action is possible, and an employer is not to be criticised because he adopts one in preference to another. It is not the duty of the tribunal to decide if they would have come to the same conclusion as the employer based on the facts which were within the employer's knowledge (*Ferodo v Barnes*), nor should the tribunal substitute their own judgment for that of the employer (*Donn v Greater London Council*), and any temptation to interfere with management prerogatives should be resisted. In *St Anne's Board Mills v Brien* four employees refused to work with another employee, who they considered had been responsible for an accident. The employers investigated the matter, came to the conclusion that that employee was not to blame, and required the four to continue to work with him. They continued to refuse, and were dismissed. After considering the facts, the tribunal decided that the other employee had been responsible for the accident, and hence the four employees had not acted unreasonably in refusing to work with him. The dismissals were therefore unfair. On appeal, it was held that the question before the tribunal was not who was responsible for the accident, but whether the employers had acted reasonably in the circumstances. They had investigated the matter thoroughly and carefully, and come to certain conclusions. They had had the choice of dismissing an employee whom they considered to be blameless, or the four employees who were (in their view, wrongfully) refusing to work with him. In the circumstances, they had not acted unreasonably in dismissing the latter.

9.27 The paramount duty of the industrial tribunal is to apply the law as laid down by Parliament. Account must be taken of the interpretation of that law as laid down by the EAT and other superior courts, but it is the statute which is paramount. In *Earl of Bradford v Jowett*, the industrial tribunal refused to follow a test of selection for redundancy as laid down by the EAT in *Vickers v Smith*. It was held that this did not constitute an error of law on the part of the tribunal. When the language of a statute is unclear or ambiguous, then the duty of the courts is to interpret the statute and thus lay down binding precedents. But when the statute is clear and unambiguous, precedents are only guides, and do not bind (*Kearney & Trecker Marwin Ltd v Varndell*). The prime duty of the industrial tribunal is to follow the words of the statute (*Anandaraajah v Lord Chancellor's Department*).

9.28 About 90% of all the decisions of the industrial tribunals are unanimous, the remainder being majority decisions of 2-1, sometimes with the two 'wingmen' joining together to outvote the legal chairman. An unusual case was *R v Industrial Tribunal, ex p Cotswold Collotype*, where one tribunal member thought that the applicant was unfairly dismissed, a second member thought the applicant was not unfairly dismissed but redundant, and the third member thought the applicant was neither unfairly dismissed nor redundant! It was held that if the voting was so inconclusive that no decision was reached, the tribunal had an inherent power to refer the matter to a differently constituted tribunal.

9.29 If the applicant fails to appear at the hearing, and does not send a representative, the industrial tribunal may adjourn to another date, or dismiss the claim (with or without an order for costs). A claim may also be struck out for want of prosecution on an application by the respondent or by the tribunal on its own motion (Industrial Tribunals (Rules of Procedure) Regulations, reg 12) but only if the respondent would be seriously prejudiced thereby (*Evans v Metropolitan Police Comr*).

9.29A If a party misbehaves at the hearing, his claim cannot be dismissed before the conclusion of the hearing on the ground that the application is vexatious or frivolous. The proper course, after due warning, is to adjourn the proceedings *sine die* (*O'Keefe v Southampton City Council*).

9.30 It is the practice of some industrial tribunals to give an oral decision immediately the hearing finishes, and then promulgate the decision in writing at a later date. In rare cases it is possible for the chairman, before such written promulgation, to announce his intention to recall the tribunal in order to reconsider some point of law which he has omitted to notice, or which was not drawn to his attention. While such practice is unusual, there is no legal objection to it (*Hanks v Ace High Productions*). However, it is not possible for an industrial tribunal to depart from their oral decision when it is reduced to writing (*Arthur Guinness (GB) Ltd v Green*).

Summary reasons

9.31 The Industrial Tribunals (Rules of Procedure) Regulations 1985 permit an industrial tribunal to give summary reasons for their decision which, in effect, will be a shortened version of their decision. Either party may apply for full reasons, either at the conclusion of the hearing or within 21 days of receiving the summary reasons. The time for lodging an appeal against the decision will be 42 days from when the full reasons are entered in the industrial tribunal register. Summary reasons will not be given in cases which relate to sex or race discrimination, equal pay, dismissal for trade union membership or non-membership, and unreasonable expulsion or exclusion from a trade union.

Full reasons

9.32 In *Meek v City of Birmingham District Council*, Bingham LJ stated the duty of an industrial tribunal as follows

> 'the decision of an industrial tribunal is not required to be an elaborate formalistic product of refined legal draftsmanship, but it must contain an outline of the story which has given rise to the complaint and a summary of the tribunal's basic factual conclusions and a statement of the reasons which have led them to reach the conclusion which they do on those basic facts. The parties are entitled to know why they won or lost. There should be sufficient account of the facts and of the reasoning to enable the EAT or, on further appeal, this court to see whether any question of law arises, and it is highly desirable that the decision of an industrial tribunal should give guidance both to the employers and trade unions as to practices which should or should not be adopted.'

Remedies

A. Reinstatement and re-engagement orders (EPCA s. 69)

9.33 If an industrial tribunal finds that the employee has been unfairly dismissed, it shall explain to him that it has the power to make an order that he be reinstated or re-engaged, and shall ask him if he wishes the tribunal to make such an order. If he expresses such a wish, the tribunal may make the necessary order. If the order is for reinstatement, the employer shall treat the employee in all respects as if he had not been dismissed, and the tribunal may specify the amount of arrears in pay payable to the employee, and rights and privileges, including seniority and pension rights, which must be restored to him, and the date by which the order must be complied with. If the employee would have benefited from an improvement in his terms and conditions of employment had he not been dismissed, the order shall require him to have those improvements. If the tribunal orders re-engagement, this is an order that the employee be re-engaged by the employer or by his successor, or an associated employer, in employment comparable to that from which he was dismissed, or other suitable employment. The tribunal will specify the terms on which the re-engagement will take place, stating the identity of the employer, the nature of the employment, the remuneration, any arrears of pay, any rights or privileges which must be restored to him (including seniority and pension rights) and the date by which the order must be complied with. If in either case the tribunal makes an order in respect of arrears of pay it will take into account (for the purpose of reducing the employer's liability) any sums received by the applicant between the date of dismissal and the date of reinstatement or re-engagement, by way of wages in lieu of notice, *ex gratia* payments, remuneration received from another employer, social security benefits, and any other benefits as the tribunal thinks appropriate. If necessary, the statutory maximum compensation limit of £11,000 can be exceeded (EPCA s. 71(1A)).

9.34 It must be stressed that the tribunal has a discretion in making either of these orders. It must first consider whether to make an order for reinstatement, and in doing so, it must take into account three considerations:

a. whether the applicant wishes to be reinstated;
b. whether it is practicable for the employer to comply with an order for reinstatement;
c. where the applicant caused or contributed to some extent to the dismissal, whether it would be just to order his reinstatement.

If the tribunal decides not to make an order, it shall then consider whether to make an order for re-engagement, and if so, on what terms. Again, there are three considerations to take into account:

a. any wish expressed by the applicant as to the nature of the order;

b. whether it is practicable for the employer or his successor or an associated employer to comply with the order;
c. where the applicant has caused or contributed to some extent to the dismissal, whether it would be just to order his re-engagement, and if so, on what terms (see *Boots Co plc v Lees Collier*).

If a re-engagement order is made, it shall, so far as is reasonably practicable, be on terms which are as favourable as an order for reinstatement, unless the tribunal takes into account the contributory fault of the applicant.

9.35 The main restriction on making reinstatement or re-engagement orders appears to be the practicability of doing so. If a permanent replacement has been engaged in place of the dismissed employee, the tribunal shall not take this into account for the purpose of deciding whether it was practicable for the employer to comply with the order unless the employer shows:
a. that it was not practicable for him to arrange for the dismissed employee's work to be done without engaging a permanent replacement; or
b. that he engaged the replacement after the lapse of a reasonable time without having heard from the dismissed employee that he wished to be reinstated or re-engaged, and that when the employer engaged the replacement, it was no longer reasonable for him to arrange for the dismissed employee's work to be done except by a permanent replacement.

9.35A It is also submitted that earlier tribunal decisions on the impracticability of making reinstatement or re-engagement recommendations (decided before the above provisions of EPCA) are still valid. For it should be noted that 'practicable' does not mean 'possible'. Thus the orders are unlikely to be made:
a. if the dismissal was in a redundancy situation, or if reinstatement would result in redundancies (*Cold Drawn Tubes Ltd v Middleton*);
b. the applicant is unfit for work (see *Rao v Civil Aviation Authority*); or
c. if there is some friction or personal animosity either with the employer or with fellow-employees (*Coleman v Magnet Joinery*); or
d. if the employer is a small firm, with few staff, reinstatement or re-engagement should only be ordered in exceptional circumstances, as there is a close personal relationship be-

tween the parties which may make such an order impracticable (*Enessy SA v Minoprio*); or

e. if there is mistrust between the parties (*Nothman v London Borough of Barnet*); or

f. if the order is likely to be ineffective (*ILEA v Gravett*).

9.35B In other words, the practicability of ordering reinstatement or re-engagement must be looked at in a subjective and pragmatic sense, bearing in mind the particular circumstances of the case. The employer is entitled to give a logical and reasonable explanation why there are no vacancies, and to make a commercial judgment about the best interests of the business. An industrial tribunal is not entitled to substitute its own views for those of management, provided the decision not to re-engage is in the bracket of reasonableness (*Port of London v Payne*). In practice, very few reinstatement or re-engagement orders are made, as very few applicants request this remedy.

B. Compensation awards (ss. 72-76)

9.36 If the order for reinstatement or re-engagement is made, but its terms are not fully complied with, the tribunal may make an award of compensation of such an amount as it thinks fit having regard to the loss sustained by the applicant in consequence of the employer's failure to comply with those terms (not subject to the statutory maximum of £11,000, see s. 71(1A)). If the order is made, but the applicant is not reinstated or re-engaged at all, then the tribunal will make an award of compensation. This will be under four headings:

a. the basic award
b. the compensatory award
c. the additional award
d. the special award.

If neither of these orders are made, then the tribunal shall make an award of compensation consisting of the basic award, the compensatory award and special award, where appropriate.

9.37 *Basic award (i)*. In two instances this will amount to two weeks' pay with a maximum of £205 per week. These are:

a. Where the employee is dismissed for reason of redundancy, but is not entitled to a redundancy payment because of the operation of EPCA s. 82(5) or (6). This section provides that an employee shall not be entitled to a redundancy payment if he unreasonably refuses the offer of alternative employment, or unreasonably terminates his new contract during the trial period of four weeks. Nonetheless, he is entitled to his basic award of two weeks' pay.

b. If the employee is not entitled to be treated as having been dismissed by virtue of s. 84 of EPCA. This provides that an employee will not be regarded as being dismissed if there is a renewal of his contract or he is re-engaged under a new contract. Thus if a contract expires, and there is an offer of renewal or re-engagement, this can still amount to a dismissal (if for reason of redundancy) and if the employee chooses to so treat it, he is entitled to two weeks' pay.

9.38 *Basic award (ii).* In all other cases the basic award will depend on the number of years in respect of which the employee has been employed. For those years of employment in which the employee was not below the age of 41, he will be entitled to one a half weeks' pay; in respect of employment below the age of 41 but not below the age of 22, he will be entitled to one week's pay; in respect of employment below the age of 22 (with no lower age limit) he will be entitled to a half of one week's pay. There is to be a maximum of 20 years' employment to be counted and the amount of the week's pay to be calculated shall not exceed £205. Thus the current maximum basic award is £6,150. If the employee is over the age of 64 there will be a reduction of one-twelfth in respect of each month after that age. For the purpose of computing the basic award, the amount is the normal week's pay, not including overtime (*Brownson v Hire Service Shops Ltd*). Where the dismissal has been held to be unfair on the grounds of trade union membership or non-membership or is a dismissal of a designated safety representative or member of a safety committee, the minimum basic award to be made is £2,700 (EPCA s. 73(4A)).

9.39 The amount of the basic award under (i) or (ii) above shall be reduced by the amount of any redundancy payment awarded by the tribunal or paid by the employer on the ground that the dismissal was for reason of redundancy. The amount of the basic award may also be reduced as the tribunal considers just and equitable if the dismissal was caused or contributed to by any act of the complainant, or because he has unreasonably refused an offer of reinstatement, or because of his conduct before the dismissal (EPCA s. 73(7B)). But no reduction in the basic award can be made on the grounds of contributory dismissal if the reason for the dismissal was redundancy unless the dismissal was unfair because of trade union membership or non-membership, in which case the excess over the ordinary basic award may be so reduced (EPCA s. 73(7C)).

9.40 The entitlement to the basic award is automatic once a dismissal is held to be unfair, and is not reduced on the ground that there is no financial loss to the applicant (*Cadbury Ltd v Doddington*). It is payable even though no compensation award is made (*BUSM v Clarke*). If the industrial tribunal decide to reduce the compensatory award (see below) on the grounds of contributory conduct, they should also decide to reduce the basic award by the same proportion, unless there are exceptional circumstances (*RSPCA v Cruden*).

9.41 *Compensatory award.* This award will be such amount as the tribunal considers just and equitable in all the circumstances, having regard to the loss sustained by the complainant, including any expenses reasonably incurred by him, and the loss of any benefit which he might reasonably be expected to have had. It is suggested that under this heading, the tribunal might consider the following headings:

a. immediate loss of wages. This could arise if the employee was dismissed summarily, or not given the length of notice to which he is entitled. In the calculation of loss of wages, net pay is taken into account, but this may be supplemented by bonuses, overtime, and pay increases had these been likely (*Mullett v Brush Electrical*);
b. the manner of dismissal will only be relevant if this causes some financial loss, for example, by making the employee less attractive to other employers;
c. loss of future earnings. If he has already obtained other employment, it will be possible to calculate the difference, if any, between his former and his present remuneration. If the latter is less than the former, it forms part of the loss, but such discrepancy cannot be expected to continue for ever, and tribunals tend to use a rule of thumb estimate of the length of time this might be expected to last. Decisions on this point vary, but there are cases where 3-4 years of such marginal loss have been taken into account. If, at the time of the hearing, the complainant has not obtained employment, a more difficult task presents itself. The tribunal must speculate on the length of time it will be before he obtains employment, taking into account their knowledge

of local employment conditions, the scarcity of jobs at different levels, the age and general employability of the complainant, and so forth. Account can also be taken of the economic climate; thus if the tribunal consider that the area is one of high unemployment, or if there is an economic recession the tribunal may base their assessment on the basis that the applicant will be unemployed for a longer period than otherwise might be the case (*MacNeilage v Arthur Roye Ltd*). On the other hand, in *Youngs of Gosport Ltd v Kendall*, the applicant was awarded 12 months' salary as compensation for unfair dismissal, even though it was recognised that the applicant would have been fairly dismissed for reasons of redundancy shortly afterwards. On appeal, it was held that the fact that there was an impending redundancy was a relevant factor to be taken into account when assessing the proper amount for loss of future earnings.

As a rough guide, it can be said that the more senior the position held by the employee, the greater the period of time which will be conjecturised by the tribunal, and the award will thus be based on this 'guesstimate'. Although an employee cannot bring a claim if he is over the normal retiring age, or over the age of 65, a compensation award can take into account the fact that an employee may continue working after those age limits have been exceeded (*Barrel Plating v Danks*). Further, anticipated overtime earnings can be taken into account when assessing the compensatory award, although this is not possible with the basic award (*Brownson v Hire Service Shops*).

9.42 The tribunal may take into account the personal characteristics of the applicant which exist at the time of the dismissal in assessing the length of time he is likely to be unemployed. Thus in *Fougere v Phoenix Motor Co Ltd* the applicant, at the time of his dismissal, was in poor health. The EAT held that loss resulting from an extended period of unemployment because of difficulties through ill-heath in finding another job was loss attributable to the fault of the employer, and therefore compensatable. But supervening events, e.g. an illness which arises after the dismissal which causes the applicant to be out of work for a long time is not a loss which is attributable to the action taken by the employer:

d. loss of any benefits. This may include loss of pension rights, car or car allowance, and any other perks enjoyed by the complainant. For loss of pension rights, reference may be made to the Government's Actuary Department's paper on the subject; also, a committee of industrial tribunal chairmen have produced a document 'Industrial Tribunals - Compensation for Loss of Pension Rights' (HMSO) to which reference may be made;

e. loss of protection against future unfair dismissal. In recent years compensation under this heading has been modest (i.e. £100, see *Muffett Ltd v Head*): however, it is possible to include a sum in respect of loss of service related notice entitlement. In *Daley v A E Dorsett* the applicant was dismissed after eight years' employment. The EAT awarded him four weeks' pay as compensation for his loss under this heading;

f. any loss of entitlement to, or expectation of, a redundancy payment, shall only include a loss referable to the amount (if any) by which a redundancy payment would exceed the basic award in respect of that dismissal. In other words, an applicant cannot have a basic award and compensation for redundancy, for the former includes the latter. Any award for redundancy is allowable only if it exceeds the basic award. Since the basic award is based on the same principles as a redundancy payment, in most cases the two will coincide, and no redundancy award will be made.

g. expenses to look for work, removal expenses incurred in taking up new employment, etc.

9.43 The industrial tribunal should deduct from the compensation award any sum paid by the employer, whether by way of *ex gratia* payments or money in lieu of notice (*Addison v Babcock FATA Ltd*; see also *Horizon Holidays Ltd v Grassi*). If the maount of any redundancy payment made exceeds the Basic Award, the excess will go to reducing any compensation award which may be payable (*Rushton v Harcros Timber and Building Supplies Ltd*).

9.43A If the employee obtained new employment after the dismissal which is at a higher rate of pay, the industrial tribunal should calculate the compensatory award on the basis of the loss suffered from the date of the dismissal up to the date when the new employment commenced, and not up to the date of the decision by the industrial tribunal to make the award (*Fentiman v Fluid Engineering Products Ltd*).

9.44 The current maximum amount of any compensatory award shall not exceed £11,000. This is the maximum which can be awarded *after* taking into account any payments already made, or any reductions made as a result of contributory conduct or failure to mitigate. In other words, the industrial tribunal should assess the compensation award, deduct any payments made etc, and then apply the statutory ceiling, if necessary (*Walter Braund (London) Ltd v Murray*). This does not, of course, include the basic award, which is additional to the compensatory award, and the combination of both awards may (in theory) exceed the statutory maximum. However, any award may be reduced on the following grounds:

a. The applicant is under a duty to mitigate against his loss so far as possible (*Scottish and Newcastle Breweries plc v Halliday*). This means that he should take reasonable steps to obtain other employment. If an employer changes his mind about a dismissal, or recognises that it is unfair, and offer reinstates or re-engagement, then if the employee refuses this offer unreasonably, it may indicate that he has not taken adequate steps to mitigate against his loss, and compensation may be reduced accordingly (*Hepworths Ltd v Comerford*). However, a failure by an employee to invoke an internal appeals machinery is not a failure to mitigate against the loss (*William Muir (Bond9) Ltd v Lamb*), for the rules relating to mitigation apply to the applicant's conduct *after* the dismissal (*McAndrew v Prestwick Circuits*). The onus of proof in respect of mitigation of loss arising from an unfair dismissal is on the employer (*Fyfe v Scientific Furnishings Ltd*);

b. *Ex gratia* payments - Since the object is to compensate for the loss suffered any *ex gratia* payment will be deducted from the compensatory award and the basic award (*Chelsea Football v Heath*);

c. Contributory conduct - If the matter to which the complaint relates was to any extent caused by or contributed to by any action of the applicant, the tribunal may reduce the compensation to the extent it thinks just and equitable. For example, in *Scottish CWS v Lloyd* a dismissal was held to be unfair because no specific warning had been given to the applicant. But he had failed to reply to complaints which had been made against him, he had failed to obey certain instructions, and failed to achieve a modest sales target. All these factors were held to be conduct which contributed to the dismissal and grounds for reducing the award. A failure to follow works rules, using company property for private purposes, unco-operative conduct, failure to apologise for a wrongful act (e.g. swearing at a manager), failure to explain adequately absences, etc, have all been held to be conduct which contributed to a dismissal and consequently grounds for making a reduction in the amount of compensation. The tribunal must ignore the technical reasons why the dismissal was unfair, and look to the realities of the situation to see to what extent the applicant contributed to his ultimate dismissal.

9.45 If the reason for the unfairness of the dismissal was a procedural irregularity, but for which the dismissal would have been fair, a high percentage of the compensatory award should be reduced on the ground of contributory conduct, to reflect the applicant's blame for the dismissal (*Nairne v Highland and Islands Fire Brigade*).

9.45A Although when determining whether a dismissal was unfair, it is proper to consider the employer's treatment of another employee who was involved in the incident, when assessing the reduction in compensation on grounds of contributory conduct it is the complainant's conduct alone which must be looked at, not the conduct of others (*Parker Foundry Ltd v Slack*).

9.46 But a reduction for contributory conduct should not necessarily be made if the employee was dismissed for incompetence, for the point about contribution is that it is made in respect of conduct over which the employee has control and for which he was blameworthy or culpable (*Nelson v BBC (No 2)*). Thus if an employee misbehaves, is guilty of misconduct, or does not try hard enough to perform his work, these are acts over which the employee has control, and therefore may contribute towards his dismissal. An employee who tries his best, but finds that his best is not good enough, cannot be said to have contributed in a blameworthy fashion to his dismissal (*Kraft Foods Ltd v Fox*). However, in *Moncur v International Paint Co Ltd* the EAT declined to treat this as an absolute proposition of law, pointing out the difficulties in determining the extent of the applicant's responsibility for his own incompetence.

9.46A Ill-health dismissals will rarely give rise to a reduction on grounds of contributory conduct. However, compensation can be reduced to reflect the period of time the applicant could have been employed had the employers dealt with the matter fairly

(*Slaughter v C Brewer & Sons Ltd*), under the 'just and equitable' provisions of s. 74(1).

9.47 A senior employee who is dismissed unfairly for gross misconduct must expect that his compensation will be reduced substantially on the ground of contributory conduct, for a higher standard of duty exists, and a higher standard of conduct is expected from him (*McPhail v Gibson*).

9.47A If the dismissal is unfair because of a failure to consult in a redundancy situation, the industrial tribunal must take into account what would have happened had there been proper consultation, and make the award accordingly (*Red Bank Manufacturing Co Ltd v Meadows*).

9.48 In the case where an applicant is dismissed on the ground of non-membership of a trade union, no reduction can be made in the compensatory award because he refused to join a union (EPCA s. 72A, see *T & GWU v Howard*).

9.49 Contributory conduct has resulted in some cases in a reduction as high as 80-90%, and for some time there was doubt as to whether it was a proper reduction to make, for there is a logical inconsistency in saying that an employee is unfairly dismissed, and yet contributed to that extent to his dismissal. It was argued that such substantial reductions should only be made when there are special factors making the dismissal unfair for technical reasons (*Maris v Rotherham Corpn*). However, in *Devis & Sons v Atkins*, the House of Lords thought that there was no particular problem in finding a dismissal unfair, and yet reducing compensation by 100%. It was stated that compensation should only be awarded when it was just and equitable to do so, and it cannot be just to award compensation when an employee has suffered no injustice by being dismissed. Nor was it inconsistent to find a dismissal unfair yet award no compensation; for example, an employee may bring about his own dismissal by his misconduct, and though this was potentially fair, it may be unfair through a failure to follow the procedure laid down in the Code of Practice. Thus a nil award or nominal compensation may well be just and equitable in the circumstances.

9.49A A constructive dismissal may give rise to a reduction on the grounds of contributory conduct in appropriate circumstances (*Polentarutti v Autokraft Ltd*).

9.50 The assessment of contributory conduct is a question of fact for the industrial tribunal to determine (*Hollier v Plysu Ltd*).

9.51 *Additional award*. It will be recalled that if an employer totally ignores a tribunal order to reinstate or re-engage the employee, an additional award can be made. This order should not be made if the employer satisfied the tribunal that it was not practicable to comply with the order, but since the tribunal will have already considered this point when making the order (see above) it will presumably be open to the employer to adduce new evidence as to why it is not practicable to do so. Otherwise, the award will be based on the following principles:

a. if the dismissal was unfair because it was an unlawful act of racial discrimination, or an act of sex discrimination, the higher additional award will be between 26 and 52 weeks' pay;
b. in any other case, the additional award will be between 13 and 26 weeks' pay. A week's pay for the purpose of the additional award shall not exceed £205.

9.52 However, in the case of a highly-paid employee, or where proceedings have been considerably delayed, the total of the maximum of the basic, compensatory and additional awards may not be adequate to meet the loss actually suffered. In such cases, s 74 of EP(C)A now enables an industrial tribunal to make a compensation award which is at least equal to the amount of pay lost between the date of dismissal and what should have been the date of reinstatement or re-engagement, to show their disapproval of the employer's decision (see *George v Beecham Group*), at the same time taking into account the employee's conduct and failure to mitigate against his loss (*Mabirizi v National Hospital for Nervous Diseases*).

9.53 *Special award*. If the applicant makes a request for re-engagement or reinstatement, and the tribunal refuses to make the order, or it makes the order but the employer refuses to comply fully, and the dismissal is then found to be unfair on the grounds of trade union membership or non-membership (*Artisian Press v Srawley and Parker*) (TULR(C)A s. 157) or because the complainant was acting as a safety representative or member of a safety committee (s. 57A(1)(a),(b)), then a special award can be made instead of the additional award. If no order for reinstatement or re-engagement is made, the special award shall be one week's pay multiplied by 104, or £13,400, whichever is the greater, except that the special award cannot exceed £26,800. The week's pay for the purpose of the special award is not subject to any statutory limit. If an order for reinstatement or re-engagement is made and not complied with, then unless the employer satisfied the industrial tribunal that it was not practicable to comply with the order, the special award will be one week's pay multiplied by 156, or £20,100, whichever is the greater. It will be noted that there is no maximum sum which can be awarded under this heading. However, if the applicant is over the age of 64 there will be a reduction of one-twelfth in respect of each month over that age, until the special award is eliminated altogether at the age of 65. The special award may also be reduced on the ground of contributory conduct by the employee, or because he has prevented an order for reinstatement or re-engagement from being complied with, or refused an offer by the employer for reinstatement.

9.54 However, if an employee has refused to join a trade union or to cease being a member, or refused to desist from union activities at an appropriate time, or refused to make a payment to a charity in lieu of joining a trade union, or refused to permit a check-off, such refusals do not constitute contributory conduct.

9.55 In theory, the total compensation which could be awarded is very high. Suppose that an employee, aged 62, was dismissed for trade union activity. He was earning £250 per week, and has had more than 20 years' continuous employment. Assume further that the employer refuses to reinstate him following a tribunal order. Compensation could then be computed as follows:

a. basic award, 20 x 1½ x £205, equals £6,150
b. compensation award, £11,000
c. special award, 156 x £250, equals £39,000.

The total compensation would amount to £56,150. If one adds two weeks' pay for failing to give written reasons for dismissal, the grand total would be £56,650.

9.56 Such an award, however, is highly theoretical. In practice, sums of a more modest nature are awarded. An award of £7,000 could be regarded as being high, while the median award is £2,500.

Interest on awards

9.56A By the Industrial Tribunals (Interest) Order 1990, interest is payable on all tribunal awards (but not the recoupment element) after 42 days from the date the decision is recorded and sent to the parties. Interest is also payable on awards made by the EAT. Any award by way of costs or expenses is excluded. If on a review or appeal the award is varied, interest accrues on the amount as varied. The rate of interest is that specified for the time being under the Judgments Act 1838 s. 17.

Recoupment of unemployment benefit

9.57 Under the heading of the compensation award, a sum of money is ascertained as the loss suffered, and the tribunal will then deduct from that sum the amount of unemployment benefit which the applicant has received. In fact, this amounts to the Government providing a subsidy to the employers, and thus regulations have been passed enabling the Government to recoup this money from the employer. The consequence is that the tribunal must ascertain the prescribed element (which is the gross loss of earnings from the date of dismissal until the date of the hearing), and this may be withheld from the applicant until the Department of Employment has served a notice on the respondent to pay the whole or part of the prescribed element to the Department. When this has been received, the DoE will pay to the applicant the sum due less the unemployment benefits he has received.

9.58 Recoupment does not apply when a settlement is reached without a tribunal hearing, because private settlements (with or without the assistance of the conciliation officer) are not within the scope of the regulations.

Reviews

9.59 An application may be made to an industrial tribunal within 14 days asking for a review of its decision. This is not an appeal, and there are limited circumstances in which the tribunal will accede to such a request. These are as follows:

a. if the decision was wrongly made as a result of an error on the part of the tribunal's staff;
b. if a party did not receive notice of the proceedings (*Hancock v Middleton*);
c. if the decision was made in the absence of a party entitled to be heard. If an employer fails to reply to a complaint by not returning the appropriate defence within the stated time he may be denied the right to be heard unless he can show some valid reason for this. But if a party is prevented from

attending a hearing through illness, then the tribunal should consider whether the absence was for a genuine reason, and it believes his story, a review should be granted (*Morris v Griffiths*). In addition to seeking a review, the person applying should state in writing his reasons not only for the application, but also for contending that the decision of the industrial tribunal was wrong. In *Drakard & Sons Ltd v Wilton*, the employers did not attend a tribunal hearing as they believed that once having made an offer of settlement to the conciliation officer, they thought that they would be contacted if any further steps were required. The EAT held that the tribunal should have granted a review. They should have enquired into the circumstances surrounding the failure to attend the hearing;

d. new evidence comes to light, which could not have been discovered before. For example, if, after the applicant has been awarded compensation for unfair dismissal, new evidence comes to light that he had been defrauding the employer during the period of employment, so that it would have been possible to have dismissed him summarily, then this will be taken into account by the tribunal when it reviews the decision, and any previous award of compensation may be altered accordingly (*McGregor v Gibbins Amusements Ltd*). It must be shown that the new evidence which has now become available could not have been presented at the original hearing, and the application should be accompanied by the substance of that new evidence, including, if possible, proofs of witnesses (*Simmons v Medway Welding Ltd*);

e. the interests of justice require a review. This general power can be illustrated by the case of *Berkeley Garage Ltd v Edmunds* where the employers were told by officers from the Department of Employment that the applicant was bringing his case out of time. Consequently, they did not bother to attend the hearing. The tribunal found that it was not practicable for the applicant to have presented the case earlier, and proceeded to hear the case on its merits. When the employers discovered this, they applied for a review and a rehearing, which the tribunal refused. On appeal this was reversed, for the interests of justice clearly required that the employers be given an opportunity to present their side of the story. Similarly, in *Help the Aged Housing Association v Vidler* the applicant was awarded £4,700 compensation for unfair dismissal, mainly on the basis that he was

60 years of age, and the tribunal thought that it would be a considerable length of time before he obtained further employment. Within two weeks of the tribunal's decision, he obtained employment. It was held on appeal that the tribunal should have exercised its powers of review and reviewed the compensation in the light of the new situation, for the original assessment was totally wrong. Because the applicant had obtained alternative employment so quickly, this altered the substratum of the tribunal's reasoning in computing the loss likely to be suffered, and hence it was in the interests of justice that there should be a review.

9.60 Before refusing an application for review, the industrial tribunal should give the applicant an opportunity to elaborate in writing the grounds which he intends to put forward (*Drakard & Sons Ltd v Wilton*).

9.60A The power to review only applies when the industrial tribunal has made a decision. There is no power to review an actual settlement reached during or at the end of proceedings, where the tribunal has not made a finding on liability (*Larkfield of Cheptstow Ltd v Milne*).

9.61 An application for review may be made on the ground that there was an error in the proceedings, but not on the ground that the decision of the industrial tribunal discloses an error of law, for that is a matter which must be dealt with on appeal to the EAT (*Trimble v Supertravel Ltd*).

Costs

9.62 An industrial tribunal has the power to award costs against a party who has acted frivolously, vexatiously or otherwise unreasonably in bringing or conducting the proceedings. Thus if an applicant or respondent knows that his case is hopeless, but still pursues it, an award of costs may be made (*Davidson v Jon Calder (Publishers) Ltd*). Costs may also be awarded if there is an unnecessary application for an adjournment or postponement, again at the discretion of the industrial tribunal.

Appeals

9.63 It has already been noted (see Chapter 1) that the Employment Appeal Tribunal will hear appeals on points of law from industrial tribunals, and on points of law and of fact from the decisions of the Certification Officer. An appeal on a point of law from the industrial tribunals must be made within 42 days from the date when the document recording the full reasons for the decision was sent to the appellant, although it is possible in exceptional circumstances to apply for an extension of time, but a good reason for the delay must be shown (*Duke v Prospect Training Services Ltd*). Legal aid is available in the EAT, but it should be noted that a delay in obtaining legal aid, or the fact that the assistance of the Equal Opportunities Commission or the Commission for Racial Equality is being sought for the purpose of pursuing an appeal are not reasons for not adhering to the 42-day time limit. In particular, a Practice Direction issued by the EAT makes it clear that if an application for a review is made to an industrial tribunal, this does not prevent the time for appealing from running (although this obviously does not prevent an appeal against the refusal of the tribunal to grant the review), and further, if an industrial tribunal makes a finding of liability, but adjourns the question of compensation, the time for appealing runs from the date of the decision, and is not suspended until the final matter of compensation has been dealt with.

9.64 An appeal from a decision of an industrial tribunal can only hope to succeed if the industrial tribunal have misdirected themselves in law, or entertained the wrong issue, or proceeded on a misapprehension or misconstruction of the evidence, or taken matters into account which were irrelevant to the decision, or reached a decision which no reasonable industrial tribunal, properly directing themselves in law, could have arrived at. In *Neale v Hereford and Worcester County Council*, Lord Justice May propounded the so-called 'Biggles' test. He stated that the EAT should not interfere with the decision of the industrial tribunal (except when they erred on a point of law) unless it was possible to say 'My goodness, that was certainly wrong!' Thus, if there is evidence to support their decision, the EAT will not normally interfere, particularly where the questions of fact and degree are at issue. The task of the EAT is to hear appeals only on points of law (*Spook Erection Ltd v Thackray*). It is not an error of law that the industrial tribunal has misunderstood the facts (*British Telecommunications plc v Sheridan*).

9.64A In *Piggott Bros & Co Ltd v Jackson* the Court of Appeal stated that a decision of the industrial tribunal can only be characterised as being perverse if it was not a permissible option. The EAT would have to identify a finding of fact which was unsupported by any evidence or a clear self-misdirection of law. However, in *East Berkshire Health Authority v Matadeen* the EAT held that in addition, 'perversity' was a free-standing basis for interfering with an industrial tribunal's decision, if that decision 'was not a permissible option' or was 'a conclusion which offends reason' or 'so outrageous in its defiance of logic or of acceptable standards of industrial relations'. In particular, the EAT thought that the lay members were there to bring their experience and industrial judgment to the application of the law and to the decision to be reached on appeal. They were entitled to use that experience to ensure that industrial tribunal decisions did not ignore generally acceptable standards.

9.64B The weight to be attached to the evidence is a matter for the industrial tribunal, and it is not permissible for the EAT to substitute their own views on this (*Eclipse Blinds Ltd v Wright*). But an industrial tribunal must consider whether a dismissal fell within the range of reasonable responses open to a reasonable employer, and not substitute their own judgment. A failure to adopt this approach may result in the decision not being a permissible option (*United Distillers v Conlin*).

9.65 The notice of appeal should state quite precisely what point of law is to be argued. It is not sufficient to make a bald statement that the industrial tribunal misdirected itself on a point of law without specifying the error or misdirection to be appealed against. As Phillips J has pointed out, to say that something is an error of law does not, without further explanation, make it so. Indeed, if it turns out that there is in fact no arguable point of law involved in the appeal, the EAT is quite likely to make an award of costs against the unsuccessful party. Further, if no arguable point is disclosed in the notice of appeal, the notice itself can be rejected by the EAT, so that the appeal will never be heard.

9.66 In a Practice Note issued in 1981 the EAT stated that copies of the notes taken by the chairman of the industrial tribunal will not normally be made available in appeal proceedings except on cause shown. More latitude will be allowed to applicants who were not legally represented at the tribunal hearing (*Webb v Anglian Water Authority*). The facts of the case will be found in the tribunal's decision, and any appeal must be based on the law as applied to those facts. However, it is permissible in argument to refer to the chairman's notes for the purpose of clarifying any ambiguity in the case. If an appeal is based on the actual conduct of the case by the chairman, or some evidence contrary to that found by the tribunal, the applicant must first inform the Registrar of the EAT, so that this can be communicated to the respondent, and the views of the chairman sought. The EAT will not interfere with an award of compensation unless it is more than a trifling matter. If the question of the amount of compensation is alleged to be an error of law, it must be of a substantial nature for the EAT to interfere (*Fougere v Phoenix Motor Co*).

9.67 The EAT does have power to hear new evidence on appeal, but only if a reasonable explanation is produced as to why the evidence was not put before the industrial tribunal. The evidence must be credible, and of such a nature that if would have had a decisive effect on the tribunal's decision had they heard it (*International Aviation Services Ltd v Jones*). It is also possible to argue a new point of law, not canvassed before the industrial tribunal, if the balance of justice so requires (*Russell v Elmdon Freight Terminal Ltd*).

9.68 If there is a complaint about the actual conduct of the industrial tribunal proceedings (e.g. that a member is falling asleep) this should be raised with the chairman at the time, and not after the tribunal has reached its conclusions (*Red Bank Manufacturing Co Ltd v Meadows*), although more serious matters, such as allegations of bias, can be raised at any time (*Peter Simper & Co Ltd v Cooke*).

Reviews

9.69 The EAT has power to review its own decision on the grounds (a) that the order was wrongly made as a result of an error on the part of the tribunal or its staff, (b) a party did not receive proper notice of the proceedings, and (c) the interests of justice require such review. However, the purpose of review is not to allow appeals to be reheard and, in particular, a review will not be granted if an appeal has been lodged to the Court of Appeal (*Blockleys plc v Miller*).

Vexatious litigants (EPCA s. 136A)

9.69A If the EAT is satisfied that any person has habitually and persistently and without reasonable grounds instituted vexatious proceedings or made vexatious applications before an industrial tribunal or the EAT, then, on an application by the Attorney General or the Lord Advocate, the EAT may make a restriction of proceedings order, the effect of which will be to debar that person from instituting proceeedings or making applications without leave from the EAT.

Further appeals

9.70 An appeal will lie from the EAT to the Court of Appeal (in Scotland the Court of Session). Leave to appeal must be given by the EAT, but if this is refused an application for leave to appeal must be made to the Court of Appeal or the Court of Session. It must be shown that there is a genuine point of law of practical consequence involved (*Campbell v Dunoon and Cowal Housing Association Ltd*). A further appeal will lie to the House of Lords.

CHAPTER 10

Redundancy

10.1 The basic purpose of the Redundancy Payments Act 1965 was to compensate a long-serving employee for the loss of a right which he has in a job. There may be other benefits or advantages, such as the need to encourage mobility of labour, redistribute economic skills, and assist in the process of rationalisation of resources, but whether such objects are being achieved must be a matter for the economist rather than the lawyer. The compensation paid is in respect of the loss suffered, and is not intended as a benefit to tide the redundant employee over a period of difficulty. Thus if a person is made redundant, he is entitled to his payment even if he obtains employment elsewhere immediately; similarly, he is entitled to unemployment pay in addition to his redundancy money.

10.2 Most of the Act has been repealed and replaced by corresponding provisions in the Employment Protection (Consolidation) Act 1978, and in this Chapter appropriate references will be made to the latter Act.

Persons covered by the Act

10.3 The Act applies to 'employees', i.e. persons who have entered into a contract of service or apprenticeship. In order to qualify generally, the employee must have at least two years' continuous employment with that employer.

10.4 The usual problem arises with the definition of the term 'employee', illustrated, perhaps, by *Challinor v Taylor* (see para

2.22), which shows one of the disadvantages of being self-employed. A partner is not an employee for redundancy purposes (*Burgess v O'Brien*), nor is a clergyman working at a Mission (*Parker v Orr*). A managing director or director of a company who has executive responsibilities may claim if he has a service contract, but this might prove to be more difficult in the case of a 'one man' company where the virtual sole shareholder in effect works for himself (*Robinson v George Sorby Ltd*). A person may pay a self-employed insurance stamp, and yet be regarded as an employee, for, as we have already seen, this fact is not conclusive evidence as to the true status. The matter is one to be decided in each case on its own special facts.

What is dismissal? (s. 83)

10.5 A dismissal takes place if:

a. the employer terminates the contract (with or without notice);
b. a fixed term contract expires without being renewed;
c. the employee terminates the contract with or without notice in circumstances which are such that he is entitled to do so by reason of the employer's conduct (*Millbrook Furnishing Industries Ltd v McIntosh*); and
d. the employment is terminated by the death, dissolution, liquidation of the employer, or the appointment of a receiver (s. 93).

10.5A We have seen in Chapter 3 that a variation of a contract may amount to a new agreement. If the variation is accepted by both sides, then there is no dismissal, and continuity of employment is preserved. But a variation unilaterally imposed by the employer may amount to a dismissal. In *Marriott v Oxford and District Co-operative Society*, a foreman was told that he would be employed at a lower status and at a reduced rate of pay. This was held to be a dismissal. If the employee accepts the changed situation for a short time under protest there will still be a dismissal, though clearly there will come a point when he will be deemed to have accepted the change if he continues in employment. If the express or implied terms of the contract permit a variation, then no dismissal takes place if the employer exercises his rights thereunder. In *McCaffrey v Jeavons & Co Ltd* an express term of the contract stated that the employee should work anywhere in the United Kingdom. He was asked to move from Bristol to Reading, but he refused. His subsequent resignation was held not to amount to a dismissal.

10.6 If the employer and employee mutually agree to 'part company' this will not be a dismissal, unless there is a clear intention to this effect. For example, some employers may call for 'volunteers' to be made redundant, and they will qualify for payments despite their willingness to be dismissed (*Burton, Allton & Johnson Ltd v Peck*) but a mutual agreement whereby the employee accepts terms for early retirement does not constitute a dismissal (*Birch and Humber v University of Liverpool*).

10.7 If an employee is told that there may be possible redundancies in the future, he may be penalised if he acts precipitously. In *Morton Sundour Fabrics v Shaw* a foreman was warned of impending redundances, and he left the firm to take other employment. His initiative went unrewarded, for it was held that as he had not been dismissed, he was not entitled to a redundancy payment (see also *International Computers v Kennedy*).

10.8 As long as the employee is on the books of the firm, he is still employed, even though he is not working or not being paid. In *Marshall v Harland & Wolff Ltd* the employee was absent from work for eighteen months because of illness. The company then decided to close down the works, and gave him four weeks' notice of dismissal. It was held that he was nonetheless entitled to a redundancy payment, for the employers had not discharged the burden of showing that the contract had come to an end by virtue of frustration through illness.

10.9 An employer may dismiss an employee with appropriate notice. If, during the period of that notice, the employee gives a written counter-notice, stating that he intends to leave before the notice expires, the employee is still regarded as having been dismissed. However, the employer is not bound to accept the counter-notice, and may (again in writing) inform the employee before the end of the counter-notice that he does not accept it, and require him to work until the expiry of the original period of notice. The sanction is that the employer may contest the redundancy payment, and the tribunal has power to reduce it either in whole or in part, as it thinks just and equitable. On the other hand, if there is a mutual agreement that the employee may leave early, this constitutes a variation of the employer's notice, not a consensual termination of the contract (see para 8.94). The employee, therefore, will still be regarded as having been dismissed. (*McAlwane v Broughton Estates Ltd*).

Dismissal for reason of redundancy

10.10 For a claim to be made, the employee must be dismissed for reason of redundancy. In *Sanders v Ernest A Neale Ltd* employees went on a work-to-rule campaign in protest against management actions. The employers sacked them, and eventually the factory closed down. It was held that they were not entitled to redundancy payments. They were dismissed because they would not give an undertaking to work normally, and the dismissals caused the redundancy, rather than the redundancy bringing about the dismissals. There is a statutory presumption (s. 91) that if an employee is dismissed, it is presumed to have been for the reason of redundancy unless the contrary is proved. But this does not mean that an employer cannot properly challenge a claim if there is any doubt as to whether or not a genuine redundancy exists (*O'Hare v Rotaprint Ltd*), for public money used to be at stake. The burden of proof is on the employer to show the reason, and if none is forthcoming, or if the tribunal does not accept the reason as a genuine one, the statutory presumption will arise. However, if the employer does show a reason other than redundancy, the question may arise as to whether the dismissal was fair or unfair, but there will be no liability to redundancy payments.

10.11 A dismissal shall be for reason of redundancy if it is wholly or mainly attributable to:

a. the fact that the employer has ceased, or intends to cease, to carry on that business for the purposes for which the employee was employed; or
b. the employer has ceased or intends to cease to carry on that business in the place where the employee was employed; or
c. the fact that the requirements of that business for employees to carry out work of a particular kind, or for them to carry out that work in the place where they were so employed, have ceased or diminished or are expected to cease or diminish. The test is not as to the work the employee was actually doing at the time of his dismissal, but as to the work he was required to perform under his contract of employment (*Nelson v BBC*).

(a) Cessation of business

10.12 This is a recognisable situation which produces a few legal problems. In *Gemmell v Darngavil Brickworks Ltd* the firm closed down temporarily for a period of thirteen weeks so that repairs could be carried out, and the dismissed employees were held to be redundant, as a temporary cessation is within the meaning of the Act. If the part of the business where the employee works is closed down, but the rest of the business (in its corporate sense) carries on, there is still a cessation of the business.

(b) The employer moving his place of business

10.13 If the employee's contract requires him to work elsewhere then a refusal to do so may mean his dismissal will be fair (*United Kingdom Atomic Energy Authority v Claydon*) and this is not a redundancy situation. Otherwise, it may be. In *O'Brien v Associated Fire Alarms Ltd* the employee worked in the Liverpool area. When work fell off, he was asked to work in Barrow-in-Furness, but refused and was dismissed. Since he was not required by his contract to change his location of work, it was held that the dismissal was for reason of redundancy.

10.14 However, if the employer moves his place of work, whether the move is sufficient to constitute a redundancy situation will be a question of fact, depending on the distance between the old and the new premises, and the resultant inconvenience caused to the employees affected. In *Managers (Holborn) Ltd v Hohne*, the applicant was the manageress of premises in Holborn. The company decided to move its premises to Regent Street, a short distance away. It was held that it could not be said that there was an implied term in her contract that she would only work in Holborn. Both premises were in Central London, and easily accessible. To hold that the employers had broken the contract would mean that it would have been a breach had the employers moved just around the corner, even though the applicant's work or her travel had been completely unaffected.

(c) Surplus labour

10.15 In this situation the employer requires fewer employees for existing work (*Carry All Motors Ltd v Pennington*), or there is less work for existing employees (*Chapman v Goonvean and Rostowrack China Clay Co*), and consequently some are redundant. The redundancy can arise because the work has been re-organised, thus requiring fewer employees to do the same work, or because of the introduction of labour-saving devices, or a change in the work pattern which requires the same number of employees but a different kind of skill, or one to whom different terms and conditions of employment will apply. But the time of day in which the work is to be performed does not make it 'work of a particular kind' so that if there is a reduction in the need for night workers, who are thus transferred to day working, this does not amount to a redundancy. In *Johnson v Nottinghamshire Combined Police Authority*, clerks were employed from 9.30 a.m. to 5.30 p.m. It was decided to introduce a shift system whereby they would work from 8.00 a.m. to 3.00 p.m. and from 1.00 p.m. to 8.00 p.m. in alternate weeks. The clerks refused to do the shift work, and were dismissed. It was held that the change in the hours was to promote greater efficiency, and they were not entitled to redundancy payments.

10.16 This reasoning was confirmed by the Court of Appeal in *Lesney Products Ltd v Nolan*, where the company reorganised its working hours so that instead of the employees working one long day shift plus overtime, they were required to work two day shifts. Employees were offered work on the double day shift, and those who refused were dismissed. It was held that they were not entitled to redundancy payments. A redundancy only arises if there is a change in the terms and conditions of employment due to the fact that the employer's need for work of a particular kind is ceasing or diminishing. A reorganisation of work which results in reduced earning does not produce a redundancy situation if there is still the need for the same number of employees doing the same over-all work, and the only change is that they earn less wages. The law should not inhibit the ability of the employer to reorganise the workforce so as to improve efficiency. The fact that overtime is reduced does not create a redundancy, if the employer's requirements for the work to be done, and the employees to do the work, are the same as before. But if an employee is on a temporary contract, which is not renewed, this can be a redundancy, even though it is known at the time of his appointment that there would be no work for him at the end of the period. Section 83(2)(b) of EPCA clearly provides that a failure to renew a fixed term contract is a dismissal for redundancy purposes, and this would be unnecessary if there was no entitlement to a redundancy payment on the expiry of such a contract (*Lee v Notts County Council*).

10.17 In *Hindle v Percival Boats* the applicant was engaged in repairing wooden boats. The amount of work was declining because of the introduction of fibreglass, and it was uneconomical to retain his services, so he was dismissed because 'he was too good and too slow'. Although he was not replaced (a fact which is sometimes used to determine whether or not a redundancy exists) his work was carried out by other employees working overtime. A majority of the Court of Appeal thought that the employers had rebutted the presumption of redundancy. In another leading case (*North Riding Garages v Butterwick*) the employee was the manager of a repair workshop. New employers took over the business, and introduced new working methods to which the employee could not adapt. He was dismissed for incompetence and inefficiency, and applied for a redundancy payment. It was held that if the new methods had so altered the nature of the work that there was a lessening of the work of a kind he was formerly employed to do, this would amount to redundancy. On the facts, however, the overall requirements of the firm had not changed. It was the inability of the employee to change and adapt to new methods which brought about his dismissal.

10.18 The EAT has expressed its concern over the way the redundancy payments scheme has been operating, saying that the interpretation of the Act has been 'clouded by a slipshod acceptance of a bottomless purse'. In *O'Hare and Rutherford v Rotaprint Ltd* a company expanded its workforce in anticipation of increased production. This never in fact materialised, and the workforce was cut by 10%. The EAT doubted that those who were dismissed were dismissed for reason of redundancy, for it can hardly be said that there is a cessation or diminution of work if an expectation of increased work never materialised. It was suggested that it would be disastrous for the national economy if employers were to be inhibited from taking justifiable risks in planning increased production and taking on more labour if they thought they would be saddled with claims for redundancy payments if they had to cut down the workforce because their expectations were not fulfilled.

Presumption of redundancy

10.19 Section 91(2) of EPCA provides that if there is a dismissal, it is presumed to be by reason of redundancy, unless the contrary is proved. Thus if two employees are dismissed, although only one is redundant, they are both entitled to rely on the statutory presumption (*Willcox v Hastings*) in the absence of evidence to the contrary.

Transferred redundancy

10.20 If an employee is redundant, and he is moved to another post thus making another employee redundant, the latter may make a claim. Such 'bumping' took place in *Elliott Turbomachinery v Bates* where a redundant employee was transferred to the applicant's department, making the latter redundant. Of course, the fact that the employer can show a redundancy situation does not mean that he is justified in dealing with it by a dismissal; he still has to show that he acted reasonably (see Chapter 8). In an appropriate case, it could be held that the employer had acted reasonably in substituting an employee who had a longer service record for the applicant who was dismissed.

Offer of suitable alternative employment (s. 82)

10.21 If the employer makes an offer (whether in writing or not) to the employee to renew the contract of employment, or to re-engage him under a new contract, which is to take effect on the expiry of the old contract or within four weeks thereafter, then:

a. if the provisions of that new contract as to capacity, place at which employed, and other terms and conditions of employment would not differ from the corresponding terms of the previous contract; or
b. these terms and conditions do differ, but the offer constitutes an offer of suitable employment, and in either case the employee unreasonably refuses that offer, then he will not be entitled to a redundancy payment.

10.22 An offer, to be of suitable employment, must take into account all the relevant details, including the nature of the work, the hours, pay, conditions, qualifications and experience of the employee. It is a question of fact and degree in each case. In *Sheppard v National Coal Board* a redundant carpenter was offered a similar job which would have involved more travelling, less overtime, and the loss of certain fringe benefits. It was held that the additional travel was not excessive, and the loss of overtime did not, by itself, render the employment less suitable. The loss of the fringe benefits was more important, and it was held that the offer was not of suitable employment.

10.23 The suitability of the offer of alternative work must be assessed objectively, whereas to assess whether or not the employee's refusal is unreasonable (whether in relation to the offer to renew the old contract on the same terms or the offer of suitable alternative employment) it is permissible to take into account subjective considerations (*Cambridge and District Co-operative Society v Ruse*). Thus the employee's own personal problems which may arise through taking up the offer are relevant factors. Domestic difficulties, inadequate or inconvenient travel facilities, lack of suitable educational facilities for children, loss of friends, have all been matters which have been held to constitute reasonable grounds for refusal of the offer (*Paton Calvert & Co Ltd v Westerside*). An employee does not act unreasonably in refusing to accept alternative employment if he feels he cannot achieve a satisfactory standard in the new post (*Spencer v Gloucestershire County Council*).

10.24-10.27 But a personal whim or fad cannot constitute a reasonable refusal. In *Fuller v Stephanie Bowman Ltd* the applicant was a secretary working in Mayfair. The employers decided to move the office to Soho. The applicant rejected the offer of employment at the new premises, for these were above a sex shop, and as she was opposed to 'money for sex' activities, she found the move too distasteful. Her application for a redundancy payment failed. The tribunal pointed out that the commercial exploitation of sex was no less in Mayfair than in Soho (except, perhaps a little more discreet), and if this was the basis of her reasoning, she should move away from London altogether. Her dislike of working near a sex shop was based on a personal fad, and thus is was held that she had unreasonably refused alternative employment.

Transfer of undertakings

10.28 The Transfer of Undertakings (Protection of Employment) Regulations 1981 gave effect to EC Council Directive 77/187 (see para 5.109). The Regulations apply to a 'relevant transfer', which is a sale or other disposition of an undertaking (but not a sale or transfer of shares).

10.29 Once a relevant transfer takes place, the contract of employment of any person employed by the transferor does not come to an end, but shall have effect as if made by the transferee. It will be recalled (para 8.185) that if the transferee then dismisses the employee who has thus been transferred, the dismissal will be unfair, unless there is an economic, technical or organisational reason entailing changes in the workforce, when the dismissal shall be for 'some other substantial reason'. But the change must be in respect of the workforce, not an individual. Thus if it is sought to change the terms and conditions of employment of an individual, this could constitute a constructive dismissal (*Berriman v Delabore Slate Ltd*). However, a change in whole job contents could come within reg 8(2) (*Crawford v Swinton Insurance Brokers Ltd*). However, in most cases a redundancy payment would be due to an employee, for redundancy is the commonest of the economic, technical or organisational reasons which would entail changes in the workforce (*Gorictree Ltd v Jenkinson*). The main problem arises when it comes to be decided whether the payment should be made by the transferor or the transferee, and it is suggested that the agreement between the parties should cover the point (*Premier Motors Ltd v Total Oil Ltd*). Otherwise, the payment will be made by the employer who dismisses.

10.30 If the employees are dismissed before the transfer - even a few hours before - the liability for the redundancy payment will fall on the transferor (*Secretary of State for Employment v Spence*). If the dismissals take place after the transfer, the transferee will be liable.

10.31 Although the employee is thus transferred to the new employer, he may terminate his employment if a substantial change is made in his working conditions to his detriment. It thus appears that he could claim constructive dismissal and obtain a redundancy payment. But if he objects to being transferred, he is not to be treated as having been dismissed by the transferor (see para 5.113).

Trial period in new employment (s. 84)

10.32 If the contract is renewed on the basis of new terms and conditions of employment, then the employee is entitled to have a trial period of four weeks, or such longer period as may be agreed between the parties for the purpose of retraining the employee under that new contract. In the latter case the new agreement must be made before the employee starts to work under the new contract, it must be in writing, specifying the length of the trial period, and specify the terms and conditions of employment which will apply after the trial period. If before or during the trial period the employee terminates the contract, or the employer does so for a reason connected with the new contract, the employee shall be treated as being dismissed on the date on which his previous contract ended, and for the reason he was dismissed under that contract (*McKindley v William Hill (Scotland) Ltd*). However, in *Hempell v W H Smith & Sons Ltd* the EAT stated that this did not preclude an enquiry under s. 57(3) to ascertain whether the dismissal during the trial period was fair or unfair. If before or during the trial period the employee unreasonably terminates the contract, he shall not be entitled to a redundancy payment by reason of his dismissal from the previous contract.

10.33 The statutory right to a trial period applies to those employees who are dismissed by the employer, or whose fixed term contract has expired. However, on several occasions the EAT have decided that an employee who is constructively dismissed has a reasonable period within which to decide whether or not to accept the repudiation by the employer or to carry on with the new contract offered. The statutory trial period of four weeks does not commence until after the expiry of that reasonable period (*Turvey v Cheney & Son Ltd*). In *Air Canada v Lee* the applicant worked as a telephonist. The employers moved their premises and she was asked to work in a basement office, with no natural light. She objected, but worked there for three months, when she left. It was held that she has been made redundant when she was asked to move: it was reasonable that she should try the new premises for three months, even though the statutory period had expired.

10.34 Since an employee has a statutory right to a trial period, a refusal to offer him one may lead to a finding that his dismissal was unfair (*Elliott v Richard Stump Ltd*). The statutory trial period of four weeks is four calendar weeks, not four working weeks (*Benton v Sanderson Kayser Ltd*).

Laying off and short-time working (s. 87)

10.35 An employer may find himself in a difficult economic situation which may be envisaged to be of a temporary nature, and he may decide, instead of dismissing his employees, to lay them off temporarily, or to put them on short-time. A lay-off is where there is no work for the employees and no remuneration provided; short-time working is defined as being where less than half the normal week's pay is earned. If the lay-off or short-time has lasted for more than four consecutive weeks, or more than six weeks in any 13, then the employee may give written notice (not more than four weeks after the lay-off or short-time has finished) that he intends to claim a redundancy payment. He must then give the requisite notice to terminate his contract, and will be entitled to be considered redundant. The employer may agree to meet the claim, or refuse to do so and serve a counter-notice within seven days on the ground that he reasonably expects to be able to provide at least 13 weeks' continuous employment without further resort to lay-offs or short-time working. If the claim or counter-notice is not withdrawn, the matter will be determined by the industrial tribunal, which will consider whether or not there was a reasonable prospect of full employment for thirteen weeks. If the counter-notice is withdrawn by the employer, or the 13 weeks' continuous employment fails to materialise, the employee is entitled to be paid redundancy money.

10.36 If the employer offers work, but the employee refuses the offer because the rate of pay is too low, the employer has still offered to provide the work, and if, had he accepted the work the employee would have earned more than half a week's pay, there is no short-time working (*Spinpress Ltd v Turner*).

10.37 But an employer has no inherent right to lay off workers as he chooses. In the absence of an express right to do so in the contract, such unilateral action can be regarded as a repudiation of the contract, and hence a dismissal. Thus (in theory) at least one week's notice should be given of such intended lay-off (*Johnson v Cross*). But if the employer reserves the right to resort to a lay-off in the contract, the employee cannot treat this as a termination.

10.38 If the employer has a contractual right to lay off for an indefinite period (e.g. in the building industry) the employee's remedy is under s. 88, and he cannot claim that the lay-off was for such an unreasonable length of time as to constitute a constructive dismissal (*Kenneth MacRae & Co Ltd v Dawson*).

Dismissal during the period of notice (s. 92)

10.39 If an employee has been given due notice that he will be dismissed for reason of redundancy, and whilst he is working out that notice, he commits an act of misconduct which is sufficiently serious to warrant his instant dismissal without notice (see s. 82(2)), and he is summarily dismissed, the question will arise as to whether or not he is entitled to his redundancy payment. On the assumption that the dismissal was justified (e.g. because the employee refused to obey a lawful order (*Cairns v Burnside Shoe Repairs Ltd*), or because the employee stole from the employer (*Jarmain v Pollard & Co Ltd*)), then the industrial tribunal shall determine whether it is just and equitable that the employee should receive the whole or part of the redundancy payment, as it thinks fit. In *Lignacite Products v Krollman* the applicant was given notice of redundancy. He was then found stealing from this employers and summarily dismissed. The industrial tribunal reduced his redundancy pay by 40%, and the EAT upheld the decision. It is difficult to reconcile these decisions with the more recent case of *Bonner v H Gilbert Ltd*.

10.40 If an employee is given notice of dismissal by reason of redundancy, and during his notice period he takes part in a strike, then although this is conduct which entitles the employer to terminate the contract without notice, the employee is not barred from getting the whole of his redundancy payment (s. 92). However, if an employee is on strike, and then is dismissed for reasons of redundancy, his claim will fail. The reason is that s. 82(2) of the Act provides that the employee will not be entitled to a redundancy payment if the employer, being entitled to terminate the contract of employment, terminates it, with or without notice. Since an employee who is on strike is in breach of this contract, the employer is entitled to terminate it. In other words, s. 92 deals with the situation when an employee is dismissed for reason of redundancy, and then goes on strike. In *Simmons v Hoover Ltd* employees who were actually on strike were dismissed for reason of redundancy, and it was held that s. 82(2) operated, and s. 92 did not operate to save their claim.

Excluded classes of employees

10.41 The following employees are not eligible for, or will not be entitled to, a redundancy payment:

a. a person employed under a fixed term contract for two years or more, if before that term expires, he agrees in writing to exclude his rights to make a claim (s. 142(2)). This is one of the very few circumstances when an employee can forgo his legal rights;

b. a miscellaneous class of employees: share fishermen, employees who work less than 16 hours per week (unless they work more than 8 hours per week, and have done so for more than 5 years), and men and women over the age of 65 or normal retiring age. Domestic servants employed in a private household *are* within the scope of the Act, unless the servant is a close relative of the employer (s. 100);

c. an employee who under his contract of employment ordinarily works outside Great Britain, unless on the date he is made redundant he is in Great Britain in accordance with instructions given to him by his employer. In *Costain Civil Engineering Ltd v Draycott* the applicant was made redundant whilst on leave from Dubai, and it was held that since he was not here in accordance with his employer's instructions, his claim failed;

d. an agreement made between an employers' organisation and a trade union may provide exemption from the Act by a ministerial order on an application by both parties thereto, provided the conditions in s. 96 are satisfied;

e. if, on the termination of his employment, the employee is entitled to an occupational pension of a periodic payment or a lump sum, the employer may serve a notice on the employee that his right to a redundancy payment is excluded or reduced. If the annual value of the pension is equal to one third of the employee's leaving salary, and is payable immediately (even though the employee decides to accept a deferred pension) the employer may exclude altogether the right to receive a redundancy payment. If the pension is less than one third of the employee's leaving salary, or if it is not payable immediately but within 90 weeks, the redundancy payment is reduced proportionately (see *Royal Ordnance plc v Pilkington*). The annual leaving salary is subject to the statutory maximum of £205 per week, times 52 weeks, i.e. £10,660 (Redundancy Payments Pensions Regulations 1965).

Claims for redundancy payments

10.42 A claim must be made to the industrial tribunal within six months from the relevant date, which is the date of the expiry of the notice to terminate the employment, or the date when the contract expires, or the date on which a fixed term contract comes to an end. The tribunal has a discretion to admit a claim which is outside the time limit if it thinks it would be just and equitable to do so, but no claim can be entertained after 12 months have lapsed. The claim, if admitted or successful, must be met by the employer. The amount of the claim will be determined by the length of time the employee has been employed, his normal week's pay, and his age.

10.43 The employee must have been continuously employed for two years or more by the same employer for more than 16 hours per week in order to qualify for payments though not necessarily under the same contract. Continuity of employment is not broken by lay-offs or short-time working, and although periods spent on strike do not count in computing the length of employment, they do not break continuity. Time off through sickness, injury, etc, is reckonable in computing the total period of continuous employment, as is any time off by arrangement or custom (e.g. the secondment of an employee to another employer).

10.44 Continuity of employment exists if an employee works for a subsidiary or associated employer of the original employer, or if there is a take-over of the business (not just its assets) and the new employer offers to re-engage the employee on suitable terms which are accepted. In *Lord Advocate v De Rosa*, the employee was employed from 1950 to 1967 by Isaac Barrie

(Transport) Ltd when the business was transferred to John Barrie (Contractor) Ltd. There was no interruption in his employment, but he did change his job from transport manager to docks manager. In 1971 he was made redundant. It was held that his redundancy payment was to be calculated with reference to both periods of employment, for continuity was preserved even though there had been a change in his terms and conditions of employment.

10.45 The week's pay is calculated on the normal rate of pay; in respect of piece-workers it will be the average of their earnings for the past four weeks, while for hourly workers it will be based on the number of normal working hours. Overtime earnings are not included in the calculations (see *Gascol Conversions v Mercer*, para 3.36) unless the employer is legally obliged to provide overtime and the employee is legally obliged to work it. If the employer is entitled, but not obliged, to call for overtime working, this does not count as normal working time, even though the employee is bound to work under the terms of his contract (*Lotus Cars Ltd v Sutcliffe*). Overtime premiums also do not count (*British Coal Corpn v Cheesbrough*). The average weekly rate of remuneration is (a) any sum paid by way of a wage or salary, (b) the value of any benefit in kind, and (c) any other profit or surplus which is a benefit in the hands of the employee. But expenses which form part of reimbursement for expenditure do not count. Therefore a car allowance and travelling expenses should normally be excluded. So, too, are other perks, such as free accommodation, use of the company's car, etc, for redundancy payments are only made on the basis of remuneration received (*Skillern v Eastwoods Froy Ltd*). The tribunal must determine as a fact in broad terms whether a sum regularly paid to the employee represents a reimbursement or a profit or surplus in the employee's hand (*S & U Stores v Wilkes*).

10.46 The amount of redundancy payment is finally determined by the age of the employee, with the following result; for each year's employment between the ages of 18 and 21, he is entitled to one half of a week's pay, between the ages of 22 and 40 he is entitled to one week's pay, and between the ages of 41 and 64 he is entitled to one and a half weeks' pay. In respect of employees over the age of 64, there is a reduction of one-twelfth in the total entitlement in respect of each month over the age of 65. All this is subject to a maximum of 20 years' reckonable employment, and a maximum week's pay of £205. Thus the maximum payment possible for an employee over the age of 60 with 20 years' continuous employment is 20 x 1½ x £205, i.e. £6,150. When making the payment, the employer shall give to the employee a written statement showing how the amount of payment is calculated and it is an offence, punishable on summary conviction by a fine not exceeding level 1 on the standard scale, not to do so (s. 102). If an employer gives a lump sum to a redundant employee without so indicating how it is made up, this may be regarded as an *ex gratia* payment, not intended to be by way of redundancy payment (*Galloway v Export Packing Services Ltd*).

Consultation provisions

10.47–10.62 For the provisions relating to consultations with trade unions on redundancies and transfers, see Chapter 15.

Notification of mass redundancies to the minister (TULR(C)A s. 193)

10.63 If an employer is proposing to make redundant more than 100 employees at one establishment within 90 days, or more than 10 employees within 30 days, he must notify the Secretary of State of his proposals within 90 or 30 days respectively, and also give a copy of this notification to the representatives of any recognised independent trade union with members affected. If there are special circumstances which make compliance not reasonably practicable, he shall take all such steps as are reasonably practicable. But a failure on the part of a person who controls the employer to provide information to the employer does not constitute a special circumstance (s. 193(7)).

10.64 An employer who fails to give the required notification to the Secretary of State may be prosecuted in the magistrates' court, and is liable on conviction to a fine not exceeding level 5 on the standard scale (TULR(C)A s. 194(1)).

10.65 The rules on consultation on redundancy (see Chapter 15) apply whether or not the employees in question are trade union members, as long as there is a recognised trade union with which to consult. However, notification to the Secretary of State applies whether there is a union presence or not.

CHAPTER 11

Duties of ex-employees

11.1 Since, as we have seen, the relationship between employer and employee is one of trust, confidence and faith, it must follow that an ex-employee does not escape entirely from those obligations merely by leaving the employment. How the law tries to achieve a balance between the conflicting interests of the individual, the employer and the State will be the subject of this chapter.

11.2 A distinction must be drawn between the duty of fidelity owed by an employee during the currency of the contract of employment (see *Marshall v Industrial Systems and Controls Ltd*, and *Laughton and Hawley v Bapp Industrial Supplies Ltd*, para 8.7) and the duty owed after the employment has ended. In *Faccenda Chicken Ltd v Fowler* (see below) the Court of Appeal made it clear that in the former case, the duty is contractual, whether as an express or implied term of the contract of employment. This means that an employee cannot properly disclose information or give assistance to a competitor, even in his own time. The obligations of an ex-employee are more limited; he may be under a duty not to disclose information which has been imparted to him in confidence, such as secret processes, trade secrets, etc, but this does not cover all information given or acquired by the employee during his employment, and does not cover information which is confidential in the sense that it would have been a breach of the employee's duty of fidelity for him to have disclosed it to a third party during the course of the employment.

11.3 To determine whether particular information falls into the category of information which ought not to be disclosed after the employment has ceased, regard must be had to all the circumstances, and in particular to:

a. the nature of the employment;
b. the nature of the information;
c. whether the employer regarded the information as being confidential and informed the employee of this;
d. whether the information could be easily isolated from other information which the employee is free to use.

11.4 Thus, in *Faccenda Chicken Ltd v Fowler*, the employer sought an injunction to restrain two former employees from using their knowledge of sales and prices information when they set up a competing business. It was held that this was not confidential information, and the application for the injunction was refused. Thus, subject to the above restrictions, an ex-employee is entitled to make use of his skill and knowledge which he has generally acquired in his previous employments (*United Sterling Corpn v Felton*), and may only be restrained by a validly worded restrictive covenant.

Disclosure of information

11.5 The ex-employee is under a duty not to disclose to any unauthorised person any confidential information he had obtained during his employment, or to use such information in an unauthorised manner. In *Robb v Green* an employee copied out a list of the employer's clients with a view to approaching them after his employment had ceased, and in *Wessex Dairies v Smith* a milk roundsman, during the last week of his employment, approached his customers to ask them if they would join a round of his own which he was proposing to start. In both cases it was held that there was a breach of contract.

11.6 It will be obvious that the rule is easier to state in theory than to enforce in practice, for it is not possible to wipe out from an employee's mind information which he has gained in the course of the employment and which he may properly place at the disposal of his new employer. A distinction must be drawn between trade secrets and confidential information on the one hand, and an employee's skill, knowledge and general familiarity with his former employer's business on the other hand (*Lock International plc v Beswick*). In *Printers and Finishers*

Ltd v Holloway the plaintiffs sought an injunction against their former works manager restraining him from disclosing certain confidential information which he had obtained during his employment. Some of this information was contained in documents which the defendant had taken with him, and an injunction was granted in respect of these. So far as confidential matters which were in his memory were concerned, which related to the know-how and general processes of the plaintiff's business, these were not readily separable from his general knowledge of the whole trade, and it would not be unreasonable for him to recall particular skills of his former employer's business and use his skills for the benefit of his new employer. Consequently, an injunction relating to these matters was refused. Nonetheless, the court ordered an enquiry to ascertain what damage, if any, had flowed from the defendant's breach of duty.

11.7 By contrast, in *Thomas Marshall Ltd v Guinle*, the defendant was appointed Managing Director of the plaintiff company under a 10 year service contract, which contained clauses against disclosing confidential information relating to the affairs, customers or trade secrets of the company, during his employment or after it ceased. He resigned after five years and set up his own competing business. The court granted an injunction against him from acting in breach of the agreement.

11.8 However, if the information obtained, though confidential, relates to a breach of the law or wrongful act by the employer, then there is an entirely different situation, for 'there is no confidence as to the disclosure of an iniquity'. In *Initial Services v Putterill* the defendant was employed as a manager by the plaintiffs. After leaving his employment he gave information to a newspaper concerning the conduct of the plaintiffs' business, in particular alleging that they had violated the Restrictive Trade Practices Act 1956 by entering into agreements with other laundries which ought to have been registered under that Act, and that they had issued circulars which were misleading to the public. The newspaper proposed to publish an article which would have made detrimental allegations about the plaintiffs' business, and an injunction was sought. It was held that the disclosure would be justified as being in the public interest, and there was no confidence attached thereto.

11.8A Nor can an employee be restrained from disclosing information to regulatory bodies (such as FIMBRA) which have a duty to investigate matters within their remit (in *Re A Company's Application*).

Garden leave clauses

11.8B We have noted (see para. 11.2) that a distinction must be drawn between a contractual term which prohibits an employee from working for another employer (usually, but not necessarily, a competitor) during the subsistence of the contract, and a restrictive covenant which restrains an employee from working for a competitor for a certain period after the contract has ended. In the former case, such work would constitute a breach of the duty of faithful service (see para 6.53), which would warrant dismissal. However, there are cases where an employee resigns his employment, sometimes by giving due notice, sometimes by giving less notice than the contract requires, and then seeks to work for a competitor. Can he be restrained from so working in breach of contract?

11.8C In *Evening Standard v Henderson*, the employee agreed that during his contract he would not work for another employer. His contract also provided that one year's notice had to be given by either side. He decided to work for a rival newspaper, and gave two months' notice to terminate his employment. The employer applied for an injunction to restrain him from working for the rival newspaper until the full year's contractual notice had expired. In the circumstances of the case, the injunction was granted. The plaintiffs were quite willing to pay the employee during the full year notice period, whether or not he worked for them. The balance of convenience was in favour of granting the injunction to enforce the very thing the contract was designed to prevent him from doing, namely working for a rival concern.

11.8D But if the employee gives lawful notice, can the employer require him not to work during the notice period, pay him his salary, and yet insist that he does not work for a rival concern during the notice period. The effect of such a 'garden leave' arrangement was considered in *Provident Financial Group plc v Hayward*, where the defendant was a financial director of an estate agency business. His contract provided that during his employment he would not work for any other person. He tendered his resignation on 1 July, and although he was bound to give 12 months' notice, it was mutually agreed that his employment would terminate at the end of December. He continued to work during the notice period until September, when the employers decided that he need no longer do any work, although they were prepared to pay him his salary until the end of December. In effect, he was on 'garden leave', at home, on full pay and with all his contractual benefits. In October, he announced that he intended starting work for another firm of estate agents, and the plaintiffs sought an injunction to restrain him from doing so. The application was refused. There were only ten weeks of the unexpired notice period left, and there was no evidence of the prospect of serious damage resulting to the plaintiffs' business if the employee took up the new job. His duties were more of an administrative nature, and he had very little confidential information in his possession which would cause the employers damage.

11.8E The matter is one for the court's discretion. In *Hayward*, the Court of Appeal made it clear that there were circumstances where it would be appropriate to restrain an employee from working during his notice period, particularly if the notice period is not excessive, and the employee is not being deprived of his opportunity to practice his skills. However, the insertion of long periods of 'garden leave' provisions in contracts of employment is capable of abuse. It is to be expected that senior employees will seek employment with someone in the same line of business, and will not take kindly to enforced idleness, even if they are being paid. Employers will also have exaggerated fears as to the damage likely to be caused to their business (see also *JA Mont (UK) Ltd v Mills*).

Covenants in restraint of trade

11.9 An employer cannot prevent an ex-employee from competing with him, nor using the knowledge, skill and experience gained during the employment. The employer can, however, extract a promise that the ex-employee will not use his personal influence over customers, or his knowledge of trade secrets, to the disadvantage of the employer (*Spafax Ltd v Harrison*), provided this is reasonably necessary for the protection of the employer's business. Thus, an employer who wishes to have protection against the disclosure of confidential information should get the employee to sign a covenant to this effect, so that the employee's future conduct is restricted once the employment comes to an end. Normally, this would be signed at the commencement of the employment, but though desirable, this is not essential. In *R S Components Ltd v Irwin* the employer asked a salesman, who was already in employment, to sign a covenant which would have prevented him from soliciting business from the firm's customers for a period of 12 months after leaving the employment. The employee refused to do so, and his consequent dismissal was held by the NIRC to have been fair on the grounds of 'some other substantial reason' (see Chapter 8).

11.10 There are several limitations on the right of the employer to impose such restraints, for the courts will look with a critical eye at any agreement which has the effect of restraining a person from earning his livelihood in the future. The employer cannot take away the employee's skill, experience and fund of knowledge which he has obtained during the employment, and, in particular, the employer cannot protect himself against future competition *per se*. For example, in *Strange v Mann*, the defendant was employed by a firm of bookmakers as a manager. Most of the betting was done by telephone, and hence the defendant had little personal contact with customers. He agreed that he would not, after leaving the employment, be engaged in a similar business within a radius of 12 miles. After leaving his job, he set up in business as a bookmaker within the prohibited area. It was held that the restriction was void. The purpose of the covenant was not to give legitimate protection to the business interests of the employer, but was a naked attempt to prevent future competition.

11.11 What, then, are the interests in respect of which the employer is entitled to have protection? Basically, there are three, the first relates to his trade secrets, the second to his customers and connections, and the third relates to working for competitors.

A. Trade secrets

11.12 If an employer could not ensure that his employees would not pass on information concerning his secret processes, it might restrict the employment relationship to an extent where commercial initiative became impossible. The employer would not be able to trust the employee; furtive attempts would have to be made to disclose some information without disclosing all, industrial espionage would flourish, and employees would attempt to sell secrets by offering themselves on the labour market at the highest bidder. Research and development would be hampered and become unprofitable. So, at least, ran the economic theories of former ages, though with the advent of patent law the modern scene might be somewhat different. Nonetheless, the legal principles remain substantially the same. Thus if a trade secret, or a secret process, exists, the employer is entitled to have his employee's promise not to divulge that information to a future employer, at least, subject to possible limitations on time and area. In *Foster & Sons Ltd v Suggett* the defendant was a works engineer concerned with a secret process in the glass-making industry. He covenanted that he would not divulge any trade secret or manufacturing process, and would not be employed by a competitor anywhere in the United Kingdom for five years after leaving his employment with the plaintiffs. It was held that the covenant was reasonable and enforceable.

11.13 It is not possible to restrain an employee from disclosing to a future employer a special method of organisation, as opposed to a secret process, for one must draw a distinction between objective knowledge, such as trade secrets and lists of customers, which are part of the employer's property, and subjective knowledge which has been acquired by the employee, such as his general knowledge of the trade or industry, or his organisational ability. In *Herbert Morris Ltd v Saxelby* an engineer covenanted not to be engaged by a competitor for seven years after leaving his employment. This was held to be void, for it was a restraint on his technical skill and knowledge which he had acquired by his own industry, observation and intelligence, and this could not be taken away from him.

B. Existing customers and connections

11.14 The nature of the employee's work may well lead him into close contact with the firm's customers, so as to build up a relationship which may lead those customers to follow the employee when he takes up new employment. This, then, is a legitimate field where the employer may seek protection. In *Plowman v Ash*, the defendant was employed as a sales representative. He covenanted not to canvass or solicit orders from any person who was a customer of the firm for a period of two years after leaving his employment. It was held that the restraint was valid, even though it extended to customers whom the employee did not know or with whom he had no contact during his period of employment. It was argued that the restraint was bad because it could apply to those customers who had ceased to do business with the firm, but the Court of Appeal thought that an employer was entitled not to abandon hope that such customers would return to do business once more.

11.15 On the other hand, if an employee does not come into contact with such customers, then it cannot be argued that he has built up a special relationship with them so as to entitle the employer to extract a covenant restraining the employee from approaching them with a view to taking business away from the employer. For example, if a firm is engaged mainly in trading in the South of England, and has few customers outside that area, a covenant restraining an employee from working in that type of business anywhere in the world must of necessity be void, as being wider than legitimately required for the protection of the employer's business (*Dowden & Pook Ltd v Pook*). In *Attwood v Lamont* a tailor's cutter in a department store agreed not to be employed by another firm which competed with his employer. Since it can hardly be said that in his position he had gained the trust and confidence of the customers so that they would follow him if he left the firm, the covenant was void. Again, if the business is such that it is not of a recurring nature, then the employer's interest in the customer ceases on the conclusion of a particular transaction, and he is not entitled to protection against poaching. In *Bowler v Lovegrove* the defendant was a negotiating clerk who worked for a firm of estate agents. He covenanted not to enter into a similar business for one year within a restricted area, but it was held that as the business was of a non-recurring nature, the employer had no interest to protect, and the covenant was void.

11.16 The position held by the employee may be relevant, too. An employer can scarcely claim that he fears competition from an ex-employee if, during the period of employment, he pays him a low wage, for this reflects the regard he has for his services (*M & S Drapers v Reynolds*). Nor is an employer entitled to restrain competition by preventing the ex-employee from approaching persons who are not his customers. In *Gledhow Autoparts v Delaney* the plaintiffs employed the defendant as a commercial traveller. It was agreed that after leaving his employment, the defendant would not seek orders from any firm within the area in which he had previously operated. The restraint was held to be void, for as worded, it would have prevented him from calling on firms who were not then customers of the plaintiffs, and was therefore a covenant designed to restrain competition.

11.16A Moreover, the personality, temperament and general make-up of an employee is his own possession, and there is thus no proprietary right in an employee's own personality which the employer can keep to himself as part of his own business (*Cantor Fitzgerald (UK) Ltd v Wallace*).

11.17 If there is a *prima facie* breach of a covenant not to deal with the employer's former customers, the employer is entitled to an injunction even though the customer has intimated that he will not do further business with the employer (*John Michael Design plc v Cooke*).

11.17A The employer's 'connections' are also a legitimate object for protection. Thus an employment agency which supplied temporary staff to business clients was held to be entitled to extract and enforce a restrictive covenant from its own staff who dealt with the temporary staff (the connection) and the clients (*Office Angels Ltd v Rainer-Thomas*).

C. Working for competitors

11.18 We have seen (para 6.1) that the courts will not grant an injunction to compel a person to work for a particular employer, for this would amount to compulsory labour. Thus if an employee agrees that after leaving his employment, he will not work for a competitor, the courts will rarely enforce such an agreement because the employee will be faced with the alternative of being forced to work for his former employer or starve! But if the latter alternative does not exist, the courts may be more willing to enforce the agreement.

11.19 In *Littlewoods Organisation Ltd v Harris*, the plaintiffs ran a mail order business, their chief rivals being Great Universal Stores (GUS). The defendant worked for the plaintiffs in a senior position, and had access to confidential information about how the business was operated. He agreed that on leaving his employment, he would not work for GUS for a period of 12 months. He then resigned his position in order to take employment with GUS, and the plaintiffs sought an injunction to restrain him. For the defendant it was argued that the covenant was too wide, and therefore void, for, as worded, it would have prevented him from being employed by GUS anywhere in the world, or by one of their companies which was not concerned with mail order. Nonetheless, the restriction was held to be valid by a majority of the Court of Appeal. It was held that where a covenant in restraint of trade was drafted in general terms, which, without alteration could be construed in a sense which was not unreasonably wide in relation to the relevant confidential information or trade secrets for which the covenantee was seeking protection, the court could construe the covenant in that sense, thereby rendering it valid and enforceable. Accordingly, the covenant should not be construed as applying to the whole range of business carried on by GUS throughout the world, but only to the mail order business carried on in the United Kingdom. So construed, it was no wider than was reasonably necessary to protect the confidential information about the mail order side of the plaintiffs' business, and it was thus enforceable. There is little doubt that this case represents a major shift in the judicial approach to the interpretation of restrictive covenants, though it is arguable that the conclusion is warranted on the special facts.

11.20 But the protection taken out by the employer must be in respect of his specific interests, and if it is too wide for this purpose, it will be void. In *Commercial Plastics Ltd v Vincent*, the plaintiffs employed the defendant to work on the production of PVC calendering sheeting for adhesive tape. The defendant agreed not to be employed by a competitor in the PVC calendering field for one year after leaving his employment. This restriction was held to be void. The protection legitimately required by the plaintiffs could only be in respect of their own business, which was the production of adhesive tape. In fact, the covenant covered the whole field of calendering sheeting, and hence was too wide.

Extent of the restraint

11.21 The legitimate interests of the employer can only be protected within their proper limits, and any restraint outside those limits will be void. Thus if the covenant is too wide in time, or too extensive in terms of the area covered, the courts will not enforce it. Covenants which are in restraint of trade will only be valid if they are reasonable, and this will depend on an examination of all the circumstances. In *Nordenfelt v Maxim Nordenfelt Guns and Ammunition Co Ltd* an inventor of guns and ammunition sold his business to a company for a substantial sum, and covenanted not to be engaged in any similar business anywhere in the world for 25 years. Considering the world-wide nature of the business, and the price which had been paid for his promise, the House of Lords held that the restraint was reasonable.

11.22 Time and area may be looked at together to assess the validity of the covenant. In *Fitch v Dewes* a solicitor's clerk was prohibited from entering into the employment of another solicitor within a radius of seven miles of Tamworth Town Hall. Although this was a lifetime restraint, the modest area enabled him to work quite openly outside the limit, and it was held to be valid. But if the covenant is too wide for its purpose, either in time or area, it will be void. In *Mason v Provident Clothing and Supply Co Ltd* a covenant restraining a canvasser from competing with his former employer anywhere within 25 miles from the centre of London was held to be void. And in *Herbert Morris v Saxelby* (above) a seven-year restraint on an engineer was equally bad.

11.23 The restriction cannot be worded in a manner which prevents the employee from obtaining non-competing employment (*Commercial Plastics Ltd v Vincent* (above)). For example, in *Fellowes & Son v Fisher* the defendant was a conveyancing clerk employed by a firm of solicitors in Walthamstow. He agreed that for five years after leaving his employment, he would not (a) be employed or concerned in the legal profession anywhere within the postal districts of Walthamstow and Chingford, or (b) solicit any person who had been a client of the firm whilst he had been with them. After leaving his employment, he commenced work with another firm of solicitors who had offices in Walthamstow. The Court of Appeal refused to grant an injunction to restrain him. A restraint of five years which covered such a thickly populated area was undoubtedly too wide in the circumstances. Further, clause (a), as worded, would have prevented him from being employed as an assistant to a justices' clerk, or in the legal department of the local authority. In *Greer v Sketchley Ltd*, the activities of the company were confined to the Midlands and London area. The employee agreed that after leaving his employment he would not work for any similar business anywhere in the United Kingdom. This was held to be void; the fact that there was a problematical and possible expansion by the company into other areas of the country was too vague to justify such a wide restraint.

11.23A An area restriction will always be considered critically by the courts, since it will frequently amount to a covenant against competition, which would generally be unenforceable. Thus if such a restriction will do little to protect the employer (e.g., because most of the orders are placed on the telephone), or if there is no functional connection with the area covered by the restriction and the areas associated with the employee's work, the restraint is likely to be void (*Office Angels Ltd v Rainer-Thomas*).

11.24 Thus if a covenant is too restrictive, it will be totally void, and the courts will not enforce it or any part of it. They will not normally validate the agreement by altering it, for the test is whether the parties have in fact made a valid agreement, not whether they could have done so, and it must stand or fall on its own merits. Exceptionally, however, the courts may relax this strict interpretation by use of a device known as 'the blue pencil' rule. If there are terms which are too wide, and others which are valid and reasonable, then the former may be struck out of the agreement altogether. If those terms which thus remain are valid, then they may be enforced. In *Lucas v Mitchell* the defendant was employed by the plaintiffs as a sales representative. He agreed that after leaving his employment he would not (a) deal in any goods similar to those which he had previously sold, or (b) solicit orders from or supply any such goods to any customer of the firm within the Manchester area. The first part of the covenant was clearly void, for this was a restraint on competition. The second part was clearly reasonable. Because there were two separate restraints, capable of being enforced separately, the excision of the first was possible without affecting the second.

11.24A Severance is possible if there is no grammatical difficulty in removing the offending words (*Business Seating Ltd v Broad*). If that which remains is reasonable, the covenant will be enforced (*Rex Stewart etc v Parker*).

11.24B In considering whether or not to grant an injunction, the court will take account of the 'balance of convenience' in accordance with the principles laid down in *American Cyanamid v Ethicon Ltd*. Three questions need to be asked; (a) is there a serious issue to be tried, (b) would damages be an appropriate remedy if the injunction is not granted, and (c) what is the likelihood of the plaintiff succeeding at a full trial. In *Lansing Linde Ltd v Kerr* it was alleged that the defendant was in breach of a covenant which was designed to prevent him from working for a competitor for a period of 12 months after leaving his employment. The Court of Appeal held that an application for an injunction was rightly refused. The trial of the action would not have taken place until most of the period for which the injunction was sought would have expired. Thus the question was not only whether there was a serious issue to be tried, but also an assessment of the plaintiff's prospect of succeeding at that hearing. The injunction, if granted, would have effectively determined the case in the plaintiff's favour, and therefore the judge had been correct in considering as an additional factor the strength of the plaintiff's claim.

11.24C It should be noted that if an employer wrongfully dismisses an employee, he cannot at the same time claim the benefit of the restrictive covenant, for the whole contract will have been repudiated by the employer (*General Billposting Co v Atkinson*). This is so even if there is an automatic termination of the employment (e.g. on the dissolution of a partnership (*Briggs v Oates*). But if a contract provides that it may be terminated by an employer on giving six months' notice or six months' pay in lieu of notice, an employer who adopts the latter option is not acting in breach of contract (*Rex Stewart etc v Parker*).

11.24D It should also be noted that if an employee has agreed to a restrictive covenant with his employers, which has the effect of restricting his activities after the employment has ended, then if the employer transfers the business in circumstances in which the Transfer of Undertakings (Protection of Employment) Regulations apply (see para 5.104), the new owner of the transferred business is entitled to enforce that covenant against the employee (*Morris Angel & Son Ltd v Hollande*, see para 5.119A).

11.25 Employers cannot agree to a restraint among themselves which would not be enforced if it was entered into by their employees. In *Kores Manufacturing Co v Kolok Manufacturing Co* two companies, both engaged in the selling of carbon paper, agreed that they would not employ any person who had been employed by the other party for a period of five years after that person had left the other's employment. Had the restraint been imposed by a company on the employees, it would have been void. It was equally void having been made by the employers themselves.

Anton Piller orders

11.26 In addition (or as an alternative) to obtaining an injunction, the aggrieved employer may seek an Anton Piller order. This permits the employer to search the employee's premises or home etc, and to remove documents, drawings, records, prototypes or other specified matter. The purpose is to prevent a defendant from destroying, hiding or removing vital evidence, and to enable the plaintiff to obtain inspection of any relevant matter in the defendant's possession. A refusal to permit the search, and/or the removal, destruction etc of the evidence not only enables the courts to draw an adverse conclusion, but may also amount to a contempt of court (*Anton Piller KG v Manufacturing Processes Ltd*). Before granting the order, the court must be satisfied (a) that there is a strong *prima facie* case, (b) the actual or potential damage to the plaintiff would be very serious, and (c) that there is clear evidence that the defendant has in his possession incriminating matter, and that there is a real possibility that he would destroy, hide, remove or otherwise dispose of it (*Lock International v Beswick*).

Training agreements

11.27 An employer may permit an employee to go on a training course (possibly with paid leave of absence) under an agreement whereby the employee agrees to serve the employer for a specified period after completing the course. Clearly, such an agreement can be for the mutual benefit of both parties. The problem arises when the employee fails to serve the employer for the specified period. In *Strathclyde Regional Council v Neil*, the defendant was employed by the plaintiffs as a trainee social worker. She was given paid leave of absence to go on a training course, and signed an agreement to serve the council for two years after completing the course. The agreement also specified that if she left her employment before completing two years' service she would refund to the council a sum of money, proportionate to the unexpired period of the contractual two years. After completing the course, she worked for the council for 15 months, and resigned her employment. It was held that the council could recover a proportion of their expenditure in respect of her salary, course fees, examination fees and book allowance. The terms of the contract were not extravagant or unconscionable.

CHAPTER 12

Health and safety at work

12.1 As a result of the recommendations of the Robens Committee, the Health and Safety at Work etc Act 1974 was passed. In considering the then existing laws and practices relating to health and safety, the Committee came to a number of interesting conclusions. It found that in fact there was too much law, that much of it was unsatisfactory and unintelligible, and there was overlapping jurisdiction between those bodies whose task it was to enforce the law. The result of this was that there was a general feeling of apathy in the day-to-day implementation of safety rules, and little interest was shown in the subject. The new Act thus lays down the general legal obligations of all concerned in a single enactment, with the enforcement under the control of a unified administration. At the time of writing, most of the old law (Factories Act 1961, Offices, Shops and Railway Premises Act 1963, etc) remains in force, although these are being progressively repealed and replaced by regulations and approved codes of practice which are designed to maintain and improve the standards of health, safety and welfare.

12.2 Several fundamental changes are brought about by the new legislation. In the first place, the Act applies to people, not to premises. It covers all employed persons (with the exception of domestic workers), wherever they work, thus bringing within the orbit of safety legislation an additional 7,000,000 employees who were hitherto outside the protection of statutory rules. In addition, the Health and Safety (Training for Employment) Regulations 1990 apply the provisions of the Act to trainees on government sponsored training schemes as if they were employees. The Act also applies to people who are not employees, in so far as they may be affected by activities which are being carried on in places of work.

12.2A The Act, when passed, excluded the Health and Safety Commission from having responsibilities for agriculture, and gave these to the Minister of Agriculture. These provisions have been repealed by the Employment Protection Act 1975 s. 116 and Sch 15, so that agriculture is treated in the same way as any other form of employment. The Act also applies (with appropriate modifications) to offshore installations and pipe lines within British territorial waters and areas designated under the Continental Shelf Act 1964, including construction work and diving activities.

12.2B Next, it will be noted that obligations are placed on employers in their different capacities as manufacturers, suppliers, and importers of articles and substances to be used at work, to ensure that these can be used in safety and without risk to health.

12.2C The emphasis of the Act is on criminal sanctions and enforcement of the law by new techniques, for the Act itself does not give rise to questions of civil liability. The inspectorate appear to be using their powers of prosecution at the rate of 2,600 per year, which is small compared with the number of offences revealed by inspections, for the emphasis is on co-operation rather than compulsion. In addition, however, the new powers of issuing improvement and prohibition notices have been widely exercised, and these are proving to have very dramatic effects. Currently, about 12,000 such notices are issued each year.

12.3 Finally, there are a number of provisions designed to bring about a greater awareness by all concerned of the need to promote safety and health at work, and thus provide the impetus to the greater self-regulatory system which the Robens Committee thought to be desirable.

12.4 Some amendments to the Act have been made by the Consumer Protection Act 1987 (Sch 3). The Act now applies to fairground equipment and micro-organisms, customs officers may detain articles and substances for the purpose of enabling enforcing officers to perform their duties, and s. 6 of the Act (see para 12.38) has been significantly improved.

12.5 We can examine the provisions of the Act under five headings.

A. Enforcement of the Act

12.6 Generally, the enforcement of the Act will be the responsibility of the Health and Safety Executive. The Secretary of State has, however, made regulations enabling the relevant statutory provisions to be the responsibility of the local authorities, and the exercise of such powers will be under the guidance of the Commission.

12.6A Neither the Secretary of State nor the Commission can instruct the Executive to enforce any particular provision or to institute proceedings in any particular case. All enforcing authorities will appoint inspectors, who will have the following powers, for the purpose of giving effect to the relevant statutory provisions:

a. at any reasonable time, or, if there is a dangerous situation at any time, to enter premises;
b. to take with him a constable if he has reasonable cause to apprehend any serious obstruction in the execution of his duty;
c. to take with him any other authorised person and any equipment or materials required for any purpose for which the power of entry is being exercised;
d. to make such examination and investigation as may be necessary;
e. to direct that any premises shall be left undisturbed so long as is reasonably necessary for the purpose of examination or investigation;
f. to take such measures and photographs and make such recordings as he considers necessary;
g. to take samples of any articles or substances found in any premises and of the atmosphere in, or in the vicinity of, such premises. The Secretary of State may make regulations concerning the procedure to be adopted in such cases;
h. in the case of any article or substance likely to cause danger to health or safety, to cause it to be dismantled or subjected to any process or test, but not to damage or destroy it unless it is for the purpose of exercising his powers. If the person who has responsibilities in relation to those premises is present, and so requests, the inspector shall exercise this power in that person's presence, unless he considers that it

would be prejudicial to the safety of the State to do so. In any case, before exercising these powers, he must consult with appropriate persons for the purpose of ascertaining what dangers, if any, there may be in doing what he proposes to do;

i. in the case of any article or substance likely to cause danger to health or safety, to take possession of it, and detain if for so long as is necessary in order to examine it, to ensure it is not tampered with before he has completed his examination, and to ensure that it is available for use as evidence in any proceedings for an offence, or in respect of matters arising out of the issuing of an improvement notice or a prohibition notice. He must leave a notice giving particulars of the article or substance, stating that he has taken possession of it, and, if practicable to do so, leave a sample with a responsible person;

j. if conducting an examination or investigation under d. above, to require any person whom he has reasonable cause to believe to be able to give any information to answer such questions as the inspector thinks fit to ask, and to sign a declaration of the truth of his answers;

k. to require the production of, inspect, and take copies of any entry in, any books or documents which are required to be kept, and any other book or document which it is necessary for him to see for the purpose of any examination or investigation under d., above;

l. to require any person to afford him such facilities and assistance within that person's control or responsibilities, as are necessary for him to exercise his powers;

m. any other power which is necessary for the purpose of exercising any of the above powers.

Improvement notices (s. 21)

12.7 If an inspector is of the opinion that a person is contravening one or more relevant statutory provisions, or has done so and the contravention is likely to be continued or repeated, he may serve on him an improvement notice, stating that opinion, specifying the relevant statutory provision, giving reasons why he is of that opinion, and requiring that person to remedy the contravention within such period as may be specified in the notice, but not less than 21 days (i.e. the period in which an appeal may be made - see below). For a specimen of an improvement notice, see Appendix E.

Prohibition notices (s. 22)

12.8 In respect of any activity covered by a relevant statutory provision, if the inspector thinks that those activities are carried on or are likely to be carried on so as to involve a risk of serious personal injury, the inspector may serve a prohibition notice. This will state his opinion, specify the provisions which give rise to that opinion, and direct that the activities to which the notice relates shall not be carried on by or under the control of that person on whom the notice was served unless the matters specified and any associated contravention are remedied. This direction takes effect at the end of the period specified in the notice or, if the notice so declares, immediately. Prohibition notices can be issued on persons, e.g. for a failure to wear protective eye shields. One notice was issued on a worker who failed to use protective spats.

12.9 In the case of an improvement notice or a prohibition notice, the notice may (but need not) include directions as to the measure to be taken to remedy the contravention, which may be by reference to any approved code of practice or afford a choice between different ways of remedying the contravention. However, in respect of an improvement notice relating to a building, this cannot impose more onerous requirements that those imposed by the building regulations unless there is a statutory provision to the contrary. Also, if the notice relates to the means of escape in the event of fire, the inspector must engage in prior consultations with the fire authorities. Any improvement notice or a deferred prohibition notice may be withdrawn by the inspector before the expiry of 21 days, and may also be extended by the inspector at any time when an appeal is not pending. For a specimen of a prohibition notice, see Appendix E, below.

Appeals against improvement or prohibition notices (s. 24)

12.10 An appeal from the imposition of an improvement notice or a prohibition notice may be made to the industrial tribunal, which can cancel or affirm it, or affirm it with such modifications as the tribunal thinks fit. For the purpose of hearing such appeals, the tribunal may include assessors specially appointed to sit with the regular members. Once an appeal has been lodged, this will suspend the operation of the improvement notice until such time as the appeal is disposed of or withdrawn; in the case of a prohibition notice, however, the lodging of an appeal will only suspend it if the tribunal so directs, and then only from the time it does so direct.

12.11 An appeal against an improvement notice or a prohibition notice can be made on a number of grounds.

12.12 First, it could be argued that there is no breach of a statutory duty. To determine this, a tribunal may refer to any relevant code of practice and guidance note. In *Sutton & Co Ltd v Davies* the employers were in breach of s. 13 of the Factories Act in not guarding transmission machinery. They appealed against an improvement notice, arguing that they had operated for 27 years without an accident. The appeal was dismissed, for the requirements of the Act are absolute. But in *Brewer & Sons v Dunston* the inspector issued a prohibition notice on a machine. No accident had occurred in 18 years of use, and the tribunal held that there was no evidence to support the contention that there was risk of imminent danger. The distinction is that for an improvement notice, the sole issue is whether or not there has been a breach of a statutory provision, whereas a prohibition notice is concerned with whether there is a risk of serious personal injury.

12.13 Secondly, an appeal may be against the time limit imposed for remedying the defect, and there the tribunal may consider any serious embarrassment which may be caused to the company, and may take into account any history of recorded accidents at the firm. A company with a good record may well be given an extension of time so as to maintain production, so long as there is no immediate risk of danger or injury, and there is a willingness to make the appropriate modifications.

12.13A A third ground for appeal may be based on the absence of any risk or danger. In *South Surbiton Co-operative Society v Wilcox*, a cracked washbasin was made the subject of an improvement notice. It was argued that the breach was trivial, there was little risk to health, and that there must be many employers who are similarly in breach and who have not been served with improvement notices. Nonetheless, the notice was confirmed by the tribunal. The requirements of the Act were absolute.

12.14 But in *Associated Dairies v Hartley*, an improvement notice required the company to issue safety shoes free of charge to employees. In the previous year, one employee had been injured when the wheel of a truck ran over his foot. The company employed 1,000 employees, with a high turnover. Free footwear would have cost £20,000 in the first year. The tribunal held that the expense of providing protective footwear was disproportionate to the risk, and the notice was cancelled. In this case, the Act only required the employer to do that which was reasonably practicable.

12.15 A final ground for appeal may be based on the financial inability of the employer to comply with the order. Such an appeal is doomed from the start. In *Harrison Ltd v Ramsey*, the company appealed against an improvement notice which required them to paint and clean the walls of the factory, in accordance with s. 1 of the Factories Act 1961. It was stated that their financial position was precarious due to difficult trading conditions, but the industrial tribunal had no hesitation in confirming the notice. To do otherwise would be to allow a firm to keep its charges low so as to undercut competitors, thus obtaining an unfair advantage over those who complied with the legal requirements. An employer cannot be relieved of his statutory duties because of financial difficulties.

12.16 Unlike other proceedings before industrial tribunals, appeals against improvement and prohibition notices may result in an order for costs being made against the unsuccessful party. Such an order is entirely at the discretion of the tribunal, who may take into account the conduct of the party in failing to remedy the breach, and the hopelessness or otherwise of the appeal. In *South Surbiton Co-operative Society v Wilcox* (above) no order for costs was made, as the tribunal considered that the breach was trivial.

A failure to observe the requirements of a prohibition or improvement notice is a criminal offence, and it is no defence in criminal proceedings to argue that the employer has done all that is reasonably practicable to comply. The proper forum in which to argue questions of practicability is the industrial tribunal (*Deary v Mansion Hide Upholstery Ltd*).

12.16A An appeal against a decision of an industrial tribunal relating to a prohibition or improvement notice must be made to the Divisional Court. The reason is that the failure to comply with such notices is a criminal offence.

Crown notices

12.17 Because there is a rule of law that the Queen cannot be prosecuted in her own courts, it is not possible to enforce prohibition and improvement notices against Crown organisations, even though they employ large numbers of employees in various government departments. Consequently, the Commission have devised the Crown Notice, which will be issued when a prohibition or improvement notice would be appropriate. Such notices have only a moral sanction, but are designed to draw attention to potential hazards, and, as copies are to be given to employees' representatives, will naturally attract publicity. About 40 such notices were issued annually. So far as the health service is concerned, a health authority is no longer to be regarded as a servant or agent of the Crown for the purpose of health and safety legislation (see National Health Service and Community Care Act 1990 s. 60). Thus the normal prohibition and improvement notices can be served on these bodies, and they may also be prosecuted for offences.

Power to deal with imminent danger (s. 25)

12.18 If the inspector finds on any premises any article or substance which he has reasonable cause to believe is a cause of imminent danger of serious personal injury, he may seize it and cause it to be rendered harmless whether by destruction or otherwise. Before doing so if it is practicable for him to do so, he will give a sample with an identifiable mark to a responsible person. Thereafter, he will prepare and sign a report giving particulars of the circumstances, and give a copy to a responsible person at those premises, and also to the owner.

Enforcement powers of the court (s. 42)

12.19 Where a person is convicted of an offence under any relevant statutory provision, the court may, in addition to, or instead of, imposing any punishment, order him to take such steps as may be specified in the order to remedy the matters specified, within such time as may be fixed. Failure to do so may amount to contempt of court, but an application may be made for an extension of the time limit. During the period given to remedy matters, the person cannot be liable for a failure to observe the provisions. After that time, if he continues with the contravention, he can be sentenced to six months' imprisonment and/or fined up to £20,000 in the magistrates' courts, or up to two years' imprisonment and/or an unlimited fine in the Crown Court.

12.20 If a person is charged with an offence in connection with the acquisition of explosives, the court may order the article or substance in question to be forfeited and either destroyed or dealt with as the court so orders. However, such order cannot be made unless the court gives the owner or any other interested party an opportunity to be heard.

Other matters

12.21 By s. 26, if an inspector exceeds his statutory powers the enforcing authority may nonetheless indemnify him against the costs, damages, or expenses incurred if it is satisfied that the inspector acted in the honest belief that the act complained of was within his powers.

12.22 By s. 28(8) an inspector is empowered to give information to employed persons (or their representatives) if it is necessary to do so for the purpose of keeping them adequately informed about matters affecting their health, safety or welfare. This may be factual information about the premises or anything going on, or information about action he has taken or is proposing to take. If he does this, he must also give the like information to the employer.

B. New statutory duties on health, safety and welfare

12.23 In general, there are three sets of guiding rules which will govern the operation of the new law. The first of these is the general duties laid down in ss. 2-9, and which must be observed by the specified persons. The second will be the new regulations, which will supplement the new law and eventually supersede the old. The third will be the Codes of Practice, to be issued and approved in the course of time. It must be borne in mind that a breach of the general duties laid down in ss. 2-9 of the Act is a criminal offence, and does not give rise to civil proceedings (s. 47), whereas a breach of the regulations will be actionable civilly unless the regulations themselves provide otherwise. However, by s. 11 of the Civil Evidence Act 1968 any conviction for a criminal offence is admissible in civil proceedings as evidence that the person so convicted committed the offence, and therefore, a claimant may point to the conviction as being relevant to the issue of civil liability.

12.24 Some of the general duties are absolute ones, which means that the person on whom the duty is placed must carry it out. Others are preceded by the words 'so far as is reasonably practicable'. This is a somewhat lesser standard. The employer must weigh, on the one hand, the time, trouble and expense, etc of meeting that duty against the risks involved and the nature of the obligation on the other hand. Also, the duty can only be performed against the background of current knowledge which the employer knows, or ought to know. However, in *Marshall v Gotham* it was suggested that a precaution which was practicable would not lightly be held to be unreasonable. In other words, a duty or obligation must be performed or carried out unless it would be unreasonable to do so. Further, s. 40 of the Act states that in any proceedings for a failure to comply with a duty or requirement, it will be for the accused to prove that it was not reasonably practicable to do more than was in fact done.

Duties of the employer owed to his employees (s. 2)

12.25 It shall be the duty of every employer to ensure, so far as is reasonably practicable, the health, safety and welfare at work of all his employees. In particular, the employer must:

a. provide and maintain plant and systems of work that are, so far as is reasonably practicable, safe and without risks to health;
b. make arrangements for ensuring, so far as is reasonably practicable, safety and absence of risks to health in connection with the use, handling, storage and transport of articles and substances (see *Page v Freight Hire (Tank Haulage) Ltd*);
c. ensure the provision of such information, instruction, training and supervision as is necessary to ensure, so far as is reasonably practicable, the health, safety and welfare at work of his employees. The employer must give such information etc. to his employees and to persons who are not his employees (e.g. to sub-contractors and their employees) if this is necessary to ensure the health and safety of the employees of the employer (*R v Swan Hunter Shipbuilders Ltd*);

d. so far as is reasonably practicable as regards any place of work under his control, ensure the maintenance of it in a condition that is safe and without risks to health, and the maintenance of means of access and egress from it that are safe and without such risks;
e. ensure the provision and maintenance of a working environment for his employees that is, so far as is reasonably practicable, safe, without risks to health, and adequate as regards facilities and arrangements for their welfare at work.

12.26 So far as the above duties are concerned, it will be noted that they bear a strong resemblance to the common law duties of care (see Chapter 6), spelt out, perhaps, in greater detail. An employer is only responsible for premises over which he has actual control, but that does not absolve him from the duty of ensuring a safe system of work on the premises of another (*General Cleaning Contractors Ltd v Christmas*). The duty to provide a safe working environment would cover noise, fumes, heat, etc; welfare at work is not defined, but would presumably cover washing and toilet facilities, drinking water, and possibly eating arrangements.

Written safety policy (s. 2(3))

12.27 Except for employers who employ less than five employees (see *Osborne v Bill Taylor of Huyton Ltd* and Employers' Health and Safety Policy Statements (Exception) Regulations 1975) it shall be the duty of every employer to prepare and revise as often as is appropriate a written statement of his general policy with respect to the health and safety at work of all his employees, and the organisation and arrangements for the time being in force for carrying out that policy, and to bring this statement to the notice of all his employees. The Act does not give any guidance on the contents of this written statement, for the object of the exercise is for each employer to sit down and think about his own safety problems and work out the necessary solutions. Clearly, this would prove to be without value if the employer merely copied out a draft scheme drawn up by someone else.

12.27A It is suggested, however, that the safety policy should at least deal with the responsibility of all employees, including the Board of Directors, all levels of management, supervisors and operatives, inspection procedures, arrangements for dealing with special hazards, emergency arrangements, including fire drill, the provision and use of safety precautions generally, supervision, training, research and consultative arrangements. In drawing up the safety policy, it may be sound procedure to seek advice from the Commission, the Executive, employers' associations, and to consult with trade union representatives, but it must be stressed that the statement is not a joint consultative document, but one for which the employer has ultimate responsibility. The Act requires the statement to be brought to the notice of all employees, but no guidance is given on how this is to be done. It would clearly not be sufficient to place the statement on the notice board, and hope that workpeople will read it as they go past, and so the more formal channels of written communication should be used. If it is known that a particular employee does not read English, presumably some other way must be found of bringing it to his notice. The employer is obliged to revise the written statement as often as may be appropriate; it is suggested that the statement should be looked at at least once a year, in the light of practical experience of operating the safety policy, and taking into account any suggestions which might be received.

Safety representatives and safety committee (s. 2(4), (6), (7))

12.28 A trade union which is recognised by an employer may appoint safety representatives from among the employees in respect of whom the union is recognised (*Cleveland County Council v Springett*). The persons so appointed need not themselves be members of the union. Subsection (5) of section 2, which provided for the election of safety representatives from the ranks of all employees, and not their appointment by trade unions, was repealed by the Employment Protection Act 1975 s. 116, but there is nothing to stop an employer from proceeding on these lines voluntarily should he so wish.

12.29 The legal requirements are contained in the Safety Representatives and Safety Committees Regulations 1977 and a Code of Practice issued and approved by the Health and Safety Commission. An independent trade union shall notify the employer in writing of the name of the safety representative, who shall hold the appointment until the union terminates it, or he ceases to be employed at the workplace, or resigns. So far as is reasonably practicable, he shall have been employed by that employer for the preceding two years, or have had at least two years' experience in similar employment.

12.30 An employer has a duty to consult with safety representatives over a wide range of issues, with a view to making and maintaining arrangements which will enable him and his employees to co-operate effectively in promoting and developing measures to ensure the health and safety at work of employees, and checking the effectiveness of those measures (s. 2(6)). In particular, there shall be consultation about the introduction of measures which may substantially affect the health and safety of employees, the arrangements for appointing or nominating the safety assistant, the provision of health and safety information, the planning and organisation of health and safety training, and the health and safety consequences of the introduction of new technologies (Management of Health and Safety at Work Regulations 1992).

Additionally, the safety representative has the following functions:

a. to investigate the potential hazards and dangerous occurrences at the workplace, and to examine the causes of accidents;
b. to investigate complaints by any employee he represents relating to that employee's health, safety, or welfare at work;
c. to make representations to the employer about the above matters;
d. to make representations to the employer on general matters affecting the health, safety and welfare at work of the employees at the workplace;
e. to carry out inspections (see below);
f. to represent employees in consultations with inspectors of the Health and Safety Executive;
g. to receive information from the inspectors; and
h. to attend meetings of safety committees in his capacity as safety representative.

12.31 In order to perform these functions adequately, the employer shall permit the safety representative to have time off work with pay during his working hours, and also for the purpose of undergoing training in aspects of those functions as may be reasonable in the circumstances (see *White v Pressed Steel Fisher Ltd*), having regard to the provisions of the Code of Practice approved by the Commission for this purpose. The safety representative is entitled to be paid his normal earnings or average hourly earnings.

12.32 Safety representatives are entitled to carry out an inspection of the workplace at least every three months (or more frequently with the employer's consent), and also further inspections if there has been some substantial change in the conditions of work (e.g. by the introduction of new working processes, or the coming to light of new information disclosing a potential hazard). Inspections may also be carried out after a notifiable accident has occurred or a notifiable disease contracted, for the purpose of determining the cause. The employer shall provide reasonable facilities and assistance, but he, or his representative, may be present during the inspection.

12.33 The employer shall establish a safety committee when at least two safety representatives make such a request. For this purpose, he shall consult with these representatives, and also those of any recognised trade unions. A notice must be posted stating the composition of the committee, which must be established within three months of the request being made.

12.34 A complaint may be made to an industrial tribunal that the employer has failed to permit a safety representative to have time off work for these purposes, or has failed to pay for such time off. If the complaint is well-founded, the tribunal shall make a declaration, and may make an award of compensation.

Right not to suffer a detriment in health and safety cases (EPCA s. 22A)

12.34A An employee is entitled not to be subjected to any detriment by an act or a failure to act by his employer on any of the following grounds:

a. having been designated by the employer to carry out activities in connection with preventing or reducing risks to health and safety at work, he carried out (or proposed to carry out) those activities;
b. being a safety representative or member of a safety committee, he performed (or proposed to perform) any functions as such;
c. if there is no safety representative or safety committee where he is, or, if there are, it is not reasonably practicable to raise such matters, he brought the employer's attention (by reasonable means) to circumstances connected with his work which he reasonably believed were harmful or potentially harmful to health or safety;

d. in circumstances of danger which he reasonably believed to be serious and imminent and which he could not reasonably be expected to avert, he left, or proposed to leave, or, while the danger persisted, he refused to return to, his place of work or any dangerous part of his place of work;
e. in circumstances of danger which he reasonably believed to be serious and imminent, he took, or proposed to take, appropriate steps to protect himself or other persons from the danger. This is to be judged by reference to all the circumstances, including his knowledge, and the facilities and advice available to him at the time. However, he will not have been subjected to a detriment if he was so negligent in the steps he took that the employer treated him as a reasonable employer would have done in those circumstances.

12.34B An employee who believes that he has suffered a detriment contrary to s. 22A may bring a complaint before an industrial tribunal within the usual time limits. If the complaint is upheld, the tribunal shall make a declaration to that effect, and also award compensation to the complainant, the amount being such as the tribunal considers to be just and equitable in all the circumstances. This will include any expenses incurred and take account of any benefits lost. The employee is expected to mitigate against his loss, and the compensation award can be reduced on the ground of contributory conduct (see para 9.44).

Dismissal in health and safety cases (EPCA s. 57A)

12.34C It will be unfair to dismiss an employee because of any of the following circumstances arising out of health and safety matters:
a. having been designated by the employer to carry out activities in connection with preventing or reducing risks to health and safety at work, he carried out (or proposed to carry out) those activities;
b. being a safety representative or member of a safety committee he performed (or proposed to perform) any functions as such;
c. if there is no safety representative or safety committee where he is, or, if there are, it is not reasonably practicable to raise such matters, he brought the employer's attention (by reasonable means) to circumstances connected with his work which he reasonably believed were harmful or potentially harmful to health or safety;

d. in circumstances of danger which he reasonably believed to be serious and imminent and which he could not reasonably be expected to avert, he left, or proposed to leave, or, while the danger persisted, he refused to return to, his place of work or any dangerous part of his place of work;
e. in circumstances of danger which he reasonably believed to be serious and imminent, he took, or proposed to take, appropriate steps to protect himself or other persons from the danger. This is to be judged by reference to all the circumstances, including his knowledge, and the facilities and advice available to him at the time. However, his dismissal shall not be regarded as being unfair if he was so negligent in the steps he took that the employer treated him as a reasonable employer would have treated him in those circumstances.

12.34D It should be noted that if a dismissal is unfair by virtue of a. or b. above, and the employer refuses to reinstate or re-engage the employee following a tribunal order, a special award (see para 9.53) can be made.

Interim relief in health and safety cases (ss. 77-79, EPCA).

12.34E If an employee is dismissed for an inadmissible reason because he has been designated to carry out health and safety activities, or is a safety representative or member of a safety committee (see para 12.34C) and he proposed to carry out activities as such, he may apply for interim relief, within seven days following the effective date of termination of his employment. The procedure and remedies are similar to the interim relief provisions contained in TULR(C)A ss. 161-166 (see para 13.82).

Duty owed to non-employees (s. 3)

12.35 It shall be the duty of every employer, and every self-employed person, to conduct his undertakings in such a way as to ensure, so far as is reasonably practicable, that persons who are not his employees who may be affected thereby are not exposed to risks to their health or safety. This duty applies not only to persons who are lawfully on the employer's premises, for example, students in an educational establishment, but also persons who are outside those premises, but who may be affected by the activities in question. Thus if there is a potential hazard on the employer's premises, he must provide information not only to his own employees, but to visitors and the employees of a sub-contractor who may be working there (*R v Swan Hunter Shipbuilders Ltd*).

Duties of controllers of premises (s. 4)

12.36 Every person who has control of premises (not being domestic premises) must ensure, as far as it is reasonable for a person in his position to ensure, that so far as is reasonably practicable, all means of access thereto or egress therefrom, and plant and substance, in the premises, shall be safe and without risks to health in respect of persons who use those premises as a place of work (*Westminster City Council v Select Managements Ltd*). A person who has, by virtue of a contract of tenancy, the obligation to maintain or repair those premises, or be responsible for the safety or absence of risks therein, shall be the person to be regarded as being in control.

Pollution control (s. 5)

12.37 It shall be the duty of every person having control of prescribed premises to use the best practicable means for preventing the emission into the atmosphere from those premises of noxious or offensive substances, and for rendering harmless and inoffensive such substances as may be emitted. However, responsibility for pollution control has been transferred from HSC to HM Inspectorate of Pollution, under the Department of the Environment.

Duties of manufacturers, etc (s. 6 as amended)

12.38 A duty is imposed on any person who designs, manufacturers, imports or supplies *any article* for use at work or *any article of fairground equipment*:

a. to ensure, as far as reasonably practicable, that the article is so designed and constructed that it will be safe and without risks to health at all times when it is being set, used, cleaned or maintained by a person at work. However, subs. 8 provides that where a person designs, manufactures, imports or supplies an article for use at work or an article of fairground equipment and does so for or to another on the basis of a written undertaking by that other that he will take specified steps to ensure, so far as is reasonably practicable, that the article will be safe and without risks to health at all the above mentioned times, the undertaking will release the designer, manufacturer, importer or supplier (as the case may be) from this duty, to such an extent as is reasonable having regard to the terms of the undertaking. For example, if a person wishes to sell second-hand machinery, it might be advisable to extract a written undertaking from the purchaser to ensure its complete overhaul before putting it to use;

b. to carry out or arrange for the carrying out of such testing and examination as may be necessary for the performance of the above duty. However, this does not require the repeating of any tests or examinations which may have been carried out by others, in so far as it is reasonable to rely on the results of those others' work;

c. to take such steps as are necessary to secure that persons supplied by that person with the article are provided with adequate information about the use for which the article has been designed or has been tested, and about any conditions necessary to ensure that it will be safe and without risks to health at all times as are mentioned above, and also when it is being dismantled or disposed of;

d. to take all such steps as are necessary to secure, so far as is reasonably practicable, that persons so supplied are provided with any revision of the above information by reason of it becoming known that anything gives rise to a serious risk to health or safety.

12.39 Similar obligations are placed upon persons who design, manufacture, import or supply articles of fairground equipment used for or in connection with the entertainment of members of the public.

12.40 There is also a duty on designers and manufacturers (but not importers or suppliers) to carry out or arrange for the carrying out of any necessary research with a view to the discovery and, so far as is reasonably practicable, the elimination or minimisation of any risks to health or safety to which the design or article may give rise, but again, this does not require the repeating of any research already carried out, if it was reasonable to rely on the results.

12.41 It is the duty of any person who erects or installs any article for use at work, or any article of fairground equipment, to ensure, so far as is reasonably practicable, that nothing about the way in which the article is erected, or installed makes it unsafe or a risk to health, when it is being set, used, cleaned or maintained by a person at work.

12.42 A duty is imposed on any person who manufactures, imports or supplies *any substance*:

a. to ensure, so far as is reasonably practicable, that the substance will be safe and without risks to health at all times when it is being used, handled, processed, stored or transported by a person at work or in premises to which s. 4 (above) applies;
b. to carry out or arrange for the carrying out of such testing and examination as may be necessary for the performance of the above duty, but again this does not require the repeating of any tests or examinations which have been carried out by others, in so far as it is reasonable to rely on the results of those others' work;
c. to take such steps as are necessary to secure that persons supplied by that person with the substance are provided with adequate information about any risks to health or safety to which the inherent properties of the substance may give rise, about the results of any relevant tests which have been carried out on or in connection with the substances, and about any conditions necessary to ensure that the substance will be safe and without risks to health at all such times as are mentioned above, and when it is being disposed of;
d. to take such steps as are necessary to secure, so far as is reasonably practicable, that persons so supplied are provided with all such revisions of information as are necessary by reason of its becoming known that anything gives rise to a serious risk to health or safety.

12.43 A manufacturer of any substance is under a duty to carry out (or arrange for the carrying out of) any necessary research with a view to the discovery and, so far as is reasonably practicable, the elimination or minimisation of any risks to health or safety to which the substance may give rise, but he need not repeat any test, examination or research done by others in so far as it was reasonable for him to rely on the results thereof.

12.44 For the purposes of s. 6, an absence of safety or a risk to health is to be disregarded in so far as it has arisen by an occurrence which could not be reasonably foreseen, and so far as the obligations placed on designers, manufacturers, importers and suppliers of articles and substances are concerned, regard may be had to any relevant information which has been provided by them to any person.

12.45 Section 6(7) provides that the above duties only extend to things done in the course of a trade, business or undertaking (whether for profit or not), and to matters within a person's control. The definition of 'article' for use at work' (see s. 53) is 'any plant designed for use or operation (whether exclusively or not) by persons at work, and any articles designed for use as a component in any such plant', a definition which may be somewhat restrictive. A substance is defined as being 'any natural or artificial substance (including micro-organisms) whether in a solid or liquid form or in the form of gas or vapour'.

12.46 An interesting point arises concerning the effect on civil contracts of the above provisions. Supposing, for example, an employer purchases a machine from a manufacturer, and this is delivered without safety instructions, or in an unguarded state. Could the employer reject the machine on the grounds that it was not fit for its purpose or not of merchantable quality, contrary to the Sale of Goods Act 1979?

Duties of employees at work (s. 7)

12.47 Every employee is under a duty while at work:

a. to take reasonable care for the health and safety of himself and of others who may be affected by his acts or omissions at work; this could mean that an employee who failed or refused to wear or use safety precautions which are provided would be in breach of his legal duty;
b. as regards any duty imposed on his employer or any other person, to co-operate with him so far as is necessary to enable that duty to be performed or complied with.

Duty not to interfere with safety provisions (s. 8)

12.48 No persons shall intentionally or recklessly interfere with or misuse anything provided in the interest of health, safety or welfare in pursuance of any relevant statutory provisions. This duty is wider than the old law, which was directed against 'wilful' conduct, defined as perverse or deliberate action. Intentional or reckless conduct does not need to be wilful.

Duty not to charge (s. 9)

12.49 An employer shall not charge any employee in respect of anything done or provided in pursuance of any relevant statutory provision (see Personal Protective Equipment at Work Regulations 1992).

C. Health and Safety Regulations (s. 15 and Sch. 3)

12.50 As has already been indicated, one of the main purposes of the Act is to replace the existing statutory provisions by regulations, and over a period of time, the 'old' law contained in the Factories Act 1961, Offices, Shops and Railway Premises Act 1963, and so forth (for a complete list, see column 3 in Sch. 1 of the Act), will gradually be phased out, and replaced with a system of regulations and Codes of Practice which, in combination with the other provisions of the Act, are designed to maintain and improve the standards of health, safety and welfare. Regulations are of three general types; first, there are those which lay down standards to be applied in most or all employment situations, second, there are those which are designed to control a particular hazard which may exist in a particular industry, and third, there are those which refer to particular hazards or risks but which may be found in a number of different industries. The view appears to be held that the use of regulations as a device for laying down legal standards is a superior method to legislation, for regulations are simpler and more flexible; they can be altered more readily in accordance with experience and technological progress, and will be more manageable to those who have to implement them.

12.51 Regulations are to be made by the Secretary of State either as a result of proposals made to him by the Commission, or on his own initiative, but in the latter case he must consult with the Commission and any other appropriate bodies. If the Commission makes the proposals, it, too, must consult with the appropriate government departments and other bodies (s. 50). Regulations may:

a. repeal or modify any existing statutory provision;
b. exclude or modify in relation to any specific class of case any of the provisions of ss. 2-9 (above) or any existing statutory provision;
c. make a specific authority responsible for the enforcement of any relevant statutory provision;

d. impose requirements by reference to the approval of the Commission or other specified body or person;
e. provide that any reference in a regulation to a specific document shall include a reference to a revised version of that document;
f. provide for exemptions from any requirement or prohibition;
g. enable exemptions to be granted by a specified person or authority;
h. specify the persons or class of persons who may be guilty of an offence;
i. provide for specified defences either generally or in specified circumstances;
j. exclude proceedings on indictment in relation to certain offences;
k. restrict the punishment which may be imposed in respect of certain offences.

12.52 In addition to the above, Sch 3 contains detailed provisions about the contents of such regulations, sufficient, it is thought, to completely replace the old law, and wide enough to enable the Secretary of State and the Commission to do almost anything in the interest of health and safety. In particular, however, we may note two further important provisions. The first is the power to prohibit the carrying on of any specified activity or the doing of any specified thing without a licence granted for that purpose, which may be subject to conditions. The second is contained in s. 235 of the Companies Act 1985, so as to enable the Secretary of State to prescribe cases whereby directors' reports will contain such information about the arrangements in force for that year for securing the health, safety and welfare at work of the employees of that company (and any subsidiary company), and for protecting other persons against risks to health resulting from the activities at work of the employees. To date, no such regulations have been made.

12.53 A breach of duty imposed by regulations is, of course, punishable as a criminal offence. Additionally, a breach may give rise to civil liability, except in so far as the regulations provide otherwise.

12.53A Since the passing of the Health & Safety at Work etc Act, a considerable number of health and safety regulations have been introduced, and the progressive repeal of 'old legislation' has continued. In recent years, however, health and safety at work has been prominent on the European agenda, and many of the recent changes owe their origin to membership of the EC. A number of Directives have been approved, and additional ones are in the process of being discussed.

12.53B The view taken by HSC is that these Directives do not involve any fundamental change in the way British law deals with these problems, but that they merely require the law to make explicit that which is implicit in the existing law. In certain instances, a lead-in period of 3-4 years has been allowed to enable employers to work towards compliance, and HSE will give as much guidance and assistance as possible.

12.53C Fundamental to the new law is the need to take proactive steps to ensure health and safety at work of employees and others. These will include risk assessment in certain specified situations, provision of information to all those who may be at risk, health surveillance, the use of safety advisers, cooperation between employers, the provision of approved equipment and personal protection equipment and so on. Employees have a duty to use the equipment etc provided in a proper manner, to report shortcomings in the employer's protection arrangements or which represent a serious and immediate danger to health and safety.

12.53D In particular, six regulations came into force on 1st January 1993. These are (a) Management of Health and Safety at Work Regulations, (b) Personal Protection Equipment at Work Regulations, (c) Provision and Use of Work Equipment Regulations, (d) Workplace (Health, Safety and Welfare) Regulations, (e) Manual Handling of Loads Regulations, and (f) Health and Safety (Display Screen Equipment) Regulations. Many 'old' regulations have been revoked, and most of the existing protective legislation, found in the Factories Act 1961, Offices, Shops and Railway Premises Act 1963 etc, have either been repealed or are scheduled for repeal in the near future.

D. Codes of practice (s. 16)

12.54 For the purpose of providing practical guidance with respect to the general duties imposed by ss. 2-7 (above), or by any regulation or any existing statutory provisions, the Commission may approve and issue Codes of Practice which are suitable for that purpose. The Commission may also approve other such suitable codes which are drawn up by other persons or organisations, and thus there is no reason why a private firm or employers' organisation should not draw up its own code and submit it for approval, should this be thought desirable. One might also expect approval to be given to the existing British Standards Institution's own codes. The Commission cannot approve a code without the consent of the Secretary of State, and prior to obtaining this, must consult with government departments and other appropriate bodies. The codes may be revised from time to time, and the Commission may, if necessary, withdraw its approval from a particular code.

12.55 A failure on the part of any person to observe the provisions contained in an approved code of practice shall not of itself render that person liable to any civil or criminal proceedings, but in any such criminal proceedings, if a person is alleged to have committed an offence concerning a matter in respect of which an approved code is in force, the provisions of that code shall be admissible in evidence, and a failure to observe it shall constitute proof of the breach of duty, or contravention of the regulation or statutory provision, unless the accused can satisfy the court that he complied with the requirements of the law in some other equally efficacious manner. The codes, therefore, will be the guides to good safety practice, and if a person follows the provisions of the codes, he cannot be successfully prosecuted for an offence. If he fails to follow the relevant code, he may be guilty of an offence unless he can show that he observed the specific legal requirement some other way.

12.56 The Act contains no guidance on the use of the codes in civil proceedings, but it is likely that a failure to observe any such provision as is contained therein may well constitute *prima facie* evidence of negligence, which can be rebutted by evidence to the contrary.

E. Penalties (s. 33)

12.57 Any person or body corporate (e.g. a company) may be charged with and convicted of an offence under the Act, and punished accordingly. In addition, if an offence committed by a body corporate is proved to have been committed with the consent of, connivance of, or attributable to any neglect on the part of, any director, manager, secretary or other similar officer, then he, as well as the body corporate may be guilty of an offence, and liable to be proceeded against and punished accordingly (s. 37).

12.58 In *Armour v Skeen*, a senior local government official was prosecuted for failing to prepare and carry out a safety policy, for this neglect of duty ultimately led to breaches of safety provisions which resulted in the death of an employee. It was held that the official was guilty of an offence under s. 37. He was in a senior position in his organisation, and was therefore responsible for the general safety policy in his department. But in *R v Boal* the accused was an assistant manager in a bookshop. Following a visit by inspectors, he was prosecuted and convicted in respect of a number of offences. On appeal, it was held that criminal liability was to be imposed on persons in authority in the company who were the 'decision makers', with the power and responsibility to decide corporate policy. As the accused was an 'underling', his conviction was quashed.

12.59 Where the commission of an offence by a person is due to the default of another person, that other person may be proceeded against, whether or not proceedings are taken against the first mentioned person (s. 36). No proceedings under the Act may be brought except by an inspector, or with the consent of the Director of Public Prosecutions.

12.60 There is an anomaly, however, in that although Crown bodies (excluding health authorities) have the same obligations under the Act as other employers, they cannot be prosecuted, and it is not possible to issue improvement or prohibition notices against the Crown. However, this rule does not prevent the prosecution of individual Crown employees.

12.61 If a person is found guilty of an offence on summary conviction in the magistrates' court, the maximum punishment is a fine of £20,000 and/or 6 months' imprisonment. If proceedings are brought on indictment (i.e. in the Crown Court before a jury), there is the possibility of an unlimited fine, and in certain specified cases, up to two years' imprisonment. The full list of offences and punishments can be found in Appendix A.

The effect of European Law

12.62 Article 118A of the Treaty of Rome provides that Member States shall pay particular attention to encouraging improvements, especially to the working environment, as regards the health and safety of workers. Under this provision, a number of Directives have been adopted or are under discussion, and those adopted are enacted into British law. In particular, the 'Framework Directive' (98/391/EEC) and five 'Daughter Directives' were given effect to by regulations recently introduced (see para 12.53D). The process is an ongoing one, in the light of the policy of harmonisation of health and safety rules throughout the Community.

CHAPTER 13

Individual trade union rights

13.1 In this chapter we shall consider the rights of an individual in respect of his trade union membership and/or non-membership. These rights exist vis-à-vis a trade union and against an actual or potential employer. The relevant statutory provisions are contained in the Employment Protection (Consolidation) Act 1978 and the Trade Union and Labour Relations (Consolidation) Act 1992, as amended by the Trade Union Reform and Employment Rights Act 1993, and reference may further be made to various common law decisions.

Rights vis-à-vis a trade union

(1) Right not to be excluded from any trade union (TULR(C)A s. 174)

13.2 An individual cannot be excluded or expelled from any trade union unless:

(a) he does not satisfy an enforceable membership requirement contained in the rules of the union. Enforceable means the restriction of membership solely by reference to employment in a specified trade, industry or profession, or occupational description, or the possession of a specified trade, industrial or professional qualification or work experience;

(b) he does not qualify for membership by reason of the union operating only in a particular part of Great Britain;

(c) the union negotiates with one particular employer (or a number of particular employers who are associated) and the applicant is no longer employed by that employer;

(d) the exclusion or expulsion is entirely attributable to the applicant's conduct. Conduct does not include being, or ceasing to be, a member of another trade union, or employment by a particular employer at a particular place, or membership of a political party, or conduct which would constitute unjustified discipline within the meaning of s. 65 (below).

13.3 If a person's application for membership of a trade union is neither granted nor rejected within a reasonable period, he shall be treated as having been excluded from the union (s. 177).

13.4 The significance of the new law is two-fold. First, at common law a trade union was entitled to lay down the description of persons who were eligible to join, and could specify any qualification for membership it desired (see *Boulting v ACTAT*), and exclude a person on any ground (see *Faramus v Film Artistes' Association*). The courts did take the view that a rule which operated arbitrarily and unreasonably was void as being against public policy (see *Nagle v Feilden*), but such cases were rare and, generally speaking, a trade union could control its own admissions, and the court had no power to order it to grant membership to any particular individual. Section 174 now overrides the common law in this respect. A trade union may lay down certain requirements for membership, as above, but otherwise must admit any person seeking to join.

13.5 The second significance of the new law is that the Bridlington Agreement, which governs inter-union disputes arising from competition for members, and applies to TUC affiliated unions, can no longer be activated. Hitherto, if a trade union commenced recruitment in an area in which another union already had a substantial membership, the TUC could order the interloper to surrender the members gained in the recruitment drive (see *Rothwell v APEX*). This is no longer possible, because the individual has an indefeasible right to join whichever union he pleases, and cannot be expelled as a result of any award made by the TUC Disputes Committee.

13.6 A union may still specify who is entitled to join as a member within the limits specified above, but it is submitted that even these requirements cannot be exercised in an arbitrary and unreasonable manner (see *Nagle v Feilden*). But if an applicant needs a trade union card because an actual or prospective employer operates a 'closed shop' he cannot otherwise be excluded from membership (*Clarke v NATSOPA (SOGAT '82)*). In any case, the aggrieved person would have a right against the actual or potential employer under the 'unfair recruitment' provisions (see para 13.29).

13.7 The remedy for a failure to admit an applicant to membership is dealt with at para 13.20.

(2) Right not to be unjustifiably disciplined (TULR(C)A s. 64)

13.8 The power of a trade union to take disciplinary action against a member, and the procedural rules which should be followed, is noted in Chapter 14, para 14.22. In addition, a member has the right not to be unjustifiably disciplined by the trade union. A member is unjustifiable disciplined if the reason for the disciplinary action was conduct by him which was:

a. a failure to participate in or support a strike or other industrial action (whether by members of that union or by others) or indicated his opposition to or lack of support for any such strike or other industrial action; or
b. something required from him by virtue of an obligation imposed by his contract of employment or other agreement made with his employer; or
c. the making of an assertion that the union, or an official or representative or trustee of the union's property has contravened or is proposing to contravene a requirement of the union's rules or any other agreement or legal provision, or attempts to vindicate any such assertion; or
d. the encouraging of any person to perform an obligation imposed by virtue of a contract of employment or any other agreement; or
e. the contravention by him of any requirement imposed by a determination which itself constitutes an infringement of his rights or of the right of any other individual; or
f. failing to agree to, or withdrawing from, a check-off agreement; or
g. resigning from a union, becoming a member of another union, or refusing to join any other union; or
h. working with individuals who are not members of the union or any other union; or
i. working for an employer who employs individuals who are not members of the union, or who are or are not members of any other union; or

j. requiring the union to do something which the union is required to do on the requisition of any member; or
k. an approach to the Commissioner for the Rights of Trade Union Members or to the Certification Officer for advice or assistance on any matter whatsoever, or involves any other person being asked for advice or assistance with respect to any assertion made under c. above; or
l. a proposal to engage in conduct outlined in paras. a. to k. above, or preparatory conduct (s. 65).

13.9 Discipline, for the purpose of this section, is a determination made under the union's rules by an official of the union, or by a number of persons including an official:
a. that an individual shall be expelled from the union (or branch or section). In *T&GWU v Webber*, it was held that a recommendation that the plaintiff be expelled was not a determination for the purpose of s. 174. Until an appeal against the recommendation had been heard, he was still a member of the union;
b. that an individual shall pay any sum to the union (or branch or section) or to any other person whatsoever;
c. that sums tendered by that individual in respect of any obligation to pay a subscription or other sums to the union (or branch or section) should be treated as unpaid or as paid for a different purpose;
d. that that individual should be deprived of, or refused access to, benefits, services or facilities which would otherwise be available to him as a member of the union. Suspending a member involves depriving him of benefits which accrue from union membership (*NALGO v Killorn*);
e. that another trade union (or branch or section) should be encouraged or advised not to accept that individual as a member; or
f. that that individual should be subjected to any other detriment. Naming a person as a 'strike breaker' in a union circular, with the intention of causing him embarrassment is to subject that person to a detriment (*NALGO v Killorn*).

13.10 However, a member will not be unjustifiably disciplined if the reason for the disciplinary action was that he made an allegation that the union, an official, a representative or a trustee had contravened the union's rules or an agreement or an enactment or rule of law, and the assertion was false, and the member knew it was false or otherwise acted in bad faith.

13.11 If a complaint relating to an expulsion is brought under s. 174, and is declared to be well-founded, no further complaint relating to that matter can be brought under s. 64 (unjustifiable discipline).

Complaints of unjustifiable discipline (TULR(C)A s. 66)

13.12 An individual who believes that he has been unjustifiably disciplined by a trade union may present a complaint to an industrial tribunal, alleging that his rights have been infringed. The complaint must be presented within three months of the alleged infringement, unless the industrial tribunal is satisfied that it was not reasonably practicable to present the complaint earlier, and that any delay in making the complaint was wholly or partially attributable to any reasonable attempts to appeal against the decision or to have it reconsidered or reviewed.

13.13 If the industrial tribunal find that the applicant has been unjustifiably disciplined contrary to s. 64, they will make a declaration that the complaint is well-founded. Thereafter, the applicant's remedies depend on what the trade union does about the situation. If, after four weeks but within six months from the date of the declaration, the determination which constituted the infringement of rights has not been revoked, (see *NALGO v Courtney-Dunn*), or the trade union fails to take such steps as are necessary for securing the reversal of anything done, an application must be made to the Employment Appeal Tribunal. If, on the other hand, the determination has been revoked, or the necessary steps have been taken to reverse anything done, the application may be made to the industrial tribunal. The EAT or the industrial tribunal may then made an award of compensation, and may also order the union to repay any sum paid to the union (or branch or section) or to any other person (e.g by way of a fine or donation etc).

13.14 The amount of compensation to be awarded will be such as is considered to be just and equitable in all the circumstances, bearing in mind the duty of the applicant to mitigate against his loss, and any reduction which may be made on the ground of contributory conduct.

13.15 If the application has been made to an industrial tribunal, the maximum compensation shall not exceed

a. 30 times one week's pay (maximum £205 per week), i.e. £6,150, plus
b. £11,000.

13.16 If the application is made to the EAT, the above maximum figures apply, but there will be an irreducible minimum of £2,700 (see *Bradley v NALGO*).

13.17 An appeal will lie from any decision of an industrial tribunal on a point of law. Any provision in an agreement which purports to take away a person's rights under these sections shall be void, but this does not preclude any agreement made under the auspices of a conciliation officer, acting under the provisions of s. 133 of EPCA.

(3) Right to resign from a trade union (TULR(C)A s. 69)

13.18 In every contract of membership of a trade union, whether made before or after the passing of the Act, there shall be an implied term conferring a right on the member, on giving reasonable notice and complying with any reasonable conditions, to terminate his membership of the union. In *Ashford v Association of Scientific, Technical and Management Staffs* (decided under the provisions of the Industrial Relations Act 1971) the applicant wrote a letter of resignation to the union, which was to take immediate effect. This was not in accordance with the union rules, and subsequently expulsion proceedings were commenced. It was held by the NIRC that as the member had failed to give reasonable notice, he was bound by the union's rules. It was suggested that although it might be reasonable to invite members to state their reasons for resignation, it would not be reasonable to make such a statement a condition of resignation.

(4) Right not to be expelled from the union (TULR(C)A s. 174)

13.19 The grounds upon which a person cannot be excluded from trade union membership (see para 13.2) apply equally to the right not to be expelled from a union. However, a person who resigns from the union because of dissatisfaction with the way the union is conducting its affairs cannot bring proceedings under s. 174, for there is no such doctrine as 'constructive expulsion' (*McGhee v T&GWU*). If a member ceases to be a member of the union on the happening of an event specified in the rules of the union, he shall be treated as having been expelled from the union (s. 177).

Remedies for wrongful exclusion or expulsion (TULR(C)A ss. 175-6)

13.20 A person who claims that he has been wrongly excluded or expelled from a trade union may present a complaint to an industrial tribunal within six months from the date of the exclusion or expulsion, or, where it was not reasonably practicable to do so, within such further period as the tribunal considers reasonable. If the tribunal find the complaint to be well-founded, it shall make a declaration to that effect. If the applicant has been admitted or re-admitted to the union, a further application may be made (after four weeks from the date of the declaration, but within six months) for compensation to be assessed by the industrial tribunal. The amount shall be such as the tribunal considers to be just and equitable in all the circumstances, and may be reduced if the applicant caused or contributed towards the exclusion or expulsion (*Saunders v Bakers, Food and Allied Workers Union*). If the applicant has not been admitted or readmitted to the union, an application may be made to the Employment Appeal Tribunal, within the same time limits, and the EAT will make an award of compensation on the same principles.

The amount of compensation shall not exceed the aggregate of:

(a) 30 times the maximum amount of a week's pay for basic awards in unfair dismissal cases (£6,150); and
(b) the maximum compensation award of £11,000.

However, if the award is made by the EAT, the award shall not be less than £5,000.

(5) Right of access to the courts (TULR(C)A s. 63)

13.21 A member who is seeking a determination or conciliation of a dispute under the union's rules should first pursue his case through the union's internal disputes procedure before seeking recourse to the courts (*White v Kuzych*). But irrespective of any provision in the union's rules, the member has an indefeasible right to apply to the courts any time after six months from when the union first receives his application to have the matter determined or conciliated. However, if the delay is attributable to the unreasonable conduct of the union member, the court can extend the six month period (i.e. to give the union more time to deal with the complaint).

13.22 The right to apply to the court after six months is of course without prejudice to a member's right to apply to the court at any time when, for example, an appeal cannot cure a defect because the action complained against is *ultra vires* or otherwise contrary to law.

(6) Right to a ballot before industrial action (TULR(C)A s. 62)

13.23 If a trade union calls on members to engage in a strike or other industrial action without the affirmative support of a ballot conducted in accordance with the stringent requirements of the Act, any member may apply to the court for an order seeking to have the authorisation or endorsement of the action withdrawn by the union. If the strike is not called by the specified person, or the Act's requirements relating to the functions of the independent scrutineer are not satisfied, or members have not been given an equal opportunity to vote, or a ballot has been held but a majority have not voted in favour, then the court will make such order as it considers appropriate for requiring the union to take steps for ensuring that there is no further inducement to take part in the action, and that no member engages in conduct after the making of the order by virtue of having been induced before the order to take part or continue to take part in the action.

13.24 The right to apply to the court for an order is thus available to an individual member of the union, whether or not the strike is actionable by anyone else (e.g. an employer, see para 15.93) and is additional to any right a member may have in respect of any breach which may have occurred of the trade union's rules. The right exists in respect of calls for any strike or other industrial action, whether or not the member is in breach of his contract of employment. Thus secondary action (see para 15.71) is covered.

13.25 A court may grant interlocutory or interim relief by ordering that the authorisation or endorsement of the industrial action is withdrawn, but it cannot order the union to hold a ballot. The right to bring an action under s. 62 applies to self-employed persons, as well as to employees (s. 62(8)).

13.26 Crown employees (who may not be employed under a contract of employment) are within the provisions of s. 62 also (s. 62(7)).

(7) Other individual rights

13.27 A member of a trade union has the right to restrain the union from indemnifying unlawful conduct (see para 14.48), to bring an action against the union's trustees in respect of unlawful application of the union's property (see para 14.50), and to bring a complaint about the conduct of the ballot in respect of a political fund (see para 14.59). He has the right to inspect the register of members (see para 14.17A) and examine the union's accounts, and can apply to the court if the union has failed to comply with the requirements relating to union elections, election addresses, appointment of a scrutineer, etc. These matters will be considered in Chapter 14.

Rights vis-à-vis an employer

13.28 An individual worker has a number of legal rights against an actual or potential employer, as follows.

(1) Access to employment (TULR(C)A s. 137)

13.29 It is unlawful to refuse a person employment:
a. because he is, or is not, a member of a trade union; or
b. because he is unwilling to accept a requirement:
   (i) to take steps to become or cease to be, or to remain or not to become, a member of a trade union; or
   (ii) to make payments or suffer deductions in the event of his not being a member of a trade union.

13.30 A person shall be taken to have been refused employment if the person to whom he is applying:
a. refuses or deliberately omits to entertain and process his application or enquiry; or
b. causes him to withdraw or cease to pursue his application or enquiry; or
c. refuses or deliberately omits to offer him employment of that description; or
d. makes him an offer of such employment the terms of which

are such that no reasonable employer who wished to fill the post would offer, and which is not accepted; or

e. makes him an offer of such employment but withdraws it or causes him not to accept it.

13.31 The law is aimed at preventing any form of discrimination against a worker on the ground of his trade union membership. The employer is quite entitled to refuse to employ someone because of that person's previous trade union activities (e.g. a well-known militant, see *Birmingham City District Council v Beyer*), because the refusal is not based on trade union membership, but disruptive conduct in his previous employment. Whether the employer thus refuses employment because of past trade union membership or past trade union activities is a question of fact for the industrial tribunal to determine in accordance with the evidence. However, once the worker has entered employment slightly different considerations may apply (see *Fitzpatrick v British Railways Board*, para 13.61).

Job advertisements (TULR(C)A s. 137(3))

13.32 Where a job advertisement (including every form of advertisement or notice, whether to the public or not), is published, which indicates (or might reasonably be understood as indicating) that the employment is only open to a person who is, or who is not, a member of a trade union, or make payments or suffer deductions (see para 13.29 above), then if a person applies for a job, and he is refused employment, it will be conclusively presumed that he was refused employment for that reason. Thus it is clear that all references to trade union membership or non-membership should be eliminated from job advertisements. However, the job advertisement *per se* is not unlawful (unlike advertisements which seek to discriminate on grounds of race or sex, see para 4.115 and para 4.57), and the only remedy is for an individual who has been refused employment to bring a personal complaint.

Unfair practices (TULR(C)A s. 137(4))

13.33 Where there is an arrangement or practice under which employment is only offered to persons put forward or approved by a trade union, a person who is not a member of the trade union, and who is refused employment because of that arrangement or practice, shall be taken to have been refused employment because he is not a member of the trade union.

Employment agencies (TULR(C)A s. 138)

13.34 The Act covers employment agencies, defined as any person who provides services for the purpose of finding employment for workers or for supplying employers with workers. In so far as the employment agency acts as an agent for an employer, the provisions of s. 137 (above) apply. In so far as the agency is acting in its own right, the identical provisions apply, and a person who has been refused the services of an employment agency (on grounds on his membership or non-membership of a trade union) will have a right to complain against the agency to an industrial tribunal. Advertisements by employment agencies are also covered by identical provisions (s. 138(3)).

Exceptions to the Act

13.35 The Act only deals with employment under a contract of service or apprenticeship. Thus it cannot apply to self-employed persons. Further, if a person is being considered for appointment or election to an office in a trade union, then s. 137 does not prevent anything done for the purpose of securing the compliance with a condition that he be or become a member of the trade union, even though this would constitute employment. Thus it is not unlawful to insist that a trade union official becomes a member of the union concerned.

13.36 The unfair recruitment provisions do not apply to members of the armed forces, police, share fishermen, employees who ordinarily work outside Great Britain, seamen registered on ships registered at ports outside Great Britain, or who are not ordinarily resident in Great Britain, and when the Minister issues an exemption certificate on the ground of national security.

Remedies under the Act (ss. 139-142)

13.37 A person who considers that his rights have been violated under the Act may make a complaint to an industrial tribunal within three months from the date of the act complained of, with the usual extension of time if it was not reasonably practicable to present it earlier. If the tribunal uphold the complaint, they must make a declaration to that effect, may award compensation, and may make a recommendation that the respondent takes action to obviate or reduce the effect on the complainant of the conduct which is the subject of the complaint. If the complaint is made against an employment agency and a prospective employer, there are provisions which permit the joinder of both parties, and any award of compensation may be apportioned between them, as the tribunal think just and equitable. It is also possible to join a third party (e.g. a trade union or shop steward) if the act complained of came about by virtue of industrial pressure.

13.38 The practical effect of legislation is that the pre-entry and post-entry closed shop is no longer lawful in Great Britain.

(2) Action short of dismissal (TULR(C)A s. 146)

13.39 Every employee has the right not to have action short of dismissal taken against him by his employer for the purpose of:

a. preventing or deterring him from being a member of an independent trade union, or penalising him for being so; or
b. preventing or deterring him from taking part in the activities of an independent trade union at the appropriate time, or penalising him for doing so; or
c. compelling him to become a member of a trade union.

The 'appropriate time' means time which is outside his working hours, or at a time within his working hours at which, in accordance with arrangements agreed with or consent given by, his employer, it is permissible for him to take part in those activities. Such consent may be express, and will frequently be implied from the conduct of the parties. However, it would be rare that consent can be implied in the case of a shop steward who is not accredited (*Marley Tile Co Ltd v Shaw*). An employee cannot just engage in trade union activities in working hours when he feels like it. Thus in *Brennan and Ging v Ellward (Lancs) Ltd* the applicants left a site on which they were working to consult their trade union official, despite a warning that if they did so they would be dismissed. Although this may have amounted to trade union activities, it was not within the appropriate time for such activities.

13.40 In *Robb v Leon Motor Services* the applicant was a long distance coach driver. He was appointed shop steward. He was then told that he would have to drive other vehicles, because of all the trouble he was causing, and he claimed that by taking him off better paid and more important work, he was being deterred from carrying out his trade union activities at an appropriate time. It was held that even though this was action taken against him short of dismissal, and even though it was done for the purpose of deterring him from taking part in trade union activities, he could not succeed. There was no attempt to stop him from taking part in union activities outside his working hours, and the activities he was engaged in within working hours were not done with any arrangement or with the consent of the employers. Consequently, he was not being deterred from taking part in trade union activity at the appropriate time.

13.41 Section 146 is designed to prevent a person from being penalised for being a member of a particular trade union as well as any trade union. In *National Coal Board v Ridgway* the employers reached an agreement with the Union of Democratic Miners which gave members of that union a wage increase, which was not paid to members of the National Union of Mineworkers. The applicant, a member of the NUM, brought a claim in the industrial tribunal, alleging that his employers were penalising him for being a member of the NUM. His claim was upheld by the Court of Appeal. A failure to pay the wage increase to members of the NUM was 'action', it was taken against the applicant 'as an individual', the purpose was to 'penalise' him for not being a member of the UDM, and the action was taken against him for being a member of the NUM, which is an independent trade union. However, it is important to note that the industrial tribunal found as a fact that the employer's purpose was to penalise the applicant for being a member of the NUM. If, in a multi-union situation, an employer offers a wage increase to members of one union for a legitimate reason, e.g. a change in working practices, his purpose would be to reward members of that union, not to penalise members of other unions.

13.42 If there is a requirement (whether contractual or not) that in the event of a failure by the employee to become or remain a member of a trade union, he must make a payment (usually to charity), and a deduction is made from the employee's wages in consequence, this shall be treated as action short of dismissal. Further, where an employee notifies the employer that he has ceased or will cease to be a member of a trade union as from a certain date, the employer will ensure that no amount representing his trade union subscription shall be deducted from the employee's pay (TULR(C)A s. 68, see below). If the employer fails to comply, the employee may seek a declaration in the county court. The court may make an order to ensure that the employer's actions are not repeated, but for any unlawful past deductions, the employee must seek a remedy in the industrial tribunal under the provisions of s. 5 of the Wages Act 1986.

13.43 Whether the activities in question are the activities of an independent trade union is an issue of fact for the industrial tribunal to determine (*Marley Tile Co Ltd v Shaw*). There must be some institutional link, with the union or an accredited shop steward being involved. Individual requests or complaints, or group meetings which have no union connection, are outside the statutory protections (*Dixon and Shaw v West Ella Developments Ltd*).

13.44 It is now established that the derecognition of a trade union is not 'action' within s. 146, because it is not taken against an individual, although it might be if the motive of the employer was prompted by an anti-union bias. In *Associated Newspapers Ltd v Wilson* the employers announced that from a given date they would no longer negotiate with a trade union, and required employees to negotiate individual contracts. Those who signed the new contracts were offered a pay rise of 4½%, but those who did not received no pay rise. The applicant claimed that this was action which 'deterred' him from joining a trade union. His claim was upheld by the industrial tribunal, but the decision was reversed by the EAT. On a further appeal, the Court of Appeal upheld the claim. It was stated that the purpose of the action was to reduce the power of the trade union so as to negate it totally, thus having the foreseeable consequence of deterring employees from being trade union members. Similarly, in *Associated British Ports v Palmer*, the employers offered personal contracts which were designed to replace terms and conditions contained in a collective agreement. Those employees who did not accept these had their wages negotiated by the trade union, but, although the work was the same, those on personal contracts ended up with higher wages. Again, the Court of Appeal held that the purpose of the action was to penalise those who refused to forgo trade union representation.

There was some doubt as to whether these two decisions were consistent with the original intentions of Parliament when the statutory provisions were first passed in 1975, and, in a climate when collective bargaining arrangements are on the decline, they make it difficult for employers to withdraw from collective bargaining arrangements. Thus the Government moved swiftly to reverse the decisions, by making a last-minute amendment to the Trade Union Reform and Employment Rights Bill, which nullified their effect, and restored the previous understanding of the law.

Section 146 (3)–(5) now states that if there is evidence that the employer's purpose in taking the action was to make a change in his relationship with his employees, and there is evidence that this purpose could also be action to deter or penalise an employee for his trade union membership, then the industrial tribunal shall regard the first purpose as being the purpose for which the employer took the action, unless the action was such that no reasonable employer would have taken it. In other words, if an employer wishes to switch from collective to individual bargaining arrangements, this is permissible, so long as it is not evidence of anti-union antipathy towards trade union membership. The purpose of the action may have the side effect of reducing trade union membership, but it is not done with the purpose of preventing, deterring or penalising such membership.

13.45 A complaint may be presented to a tribunal that an employer has taken action against an employee in violation of the above rights. The burden of proof is placed on the employer to show the purpose for which the action was taken. Moreover, no account is to be taken of any pressure which may have been exercised on the employer by way of strike or other industrial action (or threats of such), and the tribunal will determine the issue as if no such pressure has been exercised. But if the complaint is on the ground that the employer has taken action against the employee for the purpose of compelling him to be or become a member of a trade union, and the employer or employee claims that the employer was induced to take such action by such pressure, the employer or the employee may, before the hearing of the complaint, require the person who he claimed exercised the pressure to be joined as a party to the proceedings.

13.46 The industrial tribunal may then make an award of compensation to the complainant either against the employer or the party who exercised the pressure, or partly against each of them as it thinks just and equitable in the circumstances (TULR(C)A s. 150).

13.47 The complaint must be presented within three months from the date of the last action complained of (see *Adlam v Salis-*

bury and Wells Theological College), with the usual extension of time in cases where it was not reasonably practicable to present it earlier. If the tribunal upholds the complaint, it may make a compensation award as it considers just and equitable having regard to the complainant's loss, and the infringement of his rights, including any expenses incurred and any benefits he might have received but for that action. There is no limit (in theory) on the amount of compensation which can be awarded. The complainant must mitigate against his loss, and compensation is subject to a reduction on the ground of contributory conduct.

13.48 The basis of the award is to compensate the employee for any loss suffered, not for the purpose of imposing a fine on the employer. In *Brassington v Cauldron Wholesale Ltd* an employer threatened to close his business down if he was forced to recognise a trade union. The applicant claimed this was action short of dismissal taken against him for the purpose of preventing or deterring him from joining an independent trade union, and with some hesitation, the EAT agreed that this was so. But the mere infringement of a person's trade union rights would only lead to an industrial tribunal making a mandatory declaration. The compensation award can be given only if the employee can show that he has suffered a loss. This could be , for example, stress causing ill-health (see *Cheall v Vauxhall Motors Ltd*), or the loss of the benefit of trade union advice or assistance, or the inability of the trade union to negotiate a collective agreement, and so on.

(3) Time off work for trade union duties (TULR(C)A s. 168)

13.49 An employer shall permit an employee of his who is an official of a recognised independent trade union to take time off work during his working hours, for the purpose of enabling him

a. to carry out
   (i) any duties of his, as such an official, which are concerned with negotiations with the employer that are related or connected with any matters which fall within s. 244(1) of TULR(C)A (definition of 'trade dispute'), and in relation to which the trade union is recognised by the employer, or
   (ii) any other duties of his, as such an official, which are concerned with the performance, on behalf of employees of the employer, of any functions that are related to or connected with any of those matters, and that the

employer has agreed may be so performed by the trade union, or

b. to undergo training in aspects of industrial relations which is relevant to the carrying out of those duties, and which has been approved by the TUC or by his union.

13.50 Time off work for this purpose is not confined to face-to-face meetings with the employers, but can also include preparatory or co-ordinating meetings in order to discuss forthcoming negotiations, as long as these are in connection with the collective bargaining purposes outlined in s. 244 (*London Ambulance Service v Charlton*).

13.51 A trade union official wishing to take time off work for training should show a copy of the syllabus to the employer. In *Menzies v Smith & McLaurin Ltd* the applicant wished to go on a course relating to job security. The union sent a copy of the syllabus to the employers, showing that topics to be covered included import controls, North Sea Oil, EEC policies, and so on. The company decided that all this was not relevant to his trade union duties, but agreed to give him time off work (without pay) for trade union activities. He went on the course and then claimed his pay. It was held that he was not entitled to be paid. The syllabus clearly indicated that the course was not relevant to his duties as a trade union official.

13.52 The amount of time off, the purposes for which, the occasions on which, and any conditions subject to which time off may be taken are those that are reasonable in all the circumstances having regard to the relevant provisions of the Code of Practice issued by ACAS. The employer shall pay an employee who has taken time off for these purposes in accordance with his usual rate of remuneration. A failure to permit an employee to have time off under this section, or a failure to pay him for time off, may be the subject of a complaint to an industrial tribunal by the aggrieved employee. In *Blower v CEGB* the applicant, who was a night shift worker, was a member of a works committee which met during the day. His day shift colleagues were paid for attending, whereas he was not. It was held that he was not entitled to be paid. It was part of his union work that his leisure time would be eaten into; the law only requires time off to be paid for if it is during his normal working hours, not for time spent on trade union duties outside his working hours (see *Hairsine v Kingston upon Hull City Council*).

13.53 Whether it is reasonable to have time off under s. 168 is a question of fact for the industrial tribunal, and its findings cannot be challenged in the EAT unless it took into account matters which ought not to be taken into account (*Thomas Scott & Sons (Bakers) Ltd v Allen*).

(4) Time off work for trade union activities (TULR(C)A s. 170)

13.54 An employer shall permit an employee who is a member of a recognised independent trade union to take time off during the employee's working hours for the purpose of taking part in:

a. any activities of that trade union; and
b. any activities in relation to which the employee is acting as a representative of that union. This might include, for example, attendance at a conference as a union delegate, etc, but the activities for which permission is to be granted do not include anything which involved the taking of industrial action, whether or not in contemplation or furtherance of a trade dispute. Nor does the lobbying of Parliament to protest against proposed legislation come within the definition of 'trade union activities', even if the lobby is organised by a trade union, because it is intended to convey political and ideological objections to the proposed legislation, and is not as such a trade union activity (*Luce v London Borough of Bexley*).

13.55 Again, the amount of time off, the purposes, the occasions and the conditions are those that are reasonable in all the circumstances having regard to the relevant provisions in the Code of Practice issued (see *Depledge v Pye Telecommunications Ltd*). It will be noted that the employer does not have to pay an employee for time taken off for trade union activities. A failure to permit time off for these purposes may be the subject of a complaint to an industrial tribunal by the aggrieved employee.

(5) Check-off arrangements (TULR(C)A s. 68)

13.56 If a trade union and an employer have an agreement whereby the employer will deduct the union subscriptions from the worker's wages and pay this direct to the union (i.e. a check-off agreement) the employer shall ensure that the worker has authorised the deduction in a document which is signed and dated, that the amount of the deduction does not exceed the permitted amount, and that the authorisation is current on the day of the deduction. An authorisation once made will be operative for three years, unless the worker withdraws it in writing. The permitted amount is the amount of the union subscription. If the union subscription is increased, the employer must give one month's notice to the worker before he can deduct that increase. This notice must be in writing, state the amount of the increase, the total amount of the union subscription to be deducted, and further state that the worker may at any time withdraw his authorisation by giving notice in writing to the employer. Existing check-off arrangements may continue until 30 August 1994, after which time written authority under s 68 must be obtained.

13.57 The fact that the worker has given his authorisation to the deductions does not give rise to any obligation on the part of the employer to continue to make the deductions (s. 68(9)). That is clearly a matter between the employer and the trade union.

13.58 A worker may bring a complaint before an industrial tribunal that his employer has made a deduction in contravention of s. 68. The complaint must be presented within three months from the date of the last deduction, with the usual extension of time if it was not reasonably practicable to present the claim earlier.

13.59 If the tribunal find the complaint to be well-founded, it shall make a declaration to that effect, and also order the employer to pay to the worker the unauthorised deduction (or unauthorised increase in subscription).

(6) Deductions for the political fund of the union (s. 68)

13.60 If a member of a trade union informs the employer in writing that he is exempt from paying the levy to the political fund of the union, the employer shall ensure that no amount representing the contribution to the political fund is deducted from the employee's wages. If an employee claims that his employer has failed to comply with s. 68, then, somewhat curiously, he must make an application to the county court (in Scotland, the sheriff court) which will make a declaration, and an appropriate order (s. 87). Armed with such declaration, the employee may, if necessary, present a claim to an industrial tribunal under the provisions of the Wages Act s. 5 within three months from the date of the declaration (s. 88).

(7) Dismissal on the ground of trade union membership or non-membership, or trade union activities (EPCA s. 58(1))

13.61 The dismissal of an employee will be unfair if the reason (or principle reason) was because the employee:

a. was, or proposed to become, a member of an independent trade union; or

b. had taken part, or proposed to take part, in the activities of an independent trade union at an appropriate time. 'Appropriate time' means time which is outside his working hours, or time within his working hours at which, in accordance with arrangements agreed with or consent given by his employer it is permissible to take part in those activities. 'Working hours' means any time when the employee is required to work. A person is not taking part in trade union activities merely because he is a trade union activist, for one must distinguish between individual and trade union activities (*Chant v Aquaboats Ltd*). Nor do the activities of an unofficial strike committee constitute trade union activities. But enlisting the help of a trade union official to assist in negotiations of terms and conditions of employment does constitute trade union activities (*Discount Tobacco and Confectionery Ltd v Armitage*).

   If the employee is dismissed because the employer learns of his trade union activities in a previous employment (e.g. as a trade union activist), it would be inevitable that the employer was dismissing him because of the belief that he would be involved in trade union activities in his current employment, and thus the principle reason for the dismissal would be that the employee proposed to take part in trade union activities, and hence the dismissal is unfair (*Fitzpatrick v British Railways Board*). But if the trade union activist has obtained employment by deceit (e.g. by changing his name) then a dismissal for that deceit may be fair, and the reason is not because of past or proposed trade union activities (*Birmingham City District Council v Beyer*);

c. was not a member of any trade union, or a particular trade union, or had refused or proposed to refuse to become or remain a member (*Crosville Motor Services Ltd v Ashfield*). This provision gives general rights to non-unionists not to be dismissed because of their non-membership of a trade union.

13.62 If a person is dismissed for any of the above reasons, it will be an unfair dismissal, and thus it is not necessary for him to have the normal qualifying period of employment of two years before he can bring his claim (EPCA s. 64(3), and see *Carrington v Therm-A-Stor Ltd.*) Taking part in a strike may be trade union activity, but it is not at an appropriate time (see para 13.64).

(8) Dismissal in connection with industrial action (TULR(C)A ss. 237-239)

(a) Dismissal in connection with a lock-out (TULR(C)A s. 238(1)(a)

13.63 A lock-out is the closing of a place of employment, or a suspension of the work, or the refusal by the employer to continue to employ his employees, done with a view to compelling those employees to accept terms and conditions of or affecting employment (EPCA Sch 13 para 24). A lock-out by an employer is not necessarily a breach of contract by him (*Express and Star Ltd v Bunday*). If an employee claims that he has been dismissed by virtue of the lock-out, an industrial tribunal is precluded from determining whether or not such dismissal is fair or unfair unless it can be shown that (a) one or more of the relevant employees were not dismissed, or (b) if they were dismissed, they were re-engaged within three months from the date of dismissal, but the applicant was not offered re-engagement. The relevant employees are those who were directly interested in the dispute on the day of the lock-out (*H Campey & Sons v Bellwood*).

(b) Dismissals in connection with an official strike (TULR(C)A s. 238(1)(b))

13.64 If an employee is dismissed because he was taking part in a strike or other industrial action, the tribunal shall not determine whether the dismissal was fair or unfair unless it is shown that (a) one or more of those employees at the establishment where the complainant works who were taking part in the strike or other industrial action at the time of the complainant's dismissal were not dismissed, or (b) that any such employee who was dismissed was offered re-engagement within three months of the complainant's dismissal, but that he was not offered re-engagement (TULR(C)A s. 238(2)). There is no requirement that the offer to re-engage must be in writing (*Marsden v Fairey Stainless Ltd*).

13.65 Whether or not an employee is taking part in a strike or other industrial action must be determined as an objective fact. In other words, the test is 'what is the employee doing or omitting to do?' The subjective knowledge of the employer is not relevant (*Manifold Industries v Sims*).

13.66 It will be recalled that a strike is a breach of contract by the employee which entitled the employer to dismiss him. Provided the employer dismisses all the strikers, or offers all of them re-engagement after the strike is over within three months, the industrial tribunal has no jurisdiction to hear any complaint. This is the 'no picking and choosing' rule (see *McCormack v Horsepower Ltd*). But if an employer is selective in his dismissals or offers of re-engagement, those employees who have been excluded may bring claims in the industrial tribunals. To avoid a finding of unfair dismissal, the employer must show that he has acted reasonably in not taking back those strikers who were not offered re-engagement. The question will be determined by the circumstances, having regard to the equity and substantial merits of the case (*Edwards v Cardiff City Council*).

13.67 Further, the employer can re-engage an employee who has been dismissed for striking any time after three months from the time another striker was dismissed without exposing himself to a claim for unfair dismissal from the latter.

13.68 But if the employer (or an associated employer) re-engages a striker by mistake (e.g. in ignorance of the fact that he had been on strike) this gives the industrial tribunal jurisdiction to consider a claim from a striker who has not been offered re-engagement (*Bigham v GKN Kwikform Ltd*).

13.69 The three-month period is in the nature of a 'cooling off' period, designed to enable industrial disputes to be settled on honourable terms. As long as the offer of re-engagement is made within that period, the industrial tribunal has no jurisdiction to hear a claim by a person who does not wish to accept that offer (*Highland Fabricators Ltd v McLaughlin*).

13.70 But the employer will lose the protection of s. 238 if he seeks to dismiss before the strike has begun or after the strike is over. In *Heath v Longman (Meat Salesmen) Ltd* employees went out on strike, but subsequently decided to return to work. One of them informed the employer that the strike was over, but when they returned to work they were dismissed. The NIRC held that since they had returned to work, they were no longer on strike, and hence the dismissals were unfair. In *Midland Plastics Ltd v Till*, a letter was sent to the company management stating that unless certain demands were met, industrial action would commence at 11 a.m. At 9.30 a.m., the managing director spoke to four employees, who confirmed that they would abide by the decision, and they were immediately dismissed. It was held that the industrial tribunal were not precluded by s. 238 from entertaining a complaint of unfair dismissal. The threat to take part in a strike was a mere display of power by one side to a dispute which is a substantial feature of industrial relations negotiations. As the dismissals took place before the strike, s. 238 did not apply.

13.71 An employee who does not receive a letter of dismissal, and who therefore carries on working, is not a 'relevant employee' who has been dismissed and offered re-engagement so as to confer jurisdiction on an industrial tribunal to consider complaints of unfair dismissal from strikers who were not offered re-engagement. Neither is a person who is off work through sickness taking part in a strike, even though had he been at work he would have done so (*Hindle Gears Ltd v McGinty*).

13.72 The offer of re-engagement must be made to the striking employee. A general advertising campaign offering employment to those who apply does not amount to an offer of employment to any particular individual. Such a campaign merely makes available the opportunity to be offered employment (*Crosville Wales Ltd v Tracey*).

13.73 TULR(C)A does not define what is meant by 'other industrial action', and it is assumed that the term includes traditional industrial techniques such as work-to-rule campaigns, a go-slow, sit-ins, and, possibly, 'working without enthusiasm'. In *Thompson v Eaton Ltd* employees were standing around a new machine so as to prevent the employers from testing it. They refused to return to their normal place of work, and were dismissed. It was held that they were engaged in 'other industrial action', and consequently the industrial tribunal had no jurisdiction to hear the case. In *Power Packing Casemakers v Faust* the applicants were dismissed for refusing to do overtime, even though there was no contractual requirement to do so. The refusal occurred because of a dispute about wages. It was held that the applicants had been carrying out industrial action, and the industrial tribunal had no jurisdiction to hear the claim. Other examples include a 'go slow' (*Drew v St Edmundsbury Borough Council*), a 'work to rule' (*Secretary of State for Employment v ASLEF*), imposing sanctions on normal working (*Williams v*

Western Mail), etc. However, a mere threat to take other industrial action is not sufficient (*Midland Plastics Ltd v Till*). Whether or not employees are taking part in other industrial action is a question of fact for the industrial tribunal to determine (*Naylor v Orton & Smith Ltd*).

(c) Dismissal of unofficial strikers (TULR(C)A s. 237)

13.74 An employee has no right to complain that he has been unfairly dismissed if at the time of the dismissal he was taking part in an unofficial strike or other unofficial industrial action.

13.75 A strike or other industrial action will be unofficial unless:

a. he is a trade union member, and the strike or action was authorised or endorsed by the trade union; or
b. he is not a member of the trade union, but at least two of those taking part in the action are members of the union by which the action has been authorised or endorsed.

13.76 A strike or other industrial action cannot be unofficial if none of those taking part are members of a trade union. It will only become unofficial if some of those taking part are union members, but the action has not been authorised or endorsed by the union. If the trade union repudiates the official action (for which it might otherwise be deemed to be responsible, see para 15.78), the action becomes unofficial the next working day after the repudiation takes place.

(d) Exceptions in health and safety and maternity cases (TULR(C)A s. 237(1A) and s. 238(2A))

13.77 We have seen (above) that if an employee is taking part in a strike (whether official or unofficial) or the employer conducts a lock-out, an industrial tribunal has no jurisdiction to hear a claim for unfair dismissal except in the stated circumstances. However, these rules do not apply if the reason for the dismissal (or selection for redundancy) is a reason specified in s. 59A (dismissal in health and safety cases, see para 12.34C) or s. 60 (maternity dismissal, see para 5.30) of EPCA. In such circumstances, the industrial tribunal will have jurisdiction.

(9) Dismissal due to industrial pressure (EPCA s. 63)

13.78 If an employer is forced to dismiss an employee because of actual, or the threat of, industrial pressure by other employees, this may amount to an unfair dismissal. The reason is that s. 63 of the EPCA provides that for the purpose of determining whether the employer has a statutory reason for dismissing, or whether the employer acted reasonably in dismissing, no account shall be taken of any industrial pressure (i.e. strike or other industrial action) which was put on the employer, and the question must be determined as if no such pressure had been exercised. In *Hazells Offset v Luckett*, the applicant was dismissed from his managerial post after trade union representatives had indicated that they would not co-operate with him. Clearly, the principal reason for the dismissal was the industrial pressure, but this could not be advanced as a reason. Since there was no other reason, the dismissal was unfair. The tribunal thought that this did not seem right, nor fair, but it was clearly what Parliament had decided. But if the employee was partly responsible for the threat of industrial action, this could amount to contributory conduct so as to warrant a reduction in the compensation awarded. Thus if the industrial pressure is exercised because of some personal animosity, and the employee is unco-operative in a difficult situation, and, for example, refuses to move to another job, he may well have contributed to his dismissal (*Ford Motor Co v Hudson*).

13.79 However, if on a claim for unfair dismissal the employer or the applicant claims that the employer was induced to dismiss the applicant because of pressure which a trade union or other person exercised on him by way of calling, organising, procuring or financing a strike, or threatening to do so, and the pressure was exercised because the applicant was not a member of any trade union or a particular trade union, then the employer or the applicant may, before the hearing of the complaint, join that person as a party to the proceedings before the industrial tribunal. If the latter decides to make an award of compensation in favour of the applicant, but also finds that the employer was induced to dismiss him because of the pressure, the tribunal may make an award against that person instead of the employer, or partly against that person and partly against the employer. The amount shall be such as the tribunal consider to be just and equitable in all the circumstances (see EPCA s. 76A).

(10) Selection for dismissal on grounds of redundancy (EPCA s. 59)

13.80 We have seen (para 8.167) that to select a person for dismissal on grounds of redundancy will be unfair if the reason for the selection was his membership or non-membership of a trade union, or the selection was contrary to the customary procedure. No qualifying period of continuous employment is required.

(11) Compensations for dismissals (EPCA ss. 73–74)

13.81 In respect of compensation for dismissals for trade union membership or non-membership, there are rules relating to a minimum basic award, a special award, as well as the usual compensation award (see Chapter 9).

(12) Interim relief for dismissed trade unionists or non-unionists (TULR(C)A ss. 161-166)

13.82 If an employee considers that he was unfairly dismissed because he was, or proposed to become a member of an independent trade union, or had taken or proposed to take part in the activities of that union, or he was not a member of a trade union, he may present a complaint to an industrial tribunal asking for an order that he be reinstated or re-engaged by the employer or, if this cannot be agreed upon, that he be suspended on full pay pending a settlement or a determination of the complaint. The employee must present the complaint before the end of seven days from the effective date of the termination of his employment, and must, if he is claiming he was dismissed because of his trade union membership or activities, accompany his complaint with a certificate signed by an authorised official of the trade union concerned, stating that the employee was or had proposed to become a member, and that there were reasonable grounds for believing that the reason for the dismissal was the one alleged in the complaint. The signature of a trade union official is *prima facie* evidence that he is duly authorised to sign the certificate, but if this is challenged, the onus is on the employee to show that the official had actual or implied authority to sign it (*Sulemany v Habib Bank*).

13.83 The tribunal will give the employer seven days' notice before the hearing, but shall thereupon hear the complaint as soon as is practicable. If the tribunal comes to the conclusion that it is likely that it would uphold a complaint of unfair dismissal on one of the above grounds, it shall announce this preliminary finding and explain to the parties its powers. It will then ask the employer if he is willing to reinstate the employee, or re-engage him on terms and conditions which are no less favourable than he formerly enjoyed, pending the determination or settlement of the complaint. If the employer is willing to re-engage the employee in another job, and specifies the terms and conditions, the tribunal will ask the employee if he is willing to accept, and if so, an order to that effect will be made. If the employee is unwilling to accept the job on those terms and conditions, then, if his refusal is reasonable, the tribunal will make an order for the continuation of his contract of employment, but if his refusal is regarded as being unreasonable, no order will be made. If the employer fails to attend the hearing, or states that he is unwilling to reinstate or re-engage the employee, the tribunal will make an order for the continuation of the employee's contract of employment.

13.84 The effect of an order for continuation of the contract of employment is that if the employment has ceased, it will continue in force, or if it has not yet ceased, it will continue when it does so cease, until, in either case, the determination or settlement of the complaint, for the purposes of pay, seniority, pension rights, and other similar rights, and for determining for any purpose the period for which the employee has been continuously employed. The tribunal will also specify the pay due to the employee from the time of dismissal until the complaint is finally settled, but it will take into account any lump sum received in lieu of wages. At any time after making the order and before the determination by the tribunal, the employer or the employee may apply for a revocation or variation of the order on the ground that there has been a relevant change in circumstances. Also, the employee may apply to the tribunal on the ground that the employer has not complied with the terms of the order. If his complaint is that the employer has not paid the amount specified, the tribunal will determine the amount due, and make it as a separate award for any other sum it gives by way of compensation. If the complaint relates to any other breach by the employer, then it shall make an award of compensation as it thinks just and equitable having regard to the loss suffered by the complainant.

13.85 An order for continuation of employment merely preserves the employee's rights; the employer does not have to permit him to come back to work, or to allow him on the premises.

13.86 On an application for interim relief, the industrial tribunal must decide if the applicant can establish that he has a pretty good chance of succeeding at a full hearing. This is a higher degree of certainty than a mere reasonable chance of success. 'Likely' means more than 'probable', and probable itself suggests more than an even chance (*Taplin v Shippham Ltd*).

13.87 It will be extremely rare that an employer will admit that a person was dismissed because he engaged in trade union activity, and doubtless some other reason will be advanced. In *Forsyth v Fry's Metals Ltd* the tribunal considered the evidence under four headings: (a) the extent of the alleged behaviour, (b) the extent of the employer's dissatisfaction with the employee, (c) the coincidence in time between the alleged behaviour and the initial steps taken towards dismissal, and (d) the coincidence in time between the behaviour and the actual dismissal. In this case, the applicant was dismissed for alleged poor work performance. There was little direct evidence of this; on the other hand he had been instrumental in persuading most of the employees to join a trade union, and had been elected shop steward. On the facts, there was a likelihood that he would succeed in establishing his claim, and interim relief was granted.

13.88 On an application for interim relief, it is possible to join a person who is exercising pressure to bring about the dismissal (see s. 160), and such a person shall be given notice of the time, date and place of the hearing as soon as reasonably practicable (s. 162(3)).

CHAPTER 14

The law relating to trade unions

14.1 In this Chapter we shall concentrate on the law as it affects the running of a trade union. All the relevant law has now been consolidated by the Trade Union and Labour Relations (Consolidation) Act 1992, although this Act, as well as the Employment Protection (Consolidation) Act 1978, has been amended by the Trade Union Reform and Employment Rights Act 1993. All references are to the 1992 Act (as amended) unless otherwise stated. In so far as earlier reported decisions were based on provisions in earlier (now replaced) legislation, references to the relevant statutory provisions have, for the sake of convenience, been transposed to the corresponding provisions of the 1992 Act.

Definition of a trade union (TULR(C)A s. 1)

14.2 A trade union is an organisation (whether permanent or temporary) which either:

a. consists wholly or mainly of workers of one or more descriptions and whose principal purposes include the regulation of relations between workers and employers or employers' associations; or
b. consists wholly or mainly of:
   i. constituent or affiliated organisations which have those purposes; or
   ii. representatives of such constituent or affiliated organisations, and in either case whose principal purposes include the regulation of relations between workers and employers or workers' and employers' associations, or

include the regulation of relations between the constituent or affiliated organisations.

This definition disclosed two functional bodies:

a. refers to a single trade union; and
b. refers to confederated organisations, such as the Confederation of Shipbuilding and Engineering Unions or the Trades Union Congress.

14.3 Whether or not a trade union has a 'legal personality' of its own was always a matter of some controversy. Section 10 provides that a trade union shall not be a body corporate, but shall nonetheless be capable of making contracts, suing and being sued in its own name, and capable of being prosecuted for any offences committed in its name. As, however, it has no 'legal' existence, property must be held by its trustees, and any judgment, order or award shall be enforced against the property held by the trustees. This does not apply to those organisations which were on the special register created by the Industrial Relations Act 1971 (see TULR(C)A s. 117) for these were professional organisations which engaged in collective bargaining on behalf of their members, and their legal personality stemmed from their charter of incorporation, or by virtue of incorporation under the Companies Acts. Such legal personality is to continue, but other than these, any registration by a trade union under the Companies Acts, or as a friendly society or an industrial and provident society, is void.

14.4 Between 1901 and 1971, a series of legal decisions had laid down that a trade union had some form of quasi-legal personality, but this status has been clearly removed by s. 10. In *EEPTU v Times Newspapers*, it was held that a trade union, not having a legal personality, could not therefore sue for libel in respect of its reputation, for s. 10 states that a trade union shall not be 'or treated as if it were', a body corporate, and hence the plaintiff trade union did not have the personality which could be protected by an action for defamation.

Definition of employers' association (TULR(C)A s. 122)

14.5 An employers' association is defined as an organisation which either:

a. consists wholly or mainly of employers or individual proprietors, and whose principal purposes include the regulation of relations between employers and workers or trade unions; or
b. consists wholly or mainly of constituent or affiliated organisations with those purposes or representatives of such constituents or affiliated organisations, whose principal objects include the regulation of relations between employers and workers or between the constituent or affiliated organisations.

14.6 An employers' association may be incorporated under the Companies Acts, or may be an unincorporated association. In the latter case it shall nonetheless be capable of making contracts, or suing and being sued in its own name, and of being prosecuted in its own name. Its property, however, will have to be held by trustees, and any judgment, award or order would have to be enforced against that property. A trade association, which is largely concerned with the business interests of employers, is not an employers' association within the statutory definition, but if it did have as one of its purposes collective bargaining objectives, or if it regulated the relations between organisations which have such objectives, it could be an employers' association. This is because the Act requires the principal objects of an employers' association to 'include' the statutory objects, not that the principal objects 'shall be' the statutory objects.

Listing of trade unions (TULR(C)A s. 2)

14.7 The Certification Officer (a post created by the Employment Protection Act - see Chapter 1) has taken over and maintains a list of trade union organisations which were formerly held by the Registrar of Friendly Societies (s. 257). On this list there will be organisations which were registered under the pre-1971 law (or formed as a result of an amalgamation of two or more bodies which were registered), all organisations registered under the Industrial Relations Act 1971, and all TUC affiliated trade unions. Any organisation (including employers' associations) which is not listed may apply for inclusion, submitting the appropriate fee, a copy of its rules, a list of officers, the address of its head office, and details of its name. The Certification Officer will refuse to enter on the list any organisation the name of which is the same as a previously registered or listed organisation, or a name which so closely resembles any such organisation as to be likely to deceive the public. If it appears to the Certification Officer that an organisation whose name is on the list is not a trade union he may remove it from the list, but not without giving notice of his intention to do so, and considering any representations which may be made. An organisation which is aggrieved by the decision of the Certification Officer to refuse to enter it on the list, or a decision to remove it from the list, may appeal either on a question of law or of fact, to the Employment Appeal Tribunal. Copies of the list shall be available for public inspection.

14.8 There are certain advantages of being a 'listed' trade union. First, it is evidence that the body concerned satisfied the statutory definition without further proof being required. Second, there are tax reliefs on income in the union's provident funds. Third, there are procedural advantages in connection with the passing of property consequent on the change of trustees. Fourth, and perhaps the most significant of all, only a listed trade union can apply for a certificate of independence.

Listing of employers' associations (TULR(C)A s. 123)

14.8A The Act permits the employers' associations to be entered on the appropriate list, but there are few advantages of doing so. Many employers' associations are incorporated under the Companies Act, and therefore do not require trustees to hold property. They do not have provident funds, and do not require certificates of independence. Not surprisingly, less than half of employers' associations have bothered to become listed.

Certification of trade unions (TULR(C)A s. 6)

14.9 Any trade union which is on the list may apply to the Certification Officer for a certificate that it is an independent trade union. A union is independent if:

a. it is not under the domination or control of an employer or groups of employers or an employers' associations; and
b. it is not liable to interference by an employer or any such group or association arising out of the provision of financial or material support or by any other means whatsoever tending towards such control (s. 5).

If, after making enquiries the Certification Officer decides that the union is independent he will issue a certificate accordingly, otherwise he will refuse to do so, but must give reasons for his refusal. Even if he grants the certificate, he may withdraw it if he is of the opinion that the union is no longer independent, but he must notify the trade union concerned of his intention, and may take into account any relevant information supplied by any person. An appeal will lie on a point of law or fact to the Employment Appeal Tribunal against the decision of the Certification Officer to refuse to grant, or to withdraw, a certificate.

14.10 Only a trade union aggrieved by the decision not to grant a certificate may appeal. There is no general right of appeal by anyone who is aggrieved. In *General and Municipal Workers Union v Certification Officer*, a trade union objected to a decision of the Certification Officer to grant a certificate to another organisation, but it was held that the trade union had no right to appeal against that decision.

14.11 Once granted, the certificate is conclusive evidence of the independence of the trade union, and in any proceedings before any court, the Employment Appeal Tribunal, The Central Arbitration Committee, or an industrial tribunal, where the independence of the trade union is in issue and there is no certificate in force and no refusal, withdrawal or cancellation recorded, the proceedings shall be stayed until a certificate has been issued or refused by the Certification Officer.

14.12 To understand the arguments about certification, it is necessary to make a short excursus into industrial relations. Some years ago there was an expansion of unionisation, particular among to so-called 'white collar' workers and management. A considerable number of staff associations have sprung up in order to exercise the sort of industrial pressure hitherto reserved for the blue collar workers. These staff associations are looked upon as not being 'proper' trade unions, and are sometimes referred to in a derogatory tone as being 'sweetheart unions' or 'house unions'. The test of independence for certification purposes is to permit through the net those unions which can demonstrate that they are truly independent, and not just the tame adjuncts of management. A considerable number of such staff associations have applied for and obtained certificates of independence; many have not bothered, on the ground that they can obtain by negotiation all the advantages which certification confers. Those that have succeeded in obtaining a certificate are criticised for bringing about a proliferation of trade unions (at a time when a reduction in the number of unions is thought to be desirable) and for not joining in with the existing established (i.e. TUC) trade unions.

14.13 The first case to be challenged under this branch of the law was *Blue Circle Staff Association v Certification Officer*. In 1971 the staff association was formed for salaried staff at the instigation of higher management. Subsequently, changes were made to the association's constitution and an application was made for certification. It was held by the EAT that the Certification Officer was right in his refusal to grant a certificate. The association had not yet attained the freedom from domination by the employer under which it had lived since its formation. There is a heavy burden to show that it had shaken off such paternal control.

14.14 A different view of the realities of the scene was taken in *Association of HSD (Hatfield) Employees v Certification Officer*, where the association was formed with the active encouragement of the employers, who shared the opposition of the association to proposals for nationalisation. After the decision to nationalise was taken, the new head of the industry visited the factory, and was met by a hostile demonstration organised by the association. A subsequent application for a certificate of independence was refused by the Certification Officer, and the association appealed to the EAT. It was held that the certificate should be granted. Under s. 5(a) the organisation must show that it is not under the domination or control of the employer. This involves an examination of the factual situation, including finance, the extent (if any) of employer assistance or interference, the history, rules, organisation, membership base and general attitude. Under s. 5(b) there is inevitably a degree of speculation, but the Certification Officer ought not to be unduly anxious about future possibilities as he always has the power to revoke the certificate if he thinks he should do so. On the facts of the case, the EAT was clearly impressed by the hostile demonstration, and held that as the association had demonstrated that it was 'fiercely independent of management' a certificate should be granted.

14.15 The fact that an association is company based is not fatal to the association's independence, for there are many trade unions in industry which negotiate with a single employer (e.g. the Post Office, or the National Coal Board). Nor is the fact that the employer makes facilities available to a trade union destructive of its independence, for this may be seen as good industrial relations practice, and is in accordance with the Code of Practice on Time Off for Trade Union Duties and Activities. In *Squibb UK Staff Association v Certification Officer*, a certificate of independence was refused because of fears of vulnerability to employer interference. This was based largely on the extensive facilities which were provided by the employer, which included time off with pay for the officials of the association when performing their duties, free use of office accommodation and rooms for meetings, the provision of free stationery, free use of the employer's telephone, photocopying and internal mailing system, and a free check-off system. In view of the obvious limited resources of the association, and its narrow membership base, the Certification Officer thought that it would be very difficult to function effectively if these were withdrawn by the employer. The EAT held that nonetheless the certificate should be granted, but this decision was reversed by the Court of Appeal, and the original ruling of the Certification Officer was confirmed. The test of 'liability to interference' by the employer, which would be fatal to the association's independence, meant vulnerable to, or at risk of, interference. The degree of the likelihood of the risk was irrelevant as long as it was not insignificant.

14.15A If the continued existence of the staff association is dependent on the approval of the employer, then it is 'liable to interference' and hence cannot be an independent trade union (*Government Communications Staff Federation v Certification Officer*).

Advantages of certification

14.16 The advantages of having a certificate of independence are to be found mainly in the 1992 Act, and are as follows:

a. representatives of recognised independent trade unions are entitled to receive information for collective bargaining purposes (s. 181);
b. the rights of employees not to have discriminatory action taken against them (short of dismissal) apply only to members of independent trade unions (s. 146);

c. employees who are officials of recognised independent trade unions are entitled to have time off work to carry out their duties as such, or for the purpose of undergoing training in industrial relations. In doing so, they are entitled to their normal remuneration (s. 168);
d. employees who are members of recognised independent trade unions are entitled to have time off work for trade union activities, though not necessarily with pay (s. 170);
e. an employer must consult with representatives of recognised independent trade unions in the event of redundancies arising (s. 188);
f. an application for interim relief if a dismissal is alleged to be for trade union membership may be made by a member of an independent trade union (s. 161);
g. it is unfair to dismiss a person because he wishes to join an independent trade union, or take part in its activities (s. 152);
h. an independent trade union may obtain public funds for the purpose of holding various ballots (s. 115, although this right is being phased out, and will cease altogether in April 1996, see para 14.40).
i. a recognised independent trade union is entitled to be given information and be consulted under the Transfer of Undertakings (Protection of Employment) Regulations 1981;
j. a recognised independent trade union is entitled to receive information from an employer concerning occupational pension schemes (Social Security Act 1975, s. 56A);
k. an independent trade union may enter into an agreement to exclude statutory rights of unfair dismissal and substitute a dismissal procedure (EPCA s. 65);
l. an independent trade union is entitled to appoint safety representatives (Health & Safety at Work Act etc 1974, s. 2).

Register of members (s. 24)

14.17 A trade union shall maintain a register of the names and addresses of its members. The register shall be accurate, up to date, and may be kept by means of a computer.

14.17A A member is entitled to know whether there is an entry in the register relating to him, and be supplied with a copy of that entry. The person who has been appointed as an independent scrutineer for election purposes must also be permitted to inspect the register and be provided with an up-to-date copy of it (see para 14.34).

Confidentiality of the register of members (s. 24A)

14.18 A trade union shall impose a duty of confidentiality on the independent scrutineer who has been appointed to oversee any ballot held on an election for office, political resolution or resolution to approve an instrument of amalgamation or transfer. The scrutineer or independent person must not disclose any name or address on the register (except in permitted circumstances), and must take all reasonable steps to ensure that no such disclosure takes place. Disclosure will be permitted (a) when the member consents (b) where required for the purposes of the discharge of functions by the Certification Officer or of the scrutineer under the terms of his appointment, or (c) where required for the purpose of investigating crime or of criminal proceedings.

Remedies (ss. 25-26)

14.19 A member of a trade union who claims that the union has failed to comply with ss. 24 or 24A may apply to the Certification Officer for a declaration to that effect. As an alternative (or as a follow-up, because the Certification Office has no enforcement powers), an application may be made to the court, which can make an enforcement order that the union take such steps to remedy the matter, or to abstain from any acts, as may be specified in the order.

Membership of a trade union

14.20 In principle, it is for the trade union to lay down the description of persons who are eligible to join, and this will usually be laid down in the union's rules (*Boulting v ACAT*). It follows that it cannot accept for membership someone who is not within the prescribed class, and cannot create a category of membership not provided for in the rules (*Martin v Scottish Transport and General Workers' Union*). The rules may also specify a class of person who is not eligible to join (*Faramus v Film Artistes' Association*). However, a trade union cannot exclude a person from membership on arbitrary and unreasonable grounds (*Nagle v Feilden*). It is unlawful to discriminate against a woman in the terms on which it is prepared to accept her for membership, or by refusing or deliberately omitting to accept her application (Sex Discrimination Act 1975, s. 12) or to discriminate against her in the way in which it affords her access to any benefits, facilities or other services, to deprive her of membership, or subject her to any other detriment (other than benefits on death or retirement). Similar provisions relating to unlawful discrimination on grounds of race etc are contained in the Race Relations Act 1976 s. 12.

14.20A However, notwithstanding anything contained in the union's rules, a person cannot be excluded (or expelled) from a trade union unless this is permitted by the provisions of s. 174 of TULR(C)A (see para 13.19), and a person who is so excluded or expelled has the right to bring a complaint before an industrial tribunal or the EAT as appropriate.

Rules of a trade union

14.21 At common law, a trade union was tainted with illegality because its rules and/or objects were in 'restraint of trade'. In the 19th century this led to certain problems; the trade unionists were prosecuted for criminal conspiracy, and the rules of the unions were generally unenforceable. The effect of the doctrine against restraint of trade on trade unions, was nullified by the 1871 Trade Union Act, (see now TULR(C)A s. 11) which provides that the purposes of a trade union or an employers' association shall not, by reason of being in restraint of trade, make any member liable for criminal conspiracy, or make any agreement or trust void or voidable, nor shall the rules be unlawful or unenforceable by virtue of their being in restraint of trade (see *Goring v British Actors Equity Association*). This also applies to incorporated employers' associations and special register bodies in so far as the purposes or rules relate to the regulation of relations between employers or employers' organisations and workers.

14.21A As long as a trade union complies with the various statutory requirements, there are no general restrictions on the rules which it may adopt. But the rules constitute a contract between the union and its members, and must be strictly observed.

Disciplinary action

14.22 If the trade union wishes to take disciplinary action, by way of fines or forfeitures, or wishes to expel a member, such powers must be contained in the rules, otherwise they cannot be exercised. In *Spring v National Amalgamated Stevedores and Dockers' Society* the plaintiff was enrolled as a member of the defendant union contrary to the Bridlington Agreement, which was designed to prevent poaching of members among TUC affiliated unions. The TUC ordered the union to expel the members, which it did, but the expulsion was held to be void when it was discovered that the union rules contained no power of expulsion.

14.22A If the rules specify the grounds on which disciplinary action may be taken, then the union must adhere to these grounds, and not proceed on others. Moreover, the courts have in the past exercised the power to interpret the rules of the union in accordance with the courts' understanding of the rules, not the union's. In *Lee v Showmen's Guild*, the plaintiff was expelled from the defendant Guild for violating a rule designed to prevent 'unfair competition'. It was held that since the Guild had misconstrued the meaning of this term, the court could substitute its own interpretation, and the expulsion was declared void. This interpretative power is particularly important in those cases where the rules are somewhat vague (e.g. 'conduct detrimental to the union' in *Kelly v NATSOPA*), although the legitimate interests of the union will be upheld. In *Evans v National Union of Bookbinding and Printing Workers*, the rules provided that a member who acted contrary to the interests of the union might be expelled. The plaintiff absented himself from work on several occasions, contrary to an agreement between the union and the employers. As a result of such conduct, he was expelled. It was held that the expulsion was valid, for it was designed to uphold the success of the collective bargaining arrangements.

14.22B If the union rules provide for a procedure to be adopted in disciplinary cases, then that procedure must be strictly adhered to, and the smallest irregularity will be as fatal as the greatest. The rules cannot be so framed as to oust the jurisdiction of the courts by declaring that the decision of the union shall be final and binding (*Chapple v ETU*), and if there is an appeal procedure which is denied to the aggrieved member, the expulsion will be invalid (*Braithwaite v Electrical Electronics and*

Telecommunications Union). If the expulsion is void because of lack of authority or some other reason, then, as the appeal procedure cannot cure the defect, the aggrieved member may apply to the courts nonetheless, without exhausting the internal machinery. In *Porter v National Union of Journalists*, the union called a strike of provincial journalists without holding a ballot as required by its rules. An injunction was granted to restrain the union from taking disciplinary action against those members who refused to comply with the instruction, for the strike call was unconstitutional.

14.22C Although the statutory requirements that a trade union must act in accordance with the rules of natural justice have been repealed, it is submitted that the common law position remains unchanged. This means that a trade union, in the exercise of what is essentially a quasi-judicial function, cannot expel a member without giving him a hearing, notifying him of the charges against him, and giving him an opportunity to rebut them (*Lawlor v Union of Post Office Workers*). It also means that the officials of the union should avoid being placed in the position of being prosecutor, judge and jury. In *Taylor v National Union of Seamen*, the general secretary of the union dismissed the plaintiff for insubordination. When the plaintiff appealed to the executive council, the general secretary was the chairman of the meeting, and after the plaintiff had withdrawn, the meeting was treated to a long statement of matters which were not the subject of the charge, but which were prejudicial to him, and he had no opportunity of rebutting. It was held that the hearing of the appeal offended against the rules of natural justice.

14.22D However, the withdrawal of a privilege, granted outside the rules is not disciplinary action. In *Hudson v GMB*, a federated trade union nominated the plaintiff to attend a regional conference of the Labour Party. It was then alleged that she was a member of 'Militant', an organisation proscribed by the Labour Party, and so her nomination was withdrawn. She claimed that this was disciplinary action in violation of the rules of the union, as she had not been allowed to state her case. Further, she claimed that her nomination was a privilege which could not be withdrawn without proceedings taken in accordance with the principles of natural justice. Her claim failed. The withdrawal of the nomination was not a disciplinary measure relating to an office within the union's rules. Nor was the nomination made in respect of any permanent position which would involve a financial advantage. The union had no rules concerning such delegates, and the nomination could therefore be withdrawn at will.

14.22E A member who has been wrongfully expelled may apply for a declaration that he is still a member, an injunction restraining the union and its officials from acting on the purported expulsion, and damages for wrongful expulsion. In *Bonsor v Musicians' Union*, the appellant was expelled by the branch secretary, when this power could only be exercised by the branch committee. In consequence, he could not get work, and was reduced to earning a living by scraping rust off Brighton Pier. It was held that as the expulsion was void, he could recover damages for wrongful expulsion.

14.22F In addition (as already indicated) whatever the rules may or may not state, a member of a trade union has a statutory right not to be unjustifiably disciplined (see para 13.8) or expelled from a trade union (see para 13.19) unless the discipline or expulsion is not prohibited by the statute, and may seek an appropriate remedy before an industrial tribunal.

Conduct of union affairs

14.23 Membership of a trade union confers certain rights and privileges on the members, and they are entitled to damages if these are not forthcoming. If the rules provide that members shall be entitled to legal advice, then a union which fails to provide that advice, or negligently provides incorrect advice, may be sued for the loss which flows from that breach. The tremendous increase in the statutory rights of employees is bound to throw an additional burden on trade union officials, who now need to be as familiar with those rights as management. Thus it is submitted that if a trade union fails to apply for a protective award in appropriate circumstances, or negligently delays the presentation of a claim to an industrial tribunal so that it becomes out of time, the aggrieved member will have a right of action against that union for damages. The union can meet certain obligations by placing the matter in the hands of a competent solicitor (*Cross v British Iron, Steel and Kindred Trades Association*), although no breach of contract arises if the members fails to show that his action had a reasonable prospect of success (*Buckley v NUGMW*).

14.23A In the conduct of union affairs, the officials can only act within the confines of the rules. Thus in *Weakley v AEUW* the president of the union exercised a casting vote on a motion when the committee was equally divided. An injunction was granted restraining the union from acting on the motion, for, on a true construction of the rules, the president was not entitled to exercise a casting vote. But the officials may have implied power to do certain things which are in the interests of the union. In *Hill v Archbold*, two union officials brought an action in respect of matters which arose out of their employment. The actions were dismissed, but the union sought to pay the legal costs on behalf of the officials, though there was no provision in the rules for such expenditure. It was held that the union had implied power to do so, for the matter was incidental to their work as officials of the union.

14.23B A trade union which pays out strike pay which is not authorised by the rules (*Taylor v NUM (Derbyshire Area)*) or imposes a levy for a purpose which is *ultra vires* (*Hopkins v National Union of Seamen*) can be restrained from so doing by an injunction. However, allegations of electoral irregularities can be pursued under the provisions of s. 54, (see para 14.39).

Copy of the rules (s. 27)

14.23C A trade union shall supply, at the request of any person, a copy of its rules, either free or on payment of a reasonable charge.

Executive committee (TULR(C)A s. 46)

14.24 Every member of the principal executive committee of a trade union (including those members who are members by virtue of holding an office) shall be elected by a ballot at least every five years. A person who holds his membership of the principal executive committee as a result of an election may continue as a member or official for such period as may be necessary (not exceeding six months) to give effect to an election result. In such a ballot, every member of the union shall be entitled to vote, except:

a. those members who as a class are excluded by the rules from voting;

b. members not in employment;
c. members in arrears; and
d. members who are students, trainees, apprentices or new members.

If the rules permit, it is possible to have voting restricted to special classes of membership, determined by reference to:
a. trade or occupation;
b. geographical area;
c. separate sections of the union; or
d. any combination of these.

Voting at an election must be made by the marking of a ballot paper by the person voting, and every person entitled to vote (a) must be allowed to do so without interference or constraint imposed by the union or any of its members, officials or employees, and (b) so far as is reasonably practicable, be able to do so without incurring any direct cost. So far as is reasonably practicable, voting papers must be sent to voters by post, containing or accompanied by a list of candidates, and the voter must be given a convenient opportunity to vote by post. So far as is reasonably practicable, voting shall be in secret, and the result shall be determined by the counting of the number of votes cast for each candidate (with or without the transferable vote) and votes shall be fairly and accurately counted.

14.25 The above provisions do not apply to trade unions which consist of representatives of constituent or affiliated organisations, merchant seamen who are ordinarily resident outside the United Kingdom, newly formed trade unions, or to members of the principal executive committee who are near retirement.

14.26 The president and general secretary (or persons who hold equivalent positions) shall be deemed to be members of the principal executive committee (and hence subject to the balloting provisions) as will be any other persons, notwithstanding anything in the rules of the union, if they are permitted to attend and speak at the meeting of that committee, other than for the purpose of providing the committee with factual information or technical or professional advice.

14.27 However, a person who is the president or general secretary of the union, and who is neither a voting member of the principal executive committee, nor an employee of the union, is not required to be elected in the above manner if he holds his office for a period of less than 13 months.

14.28 Elections for the members of the principal executive committee shall be by means of postal ballot, and no other method, except that there is no need to hold a ballot if the election is uncontested.

Election of candidates (TULR(C)A s. 47)

14.29 No member of a trade union shall be unreasonably excluded from standing as a candidate for election to the principal executive committee, and no candidate shall be required to be a member of a political party.

Election addresses (TULR(C)A s. 48)

14.30 Every candidate in an election for the principal executive committee must be provided with an opportunity of preparing an election address, in his own words, and submitting it to the union to be distributed to those who are entitled to vote. Such election addresses are to be sent out with the voting paper, and the candidates are not required to bear any expense for the production of these copies. The election address shall be sent out without any modification except at the request of or with the consent of the candidate, or where the modification is necessarily incidental to the method adopted for the production of the copy. The same method of production is to be used for the election addresses of all candidates. A trade union may determine that election addressees may not exceed a certain length (but must permit a minimum of 100 words), and may incorporate only such photographs or other matter as the union may determine. So far as is reasonably practicable, the union must ensure that the same facilities and restrictions with respect to the preparation, submission, length and modifications, and the incorporation of photographs or other matter not in words are provided or applied equally to each of the candidates.

14.31 No person other than the candidate himself shall be subject to any criminal or civil liability in respect of the publication of a candidate's election address made under s. 48.

Independent scrutineer (ss, 49, 75, 100A, 226B)

14.32 Before an election is held for positions in the principal executive committee, or a ballot is held on the approval of a political fund, or approving an instrument of amalgamation or transfer, or a ballot on the holding of industrial action, the trade union must appoint a qualified independent person as a scrutineer, who will carry out his functions without interference. A person will be eligible for such appointment if he satisfies the conditions laid down in the Trade Union Ballots and Elections (Independent Scrutineers Qualifications) Order 1988.

14.33 However, a scrutineer need not be appointed if there is a ballot on the holding of industrial action, and the number of members entitled to vote does not exceed 50 (s. 226C).

14.34 The union will supply the scrutineer with a copy of the register of members, which he will inspect as appropriate, and in particular if requested to do so by a member or candidate who suspects that it was not accurate or up to date. The name of the independent scrutineer must be sent to every member of the union by notice, or communicated to members in the same manner as when matters of general interest are brought to their attention. His name must also appear on any ballot paper.

14.35 The storage, distribution and counting of ballot papers must be undertaken by an independent person, who may be the scrutineer or other person whose competence and independence is not in doubt (s. 51A). The scrutineer must supervise the production and distribution of all voting papers, which are to be returned to him by those voting. He will retain them for one year after the announcement of the result of the election or ballot or, if the result is challenged before the Certification Officer or a court, until disposal is authorised.

14.36 As soon as is reasonably practicable after the last date for the return of the voting papers, the scrutineer shall make a report to the union, stating:

a. the number of voting papers distributed;
b. the number of voting papers returned to him;
c. the number of valid votes cast in the election for each candidate, or, in a ballot, for each proposition;
d. the number of invalid or spoiled votes returned; and

e. the name of the person (if any) appointed as an independent person to count the votes.

14.37 The report will also state if he is satisfied that there was no contravention of any requirement imposed by law, that the arrangements for the ballot or election (including any security arrangements) minimised the risk of any unfairness or malpractice, and that he was able to carry out his functions without interference or anyone calling his independence into question. He will also state if he has inspected the register of members, and whether any such inspection has revealed any matter which should be brought to the attention of the union in order to ensure that it is accurate and up to date (s. 52).

14.38 Within three months of receiving the scrutineer's report on an election (s. 52(4)), on a political fund resolution (s. 78(4)), or on an amalgamation or transfer resolution (s. 100E(6)), the trade union shall send a copy to every member to whom it is reasonably practicable to send such a copy, or take all such steps for notifying the contents of the report to members of the union as it is the practice for the union to take when matters of general interest need to be brought to the members' attention. So far as ballots on industrial action are concerned, any person entitled to vote in the ballot, and the employer of any such person, is entitled to be supplied with a copy of the scrutineer's report on request. This may be supplied free of charge or on the payment of a reasonable fee.

Remedies (s. 54)

14.39 Any member may apply to the High Court (or Court of Session) or the Certification Officer for a declaration that the trade union has failed to comply with any requirement of the Act relating to secret ballots for trade union elections or relating to election addresses or to scrutineers. The court may make an enforcement order specifying the action which the trade union shall take in consequence of its failure to comply with the Act. The Certification Officer has no such powers, but may specify the steps to be taken by the union to remedy the declared failure. The observations of the Certification Officer may be brought to the attention of the court in any subsequent proceedings relating to the same matter. The application must be made within one year from the last day on which the votes were cast in the ballot.

Public funds for ballots (TULR(C)A s. 115)

14.40 The Secretary of State is empowered to make regulations for a scheme whereby the Certification Officer may make payment towards the expenditure incurred by an independent trade union in respect of certain ballots held by them. The statutory purposes for which the ballots may be held are:

a. obtaining a decision or ascertaining the views of members as to the calling or ending of a strike or other industrial action;
b. carrying out an election provided for by the rules of a trade union, or for the election of the principal executive committee, president, chairman, secretary or treasurer, or to any position which the person elected will hold as an employee of the union;
c. electing a worker who is a member of a trade union to be a representative of other members also employed by his employer;
d. amending the rules of the union (*see R v Certification Officer, ex p Royal College of Nursing*);
e. voting on a decision to amalgamate with another union;
f. obtaining a decision of members as to the acceptance or rejection of a proposal by an employer relating to the contractual terms and conditions;
g. obtaining a decision on the creation or continuation of the political fund.

Ballots must be held in secret, confined to members of the union, and comply with the requirements of TULR(C)A. The circumstances in which, and the conditions subject to which, payments can be made are laid down in the Funds for Trade Union Ballots Regulations 1984-90 (see *R v Certification Officer, ex p EPEA*).

14.41 However, financial assistance towards expenditure on ballots and elections will cease to have effect as from April 1996. In the meantime, funding available for such ballots is to be reduced by 25% each year over the next four years (Funds for Trade Union Ballots Regulations (Revocation) Regulations 1993).

Ballots on employer's premises (TULR(C)A s. 116)

14.41A An independent trade union is entitled to use an employer's premises for the purpose of holding ballots, but in practice this provision is otiose, as most ballots are now required to be postal. Further, this provision will cease to have effect after 1 April 1996.

Accounts, records, etc (TULR(C)A s. 28)

14.42 Every trade union and employers' association shall keep proper records, and establish a satisfactory system of control over its cash holdings, receipts and remittances. An annual return must be sent to the Certification Officer, with accounts duly audited. There are provisions in ss. 32-42 detailing the matters which must be contained in the annual return including the salaries paid to, and the benefits provided for, the president, general secretary and members of the executive committee, together with the qualifications, appointment, functions, and removal of auditors, and for the control over members' superannuation schemes. Any person who refuses or wilfully neglects to perform a duty imposed by these provisions, or who alters a document required for those purposes, shall be guilty of an offence, punishable by a fine of up to level 3 and 5 on the standard scale respectively.

14.43 An annual statement must be sent to all members of the union (or otherwise communicated to them) giving details of the union's income and expenditure, salaries paid to the president, general secretary and executive members, and the income and expenditure of the political fund. The statement will also include prescribed information on the remedies to members who are concerned about any irregularities in the conduct of the union's affairs (s. 32A).

Right to inspect accounts (ss. 29-31)

14.44 A trade union shall keep its accounting records available for inspection for six years from 1st January following the end of the period to which those records relate.

14.45 Any member of a trade union may request to be permitted access to those records in respect of any period when he was a member. Such access shall be permitted within 28 days of the request and, unless otherwise agreed, at a reasonable hour and at the place where the records are normally kept. The member is entitled to take an accountant with him, and to take, or be supplied with, such copies or extracts from those records as he may require. The trade union may make a charge in respect of reasonable administrative expenses incurred (s. 30).

14.46 If the trade union fails to comply with the member's request for access to the accounting records, the member may apply to the court, which may make such order as is considered appropriate for ensuring that that person:

a. is allowed to inspect the records;
b. is allowed to be accompanied by an accountant; and
c. is allowed to take, or is supplied with, such copies of or extracts from those records as he may require (s. 31).

14.47 The Certification Officer has the power to require the production of documents, take copies etc and appoint an inspector to investigate the financial affairs of the union, if he suspects that the financial affairs of the union have been conducted in a fraudulent manner, or a person managing its affairs has been guilty of fraud, or the union has failed to comply with a provision of the Act or its own rules with relation to the conduct of its financial affairs (TULR(C)A s. 37B). The inspector has wide powers of investigation, and will report back to the Certification Officer. It is an offence for a person to fail to produce a document in his possession, or to destroy or alter it, or make false statements etc, punishable by a fine or, in certain circumstances, a term of six months' imprisonment (ss. 45-45A). A person who has been convicted may not hold office as a president, general secretary or executive member for a period of five or ten years, depending on the offence (s. 45B).

Indemnifying unlawful conduct (s. 15)

14.48 It is unlawful for any property of a trade union to be applied towards the payment for any individual, or towards the provision of anything for indemnifying an individual, in respect of any penalty which has been imposed on him for a relevant offence, or for contempt of court. A 'relevant offence' is any offence other than one which has been designated as an offence by the Secretary of State in relation to which s. 15 does not apply.

14.49 If property has been so applied in contravention of this section, the equal amount of any payment is recoverable from the individual concerned by the trade union, and in the case of property, the individual shall be liable to account for its value. If the trade union unreasonably fails to make a claim against the individual, any member may apply to the court for authorisation to bring or continue proceedings on the union's behalf and at the union's expense.

Remedies against trustees (s. 16)

14.50 If a member of a trade union considers that the trustees of the union's property are carrying out their functions so as to permit an unlawful application of the union's property, or are complying with an unlawful direction which has been given to them under the union's rules, he may apply to the court for an order. If the court is satisfied that the application is well-founded, it may make such orders as it deems appropriate, including:

a. requiring the trustees of the union to take all such steps as may be specified for the purpose of protecting or recovering the union's property;
b. appointing a receiver (or judicial factor) of/on the union's property;
c. the removal of one or more trustees.

14.51 Should the trustees act in contravention of the court's order, the court may remove all the trustees except those who can satisfy the court that there is good reason to allow them to remain a trustee.

Political fund and political objects (TULR(C)A ss. 71-74)

14.52 The Act lays down the necessary requirements before a trade union can have a political fund and pursue political objects. A resolution to establish a political fund must be passed at least every ten years by a ballot of all the union's members, and if approved, a separate political fund may be created. The ballot must be by the use of a voting paper, and every person entitled to vote must be allowed to do so without interference from or constraint imposed by the trade union or any of its members, officials or employees. The member must be able to vote without incurring any direct cost.

14.53 So far as is reasonably practicable, every person who is entitled to vote on a ballot concerning the establishment of a political fund must have the voting papers sent to him at his home or postal address, and be given a convenient opportunity to vote by post. The voting must be in secret, and the votes fairly and accurately counted (s. 77).

14.54 If the political fund is established, no property of the trade union shall be added to that fund other than sums representing contributions made to the fund by the members or any other person and property accruing to the fund in the course of administering its assets. No liability of the political fund shall be met out of any other fund of the trade union. If there is no resolution in force establishing the political fund, no property shall be added to an existing fund (other than that which accrues in the course of administering the fund) and no union rule shall require any member to contribute towards the fund. The union may transfer the whole or part of the assets of an existing fund to such other fund of the trade union as it thinks fit. Where a resolution is passed rescinding an existing fund, the trade union may use the fund for a period of six months, but not so as to put the fund in deficit.

14.55 If a resolution to have a political fund ceases to have effect, the union shall take such steps to ensure that the collection of contributions to the fund is discontinued as soon as is reasonably practicable, and any contribution collected after the resolution ceases to have effect may be paid to any other fund of the trade union. If the trade union continues to collect contributions these are refundable at the members' request.

14.56 Any member of a trade union who wishes to contract out of a political fund must be free to do so, and if he does, he shall not in consequence be excluded from any benefit or disqualified from holding any office other than a position connected with the management of the political fund. Contributing towards the fund must not be a condition of membership.

14.57 The TUC has issued a 'Statement of Guidance' on political funds. It advises trade unions to draw up 'information sheets' about their political funds, and inform members why it has a fund, make clear members' legal rights to opt out, state the current amount of the levy, and provide information on how members may contract out.

14.58 The political fund may be used for the following purposes:

a. any contribution to the funds of, or the payment of any expense incurred by, a political party;
b. the provision of any services or property for the use by or on behalf of a political party;
c. the registration of electors, the candidature of any person, the selection of any candidate, or the holding of a ballot by the union in connection with any election to a political office;
d. the maintenance of any holder of a political office;
e. the holding of any conference or meetings by or on behalf of a political party, or any other meetings the main purpose of which is the transaction of business in connection with a political party;
f. the production, publication or distribution of any literature, document, film, sound recording or advertisement the main purpose of which is to persuade people to vote for a political party or candidate or not to vote for it or him.

Complaints over political fund ballots (TULR(C)A ss. 79-81)

14.59 A member of a trade union who complains that a ballot on the political fund was taken otherwise than in accordance with the rules approved by the Certification Officer, or that there has been a failure to comply with those rules, may apply to the Certification Officer or to the court for a declaration. The application must be made within one year from the date when the result of the ballot was announced.

14.60 The court may make an enforcement order, specifying the action which the trade union shall take in consequence of its failure to comply with the Act. The Certification Officer has no such power, but may specify the steps to be taken by the trade union, and his observations are admissible before the court in any subsequent proceedings arising from the same matter.

Other breaches of rules

14.61 An allegation that a trade union has broken a rule as to the use to which the political fund may be put may be the subject of an investigation by the Certification Officer. In *Richards v NUM* a complaint was made that the union had spent money from the general fund sending members on a lobby of Parliament organised by the Labour Party, and had also paid money to a trade union consortium which was developing Labour Party headquarters. It was held by the Certification Officer that such expenditure was in furtherance of political objects, and he ordered that the money should come from the political funds of the union, not the general funds. Similarly, a complaint relating to a breach of the rules in taking a vote on a resolution to approve an instrument of transfer or amalg–amation made under s. 103 may be made to the Certification Officer. In either case, appeals on a question of law will lie to the Employment Appeal Tribunal.

Amalgamation and transfers (ss. 97-105)

14.62 Two or more trade unions may decide to amalgamate into one union, or a union may wish to transfer its engagements to another union. In both cases, the instrument of amalgamation or transfer must first be submitted to the Certification Officer for approval, and then voted upon by the members of the amalgamating unions or transferor union, as the case may be. The union must give the members a notice in writing, which either sets out the instrument of amalgamation or transfer, or gives an account of it so as to enable the member to form a reasonable judgment of its main effects. Section 100 of the Act provides that the instrument may be approved by a simple majority of votes recorded, unless the rules of the union specifically exclude this provision, in which case some other specified proportion of members will be required to approve.

14.63 An independent scrutineer must be appointed, who will supervise the production and distribution of the voting papers, inspect the register of members, and generally report to the union after the ballot has been concluded. Voting in the ballot shall be accorded equally to all members of the union, the ballot papers will be numbered consecutively, and sent to members' homes or postal address. The notice sent to members shall not contain any statement making a recommendation or expressing an opinion about the proposed transfer or amalgamation. A copy of the scrutineer's report must be sent to every member or otherwise suitably published.

CHAPTER 15

Law relating to industrial relations

15.1 In this Chapter we will consider the collective aspect of employment law, with reference to the rights and duties of trade unions and employers. No subject has caused greater political controversy in recent years than a consideration of the extent to which the law should play a role in the control of trade unions and industrial relations, and the precise nature of that law. It is not possible to understand the present legal position without some reference to the previous law on this topic, though it is intended to keep such excursus to a minimum. In particular it will be necessary to examine certain common law rules which, though they may now be of historical importance, have shaped the legislative provisions.

Disclosure of information (TULR(C)A s. 181)

15.2 For the purpose of all stages of collective bargaining it shall be the duty of the employer, on request, to disclose to representatives of a recognised independent trade union all such information relating to his undertaking as is in his possession, and is information without which the representatives would to a material extent be impeded in carrying on such bargaining, and is information which it would be in accordance with good industrial relations practice that he should disclose. In one of its earliest findings, the CAC held that the test of 'materially impeded' meant that the information should be both relevant and important (*Institute of Journalists v Daily Telegraph*). The employer need only make the disclosure to unions which are recognised by him. In determining what is good industrial relations practice, regard will be had to any Code of Practice issued by ACAS. If the trade union representatives so request the employer will disclose or confirm the information in writing, but he need not disclose:

a. information the disclosure of which would be contrary to the national interest;
b. any information which he could not disclose without breaking the law;
c. information which he received in confidence;
d. information relating to an individual, unless he has consented to the disclosure;
e. information the disclosure of which would cause substantial injury to the employer's business for reasons other than its effect on collective bargaining;
f. information obtained by the employer for the purpose of bringing or defending any legal proceedings.

15.3 The employer is not bound to produce, or allow the inspection of, any document, or to compile information where this would involve an amount of work or expenditure out of all reasonable proportion to its value in the conduct of collective bargaining.

15.4 If an independent trade union wishes to make a complaint that an employer has failed to disclose information which he is required to produce, it may report the matter to the Central Arbitration Committee. If that body thinks that the complaint can be settled by conciliation it will refer the matter to ACAS, which will try to promote a settlement. If this does not prove possible, or if the complaint is not so referred, the Committee will hear and determine the complaint. If it finds the complaint is wholly or partly well-founded, it will issue a declaration, stating:

a. the information in respect of which the complaint is well-founded;
b. the date on which the employer refused or failed to disclose the information; and
c. a period (being more than one week from the date of the declaration) within which the employer ought to disclose the information. If, at the end of that period, the employer still fails to disclose, a further complaint may be made by the trade union.

15.5 The complaint may be accompanied by a claim relating to the terms and conditions of the employees, and if the employer still persists in his refusal, the Committee may make an award that in respect of the employees of any description specified in the claim, the employer shall observe the terms and conditions demanded, or other terms and conditions which the Committee considers to be appropriate. These will form part of the contracts of employment of those employees from a date specified in the award, until varied or superseded by a further award or a subsequent collective agreement, or an express or implied agreement made between the employer and the employees which is an improvement on the award. As a general rule, CAC would consider the likely loss which flows from the failure to give the union the relevant information, and make an award accordingly.

Consultations on redundancies (TULR(C)A ss. 188-192)

15.6 If an employer recognises an independent trade union, he must, at the earliest opportunity, consult with representatives of that union about any proposal to dismiss as being redundant any employee who is covered by that recognition agreement. In particular, if the employer proposes to dismiss as being redundant more than 100 employees at one establishment within a period of 90 days or less, then he must consult with those union representatives at least 90 days before the first dismissals take effect. If he proposes to make ten or more employees redundant at one establishment within 30 days or less, he must enter into consultation at least 30 days before the first of those dismissals takes effect. Consultations must take place even though the employees concerned are employed for less than 16 hours per week, but not if they have contracts for less than 12 weeks (*NATFHE v Manchester City Council*).

When is a union recognised?

15.7 There is no statutory definition of what constitutes recognition, and the industrial tribunals appear to operate under the general rule that it is for the trade union to show that there is some formal agreement (not necessarily in writing) that it is recognised for collective bargaining purposes (*T&GWU v Dyer*). The mere fact that there are employees who are trade union members, and that one of them negotiates, but without specific trade union authority, will not constitute recognition (*AUEW v*

Sefton Engineering). Negotiations which may lead to recognition do not themselves constitute recognition (*T&GWU v Stanhope Engineering*). Nor can recognition be inferred if a full-time union official represents an individual in a disciplinary proceeding, for this is not recognition for the purpose of collective bargaining (*T&GWU v Courtenham Products*). The fact that an employer is a member of an association which negotiates with a trade union does not mean that the individual employer recognises the union (*NUGSAT v Albury Bros*). Nor does recognition by a former employer by itself constitute recognition by a successor (*UCATT v Burrage*). In *NUTGW v Charles Ingram & Co Ltd* five propositions were established: (1) recognition is a mixed question of law and fact; (2) recognition requires mutuality; (3) there must be an express or implied agreement for recognition; (4) if the agreement was implied, there must be clear and unequivocal acts or conduct, usually over a period of time; (5) there may be partial recognition, for some, but not all purposes. Recognition for representation purposes only is not the same thing as recognition for negotiating purposes (*USDAW v Sketchley Ltd*).

What is an 'establishment'?

15.8 The term 'establishment' is not defined in the Act, and has thus been the subject of interpretation by the tribunals. In *Clarks of Hove Ltd v Bakers Union* it was held that separate premises can amount to one establishment, if there is no separate accounting, management or trading. In *Barratt Developments Ltd v UCATT* the company, which had its headquarters in Bradford, operated 14 building sites in Lancashire. On each site there was a temporary shed, with a telephone link to the headquarters. It was decided to reduce the labour force, and 24 employees were made redundant, being selected from eight different sites. It was held that all 14 sites were part of one establishment, and as there had been a failure to consult with the trade union, a protective award would be made.

The consultation provisions

15.9 An employer is 'proposing to dismiss' employees as redundant (thus triggering the consultation provisions of the Act) when, 'following a diagnosis of the problem, specific proposals are formulated, with redundancies as one of the available options' (*Hough v Leyland DAF Ltd*).

15.10 The actual notice of dismissals can be issued during the consultation period, provided that the dismissals do not take effect until after the consultation period has elapsed. But if an employer issues dismissal notices the day after consultations begin, it may be thought that he does not intend meaningful consultations to take place (*NUT v Avon County Council*). Similarly, if the employer does not give the trade union sufficient time to consider the proposals before they are implemented, meaningful consultation is being denied (*T&GWU v Ledbury Preserves (1928) Ltd*).

15.11 In such consultations, the employer must disclose:

a. the reasons for his proposals;
b. the numbers and descriptions of employees whom it is proposed to dismiss as being redundant;
c. the total number of employees of that description employed by the employer at that establishment;
d. the proposed method of selecting the employees who are to be dismissed;
e. the proposed method of carrying out the dismissals, with due regard to agreed procedure, including the period over which dismissals are to take effect; and
f. the proposed method for calculating any redundancy payments to be made, other than statutory redundancy pay (s. 188(4)).

15.12 The consultations shall be about ways of avoiding the dismissals, reducing the numbers to be dismissed, and mitigating the consequences of the dismissals, and shall be undertaken by the employer with a view to reaching agreement with the union representatives (TULR(C)A s. 188(6)). Consultations, therefore, must be meaningful and genuine.

15.13 Having provided the above information, the employer must consider any representations made by that trade union, and reply to them. If he rejects any of those representations, he must state his reasons. It must be stressed that the employer's duty is to consult with the union. He does not have to reach any agreement, and the final decision is his. In *Perez v Mercury Display Ltd* the employer consulted with a trade union about a redundancy. The employer wanted selection to take place on the basis of LIFO, but the union wanted volunteers to be selected. The employer gave to the union his reasons for rejecting the representations, and dismissed the employees on the basis of LIFO. It was held that the employer had complied with his statutory obligations.

15.14 If there are special circumstances which render it not reasonably practicable for the employer to comply with any of the above provisions relating to consultation or considering representations, he shall take all such steps as are reasonably practicable in the circumstances. Special circumstances may exist if a company becomes insolvent but insolvency *per se* is not a special circumstance, for reasonable and prudent management may well foresee such a possibility (*Clarks of Hove Ltd v Bakers' Union*). The sudden appointment of a receiver would be a special circumstance (*FTATU v Lawrence Cabinet*). The loss of a key order (*AUEW v Cooper Plastics*) and the unexpected failure to obtain a renewal of an important contract (*NUPE v General Cleaning Contractors*) have also come within this defence. But the fact that the employer genuinely believes that he has not recognised a trade union for the purpose of collective bargaining does not constitute a special circumstance which would render it not reasonably practicable to comply with the obligation to consult (*Joshua Wilson & Bros Ltd v USDAW*). Special circumstances may also be said to exist if delicate negotiations are taking place which may be prejudiced if consultations are carried on with the union (*APAC v Kirvin Ltd*). A circumstance is likely to be special if it is sudden, as opposed to being gradual or foreseeable with reasonable prudence (*USDAW v Leancut Bacon Ltd*).

15.15 The dismissal of employees in order to make the sale of a business more attractive to buyers, or the absence of orders, are not special circumstances within the meaning of the Act (*GMB v Rankin and Harrison*). A failure on the part of a person who controls the employer (e.g. a multi-national corporation in control of a subsidiary) to provide information to the employer also does not constitute a special circumstance (s. 193(7)).

15.16 An employer does not fail to consult if he deals only with an accredited shop steward, for there is no requirement that the information should be conveyed to a full-time union official (*GMWU v Wailes Dove Bitumastic*).

Protective award

15.17 If an employer fails to consult as above, a trade union may present a complaint to an industrial tribunal. If the employer wishes to plead that it was not reasonably practicable for him to comply with these provisions, he must show that this was so, and that he took all reasonably practicable steps in the circumstances. Otherwise, if the tribunal finds the complaint to be well-founded, it will make a declaration to that effect, and may also make a protective award, which is remuneration for a protected period for those employees who were dismissed (or whose dismissal was being proposed) and in respect of whom the employer has failed to comply with the legal requirements. The protected period is such time as the tribunal considers to be just and equitable, having regard to the seriousness of the employer's default, but:

a. in the case where it was proposed to make 100 or more employees redundant within 90 days, the protected period shall not exceed 90 days;
b. in the case where it was proposed to make ten or more employees redundant within 30 days, the protected period is 30 days;
c. in any other case (e.g. if less than ten employees are being made redundant) the protected period is 28 days.

15.18 If a protective award is made, every employee to whom it relates shall be entitled to one week's pay for each week of the protected period, with proportionate reductions in respect of a period which is less than one week. If the employer has already made any payment to the employee in respect of any period falling within the protected period, or by way of damages for breach of contract, this will no longer go towards reducing the employer's liability to pay remuneration under the protective award, and conversely, any payment made under a protective award will not go towards reducing any liability to pay any sum due in respect of a breach of contract by the employer for that period.

15.19 If an industrial tribunal finds that the employer is in default of the consultation provisions, then the making of a declaration to that effect is mandatory, but the amount of the protective award is discretionary (*UCATT v Rooke & Sons Ltd*), and it should not be such as to register the tribunal's disapproval of the employer's conduct. Rather it should reflect the loss suffered by the employees. To use the protective award as a method of imposing a penalty for bad behaviour is inconsistent with modern legislation (*Talke Fashions Ltd v ASTWKT*). Subject to that, the award is a matter for the discretion of the industrial tribunal (*Sovereign Distribution Services Ltd v T&GWU*).

15.20 As a result of consultations with the appropriate trade union, there may well be an agreement that employees will leave the firm before the appropriate period of 90 or 30 days has expired. Whether the agreement has been reached with the trade union or employees on an individual basis, it is probably void by virtue of s. 288 of TULR(C)A which prevents the contracting out of the various statutory rights. It is clear therefore that the dismissals will take effect before the end of the consultations periods, and there will be a breach of the Act. However, on a complaint that the employer has failed to consult within the statutory period, the industrial tribunal will make the mandatory declaration, but not a protective award (*ASTMS v Hawker Siddeley Aviation*).

15.21 If, during the protected period, the employee is fairly dismissed for some reason other than redundancy, or if he unreasonably resigns, then his entitlement to the protective award shall cease from the time his contract is terminated. If the employer makes an offer to renew the contract, or to re-engage under a new contract, so that the renewal or re-engagement would take effect before or during the protected period, or the offer constitutes an offer of suitable employment, and the employee unreasonably refuses that offer, then he shall not be entitled to any payment under the protective award in respect of any period during which but for the refusal he would have been employed.

15.22 Only an independent trade union which is recognised by the employer in respect of the affected employees may apply for a protective award. Once this has been granted, then any individual employee may present a complaint to a tribunal that the employer has failed, in whole or in part, to pay him the remuneration under that award. If the complaint is well-founded, the tribunal shall order the employer to make that payment.

15.23 The fact that the employer has failed to consult in accordance with the above provisions is irrelevant to the issue as to whether a particular employee's redundancy is fair or unfair (*Forman Construction v Kelly*).

15.24 It should be noted that, for the purpose of the consultations provisions only, the definition of redundancy is not the same as the one laid down in s. 81 of EPCA. Under TULR(C)A s. 195, when considering the consultation provisions, references to dismissals for reason of redundancy are references to a dismissal not related to the individual concerned (or for a number of reasons not so related). This wider definition throws out some interesting possibilities. For example, suppose an employer decides to give lawful notice to all his employees, coupled with an offer to re-engage them all on changed terms of employment. Since this 'dismissal' is not related to an individual, it is submitted that period consultations with recognised trade unions are required under s. 195 of TULR(C)A.

Consultations on transfers

15.25 On the transfer of an undertaking, it is clear that employees of the transferor or transferee may be affected in some way. The Transfer of Undertakings (Protection of Employment) Regulations provided that the employer (i.e. transferor or transferee, as the case may be) shall inform the representatives of any recognised trade union of:

a. the fact that the relevant transfer is to take place, when (approximately) it will take place, and the reasons for the transfer;
b. the legal, economic and social implications of the transfer for the affected employees;
c. the measures (if any) which the employer envisages he will take in relation to the affected employees; and
d. the measures which the transferor envisages the transferee will take (if any) in relation to the affected employees. For this purpose, the transferee shall give to the transferor such information as will enable the transferor to perform this duty.

15.26 This information shall be given to the recognised independent trade union long enough before the relevant transfer to enable consultations to take place. If either employer envisages that he will be taking measures in respect of such employees who are represented by a recognised independent trade union, he shall enter into consultations with that union with a view to seeking their agreement to the measures to be taken, consider any representations made and reply to them, and if he rejects any of those representations, he shall state his reasons. However, it it is not reasonably practicable for him to consult as stated, he shall take all such steps as are reasonably practicable in the circumstances.

15.27 If an employer fails to inform or consult as required, the union may present a complaint to an industrial tribunal. If the employer intends to rely on the defence that it was not reasonably practicable for him to perform the duty, he will need to show that there were special circumstances which rendered it not reasonably practicable to do so, and that he took all steps which were reasonably practicable. If the transferor intends to rely on the defence that the transferee failed to give him the required information within the requisite time, he must give notice of that fact to the transferee, thus making him a party to the proceedings.

15.28 If the complaint is upheld, the industrial tribunal shall make a declaration to that effect, and may award 'appropriate compensation', which in practice means not more than four weeks' pay to the affected employees. If at the same time, there is a complaint that the employer has failed to comply with s. 188 of TULR(C)A (see para 15.6), any amount payable under these Regulations will no longer go towards reducing any protective award made under that Act (see Trade Union Reform and Employment Rights Act 1993 s. 29(5)).

Legal liabilities and legal proceedings

15.29 At common law it is impossible for a trade union to engage in any effective industrial relations activity without falling foul of some well-established legal rule. An understanding of those liabilities is necessary in order to understand and appreciate the statutory protections which have been developed over the years.

A. Inducing or procuring a breach of contract

15.30 It is a tort (civil wrong) for a person to induce another to break a contract to which the other is a party, or to procure a breach of that contract. In *Lumley v Gye*, an opera singer contracted to sing at a theatre owned by the plaintiff. The defendant induced her to break that contract and sing for him instead.

Clearly, the singer was liable for her own breach of contract, but it was held that the plaintiff could successfully sue the defendant for inducing her to break the contract. In terms of industrial relations, the tort is peculiarly appropriate (see, for example, the recent County Court decision in *Falconer v ASLEF and NUR*). An employer has a contract (of employment) with an employee. If a trade union official calls upon that employee to strike, the employee is breaking the contract (for which he can be dismissed - see Chapter 8) but the union official (and possibly the union also) could be held liable for inducing a breach of that contract. Equally, if a trade union was to call for a secondary boycott, it may be furthering strike action, but it is also inducing (or procuring) a breach of a commercial contract. In *Torquay Hotel Co v Cousins*, a trade union was in dispute with an hotel. A union official informed a company which was supplying oil to the hotel of the existence of the dispute, and instructed its members not to deliver oil supplies. It was held that an injunction would lie restraining the union officials from causing any fuel supplier to breach its contract to supply oil.

15.31 If a shop steward has express or implied authority to act on behalf of a trade union, then the union may be responsible for his actions unless it can shelter behind some legal protection (*Heatons Transport v T&GWU*). But a union cannot be responsible for activities of unofficial committees of shop stewards, particularly when they are pursuing policies which are contrary to those of the union, and where union officials are trying to solve problems through machinery for negotiation and conciliation, while the shop stewards are taking militant industrial action (*General Aviation Services Ltd v T&GWU*). However, in such a situation, the union must repudiate the activities in question (see para 15.80) if it wishes to retain its immunities.

B. Conspiracy

15.32 A conspiracy is a combination of two or more persons to do an unlawful act, or a lawful act by unlawful means. Such acts could lead to a prosecution for criminal conspiracy (i.e. where the conspirators combine in order to pursue criminal objects) or an action for civil conspiracy where the alleged act constitutes a tort. Since trade unions are by necessity combinations, it is not surprising that they are particularly vulnerable to this form of legal constraint. For example, in *Quinn v Leathem*, Leathem was a butcher who employed non-union labour. The union called upon him to dismiss them, but he refused to do so. Instead, he offered to pay the men's arrears of subscriptions if they were admitted into the union. This offer was rejected by the union officials, who wanted to teach the non-unionists a lesson 'and make them walk the streets for twelve months'. Munce supplied meat to Leathem, and the union threatened to call a strike of Munce's men unless supplies of meat to Leathem were cut off, and Munce complied with this request. It was held that the union officials had conspired together to cause harm to Leathem without lawful jurisdiction. Their legitimate trade union objectives could have been achieved by accepting Leathem's offer and admitting the men to membership, but in fact their subsequent conduct had been motivated by vindictiveness.

15.33 But the mere fact that an act causes harm does not, by itself, amount to a conspiracy. Clearly, a strike causes harm to an employer, but if the object is a legitimate one, e.g. obtaining higher wages, no actionable conspiracy exists (*Crofter Hand Woven Harris Tweed Co v Veitch*). In *Scala Ballroom (Wolverhampton) Ltd v Ratcliffe,* the plaintiffs operated a colour bar at their dance hall. Officials of the Musicians' Union placed a boycott on the premises in protest. It was held that this was not a conspiracy to injure, for the combination was a legitimate furtherance of the union's interests.

C. Intimidation

15.34 This 'obscure and unfamiliar' tort was resurrected from oblivion in the controversial case of *Rookes v Barnard*, where a shop steward threatened to call a strike at Heathrow Airport unless the plaintiff, a non-unionist, was dismissed. This 'threat' constituted a breach of contract, which was held to be an unlawful act (i.e. in the same way that a threat to commit an act of violence would be unlawful) and the defendants were held liable for intimidation.

D. Other tort liabilities

15.35 There are a number of other possible headings of legal liabilities which trade unions may run up against, including such headings as unlawful interference with trade business or employment, interference with future contracts, and so forth. Such torts are to be found in judicial hints rather than actual-ity, and the fear was of their emergence rather than their existence. With the increased statutory control over the conduct of trade unions, it is unlikely that these obscure torts will be revived.

15.36 But if there are unlawful acts committed by a trade union, an injured party may apply for an injunction to restrain the commission of such acts, and sue for damages in respect of any loss suffered, including, if necessary, exemplary damages (*Messenger Newspapers Group Ltd v NGA*). A trade union can only defend itself if it can rely on the statutory protections.

Legal protections

15.37 It is clear from the above that if trade unions are to carry out their legitimate functions in industrial relations, they require protection from these headings of common law liability, and arguably against judicial ingenuity in developing new case law which would restrict their activities. This has been the object of statute law since 1906; it was a process which was carried on by the Industrial Relations Act 1971, and has been continued in TULR(C)A. But the statutory immunities are not a licence to do anything; they only provide a protective cover for trade unions when legitimate objectives are being pursued. These objectives are limited to acts done in furtherance or contemplation of a trade dispute, and it is to the wide meaning of this phrase that we must now turn.

A. 'Trade dispute' (TULR(C)A s. 244)

15.38 A trade dispute means a dispute between workers and their employers which relates wholly or mainly to one or more of the following:

a. terms and conditions of employment, or the physical conditions in which any workers are required to work;
b. the engagement or non-engagement or termination or suspension of employment or the duties of employment, of one or more workers;
c. the allocation of work or the duties of employment between workers or groups of workers;
d. matters of discipline;
e. membership or non-membership of a trade union on the part of a worker;

f. facilities for officials of trade unions;
g. machinery for negotiations or consultation, and other matters relating to the foregoing (i.e. a-f above), including recognition by employers or employers' associations of the right of a trade union to represent workers in any such negotiations or consultations or in the carrying out of such procedures.

15.39 The important change made by the Employment Act 1982 is that the dispute must relate 'wholly or mainly' to the above matters. In *Mercury Communications Ltd v Scott-Garner*, the plaintiffs were granted a licence by the Government to run a telecommunications system (the 'liberalisation' agreement), which effectively broke the Post Office monopoly. The Government also proposed to privatise British Telecommunications. The Post Office Engineering Union opposed both the liberalisation and privatisation of the work, and gave instructions to its members not to do work which would enable the plaintiffs to connect to the British Telecommunications network. The plaintiffs applied for an injunction to restrain the union from inducing a breach of contractual relations between themselves and British Telecommunications. The Court of Appeal granted the injunction. It was unlikely that the union would be able to establish at the trial that there was a trade dispute within the statutory definition. There was little evidence to support the union's contention that there was a dispute about the risk of loss of jobs. The reality was that the union was waging a campaign against the political decisions to liberalise and privatise the industry.

15.40 In addition, there are three other circumstances to consider. First, a trade dispute will exist between a Minister of the Crown and a group of workers notwithstanding that the Minister is not the employer of those workers, if the dispute relates to matters which have been referred for consideration to a joint body on which that Minister is bound by statute to be represented, and which cannot be settled without the Minister exercising a power.

15.41 For example, in *Wandsworth London Borough Council v National Association of School Masters and Union of Women Teachers*, the defendants wished to ballot their members to protest against the excessive workload caused by the assessment requirements of the national curriculum, which had been imposed by the Government. A local authority sought an injunction against the unions, arguing that the dispute was not about terms and conditions of employment, but about the very idea of the national assessment, and this was a matter which could only be resolved by the Secretary of State exercising a power conferred by statute. It was held that the dispute was wholly or mainly about the workload imposed on teachers and, therefore, since it was about the terms and conditions of employment, the statutory protection (see below) applied, and the application for an injunction was refused.

15.42 Second, there is a trade dispute even though it relates to matters occurring outside the United Kingdom as long as the persons who are taking action are likely to be affected in respect of one or more of the matters mentioned above. The third situation is more curious. In *Cory Lighterage v T&GWU*, a lighterman named Shute decided to leave the union, and the employers were informed that none of the crew would sail if he did not pay his union dues. The employers had no quarrel with the union, for they accepted the principle of 100% unionisation, but they could not dismiss Shute under the Dock Workers Employment Scheme, so they sent him home on full pay. It was held that as there was no dispute between the employers and the union, the statutory protections did not apply. The employers did not resist the demands of the union, but rather acceded to them by taking Shute off the lighter. In line with the policy of giving the widest possible protection to trade unions in all actual and potential conflict situations, TULR(C)A s. 244(4) provides that an act, threat or demand done or made by one party or organisation against another which, if resisted, would have led to a trade dispute with that other, shall, notwithstanding that because that other submits to the act or threat or accedes to the demand no dispute arises, be treated as done or made in contemplation or furtherance of a trade dispute.

15.43 But a strike called for political reasons is not a trade dispute. In *BBC v Hearn*, the Association of Broadcasting Staff threatened to stop a transmission of the Cup Final by satellite to South Africa, in protest of the alleged racist policies of the Government of that country. This would also have affected a number of other countries throughout the world. The Court of Appeal held that there was no trade dispute, and granted an injunction restraining the union from telling its members to break their contracts of employment, and from inducing the

BBC to break its contracts with other countries. In *Express Newspapers v Keys*, three trade unions instructed their members to strike in response to a call sent out by the TUC for a one day national stoppage in protest against Government policies. It was held that this was a political strike, not in connection with a trade dispute, and injunctions were granted restraining the unions from inducing or procuring breaches of contract between the plaintiffs and their employees.

15.44 In *Examite Ltd v Whittaker*, a trade union called a strike against a firm called Baldwins Industrial Services, with the result that the company's business came to a standstill. A new company called Examite was formed, with two shares being issued, and it took over the business of Baldwins and engaged some of its former employees. The union continued the strike against the new company, as it was considered to be a sham, and the company sought an injunction to restrain the union officials from intimidating the employees and to restrain them from procuring a breach of contract. It was held that a trade dispute existed between the union and Examite. There was sufficient evidence to show that the company had been formed to take over the business formerly carried on by Baldwins. The 'hat' worn by the employer was irrelevant. The truth was that the new company was carried on by the same people who ran the old one, and the legal form it took was irrelevant.

B. 'In contemplation of'

15.45 Having obtained the formula for a trade dispute, for an act to come within the statutory protection, it must be in contemplation of that dispute. The act may be so done if it is committed before the dispute arises, but is imminent. However, the dispute must be more than a mere possibility. In *Bents Brewery v Hogan* managers of a brewery were asked by a trade union official to obtain information about the firm's salaries, sales, etc. In providing this, the managers were in breach of their contract not to disclose confidential information to unauthorised persons (see Chapter 6). The union official was clearly inducing a breach of that contract, and it was held that his action was not in contemplation of a trade dispute, even though one may well have arisen at some future date. His actions may have been preparatory to the dispute, but were not in contemplation of one.

C. 'In furtherance of'

15.46 The act committed must also be in furtherance of the trade dispute, and not in furtherance of some other issue. In *Conway v Wade* a union official informed employers that unless a worker was dismissed there would be a strike. This was untrue, and the union official's actions were prompted by his desire to get the worker to pay a fine which was due to the union. It was held that although a trade dispute existed, the act was not done in furtherance of that dispute, but for some other motive. A more difficult problem arises when there is more than one motive for the acts in question, and some of the pre-1971 cases, which were decided on a much narrower definition of the term 'trade dispute' must now be viewed with greater care. For example, in *Huntley v Thorton* the plaintiff was recommended for expulsion by the branch committee of a trade union, but this was not upheld by the national executive. Nonetheless, the local officials regarded him as being expelled, and took steps to ensure that he did not obtain employment. The judge thought that there was no trade dispute, but such conduct would nowadays clearly be covered by the new, wider definition. More interesting was the finding that some of the officials were not acting in furtherance of a trade dispute, but in furtherance of a personal grudge, and their actions were in the nature of a vendetta. In other words, if protection is sought for acts done in furtherance of a trade dispute, the predominant motive must be the advancement of legitimate objects, and trade unionists cannot use the cover of the statutory protection to pursue improper aims.

15.47 But not every action which flows from a trade dispute is necessarily in furtherance of that dispute. In *Beaverbrook Newspapers v Keys*, a trade dispute existed between the Daily Mirror newspaper and a trade union, which resulted in a complete stoppage of production. The *Daily Express* decided to print more copies to cater for the increase in demand, but the general secretary of the printing union told his members not to handle the additional copies. The plaintiffs applied for an injunction to restrain the union from inducing their employees to break their contracts of employment. It was held that the injunction would be granted. There was no trade dispute between the members of the defendant's union and the plaintiffs, and the action would not further the dispute between the Daily Mirror and its employees.

15.48 Armed with the 'golden formula', we can now consider those statutory protections, and consider when the immunities will be lost.

The provisions of TULR(C)A s. 219

15.49 Subsection (1) provides that an act done by a person in contemplation or furtherance of a trade dispute shall not be actionable in tort on the ground only (a) that it induces another person to break a contract or interferes or induces any other person to interfere with its performance; or (b) that it consists of his threatening that a contract (whether one to which he is party or not) will be broken or its performance interfered with, or that he will induce another person to break a contract or to interfere with its performance.

15.50 This subsection does three things. First, it gives immunity against legal action to anyone who calls a strike or other industrial action and thus induces a breach of contract (of employment) by the strikers, or a breach of a commercial contract by any other person. It also covers any inducement which interferes with the performance of a contract. Second, the subsection provides immunity where a threat of strike or other industrial action is made, whether this is done by the actual strikers or some other person, e.g. a trade union official. Thus, the threat to call a strike - the unlawful act in *Rookes v Barnard* - is no longer actionable. Third, it protects those who threaten to induce a breach of contract or to interfere with its performance.

15.51 Section 219(2) provides that an agreement or combination of two or more persons to do or procure the doing of an act in contemplation or furtherance of a trade dispute shall not be actionable in tort if the act is one which, if done without such agreement or combination, would not be so actionable. This subsection is designed to nullify the law of conspiracy as applied to trade disputes (above). If an act in contemplation or furtherance of a trade dispute would be actionable if done by one person, then a civil conspiracy would be committed if a group of persons did it. For example, if strikers commit a trespass by engaging in a sit-in, or commit a nuisance, or libel someone by picketing with defamatory placards, such conduct would be actionable if done by one person, and therefore no statutory protection exists.

15.52 Thus, in *News Group Newspapers Ltd v SOGAT '82* the defendants were responsible for organising mass picketing at the plaintiff's premises at Wapping. This was held to be a public nuisance, intimidation and an interference with commercial contracts, and injunctive relief was granted. But if the act was lawful if done by one person, it does not become an actionable conspiracy merely because a group of persons do it. Thus it is not unlawful for one person to threaten to strike or to go on strike. It therefore cannot be a conspiracy if more than one person does so. It is unlawful for one person to use violence; it will be a conspiracy for a group of persons to agree to use violence or to actually use it in a strike situation, and civil, as well as potential criminal liability, may arise.

15.53 However, it was suggested in *Meade v Haringey London Borough Council* that the immunity of a trade union from actions in tort based on conspiracy may not apply if there is an inducement to break a duty laid down by statute. Thus, if a local authority is forced to close a school (which it is under a statutory duty to keep open) because of trade union pressure, the union officials may be liable for inducing a breach of statutory duty and will not be protected by TULR(C)A. But if the statutory duty can be re-arranged so that it can still be carried out, injunctive relief will not be granted (*Barretts and Baird (Wholesale) Ltd v IPCS*). Also, if there is no statutory obligation to break, a trade union cannot be liable for inducing an alleged breach (*ABP v T&GWU*).

Loss of immunities

15.54 In recent years, the tactics adopted by trade unions in industrial disputes have not always attracted universal approval, and Parliament has intervened to place restrictions on certain types of activities, by limiting the immunity conferred by s. 219 of TULR(C)A. The objects are twofold: first, to ensure greater democracy in trade unions by requiring secret ballots to be held before strikes or other industrial action are called, so as to negate decisions made at mass meetings by show of hands, or calls for action which may be unsupported by the rank and file; second, to prevent unnecessary hardship caused by industrial action to third parties who are in no way involved with or connected with the dispute. The primary purpose is to regulate official trade union action; unofficial action, though covered by the law, is seldom the subject of court proceedings (but see para 15.70).

Consequently, the immunity provided by s. 219 of TULR(C)A will be lost in the following circumstances.

Secret ballots before industrial action (TULR(C)A s. 226 (as amended))

15.55 An act done by a trade union to induce a person to take part, or to continue to take part, in industrial action is not prevented by s. 219 from being actionable in tort unless:
(a) it has the support of a ballot; and
(b) the employer has been notified (seven days before the opening of the ballot):
    (i) that the union intend to hold a ballot;
    (ii) the opening day of the ballot; and
    (iii) the description of the employees of the employer who will be entitled to vote in the ballot.

Also, a sample of the voting paper is to be received by the employer at least three days prior to the opening of the ballot.

15.56 In other words, the civil immunity of a trade union is removed so far as official strikes are concerned, unless a postal ballot is held among those who are being called upon to take such action (see *Boxfoldia v National Graphical Association*). The authorisation or endorsement of the action must satisfy the requirements of s. 20 (see below).

15.57 All those members of the trade union who it is reasonable (at the time of the ballot) to believe will be induced to take part in the strike or other industrial action must be balloted, and no other person. If a member is denied entitlement to vote in the ballot, and is subsequently induced to take part in the industrial action, the trade union will lose its civil immunity. However, the inadvertent deprivation of one member of the opportunity to vote will not necessarily invalidate the whole ballot (*British Railways Board v NUR*).

15.58 Voting must be by means of the marking of a voting paper, which must contain a question, however framed, requiring the member to answer 'Yes' or 'No' whether he is prepared to take part (or continue to take part) in a strike or other industrial action. If a trade union wishes to ascertain the views of its members on whether they would be willing to take part in a strike or other industrial action, these are two separate questions, and to obtain the statutory immunity, the union must obtain the requisite majority in favour of the particular course of action adopted (s. 229(2)). After all, a member might be willing to take part in a strike, but not other industrial action, and *vice versa* (*Post Office v Union of Communication Workers*).

15.59 Every voting paper must contain the name of the independent scrutineer (see Chapter 14), the address to which and the date by which it is to be returned, and marked with a number which is one of a series of consecutive whole numbers (s. 229(1A)).

15.60 The question put on the ballot paper must relate to the trade dispute (within the statutory definition) and not to matters in respect of which no statutory immunity applies (*London University Ltd v National Union of Railwaymen*). Further, the following statement must appear on the voting paper, without being qualified or commented on 'If you take part in a strike or other industrial action, you may be in breach of your contract of employment' (s. 229(4)).

15.61 So far as is reasonably practicable, the ballot paper must be supplied to the member at his home address (or other notified address) and he must be given a convenient opportunity to vote by post (s. 230(2)). (Merchant seamen who are at sea or outside Great Britain when the votes are cast, may vote on board the ship or at a place where the ship is.)

15.62 The voting paper must specify the person who is authorised to call upon the members to take part in the strike or other industrial action, and this person must be one of those specified in s. 20(3), i.e.:

a. the principal executive committee;
b. any person authorised by the rules to call or authorise the act;
c. the president or general secretary;
d. any employed official;
e. any committee of the union to whom an employed official of the union regularly reports.

15.63 As soon as is reasonably practicable, the trade union shall inform all persons entitled to vote of the number of:
a. votes cast;
b. individuals voting 'yes';
c. individuals voting 'no'; and
d. spoilt papers.

The union will also ensure that every relevant employer receives this information (s. 231A).

15.64 A ballot will be ineffective in so far as it relates to a call for strike or other industrial action before the date of the ballot, or any such call after the ballot ceases to be effective. In other words, industrial action cannot be subsequently validated by a ballot (s. 233). But this does not require the union to adopt a 'neutral stance' on the matter, and if the union urges its members to vote in favour of strike action, this is not the same thing as calling on them to strike (*Newham London Borough Council v NALGO*).

15.65 A ballot will also cease to be effective at the end of four weeks, although it will validate any industrial action which commenced within the four-week period. If, during the four-week period, industrial action is prohibited by a court order (e.g. on an application for a temporary injunction) and the court order is subsequently discharged, or it lapses, the trade union may request the court to order that the period during which the prohibition had an effect shall not count towards the four-week period. But no such application shall be made after eight weeks from the date of the ballot (TULR(C)A s. 234). The court will not make the necessary order if it thinks that the ballot no longer represents the views of the union members, or an event is likely to occur as a result of which the members would be likely to vote against industrial action if another ballot were to be held.

Ballots for overseas members

15.66 Generally, a trade union can ignore overseas members for balloting purposes (i.e. members who are outside Great Britain). However, it the ballot relates to industrial action involving Great Britain and Northern Ireland, members in both countries must be balloted (TULR(C)A s. 232).

Separate workplace ballots (TULR(C)A s. 228)

15.67 Certain conditions must be satisfied by a trade union if it wishes to call aggregated ballots at different places of work. The union must believe that each union member entitled to vote has a factor, relating to his terms of conditions of employment, in common with other members who are entitled to vote, which he does not have in common with members employed by the same employer who are not entitled to vote. If these conditions are not satisfied, the trade union must conduct separate ballots for each place of work where members who are entitled to vote work. The purpose is to prevent a trade union from unduly 'weighting' strike ballots by limiting the ballot to certain sections of the workforce.

Notice of industrial action to employers (s. 234A)

15.68 An act done by a trade union to induce a person to take part in industrial action shall not be prevented from being actionable in tort by s. 219 unless the union takes such steps as are reasonably necessary to ensure that the employer receives a relevant notice of the industrial action. The notice must be in writing, and must:

(a) describe the employees of the employer who the union intend to induce to take part in the industrial action; and
(b) state whether the action is intended to be continuous or discontinuous.

If the action is to be continuous, the notice must specify the date when it is to start; if discontinuous, it must state the intended dates. The notice must be given any time after the employer has been informed of the result of the ballot and seven days before the date on which the industrial action is to commence.

Industrial action to enforce a closed shop (TULR(C)A s. 222)

15.69 Section 219 shall not provide an immunity in tort for acts done in furtherance or contemplation of a trade dispute if the reason for the act is that the employer is employing or proposes to employ a person who is not a member of a trade union or of a particular trade union. Immunity is also removed if the action is designed to put pressure on an employer into treating persons less favourably on grounds of their non-membership of a trade union.

Industrial action in support of unofficial strikers (TULR(C)A s. 223)

15.70 We have noted that if a person goes on unofficial strike, and is dismissed, he has no right to claim that he has been unfairly dismissed (see para 13.74). Section 223 provides that s. 219 will not prevent an act from being actionable in tort, if the reason for the action was that an employer had lawfully dismissed unofficial strikers.

Secondary action (TULR(C)A s. 224)

15.71 The immunities conferred by s. 219 will only apply when a trade union takes industrial action (supported by the appropriate ballot) vis-à-vis an employer with whom there is a trade dispute. In recent years, it became an increasingly popular technique to strengthen the effectiveness of such action by extending it to employers who were not themselves parties to the dispute, in the hope that pressure (direct or indirect) would be thereby exerted on the employer with whom there was a dispute. This is known as secondary action (see, e.g. *Duport Steels Ltd v Sirs*).

15.72 Secondary action is defined as when a person:

a. induces another to break a contract of employment; or
b. interferes or induces another to interfere with its performance; or
c. threatens that a contract of employment under which he or another is employed will be broken, or its performance interfered with; or
d. threatens that he will induce another to break a contract of employment, or to interfere with its performance,

and the employer under the contract of employment is not the employer party to the dispute (s. 224(2)).

15.73 In these circumstances, nothing in s. 219 shall prevent an act from being actionable in tort where one of the facts relied upon for the purpose of establishing such liability amounts to secondary action which is not lawful picketing.

15.74 The current definition of secondary action is wider than the original definition contained in the Employment Act 1980, and thus there are greater pitfalls for those who engage in such action. Secondary action must result in a breach of a contract of employment, whether or not there is a breach of a commercial contract. Further, the present definition extends the meaning of contract of employment to include the contract of a self-employed person who contracts personally to do work or perform services for another, thus closing a loophole revealed in *Shipping Co Uniform Inc v ITWF*.

15.75 The only type of secondary action which now remains lawful is peaceful picketing, as laid down in s. 220 of TULR(C)A (see para 15.100), i.e. by workers who are (or were) employed by the employer who is a party to the dispute, and by a trade union official whose attendance is lawful by virtue of s. 220(4) of the Act. Secondary picketing (i.e. at the gate of an employer who is a customer or supplier to the employer who is a party to the dispute) is not lawful.

Pressure to impose union recognition requirement (s. 225)

15.76 An act will not be protected by s. 219 if it constitutes an inducement of a person to incorporate into a contract a term requiring a party to a contract for goods or services to recognise a trade union for the purpose of negotiating on behalf of workers employed by him, or to negotiate or consult with an official of a trade union (such a contract term would be void be reason of s. 186, see para 15.114). Nor will an act be protected if it interferes with the supply of goods or services, by inducing another person to break a contract of employment, and the reason being that the supplier does not recognise or negotiate or consult with a trade union (see para 15.113).

Immunity of trade unions (TULR(C)A s. 20)

15.77 Section 14 of TULRA 1974 (which re-enacted provisions dating from the Trade Disputes Act 1906) conferred total legal immunity on trade unions in respect of most actions in tort. This immunity was repealed by the Employment Act 1982, and nowadays a trade union will be liable in tort if the protection of s. 219 of TULR(C)A is not available. However, a trade union cannot be responsible for everything which is done in its name by its members, shop stewards or officers, but only for those actions which have been authorised or endorsed.

15.78 A trade union will only be liable for inducing breaches of contract, or threatening that a contract will be broken, or for actions for conspiracy, if the act in question is authorised or endorsed by the union. An act shall be taken to have been endorsed or authorised by the trade union if it was done or authorised or endorsed by:

a. any person empowered by the rules to do, authorise or endorse the act; or
b. the principal executive committee or the president or general secretary of the union; or
c. by any other committee of the union, or any other official of the union (whether employed by the union or not).

15.79 Thus, under the current law, a trade union may be held to be legally liable not only for the acts of its full-time officials, but also for its shop stewards if they are authorised to do an act. Further, the liability arises for the acts of any committee (set up in accordance with the union's rules) and also for the acts of any group of members of which a shop steward was a member, and the purpose of which included the organising or co-ordinating of industrial action (TULR(C)A s. 20(4)). This is so notwithstanding anything in the rules of the union, or any contract or rule of law subject to the repudiation provisions, below.

15.80 However, the union will not be liable if the act was repudiated by the principal executive committee or president or general secretary as soon as was reasonably practicable. Written notice must be given to the committee or official in question, without delay, and the union must do its best to give written notice of the fact and date of repudiation, without delay, to every member whom the union believe is taking part in the industrial action, and to the employer of every such member (s. 21).

15.81 The written notice must be in the following form. 'Your union has repudiated the call (or calls) for industrial action to which this notice relates and will give no support to unofficial industrial action taken in response to it (or them). If you are dismissed while taking industrial action, you will have no right to complain of unfair dismissal.'

15.82 The repudiation will not be effective if the principal executive, president or general secretary behave in a manner inconsistent with the repudiation (see *Richard Read (Transport) Ltd v National Union of Mineworkers*). If, within three months of the purported repudiation, a person who is a party to a commercial contract which has been interfered with by the unofficial industrial action so requests, the union must confirm the repudiation in writing.

The effect of the Act

15.83 If a trade union calls for a strike or other industrial action in violation of the balloting provisions of the Act, or for a reason which is not permitted by the Act, it can be sued, and will not have the immunity conferred by s. 219. An application may be made by an aggrieved person to the court for an injunction (*Solihull Metropolitan Borough Council v NUT*) and a failure to comply constitutes contempt of court, which would lead to a fine or imprisonment being imposed (*Express and Star Ltd v NGA*) or sequestration of property (*Kent Free Press v NGA*). Additionally, an action for damages could be brought against the trade union, subject to the limits on the amount which can be awarded, depending on the size of the trade union.

Amount of damages (TULR(C)A s. 22)

15.84 If a trade union is sued successfully in tort, there are limits to the amount of damages which may be awarded. These limits are dependent on the size of the union's membership and are as follows:

less than 5,000 members, the limit is £10,000
5,000 or more, but less than 25,000, the limit is £50,000
25,000 or more, but less than 100,000, the limit is £125,000
100,000 or more, the limit is £250,000.

15.85 These limits are applicable in each claim brought against the union, and are not global limits on each incident.

Thus, if a trade union calls a strike in circumstances where it lacks legal immunity under s. 219, each employee who has suffered damage may sue the union for the maximum sum, depending on the number of members it has. In addition, interest may be added to the award (*Boxfoldia Ltd v NGA*).

15.86 The limits do not apply to any action in tort in respect of personal injury caused by negligence, nuisance or breach of statutory duty, nor to any breach of duty in connection with the ownership, occupation, possession, control or use of property.

15.87 If damages, costs or expenses are awarded against a trade union, these cannot be enforced against the 'protected property' i.e. property which belongs to trustees other than in their capacity as trustees of the union, property owned by members in association with other members (i.e. common property), the property of an official who is not a member or trustee, political funds and provident benefit funds.

Injunctions and interdicts (TULR(C)A s. 221)

15.88 An *ex parte* injunction is an application for a temporary injunction to restrain the commission of some act. It is usually made in great haste, and thus only the party applying will have the time and opportunity to argue the case and be represented. Section 221 states that the court shall not grant such an application if the party against whom the injunction is sought claims, or the court thinks he might claim, that the act was done in contemplation or furtherance of a trade dispute, unless all reasonable steps have been taken to give that person notice of the hearing and an opportunity has been given for that party to be heard.

15.89 If an application is made for an interlocutory injunction (i.e. restraining an act until the matter comes to trial), and the party against whom the injunction is sought claims that he acted in contemplation or furtherance of a trade dispute, the court shall, in exercising its discretion whether or not to grant the injunction, assess the likelihood of success of any defence which may be raised that the act complained of will be protected by the statutory immunities (s. 221(2)). This provision does not apply in Scotland.

Injunctive relief (TULR(C)A s. 20(6))

15.90 If a trade union is responsible for official or unofficial strike action under the provisions of s. 20 then in any court proceedings arising out of the act in question, the court may grant an injunction requiring the trade union to take such steps as the court thinks appropriate for ensuring:

a. that there is no, or no further, inducement of persons to take part in industrial action; and
b. that no person engage in any conduct after the granting of the injunction because he was induced to take part in industrial action before the injunction was granted.

15.91 This appears to give the court power to order a trade union to take disciplinary action against those who continue to induce or take part in industrial action after it has been repudiated by the union. However, no court shall make an order of specific performance or grant an injunction if the effect is to compel an employee to work or attend any place for the doing to any work (s. 236).

15.92 A failure by a trade union (or any other person) to observe the terms of an injunction amounts to contempt of court, in respect of which a fine and/or imprisonment or sequestration of property may be ordered (*Kent Free Press v NGA*).

Industrial action affecting an individual (s. 235A)

15.93 Any individual, who claims that industrial action has been called by a trade union which is actionable in tort or which has not been supported by a ballot under s. 226, and the effect of which is to prevent or delay the supply of goods or services, or reduce their quality, may make an application to the High Court or Court of Session. It is immaterial that the individual in question is entitled to be supplied with the goods or services in question. If the court is satisfied that the claim is well-founded, it shall make such order as it considers appropriate for requiring the union to take steps for ensuring that no further act is done by him to induce any person to take part in the industrial action, and that no person engages in any conduct before the making of the order because he has been induced before the making of the order to take part in industrial action.

This section also applies to Crown employment even though no contract of employment may exist.

15.94 The situation may sometimes arise where a trade union calls for industrial action which would otherwise be actionable in tort because the various statutory provisions have not been complied with, but, (for whatever reason) the employer (or union members) are unwilling to seek to restrain the industrial action. In such circumstances, any individual, whether affected by the industrial action or not, can bring an application to the court, seeking an appropriate order. For this purpose, assistance may be sought from the Commissioner for the Protection Against Unlawful Industrial Action (see para 1.35).

Legal effect of collective agreements (TULR(C)A s. 178-179)

15.95 A collective agreement is any agreement or arrangement made by or on behalf of a trade union on the one part, and one or more employers or employers' associations on the other part, relating to one or more of the matters contained above in the definition of a trade dispute. In essence, a collective agreement performs two functions. First, it lays down the guiding procedures which will govern the relationship between the signatory parties, by providing, for example, for the constitution of any joint body, or the procedure to be adopted in the event of a dispute or disagreement. Second, it will lay down patterns of terms and conditions of employment which are to cover union members, and possibly others as well, and which are to be observed by all federated and some assenting non-federated firms. Such terms and conditions are usually the minimum, not the maximum rate, so if national bargaining results in a particular award, this may frequently be supplemented at a local level by a further bout of negotiations.

15.96 So far as legal enforceability of these agreements is concerned, s. 179 provides that any agreement shall be conclusively presumed not to have been intended by the parties to be a legally enforceable contract, unless the agreement is in writing, and contains a provision stating that the parties do intend the agreement to be legally binding (*Universe Tankships Inc of Monrovia v International Transport Workers' Federation*). It is possible for the parties to state expressly that only part of the agreement is intended to be legally binding, and part not, in which case, the parties' intentions will be given effect to, though it is possible to look at a non-legally binding part for the purpose of interpreting a part which is legally binding.

15.97 There must be an express statement to the effect that the parties intend the collective agreement to be legally enforceable. If the agreement states that the parties intend to be bound by it, this may indicate that it is intended to be binding in honour only, which would not satisfy the provisions of s. 18 (*National Coal Board v NUM*).

15.98 The extent to which, and the circumstances in which, the terms of a collective agreement can be incorporated into the contract of employment of an individual employee have already been examined in Chapter 3. Section 180 lays down one further important rule. If a collective agreement, whether legally binding or not, contains a clause prohibiting or restricting the right of workers to engage in a strike or other industrial action, this particular clause shall not be incorporated into the individual contract of employment of any worker, unless the collective agreement:

a. is in writing;
b. contains a provision expressly stating that such term shall be or may be incorporated into such contract;
c. is reasonably accessible at the place of work of such a worker, and is available for him to consult during working hours; and
d. is one made by an independent trade union.

It should have been noted that this rule applies notwithstanding any agreement to the contrary, whether contained in a collective agreement or an individual contract of employment.

15.99 Thus, if a collective agreement provides that 'the union will not call a strike until the disputes procedure is exhausted', a breach of this clause would be governed by the law relating to the legal effect of the agreement, as mentioned above. If the collective agreement states: 'The employees will not go on strike until the disputes procedure is exhausted', then this clause will only form part of the individual contract of employment if the above conditions are fulfilled. The matter, however, is not really important, for a strike is likely to be a breach of most individuals' contracts of employment (whether or not it is in breach of the terms of a collective agreement) as it is a breach of the duty of faithful service (see Chapter 6) and a breach of contract of such importance that a striker may be dismissed.

Peaceful picketing (TULR(C)A s. 220)

15.100 It shall be lawful for a person in contemplation or furtherance of a trade dispute to attend:

a. at or near his own place of work; or
b. if he is an official of a trade union, at or near the place of work of a member of that union whom he is accompanying and whom he represents;

for the purpose only of peacefully obtaining or communicating information, or peacefully persuading any person to work or to abstain from working. If a person works at more than one place, or at a place where it is impracticable to picket because of its location, his place of work shall be any premises from which he works, or from which his work is administered. A person whose employment has been terminated because of a trade dispute is allowed to picket at his former place of work.

15.101 A trade union official who has been elected or appointed to represent some of the members shall be regarded as representing only those members. Otherwise, a union official shall be regarded as representing all its members (s. 220(4)). The purpose of this provision is to draw a distinction between officials who are shop stewards and full-time officials.

15.102 An employee's 'place of work' means his principal place of work or base. It does not refer to premises which, during his work, he may visit from time to time (*Union Traffic v T&GWU*).

15.103 Whether the picketing has taken place at or near the place of work is a question of fact and degree. In *Rayware Ltd v T&GWU*, pickets stood at the entrance of a private estate, about $\frac{3}{10}$th of a mile from the employers' premises. An application by the employers for an injunction to restrain unlawful picketing failed. The pickets could not get any nearer to their place of work without trespassing, and thus they were picketing lawfully near their place of work.

15.104 Section 220 only makes lawful the above acts. If something else is done, the section provides no protection. Thus in

Piddington v Bates, a policeman wished to restrict the number of pickets who were outside a factory. When a striker tried to join the picket line, he was arrested, and charged with obstructing the policeman in the course of his duty. A conviction was upheld, for the policeman had acted on reasonable grounds that a breach of the peace might have occurred. In *Tynan v Balmer*, a group of pickets walked in a circle at the entrance of a factory in order to prevent traffic from entering and this was held to be an obstruction of the highway and a nuisance.

15.105 Nor do pickets have the power to stop vehicles, for traffic control is a matter for the police. In *Broome v DPP* a trade union official stood in front of a lorry and attempted to persuade the driver not to deliver goods to a factory where a dispute was on. The police told him to get out of the way, but he refused, and he was arrested and charged with obstructing the highway, an offence under the Highways Act 1959. It was held that he was guilty of the offence. Views were expressed in *Broome's* case that the law gave no right to pickets to stop persons or vehicles, for that would indicate that those persons were under a duty to stop and listen. The purpose of the statute was to make attendance at a picket line lawful, and then only for the statutory purposes of peacefully communicating information, etc.

15.106 Mass picketing can also amount to the tort of public nuisance (unreasonable obstruction of the highway), private nuisance (interference with access to the highway) and intimidation (see *News Group Newspapers v SOGAT '82*). Thus under the new law, 'flying pickets' and mass demonstrations are clearly unlawful, the former because they will not normally be picketing at their own place of work, the latter because it is unlikely that it is for the purpose of peacefully persuading. In *Thomas v National Union of Mineworkers (South Wales Area)*, it was held that mass picketing constituted a common law nuisance (as well as an offence under TULR(C)A s. 241(1)), for all citizens had the right to use the highway without harassment or unreasonable interference. Accordingly, injunctions were granted against various trade union officials to prevent them from organising, encouraging, etc., members of the union congregating at coal mines, other than for the statutory purpose of peacefully communicating information, numbers in such cases being restricted to six.

15.107 Section 219(s) of TULR(C)A now provides that if an act is done in the course of picketing which is not lawful then s. 219

will not provide a defence to any action which may be brought. Thus, if a picket induces workers to break their contracts of employment, and he is picketing at some place other than his own place of work, he can be sued in tort, and the statutory immunity of s. 219 will not be available to him. Thus, unlawful picketing may now attract civil, as well as criminal liabilities. A Code of Practice on picketing has been approved by Parliament laying down the parameters for peaceful picketing.

15.108 If a tort is committed by picketing, s. 220 will provide a trade union with legal protection provided the picketing is lawful within that section. But if no tort has been committed, the statutory rules are basically irrelevant. Thus, in *Middlebrook Mushrooms Ltd v T&GWU*, the employers were mushroom producers, employing some 300 workers. They wished to introduce certain cost-saving measures, but these were not agreed to, and the union called a strike. The employer then dismissed all those employees who went on strike.

The union then urged its members to attend at supermarkets which were supplied with the mushrooms by the employers, and hand out leaflets to members of the public, asking them not to buy the employers' mushrooms. The employers brought an action for an interlocutory injunction restraining the union and its officials from organising the 'pickets' outside the supermarkets. The judge held that there was a direct interference with the contracts between the employers and the supermarkets, and granted the injunction.

However, the Court of Appeal reversed the decision. There was nothing in the leaflets which were handed out to members of the public which was aimed at the managers of the supermarket who placed orders with the employers. Thus the union was not seeking to persuade a party to the contract (i.e. the employers and the supermarkets) but members of the public, who, of course, had no contractual relations with the employers. It may well be that the managers of the supermarket might react to the reaction of the public (not to the picketing), but this, at most, would amount to an indirect inducement not to enter into future contracts, and, as no unlawful means had been used, the application for an injunction was dismissed.

Sit-in

15.109 Workers who engage in a sit-in or work-in are in breach of their contractual licence to remain on the employers' premises

(*City and Hackney Health Authority v National Union of Public Employees*), and as such, if they refuse to leave after being given reasonable notice to do so are committing the tort of trespass and interfering with business by unlawful means (*Norbrook Laboratories Ltd v King*). It is possible to obtain an injunction against those involved, and also an employer may use the special expedited procedure to obtain possession of the property (see Ord. 113 of the Rules of the Supreme Court).

15.110 If a trade union called for or authorised the sit-in or work-in, it would not be protected by the immunity conferred by s. 219, even if a ballot was held, because the immunity in respect of interference with business by unlawful means was removed with the repeal of earlier legislation.

Union or non-union members only contracts (TULR(C)A s. 144)

15.111 Any term or condition in a contract for the supply of goods or services shall be void in so far as it purports to require that the whole or part of the work shall be done by persons who are not members of a trade union (or a particular trade union), or who are members of a trade union (or a particular trade union).

15.112 It will be a tort of breach of statutory duty if, on the grounds of union membership or non-membership, a person:

a. fails to include a particular person's name on a list of approved suppliers of goods or services;
b. terminates a contract for the supply of goods or services;
c. excludes a person from tendering for the supply of goods or services;
d. fails to permit a person to submit a tender; or
e. otherwise determines not to enter into a contract for the supply of goods or services.

15.113 Thus any person who suffers damage through the failure or refusal of another to enter into a contract with him for the supply of goods or services on the grounds of union membership or non-membership may sue for breach of statutory duty, and will be able to recover damages (subject to any general defences which may exist to such an action). Further, if there is pressure from any person to induce another to incorporate into a contract to which that other is a party any term or condition which would be void by the above provisions then s. 219 shall not be a defence. Nor will s. 219 be a defence if a person induces or threatens to induce another person to break a duty imposed by s. 144. Thus if trade unionists threaten to strike unless an employer enters into a union labour only contract, or unless he removes non-union sub-contractors from a site, such acts will be actionable despite the general immunity of s. 219 (see s. 222(3)).

Prohibition on union recognition requirements (TULR(C)A s. 186)

15.114 Any term or condition of a contract for the supply of goods or services shall be void in so far as it purports to require any party to the contract

a. to recognise one or more trade unions, or
b. to negotiate or consult with any official of a trade union.

Refusal to deal on union exclusion grounds (TULR(C)A s. 187)

15.115 If a person maintains a list of approved suppliers of goods or services, or list of persons from whom tenders may be invited, and fails to include on that list a person who does not recognise trade unions, or terminates a contract for the supply of goods or services on that ground, or does other acts which prevent a person from being able to enter into a contract for the supply of goods or services because he does not recognise trade unions, such action will amount to a breach of statutory duty, and is actionable accordingly (subject to any relevant defences) by the person against whom the action was taken or by any other person adversely affected.

15.116 An act will not be protected by s. 219 if it consists of inducing a person to impose a union recognition requirement contrary to ss. 186-187 (see s. 225).

Criminal liabilities

15.117 Members of the armed forces and policemen have no right to strike. Merchant seaman may lawfully terminate their contracts and give 48 hours' notice of strike action provided their ship is in a safe berth in the United Kingdom. Industrial action by post office workers may involve criminal liability (see *Gouriet v Union of Post Office Workers*) and there are restrictions on aliens who promote industrial action.

15.118 Sections 240-241 of TULR(C)A enacts two provisions which may be relevant in trade disputes generally. The first is contained in s. 240 of the Act, which provides that where any person wilfully and maliciously breaks a contract of service of hiring, knowing or having reasonable cause to believe that the probable consequences of his doing so, either alone or in combination with others, will be to endanger human life, or cause serious bodily injury, or to expose valuable property whether real or personal to destruction or serious injury, he shall, on conviction, be liable to a fine or to imprisonment for a term not exceeding three months.

15.119 The second provision is contained in s. 241 of the Act. This states that every person who, with a view to compelling any person to abstain from doing an act which he has a legal right to do:

a. uses violence to or intimidates such other person or his wife or children, or injures his property; or
b. persistently follows such other persons from place to place; or
c. hides any tools, clothes or other property owned or used by such other person, or deprives him of or hinders him in the use thereof; or
d. watches or besets the house or other place where such person resides, or works, or carries on business, or happens to be, or the approach to such house or place; or
e. follows such other person with two or more other persons in a disorderly manner along any street or road,

then he shall be liable to a fine not exceeding level 5 on the standard scale or a term of imprisonment not exceeding six months, or both.

15.120 Section 241 was considered in the recent case of *Galt v Philp*, where workers engaged in a 'sit-in', during which they locked and barricaded laboratories, thus preventing other employees from entering the rooms. This was held to be 'besetting' within the meaning of s. 241(1)(a) and the individuals concerned were found guilty of an offence under the Act.

15.121 It must be remembered that s. 219 of TULR(C)A only protects a person from civil liability, and does not give any immunity in respect of criminal acts.

Public Order Act 1986

15.122 This Act abolished the common law offences of riot, rout, unlawful assembly and affray, and repealed the provisions of the Public order Act 1936, relating to threatening behaviour likely to provoke a breach of the peace. A number of statutory criminal offences have been introduced by the new Act, which may be invoked when the conduct of industrial disputes gets out of hand. These are:

a. *Riot* (s.1). This is where 12 or more people use or threaten to use violence for a common purpose which would cause a person of reasonable firmness to fear for his personal safety;
b. *Violent disorder* (s.2). This has the same elements as *riot*, except that it applies when three or more persons are taking part;
c. *Affray* (s.3). This also has the same elements as *riot*, except that only one person need be involved, and threats, by themselves, would not be sufficient;
d. *Fear or provocation of violence* (s.4). It is an offence to use threatening, abusive or insulting words or behaviour or to distribute or display any visual representation which is threatening, abusive or insulting, where the act is intended or likely to make a person fear immediate violence, or to provoke immediate violence;
e. *Harassment, alarm or distress* (s.5). This has almost the same elements as *fear or provocation of violence*, but the accused may defend himself by arguing that he had no reason to believe that a person alarmed was within his hearing or sight, or that his conduct was reasonable.

15.123 The Act also lays down new rules for marches, processions, demonstrations and public assemblies.

Appendices

Contents

A Penalties under the Health and Safety at Work Act 531
B Redundancy Pay Calculation Table 535
C Enforcement of Statutory Rights 537
Table 1: No hours condition, no continuous employment condition 538
Table 2: Hours condition, no continuous employment condition 540
Table 3: Hours condition, continuous employment condition 541
Table 4: Rights by and against trade unions 543
D Forms IT1 and IT3 (Industrial Tribunals) 544
E Improvement and Prohibition Notices (Health and Safety Executive) 550
F Names and Addresses 554
G Discipline at Work (ACAS Advisory Handbook) 556
H Main Legislative Provisions 1980-1993 588
I Codes of Practice
(a) Disciplinary Practices and Procedure in employment 593
(b) Disclosure of information to trade unions for collective bargaining purposes 599
(c) Time off for trade union duties and activities 605
(d) For the elimination of sex and marriage discrimination 613
(e) For the elimination of racial discrimination 626
(f) Picketing 648

Penalties under the Health and Safety at Work Act

	Offence	*Summary conviction*	*On indictment*
1.	Failure to discharge a duty under ss. 2-6	£20,000	Fine
2.	Contravening ss. 7-9	£5,000	Fine
3.	Contravening Health and Safety Regulations	£5,000	Fine
4.	Contravening any requirement made by regulations relating to investigations or enquiries made by the Commission, etc under s. 14, or obstructing anyone exercising his powers	£5,000	
5.	Contravening any requirement under s. 20 (powers of inspectors)	£5,000	
6.	Contravening any requirement under s. 25 (power of the inspector to seize and render harmless articles or substances likely to cause imminent danger)	£5,000	Fine

	Offence	*Summary conviction*	*On indictment*
7.	Preventing a person from appearing before an inspector or from answering questions under s. 20(2)(j) (examinations and investigations)	£5,000	
8.	Contravening a requirement or prohibition imposed by an improvement notice	£20,000 and/or six months' imprison - ment	Fine and/or 2 years' imprison - ment
9.	Contravening a requirement or prohibition imposed by a prohibition notice	£20,000 and/or 6 months' imprison - ment	Fine and/or 2 years' imprison - ment
10.	Intentionally obstructing an inspector or obstructing a customs officer in the exercise of his powers under s. 25A	£5,000	
11.	Contravening a notice served by the Commission under s. 27(1) requiring information	£5,000	Fine
12.	Using or disclosing information in contravention of s. 27(4) (disclosure by the Crown or certain Government agencies of information to the Commission or Executive)	£5,000	Fine and/or 2 years' imprison - ment

	Offence	*Summary conviction*	*On indictment*
13.	Disclosure of information obtained under s. 27(1) or pursuant to any statutory provision, not within the exceptions of s. 28	£5,000	Fine
	Offence	Summary conviction	On indictment
14.	Making a false or reckless statement in purported compliance with a statutory provision, or for the purpose of obtaining the issuance of a document under any statutory provision	£5,000	Fine
15.	Intentionally making a false entry in any register, book, or other document required to be kept, or to making use of such entry, knowing it to be false	£5,000	Fine
16.	Forging document, or, with intent to deceive, using a forged document	£5,000	Fine
17.	Pretending to be an inspector	£5,000	
18.	Failing to comply with an order of the court under s. 42 (order to remedy)	£20,000 and/or six months' imprison - ment	Fine and/or 2 years' imprison - ment
19.	Acting without a licence which is necessary under a relevant statutory provision	£5,000	Fine and/or 2 years' imprison - ment

	Offence	*Summary conviction*	*On indictment*
20.	Contravening the terms of such licence	£5,000	Fine and/or 2 years' imprison - ment
21.	Acquiring, using or possessing explosives contrary to the relevant statutory provisions	£5,000	Fine and/or 2 years' imprison - ment
22.	Breach of regulations made under the Offshore Safety Act	£5,000	Fine and/or 2 years' imprison - ment

Redundancy Pay Calculation Table

1. Read off the employee's age and number of complete years' employment.
2. Multiply the relevant factor by the employee's week's pay (current maximum to be applied is £205 per week).
3. For men and women over the age of 64, reduce the entitlement by 1/12th for each month over that age, until entitlement ceases altogether at the age of 65.
4. The table may be used to calculate the Basic Award, it being noted that there is no lower age limit, and employment below the age of 18 will therefore count.

Service (years)

Age (years)	2	3	4	5	6	7	8	9	10	11	12	13	14	15	16	17	18	19	20
20	1	1	1	1	–														
21	1	1½	1½	1½	1½	–													
22	1	1½	2	2	2	2	–												
23	1½	2	2½	3	3	3	3	–											
24	2	2½	3	3½	4	4	4	4	–										
25	2	3	33½	4	4½	5	5	5	5	–									
26	2	3	4	4½	5	5½	6	6	6	6	–								
27	2	3	4	5	5½	6	6½	7	7	7	7	–							
28	2	3	4	5	6	6½	7	7½	8	8	8	8	–						
29	2	3	4	5	6	7	7½	8	8½	9	9	9	9	–					
30	2	3	3	4	5	6	7	8	8½	9	9½	10	10	10	10	–			
31	2	3	4	5	6	7	8	9	9½	10	10½	11	11	11	11	–			
32	2	3	4	5	6	7	8	9	10	10½	11	11½	12	12	12	12	–		
33	2	3	4	5	6	7	8	9	10	11	11½	12	12½	13	13	13	13	–	
34	2	3	4	5	6	7	8	9	10	11	12	12½	13	13½	14	14	14	14	–
35	2	3	4	5	6	7	8	9	10	11	12	13	13½	14	14½	15	15	15	15
36	2	3	4	5	6	7	8	9	10	11	12	13	14	14½	15	15½	16	16	16
37	2	3	4	5	6	7	8	9	10	11	12	13	14	15	15½	16	16½	17	17

Service (years)

	2	3	4	5	6	7	8	9	10	11	12	13	14	15	16	17	18	19	20
Age (years)																			
38	2	3	4	5	6	7	8	9	10	11	12	13	14	15	16	17	17½	18	
39	2	3	4	5	6	7	8	9	10	11	12	13	14	15	16	17	17½	18	18½
40	2	3	4	5	6	7	8	9	10	11	12	13	14	15	16	17	18	18½	19
41	2	3	4	5	6	7	8	9	10	11	12	13	14	15	16	17	18	19	19½
42	2½	3½	4½	5½	6½	7½	8½	9½	10½	11½	12½	13½	14½	15½	16½	17½	18½	19½	20½
43	3	4	5	6	7	8	9	10	11	12	13	14	15	16	17	18	19	20	21
44	3	4½	5½	6½	7½	8½	9½	10½	11½	12½	13½	14½	15½	16½	17½	18½	19½	20½	21½
45	3	4½	6	7	8	9	10	11	12	13	14	15	16	17	18	19	20	21	22
46	3	4½	6	7½	8½	9½	10½	11½	12½	13½	14½	15½	16½	17½	18½	19½	20½	21½	22½
47	3	4½	6	7½	9	10	11	12	13	14	15	16	17	18	19	20	21	22	23
48	3	4½	6	7½	9	10½	11½	12½	13½	14½	15½	16½	17½	18½	19½	20½	21½	22½	23½
49	3	4½	6	7½	9	10½	12	13	14	15	16	17	18	19	20	21	22	23	24
50	3	4½	6	7½	9	10½	12	13½	14½	15½	16½	17½	18½	19½	20½	21½	22½	23½	24½
51	3½	4½	6	7½	9	10½	12	13½	15	16	17	18	19	20	21	22	23	24	25
52	3	4½	6	7½	9	10½	12	13½	15	16½	17½	18½	19½	20½	21½	22½	23½	24½	25½
53	3	4½	6	7½	9	10½	12	13½	15	16½	18	19	20	21	22	23	24	25	26
54	3	4½	6	7½	9	10½	12	13½	15	16½	18	19½	20½	21½	22½	23½	24½	25½	26½
55	3	4½	6	7½	9	10½	12	13½	15	16½	18	19½	21	22	23	24	25	26	27
56	3	4½	6	7½	9	10½	12	13½	15	16½	18	19½	21	22½	23½	24½	25½	26½	27½
57	3	4½	6	7½	9	10½	12	13½	15	16½	18	19½	21	22½	24	25	26	27	28
58	3	4½	6	7½	9	10½	12	13½	15	16½	18	19½	21	22½	24	25	26½	27½	28½
59	3	4½	6	7½	9	10½	12	13½	15	16½	18	19½	21	22½	24	25½	27	28	29
60	3	4½	6	7½	9	10½	12	13½	15	16½	18	19½	21	22½	24	25½	27	28½	29½
61	3	4½	6	7½	9	10½	12	13½	15	16½	18	19½	21	22½	24	25½	27	28½	30
62	3	4½	6	7½	9	10½	12	13½	15	16½	18	19½	21	22½	24	25½	27	28½	30
63	3	4½	6	7½	9	10½	12	13½	15	16½	18	19½	21	22½	24	25½	27	28½	30
64	3	4½	6	7½	9	10½	12	13½	15	16½	18	19½	21	22½	24	25½	27	28½	30

APPENDIX C

Enforcement of Statutory Rights

Table 1 deals with those statutory rights in respect of which an employee is not required to show that s/he has been employed for a certain period of time, or for a minimum number of hours per week.

Table 2 deals with those statutory rights in respect of which the employee must show that s/he has been employed under a contract of employment of 16 hours or more per week, or between 8 hours and less than 16 hours per week for more than 5 years.

Table 3 deals with those statutory rights in respect of which the employee must show that s/he satisfied the hours conditions (as in Table 2), and also show that s/he has been employed for the relevant period of continuous employment. For Guarantee Payments, Medical Suspension Payments, right not to be dismissed because of Medical Suspension, and Minimum Periods of Notice, the employee must be employed for more than one month. For the right to have a Written Statement of Terms and Conditions, s/he must be employed for more than 8 weeks. All other rights require 2 years' continuous employment.

Table 4 deals with statutory rights of and against trade unions.

Table 1

(no hours condition; no period of employment condition)

Statutory claim	*Statutory reference*	*Time limit for bringing claim*	*Maximum criteria for award*	*Maximum award*
1. Equal Pay	EqPA 1970 s. 2(4)	6 months from termination of employment	Differences in pay between applicant and comparator	Arrears of pay for up to 2 years
2. Sex Discrimination	SDA 1975 s. 65(2)	3 months from incident	Compensation for loss suffered (including injury to feelings)	£11,000
3. Race Discrimination	RRA 1976 s. 56(2)	3 months from incident	Compensation for loss suffered (including injury to feelings)	£11,000
4. Dismissal for union or non-union membership	TULR(C)A ss. 152, 156-158	3 months from effective date of termination	£205 per week	(a) *Reinstatement / re-engagement not sought* (i) Basic award £6,150 (minimum award £2,700) (ii) Compensation award, £11,000 (b) *Reinstatement / re-engagement sought but IT makes no order* (i) Basic award £6,150 (minimum £2,700) (ii) Compensation award, £11,000

			no limit	(iii) Special award 104 weeks pay (minimum £13,400 maximum £26,800)
5. Refusal to employ on ground of union membership or non-membership	TULR(C)A s. 137	3 months from refusal	Compensation for loss suffered (including injury to feelings)	£11,000
6. Action short of dismissal	TULR(C)A s. 146	3 months from the action complained of	no limits	Just and equitable
7. Interim relief	EPCA s. 77 TULR(C)A s. 161	7 days from effective date of termination	no award	no award
8. Unlawful deduction from wages	Wages Act 1986 s. 5	3 months from the date of deduction or non-payment	amount of deduction or non-payment	—
9. Time off work for ante-natal care	EPCA 1978 s. 31A	3 months from the date of the appointment	appropriate hourly rate or amount due	—
10. Time off work for safety representatives	Safety Reps etc Reg 1977	3 months from the failure to permit or failure to pay	just and equitable or amount due	—
11. Rights in insolvency	EPCA 1978 s. 122	3 months from the decision of the Secretary of State not to pay	(a) arrears of pay £205 per week (b) holiday pay £205 per week	8 weeks' pay (£1,640 maximum) 6 weeks' holiday pay (£1,230 maximum)
12. Unfair dismissal because of pregnancy or childbirth, or assertion of a statutory right	EPCA s. 60, s. 60A	3 months from effective date of termination	Basic award (£205 per week max.) Compensation award	£6,150 £11,000

Table 2

(Must be employed for more than 16 hours per week, or more than 8 hours per week for more than 5 years. No period of employment condition)

Statutory claim	*Statutory reference*	*Time limit for bringing the claim*	*Criteria for award*	*Maximum award*
1. Itemised pay statement *	EPCA 1978 s. 11(9)	3 months from effective date of termination	—	Unnotified deduction for 13 weeks prior to application
2. Time off for trade union duties	TULR(C)A s. 168	3 months from the failure to permit time off work	just and equitable *or* amount which should have been paid	—
3. Time of for trade union activities	TULR(C)A s. 170	3 months from the failure to permit time off work	just and equitable	—
4. Time off work for public duties	EPCA 1978 s 30	3 months from the failure to permit time off work	just and equitable	—

*** Eight hours employment per week if the employer employs 20 or more employees**

Table 3

(Must be employed (a) 16 or more hours per week, or between 8 and 16 hours per week for more than 5 years *and* (b) for the relevant period of continuous employment)

Statutory claim	*Statutory reference*	*Relevant period of continuous employment*	*Time limit for bringing claim*	*Criteria for award*	*Award limits*
1. Guarantee pay	EPCA 1978 s. 17	1 month (with exceptions, see s. 13(2))	3 months from the day for which it is claimed	£14.10 per day	5 days in any period of 3 months (i.e. £70.50)
2. Medical suspension pay	EPCA s. 22	1 months (with exceptions, see s. 20)	3 months from day for which it is claimed	Actual pay due	26 weeks' pay
3. Unfair dismissal as a result of medical suspension	EPCA s. 64(2)	1 month	3 months from effective date of termination	Basic award (£205 per week max.) Compensation award	£6,150 £11,000
4. Written particulars of employment*	EPCA s. 1	2 months	—	—	—
5. Right to return to work after maternity leave	EPCA s. 39	2 years prior to 11th week prior to expected week of confinement	3 months from date of refusal by employer	basic award (£205 per week max.) Compensation award	£6,150 £11,000

* Only eight hours employment required.

6. Redundancy payment	EPCA s. 81	2 years (service prior to 18th birthday doesn't count)	6 months from relevant date	Dependent on age, length of service, and week's pay (£205 per week max)	£6,150
7. Unfair dismissal	EPCA ss. 54, 59	2 years	3 months from effective date of termination	Basic award (£205 per week max.) Compensation award	£6,150 £11,000
8. Time off to look for work	EPCA s. 31	2 years	3 months from date of refusal	Amount which should have been paid	2 days' pay
9. Written reasons for dismissal	EPCA s. 53	2 years	3 months from effective date of termination	2 weeks' actual pay	No limit
10. Rights in insolvency (pay in lieu of notice)	EPCA s. 122(3)(b)	4 weeks	3 months from Secretary of State's decision	Up to 12 weeks' statutory notice pay (£205 per week max.)	£2,440
11. Unfair dismissal (unfair selective re-engagement)	EPCA s. 62	2 years	6 months from the date of dismissal	Basic award (£205 per week max.) Compensation award	£6,150 £11,000

Table 4

Statutory rights by and against trade unions

Statutory right	*Statutory reference*	*Time limit for presenting complaint*	*Maximum criteria for award*	*Award limits*
1. Failure to consult trade union on redundancies	TULR(C)A s. 189	3 months from date dismissals took effect	£205 per week maximum	28, 30, 90 days protective award, depending on the numbers made redundant
2. Failure to inform or consult on transfers	Transfers of Undertakings Regulations	3 months from date the transfers were completed	Appropriate compensation £205 per week maximum	Four weeks' pay
3. Unreasonable exclusion or expulsion from a trade union	TULR(C)A s. 174	6 months from the exclusion or expulsion	(a) *if admitted or re-admitted to union* just and equitable (b) *if not admitted or re-admitted* just and equitable (EAT) minimum £5,000	£16,150 £26,810
4. unjustifiable discipline by a trade union	TULR(C)A s. 64	3 months from date of decision	Just and equitable (IT) Just and equitable (EAT, minimum £2,700)	£16,150 £16,150

APPENDIX D

Industrial Tribunal Forms

Application to an Industrial Tribunal

Notes for Guidance

Before filling in this form please read:

- **these guidance notes**
- **Leaflet ITL1 which you were given with this form**
- **the correct booklet for your type of case**

Information

There are many things you can complain to a Tribunal about. Leaflet ITL1 tells you what they are, which law (an Act of Parliament) covers your complaint and which booklet you should get. Each of the booklets explains the law in simple terms. You can get the booklets free from any employment office, Jobcentre or Unemployment Benefit Office. If you are in doubt, your Trade Union or a Citizens' Advice Bureau may be able to give you further advice or information.

Time Limits

You must send in your application form so that it arrives at the Central Office of the Industrial Tribunals within the time limit. The time limit depends on which complaint you are making; for example, for unfair dismissal complaints it is three months beginning with the date of dismissal. So if you were dismissed on 10th January, the form must arrive by 9th April.

Qualifying periods

There are rules about how long you have to work for an employer before you can bring a case to a Tribunal. These rules are explained in the booklets.

If you are in any doubt about the time limits or qualifying periods, please contact your local employment office, Jobcentre or Unemployment Benefit Office; or get in touch with the Advisory Conciliation and Arbitration Service (ACAS) - see leaflet ITL1 for addresses and telephone numbers.

Representatives

You can present your own case at the Tribunal. If you want someone else to present your case, try to consult him or her before you complete your application form, but remember your form must arrive within the **time limit. If you name a representative, all future dealings will be with him or her and not with you.** If you name a representative, you should ask him or her any questions you have about the progress of your case and when the Tribunal hearing will be.

If your complaint concerns equal pay or sex discrimination, you may wish to contact the Equal Opportunities Commission for advice or representation. If your complaint is about racial discrimination, you may wish to contact the Commission for Racial Equality for advice or representation.

Help for people with disabilities

If you, or anyone who needs to visit a Tribunal, are disabled and may have difficulty getting in or out of the office, or using normal seating or toilets, please inform our staff at the office where your case is being handled. They will do all they can to help.

Data Protection Act 1984

We may put some of the information you give in this form on to a computer. This helps us to monitor progress and produce statistics. We may also give information :

- to the other party in the case;
- for the same purposes, to other parts of the Employment Department Group and organisations such as the Advisory, Conciliation and Arbitration Service (ACAS), the Equal Opportunities Commission or the Commission for Racial Equality.

Filling in the form

Help
Your Trade Union or local Citizens' Advice Bureau may be able to help you fill in the form if you have any problems, but make sure your form arrives within the **time limit.**

Questions to answer
Try to complete all the boxes that apply in your case. You must answer the questions in boxes 1, 2, 4, 8 and 10.

Be clear
This form has to be photocopied, so please use black ink, or type your answers, and use **CAPITAL LETTERS** for names and addresses. Where boxes appear in this form which give you a choice of answer(s), please tick those that apply. If there is not enough space for your answer, please continue on a separate sheet of paper and attach it to this form.

Box 1
Put here the type of complaint you want the Tribunal to decide (for example, unfair dismissal, redundancy payment, equal pay etc). A full list of types of complaint is given in leaflet ITL 1. If there is more than one complaint you want the Tribunal to decide, please say so. Give the details of your complaints in Box 10.

Box 2
Give your name and address and date of birth, and if possible a telephone number where the Tribunal or ACAS can contact you during the day about your application.

Box 4
Give details of the employer, body or person (the "respondent") you wish to complain about. In the second box, give the place where you worked or applied for work, if different from that of the respondent you have named. (For example, complete both boxes if you have named a liquidator, the Secretary of State for Employment, or your employer's Head Office as the respondent).

Box 10
Give full details of your complaint. If there is not enough room on the form, continue on a separate sheet and attach it to the form. Do NOT send any other documents or evidence in support of your complaint at this stage. Your answer may be used in an initial assessment of your case, so make it as complete and accurate as you can. (See **Help** above).

When you have finished:

- **sign and date the form**
- **keep these guidance notes and a copy of your answers**
- **send the form to:**

ENGLAND AND WALES
The Secretary of the Tribunals,
Central Office of the Industrial Tribunals,
100 Southgate Street,
Bury St Edmunds,
Suffolk,
IP33 2AQ.
Telephone 0284 762300

SCOTLAND
The Secretary of the Tribunals,
Central Office of the Industrial Tribunals (Scotland),
St Andrew House,
141 West Nile Street,
Glasgow,
G1 2RU.
Telephone 041 331 1601

FOR COIT USE ONLY

Received at COIT	Case Number	Code
	Initials	ROIT

Application to an Industrial Tribunal

Please read the notes opposite before filling in this form

1. Say what type of complaint(s) you want the tribunal to decide *(see note opposite)*.

2. Please give your name and address in CAPITALS

Mr ☐ Mrs ☐ Miss ☐ Ms ☐

Surname

First name(s)

Address

Postcode

Telephone

Date of birth

3. Please give the name and address of your representative, if you have one.

Name

Address

Postcode

Telephone

4. Please give the details of the employer or body (the respondent) you are complaining about *(see note opposite)*.

Name

Address

Postcode

Telephone

Please give the place where you worked or applied for work, if different from above.

Name

Address

Postcode

Telephone

5. Please say what job you did for the employer (or what job you applied for). If this does not apply, please say what your connection was with the employer.

IT 1 and IT 1(Scot) (Revised Feb 1991) **Over ▶**

6. Please give the number of normal basic hours you worked per week.

Hours [ ] per week

8. Please give the dates of your employment. *(if applicable)*

Began on [ ]

Ended on [ ]

7. Basic wage/ salary £ [ ] per [ ]

Average take home pay £ [ ] per [ ]

Other bonuses or benefits £ [ ] per [ ]

9. If your complaint is not about dismissal, please give the date when the action you are complaining about took place (or the date when you first knew about it).

Date [ ]

10. Please give full details of your complaint *(see notes attached)*:

11. Unfair dismissal claimants only *(Please tick a box to show what you would want if you win your case)*

[ ] **Reinstatement:** to carry on working in your old job as before.

[ ] **Re-engagement:** to start another job, or a new contract, with your old employer.

→ Orders for re-instatement or re-engagement normally include an award of compensation for loss of earnings.

[ ] **Compensation only:** to get an award of money.

You can change your change your mind later. The Tribunal will take your preference into account, but will not be bound by it.

12. Have you already sent us a copy of this application by facsimile transmission (fax)?

Yes [ ] **No** [ ]

Signed [ ] Date [ ]

1797 13.9.2MKS

Industrial Tribunals

Case number:

Notice of Appearance by Respondent

1 Please give the following details

Mr ☐ Mrs ☐ Miss ☐ Ms ☐

Other title

(Or give the name of the company or organisation)

Name

Address

Telephone

2 Do you intend to resist the application made by

YES ☐ NO ☐

3 Was the applicant dismissed?

YES ☐ NO ☐

If 'YES', what was the reason?

4 Are the dates of employment given by the applicant correct?

YES ☐ NO ☐

If 'NO', please give the correct dates

Began on

Ended on

5 If a representative is acting for you, please give his/her name and address (NOTE. *All further communications will be sent to him or her, not to you)*

Name

Address

Telephone

Reference

6 Are the details given by the applicant about wages/salary or other payments or benefits correct?

YES ☐ NO ☐

If 'NO', or if details were not given, please give the correct details:

Basic wage/salary

£ per

Average take home pay

£ per

Other bonuses/benefits

£ per

7 Maternity rights cases only

When the applicant's absence began did you have more than five employees?

YES ☐ NO ☐

Please continue overleaf ►

IT 3

8 If you answered 'YES' to question **2**. please give below sufficient details to show the grounds on which you intend to resist the application: ***(continue on a separate sheet if there is not enough space for your answer)***

9

Signed ______________________

Date ______________

10 Please send this form to:
The Assistant Secretary

REGIONAL OFFICE OF THE
INDUSTRIAL TRIBUNALS
SOUTHGATE STREET
BURY ST. EDMUNDS
IP33 2AQ.
TEL : 0284 762171
FAX : 0284 706064

For official use

Date received ______________________ Initials ______________

IT 3 (Reverse)

EQ2.12.87

APPENDIX E

Improvement and Prohibition Notices

HSE
Health & Safety Executive

Health and Safety at Work etc Act 1974, Sections 21, 23, and 24

Serial number

Improvement notice

Name

Address

Trading as*

Inspector's full name — I,

Inspector's official designation — one of Her Majesty's Inspectors of

Being an Inspector appointed by an instrument in writing made pursuant to section 19 of the said Act and entitled to issue this notice

Official address — of

Telephone number

hereby give you notice that I am of the opinion that

Location of premise or place of activity — at

you, as an employer / a self employed person / a person wholly or partly in control of the premises / other*

are contravening / have contravened in circumstances that make it likely that the contravention will continue or be repeated* the following statutory provisions :

The reasons for my said opinion are :

and I hereby require you to remedy the said contraventions or, as the case may be, the matters occasioning them by (and I direct that the measures specified in the Schedule which forms part of this notice shall be taken to remedy the said contraventions or matters)*

Signature Date

An Improvement Notice is also being served on

of

related to the matters contained in the notice.

Environment and Safety Information Act 1988 — This is a relevant notice for the purposes of the Environment and Safety Information Act 1988 YES / NO*
This page only will form the register entry*.

Signature Date

LP1 (rev 3 / 92) *SEE NOTES OVERLEAF* ** delete as appropriate*

1. Failure to comply with this Improvement Notice is an offence as provided by section 33 (1) (g) of the Health and Safety at Work etc Act 1974 and section 33 (2A) of this Act renders the offender liable on summary conviction, to imprisonment for a term not exceeding 6 months, or to a fine not exceeding £20,000, or both, or, on conviction on indictment, to imprisonment for a term not exceeding 2 years, or a fine, or both.

2. An Inspector has power to withdraw an Improvement Notice or to extend the period specified in the notice before the end of the period specified in it. If you wish this to be considered you should apply to the Inspector who issued the notice, but you must do so before the end of the period given in it. Such an application is not an appeal against this notice.

3. The issue of this notice does not relieve you of any legal liability for failing to comply with any statutory provision referred to in the notice or to perform any other statutory or common law duty resting on you.

4. Your attention is drawn to the provision for appeal against this notice to an Industrial Tribunal. Details of the method of making an appeal are given below, see also Section 24 of this Act. The appeal should be sent to : The Secretary of the Tribunals, Central Office of the Industrial Tribunals, Southgate Street, Bury St. Edmunds, Suffolk IP33 2AQ. (for England and Wales) or the Secretary of the Tribunals, Central Office of the Industrial Tribunals, Saint Andrews House , 141 West Nile Street, Glasgow G1 2RU (for Scotland only).

The appeal must be commenced by sending in writing to the Secretary of the Tribunals a notice containing the following particulars :

(a) the name of the appellant and his address for the service of documents ;

(b) the date of the notice, or notices, appealed against and the address of the premises or place concerned ;

(c) the name and address, as shown on this notice, of the respondent ;

(d) particulars of the requirements or directions appealed against; and

(e) the grounds of the appeal.

A form which may be used for appeal is attached.

Time limit for appeal

A notice of appeal must be sent to the Secretary of the Tribunals within 21 days from the date of service on the appellant of the notice, or notices, appealed against, or within such further period as the tribunal considers reasonable in a case where it is satisfied that it was not reasonably practicable for the notice of appeal to be presented within the period of 21 days. If posted the appeal should be sent by recorded delivery.

The entering of an appeal suspends the Improvement Notice until the appeal has been determined, but does not automatically alter the date given in this notice by which the matters contained in it must be remedied.
The rules for the hearing of an appeal are given in The Industrial Tribunals (Improvement and Prohibition Notices Appeals) Regulations 1974 (SI 1974 No 1925) for England and Wales and The Industrial Tribunals (Improvement and Prohibition Notices Appeals) (Scotland) Regulations 1974 (SI 1974 No 1926) for Scotland.

ENVIRONMENT AND SAFETY INFORMATION ACT 1988

1. A notice which is relevant for the purposes of this Act (see overleaf) will be included as an entry in a public register which will be kept by the Health and Safety Executive. A relevant notice is one which does not impose requirements or prohibitions solely for the protection of persons at work.

2. The register entry shall be made within 14 days of either the right of appeal against the notice expiring , or of such an appeal being disposed of. Where a notice is cancelled on appeal no entry shall be made.

3. When an Inspector is satisfied a relevant notice has been complied with an entry shall be made in the register to show this. If a notice is withdrawn or amended the entry shall be deleted or amended. These alterations of the register shall be made within 7 days.

4. Entries shall be kept in the register for a period of at least 3 years.

5. If you think that the entry for this notice on the register will disclose information about a trade secret or secret manufacturing process you should give written notification to the Health and Safety Executive within 14 days. The Health and Safety Executive will then draft an entry which in its opinion will not reveal the secret, and serve this on you.

6. If you are not satisfied with this draft entry you may appeal within 14 days to the Secretary of State who may decide that the entry should be made as drafted, or, if it is considered it does not afford reasonable protection to the secret, the Secretary of State may specify the form the entry should take.

7. If you make a written notification the Health and Safety Executive will not make an entry in relation to the notice other than one which only specifies your name and address, identifies any place involved and specifies the relevant legal provisions. A fuller entry will only be made when a) you give your written consent to the draft, or b) where no consent is given the time allowed for appeal to the Secretary of State has expired, or c) on appeal the Secretary of State has directed that an entry shall be made.

HSE Health & Safety Executive

Health and Safety at Work etc Act 1974, Sections 22,23, and 24

Serial Number
P

Prohibition notice

Name

Address

Trading as*

Inspector's full name
I,

Inspector's official designation
one of Her Majesty's Inspectors of
Being an Inspector appointed by an instrument in writing made pursuant to section 19 of the said Act and entitled to issue this notice

Official address
of

Telephone number

hereby give you notice that I am of the opinion that the following activities namely :

which are being carried on by you / likely to be carried on by you / under your control* at

Location of premises or place of activity

involve, or will involve, a risk of serious personal injury, and that the matters which give rise / will give rise* to the said risks are :

and that the said matters involve / will involve* contravention of the following statutory provisions :

because

and I hereby direct that the said activities shall not be carried on by you or under your control immediately / after* unless the said contraventions and matters have been remedied.

I further direct that the measures specified in the schedule which forms part of this notice shall be taken to remedy the said contraventions or matters.*

Signature Date

* A Prohibition Notice is also being served on

of

related to the matters contained in this notice.

Environment and Safety Information Act 1988
This is a relevant notice for the purposes of the Environment and Safety Information Act 1988 YES / NO*
This page only will form the register entry*.

Signature Date

LP2 (rev 3 / 92) *SEE NOTES OVERLEAF* ***delete as appropriate**

1 Failure to comply with this Prohibition Notice is an offence as provided by section 33(1) (g) of the Health and Safety at Work etc Act 1974 and section 33(2A) of this Act renders the offender liable on summary conviction, to imprisonment for a term not exceeding 6 months, or to a fine not exceeding £20,000, or both, or, on conviction on indictment, to imprisonment for a term not exceeding 2 years, or a fine, or both.

2 Except for an immediate Prohibition Notice, an Inspector has power to withdraw a notice or to extend the period specified in the notice, before the end of the period specified in it. If you wish this to be considered you should apply to the Inspector who issued the notice, but you must do so before the end of the period given in it. Such an application is not an appeal against this notice.

3 The issue of this notice does not relieve you of any legal liability for failing to comply with any statutory provisions referred to in the notice or to perform any other statutory or common law duty resting on you.

4 Your attention is drawn to the provision for appeal against this notice to an Industrial Tribunal. Details of the method of making an appeal are given below, see also section 24 of this Act. The appeal should be sent to : The Secretary of the Tribunals, Central Office of the Industrial Tribunals, Southgate Street, Bury St Edmunds, Suffolk. IP33 2AQ. (for England and Wales) or the Secretary of the Tribunals, Central Office of the Industrial Tribunals, St Andrew House, 141 West Nile Street, Glasgow G1 2RU (for Scotland only).

The appeal must be commenced by sending in writing to the Secretary of the Tribunals a notice containing the following particulars :

(a) the name of the appellant and his address for the service of documents;

(b) the date of the notice, or notices, appealed against and the address of premises or place concerned;

(c) the name and address, as shown on this notice, of the respondent;

(d) particulars of the requirements or directions appealed against; and

(e) the grounds of appeal.

A form which may be used for appeal is attached.

Time limit for appeal

A notice of appeal must be sent to the Secretary of the Tribunals within 21 days from the date of service on the appellant of the notice, or notices, appealed against, or within such further period as the tribunal considers reasonable in a case where it is satisfied that it was not reasonably practicable for the notice of appeal to be presented within the period of 21 days. If posted the appeal should be sent by recorded delivery.

The entering of an appeal does not have the effect of suspending this notice. Application can be made for the suspension of this notice to the Secretary of the Tribunals, but the notice continues in force until a tribunal otherwise directs.

An application for suspension of the notice must be in writing and must set out :

(a) the case number of the appeal, if known, or particulars sufficient to identify it; and

(b) the grounds on which the application is made. (It may accompany the appeal .)

The rules for the hearing of an appeal are given in The Industrial Tribunals (Improvement and Prohibition Notices Appeals) Regulations 1974 (SI 1974 No 1925) for England and Wales and the Industrial Tribunals (Improvement and Prohibition Notices Appeals) (Scotland) Regulations 1974 (SI 1974 No 1926) for Scotland.

ENVIRONMENT AND SAFETY INFORMATION ACT 1988

1 A notice which is relevant for the purposes of this Act (see overleaf) will be included as an entry in a public register which will be kept by the Health and Safety Executive. A relevant notice is one which does not impose requirements or prohibitions solely for the protection of persons at work.

2 The register entry shall be made within 14 days of either the right of appeal against the notice expiring, or of such an appeal being disposed of.Where a notice is cancelled on appeal no entry shall be made.

3 When an inspector is satisfied a relevant notice has been complied with an entry shall be made in the register to show this. If a notice is withdrawn or amended the entry shall be deleted or amended. These alterations of the register shall be made within 7 days.

4 Entries shall be kept in the register for a period of at least 3 years.

5 If you think that the entry for this notice on the register will disclose information about a trade secret or secret manufacturing process you should give written notification to the Health and Safety Executive within 14 days. The Health and Safety Executive will then draft an entry which in its opinion will not reveal the secret, and serve this on you.

6 If you are not satisfied with this draft entry you may appeal within 14 days to the Secretary of State who may either decide that the entry should be made as drafted, or, if it is considered it does not afford reasonable protection to the secret, the Secretary of State may specify the form the entry should take.

7 If you make a written notification the Health and Safety Executive will not make an entry in relation to the notice other than one which only specifies your name and address, identifies any place involved and specifies the relevant legal provisions. A fuller entry will only be made when a) you give your written consent to the draft, or b) where no consent is given the time allowed for appeal to the Secretary of State has expired, or c) on appeal the Secretary of State has directed that an entry shall be made.

Names and Addresses

Department of Employment
Caxton House
Tothill Street
London SW1H 9NA
071-273 3000

Advisory, Conciliation and Arbitration Service
27 Wilton Street
London SW1X 7AZ
071-210 3645
(Regional Offices can be found in Newcastle-upon-Tyne, Leeds, London, Bristol, Brimingham, Manchester, Glasgow and Cardiff)

Central Office of the Industrial Tribunals
Southgate Street
Bury St Edmunds
Suffolk IP33 2AQ
0284 762300
Fax: 0284 766334

Central Office of Industrial Tribunals
St Andrew's House
141 West Nile Street
Glasgow G1 2RG
041-331 1601
Fax: 041-332 3316

Certification Officer
27 Wilton Street
London SW1X 7AZ
071-210 3734

Central Arbitration Committee
39 Grosvenor Place
London SW1X 7BD
071-210 3738

Commission for Racial Equality
Elliot House
10-12 Allington Street
London SW1E 5EH
071-828 7022

Health and Safety Executive
Baynards House
1 Chepstow Place
Westbourne Grove
London W2 4TF
071-221 0870

Equal Opportunities Commission
Overseas House
Quay Street
Manchester M3 3HN
061-833 9244

Employment Appeal Tribunal
58 Victoria Embankment
London EC4Y 0DS
071-273 1041
Fax:071-273 1045

11 Melville Crescent
Edinburgh
031-225 3963
Fax: 031-220 6694

Commissioner for the Rights of Trade Union Members and **Commissioner for the Protection against Unlawful Industrial Action**
First Floor
Bank Chambers
2A Rylands Street
Warrington
Cheshire WA1 1EN
0925 415771

APPENDIX G

Discipline at Work

ACAS ADVISORY HANDBOOK

1 Checklist for handling a disciplinary matter

This checklist sets out the key steps which employers should consider when handling a disciplinary matter. All employers, regardless of size, should observe the principles of natural justice embodied below:

1 Gather all the relevant facts:
- promptly before memories fade
- take statement, collect documents
- in serious cases consider suspension with pay while any investigation is conducted.

2 Be clear about the complaint
- is action needed at this stage?

3 If so, decide whether the action should be:
- advice and counselling
- formal disciplinary action.

4 If formal action is required, arrange a disciplinary interview:
- ensure that the individual is aware of the nature of the complaint and that the interview is a disciplinary one
- tell the individual where and when the interview will take place and of a right to be accompanied
- try to arrange for a second member of management to be present.

5 Start by introducing:

- those present and the purpose of the interview
- the nature of the complaint
- the supporting evidence.

6 Allow the individual to state his/her case:
- consider and question any explanations put forward.

7 If any new facts emerge:
- decide whether further investigation is required
- if it is, adjourn the interview and reconvene when the investigation is completed.

8 Except in very straightforward cases, call an adjournment before reaching a decision:
- come to a clear view about the facts
- if they are disputed, decide on the balance of probability what version of the facts if true.

9 Before deciding the penalty consider:
- the gravity of the offence and whether the procedure gives guidance
- the penalty applied in similar cases in the past
- the individual's disciplinary record and general service
- any mitigating circumstances
- whether the proposed penalty is reasonable in all the circumstances.

10 Reconvene the disciplinary interview to:
- clearly inform the individual of the decision and the penalty, if any
- explain the right of appeal and how it operates
- in the case of a warning, explain what improvements are expected, how long the warning will last and what the consequences of failure to improve may be.

11 Record the action taken:
- if other than an oral warning, confirm the disciplinary action to the individual in writing
- keep a simple record of the action taken for future reference.

12 Monitor the individual's performance:
- disciplinary action should be followed up with the object of encouraging improvement
- monitor progress regularly and discuss it with the individual.

2 The need for rules and disciplinary procedures

Key points:

Rules are necessary because they set standards. A good disciplinary procedure will help employees to keep them and help employers to deal fairly with those who do not.

Rules should normally cover issues such as absence, health and safety, misconduct, sub-standard performance, use of company facilities, timekeeping and holiday arrangements.

Rules and procedures should be clear and usually in writing and should be known and understood by all employees.

Every employee should have access to a copy of the rules and disciplinary procedure.

Management should aim to secure the involvement of employees and any recognised trade union when disciplinary procedures are introduced or revised.

Rules should be reviewed from time to time.

Management should ensure that those responsible for operating disciplinary rules understand them and receive appropriate training.

Why have rules?

Clear rules benefit both employers and employees. They set standards of conduct at work and make clear to employees what is expected of them.

How should rules be drawn up and communicated?

- They should generally be written down to ensure that employees know what is required of them and to avoid misunderstanding
- Care should be taken to ensure that they are non-discriminatory and are applied irrespective of sex, marital status or racial group[1]

1 Further guidance can be obtained from the Codes of Practice produced by the Equal Opportunities Commission and the Commission for Racial Equality. The Race Relations Employment Advisory Service (RREAS) of the Department of Employment is also available to give assistance and can be contacted at St Vincent House, Orange Street, London WC2H YHH.

- They should be readily available and managers should take all reasonable steps to ensure that all employees know and understand them
- An explanation of the rules should be given to all new employees when they join. Section 1 of the Employment Protection (Consolidation) Act 1978 requires employers to provide employees with a written statement covering their main terms and conditions of employment and disciplinary rules
- Special attention should be paid to ensure that rules are understood by young people with little experience of working life and by employees whose English is limited
- Where a rule has fallen into disuse or has not been applied consistently, employees should always be told before there is any change in practice.

What should rules cover?

The following are examples of the kinds of issue which rules should cover. An example of the sort of rules which might be appropriate in a small company is given in Appendix 2.

Timekeeping:

- are employees required to 'clock-in'
- what rules apply to lateness?

Absence:

- who authorises absence
- who approves holidays
- who should employees notify when they are absent from work
- when should notification of absence take place
- when is a medical self-certificate sufficient
- when will a doctor's certificate be necessary?

Health and safety:

- are there special requirements regarding personal appearance or cleanliness, e.g. length of hair, jewellery, protective clothing
- are there special hazards
- are there non-smoking areas
- is alcohol prohibited?

Gross misconduct:

- are the kind of offences regarded as gross misconduct and which could lead to dismissal without notice clearly specified?

Use of company facilities:

- are private telephone c:alls permitted
- are employees allowed to be on company premises outside working hours
- is company equipment generally available for personal use?

Discrimination:

- is it clear that racial and sexual abuse or harassment will be treated as disciplinary offences
- is there a rule about clothing or uniform which is disproportionately disadvantageous to a racial group and which cannot be justified on non-racial grounds
- is there a rule requiring higher language standards than are needed for safe and effective performance of the job
- is there a requirement about mobility of employment which cannot be justified on operational grounds and is disadvantageous to one sex?

It is helpful if rules are written down so that both managers and employees are clearly aware what is expected of them. The rules should be made clear to any new employees and ideally they should be given their own copy. In the small firm it may be sufficient for rules to be displayed in a prominent place. In large firms it is good practice to include a section on rules in the company handbook and to discuss them during the induction programme.

Employees will more readily accept rules if care is taken to explain why they are necessary. They should be presented as giving information rather than as warnings; for example ... 'For reasons of safety and security, you may not bring visitors on to company premises without the express permission of your manager'.

Unless there are valid reasons why different sets of rules should apply to different groups of workers - perhaps for health and safety reasons - rules should generally apply to all employees, be they management or shop-floor, full-time or part-time.

Why have a disciplinary procedure?

A disciplinary procedure is the means by which rules are observed and standards are maintained. It provides a method of dealing with any shortcomings in conduct or performance and can help an undisciplined or poorly performing employee to become effective again. The consistent application of a fair and effective disciplinary procedure will help to minimise disagreements about disciplinary matters and reduce the need for dismissals.

What should disciplinary procedures contain?

Paragraph 10 of the *Code of Practice* reproduced below recommends what disciplinary procedures should contain:

10 Disciplinary procedures should:

(a) Be in writing.
(b) Specify to whom they apply.
(c) Provide for matters to be dealt with quickly.
(d) Indicate the disciplinary actions which may be taken.
(e) Specify the levels of management which have the authority to take the various forms of disciplinary action, ensuring that immediate superiors do not normally have the power to dismiss without reference to senior management.
(f) Provide for individuals to be informed of the complaints against them and to be given an opportunity to state their case before decisions are reached.
(g) Give individuals the right to be accompanied by a trade union representative or by a fellow employee of their choice.
(h) Ensure that, except for gross misconduct, no employees are dismissed for a first breach of discipline.
(i) Ensure that disciplinary action is not taken until the case has been carefully investigated.
(j) Ensure that individuals are given an explanation for any penalty imposed.
(k) Provide a right of appeal and specify the procedure to be followed.

In addition disciplinary procedures should:

- apply to all employees, irrespective of their length of service
- be non-discriminatory and applied irrespective of sex, marital status or race
- ensure that any investigatory period of suspension is with pay and specify how pay is to be calculated during such pe-

riod (if, exceptionally, suspension is to be without pay this should be provided for in the contract of employment)

- ensure that, where the facts are in dispute, no disciplinary penalty is imposed until the case has been carefully investigated and it is concluded on the balance of probability that the employees committed the act in question.

Two examples of a disciplinary procedure are shown in Appendix 3. The first can be used by an organisation with formal relations with trade union(s) but the second example may be better suited to the needs of smaller firms.

Training

Those responsible for applying disciplinary rules and procedures should be trained for the task. If the provisions of an agreed disciplinary procedure are ignored when dismissing an employee, then this in itself is likely to have a bearing on the outcome of any subsequent complaint of unfair dismissal. Senior management should ensure that, wherever practicable, managers and supervisors have a thorough knowledge of their disciplinary rules and procedures and that they know how to prepare for and conduct a disciplinary interview. Where unions are recognised, consideration might be given to training managers and trade union representatives jointly.

3 Handling a disciplinary matter

Key points:

Remember that disciplinary action is intended to encourage an unsatisfactory employee to improve.

Handle the matter promptly and gather all the relevant facts.

Be firm, it is a manager's responsibility to maintain satisfactory standards.

Consider suspension with pay while the case is investigated.

Be objective, fair and consistent.

Consider each case on its merits and avoid snap decisions made in the heat of the moment.

Follow the disciplinary procedure.

Encourage improvement

The main purpose of the disciplinary procedure is to encourage an employee whose standard of work or conduct is unsatisfactory to improve.

Handle promptly

Problems dealt with early enough can be 'nipped in the bud', whereas delay can make things worse. In all cases interviews should be arranged as soon as possible.

Gather facts

The manager should find out all the relevant facts promptly before memory fades, including anything the employee wishes to say. If in serious disciplinary cases there are witnesses, statements should be obtained from them at the earliest opportunity. The manager should be clear precisely what the complaint is. Personal details such as age, length of service, past disciplinary history and any current warnings should be obtained before the hearing as well as any necessary records or relevant documents.

Be firm

The disciplinary procedure is there to provide a fair and consistent method of dealing with problems of conduct or work performance. Maintaining satisfactory standards and dealing with disciplinary issues requires firmness on the part of the manager.

Suspension with pay

In cases which appear to involve serious misconduct, a brief period of suspension should be considered while the case is being investigated. This should be with pay unless the contract of employment provides for suspension without pay in such circumstances. A suspension without pay should be exceptional as this in itself may amount to a disciplinary penalty. Where there has been physical violence, or where tempers have been raised, it is often wise to get those concerned off the premises as quickly as possible while the matter is investigated. They should be told clearly that they are suspended, that it will be for as short a period as possible and that they will be called back for interview.

Stay calm

Enquiries and proceedings should always be conducted with thought and care. Snap decisions made in the heat of the moment should be avoided. The disciplining of an employee is a serious matter and should never be regarded lightly or dealt with casually.

Be fair

Maintaining standards of acceptable conduct and work performance calls for objectivity and fairness. It is important to keep an open mind and not prejudge the issues.

Be consistent

The attitude and conduct of employees who obey rules will be seriously affected if management fails to apply the same rules and considerations to each case. Management should try to ensure that all employees are aware of the normal company practice for dealing with the misconduct or poor performance under consideration.

Consider each case on its merits

While consistency is important, it is essential to take account of the situations and people involved. Any decision to discipline an employee must be reasonable in all the circumstances.

Follow the disciplinary procedure

The disciplinary procedure should be followed and the supervisor or manager should never exceed the limits of his or her authority.

Is disciplinary action necessary?

Having gathered all the facts the manager or supervisor should decide whether to:

Drop the matter. There may be no case to answer or the matter may be so trivial that it is better to overlook it.

Arrange counselling. This is an attempt to correct a situation and prevent it from getting worse without using the disciplinary procedure.

Arrange a disciplinary interview. This will be necessary when the matter is more serious and it appears that there has been a disciplinary offence which requires appropriate disciplinary action.

4 Counselling

Key points:

Counselling may often be a more satisfactory method of resolving problems than a disciplinary interview.

It should take the form of a discussion with the objective of encouraging and helping the employee to improve.

The employee should fully understand the outcome.

A note of any counselling should be kept for reference purposes.

What is counselling?

In many cases the right word, at the right time and in the right way may be all that is needed, and will often be a more satisfactory method of dealing with a breach of discipline than a formal interview.

How should it be done?

- Wherever possible hold the discussion out of hearing of other employees. It should be a two-way discussion, aimed at pointing out any shortcomings in conduct or performance and encouraging improvement. Criticism should be constructive, and the emphasis should be on finding ways in which the employee can remedy any shortcomings.
- Listen to any explanation put forward by the employee. If it becomes evident that there is no case to answer this should be made clear to the employee.
- Where an improvement is required make sure that the employee understands what needs to be done, how performance or conduct will be reviewed, and over what period. The employee should be told that if there is no improvement the next stage will be the formal disciplinary procedure.
- Take care that a counselling interview does not turn into a formal disciplinary hearing as this may unintentionally deny the employee certain things, such as the right to be

accompanied. If during the meeting it becomes obvious that the matter is more serious, the discussion should be adjourned. It should be made clear that the matter will be pursued under the formal disciplinary procedure.

- Keep a brief note of any counselling for reference purposes. It should not be confused with action taken under the formal disciplinary procedure.

5 Holding a disciplinary interview

Key points:

Prepare for a disciplinary interview carefully and ensure all the relevant facts are available.

Tell the employee what is being alleged and advise him or her of any rights under the disciplinary procedure.

Give the employee time to prepare and an opportunity to state his or her case.

Carry out sufficient investigation and come to a clear view about the facts.

Consider adjourning the hearing before deciding on any disciplinary penalty to allow proper consideration of all the matters raised.

Preparing for the interview

- Prepare carefully and ensure you have all the facts.
- Tell the employee of the complaint, the procedure to be followed and that he or she is required to attend a disciplinary interview.
- Tell the employee that he or she is entitled to be accompanied at the interview.
- Find out if there are any special circumstances to be taken into account. (For example, are there personal or other outside issues affecting performance or conduct?)
- Are the standards of the other employees acceptable or is this employee being unfairly singled out?
- Consider what explanations may be offered by the employee and, if possible, check them out beforehand.
- Allow the employee time to prepare his or her case. In complex cases it may be useful and save time at the interview

if copies of any relevant papers are given to the employee in advance.

- If the employee concerned is a trade union official ensure that no disciplinary action beyond an oral warning is taken until the circumstances of the case have been discussed with a trade union representative or full-time official. This is because the action may be seen as an attack on the union's function.
- Arrange a time and, if possible, a quiet place for the interview with adequate seating, where there will be no interruptions.
- Ensure that all the relevant facts are available, such as personal details, disciplinary record and any current warnings, other relevant documents (e.g., absence or sickness records) and, where appropriate, written statements from witnesses.
- Establish what disciplinary action was taken in similar circumstances in the past.
- Where possible arrange for a second member of management to be present to take note of the proceedings and to act as a witness, particularly if the employee is to be accompanied.
- Where possible ensure that any witnesses who can do so attend the interview, unless the employee accepts in advance that the witness statements are statements of fact.
- If the witness is someone from outside the company who is not prepared to attend the interview, try to get a written statement from him or her.
- If there are likely to be language difficulties consider whether a friend of the employee can assist as an interpreter or other arrangements can be made.
- Consider how the interview will be structured and make notes of the points which need to be covered.

How should a disciplinary interview be conducted?

Interviews rarely proceed in neat, orderly stages but the following guidelines should help:

- introduce those present to the employee and explain why they are there
- explain that the purpose of the interview is to consider whether disciplinary action should be taken in accordance with the company's disciplinary procedure
- explain how the interview will be conducted.

Statement of the complaint

- state precisely what the complaint is and outline the case briefly by going through the evidence that has been gathered. Ensure that the employee and his or her representative is made aware of witness statements and of the contents of any relevant records
- remember that the object of the interview is to discover the truth, not to catch people out. Establish whether the employee is prepared to accept that he or she has done something wrong. Then agree the steps which should be taken to remedy the situation.

Employee's reply

- give the employee the opportunity to state his or her case, ask questions, present evidence and call witnesses. Listen attentively and be sensitive to silence as this can be a constructive way of encouraging the employee to be more forthcoming
- if it not practical for witnesses to attend, consider proceeding if it is clear that there evidence will not affect the substance of the complaint.

General questioning and discussion

- use this stage to establish all the facts
- adjourn the interview if further investigation is necessary or, if appropriate, at the request of the employee's representative
- ask the employee if he or she has any explanation for the misconduct or failure to improve or if there are any special circumstances to be taken into account
- if it becomes clear during this stage that the employee has provided an adequate explanation or there is no real evidence to support the allegation, stop the proceedings
- keep the approach formal and polite but encourage the employee to talk freely with a view to establishing all the facts. A properly conducted disciplinary interview should be a two-way process. Use questions to clarify all the issues and to check that what has been said is understood. Ask open-ended questions (e.g. What happened then?) to get the broad picture. Ask precise, closed questions requiring a yes/no answer only when specific information is needed

- try not to get involved in arguments and do not make personal or humiliating remarks. Avoid physical contact or gestures which the employee might regard as threatening.

Summing up

After general questioning and discussion summarise the main points concerning the offence, the main points raised by the employee and any matters that need to be checked. This will ensure that nothing has been missed and will help demonstrate to the employee that he or she has been given a fair hearing.

Adjournment

It is generally good practice to adjourn before a decision is taken about a disciplinary penalty. This allows proper consideration of all the matters raised.

Do any further checking that is necessary and come to a clear view about what took place. Where the facts are in dispute, decide which version is the most probable. If new facts emerge, consider whether the disciplinary interview needs to be reconvened.

What problems may arise and how should they be handled?

Not every disciplinary interview will go smoothly. Where problems are expected it is particularly important to ensure where–ver possible, that a second member of management and, where requested, an employee representative are present.

If the employee becomes emotionally distressed during the interview, allow time for the employee to become composed before continuing. The issues however cannot be avoided. If the employee continues to be so distressed that the interview cannot continue, it should be adjourned and resumed at a later date.

During the interview a certain amount of 'letting off steam' may be inevitable. This may be no bad thing and may be helpful in finding out and understanding precisely what happened. However, if misconduct or gross misconduct - for example abusive language or threatened physical violence - takes place during the interview treat it as such. Adjourn the interview and reconvene it at a later date when this offence can be considered as well. Consider suspending the employee with pay to allow time for him or her to calm down and to allow a full investigation.

6 Deciding and implementing disciplinary action

Key points:

Before deciding whether a disciplinary penalty is appropriate consider the employee's disciplinary and general record, whether the disciplinary procedure points to the likely penalty, action taken in previous cases, any explanations and circumstances to be considered and whether the penalty is reasonable.

Dismissal for gross misconduct without warnings or notice should only be for very serious offences (examples of which should be specified in the rules) and should only occur after a normal disciplinary investigation and interview.

Leave the employee in no doubt as to the nature of the disciplinary penalty, the improvement expected and the method of appeal.

Except in the event of an oral warning give the employee written details of any disciplinary action.

Keep records of disciplinary action secure and confidential.

Do not normally allow disciplinary action to count against an employee indefinitely.

What should be considered before deciding any disciplinary penalty?

When deciding whether a disciplinary penalty is appropriate and what form it should take, consideration should be given to:

- whether the disciplinary procedure indicates what the likely penalty will be as a result of the particular misconduct
- the penalty imposed in similar cases in the past
- any special circumstances which might make it appropriate to lessen the severity of the penalty
- the employee's disciplinary record, general record, age, position, and length of service
- whether the proposed penalty is reasonable in view of all the circumstances.

It should be clear what the normal company practice is for dealing with the kind of misconduct or poor performance under consideration. This does not mean that similar offences will always call for similar disciplinary action; each case must be looked at on its merits and any relevant circumstances taken into account. These may include health or domestic problems, provocation, ignorance of the rule or standard involved or inconsistent treatment in the past.

If there is doubt about what disciplinary action to take, consider consulting other managers or the personnel department if there is one. If guidance is needed on formal disciplinary action seek advice, where possible, from someone who will not be involved in hearing any potential appeal.

Imposing the disciplinary penalty

- In the case of minor offences, the individual should be given a formal oral warning and told that a note that it was given will be kept for reference purposes.
- In the case of more serious offences or where there is an accumulation of minor offences the individual should be given a formal written warning.
- If the employee has received a previous warning, further misconduct may warrant a final written warning or consideration of a disciplinary penalty short of dismissal (including disciplinary transfer, disciplinary suspension without pay,[2] demotion, loss of seniority, or loss of increment provided these penalties are allowed for by an express or implied term of the contract of employment).
- There may be occasions when misconduct is considered not to be so serious as to justify dismissal but serious enough to warrant only one written warning which will be both the first and final.
- A final written warning should contain a statement that any further misconduct will lead to dismissal.
- If all previous stages have been observed, the final step will be dismissal.

It will be seen that a three stage procedure is recommended before dismissal namely: formal oral warning, first written warning, and final written warning. This does not however mean that three warnings must always be given before any dismissal is considered. There may be occasions when, depending on the seriousness of the misconduct involved, it will be appropriate to enter the procedure at stage 2 (written warning) or stage 3 (final written warning). There also may be occasions when dismissal without notice is applicable (see below).

2 Special consideration should be given before imposing disciplinary suspension without pay. Where it is imposed, it should not exceed any period indicated in the contract nor be unreasonably prolonged since it would then be open to the employee to sue for breach of contract or resign and claim constructive dismissal.

Dismissal with notice

Dismissal should be the final step and only taken if, despite warnings, conduct or performance does not improve. It must be reasonable in all the circumstances of the case.

Unless the employee is being dismissed for reasons of gross misconduct (see below), he or she should receive the appropriate period of notice or payment in lieu of notice. This should include payments to cover the value of any fringe benefits such as use of company cars, medical insurance, subsidised meals and any commission which the employee might otherwise have earned. Minimum periods of notice are laid down by law. Employees are entitled to at least one week's notice if they have worked for a month but less than two years. This increases by one week (up to maximum of 12) for each completed year of service. If the contract of employment gives rights to more notice than the statutory minima, then the longer period of notice applies.[3]

Dismissal without notice

Employers should give all employees a clear indication of the type of misconduct which, in the light of the requirements of the employer's business, will warrant dismissal without the normal period of notice or pay in lieu of notice. So far as possible the types of offence which fall into this category (gross misconduct) should be clearly specified in the rules.

A dismissal for gross misconduct should only take place after the normal investigation to establish all the facts. The employee should be told of the complaint and be given an opportunity to state his or her case and be represented.

Gross misconduct is generally seen as misconduct serious enough to destroy the employment contract between the employer and the employee and make any further working relationship and trust impossible. It is normally restricted to very serious offences - for example physical violence, theft or fraud - but may be determined by the nature of the business or other circumstances.

3 Further guidance on employee's rights to notice are provided in the Department of Employment's free booklet *Rights on termination of employment*, Employment Legislation Booklet No. 14, PL707, which is available free from any DE office, Jobcentre, or Unemployment Benefit Office.

How should an employee be informed of the disciplinary decision?

The employee should be informed orally of the decision in all cases. If further investigations have taken place during the adjournment the employee should be told about the result of these before announcing the decision. The reasons for the decision should be given and the employee left in no doubt as to what action is being taken under the disciplinary procedure. If, for example, an oral warning is being given it should be made clear to the employee that this is not just a reprimand. The period of time that any warning will remain in force should also be explained. The employee should be told clearly what improvement is required, over what period and how it will be assessed.

Written notification of disciplinary action

Except in the event of an oral warning, details of any disciplinary penalty should be given in writing to the employee. A copy should be retained by the employer. The written notification should specify:

- the nature of the misconduct
- any period of time given for improvement and the improvement expected
- the disciplinary penalty and, where appropriate, how long it will last
- the likely consequences of further misconduct
- the timescale for lodging an appeal and how it should be made

Written reasons for dismissal

Full-time employees with six months' service have a right to request a 'written statement of reasons for dismissal'. Employers are required by law to comply within 14 days of the request being made,[4] unless it is not reasonably practicable, and the written statement can be used in evidence in any subsequent proceedings, for example in relation to a complaint of unfair dismissal.

4 Section 53 of the Employment Protection (Consolidation) Act 1978 refers. Fuller details of employee's rights to written reasons for dismissal are given in the Department of Employment's free booklet: *Rights on termination of employment*, Employment Legislation Booklet No. 14, PL707.

What records should be kept?

Consistent handling of disciplinary matters will be impracticable unless simple records of earlier decisions are kept. These records should be confidential, detailing the nature of any breach of disciplinary rules, the action taken and the reasons for it, the date action was taken, whether an appeal was lodged, its outcome and any subsequent developments.

Time limits for warnings

Except in special circumstances any disciplinary action taken should be disregarded for disciplinary purposes after a specified period of satisfactory conduct. This period should be established clearly when the disciplinary procedure is being drawn up. Normal practice is for different periods for different types of warnings. In general, warnings for minor offences may be valid for up to six months, whilst final warnings may remain in force for 12 months or more.

Warnings should cease to be 'live' following the specified period of satisfactory conduct and should be disregarded for future disciplinary purposes. There may however be occasions where an employee's conduct is satisfactory throughout the period the warning is in force only to lapse very soon thereafter.

Where a pattern emerges and there is evidence of abuse, the employee's disciplinary record should be borne in mind in deciding how long any current warning should last.

Exceptionally, there may be circumstances where the misconduct is so serious - verging on gross misconduct - that it cannot realistically be disregarded for future disciplinary purposes. In such circumstances it should be made very clear that the final written warning can never be removed and that any recurrence will lead to dismissal.

7 Holding an appeal

Key points:

Provide for appeals to be dealt with speedily.

Wherever possible, use a procedure which is separate from the general grievance procedure.

Wherever possible, provide for the appeal to be heard by an authority higher than that taking the disciplinary action.

Pay particular attention to any new evidence introduced at the hearing and allow the employee to comment on it.

Examine all the issues fully and do not be afraid to overturn a wrong decision.

What should an appeals procedure contain?

It should:

- Specify any time-limit within which the appeal should be lodged.
- Provide for appeals to be dealt with speedily, particularly those involving suspension without pay or dismissal.
- Wherever possible, provide for the appeal to be heard by an authority higher than that taking the disciplinary action.
- Spell out the action which may be taken by those hearing the appeal.
- Provide that the employee, or a representative if the employee so wishes, has an opportunity to comment on any new evidence arising during the appeal before any decision is taken.

Small firms

In small firms there may be no authority higher than the manager who decided the disciplinary action. If this is the case the same person who took the disciplinary action should hear the appeal and act as impartially as possible. The occasion should be seen as an opportunity to review the original decision in an objective manner and at a quieter time. This can be more readily achieved if some time is allowed to elapse before the appeal hearing.

How should an appeal hearing be conducted?

Action prior to the appeal

- Inform the employee of the arrangements for the appeal hearing and his or her rights under the procedure.
- Ensure that the relevant records are available and study them prior to the appeal hearing.

The appeal hearing

- Introduce those present to the employee.
- Explain the purpose of the hearing, how it will be conducted and what powers the appeal panel has.

- Ask the employee why he or she is appealing against the disciplinary penalty.
- Pay particular attention to any new evidence that has been introduced, and ensure the employee has the opportunity to comment on it.
- Once all the relevant issues have been thoroughly explored, summarise the facts and call an adjournment to consider what decision to come to.
- Do not be afraid to overturn a previous decision if it becomes apparent that this was not soundly based and do not regard such action as undermining authority. In practice it should help ensure that a correct decision is made next time.[5]
- Inform the employee of the results of the appeal and the reasons for the decision and confirm it in writing. Make it clear, if it is the case, that the decision is final.

Industrial tribunal time limits

Subject to the satisfaction of certain conditions, employees who feel that they have been unfairly dismissed have a legal right to make a complaint of unfair dismissal to an industrial tribunal. Such complaints must normally be received by the tribunal within three months of the employee's last day of work.

In most cases decisions of an internal appeal procedure will be reached well within this three month period. In exceptional cases a decision may take longer than three months. Where this seems likely to happen employees should consider whether to present an application to the industrial tribunal and ask that the case is not set down for hearing until the outcome of the internal appeal is known. Employers should not regard this action as affecting the internal appeal in any way.

8 Particular cases

Key points:

Consider how disciplinary matters should be handled when management and union representatives are not immediately available.

In normal circumstances take no disciplinary action, beyond

5 Discuss successful appeals with subordinate managers and explain the reasons. Consider whether further training is appropriate.

an oral warning, against a trade union official until the case has been discussed with a senior trade union representative or full-time official.

In criminal cases:

Do not dismiss or discipline an employee merely because he or she has been charged with or convicted of a criminal offence. Decide whether the employee's conduct affects ability or suitability for continued employment. If it does, use normal disciplinary rules. If it does not, decide whether in the light of the needs of the business, the employee's job can be kept open throughout the period of absence.

Base any decision on a reasonable belief following a reasonable investigation into the circumstances of the case.

Where a criminal charge has been made, do not defer taking fair and reasonable disciplinary action, if appropriate, merely because the outcome of the prosecution is not known.

What types of case require particular consideration?

Paragraph 15 of the *Code of Practice* recommends that certain cases may need special consideration. Employers may find the following additional advice helpful, particularly in relation to alleged criminal offences.

Employees to whom the full procedure is not immediately available

It may be sensible to allow time off with pay, so that employees who work in isolated locations or on shifts can attend a disciplinary interview on the main site during normal working hours. Alternatively, if a number of witnesses need to attend, it may be better to hold the disciplinary interview on the nightshift or at the particular location.

Trade union officials

Although normal disciplinary standards should apply to their conduct as employees, disciplinary action against a trade union official can be misconstrued as an attack on the union. Such problems can be avoided by early discussion with a full-time official.

Criminal offences

An employee should not be dismissed or otherwise disciplined merely because he or she had been charged with or convicted of a criminal offence. The question to be asked in such cases is whether the employee's conduct warrants action because of its employment implications.

Where it is thought that the conduct warrants disciplinary action, the following guidance should be borne in mind:

- The employer should investigate the facts as far as possible, come to a view about them and consider whether the conduct is sufficiently serious to warrant instituting the disciplinary procedure.
- Where the conduct requires prompt attention, the employer need not await the outcome of the prosecution before taking fair and reasonable action.
- Where the police are called in they should not be asked to conduct any investigation on behalf of the employer; nor should they be present at any disciplinary hearing or interview.

In some cases the nature of the alleged offence may not justify disciplinary action, for example, off-duty conduct which has no bearing on employment, but the employee may not be available for work because he or she is in custody or on remand. In these cases employers should decide whether in light of the needs of the business, the employee's job can be kept open. Where following a criminal conviction employment in a particular job would be illegal, employers should consider whether suitable alternative work is available.

Where an employee, charged with or convicted of a criminal offence, refuses to co-operate with the employer's disciplinary investigations and proceedings, this should not deter an employer from taking action. The employee should be advised in writing that unless further information is provided a disciplinary decision will be taken on the basis of the information available and could result in dismissal.

Where there is little likelihood of an employee returning to employment, it may be argued that the contract of employment has been terminated through 'frustration'.[6] The doctrine is normally only accepted by the court where the frustrating event

[6] There are circumstances where operation of law terminates a contract of employment, in particular the 'doctrine of frustration', without a dismissal taking place. In law 'frustration' occurs when, without the fault of either party, some event, which was not reasonably foreseeable at the time of the contract renders future performance either impossible or something radically different from what was contemplated originally. The doctrine is usually invoked in cases of sickness or imprisonment of the employee.

renders all performance of the employment contract clearly impossible.

An employee who has been charged with, or convicted of, a criminal offence may become unacceptable to colleagues, resulting in workforce pressure to dismiss and threats of industrial action. Employers should bear in mind that they may have to justify the reasonableness of any decision to dismiss. They should consider all relevant factors, which may include disruption to production, before reaching a reasonable decision.

9 Absence

Key points:

Before any action is taken to dismiss an employee who is absent from work always:

- carry out a full investigation into the reasons for the absence
- give the employee an opportunity to state his or her case and be accompanied
- issue warnings and give time for improvement where appropriate
- consider whether suitable alternative employment is available
- act reasonably in all the circumstances.

This section considers how to handle problems of absence and gives guidance about short-term and long-term absences.[7] A distinction should be made between absence on grounds of illness or injury and absence for reasons which may call for disciplinary action. Where disciplinary action is called for, the normal disciplinary procedure should be used. Where the employee is absent because of illness or injury the guidance in this section of the booklet should be followed.

Records showing lateness and the duration of and reasons for all spells of absence should be kept to help monitor absence levels. These enable management to check levels of absence or lateness so that problems can be spotted and addressed at an early stage.[8]

[7] Further guidance on the subject is given in the ACAS Advisory Booklet No 5: *Absence*, available free from any ACAS office.

[8] Guidance on the subject of personnel records is given in the ACAS Advisory Booklet No. 3: *Personnel Records*, available free from any ACAS office.

How should frequent and persistent short-term absence be handled?

- Absences should be investigated promptly and the employee asked to give an explanation.
- Where there is no medical advice to support frequent self-certified absences, the employee should be asked to consult a doctor to establish whether medical treatment is necessary and whether the underlying reason for absence is work-related.
- If after investigation it appears that there were not good reasons for the absences, the matter should be dealt with under the disciplinary procedure.
- Where absences arose from temporary domestic problems, the employer in deciding appropriate action should consider whether an improvement in attendance is likely.
- In all cases the employee should be told what improvement in attendance is expected and warned of the likely consequences if this does not happen.
- If there is no improvement, the employee's age, length of service, performance, the likelihood of a change in attendance, the availability of suitable alternative work and the effect of past and future absences on the business should all be taken into account in deciding the appropriate action.

It is essential that persistent absence is dealt with promptly, firmly and consistently in order to show both the employee concerned and other employees that absence is regarded as a serious matter and may result in dismissal. An examination of records will identify those employees who are regularly absent and may show an absence pattern. In such cases employers should make sufficient enquiries to determine whether the absence is because of genuine illness or for other reasons.

How should longer-term absence through ill-health be handled?

- The employee should be contacted periodically and in turn should maintain regular contact with the employer.
- The employee should be kept fully informed if employment is at risk.
- The employee's GP should be asked when a return to work is expected and what type of work the employee will be capable of: the letter of enquiry reproduced in Appendix 4 (vii), and approved by the British Medical Association, may be used and the employee's permission to the enquiry should be attached to the letter.

- On the basis of the GP's report the employer should consider whether alternative work is available.
- The employer is not expected to create a special job for the employee concerned, nor to be a medical expert, but to take action on the basis of the medical evidence.
- Where there is reasonable doubt about the nature of the illness or injury, the employee should be asked if he or she would agree to be examined by a doctor to be appointed by the company.
- Where an employee refuses to co-operate in providing medical evidence or to undergo an independent medical examination, the employee should be told in writing that a decision will be taken the basis of the information available and that it could result in dismissal.
- Where the employee is allergic to a product used in the workplace, the employer should consider remedial action or a transfer to alternative work.
- Where the employee's job can no longer be kept open and no suitable alternative work is available, the employee should be informed of the likelihood of dismissal.
- Where dismissal action is taken, the employee should be given the period of notice to which he or she is entitled and informed of any right of appeal.

Where an employee has been on long-term sick absence and there is little likelihood of he or she becoming fit enough to return, it may be argued that the contract of employment has been terminated through 'frustration'. (See Section 8 on particular cases). However, the doctrine of frustration should not be relied upon since the courts are generally reluctant to apply it where a procedure exists for termination of the contract. It is therefore better for the employer to take dismissal action.

Where it is decided to dismiss an employee who has been on long-term sick absence, the normal conditions for giving notice will apply, even though in practice the employee will be unable to work the notice. In such circumstances, the employee should receive wages throughout the notice period or wages in lieu of notice as a lump sum.

Employees with special health problems

Consideration should be given to introducing measures to help employees, regardless of status or seniority, who are suffering from alcohol or drug abuse. The aim should be to identify employees affected and encourage them to seek help and treatment.

There are a number of symptoms related to alcohol or drug abuse including poor performance, changes in personality, irritability, slurred speech, impaired concentration and memory, deterioration in personal hygiene, anxiety and depression. Where it is established that an employee is suffering from alcohol or drug abuse, employers should consider whether it is appropriate to treat the problem as a medical rather than a disciplinary matter. In all cases the employee should be encouraged to seek appropriate medical assistance.[9]

Where an employee suffers from, or is thought to suffer from, a medical condition which makes him or her unacceptable to work colleagues,[10] there may be workforce pressure to dismiss or threats of industrial action. Employers should bear in mind that they may have to justify to an industrial tribunal the reasonableness of any decision to dismiss. Before taking any decision, the nature of the medical condition, working relationships, disruption to the business and the possibility of alternative work should all be considered.

Failure to return from extended leave on the agreed date

Employers may have policies which allow employees extended leave of absence without pay, for example to visit relatives in their countries of origin or relatives who have emigrated to other counties, or to nurse a sick relative. There is no general statutory right to such leave without pay and whether it is granted is a matter for agreement between employers and their employees, or where appropriate, their trade unions.

Where a policy on extended leave is in operation, the following points should be borne in mind:

- The policy should apply to all employees, irrespective of their sex, marital status and racial group.
- Any conditions attached to the granting of extended leave should be carefully explained to the employee and the employee's signature should be obtained as an acknowledgement that he or she understands and accepts them.

9 In some areas there are specialist advice centres which can provide assistance.

10 DE and HSE have issued a booklet entitled *AIDS and employment* which explains that person-to-person transmission of the AIDS virus does not occur during normal work activities. There is no risk of becoming infected in most jobs and there are generally no grounds for dismissing or otherwise discriminating against an employee purely on the basis of infection or suspected infection.

- If an employee fails to return on the agreed date this should be treated as any other failure to abide by the rules and the circumstances should be investigated in the normal way as fully as possible.
- Care should be taken to ensure that foreign medical certificates are not treated in a discriminatory way: employees can fall ill while abroad just as they can fall ill while in this country.
- Before deciding to dismiss an employee who overstays leave, the employee's age, length of service, reliability record and any explanation given should all be taken into account.

Agreement that an employee should return to work on a particular date will not prevent a complaint of unfair dismissal to an industrial tribunal if an employee is dismissed for failing to return as agreed.[11] In such cases all the factors mentioned above and the need to act reasonably should be borne in mind before any dismissal action is taken.

10 Sub-standard work

Key points:

Careful recruitment, selection and training will minimise the risk of poor performance.

When employment begins, the standards of work required, the consequences of failure to meet them and conditions attaching to any probationary period should be fully explained.

Where warnings are in operation an employee should be given both time to improve and, where appropriate, training.

The availability of suitable alternative work should be considered before dismissal action is taken.

Any deductions from pay must comply with the provisions of the Wages Act.

This section considers how to handle problems concerning poor performance and provides guidance on how to encourage improvement.

Setting standards of performance

Employees have a responsibility to achieve a satisfactory level of performance and should be given help and encouragement

[11] S. 140 of the Employment Protection (Consolidation) Act 1978.

to reach it. In all cases employers should point out in what way current performance fails to meet the required standard. They should also consider whether any shortfall in performance is due to unreasonable expectations or lack of proper explanation on the part of management.

Consideration should be given to whether performance might be improved by suitable training, either internally or from external sources.

Standards of performance provide a means of judging what is acceptable. They should be realistic and measurable in respect of quality, quantity, time and cost. Careful recruitment, selection and training will minimise the risk of poor performance.

The following principles should be observed when employment begins.[12]

- The standard of work required should be explained and employees left in no doubt about what is expected of them. Special attention should be paid to ensuring that standards are understood by employees whose English is limited and by young persons with little experience of working life.
- Where job descriptions are prepared they should accurately convey the main purpose and scope of each job and the tasks involved.
- Employees should be made aware of the conditions which attach to any probation period.
- The consequences of any failure to meet the required standards should be explained.
- Where an employee is promoted, the consequences of failing 'to make the grade' in the new job should be explained.

What is the role of training and supervision?

Proper training and supervision are essential to the achievement of satisfactory performance. Performance should be discussed regularly with employees, either formally or informally. Steps should be taken to ensure that inadequate performance, particularly during probation periods, is identified as soon as possible, so that appropriate remedial action can be taken.

[12] Further guidance is available in the ACAS Advisory Booklet No. 6: *Recruitment and Selection*, available from any ACAS office.

Appraisal systems

An appraisal system is a systematic method of obtaining and analysing information to evaluate an employee's performance in a job and assess his or her training and development needs and potential for future promotion. It is essential that appraisal is carried out in a fair and objective manner. Assessment criteria should be non-discriminatory and should be applied irrespective of racial group, sex or marital status. They should be relevant to the requirements of the job. Staff who are responsible for carrying out appraisals should be made aware of the dangers of stereotyping and of making assumptions based on inadequate knowledge.

Negligence or lack of ability

Negligence usually involves a measure of personal blame arising, for example, from lack of motivation or inattention for which some form of disciplinary action will normally be appropriate. Lack of ability, on the other hand, is due to lack of skill or experience and may point to poor recruitment procedures or inadequate training. Where skills have become outmoded by new technology, employers should consider whether new skills could be achieved through training.

How should poor performance be dealt with?

In all cases the cause of poor performance should be investigated. The following guidelines will help to identify the cause and help to ensure that appropriate action is taken:

- The employee should be asked for an explanation and the explanation checked.
- Where the reason is a lack of the required skills, the employee should, wherever practicable, be assisted through training and given reasonable time to reach the required standard of performance.
- Where despite encouragement and assistance the employee is unable to reach the required standard of performance, consideration should be given to finding suitable alternative work.
- Where alternative work is not available, the position should be explained to the employee before dismissal action is taken.

- An employee should not normally be dismissed because of poor performance unless warnings and a chance to improve have been given.
- If the main cause of poor performance is the changing nature of the job, employers should consider whether the situation may properly be treated as a redundancy matter rather than a capability or conduct issue.[13]

Action in serious cases

Where an employee commits a single error and the actual or potential consequences of that error are extremely serious, warnings will not normally be appropriate. The disciplinary procedure should indicate that dismissal action may be taken in such circumstances.

Dismissal

If employees are unable to achieve a satisfactory level of performance even after an opportunity to improve and with training assistance, the availability of suitable alternative work should be considered. If such work is not available, the situation should be explained sympathetically to the employee before dismissal action is taken.

When are deductions from pay lawful?

The law regarding deductions from pay was changed by the Wages Act 1986 which gives new statutory protection against unlawful pay deductions and which unifies, for the first time, the position of manual and non-manual workers.[14] The Act does not apply to the recovery of an overpayment of wages but it does allow for other deductions from pay in three specified circumstances:

- Where the deduction is required or authorised by statute, for example, income tax and national insurance deductions; or

13 In this context 'redundancy' has technical meaning defined in s. 81(2) of the Employment Protection (Consolidation) Act 1978. Also see the free booklet No. 16: *Redundancy Payments* produced by the Department of Employment.

14 Further guidance is provided in a free booklet produced by the Department of Employment entitled *The Law on the Payment of Wages and Deductions - A guide to Part 1 of the Wages Act 1986.*

- Where it is required or authorised by a relevant provision of the worker's contract; or
- Where the worker has signified advance agreement to the deduction in writing.

The Act covers the situation where the employer might demand payment of a fine from the worker instead of making a direct deduction. Such a payment must also satisfy one of the conditions outlined above. Deductions made or payments demanded unlawfully cannot be 'legitimised' by later agreement or consent.

The Act provides additional protection for those who work in retail employment[15] when the employer makes a deduction or requires payment because of cash shortages or stock deficiencies. Any such deduction is limited to 10 per cent of the gross amount of the wages payable on any day (including any deductions due to alleged dishonesty). The employer must, before receiving the first payment for any particular shortage, let the workers know in writing of the full amount owed. Any demand for payment must not be made more than 12 months after the shortage was (or ought reasonably to have been) established. The 10 per cent limit on deductions does not apply to the worker's final payment of wages on termination.

Employers should be aware that there are a number of more effective measures which can be taken to minimise till and stock losses. These include greater care with staff selection, appropriate training, improved supervision and better organisation of the work.

Any worker who thinks an employer has not followed the provisions of the Act has a right to complain to an industrial tribunal. The complaint must normally by presented within three months of the alleged unlawful deduction of payment. Where a tribunal finds a complaint justified it must order the employer to reimburse the worker accordingly.

15 There is a wide definition given to retail employment. It is employment involving, whether on a regular basis or not, the carrying out of retail transactions or collecting money in respect of the sale or supply of goods or the supply of services (including financial services) directly with the public, fellow workers or other individuals.

APPENDIX H

Main Legislative Provisions: 1980-1993

1. Employment Act 1980

Enabled the payment of public funds to be made for ballots held by trade unions; independent trade unions were entitled to hold ballots on an employer's premises; the Secretary of State was empowered to issue Codes of Practice (Codes on Picketing and Trade Union Ballots have been issued; the Code on Closed Shop Agreements and Arrangements has been revoked); there is a right not to be unreasonably excluded or expelled from a trade union, but this applied only where there was a union membership agreement in force - somewhat limited because of the provisions of the Employment Act 1990, see below; the burden of proof in unfair dismissal cases was neutralised as between the parties; a dismissal for non-membership of a trade union where there was a union membership agreement was to be unfair unless a ballot was held, or if the employee objected to joining on grounds of conscience or deeply-held conviction (this provision has since been repealed); minor changes were made to the provisions on unfair dismissal and maternity leave of absence and guarantee payments; the Act provided for time off work for ante-natal care, redefined peaceful picketing, and dealt with liability in tort for secondary action (since repealed).

2. Employment Act 1982

Companies were required to deal with the employee involvement in their annual reports; new rules were laid down when a person was dismissed because of union or non-union membership, and on ballots for union membership agreement (since repealed); the Act provided for a minimum basic award and a special award and for a contribution against third parties when dismissal was on the ground of trade union membership or non-membership; changes were made when dismissal was in connection with a strike or other industrial action, and terms in contracts requiring work to be done by union or non-union workers were stated to be void; the immunity of trade unions from actions in tort was removed, but a trade union would only be liable if the act was authorised or endorsed by a responsible person (since amended); the Act provided for limits on damages awarded against trade unions, and the definition of 'trade dispute' was altered.

3. Trade Union Act 1984

Trade unions are required to hold ballots for certain posts, and the immunity of trade unions from actions in tort was removed unless the industrial action was supported by a secret ballot (since amended); ballots have to be held to establish the political fund.

4. Sex Discrimination Act 1986

The first six sections of this Act altered the Sex Discrimination Act 1975 and the Equal Pay Act 1970 in consequence of rulings by the European Court of Justice to the effect that British law did not comply with the Equal Treatment Directive (76/207/EEC). The exemption in favour of an employer who employed five or fewer employees was repealed, and the definition of genuine occupational qualification for private household employment was altered; the upper age limit for unfair dismissal was equalised; discriminatory terms of employment in collective agreements were declared to be void, and certain restrictions on working hours and conditions of employment of women were removed.

5. Wages Act 1986

Repealed the Truck Acts 1831-1940 and other legislation relating to the payment of wages. The Act provides for a remedy in respect of unlawful deductions from wages, with special provisions for retail employment; the functions of Wages Councils were restricted; redundancy rebates were limited to employers who employed less than ten employees (since repealed).

6. Employment Act 1988

A trade union member can obtain a court order restraining the union from calling a strike without holding a ballot; he also has the right not to be unjustifiably disciplined by the union; other provisions gave greater control to members of the affairs of the union; it became thus automatically unfair to dismiss a person because he was not a member of a trade union; industrial action to enforce a closed shop would no longer attract immunity; changes were made to the law on trade union ballots and elections; the post of Commissioner for the Rights of Trade Union Members was created, and given power to provide assistance to trade union members in taking certain legal actions; there must be an independent scrutineer appointed for certain ballots, and mandatory postal ballots for union elections and political fund ballots.

7. Employment Act 1989

This Act further amended the Sex Discrimination Act, so as to bring British law in line with the European Directive on the implementation of the principle of equal treatment for men and women as regards access to employment, vocational training, promotion and working conditions; it repealed many provisions of protective legislation which laid down different treatment for men and women, and removed restrictions relating to the employment of young persons; Sikhs were exempted from the requirement to wear safety helmets on construction sites; minor changes were made to the Employment Protection (Consolidation) Act (written statement under s. 1, time off for trade union duties, two years' qualifying employment for written reasons for dismissal), and the age up to which women and men could receive redundancy payment was assimilated; the redundancy rebate was abolished together; the Secretary of State was given power to provide for pre-hearing assessment); the Training Commission was dissolved.

8. Employment Act 1990

This Act made it unlawful to refuse a person employment because he was or was not a member of a trade union (being the final nail in the coffin of the closed shop); immunity in respect of secondary action was abolished, minor amendments were made to the law on trade union ballots and the responsibility of a trade union for the acts of its officials; a ballot on industrial action ceases to be effective after four weeks, though this period is extended if there are court proceedings; unofficial strikers lost their right to bring a claim for unfair dismissal, the powers of the Commissioner for the Rights of Trade Union Members were increased; the Act made provision for the revision of Codes of Practice.

9. Trade Union and Labour Relations (Consolidation) Act 1992

This Act consolidates all the relevant law on trade unions and labour relations, including provisions from the Conspiracy and Protection of Property Act 1975, Trade Union Act 1913, Trade Union (Amalgamations) Act 1964, Trade Union and Labour Relations Act 1974, Employment Protection Act 1975, Trade Union and Labour Relations (Amendment) Act 1976, Employment Protection (Consolidation) Act 1978, Trade Union Act 1984, and the Employment Acts of 1980, 1982, 1988, 1989 and 1990.

10. Trade Union Reform and Employment Rights Act 1993

This Act amends the Employment Protection (Consolidation) Act 1978 and the Trade Union and Labour Relations (Consolidation) Act 1992, and makes further changes in the law. The independent scrutineer appointed for trade union elections and ballots is given more powers, voting is to be fully postal, funds for trade union ballots are to be phased out, and ballots may no longer be carried out on employers' premises. An individual cannot be excluded or expelled from a trade union except on specific grounds, employers must not make unauthorised deductions from a worker's pay in respect of union subscriptions, and the right not to be unjustifiably disciplined is extended. To be protected from being sued in respect of industrial action, a trade union must send a copy of the ballot paper to the employer before the date of the ballot, and inform the employer of the result. Notice of industrial action must be given to an employer. Any individual may apply to the High Court claiming that industrial action is unlawful, and he may receive assistance from a new Commissioner for Protection Against Unlawful Industrial Action. There is a new general right to maternity leave for pregnant employees, and a woman dismissed on grounds connected with pregnancy or childbirth no longer requires two years' qualifying employment before she can present a claim of unfair dismissal. Protection is given to persons in health and safety cases, consultations with trade unions on redundancies must be carried out with a view to reaching agreement. Amendments are made to the written statement to be given to every employee within eight weeks of commencing employment. Wages Councils are abolished. The constitution and jurisdiction of industrial tribunals and the Employment Appeal Tribunal is altered. ACAS is given power to make charges for advice, women dismissed on grounds of pregnancy or childbirth are to be given written reasons for their dismissal without the need to request them, certain compensation awards are increased, and interim relief will apply in health and safety cases. It is unfair to dismiss an employee on the ground that he asserted a statutory right.

APPENDIX I

Codes of Practice

(a) ACAS Code of Practice 1

Disciplinary Practice and Procedures in Employment

Introduction

1 This document gives practical guidance on how to draw up disciplinary rules and procedures and how to operate them effectively. Its aim is to help employers and trade unions as well as individual employees - both men and women - wherever they are employed regardless of the size of the organisation in which they work. In the smaller establishments it may not be practicable to adopt all the detailed provisions, but most of the features listed in paragraph 10 could be adopted and incorporated into a simple procedure.

Why have disciplinary rules and procedures?

2 Disciplinary rules and procedures are necessary for promoting fairness and order in the treatment of individuals and in the conduct of industrial relations. They also assist an organisation to operate effectively. Rules set standards of conduct at work; procedure helps to ensure that the standards are adhered to and also provides a fair method of dealing with alleged failure to observe them.

3 It is important that employees know what standards of conduct are expected of them and the Contracts of Employment Act

1972 (as amended by the Employment Protection Act 1975) requires employers to provide written information for their employees about certain aspects of their disciplinary rules and procedures.

4 The importance of disciplinary rules and procedures has also been recognised by the law relating to dismissals, since the grounds for dismissal and the way in which the dismissal has been handled can be challenged before an industrial tribunal. Where either of these is found by a tribunal to have been unfair the employer may be ordered to reinstate or re-engage the employees concerned and may be liable to pay compensation to them.

Formulating policy

5 Management is responsible for maintaining discipline within the organisation and for ensuring that there are adequate disciplinary rules and procedures. The initiative for establishing these will normally lie with management. However, if they are to be fully effective the rules and procedures need to be accepted as reasonable both by those who are to be covered by them and by those who operate them. Management should therefore aim to secure the involvement of employees and all levels of management when formulating new or revising existing rules and procedures. In the light of a particular circumstance in different companies and industries trade union officials may or may not wish to participate in the formulation of the rules but they should participate fully with management in agreeing the procedural arrangements which will apply to their members and in seeing that these arrangements are used consistently and fairly.

Rules

6 It is unlikely that any set of disciplinary rules can cover all circumstances that may arise: moreover the rules required will vary according to particular circumstances such as the type of work, working conditions and size of establishment. When drawing up rules the aim should be to specify clearly and concisely those necessary for the efficient and safe performance of work and for the maintenance of satisfactory relations within the workforce and between employees and management. Rules should not be so general as to be meaningless.

7 Rules should be readily available and management should make every effort to ensure that employees know and understand them. This may be best achieved by giving every employee a copy of the rules and by explaining them orally. In the case of new employees this should form part of an induction programme.

8 Employees should be made aware of the likely consequences of breaking rules and in particular they should be given a clear indication of the type of conduct which may warrant summary dismissal.

Essential features of disciplinary procedures

9 Disciplinary procedures should not be viewed primarily as a means of imposing sanctions. They should also be designed to emphasise and encourage improvements in individual conduct.

10 Disiplinary procedures should:

a. Be in writing.
b. Specify to whom they apply.
c. Provide for matters to be dealt with quickly.
d. Indicate the disciplinary actions which may be taken.
e. Specify the levels of management which have the authority to take the various forms of disciplinary action, ensuring that immediate superiors do not normally have the power to dismiss without reference to senior management.
f. Provide for individuals to be informed of the complaints against them and to be given an opportunity to state their case before decisions are reached.
g. Give individuals the right to be accompanied by a trade union representative or by a fellow employee of their choice.
h. Ensure that, except for gross misconduct, no employees are dismissed for a first breach of discipline.
i. Ensure that disciplinary action is not taken until the case has been carefully investigated.
j. Ensure that individuals are given an explanation for any penalty imposed.
k. Provide a right of appeal and specify the procedure to be followed.

The procedure in operation

11 When a disciplinary matter arises, the supervisor or manager should first establish the facts promptly before recollections fade, taking into account the statements of any available witnesses. In serious cases consideration should be given to a brief period of suspension while the case is investigated and this suspension should be with pay. Before a decision is made or penalty imposed the individual should be interviewed and given the opportunity to state his or her case and should be advised of any rights under the procedure, including the right to be accompanied.

12 Often supervisors will give informal oral warnings for the purpose of improving conduct when employees commit minor infringements of the established standards of conduct. However, where the facts of a case appear to call for disciplinary action, other than summary dismissal, the following procedure should normally be observed:

a. In the case of minor offences the individual should be given a formal oral warning or if the issue is more serious, there should be a written warning setting out the nature of the offence and the likely consequences of further offences. In either case the individual should be advised that the warning constitutes the first stage of the procedure.
b. Further misconduct might warrant a final written warning which should contain a statement that any recurrence would lead to suspension or dismissal or some other penalty, as the case may be.
c. The final step might be disciplinary transfer, or disciplinary suspension without pay (but only if these are allowed for by an express or implied condition of the contract of employment), or dismissal, according to the nature of the misconduct. Special consideration should be given before imposing disciplinary suspension without pay and it should not normally be for a prolonged period.

13 Except in the event of an oral warning, details of any disciplinary action should be given in writing to the employee and if desired, to his or her representative. At the same time the employee should be told of any right of appeal, how to make it and to whom.

14 When determining the disciplinary action to be taken the supervisor or manager should bear in mind the need to satisfy the test of reasonableness in all the circumstances. So far as possible, account should be taken of the employee's record and any other relevant factors.

15 Special consideration should be given to the way in which disciplinary procedures are to operate in exceptional cases. For example:

a. *Employees to whom the full procedure is not immediately available.* Special provisions may have to be made for the handling of disciplinary matters among nightshift workers, workers in isolated locations or depots or others who may pose particular problems for example because no one is present with the necessary authority to take disciplinary action or no trade union representative is immediately available.
b. *Trade union officials.* Disciplinary action against a trade union official can lead to a serious dispute if it is seen as an attack on the union's functions. Although normal disciplinary standards should apply to their conduct as employees, no disciplinary action beyond an oral warning should be taken until the circumstances of the case have been discussed with a senior trade union representative or full-time official.
c. *Criminal offences outside employment.* These should not be treated as automatic reasons for dismissal regardless of whether the offence has any relevance to the duties of the individual as an employee. The main considerations should be whether the offence is one that makes the individual unsuitable for his or her type of work or unacceptable to other employees. Employees should not be dismissed solely because a charge against them is pending or because they are absent through having been remanded in custody.

Appeals

16 Grievance procedures are sometimes used for dealing with disciplinary appeals though it is normally more appropriate to keep the two kinds of procedures separate since the disciplinary issues are in general best resolved within the organisation and need to be dealt with more speedily than others. The external stages of a grievance procedure may, however, be the appropriate machinery for dealing with appeals against disciplinary action where a final decision within the organisation is contested or where the matter becomes a collective issue between management and a trade union.

17 Independent arbitration is sometimes an appropriate means of resolving disciplinary issues. Where the parties concerned agree, it may constitute the final stage of procedure.

Records

18 Records should be kept, detailing the nature of any breach of disciplinary rules, the action taken and the reasons for it, whether an appeal was lodged, its outcome and any subsequent developments. These records should be carefully safeguarded and kept confidential.

19 Except in agreed special circumstances breaches of disciplinary rules should be disregarded after a specified period of satisfactory conduct.

Further action

20 Rules and procedures should be reviewed periodically in the light of any developments in employment legislation or industrial relations practice and, if necessary, revised in order to ensure their continuing relevance and effectiveness. Any amendments and additional rules imposing new obligations should be introduced only after reasonable notice has been given to all employees and, where appropriate, their representatives have been informed.

(b) ACAS Code of Practice 2

Disclosure of information to Trade Unions for Collective Bargaining Purposes

Introduction

1 Under the Employment Protection Act 1975 the Advisory Conciliation and Arbitration Service (ACAS) may issue the Codes of Practice containing such practical guidance as the Service thinks fit for the purpose of promoting the improvement of industrial relations. In particular, the Service has a duty to provide practical guidance on the application of sections 17 and 18 of the Act in relation to the disclosure of information by employers to trade unions for the purpose of collective bargaining.

2 The Act and the Code apply to employers in operating in both the public and private sectors of industry. They do not apply to collective bargaining between employers' associations and trade unions, although the parties concerned may wish to follow the guidelines contained in the Code.

3 The information which employers may have a duty to disclose under section 17 is information which it would be in accordance with good industrial relations practice to disclose. In determining what would be in accordance with good industrial relations practice regard is to be had to any relevant provisions of the Code. However, the Code imposes no legal obligations on an employer to disclose any specific item of information. Failure to observe the Code does not by itself render anyone liable to proceedings, but the Act requires any relevant provisions to be taken into account in proceedings before the Central Arbitration Committee.

This Code supersedes paragraphs 96-98 (inclusive) of the Code of Practice in effect under Part 1 of Schedule 1 to the Trade Union and Labour Relations Act 1974, which paragraphs shall cease to have effect on the date on which this Code comes into effect.

Provisions of the Act

4 The Act places a general duty on an employer to disclose at all stages of collective bargaining information requested by rep-

resentatives of independent trade unions. The unions must be either recognised by the employer for collective bargaining purposes, or fall within the scope of an ACAS recommendation for recognition. The representative of the union is an official or other person authorised by the union to carry on such collective bargaining.

5 The information requested has to be in the employer's possession, or in the possession of an associated employer, and must relate to the employer's undertaking. The information to be disclosed is that without which a trade union representative would be impeded to a material extent in bargaining and which it would be in accordance with good industrial relations practice to disclose for the purpose of collective bargaining. In determining what is in accordance with good industrial relations practice, any relevant provisions of this Code are to be taken into account.

6 No employer is required to disclose any information which: would be against the interests of national security; would contravene a prohibition imposed by or under an enactment; was given to an employer in confidence, or was obtained by the employer in consequence of the confidence reposed in him by another person; relates to an individual unless he has consented to its disclosure; would cause substantial injury to the undertaking (or national interest in respect of Crown employment) for reasons other than its effect on collective bargaining; or was obtained for the purpose of any legal proceedings.

7 In providing information the employer is not required to produce original documents for inspection or copying. Nor is he required to compile or assemble information which would entail work or expenditure out of reasonable proportion to the value of the information in the conduct of collective bargaining. The union representative can request that the information be given in writing by the employer or be confirmed in writing. Similarly, an employer can ask the trade union representative to make the request for information in writing or confirm it in writing.

8 If the trade union considers that an employer has failed to disclose to its representatives information which he was required to disclose by section 17 of the Act, it may make a complaint to the Central Arbitration Committee. The Committee may ask the Advisory, Conciliation and Arbitration Service to conciliate. If conciliation does not lead to a settlement of the complaint the Service shall inform the Committee accordingly who shall proceed to hear and determine the complaint. If the complaint is upheld by the Committee it is required to specify the information that should have been disclosed and a period of time within which the employer ought to disclose the information. If the employer does not disclose the information within the specified time the union may present a further complaint to the Committee and may also present a claim for improved terms and conditions. If the further complaint is upheld by the Committee an award, which would have effect as part of the contract of employment, may be made against the employer on the terms and conditions specified in the claim, or other terms and conditions which the Committee considers appropriate.

Providing information

9 The absence of relevant information about an employer's undertaking may to a material extent impede trade unions in collective bargaining; particularly if the information would influence the formulation, presentation or pursuance of a claim, or the conclusion of an agreement. The provision of relevant information in such circumstances would be in accordance with good industrial relations practice.

10 To determine what information will be relevant negotiators should take account of the subject-matter of the negotiations and the issues raised during them; the level at which negotiations take place (department, plant, division, or company level); the size of the company; and the type of business the company is engaged in.

11 Collective bargaining within an undertaking can range from negotiations on specific matters arising daily at the work place affecting particular sections of the workforce, to extensive periodic negotiations on terms and conditions of employment affecting the whole workforce in multiplant companies. The relevant information and the depth, detail and form in which it could be presented to negotiators will vary accordingly. Consequently, it is not possible to compile a list of terms that should be disclosed in all circumstances. Some examples of information relating to the undertaking which could be relevant in certain collective bargaining situations are given below:

i. *Pay and benefits*: principles and structure of payment systems; job evaluation systems and grading criteria; earnings and hours analysed according to work-group, grade, plant, sex, out-workers and homeworkers, department or division, giving where appropriate, distributions and make-up of pay showing any additions to basic rate or salary; total pay bill; details of fringe benefits and non-wage labour costs.
ii. *Conditions of service*: policies of recruitment, redeployment, redundancy, training, equal opportunity, and promotion; appraisal systems; health, welfare and safety matters.
iii. *Manpower*: numbers employed analysed according to grade, department, location, age and sex; labour turnover; absenteeism; overtime and short-time, manning standards; planning changes in work methods, materials, equipment or organisation; available manpower plans; investment plans.
iv. *Performance*: productivity and efficiency data; savings from increased productivity and output; return on capital investment; sales and state of order book.
v. *Financial*: cost structures; gross and net profits; sources of earnings; assets; liabilities; allocation of profits; details of government financial assistance; transfer prices; loans to parent or subsidiary companies and interest charged.

12 These examples are not intended to represent a check list of information that should be provided for all negotiations. Nor are they meant to be an exhaustive list of types of information as other items may be relevant in particular negotiations.

Restrictions on the duty to disclose

13 Trade unions and employers should be aware of the restrictions on the general duty to disclose information for collective bargaining.

14 Some examples of information which if disclosed in particular circumstances might cause substantial injury are: cost information on individual products; detailed analysis of proposed investment; marketing or pricing policies; and price quotas or the make-up of tender prices. Information which has to be made available publicly, for example under the Companies Acts, would not fall into this category.

15 Substantial injury may occur if, for example, certain customers would be lost to competitors, or suppliers would refuse to supply necessary materials, or the ability to raise funds to finance the company would be seriously impaired as a result of disclosing certain information. The burden of establishing a claim that disclosure of certain information would cause substantial injury lies with the employer.

Trade union responsibilities

16 Trade unions should identify and request the information they require for collective bargaining in advance of negotiations whenever practicable. Misunderstandings can be avoided, costs reduced, and time saved, if requests state as precisely as possible all the information required, and the reasons why the information is considered relevant. Requests should conform to an agreed procedure. A reasonable period of time should be allowed for employers to consider a request and to reply.

17 Trade unions should keep employers informed of the names of the representatives authorised to carry on collective bargaining on their behalf.

18 Where two or more trade unions are recognised by an employer for collective bargaining purposes they should co-ordinate their requests for information whenever possible.

19 Trade unions should review existing training programmes or establish new ones to ensure negotiators are equipped to understand and use information effectively.

Employers' responsibilities

20 Employers should aim to be as open and helpful as possible in meeting trade union requests for information. Where a request is refused, the reasons for the refusal should be explained as far as possible to the trade union representatives concerned and be capable of being substantiated should the matter be taken to the Central Arbitration Committee.

21 Information agreed as relevant to collective bargaining should be made available as soon as possible once a request for the information has been made by an authorised trade union representative. Employers should present information in a form and style which recipients can reasonably be expected to understand.

Joint arrangements for disclosure of information

22 Employers and trade unions should endeavour to arrive at a joint understanding on how the provisions on the disclosure of information can be implemented most effectively. They should consider what information is likely to be required, what is available, and what could reasonably be made available. Consideration should also be given to the form in which the information will be presented, when it should be presented and to whom. In particular, the parties should endeavour to reach an understanding on what information could most appropriately be provided on a regular basis.

23 Procedures for resolving possible disputes concerning any issues associated with the disclosure of information should be agreed. Where possible such procedures should normally be related to any existing arrangements within the undertaking or industry and the complaint, conciliation and arbitration procedure described in the Act.

(c) ACAS Code of Practice 3

Time off for Trade Union Duties and Activities

Introduction

1 Under section 6 of the Employment Protection Act 1975 (referred to hereafter as the Act) the Advisory, Conciliation and Arbitration Service (ACAS) has a duty to provide practical guidance on the time off to be permitted by an employer
a. to a trade union official in accordance with section 57 of the Act; and
b. to a trade union member in accordance with section 58 of the Act. This Code is intended to provide such guidance.

2 Section 57 of the Act requires an employer to permit an employee of his or hers, who is an official of an independent trade union which is recognised by the employer, to take reasonable paid time off during the employee's working hours for the purpose of enabling the employee
a. to carry out those duties which are concerned with industrial relations between his or her employer and any associated employer and their employees; or
b. to undergo training in aspects of industrial relations which is
 (i) relevant to the carrying out of those duties; and
 (ii) approved by the Trades Union Congress or by the independent trade union of which he or she is an official.

3 An employer who permits an employee time off under this section is required to pay him or her for the time off taken. Where the employee's pay does not vary with the amount of work done, the employer is required by the Act to pay the employee as if he or she had worked during the period when the time off was taken. Where the employee's pay does vary according to the amount of work done then payment for the time off permitted is to be calculated by reference to the average hourly earnings for the work the employee is employed to do.

4 For the purposes of section 57 of the Act the word 'official' means an employee who has been elected or appointed in accordance with the rules of the union to be a representative of all or some of the union's members in a particular company or workplace.

5 Section 58 of the Act requires an employer to permit an employee of his or hers who is a member of an appropriate trade union to take reasonable time off during the employee's working hours for the purpose of taking part in any trade union activity to which the section applies. Trade union activities to which the section applies are any activities of an appropriate trade union of which the employee is a member; and any activities in relation to which the employee is acting as a representative of such a union; but excluding activities which themselves consist of industrial action whether or not in contemplation or furtherance of a trade dispute. There is no requirement under section 58 that union members or representatives be paid for time off taken on union activities.

6 The amount of time off under sections 57 and 58 of the Act, the purposes for which, the occasions on which and any conditions subject to which time off may so be taken are those that are reasonable in all the circumstances having regard to any relevant provisions of this Code of Practice.

7 Sections 57 and 58 of the Act provide that a trade union official or member may present a complaint to an industrial tribunal that his or her employer has failed to permit the taking of time off as required by these sections or, in the case of an official, to pay him or her the whole or part of any amount required by the Act to be paid. Such complaints may be resolved by conciliation by ACAS, and if such a resolution is achieved no tribunal hearing will be necessary. This Code will be taken into account in determining any question arising during tribunal proceedings on sections 57 and 58, although failure to observe any provision of the Code will not of itself render a person liable to any proceedings.

General considerations for time off arrangements

8 The general purpose of the statutory provisions on time off for trade union duties and activities is to aid and improve the conduct of industrial relations. These provisions apply to all employers without exception as to size or type of business or service. But trade unions should be aware of the wide variety of circumstances and the different operations requirements which will have to be taken into account in any arrangements for dealing with time off. For example, some employers face particular exigencies of production, services and safety in process industries. Others operate in the special circumstances of the small firm. In enterprises large and small the workforce may be fragmented. Proper regard will therefore have to be paid to particular operations requirements and obligations of different industries and services.

9 Union officials and members may face particular problems of effective representation and communication, and employers in their turn should be aware of these. They may arise, for example, from the differing hours or shifts worked by members in a single negotiating area; from employment part-time; from the scattered or isolated locations of workplaces and, particularly in the case of some married women, from domestic commitments which limit the possibilities of active participation in their union outside the workplace and outside the hours of normal day working.

10 To take account of this wide variety of circumstances and problems, employers and unions should reach agreement on arrangements for handling time off in ways appropriate to their own situations. Subsequent advice in the Code should be read in the light of this primary point of guidance which ACAS considers fundamental to the proper operation of time off facilities. The absence of a formal agreement dealing specifically with time off for trade union duties and activities should not of itself preclude the granting of release.

11 Employers and unions, at the appropriate level, will need to review jointly their current time off provisions bearing in mind the statutory requirements, this Code of Practice and the particular workplace circumstances. Where existing arrangements meet these requirements and are working to the satisfaction of both parties they need not be changed. In some situations time off arrangements will have to be revised and it may be helpful to set out any such revised arrangements in formal agreements.

12 Arrangements for the handling of time off for union duties, industrial relations training and union activities should accord with agreed procedures for negotiations, consultation, grievance handling and dispute settlement. Agreements on time off and on other facilities for union representation should be consistent with wider agreements which should deal with such matters of workplace representation as constituencies, number of representatives and the form of any joint credentials.

Trade union officials' duties concerned with industrial relations

13 In addition to his or her work as an employee a trade union official may have important duties concerned with industrial relations. An official's duties are those duties pertaining to his or her role in the jointly agreed procedures or customary arrangements for consultation, collective bargaining and grievance handling, where such matters concern the employer and any associated employer and their employees. To perform these duties properly an official should be permitted to take reasonable paid time off during working hours for such purposes as

a. collective bargaining with the appropriate level of management;
b. inform constituents about negotiations or consultations with management;
c. meetings with other lay officials or with full-time union officers on matters which are concerned with industrial relations between his or her employer and any associated employer and their employees;
d. interviews with or on behalf of constituents on grievance and discipline matters concerning them and their employer;
e. appearing on behalf of constituents before an outside official body, such as an industrial tribunal, which is dealing with an industrial relations matter concerning the employer; and
f. explanations to new employees whom he or she will represent of the role of the union in the workplace industrial relations structure.

Training of officials in aspects of industrial relations

14 To carry out their duties effectively officials need to possess skills and knowledge. In addition to the practical experience obtained from holding office officials should undertake training in relevant subjects where necessary.

15 Training should be relevant to the industrial relations duties of an official. It should be approved by the TUC or the official's union. An official's industrial relations duties will vary according to the collective bargaining arrangements at the place of work, the structure of the union and the role of the official. Accordingly there is no universally applicable syllabus for training.

16 An official who has duties concerned with industrial relations should be permitted to take reasonable paid time off work for initial basic training and such training should be arranged as soon as possible after the official is elected or appointed.

17 An official should be permitted to take reasonable paid time off work for further training relevant to the carrying out of his or her duties concerned with industrial relations where he or she has special responsibilities or where such training is necessary to meet circumstances such as changes in the structure or topics of negotiation at the place of employment or legislative changes affecting industrial relations.

18 When the trade union has identified a need for basic or further training and wishes an official to receive training it should inform management what training it has approved for the purpose and, if the employer asks for it, supply a copy of the syllabus or prospectus indicating the contents of the training course or programme.

19 The number of officials receiving training from any one place of employment at any one time should be that which is reasonable in the circumstances, bearing in mind such factors as the operational requirements of the employer and the availability of relevant courses. Trade unions should normally give at least a few weeks' notice of their nominations for training.

20 Unions and management should endeavour to reach agreement on the appropriate numbers and arrangements and should refer any problem which may arise to the relevant procedure.

Trade union activities

21 To operate effectively and democratically trade unions need the active participation of members in certain union activities. A member should therefore be permitted to take reasonable time off during working hours for union activities such as taking part, as a representative, in meetings of official policy-making bodies of the union such as the executive committee or annual conference, or representing the union on external bodies such as the committees of industrial training boards.

22 Members should be permitted to take reasonable time off during working hours for such purposes as voting at the workplace in union elections. Also there may be occasions when it is reasonable for unions to hold meetings of members during working hours because of the urgency of the matter to be discussed or where to do so would not adversely affect production or services. Employers may also have an interest in ensuring that meetings are representative.

Conditions relating to time off

23 For time off arrangements to work satisfactorily the trade union should ensure that its officials are fully aware of their role, responsibilities and functions. The unions should inform management, in writing, as soon as possible after officials are appointed or have resigned and should ensure that officials receive any appropriate written credentials promptly. Management at all levels should be familiar with agreements and arrangements relating to time off.

24 Management should make available to officials the facilities necessary for them to perform their duties efficiently and to communicate effectively with members, fellow lay officials and full-time officials. Such facilities may include accommodation for meetings, access to a telephone, notice boards and, where the volume of the official's work justifies it, the use of office facilities.

25 Management is responsible for maintaining production and service to customers, and for making the operational arrangements for time off. Union officials should bear in mind management's problems in discharging these responsibilities. The union official who seeks time off should ensure that the appropriate management representative is informed as far in advance as is reasonable in the circumstances. The official should indicate the nature of the business for which time off is required, the intended location and the expected period of absence. Management and the union should seek to agree arrangements, where necessary, for other employees to cover the work of officials or members taking time off.

26 Where it is necessary for the union to hold meetings of members during working hours it should seek to agree the arrangements with management as far in advance as is practicable. Where such meetings necessarily involve a large proportion of employees at the workplace at any one time, management and unions should agree on a convenient time which minimises the effects on production or service - for example, towards the end of the shift or the working week or just before or after a meal break.

27 When a number of members need time off at any one time there should be agreement to leave at work such members as are essential for safety or operational reasons - for example, to keep premises open to the public or to provide necessary manning in a continuous process form.

28 Management may want time off work for union duties or activities to be deferred because, for example, problems of safety or of maintenance of production or service would ensue if time off were taken at a particular time. The grounds for postponement should be made clear and parties should endeavour to agree on an alternative time for the union duty or activity. In considering postponement parties should weigh the urgency of the matter for which time off is required against the seriousness of any problems arising.

29 The union official and union member should not unduly or unnecessarily prolong the time they are absent from work on union duties or activities.

30 A dispute or grievance in relation to time off work for union duties or activities should be referred to the relevant procedure.

Industrial action

31 Management and unions have a responsibility to use agreed procedures to resolve problems constructively and avoid industrial action. Time off should be provided for this purpose. Satisfactory time off arrangements are particularly needed where communication and co-operation between management and unions are in danger of breaking down. Where industrial action has not occurred employers and unions should avoid hastily altering these arrangements since to do so may damage relationships.

32 A distinction should be made between situations where an official is engaged in industrial action along with his or her constituents and those where the official is not - for example, where only some of the constituents are taking unofficial action. Where an official is not taking part in industrial action but represents members involved, normal arrangements for time off with pay for the official should apply.

33 There is no obligation on employers to permit time off for union activities which themselves consist of industrial action but where a group of members not taking part in such action is directly affected by other people's industrial action these members and their officials may need to seek the agreement of management to time off for an emergency meeting.

(d) EOC Code of Practice

For the elimination of sex and marriage discrimination

INTRODUCTION

1 The EOC issues this Code of Practice for the following purposes:

a. for the elimination of discrimination in employment
b. to give guidance as to what steps it is reasonably practicable for employers to take to ensure that their employees do not in the course of their employment act unlawfully contrary to the Sex Discrimination Act (SDA)
c. for the promotion of equality of opportunity between men and women in employment.

The SDA prohibits discrimination against men, as well as against women. It also requires that married people should not be treated less favourably than single people of the same sex.

It should be noted that the provisions of the SDA - and therefore of this Code - apply to the UK-based subsidiaries of foreign companies.

2 The Code gives guidance to employers, trade unions and employment agencies on measures which can be taken to achieve equality. The chances of success of any organisation will clearly be improved if it seeks to develop the abilities of all employees, and the Code shows the close link which exists between equal opportunities and good employment practice. In some cases, an initial cost may be involved, but this should be more than compensated for by better relationships and better use of human resources.

Small businesses

3 The Code has to deal in general terms and it will be necessary for employers to adapt it in a way appropriate to the size and structure of their organisations. Small businesses, for example, will require much simpler procedures than organisations with complex structures and it may not always be reasonable for them to carry out all the Code's detailed recommendations. In adapting the Code's recommendations, small firms should, however, ensure that their practices comply with the Sex Discrimination Act.

Employers' responsibility

4 The primary responsibility at law rests with each employer to ensure that there is no unlawful discrimination. It is important, however, that measures to eliminate discrimination or promote equality of opportunity should be understood and supported by all employees. Employers are therefore recommended to involve their employees in equal opportunity policies.

Individual employee's responsibility

5 While the main responsibility for eliminating discrimination and providing equal opportunity is that of the employer, individual employees at all levels have responsibilities too. They must not discriminate or knowingly aid their employer to do so.

TRADE UNION RESPONSIBILITY

6 The full commitment of trade unions is essential for the elimination of discrimination and for the successful operation of an equal opportunities policy. Much can be achieved by collective bargaining and throughout the Code it is assumed that all the normal procedures will be followed.

7 It is recommended that unions should co-operate in the introduction and implementation of equal opportunities policies where employers have decided to introduce them, and should urge that such policies be adopted where they have not yet been introduced.

8 Trade unions have a responsibility to ensure that their representatives and members do not unlawfully discriminate on grounds of sex or marriage in the admission or treatment of members. The guidance in this Code also applies to trade unions in their role as employers.

Employment agencies

9 Employment agencies have a responsibility as suppliers of job applicants to avoid unlawful discrimination on the grounds of sex or marriage in providing services to clients. The guidance in this Code also applies to employment agencies in their role as employers.

Definitions

10 For ease of reference, the main employment provisions of the Sex Discrimination Act, including definitions of direct and indirect sex and marriage discrimination, are provided in a Legal Annex to this Code.

PART 1

The role of good employment practices in eliminating sex and marriage discrimination

11 This section of the Code describes those good employment practices which will help to eliminate unlawful discrimination. It recommends the establishment and use of consistent criteria for selection, training, promotion, redundancy and dismissal which are made known to all employees. Without this consistency, decisions can be subjective and leave the way open for unlawful discrimination to occur.

Recruitment

12 It is unlawful: UNLESS THE JOB IS COVERED BY AN EXCEPTION*: TO DISCRIMINATE DIRECTLY OR INDIRECTLY ON THE GROUNDS OF SEX OR MARRIAGE

- IN THE ARRANGEMENTS MADE FOR DECIDING WHO SHOULD BE OFFERED A JOB
- IN ANY TERMS OF EMPLOYMENT
- BY REFUSING OR OMITTING TO OFFER A PERSON EMPLOYMENT

[*Section* 6(1)(*a*); 6(1)(*b*); 6(1)(*c*)]°

13 It is therefore recommended that:

a. each individual should be assessed according to his or her personal capability to carry out a given job. It should not be assumed that men only or women only will be able to perform certain kinds of work;
b. any qualifications or requirements applied to a job which effectively inhibit applications from one sex or from mar-

* There are a number of exceptions to the requirements of the SDA, that employers must not discriminate against their employees or against potential employees. The main exceptions are mentioned on pages 17/18 of the Legal Annex.

° For the full text of section 6 of other sections of the Sex Discrimination Act referred to in this Code, readers are advised to consult a copy of the Act which is available from Her Majesty's Stationery Office.

ried people should be retained only if they are justifiable in terms of the job to be done:
[*Section* 6(1)(*a*), *together with section* 1(1)(*b*) or 3(1)(*b*)];
c. any age limits should be retained only if they are necessary for the job. An unjustifiable age limit could constitute unlawful indirect discrimination, for example, against women who have taken time out of employment for child-rearing;
d. where trade unions uphold such qualifications or requirements as union policy, they should amend that policy in the light of any potentially unlawful effect.

Genuine occupational qualifications (GOQs)

14 It is unlawful: EXCEPT FOR CERTAIN JOBS WHEN A PERSON'S SEX IS A GENUINE OCCUPATIONAL QUALIFICATION (GOQ) FOR THAT JOB to select candidates on the ground of sex.
[*Section* 7(2); 7(3) *and* 7(4)]

15 There are very few instances in which a job will qualify for a GOQ on the ground of sex. However, exceptions may arise, for example, where considerations of privacy and decency or authenticity are involved. The SDA expressly states that the need of the job for strength and stamina does not justify restricting it to men. When a GOQ exists for a job, it applies also to promotion, transfer, or training for that job, but cannot be used to justify a dismissal.

16 In some instances, the GOQ will apply to some of the duties only. A GOQ will not be valid, however, where members of the appropriate sex are already employed in sufficient numbers to meet the employer's likely requirements without undue inconvenience. For example, in a job where sales assistants may be required to undertake changing room duties, it might not be lawful to claim a GOQ in respect of all the assistants on the grounds that any of them might be required to undertake changing room duties from time to time.

17 It is therefore recommended that:
— A job for which a GOQ was used in the past should be re-examined if the post falls vacant to see whether the GOQ still applies. Circumstances may well have changed, rendering the GOQ inapplicable.

Source of recruitment

18 It is unlawful; UNLESS THE JOB IS COVERED BY AN EXCEPTION;
- TO DISCRIMINATE ON GROUNDS OF SEX OR MARRIAGE IN THE ARRANGEMENTS MADE FOR DETERMINING WHO SHOULD BE OFFERED EMPLOYMENT WHETHER RECRUITING BY ADVERTISEMENTS, THROUGH EMPLOYMENT AGENCIES, JOBCENTRES, OR CAREER OFFICES.
- TO IMPLY THAT APPLICATIONS FROM ONE SEX OR FROM MARRIED PEOPLE WILL NOT BE CONSIDERED.

[*Section* 6(1)(*a*)]

- TO INSTRUCT OR PUT PRESSURE ON OTHERS TO OMIT TO REFER FOR EMPLOYMENT PEOPLE OF ONE SEX OR MARRIED PEOPLE UNLESS THE JOB IS COVERED BY AN EXCEPTION.

[*Section* 39 *and* 40]

It is also unlawful WHEN ADVERTISING JOB VACANCIES,
- TO PUBLISH OR CAUSE TO BE PUBLISHED AN ADVERTISEMENT WHICH INDICATES OR MIGHT REASONABLY BE UNDERSTOOD AS INDICATING AN INTENTION TO DISCRIMINATE UNLAWFULLY ON GROUNDS OF SEX OR MARRIAGE.

[*Section* 38]

19 It is therefore recommended that:

Advertising

a. job advertising should be carried out in such a way as to encourage applications from suitable candidates of both sexes. This can be achieved both by wording of the advertisements and, for example, by placing advertisements in publications likely to reach both sexes. All advertising materials and accompanying literature relating to employment or training issues should be reviewed to ensure that it avoids presenting men and women in stereotyped roles. Such stereotyping tends to perpetuate sex segregation in jobs and can also lead people of the opposite sex to believe that they would be unsuccessful in applying for particular jobs;
b. where vacancies are filled by promotion or transfer, they should be published to all eligible employees in such a way that they do not restrict applications from either sex;

c. recruitment solely or primarily by word of mouth may unnecessarily restrict the choice of applicants available. The method should be avoided in a workforce predominantly of one sex, if in practice it prevents members of the opposite sex from applying;
d. where applicants are supplied through trade unions and members of one sex only come forward, this should be discussed with the unions and an alternative approach adopted.

Careers service/schools
20 When notifying vacancies to the Careers Service, employers should specify that these are open to both boys and girls. This is especially important when a job has traditionally been done exclusively or mainly by one sex. If dealing with single sex schools, they should ensure, where possible, that both boys' and girls' schools are approached; it is also a good idea to remind mixed schools that jobs are open to boys and girls.

Selection methods

Tests
21 a. If selection tests are used, they should be specifically related to a job and/or career requirements and should measure an individual's actual or inherent ability to do or train for the work or career.
b. Tests should be reviewed regularly to ensure that they remain relevant and free from any unjustifiable bias, either in content or in scoring mechanism.

Applications and interviewing
22 It is unlawful: UNLESS THE JOB IS COVERED BY AN EXCEPTION;

TO DISCRIMINATE ON GROUNDS OF SEX OR MARRIAGE BY REFUSING OR DELIBERATELY OMITTING TO OFFER EMPLOYMENT.
[*Section 6(1)(c)*]

23 It is therefore recommended that:
a. employers should ensure that personnel staff, line managers and all other employees who may come into contact with job applicants, should be trained in the provisions of the SDA, including the fact that it is unlawful to instruct or put pressure on others to discriminate;

b. applications from men and women should be processed in exactly the same way. For example, there should not be separate lists of male and female or married and single applicants. All those handling applications and conducting interviews should be trained in the avoidance of unlawful discrimination and records of interviews kept, where practicable, showing why applicants were or were not appointed;
c. questions should relate to the requirements of the job. Where it is necessary to assess whether personal circumstances will affect the performance of the job (for example, where it involves unsocial hours or extensive travel) this should be discussed objectively without detailed questions based on assumptions about marital status, children and domestic obligations. Questions about marriage plans or family intentions should not be asked, as they could be construed as showing bias against women. Information necessary for personnel records can be collected after a job offer has been made.

Promotion, transfer and training

24 It is unlawful: UNLESS THE JOB IS COVERED BY AN EXCEPTION FOR EMPLOYERS TO DISCRIMINATE DIRECTLY OR INDIRECTLY ON THE GROUNDS OF SEX OR MARRIAGE IN THE WAY THEY AFFORD ACCESS TO OPPORTUNITIES FOR PROMOTION, TRANSFER OR TRAINING.
[*Section* 6(2)(*a*)]

25 It is therefore recommended that:
a. where an appraisal system is in operation, the assessment criteria should be examined to ensure that they are not unlawfully discriminatory and the scheme monitored to assess how it is working in practice;
b. when a group of workers predominantly of one sex is excluded from an appraisal scheme, access to promotion, transfer and training and to other benefits should be reviewed, to ensure that there is no unlawful discrimination;
c. promotion and career development patterns are reviewed to ensure that the traditional qualifications are justifiable requirements for the job to be done. In some circumstances, for example, promotion on the basis of length of service could amount to unlawful indirect discrimination, as it may unjustifiably affect more women than men.

d. when general ability and personal qualities are the main requirements for promotion to a post, care should be taken to consider favourably candidates of both sexes with differing career patterns and general experience;
e. rules which restrict or preclude transfer between certain jobs should be questioned and changed if they are found to be unlawfully discriminatory. Employees of one sex may be concentrated in sections from which transfers are traditionally restricted without real justification;
f. policies and practices regarding selection for training, day release and personal development should be examined for unlawful direct and indirect discrimination. Where there is found to be an imbalance in training as between sexes, the cause should be identified to ensure that it is not discriminatory;
g. age limits for access to training and promotion should be questioned.

Health and safety legislation

26 Equal treatment of men and women may be limited by statutory provisions which require men and women to be treated differently. For example, the Factories Act 1961 places restrictions on the hours of work of female manual employees, although the Health and Safety Executive can exempt employers from these restrictions, subject to certain conditions. The Mines and Quarries Act 1954 imposes limitation on women's work and there are restrictions where there is special concern for the unborn child (e.g. lead and ionising radiation). However, the broad duties placed on employers by the Health and Safety at Work etc Act, 1974 makes no distinction between men and women. Section 2(1) requires employers to ensure, so far as is reasonably practicable, the health and safety and welfare at work of *all* employees.

SPECIFIC HEALTH AND SAFETY REQUIREMENTS UNDER EARLIER LEGISLATION ARE UNAFFECTED BY THE ACT.

(It is therefore recommended that

- company policy should be reviewed and serious consideration given to any significant differences in treatment between men and women, and there should be well-founded reasons if such differences are maintained or introduced.

Terms of employment, benefits, facilities and services

27 It is unlawful: UNLESS THE JOB IS COVERED BY AN EXCEPTION TO DISCRIMINATE ON THE GROUNDS OF SEX OR MARRIAGE, DIRECTLY OR INDIRECTLY, IN THE TERMS ON WHICH EMPLOYMENT IS OFFERED OR IN AFFORDING ACCESS TO ANY BENEFITS*, FACILITIES OR SERVICES.
[*Sections* 6(1)(*b*); 6(2)(*a*); 29]

28 It is therefore recommended that:

a. all terms of employment, benefits, facilities and services are reviewed to ensure that there is no unlawful discrimination on grounds of sex or marriage. For example, part-time work, domestic leave, company cars and benefits for dependants should be available to both male and female employees in the same or not materially different circumstances.

29 In an establishment where part-timers are solely or mainly women, unlawful indirect discrimination may arise if, as a group, they are treated less favourably than other employees without justification.

It is therefore recommended:

b. where part-time workers do not enjoy pro-rata pay or benefits with full-time workers, the arrangements should be reviewed to ensure that they are justified with regard to sex.

Grievances, disciplinary procedures and victimisation

30 It is unlawful: TO VICTIMISE AN INDIVIDUAL FOR A COMPLAINT MADE IN GOOD FAITH ABOUT SEX OR MARRIAGE DISCRIMINATION OR FOR GIVING EVIDENCE ABOUT SUCH A COMPLAINT.
[*Section* 4(1); 4(2); *and* 4(3)]

31 It is therefore recommended that:

a. particular care is taken to ensure that an employee who has in good faith taken action under the Sex Discrimination Act or the Equal Pay Act does not receive less favourable treatment than other employees, for example by being disciplined or dismissed;

b. employees should be advised to use the internal procedures, where appropriate, but this is without prejudice to the in-

* Certain provisions relating to death and retirement are exempt from the Act.

dividual's right to apply to an industrial tribunal within the statutory time limit, i.e. before the end of the period of three months beginning when the act complained of was done;

c. particular care is taken to deal effectively with all complaints of discrimination, victimisation or harassment. It should not be assumed that they are made by those who are over-sensitive.

Dismissals, redundancies and other unfavourable treatment of employees

32 It is unlawful: TO DISCRIMINATE DIRECTLY OR INDIRECTLY ON GROUNDS OF SEX OR MARRIAGE IN DISMISSALS OR BY TREATING AN EMPLOYEE UNFAVOURABLY IN ANY OTHER WAY.
[*Section* 6(2)(*b*)]

It is therefore recommended that:

a. care is taken that members of one sex are not disciplined or dismissed for performance or behaviour which would be overlooked or condoned in the other sex;
b. redundancy procedures affecting a group of employees predominantly of one sex should be reviewed, so as to remove any effect which could be disproportionate and unjustifiable;
c. conditions of access to voluntary redundancy benefit* should be made available on equal terms to male and female employees in the same or not materially different circumstances;
d. where there is down-grading or short-time working (for example, owing to a change in the nature or volume of an employer's business) the arrangements should not unlawfully discriminate on the ground of sex;
e. all reasonably practical steps should be taken to ensure that a standard of conduct or behaviour is observed which prevents members of either sex from being intimidated, harassed or otherwise subjected to unfavourable treatment on the ground of their sex.

* Certain provisions relating to death and retirement are exempt from the Act.

PART 2

The role of good employment practices in promoting equality of opportunity

33 This section of the Code describes those employment practices which help to promote equality of opportunity. It gives information about the formulation and implementation of equal opportunities policies. While such policies are not required by law, their value has been recognised by a number of employers who have voluntarily adopted them. Others may wish to follow this example.

Formulating an equal opportunities policy

34 An equal opportunities policy will ensure the effective use of human resources in the best interests of both the organisation and its employees. It is a commitment by an employer to the development and use of employment procedures and practices which do not discriminate on grounds of sex or marriage and which provide genuine equality of opportunity for all employees. The detail of the policy will vary according to the size of the organisation.

Implementing the policy

35 An equal opportunities policy must be seen to have the active support of management at the highest level. To ensure that the policy is fully effective, the following procedure is recommended:

a. the policy should be clearly stated and, where appropriate, included in a collective agreement;
b. overall responsibility for implementing the policy should rest with senior management;
c. the policy should be made known to all employees and, where reasonably practicable, to all job applicants.

36 Trade unions have a very important part to play in implementing genuine equality of opportunity and they will obviously be involved in the review of established procedures to ensure that these are consistent with the law.

Monitoring

37 It is recommended that the policy is monitored regularly to ensure that it is working in practice. Consideration could be given to setting up a joint Management/Trade Union Review Committee.

38 In a small firm with a simple structure it may be quite adequate to assess the distribution and payment of employees from personal knowledge.

39 In a large and complex organisation a more formal analysis will be necessary, for example, by sex, grade and payment in each unit. This may need to be introduced by stages as resources permit. Any formal analysis should be regularly updated and available to Management and Trade Unions to enable any necessary action to be taken.

40 Sensible monitoring will show, for example, whether members of one sex:

a. do not apply for employment or promotion, or that fewer apply than might be expected;
b. are not recruited, promoted or selected for training and development or are appointed/selected in a significantly lower proportion than their rate of application;
c. are concentrated in certain jobs, sections or departments.

Positive Action

Recruitment, training and promotion

41 Selection for recruitment or promotion must be on merit, irrespective of sex. However, the Sex Discrimination Act does allow certain steps to redress the effects of previous unequal opportunities. Where there have been few or no members of one sex in particular work in their employment for the previous 12 months, the Act allows employers to give special encouragement to and provide specific training for the minority sex. Such measures are usually described as Positive Action.
[*Section* 48]

42 Employers may wish to consider positive measures such as:

a. training their own employees (male and female) for work which is traditionally the preserve of the other sex, for example, training women for skilled manual or technical work;
b. positive encouragement to women to apply for management posts - special courses may be needed;

c. advertisements which encourage applications from the minority sex, but make it clear that selection will be on merit without reference to sex;
d. notifying job agencies, as part of a Positive Action Programme that they wish to encourage members of one sex to apply for vacancies, where few or no members of that sex are doing the work in question. In these circumstances, job agencies should tell both men and women about the posts and, in addition, let the under-represented sex know that applications from them are particularly welcome. Withholding information from one sex in an attempt to encourage applications from the opposite sex would be unlawful.

Other working arrangements

43 There are other forms of action which could assist both employer and employee by helping to provide continuity of employment to working parents, many of whom will have valuable experience or skills.

Employers may wish to consider with the employees whether:
a. certain jobs can be carried out on a part-time or flexi-time basis;
b. personal leave arrangements are adequate and available to both sexes. It should not be assumed that men may not need to undertake domestic responsibilities on occasion, especially at the time of child-birth;
c. child-care facilities are available locally or whether it would be feasible to establish nursery facilities on the premises or combine with other employers to provide them;
d. residential training could be facilitated for employees with young children. For example, where this type of training is necessary, by informing staff who are selected well in advance to enable them to make childcare and other personal arrangements; employers with their own residential training centres could also consider whether childcare facilities might be provided;
e. the statutory maternity leave provisions could be enhanced, for example, by reducing the qualifying service period, extending the leave period, or giving access to part-time arrangements on return.

These arrangements, and others, are helpful to both sexes but are of particular benefit to women in helping them to remain in gainful employment during the years of child-rearing.

(e) Code of Practice

Race Relations

INTRODUCTION

1 The purpose of this status of the code

1.1 This Code aims to give practical guidance which will help employers, trade unions, employment agencies and employees to understand not only the provisions of the Race Relations Act and their application, but also how best they can implement policies to eliminate racial discrimination and to enhance equal-
s. 47(1) ity of opportunity.
s. 47(10)
s. 47(11)
s. 32

1.2 The Code does not impose any legal obligations itself, nor is it an authoritative statement of the law - that can only be provided by the courts and tribunals. If, however, its recommendations are not observed this may result in breaches of the law where the act or omission falls within any of the specific prohibitions of the Act. Moreover its provisions are admissible in evidence in any proceedings under the Race Relations Act before an Industrial Tribunal and if any provision appears to the Tribunal to be relevant to a question arising in the proceedings it must be taken into account in determining that question. If employers take the steps that are set out in the Code to prevent their employees from doing acts of unlawful discrimination they may avoid liability for such acts in any legal proceedings brought against them.

References to the appropriate sections of the Race Relations Act 1976 are therefore given in the margin to the Code.

1.3 Employees of all racial groups have a right to equal opportunity. Employers ought to provide it. To do so is likely to involve some expenditure, at least in staff time and effort. But if a coherent and effective programme of equal opportunity is developed it will help industry to make full use of the abilities of its entire workforce. It is therefore particularly important for all those concerned - employers, trade unions and employees alike - to co-operate with goodwill in adopting and giving effect to measures for securing such equality. We welcome the commitment already made by the CBI and TUC to the principle of equal opportunity. The TUC has recommended a model equal opportunity clause for inclusion in collective agreements and the CBI has published a statement favouring the application by companies of constructive equal opportunity policies.

1.4 A concerted policy to eliminate both race and sex discrimination often provides the best approach. Guidance on equal opportunity between men and women is the responsibility of the Equal Opportunities Commission.

2. The application of the code

2.1 The Race Relations Act applies to all employers. The Code itself is not restricted to what is required by law, but contains recommendations as well. Some of its detailed provisions may need to be adapted to suit particular circumstances. Any adaptations that are made, however, should be fully consistent with the Code's general intentions.

2.2 Smaller firms

In many small firms employers have close contact with their staff and there will therefore be less need for formality in assessing whether equal opportunity is being achieved, for example, in such matters as arrangements for monitoring. Moreover it may not be reasonable to expect small firms to have the resources and administrative systems to carry out the Code's detailed recommendations. In complying with the Race Relations Act, small firms should, however, ensure that their practices are consistent with the Code's general intentions.

3. Unlawful discrimination

3.1 The Race Relations Act 1976 makes it unlawful to discriminate against a person, directly or indirectly, in the field of employment. s. 4

Direct discrimination consists of treating a person, on racial grounds*, less favourably than others are or would be treated in the same or similar circumstances. s. 1(1)(a)

* *Racial grounds are the grounds of race, colour, nationality - including citizenship - or ethnic or national origins and groups defined by reference to these grounds are referred to as racial groups.*

s. 1(2) Segregating a person from others on racial grounds constitutes less favourable treatment.

3.2 Indirect discrimination consists of applying in any circumstances covered by the Act a requirement or condition which, although applied equally to persons of all racial groups, is such s.1(2) that a considerably smaller proportion of a particular racial group can comply with it and it cannot be shown to be justifiable on other than racial grounds. Possible examples are:

- a rule about clothing or uniforms which disproportionately disadvantages a racial group and cannot be justified;
- an employer who requires higher language standards than are needed for safe and effective performance of the job.

3.3 The definition of indirect discrimination is complex, and it will not be spelt out in full in every relevant Section of the Code. Reference will be only to the terms 'indirect discrimination' or 'discriminate indirectly'.

s. 2 **3.4** Discrimination by victimisation is also unlawful under the Act. For example, a person is victimised if he or she is given less favourable treatment than others in the same circumstances because it is suspected or known that he or she has brought proceedings under the Act, or given evidence or information relating to such proceedings, or alleged that discrimination has occurred.

4. The code and good employment practice

Many of the Code's provisions show the close link between equal opportunity and good employment practice. For example, selection criteria which are relevant to job requirements and carefully observed selection procedures not only help to ensure that individuals are appointed according to their suitability for the job and without regard to racial group; they are also part of good employment practice. In the absence of consistent selection procedures and criteria, decisions are often too subjective and racial discrimination can easily occur.

5. Positive action

Opportunities for employees to develop their potential through encouragement, training and careful assessment are also part of good employment practice. Many employees from the racial

minorities have potential which, perhaps because of previous discrimination and other causes of disadvantage, they have not been able to realise, and which is not reflected in their qualifications and experience. Where members of particular racial groups have been under-represented over the previous twelve s. 37
months in particular work, employers and specified training &
bodies are allowed under the Act to encourage them to take s. 38
advantage of opportunities for doing that work and to provide training to enable them to attain the skills needed for it. In the case of employers, such training can be provided for persons currently in their employment (as defined by the Act) and in certain circumstances for others too, for example if they have been designated as training bodies. This Code encourages employers to make use of these provisions, which are covered in detail in paragraphs 1.44 and 1.45.

6. Guidance papers

The guidance papers referred to in the footnotes contain additional guidance on specific issues but do not form part of the statutory Code.

PART 1 THE RESPONSIBILITIES OF EMPLOYERS

1.1 Responsibility for providing equal opportunity for all job applicants and employees rest primarily with employers. To this end it is recommended that they should adopt, implement and monitor an equal opportunity policy to ensure that there is no unlawful discrimination and that equal opportunity is genuinely available.*

1.2 This policy should be clearly communicated to all employees - e.g. through notice boards, circulars, contracts of employment or written notifications to individual employees.

Equal opportunity policies

1.3 An equal opportunity policy aims to ensure:

a. *that no job applicant or employee receives less favourable treatment than another on racial grounds*;

* *The CRE has issued guidance papers on equal opportunity policies: 'Equal opportunity in Employment' and 'Monitoring an Equal Opportunity Policy'.*

b. *that no applicant or employee is placed at a disadvantage by requirements or conditions which have a disproportionately adverse effect on his or her racial group and which cannot be shown to be justifiable on other than racial grounds*;
c. *that where appropriate and where permissible under the Race Relations Act, employees of under-represented racial groups are given training and encouragement to achieve equal opportunity within the organisation.*

1.4 In order to ensure that an equal opportunity policy is fully effective, the following action by employers is recommended:
a. allocating overall responsibility for the policy to a member of senior management;
b. discussing and, where appropriate, agreeing with trade union or employee representatives the policy's contents and implementation;
c. ensuring that the policy is known to all employees and if possible, to all job applicants;
d. providing training and guidance for supervisory staff and other relevant decision makers, (such as personnel and line managers, foremen, gatekeepers and receptionists) to ensure that they understand their position in law and under company policy;
e. examining and regularly reviewing existing procedures and criteria and changing them where they find that they are actually or potentially unlawfully discriminatory;
f. making an initial analysis of the workforce and regularly monitoring the application of the policy with the aid of analyses of the ethnic origins of the workforce and of job applicants in accordance with the guidance in paragraphs 1.34-1.35.

Recruitment, promotion, transfer, training & dismissal

Sources of recruitment

Advertisements

1.5 *When advertising job vacancies it is unlawful for employers:*

s. 29 *to publish an advertisement which indicates, or could reasonably be understood as indicating, an intention to discriminate against applicants from a particular racial group. (For exceptions see the Race Relations Act.)*

1.6 It is therefore recommended that:

a. employers should not confine advertisements unjustifiably to those areas of publications which would exclude or disproportionately reduce the numbers of applicants of a particular racial group; s. 30

b. employers should avoid prescribing requirements such as length of residence or experience in the UK and where a particular qualification is required it should be made clear that a fully comparable qualification obtained overseas is as acceptable as a UK qualification. s. 31

1.7 In order to demonstrate their commitment to equality of opportunity it is recommended that where employers send literature to applicants, this should include a statement that they are equal opportunity employers.

Employment agencies

1.8 When recruiting through employment agencies, job centres, careers offices and schools, it is unlawful for employers:

a. *to give instructions to discriminate, for example by indicating that certain groups will or will not be preferred. (For exceptions see the Race Relations Act)*;

b. *to bring pressure on them to discriminate against members of a particular racial group. (For exceptions, as above).*

1.9 In order to avoid indirect discrimination it is recommended that employers should not confine recruitment unjustifiably to those agencies, job centres, careers office and schools which, because of their particular source of applicants, provide only or mainly applicants of a particular racial group.

Other sources

1.10 *It is unlawful to use recruitment methods which exclude or disproportionately reduce the numbers of applicants of a particular racial group and which cannot be shown to be justifiable.* It is therefore recommended that employers should not recruit through the following methods:

a. recruitment, solely or in the first instance, through the recommendations of existing employees where the workforce concerned is wholly or predominantly white or black and the labour market is multi-racial;

b. procedures by which applicants are mainly or wholly supplied through trade unions where this means that only members of a particular racial group, or a disproportionately high number of them, come forward.

Sources for promotion and training

1.11 *It is unlawful for employers to restrict access to opportunities for promotion or training in a way which is discriminatory*. It is therefore recommended that:

s. 4 & s. 28

– job and training vacancies and the application procedure should be made known to all eligible employees, and not in such a way as to exclude or disproportionately reduce the numbers of applicants from a particular racial group.

Selecion for recruitment, promotion, transfer, training & dismissal

1.12 *It is unlawful to discriminate*, not only in recruitment, promotion, transfer and training, but also in the arrangements made for recruitment and in the ways of affording access to opportunities for promotion, transfer or training.*

Selection criteria and tests

s. 24 & s. 28

1.13 In order to avoid direct or indirect discrimination it is recommended the selection criteria and tests are examined to ensure that they are related to job requirements and are not unlawfully discriminatory (see Introduction para. 3.2). For example:

a. a standard of English higher than that needed for the safe and effective performance of the job or clearly demonstrable career pattern should not be required, or a higher level of educational qualification than is needed;
b. in particular, employers should not disqualify applicants because they are unable to complete an application form unassisted unless personal completion of the form is a valid test of the standard of English required for safe and effective performance of the job;
c. overseas degrees, diplomas and other qualifications which are comparable with UK qualifications should be accepted as equivalents, and not simply be assumed to be of an inferior quality;

* *It should be noted that discrimination in selection to achieve 'racial balance' is not allowed. The clause in the 1968 Race Relations Act which allowed such discrimination for the purpose of securing or preserving a reasonable balance of persons of different racial groups in the establishment is not included in the 1976 Race Relations Act.*

d. selection tests which contain irrelevant questions or exercises on matters which may be unfamiliar to racial minority applicants should not be used (for example, general knowledge questions on matters more likely to be familiar to indigenous applicants);
e. selection tests should be checked to ensure that they are related to the job's requirements, i.e. an individual's test markings should measure ability to do or train for the job in question.

Treatment of applicants: shortlisting, interviewing and selection

1.14 In order to avoid direct or indirect discrimination it is recommended that:

a. gate, reception and personnel staff should be instructed not to treat casual or formal applicants from particular racial groups less favourably than others. These instructions should be confirmed in writing:
b. in addition, staff responsible for shortlisting, interviewing and selection of candidates should be:
   - clearly informed of selection criteria and of the need for their consistent application;
   - given guidance or training on the effects which generalised assumptions and prejudices about race can have on selection decisions;
   - made aware of the possible misunderstandings that can occur in interviews between persons of different cultural background;
c. where possible, shortlisting and interviewing should not be done by one person alone but should at least be checked at a more senior level.

Genuine occupational qualification

1.15 *Selection on racial grounds is allowed in certain jobs where* s. 5
being of a particular racial group is a genuine occupational s. 5(2)(d
qualification for that job. An example is where the holder of a particular job provides persons of a racial group with personal services promoting their welfare, and those services can not effectively be provided by a person of that group.

Transfers and training

1.16 In order to avoid direct or indirect discrimination it is recommended that:

a. staff responsible for selecting employees for transfer to other jobs should be instructed to apply selection criteria without unlawful discrimination;

b. industry or company agreements and arrangements of custom and practice on job transfers should be examined and amended if they are found to contain requirements or conditions which appear to be indirectly discriminatory. For example, if employees of a particular racial group are concentrated in particular sections, the transfer arrangements should be examined to see if they are unjustifiably and unlawfully restrictive and amended if necessary;

c. staff responsible for selecting employees for training, whether induction, promotion or skill training should be instructed not to discriminate on racial grounds;

d. selection criteria for training opportunities should be examined to ensure that they are not indirectly discriminatory.

Dismissal (including redundancy) and other detriment

4(2)(c) **1.17** *It is unlawful to discriminate on racial grounds in dismissal, or other detriment to an employee.* It is therefore recommended that:

a. staff responsible for selecting employees for dismissal, including redundancy, should be instructed not to discriminate on racial grounds;

b. selection criteria for redundancies should be examined to ensure that they are not indirectly discriminatory.

Performance appraisals

4(2)(b) **1.18** *It is unlawful to discriminate on racial grounds in appraisals of employee performance.*

1.19 It is recommended that:

a. staff responsible for performance appraisals should be instructed not to discriminate on racial grounds;

b. assessment criteria should be examined to ensure that they are not unlawfully discriminatory.

Terms of employment, benefits, facilities and services

s. 4(2) **1.20** *It is unlawful to discriminate on racial grounds in affording terms of employment and providing benefits, facilities and services for employees.* It is therefore recommended that:

a. all staff concerned with these aspects of employment should be instructed accordingly;

b. the criteria governing eligibility should be examined to ensure that they are not unlawfully discriminatory.

1.21 In addition, employees may request extended leave from time to time in order to visit relations in their countries of origin or who have emigrated to other countries. Many employers have policies which allow annual leave entitlement to be accumulated, or extra unpaid leave to be taken to meet these circumstances. Employers should take care to apply such policies consistently and without unlawful discrimination.

Grievance, disputes and disciplinary procedures

1.22 It is unlawful to discriminate in the operation of grievance, disputes and disciplinary procedures, for example by victimising an individual through disciplinary measures because he or she has complained about racial discrimination, or given evidence about such a complaint. Employers should not ignore or treat lightly grievances from members of particular racial groups on the assumption that they are over-sensitive about discrimination. s.4(2) & s. 2

1.23 It is recommended that:

in applying disciplinary procedures consideration should be given to the possible effect on an employee's behaviour of the following:
— racial abuse or other racial provocation;
— communication and comprehension difficulties;
— differences in cultural background or behaviour.

Cultural and religious needs

1.24 Where employees have particular cultural and religious needs which conflict with existing work requirements, it is recommended that employers should consider whether it is reasonably practicable to vary or adapt these requirements to enable such needs to be met. For example, it is recommended that they should not refuse employment to a turbanned Sikh because he could not comply with unjustifiable uniform requirements. Other examples of such needs are:

a. observance of prayer times and religious holidays*;
b. wearing of dress such as sarees and trousers worn by Asian women.

* *The CRE has issued a guidance paper entitled - 'Religious Observance by Muslim Employees'.*

s. 4 & s. 28 **1.25** *Although the Act does not specifically cover religious discrimination, work requirements would generally be unlawful if they have a disproportionately adverse effect on particular racial groups and cannot be shown to be justifiable.*+

Communications and language training for employees

1.26 Although there is no legal requirement to provide language training, difficulties in communications can endanger equal opportunity in the workforce. In addition, good communications can improve efficiency, promotion prospects and safety and health and create a better understanding between employer, employees and unions. Where the workforce includes current employees whose English is limited it is recommended that steps are taken to ensure that communications are as effective as possible.

1.27 These should include, where reasonably practicable:

a. provision of interpretation and translation facilities, for example, in the communication of grievance and other procedures, and of terms of employment;
b. training in English language and in communication skills*;
c. training for managers and supervisors in the background and culture of racial minority groups;
d. the use of alternative or additional methods of communication, where employees find it difficult to understand health and safety requirements for example:
   — safety signs, translations of safety notices;
   — instructions through interpreters;
   — instructions combined with industrial language training.

Instructions and pressure to discriminate

1.28 *It is unlawful to instruct or put pressure on others to discriminate on racial grounds.*

\+ *Genuinely necessary safety requirements may not constitute unlawful discrimination.*

* *Industrial language training is provided by a network of Local Educational Authority units throughout the country. Full details of the courses and the comprehensive services offered by these units are available from the National Centre for Industrial Language Training, The Havelock Centre, Havelock Road, Southall, Middx.*

a. An example of an unlawful instruction is:
   — an instruction from a personnel or line manager to junior staff to restrict the number of employees from a particular racial group in any particular work;
b. An example of pressure to discriminate is:
   — an attempt by a shop steward or group of workers to induce an employer not to recruit members of particular racial groups, for example by threatening industrial action.

1.29 It is also unlawful to discriminate in response to such instructions or pressure.

1.30 The following recommendations are made to avoid unlawful instructions and pressure to discriminate:
a. guidance should be given to all employees, and particularly those in positions of authority or influence on the relevant provisions of the law;
b. decision-makers should be instructed not to give way to pressure to discriminate;
c. giving instructions or bringing pressure to discriminate should be treated as a disciplinary offence.

Victimisation

1.31 *It is unlawful to victimise individuals who have made allegations or complaints of racial discrimination or provided information about such discrimination, for example, by disciplining them or dismissing them.* (See Introduction, para. 3.4).

1.32 It is recommended that:
— guidance on this aspect of the law should be given to all employees and particularly to those in positions of influence or authority.

Monitoring equal opportunity*

1.33 It is recommended that employers should regularly monitor the effects of selection decisions and personnel practices and procedures in order to assess whether equal opportunity is being achieved.

* *See the CRE's guidance paper on 'Monitoring an Equal Opportunity Policy'.*

1.34 The information needed for effective monitoring may be obtained in a number of ways. It will best be provided by records showing the ethnic origins of existing employees and job applicants. It is recognised that the need for detailed information and the methods of collecting it will vary according to the circumstances of individual establishments. For example, in small firms or in firms in areas with little or no racial minority settlement it will often be adequate to assess the distribution of employees from personal knowledge and visual identification.

1.35 It is open to employers to adopt the method of monitoring which is best suited to their needs and circumstances, but whichever method is adopted, they should be able to show that it is effective. In order to achieve the full commitment of all concerned the chosen method should be discussed and agreed, where appropriate, with the trade union or employee representatives.

1.36 Employers should ensure that information on an individual's ethnic origins is collected for the purpose of monitoring equal opportunity alone and is protected from misuse.

1.37 The following is the comprehensive method recommended by the CRE*.

Analyses should be carried out of:

a. the ethnic composition of the workforce of each plant, department, section, shift and job category, and changes in distribution over periods of time;
b. selection decisions for recruitment, promotion, transfer and training, according to the racial group of candidates, and reasons for these decisions.

1.38 Except in cases where there are large numbers of applicants and the burden on resources would be excessive, reasons for selection and rejection should be recorded at each stage of the selection process, e.g. initial shortlisting and final decisions. Simple categories of reasons for rejection should be adequate for the early sifting stages.

* *This is outlined in detail in 'Monitoring an Equal Opportunity Policy'.*

1.39 Selection criteria and personnel procedures should be reviewed to ensure that they do not include requirements or conditions which constitute or may lead to unlawful indirect discrimination.

1.40 This information should be carefully and regularly analysed and, in order to identify areas which may need particular attention, a number of key questions should be asked.

1.41 Is there evidence that individuals from any particular racial group:

a. do not apply for employment or promotion, or that fewer apply than might be expected?
b. are not recruited or promoted at all, or are appointed in a significantly lower proportion that their rate of application?
c. are under-represented in training or in jobs carrying higher pay, status or authority?
d. are concentrated in certain shifts, sections or departments?

1.42 If the answer to any of these questions is yes, the reasons for this should be investigated. If direct or indirect discrimination is found action must be taken to end it immediately.

1.43 It is recommended that deliberate acts of unlawful discrimination by employees are treated as disciplinary offences.

Positive action*

1.44 *Although they are not legally required, positive measures are allowed by the law to encourage employees and potential employees and provide training for employees who are members of particular racial groups which have been under-represented+ in particular work.* (See Introduction, para. 5). Discrimination at the point of selection for work, however, is not permissible in these circumstances.

* *The CRE has issued a guidance paper on Positive Action, entitled 'Equal Opportunity in Employment Why Positive Action?'*

\+ *A racial group is under-represented if, at any time during the previous twelve months, either there was no one of that group doing the work in question, or there were disproportionately few in comparison with the group's proportion in the workforce at that establishment, or in the population from which the employer normally recruits for work at that establishment.*

1.45 Such measures are important for the development of equal opportunity. It is therefore recommended that, where there is under-representation of particular racial groups in particular work, the following measures should be taken wherever appropriate and reasonably practicable:

a. job advertisements designed to reach members of these groups and to encourage their applications: for example, through the use of the ethnic minority press, as well as other newspapers;
b. use of the employment agencies and careers offices in areas where these groups are concentrated;
c. recruitment and training schemes for school leavers designed to reach members of these groups;
d. encouragement to employees from these groups to apply for promotion or transfer opportunities;
e. training for promotion or skill training for employees of these groups who lack particular expertise but show potential: supervisory training may include language training.

PART 2 THE RESPONSIBILITIES OF INDIVIDUAL EMPLOYEES

2.1 While the primary responsibilities for providing equal opportunity rests with the employer, individual employees at all levels and of all racial groups have responsibilities too. Good race relations depend on them as much as on management, and so their attitudes and activities are very important.

2.2 *The following actions by individual employees would be unlawful*:

s. 4 & s. 33 a. *discrimination in the course of their employment against fellow employees or job applicants on racial grounds*, for example, in selection decisions for recruitment, promotion, transfer and training;

s. 31 b. *inducing, or attempting to induce other employees, unions or management to practise unlawful discrimination*. For example, they should not refuse to accept other employees from particular racial groups or refuse to work with a supervisor of a particular racial group;

c. *victimising individuals who have made allegations or complaints of racial discrimination or provided information about such discrimination*. (See Introduction, para. 3.4).

2.3 To assist in preventing racial discrimination and promoting equal opportunity it is recommended that individual employees should:

a. co-operate in measures introduced by management designed to ensure equal opportunity and non-discrimination;
b. where such measures have not been introduced, press for their introduction (through their trade union where appropriate);
c. draw the attention of management and, where appropriate, their trade unions to suspected discriminatory acts or practices; s. 2
d. refrain from harassment or intimidation of other employees on racial grounds, for example, by attempting to discourage them from continuing employment. Such action may be unlawful if it is taken by employees against those subject to their authority.

2.4 In addition to the responsibilities set out above individual employees from the racial minorities should recognise that in many occupations advancement is dependent on an appropriate standard of English. Similarly an understanding of the industrial relations procedures which apply is often essential for good working relationships.

2.5 They should therefore:
a. where appropriate, seek means to improve their standards of English;
b. co-operate in industrial language training schemes introduced by employers and/or unions;
c. co-operate in training and other schemes designed to inform them of industrial relations procedures, company agreements, work rules, etc;
d. where appropriate, participate in discussions with employers and unions, to find solutions to conflicts between cultural or religious needs and production needs.

PART 3 THE RESPONSIBILITIES OF TRADE UNIONS

3.1 Trade unions, in common with a number of other organisations, have a dual role as employers and providers of services specifically covered by the Race Relations Act.

3.2 In their role as employer, unions have the responsibilities set out in Part 1 of the Code. They also have a responsibility to ensure that their representatives and members do not discriminate against any particular racial group in the admission or s. 11

treatment of members, or as colleagues, supervisors or subordinates.

3.3 In addition, trade union officials at national and local level and shopfloor representatives at plant level have an important part to play on behalf of their members in preventing unlawful discrimination and in promoting equal opportunity and good race relations. Trade unions should encourage and press for equal opportunity policies so that measures to prevent discrimination at the workplace can be introduced with the clear commitment of both management and unions.

Admission of members

3.4 *It is unlawful for trade unions to discriminate on racial grounds*:

a. *by refusing membership*;

s. 11 b. *by offering less favourable terms of membership.*

Treatment of members

s. 11(3) **3.5** *It is unlawful for trade unions to discriminate on racial grounds against existing members*:

a. *by varying their terms of membership, depriving them of membership or subjecting them to any other detriment*;

b. *by treating them less favourably in the benefits facilities or services provided*. These may include:
training facilities;
welfare and insurance schemes;
entertainment and social events;
processing of grievances;
negotiations;
assistance in disciplinary or dismissal procedures.

3.6 In addition, it is recommended that unions ensure that in cases where members of particular racial groups believe that they are suffering racial discrimination, whether by the employer or the union itself, serious attention is paid to the reasons for this belief and that any discrimination which may be occurring is stopped.

Disciplining union members who discriminate

3.7 It is recommended that deliberate acts of unlawful discrimination by union members are treated as disciplinary offences.

Positive action

3.8 *Although they are not legally required, positive measures are allowed by the law to encourage and provide training for members of particular racial groups which have been under-represented* in trade union membership or in trade union posts.* (Discrimination at the point of selection, however, is not permissible in these circumstances.) s. 38 (4) & (5)

3.9 It is recommended that, wherever appropriate and reasonably practicable, trade unions should:

a. encourage individuals from these groups to join the union. Where appropriate, recruitment material should be translated into other languages;
b. encourage individuals from these groups to apply for union posts and provide training to help fit them for such posts.

Training and information

3.10 Training and information play a major part in the avoidance of discrimination and the promotion of equal opportunity. It is recommended that trade unions should:

a. provide training and information for officers, shop stewards and representatives on their responsibilities for equal opportunity. This training and information should cover:
   the Race Relations Act and the nature and causes of discrimination;
   the backgrounds of racial minority groups and communication needs;
   the effects of prejudice;
   equal opportunity policies;
   avoiding discrimination when representing members.
b. ensure that members and representatives, whatever their racial group, are informed of their role in the union, and of industrial relations and union procedures and structures. This may be done, for example:

* *A racial group is under-represented in trade union membership if at any time during the previous twelve months no persons of that group were in membership, or disproportionately few in comparison with the proportion of persons of that group among those eligible for membership.* s. 38(4) *Under-representation in trade union posts applies under the same twelve month criteria, where there were no persons of a particular racial group in those posts or disproportionately few in comparison with the proportion of that group in the organisation.* s. 38(4)

through translation of material;
through encouragement to participate in industrial relations courses and industrial language training.

Pressure to discriminate

s. 31 **3.11** *It is unlawful for trade union members or representatives to induce or to attempt to induce those responsible for employment decisions to discriminate*:
a. *in the recruitment, promotion, transfer, training or dismissal of employees*;
b. *in terms of employment, benefits, facilities or services*.

3.12 For example, they should not:
a. restrict the numbers of a particular racial group in a section, grade or department;
b. resist changes designed to remove indirect discrimination, such as those in craft apprentice schemes, or in agreement concerning seniority rights or mobility between departments.

Victimisation

s. 2 **3.13** *It is unlawful to victimise individuals who have made allegations or complaints of racial discrimination or provided information about such discrimination*. (See Introduction, para 3.4).

Avoidance of discrimnation

s. 31 & s. 33 **3.14** *Where unions are involved in selection decisions for recruitment, promotion, training or transfer, for example through recommendation or veto, it is unlawful for them to discriminate on racial grounds*.

3.15 It is recommended that they should instruct their members accordingly and examine their procedures and joint agreements to ensure that they do not contain indirectly discriminatory requirements or conditions, such as:
unjustifiable restrictions on transfers between departments or irrelevant and unjustifiable selection criteria which have a disproportionately adverse effect on particular racial groups.

Union involvement in equal opportunity policies

3.16 It is recommended that:

a. unions should co-operate in the introduction and implementation of full equal opportunity policies, as defined in paras. 1.3 and 1.4;
b. unions should negotiate the adoption of such policies where they have not been introduced or the extension of existing policies where these are too narrow;
c. unions should co-operate with measures to monitor the progress of equal opportunity policies, or encourage management to introduce them where they do not already exist. Where appropriate (see paras. 1.33-1.35) this may be done through analysis of the distribution of employees and job applicants according to ethnic origin;
d. where monitoring shows that discrimination has occurred or is occurring, unions should co-operate in measures to eliminate it;
e. although positive action* is not legally required, unions should encourage management to take such action where there is under-representation of particular racial groups in particular jobs, and where management itself introduces positive action representatives should support it;
f. similarly, where there are communication difficulties management should be asked to take whatever action is appropriate to overcome them.

PART 4 THE RESPONSIBILITIES OF EMPLOYMENT AGENCIES

4.1 Employment agencies, in their role as employers, have the responsibilities outlined in Part 1 of the Code. In addition, they have responsibilities as suppliers of job applicants to other employers.

4.2 *It is unlawful for employment agencies: (for exceptions see Race Relations Act)*

a. *to discriminate on racial grounds in providing services to clients;* s. 14(1)
b. *to publish job advertisements indicating, or which might be understood to indicate that applications from any particular group will not be considered or will be treated more favourably or less favourably than others;* s. 29

* *See 1.44 - Positive Action recommendations.*

s. 14(1) c. *to act on directly discriminatory instructions from employers to the effect that applicants from a particular racial group will be rejected or preferred so that their numbers should be restricted;*

. 14(1) & s. 1(1)(b) d. *to act on indirectly discriminatory instructions from employers i.e. that requirements or conditions should be applied that would have a disproportionately adverse effect on applicants of a particular racial group and which cannot be shown to be justifiable.*

4.3 It is recommended that agencies should also avoid indicating such conditions or requirements in job advertisements unless they can be shown to be justifiable. Examples in each case may be those relating to educational qualifications or residence.

4.4 It is recommended that staff should be given guidance on their duty not to discriminate and on the effect which generalised assumptions and prejudices can have on their treatment of members of particular racial groups.

4.5 In particular staff should be instructed:

a. not to ask employers for racial preferences;

b. not to draw attention to racial origin when recommending applicants unless the employer is trying to attract applicants of a particular racial group under the exceptions in the Race Relations Act;

c. to report a client's refusal to interview an applicant for reasons that are directly or indirectly discriminatory to a supervisor, who should inform the client that discrimination is unlawful. If the client maintains this refusal the agency should inform the applicant of his or her right to complain to an industrial tribunal and to apply to the CRE for assistance. An internal procedure for recording such cases should be operated;

d. to inform their supervisor if they believe that an applicant, though interviewed, has been rejected on racial grounds. If the supervisor is satisfied that there are grounds for this belief, he or she should arrange for the applicant to be informed of the right to complain to an industrial tribunal and to apply to the CRE for assistance. An internal procedure for recording such cases should be operated;

e. to treat job applicants without discrimination. For example, they should not send applicants from particular racial groups to only those employers who are believed to be willing to accept them, or restrict the range of job opportunities for such applicants because of assumptions about their abilities based on race or colour.

4.6 It is recommended that employment agencies should discontinue their services to employers who give unlawful discriminatory instructions and who refuse to withdraw them.

4.7 It is recommended that employment agencies should monitor the effectiveness of the measures they take for ensuring that no unlawful discrimination occurs. For example, where reasonably practicable they should make periodic checks to ensure that applicants from particular racial groups are being referred for suitable jobs for which they are qualified at a similar rate to that for other comparable applicants.

(f) Code of Practice

Picketing

Section B Picketing and the Civil Law

9. The law sets out the basic rules which must be observed if picketing is to be carried out, or organised, lawfully. To keep to these rules, attendance for the purpose of picketing may only:

(i) be undertaken in contemplation or furtherance of a trade dispute;

(ii) be carried out by a person attending at or near his own place of work; a trade union official, in addition to attending at or near his own place of work, may also attend at or near the place of work of a member of his trade union whom he is accompanying on the picket line and whom he represents.

Furthermore, the only purpose involved must be peacefully to obtain or communicate information, or peacefully to persuade a person to work or not to work.

10. Picketing commonly involves persuading workers to break, or interfere with the performance of, their contacts of employment by not going to work. Picketing can also disrupt the business of the employer who is being picketed by interfering with the performance of a commercial contract which the employer has with a customer or supplier. If pickets follow the rules outlined in paragraph 9, however, they may have the protection against civil proceedings afforded by the 'statutory immunities'. These rules, and immunities, are explained more fully in paragraphs 11 to 30 below.

In contemplation or furtherance of a trade dispute

11. Picketing is lawful only if it is carried out in contemplation or furtherance of a 'trade dispute'. A 'trade dispute' is defined in law so as to cover the matters which normally occasion disputes between employers and workers - such as terms and conditions of employment, the allocation of work, matters of discipline, trade union recognition.

'Secondary' action

12. The 'statutory immunities' do not apply to protect a threat of, or a call for or other inducement of 'secondary' industrial

action. The law defines 'secondary' action - which is sometimes referred to as 'sympathetic' or 'solidarity' action - as that by workers whose employer is not a party to the trade dispute to which the action relates.

13. However, a worker employed by a party to a trade dispute, picketing at his own place of work may try to persuade another worker, not employed by that employer, to break, or interfere with the performance of, the second worker's contract of employment, and/or to interfere with the performance of a commercial contract. This could happen, for example, if a picket persuaded a lorry driver employed by another employer not to cross the picket line and deliver goods to be supplied, under a commercial contract, to the employer in dispute. Such an act by a picket would be an unlawful inducement to take secondary action unless provision was made to the contrary.

14. Accordingly, the law contains provisions which make it lawful for a peaceful picket, at the picket's own place of work, to seek to persuade workers other than those employed by the picket's own employer not to work, or not to work normally. To have such protection, the peaceful picketing must be done:

a. by a worker employed by the employer who is party to the dispute[1]; or
b. by a trade union official whose attendance is lawful (see paragraphs 22-23 below).

15. Where an entrance or exit is used jointly by the workers of more than one employer, the workers who are not involved in the dispute to which a picket relates should not be interfered with by picketing activities. Particular care should be taken to ensure that a picketing does not involve calls for a breach, or interference with the performance, of contracts by employees of the other employer(s) who are not involved in the dispute. Observing this principle will help avoid consequences which might otherwise be damaging and disruptive to good industrial relations.

Attendance at or near a picket's own place of work

16. It is lawful for a person to induce breach, or interference with the performance, of a contract in the course of attendance

1 However, the peaceful picketing may be done by a worker who is not in employment but was last employed by the employer in dispute in certain circumstances - see paragraph 20.

for the purpose of picketing only if he pickets at or near his own place of work.

17 The expression 'at or near his own place of work' is not further defined in statute law. The provisions mean that, except for those covered by paragraphs 22 and 23 below, lawful picketing must be limited to attendance at, or near, an entrance to or exit from the factory, site or office at which the picket works. Picketing should be confined to a location, or locations, as near as practicable to the place of work.

18 The law does not enable a picket to attend lawfully at an entrance to, or exit from, *any* place of work other than his own. This applies even, for example, if those working at the other place of work are employed by the same employer, or are covered by the same collective bargaining arrangements as the picket.

19. The law identifies two specific groups in respect of which particular arrangements apply. These groups are:

- those (eg mobile workers) who work at more than one place; and
- those for whom it is impracticable to picket at their own place of work because of its location.

The law provides that it is lawful for such workers to picket those premises of their employer from which they work, or those from which their work is administered. In the case of lorry drivers, for example, this will usually mean, in practice, the premises of their employer from which their vehicles operate.

20. Special provisions also apply to people who are not in work, and who have lost their jobs for reasons connected with the dispute which has occasioned the picketing. This might arise, for example, where the dismissal of a group of employees has led directly to the organisation of a picket, or where an employer has dismissed employees because they refuse to work normally, and some or all of those dismissed then wish to set up a picket. In such cases the law provides that it is lawful for a worker to picket at his former place of work. This special arrangement ceases to apply, however to any worker who subsequently takes a job at another place of work.

21. The law does not protect anyone who pickets without permission on or inside any part of premises which are private

property. The law will not, therefore, protect pickets who trespass, or those who organise such trespass, from being sued in the civil courts.

Trade union officials

22. For the reasons described in Section F of this Code, it may be helpful to the orderly organisation and conduct of picketing for a trade union official[2] to be present on a picket line where his members are picketing. The law provides that it is lawful for a trade union official to picket at any place of work provided that:

(i) he is accompanying members of his trade union who are picketing lawfully at or near their own place of work; and

(ii) he personally represents those members.

23. If these conditions are satisfied, then a trade union official has the same legal protection as other pickets who picket lawfully at or near their own place of work. However, the law provides that an official - whether a lay official or an employee of the union - is regarded for this purpose as representing only those members of his union whom he has been specifically appointed or elected to represent. An official cannot, therefore, claim that he represents a group of members simply because they belong to his trade union. He must represent and be responsible for them in the normal course of his trade union duties. For example, it is lawful for an official at a particular place of work - such as a shop steward - who represents members at a particular place of work to be present on a picket line where those members are picketing lawfully; for a branch official to be present only where members of his branch are lawfully picketing; for a regional official to be present only where members of his region are lawfully picketing; for a national official who represents a particular trade group or section within the union, to be present wherever members of that trade group or section are lawfully picketing; and for a national official such as a general secretary or president who represents the whole union to be present wherever any members of his union are picketing lawfully.

2 The law defines an 'official of the union' as a person who is an officer of the union (or of a branch or section of the union), or who, not being such an officer, is a person elected or appointed in accordance with the rules of the union to be a representative of its members (or some of them), including any person so elected or appointed who is an employee of the same employer as the members, or one or more of the members, whom he is elected to represent. This could include, for example, a shop steward.

Lawful purposes of picketing

24. In no circumstances does a picket have power, under the law, to require other people to stop, or to compel them to listen or to do what he asks them to do. A person who decides to cross a picket line *must* be allowed to do so. In addition, the law provides a remedy for any union member who is disciplined by his union because he has crossed a picket line.[3]

25. The ***only*** purposes of picketing declared lawful in statute are:

- peacefully obtaining and communicating information: and
- peacefully persuading a person to work or not to work.

26. The law allows pickets to seek to explain their case to those entering or leaving the picketed premises, and/or to ask them not to enter or leave the premises where the dispute is taking place. This may be done by speaking to people, or it may involve the distribution of leaflets or the carrying of banners or placards putting the pickets' case. **In all cases, however, any such activity must be carried out *peacefully*.**

27. The law protects peaceful communication and persuasion. It does not give pickets, anyone organising or participating in any activity associated with picketing, or anyone organising a picket, protection against civil proceedings being brought against them for any conduct occurring during the picketing, or associated activity, which amounts to a separate civil wrong such as:

- unlawful threat or assault;
- harassment (ie threatening or unreasonable behaviour causing fear or apprehension to those in the vicinity);
- obstruction of a path, road, entrance or exit to premises;
- interference (eg because of noise or crowds) in the rights of those in neighbouring properties (ie 'private nuisance');
- trespassing on private property.

28. Both individual pickets, and anyone - including a union - organising a picket or associated activity, should be careful not to commit such civil wrongs. It is possible, for example, that material on placards carried by pickets - or, for that matter, by

3 A member disciplined for crossing a picket line is 'unjustifiably disciplined'; the remedy for unjustifiable discipline is by complaint to an industrial tribunal. (See also paragraphs 60-61 in Section F of this Code.)

those involved in activities associated with picketing - could be defamatory or amount to a threat or harassment. Pickets will also have no legal protection if they do or say things, or make offensive gestures at people, which amount to unlawful threat or harassment. Section C of this Code explains that such actions may also give rise to prosecution under the criminal law.

29. Similarly, if the noise or other disturbance caused to residents of an area by pickets, or by those associated with picketing activity, amounts to a civil wrong, those involved or responsible are not protected by the law from proceedings being brought against them.

30. Similar proceedings apply in respect of any breach of the criminal law by pickets, or their organiser. As explained in Section C of this Code, a picket, or anyone involved in an associated activity, who threatens or intimidates someone, or obstructs an entrance to a workplace, or causes a breach of the peace, commits a criminal offence. Where pickets commit a criminal offence, then in many circumstances they will not be acting peacefully; consequently, any immunity under the civil law will be lost.

Seeking redress

31. An employer, a worker, or anyone else who is party to a contract which is, or may be, broken or interfered with by unlawful picketing has a civil law remedy. He may apply to the court for an order[4] preventing, or stopping, the unlawful picketing, or its organisation. Such a person may also claim damages from those responsible where the activities of the unlawful picket have caused him loss. An order can be sought against the person - which could include a particular trade union or unions - on whose instructions or advice the unlawful picketing is taking place, or will take place.

32. In making an order, the court has authority to require a trade union which has acted unlawfully to take such steps as are considered necessary to ensure that there is no further call for, or other organisation of, unlawful picketing. An order may be granted by the court on an interim basis, pending a full hearing of the case.

4 An injunction in England and Wales; an interdict in Scotland.

33. If a court order is made, it can apply not only to the person or union named in the order, but to anyone else acting on his behalf or on his instructions. Thus an organiser of unlawful picketing cannot avoid liability, for example, merely by changing the people on the unlawful picket line from time to time.

34. Similarly, anyone who is wronged in any other way by a picket can seek an order from the court to get the unlawful act stopped or prevented, and/or for damages. Thus, for example, if picketing, or associated activities, give rise to unlawful disturbance to residents in the vicinity, one or more of the residents so affected can apply to the court for such an order and/or for damages. Such proceedings might be taken against individual pickets, or the person - including a union where applicable - responsible for the unlawful act.

35. If a court order is not obeyed, or is ignored, those who sought it can go back to court and ask to have those concerned declared in contempt of court. Anyone who is found to be in contempt of court may face heavy fines, or other penalties, which the court may consider appropriate. For example, a union may be deprived of its assets through sequestration, where the union's funds are placed in the control of a person appointed by the court who may, in particular, pay any fines or legal costs arising from the court proceedings. Similarly, if a person knows that such an order has been made against someone, or some union, and yet aids and abets that person to disobey or ignore the order, he may also be found to be acting in contempt of court and liable to be punished by the court.

Determining whether a union is responsible

36. Pickets will usually attend at a place of work for the purpose of persuading others not to work, or not to work normally, and may thereby be inducing them to breach, or interfere with the performance of, contracts. The law lays down rules which determine whether a union will be held liable for any such acts of inducement which are unlawful.

37. The law provides that a union will be held responsible for such an unlawful act if it is done, authorised or endorsed by:

a. the union's principal executive committee, president, or general secretary;
b. any person given power under the union's own rules to do, authorise or endorse acts of the kind in question; or

c. any other committee of the union, or any official of the union[5] - including those who are employed by the union, and those, like shop stewards, who are not.[6]

A union will be held responsible for such an act by such a body or person regardless of any provisions to the contrary in its own rules, or anything in any other contract or rule of law.

38. Pickets may, of course, commit civil wrongs other than inducing breach, or interference with the performance, of contracts. The question of whether a union will be held responsible for those wrongs will be determined according to common law principles of liability, rather than by reference to the rules described in paragraph 37 above.

The need for a ballot

39. If what is done in the course of picketing amounts to a call for industrial action, and is an act for which the union is responsible in law, the union can only have the protection of statutory immunity if it has first held a properly-conducted secret ballot.

40. The law requires that entitlement to vote in such a ballot must be given to all the union's members who it is reasonable at the time of the ballot for the union to believe will be called upon to take part in, or continue with, the industrial action, and

5 See footnote to paragraph 22 for the relevant definition of 'official'. In this case, however, an act will also be taken to have been done by an 'official of the union' if it was done (or authorised or endorsed) by a group of persons, or any member of a group, to which such an official belonged at the relevant time if the group's purposes included organising or co-ordinating industrial action.

6 However, if an act which is done (or authorised or endorsed) by a union committee or official is 'effectively repudiated' by the union's principal executive committee, president or general secretary, the union will not be held responsible in law. In order to avoid liability in this way, the act concerned must be repudiated by any of these as soon as reasonably practicable after it has come to their knowledge. In addition, the union must, without delay:

a. give written notice of the repudiation to the committee or official in question; and
b. do its best to give individual written notice of the fact and date of the repudiation to: (i) every member of the union who it has reason to believe is taking part - or might otherwise take part - in industrial action as a result of the act; and (ii) the employer of every such member.

to no other member. The ballot must produce a majority of those voting which is in favour of taking, or continuing with, industrial action. These, and other requirements of the law in respect of such ballots, are restated in the statutory Code of Practice 'Trade Union Ballots on Industrial Action (1st Revision).'

Section C Picketing and the criminal law

41. If a picket commits a criminal offence he is just as liable to be prosecuted as any other member of the public who breaks the law. The immunity provided under the civil law does not protect him in any way.

42. The criminal law protects the right of every person to go about his lawful daily business free from interference by others. No one is under any obligation to stop when a picket asks him to do so, or if he does stop, to comply with a request, for example, not to go into work. Everyone has the right, if he wishes to do so, to cross a picket line in order to go into his place of work or to deliver or collect goods. A picket may exercise peaceful persuasion, but if he goes beyond that and tries by means other than peaceful persuasion to deter another person from exercising those rights he may commit a criminal offence.

43. Among other matters, it is a criminal offence for pickets (as for others):

- to use threatening, abusive or insulting words or behaviour, or disorderly behaviour within the sight or hearing of any person - whether a worker seeking to cross a picket line, an employer, an ordinary member of the public, or the police - likely to be caused harassment, alarm or distress by such conduct;
- to use threatening, abusive or insulting words or behaviour towards any person with intent to cause fear of violence or to provoke violence;
- to use or threaten unlawful violence;
- to obstruct the highway or the entrance to premises or to seek physically to bar the passage of vehicles or persons by lying down in the road, linking arms across or circling in the road, or jostling or physically restraining those entering or leaving the premises;
- to be in possession of an offensive weapon;
- intentionally or recklessly to damage property;
- to engage in violent, disorderly or unruly behaviour or to

take any action which is likely to lead to a breach of the peace;
- to obstruct a police officer in the execution of his duty.

44. A picket has no right under the law to require a vehicle to stop or to be stopped. The law allows him only to ask a driver to stop by words or signals. A picket may not physically obstruct a vehicle if the driver decided to drive on or, indeed, in any other circumstances. A driver must - as on all other occasions - exercise due care and attention when approaching or driving past a picket line, and may not drive in such a manner as to give rise to a reasonably foreseeable risk of injury.

Section D Role of the police

45. It is not the function of the police to take a view of the merits of a particular dispute. They have a general duty to uphold the law and keep the peace, whether on the picket line or elsewhere. The law gives the police discretion to take whatever measures may reasonably be considered necessary to ensure that picketing remains peaceful and orderly.

46. The police have **no** responsibility for enforcing the **civil law**. An employer cannot require the police to help in identifying the pickets against whom he wishes to seek an order from the civil court, nor is the job of the police to enforce the terms of an order. Enforcement of an order on the application of a plaintiff is a matter for the court and its officer. The police may, however, decide to assist the officers of the court if they think there may be a breach of the peace.

47. As regards the criminal law the police have considerable discretionary powers to limit the number of pickets at any one place where they have reasonable cause to fear disorder.[7] The law does not impose a specific limit on the number of people who may picket at any one place; nor does this Code affect in any way the discretion of the police to limit the number of people on a particular picket line. It is for the police to decide, taking into account all the circumstances, whether the number of pickets at any particular place provides reasonable grounds for the

7 In *Piddington v Bates* (1960) the High Court upheld the decision of a police constable in the circumstances of that case to limit the number of pickets to two.

belief that a breach of the peace is likely to occur. If a picket does not leave the picket line when asked to do so by the police, he is liable to be arrested for obstruction either of the highway or of a police officer in the execution of his duty if the obstruction is such as to cause, or be likely to cause, a breach of the peace.

Section E Limiting numbers of pickets

48. Violence and disorder on the picket line is more likely to occur if there are excessive numbers of pickets. Wherever large numbers of people with strong feelings are involved there is a danger that the situation will get out of control, and that those concerned will run the risk of committing an offence, with consequent arrest and prosecution, or of committing a civil wrong which exposes them, or anyone organising them, to civil proceedings.

49. This is particularly so whenever people seek by sheer weight of numbers to stop others going into work or delivering or collecting goods. In such cases, what is intended is not peaceful persuasion, but obstruction or harassment - if not intimidation. Such a situation is often described as 'mass picketing'. In fact, it is not picketing in its lawful sense of an attempt at peaceful persuasion, and may well result in a breach of the peace or other criminal offences.

50. Moreover, anyone seeking to demonstrate support for those in dispute should keep well away from any picket line so as not to create a risk of breach of the peace or other criminal offence being committed on that picket line. Just as with a picket itself, the numbers involved in any such demonstration should not be excessive, and the demonstration should be conducted lawfully. Section 14 of the Public Order Act 1986 provides the police with the power to impose conditions (for example, as to numbers, location and duration) on public assemblies of 20 or more people where the assembly is likely to result in serious public disorder; or serious damage to property; or serious disruption to the life of the community; or if its purpose is to coerce.

51. Large numbers on a picket line are also likely to give rise to fear and resentment amongst those seeking to cross that picket line, even where no criminal offence is committed. They exacerbate disputes and sour relations not only between management

and employees but between the pickets and their fellow employees. **Accordingly pickets and their organisers should ensure that in general the number of pickets does not exceed six at any entrance to, or exit from, a workplace; frequently a smaller number will be appropriate.**

Section F Organisation of picketing

52. Sections B and C of this Code outline aspects of the civil law and the criminal law, as they may apply to pickets, and to anyone, including a trade union, who organises a picket. While it is possible that a picket may be entirely 'spontaneous', it is much more likely that it will be organised by an identifiable individual or group.

53. Paragraphs 36-38 in Section B of this Code describe how to identify whether a trade union is, in fact, responsible in terms of civil law liability, for certain acts. As explained in these paragraphs, the law means, for example, that if such an act takes place in the course of picketing, and if a trade union official has done, authorised or endorsed the act, then the official's union will be responsible in law unless the act is 'effectively repudiated' by the union's national leadership.

Functions of the picket organiser

54. Wherever picketing is 'official' (ie organised by a trade union), an experienced person, preferably a trade union official who represents those picketing, should always be in charge of the picket line. He should have a letter of authority from his union which he can show to the police officers or to people who want to cross the picket line. Even when he is not on the picket line himself he should be available to give the pickets advice if a problem arises.

55. A picket should not be designated as an 'official' picket unless it is actually organised by a trade union. Nor should pickets claim the authority and support of a union unless the union is prepared to accept the consequent responsibility. In particular, union authority and support should not be claimed by the pickets if the union has, in fact, repudiated calls to take industrial action made, or being made, in the course of the picketing.

56. Whether a picket is 'official' or 'unofficial', an organiser of pickets should maintain close contact with the police. Advance

consultation with the police is always in the best interests of all concerned. In particular the organiser and the pickets should seek directions from the police on the number of people who should be present on the picket line at any one time and on where they should stand in order to avoid obstructing the highway.

57. The other main functions of the picket organiser should include ensuring that:

- the pickets understand the law and are aware of the provisions of this Code, and that the picketing is conducted peacefully and lawfully;
- badges or armbands, which authorised pickets should wear so that they are clearly identified, are distributed to such pickets and are worn while they are picketing;
- workers from other places of work do not join the picket line, and that any offers of support on the picket line from outsiders are refused;
- the number of pickets at any entrance to, or exit from, a place of work is not so great as to give rise to fear and resentment amongst those seeking to cross that picket line (see paragraph 51 in Section E of this Code);
- close contact with his own union office (if any), and with the offices of other unions if they are involved in the picketing, is established and maintained;
- such special arrangements as may be necessary for essential supplies, services or operations (see paragraphs 62-64 in Section G of this Code) are understood and observed by the pickets.

Consultation with other trade unions

58. Where several unions are involved in a dispute, they should consult each other about the organisation of any picketing. It is important that they should agree how the picketing is to be carried out, how many pickets there should be from each union, and who should have overall responsibility for organising them.

Right to cross picket lines

59. Everyone has the right to decide for himself whether he will cross a picket line. Disciplinary action should not be taken or threatened by a union against a member on the grounds that he has crossed a picket line.

60. If a union disciplines any member for crossing a picket line, the member will have been 'unjustifiably disciplined'. In such a case, the individual can make a complaint to an industrial tribunal. If the tribunal finds the complaint well-founded, it will make a declaration to that effect.

61. If the union has not lifted the penalty imposed on the member, or if it has not taken all necessary steps to reverse anything done in giving effect to the penalty, an application for compensation should be made to the Employment Appeal Tribunal (EAT). In any other case, the individual can apply to an industrial tribunal for compensation. The EAT or tribunal will award whatever compensation it considers just and equitable in all the circumstances, subject to a specified maximum amount. Where the application is made to the EAT, there will normally be a specified minimum award.

Section G Essential supplies, services and operations

62. Pickets, and anyone organising a picket should take very great care to ensure that their activities do not cause distress, hardship or inconvenience to members of the public who are not involved in the dispute. Particular care should be taken to ensure that the movement of essential goods and supplies, the carrying out of essential maintenance of plant and equipment, and the provision of services essential to the life of the community are not impeded, still less prevented.

63. The following list of essential supplies and services is provided as an illustration of the kind of activity which requires special protection to comply with the recommendations in paragraph 62 above. However, **the list is not intended to be comprehensive**. The supplies and services which may need to be protected in accordance with these recommendations could cover different activities in different circumstances. Subject to this *caveat*, 'essential supplies, services and operations' include:

- the production, packaging, marketing and/or distribution of medical and pharmaceutical products;
- the provision of supplies and services essential to health and welfare institutions, eg hospitals, old peoples' homes;
- the provision of heating fuel for schools, residential institutions, medical institutions and private residential accommodation;

- the production and provision of other supplies for which there is a crucial need during a crisis in the interests of public health and safety (eg chlorine, lime and other agents for water purification; industrial and medical gases; sand and salt for road gritting purposes);
- activities necessary to the maintenance of plant and machinery;
- the proper care of livestock;
- necessary safety procedures (including such procedures as are necessary to maintain plant and machinery);
- the production, packaging, marketing and/or distribution of food and animal feeding stuffs;
- the operation of essential services, such as police, fire, ambulance, medical and nursing services, air safety, coastguard and air sea rescue services, and services provided by voluntary bodies (eg Red Cross and St John's ambulances, meals on wheels, hospital car services), and mortuaries, burial and cremation services.

64. Arrangements to ensure these safeguards for essential supplies, services and operations should be agreed in advance between the pickets, or anyone organising the picket, and the employer, or employers, concerned.

Index

References are to paragraph numbers

Abroad,
worker ordinarily working, 8.18
Access to medical report, 5.71–5.75
Accounts,
trade union, of, 14.42–14.44
Advertising,
discrimination in, 4.19–4.20, 4.57–4.58, 4.115
intention to discriminate, 4.57, 4.58
statements in advertisement, 3.11
Advice. *See* ADVISORY, CONCILIATION AND ARBITRATION SERVICE
Advisory, Conciliation and Arbitration Service,
advice, 1.4
advisory handbook, Appendix I
annual report, 1.2
arbitration, reference to, 1.12, 1.17
codes of practice, 1.14–1.15A
conciliation, 1.5–1.11A
conciliation officers, 1.7–1.11
constitution and duties of, 1.1
discipline, advisory handbook on, Appendix I
disclosure of information to trade unions, Appendix I
enquiries by, 1.13
functions, 1.2, 1.3
staff, 1.2
statutory basis of, 1.1
time off for trade union duties and activities, Appendix I
trade disputes, 1.5–1.6
Affray,
abolition of common law offence, 15.122
Agency,
workers provided by, 2.47
Alternative employment,
redundancy, in place of, 10.21–10.24
Anton Piller orders, 11.26
Appeal. *See also* EMPLOYMENT APPEAL TRIBUNAL
improvement or prohibition, against, 12.10–12.16
industrial training levy, against 1.41
tribunal, from. *See* INDUSTRIAL TRIBUNAL
Apprenticeship,
contract of, 4.5–4.6
dancer, deed held void, 4.2
expiry of agreement, 4.7
minor lapses in conduct, 4.5
protection of new laws, 4.6
redundancy legislation applicable to apprentices, 10.3
wrongful dismissal of apprentice, 4.5
Arbitration. *See* ADVISORY, CONCILIATION AND ARBITRATION SERVICE: CENTRAL ARBITRATION COMMITTEE
Armed Forces Reserves,
employment protection, 5.65–5.70
Associate,
employee, as, 2.10

Attachment of earnings,
self-employed person, order not applicable to, 2.44
Author,
whether 'worker', 2.3
Award,
additional, 9.51–9.52
compensation, 9.36–9.40
compensatory, 9.41–9.50
special, 9.53–9.56

Ballot,
different places of work, at, 15.67
industrial action, before, 15.55–15.66
overseas members, for, 15.66
political fund, 14.52–14.60
public funds for, 14.40
Bribe,
secret, employee not to accept, 6.62–6.63
Business consultant,
whether employee, 2.9

Cashless pay. *See* WAGES
Central Arbitration Committee,
appointment and functions, 1.17
constitution, 1.17
determination of claims by, 1.17
failure of employer to disclose information, 15.4
generally, 1.17
reference of disputes to, generally, 1.12
Certification,
advantages of certificate of independence, 14.16
trade unions, of, 14.9–14.15
Certification officer,
annual report, 1.16
appointment and functions, 1.16, 14.7
Commissioner for Rights of Trade Union Members, assistance by, 1.34
documents—
custody, 1.16
public inspection, 1.16
Childbirth. *See* MATERNITY
Children,
employment of, 4.4, 4.4A
meaning, 4.4
part-time work by, 4.4
unborn, employer's duty to, 6.28
Civil servants,
position of, 2.14, 2.15
Clergyman,
contract of employment not applicable to, 2.3
Code of practice,
Advisory, Conciliation and Arbitration Service, 1.14–1.15A, Appendix I
failure to observe, 1.15
future issue of, in safety, health and welfare matters, 12.23, 12.54–12.56
Collective agreement,
conflicting agreements, 3.36
employment terms—
custom as source of, 3.39–3.41A
what are, 3.37–3.38
equal pay legislation, effect of, 4.94
express incorporation of terms of, 3.25–3.29
implied incorporation of terms, 3.30–3.32A
legal effect of, 15.95–15.99
meaning, 3.25
non-unionists and, 3.33–3.35
'normative' terms of, 3.26
suspension, grounds for, may be incorporated in, 7.42
when binding in law, 3.25
Collective bargaining,
information, disclosure by employers, 15.2–15.5
Commission,
employee not to accept, 6.62–6.63
Commission for Racial Equality,
code of practice, 1.45
establishment and functions, 1.45
proceedings by, 4.118, 4.125
Commissioner for Rights of Trade Union Members,
annual report, 1.28
appointment, 1.28
certification officer, application to, 1.33
expenses, 1.32
functions, 1.28A–1.34
Company,
control, 8.38
meaning, 8.39
Company director. *See* DIRECTOR
Compensation award,
additional award, 9.51–9.52
basic award, 9.36–9.40

Compensation award—*contd*
compensatory award, 9.41–9.50
special award, 9.53–9.56
unemployment benefit, recoupment of, 9.57–9.58
where re-instatement or re-engagement order not complied with, 9.36–9.56
Compensatory award,
making of, by industrial tribunal, 9.41–9.50
maximum amount of, 9.44
Competitors,
working for, duties of ex-employees, 11.18–11.20
Complaint. *See* INDUSTRIAL TRIBUNAL
Conciliation. *See* ADVISORY, CONCILIATION AND ARBITRATION SERVICE
Conciliation officer,
appointment of, 1.7
confidential nature of work of, 9.10
duties of, 1.7–1.11A
impartiality, need for, 1.10
intervention of, cases settled through, 1.7
privileged documents, 9.10
settlement under auspices of, 9.11
Confederation of Shipbuilding and Engineering Unions,
example of confederated organisation, as, 14.2
Conspiracy,
actions for, 15.32
legitimate strike is not, 15.33
meaning, 15.32
trade union officials, by, 15.32
Constructive dismissal,
effective date of termination, 9.8A
explained, 3.24, 8.62–8.78
failure to pay minimum wage, 8.66A
reasonable notice of transfer, and, 8.67B
Constructive resignation,
breach of contract as, 3.15
Consultant,
whether employee, 2.9
Continuous employment,
change of employer, 8.33–8.45
computation of, 8.21–8.25
effect of continuity rules, 8.46
generally, 8.20, 10.43–10.44
Continuous employment—*contd*
necessity for employee to have appropriate period of, 8.20
preservation of continuity, 8.26–8.32
sickness or injury, effect of, 8.27
strike does not break continuity, 8.32
Contract,
apprenticeship, of, 4.5–4.6
capability of trade union to make, 14.3
fixed-term—
exclusion of redundancy provisions, 10.41
meaning, 8.60
frustration of, 8.87–8.93
inducing or procuring breach of, 15.30–15.31
service, between company and director, 2.6, 2.7
union or non-union members only, 15.111–15.113
Contract of employment,
breach of contractual term, 3.14
business consultants, 2.9
children, 4.4
clergyman not engaged under, 2.3
contract of service. *See* CONTRACT OF SERVICE
defences to action based on common law negligence—
contributory negligence, 6.48
denial of negligence, 6.43–6.44
generally, 6.42
injury sole fault of employee, 6.45–6.47
disciplinary and grievance procedures, 3.47–3.49
duty to insure, and, 6.19A
formation—
collective agreement—
conflicting, 3.36
employment terms, which terms are, 3.37–3.38
express incorporation of terms, 3.25–3.29
implied incorporation of terms, 3.30–3.22A
non-unionists and, 3.33–3.35
custom as source of employment terms, 3.39–3.41
employment protection. *See* EMPLOYMENT

Contract of employment—*contd*
formation—*contd*
express terms, 3.9–3.16
generally, 3.1–3.5
holidays, 3.71–3.73
illegality, 3.1C
implied terms, 3.17–3.24
intention to create legal relations, 3.1B
itemised pay statements, 3.69–3.70
job descripton, 3.50
legal constraints on terms and conditions, 4.1 *et seq.*
offer and acceptance, 3.1A
terms and conditions, 3.7–3.8
variation of contractual terms, 3.51–3.59
works and staff rules, 3.42–3.46
written particulars, 3.60–3.68
frustration of, 8.87–8.93
global, 2.66
implied duties of employer—
generally, 6.7
indemnity, 6.18–6.19
mutual respect, 6.8–6.10
references, 6.20–6.22
safety, as to, 6.23–6.27
wages or remuneration, to pay, when no work, 6.13–6.17
work, to provide, 6.11–6.12
implied obligations of employee—
bribes or commission not to be accepted, 6.62–6.63
competitor, duty not to work for, 6.71
confidential information not to be disclosed, 6.64–6.65
disclosure, duty of, 6.72
faithful service, 6.53–6.55
'moonlighting', 6.70–6.71, 8.151
obedience to orders, 6.56–6.60
patents, inventions and copyright, 6.66–6.69
punctuality, 6.53
skill and care, duty to use, 6.61
importance of agreeing terms, 3.5
job description document, 3.50
methods of entering into, 3.1
ministers of religion, 2.13
minors, 4.2–4.3, 4.4

Contract of employment—*contd*
nature of—
agency workers, 2.47
business consultants, 2.9
common law remedies, 2.67
Crown employees, 2.14–2.15, 2.64–2.65
directors, 2.6–2.8
domestic servants, 2.58
employees, 2.22–2.24
employers, 2.5
foreign employees, 2.59
generally, 2.1
global contracts, 2.66
Health Service employees, 2.16
national security, 2.64–2.65
office holders, 2.11–2.12
overseas employment, 2.60–2.62A
partners, 2.10
part-time employees, 2.49–2.52C
police, 2.17–2.19
probationary employees, 2.53–2.55
public law remedies, 2.68–2.70
retainers, 2.63
secondment of employees, 2.45–2.46
self-employed and employees, distinction between, 2.25–2.25A, 2.37–2.44
status, 2.20–2.21
temporary employees, 2.48
trainees, 2.56–2.57
workers, 2.2–2.4
performance, 6.1 *et seq.*
personal nature of, 6.1–6.6
race relations, 4.156
remedies—
common law, 2.67
public law, 2.68–2.70
Royal Commission on Civil Liability, 6.50–6.52
separate, with same employer, 2.24
termination—
consensual, 8.94–8.95
constructive resignation, 8.84–8.85
frustration, 8.87–8.93
methods, 8.80
project, 8.96
resignation, 8.81–8.83

Contract of employment—*contd*
terms and conditions, legal constraints on, 4.1 *et seq.*
transfers of undertakings, 10.29
unilateral variation of, 3.51, 3.52
variation of, 3.51–3.59
written particulars of, 3.60–3.68
Contract of service,
contract for services distinguished, 2.25–2.35
control test, 2.26–2.27
generally, 2.25–2.25A
meaning, 2.28
multiple test, 2.29–2.35
organisational test, 2.28
Contract worker,
discrimination against, 4.112
Contributory negligence,
defence of, 6.48
Controller of premises,
duties of, 12.36
Conviction,
employee, of, for offence outside employment, 7.61–7.62, 8.149–8.150
Copyright,
work written in course of employment, 6.69
Costs,
industrial tribunal, 1.23, 9.62
Counter-notice,
following notice of dismissal, 10.9
Covenant,
restraint of trade. *See* RESTRAINT OF TRADE
Criminal liabilities,
trade disputes, 15.117–15.121
Crown employees,
employment protection, 2.14
national security, 2.64–2.65
position of, 2.14–2.15
Crown notice,
issue of, 12.17
Custom,
employment terms, as source of, 3.39–3.41
Customers,
ex-employee soliciting, as breach of contract, 11.5
protection against soliciting of, 11.14–11.17

Damages,
trade unions, and, 15.84–15.87
Damages—*contd*
wrongful dismissal, 7.9
Danger,
imminent, power to deal with, 12.18
unknown and unforeseen by employer, 6.25
Danger money,
payment of, 6.46
Death,
employer or employee, of, 5.92
Deductions,
exceptions, 5.136
general restrictions, 5.129–5.130
negligent work, for, 7.38–7.40
retail employment, 5.137–5.140
Demonstration,
new rules, 15.128
Demotion,
disciplinary grounds, on, 7.58
equivalent to dismissal, 7.57–7.58, 7.61
Department of Employment,
codes of practice, issue of, 1.42
employment and training schemes, 1.43
responsibility and duties of, 1.42
Dermatitis,
precautions against, 6.43, 6.44
Director,
one-man business of, whether entitled to redundancy payment, 2.6
whether employee, 2.6–2.8
Disabled persons,
Code of Practice, 4.129
provision of jobs for, 4.126–4.129
Disciplinary powers,
ACAS advisory handbook, Appendix I
demotion, 7.58
management, of, *See* MANAGEMENT
Disclosure
employee's duty of, 6.72
occupational pension scheme, 3.75–3.77
Discovery of documents,
confidential documents, 9.16
disclosure, 1.25
improper use of documents disclosed, 1.25
privileged documents, 9.10

Discrimination. *See* RACIAL DISCRIMATION; SEX DISCRIMINATION
Dismissal. *See also* FAIR DISMISSAL: UNFAIR DISMISSAL
appeal against, 7.10–7.16
asserting statutory right, for, 8.187–8.192
beard, for wearing, 3.45
breach of contractual term, 3.14
conciliation officers, functions of, 1.9
conduct contributing to, 9.44–9.49
constructive, 3.24, 8.62–8.78
consultation, lack of, 8.159–8.161
counter-notice following notice, 10.9
deemed, 8.79
demotion equivalent to, 7.57–7.58, 7.61
evidence as to reasons for, 9.21–9.22
failure to return to work after maternity leave, 8.96A
fair. *See* FAIR DISMISSAL
former law, 8.1–8.2
generally, 8.1–8.3
how effected—
constructive dismissal, 3.24, 8.62–8.78
deemed dismissal, 8.79
employee resigning by reason of employer's conduct, 8.62–8.78
expiry of fixed term without renewal, 8.58–8.61
termination by employer with or without notice, 8.48–8.57
instant. *See* 'summary' *post*
intention more important than words, 8.56
invited by employee, 8.52
lawful, 8.11–8.14
misconduct, acts constituting, 8.136, 8.142
mutual agreement to part company is not, 8.49, 10.6
national security, 8.206
neglectful incompetence, 8.110–8.114
non-renewal of contract, 8.58–8.61
notice, length of, 8.11–8.14
payment in lieu of notice, 9.7
period of notice, during, 10.39–10.40

Dismissal—*contd*
police, of, 2.17, 2.19
post, notice sent by, 8.18
qualifications, lack of, 8.130–8.132
redundancy, by reason of—
cessation of business, 10.12
generally, 10.10–10.11
moving of place of business, 10.13–10.14
surplus labour, 10.15–10.18
See also REDUNDANCY
references given after, 6.20–6.22
repudiatory conduct of employer, 8.62–8.78
resignation is not, unless constructive dismissal, 8.48
summary—
bad language, 8.5
dishonest conduct, 8.5
drinking, smoking, etc., 8.6
express term of contract, breach, of, 8.6
generally, 8.4
go-slow or work-to-rule, 8.9
immediate effect, 8.10
negligence, 8.8
night-watchman's absence, 8.5
standards to be applied, 8.4
unpunctuality, etc., 8.9
works rules, breach of provision in, 8.6
unfair. *See* UNFAIR DISMISSAL
vandalism, for, 7.17
victimisation causing resignation, 4.17, 4.104
what constitutes, 10.5–10.9
without notice, 9.7
words used to denote, 8.53–8.54
written reasons for, 8.207–8.213
wrongful, action for, 8.17
Dispute. *See* TRADE DISPUTE
Dock workers,
legal status of, 2.20
Domestic servants,
position of, 2.58
redundancy provisions, 10.41
Duty of care. *See* SAFETY

Employee,
agency workers, 2.47
application of redundancy legislation to, 10.3
'associate' as, 2.10
business consultant, 2.9

Employee—*contd*
cannot opt out of statutory rights, 9.11
capability, meaning, 8.97
commission not to be accepted, 6.62–6.63
confidential information not to be disclosed by, 6.64–6.65
conflict with employer's interests, 6.70
contract of service. *See* CONTRACT OF SERVICE
control test, 2.26–2.27
conviction of, for offence outside employment, 7.61–7.62, 8.149–8.150
Crown employees, 2.14–2.15
death of, effect, 5.92
demotion of, 7.57–7.58, 7.61
detriment, subjection to, 4.30
director may be, 2.6–2.8
disciplinary rules applicable to, 3.62
disclosure, duty of, 6.72
domestic servants, 2.58
employed whilst on books of firm, 10.8
employer's duty to engage competent fellow-employees, 6.41
ex-employees, duties of. *See* EX-EMPLOYEE
expenses incurred by, employer's duty to indemnify, 6.18–6.19
explanation of conduct by, 8.135
flexi-time, withdrawal of, 7.60
foreign, 2.59
foreigner unable to understand English, 6.31
gifts not to be accepted, 6.62–6.63
Health Service, 2.16
hours of work, not possible to aggregate, 2.24
implied obligations of, 6.53–6.72
incompetence, neglectful, 8.110–8.114
injury due to fault of, 6.45–6.47
invention by, 6.66–6.68
lateness, persistent, 7.60
meaning, 2.4, 2.22
misconduct by, 8.136, 8.142–8.143
'moonlighting' by, 6.70–6.71, 8.151
mutual respect, duty of, 8.67
not every worker is, 2.3

Employee—*contd*
office holder, 2.11–2.12
overseas employment, 2.60–2.62A
part-time—
custom and practice, 2.52
generally, 2.49
hours per week, 2.50
pay variation, 4.89
work at home, 2.51
police, 2.17–2.19
probationary, 2.53–2.55
property of, 3.13, 3.23
qualifications meaning, 8.97
refusal to obey lawful order, 6.56–6.60
refusal to transfer place of employment, 6.56
resignation—
constructive, 8.84–8.85
generally, 8.81–8.83
without notice, 8.76
retiring age, having reached, 8.18
safety of, employer's duty to ensure, 6.23–6.27
secondment of, 2.45–2.46
secret bribes not to be accepted, 6.62–6.63
self-employed person distinguished, 2.25–2.25A, 2.37–2.44
skill and care, 6.61
status, 2.20–2.21
temporary—
contract, acceptance of, 10.16
engaged in place of suspended employee, 5.8
rights, 2.48
time worked at home, additional, 2.51
trainees, 2.56–2.57
training agreements, 11.27
transfer—
disciplinary, 7.59, 8.74
from one employer to another, 8.38
reasons for, 7.59
two or more employers, with, 2.23
unlawful order, refusal to obey, 6.57
unreasonable conduct, 8.72
victimisation of, 4.17, 4.104
work—
competitor, for, 6.71

Employee—*contd*
work—*contd*
done in unlawful manner by, 6.19
worker, 2.2–2.4
Employer,
associated, 8.38
change of, continuous employment where, 8.33–8.45
compulsory insurance to cover liability for injuries, 6.35
criminal law, liability under, 6.82
danger unknown and unforeseen by, 6.25
death of, effect, 5.92
duty to ensure safety of employees, 6.23–6.27, 12.25–12.26
implied duties of, 6.7–6.27
investigations by, 7.17–7.23D
management, acts of, 2.5
meaning, 2.5
no obligation to provide work, 6.12
personal nature of duty, 6.29–6.32
protection of commercial interests of, 8.175
references, not obliged to give, 6.20
reply to industrial tribunal, 9.12
statutory sick pay. *See* EMPLOYERS' STATUTORY SICK PAY
threefold nature of duty, 6.33–6.41
unborn children, duty to, 6.28
unlawful acts, liability for, 4.61
vicarious liability of, 6.73–6.82
Employers' association,
incorporation, 14.5–14.6
listing of, 14.8A
meaning, 14.5–14.6
property and liabilities, 14.6
Employers' statutory sick pay,
amount, 5.79
conditions, 5.78
enforcement, 5.84–5.85
entitlement, 5.79
exclusions from entitlement, 5.81
industrial injuries claims, abolition of, 5.83
leaver's statement, 5.82
provisions, 5.76–5.80
Employment,
alternative, in place of redundancy, 10.21–10.24
children, of, 4.4
consensual termination of, 8.94–8.95
Employment—*contd*
continuity of, 8.20, 10.43–10.44
continuous—
computation of, 8.21–8.25
necessity for appropriate period of, 8.20
contract of. *See* CONTRACT OF EMPLOYMENT
convictions, previous, disclosure of, 4.130–4.136
'course of employment', 6.75
custom as source of terms, 3.39–3.41
effective date of termination, 9.5–9.8
equal pay. *See* EQUAL PAY
legal constraints on terms and conditions, 4.1 *et seq.*
new, trial period in, 10.32–10.34
overseas, 2.60–2.62A
project termination, 8.96
protection of—
death of employer or employee, 5.92
generally, 5.1.
guarantee payments, 5.2–5.6
industrial injuries claims, 5.83
insolvency, rights in, 5.87
leaver's statement, 5.82
self certification of illness, 5.86
statutory sick pay, 5.76–5.80
suspension on medical grounds, 5.7–5.8
time off work—
agreement of employer, with, 5.64
ante-natal care, 5.62
jury service, 5.63
new work, to look for, 5.59–5.60
public duties, 5.55–5.58
unauthorised, 5.64
wages. *See* WAGES
qualifying periods of, Appendix C
racial discrimination in, 4.110
rehabilitated persons, 4.130–4.136
retail, deductions and payments, 5.137–5.140
sex discrimination in. *See* SEX DISCRIMINATION
unlawful, 3.1B
works and staff rules, 3.42–3.46
Employment Act 1980, Appendix H
Employment Act 1982, Appendix H

Employment Act 1988,
Appendix H
Employment Act 1989, Appendix H
Employment Act 1990, Appendix H
Employment appeal tribunal,
appeal to, 1.18, 9.63–9.70
appearance before, 1.18
jurisdiction, 1.18–1.19B
membership, 1.18
sittings, 1.18
superior court of record, as, 1.18
Employment protection,
Armed Forces reserves, 5.65–5.70
Enforcement of statutory rights,
Appendix C
Equal Opportunities Commission,
codes of practice, 1.44, Appendix I
establishment, 1.44
functions, 1.44
guidance of employment advertising practice, 4.57
membership, 1.44
Equal pay,
burden of proof, 4.70A
different duties, 4.74
different hours, 4.75–4.76
different responsibilities, 4.77
discrimination to be eliminated from pay structures, 4.94
equality clause deemed included in contract, 4.71
European Court of Justice, 4.69, 4.69A
'in the same employment', 4.70B
like work, considerations determining, 4.72–4.77
purpose and effect of 1970 Act, 4.68
remedies under 1970 Act, 4.95–4.97A
work—
equal value, 4.80–4.83A
genuine material factor, 4.84–4.93
rated as being equivalent, 4.78–4.79
Equipment,
defective, liability for, 6.35, 6.36
European Charter for Fundamental Social Rights,
1.70–1.74
European Community,
Articles of Treaty of Rome, 1.52
European Community—*contd*
Directives, 1.53–1.64
Acquired Rights, 1.59
Collective Redundancies, 1.58
Employers' Insolvency, 1.63
Equal Pay, 1.56
Equal Treatment, 1.57
Equal Treatment for Self-employed, 1.62
Equal Treatment in Occupational Pension Schemes, 1.61
Equal Treatment in Social Security Matters, 1.60
impact of, 1.50
law, 1.51
recommendations, 1.65, 1.66
European Court of Human Rights,
access to, 1.69
European Court of Justice, 1.67, 1.68
equal pay, and, 4.69, 4.69A
jurisdiction, 1.67
European law,
health and safety, and, 12.62
Evidence,
industrial tribunals, before, 9.21–9.25
reasons for dismissal, as to, 9.21
theft, of, 9.24
Ex-employee,
Anton Piller orders, 11.26
duties of—
competitors, working for, 11.18–11.20
covenants in restraint of trade, 11.9–11.20
customers and connections, as to, 11.14–11.17
extent of restraint, 11.21–11.25
fidelity, 11.2
garden leave clauses, 11.8B–11.8E
generally, 11.1–11.4
information, not to disclose, 11.5–11.8A
obligations, 11.1
trade secrets, not to disclose, 11.12–11.13
training agreements, 11.27
Express terms,
agreement of, 3.8, 3.9–3.16

Fair dismissal,
commercial reasons, 8.174–8.177
conduct of employee—
inside employment, 8.133–8.148
'moonlighting', 8.151
obstruction, 8.144
outside employment, 8.149–8.153
refusal to work overtime, 8.144
employment barred by statute, 8.172–8.173
employment terms, refusal to accept change, 8.177
evidence as to whether, 9.24–9.25
husband of employee starting rival business, 8.174
inherent inability, 8.106–8.109
long-term sickness, 8.115–8.123
manager moving away from district, 8.174
neglectful incompetence, 8.110–8.114
qualifications, lack of, 8.130–8.132
reasons whereby dismissal may be, 8.97–8.105
redundancy. *See* REDUNDANCY
refusal to change working hours, 8.176
restrictive covenant, refusal to sign, 8.176
substantial reasons, 8.174–8.184
variation in contract, refusal to accept, 8.176
Fines,
negligent work, for, 7.38–7.40
Fishermen,
master and crew of fishing vessel excluded from unfair dismissal provisions, 8.18
share fishermen, redundancy legislation not applicable to, 10.41
Frustration,
contract of employment, of, 8.87–8.93
imprisonment, effect of, 8.87
sickness, by, 8.89

Gifts,
employee not to accept, 6.62–6.63
tips are not, 6.62
what may constitute, 6.63
Global contract,
existence of, 2.66
Go-slow,
breach of contract, as, 8.9
Guarantee payments,
collective agreement relating to, 5.6
guaranteed week agreement, 5.4
payment of, by employer, 5.2–5.6
provision for, when coming into effect, 5.2
strike, effect of, 5.3

Harassment,
sexual, 4.37–4.40
Health,
absolute and other duties, 12.24
codes of practice to be issued, 12.23, 12.54–12.56
consultation with employee as to, 8.116
controllers of premises, duties of, 12.36
Crown Notices, 12.17
duties, statutory, guiding rules as to, 12.23–12.26
employees at work, duties of, 12.47
employer, duties of, owed to employees, 12.25–12.26
enforcement—
powers of court, 12.19–12.20
statutory provisions, of, 12.6
European law, and, 12.62
former law, progressive repeal of, 12.1
generally, 12.1–12.5
Health and Safety Commission. *See* HEALTH AND SAFETY COMMISSION
ill-health. *See* ILL-HEALTH
improvement notice—
appeal against, 12.10–12.16
form, appendix E
service of, 12.7
inspectors—
appointment of, 12.6
powers of, 12.6, 12.21–12.22
interference with provisions relating to, 12.48
manufacturers, duty of, 12.38–12.46
non-employees, duty to, 12.35
penalties for statutory offences, 12.57–12.61, Appendix A
pollution control, 12.37

Health—*contd*
prohibition notice—
appeal against, 12.10–12.16
contents, 12.9
form, appendix E
service, 12.8
regulations—
generally, 12.50–12.53
new, to supersede old, 12.23
written policy, preparation and revision of, 12.27–12.27A
Health and Safety Commission,
arrangements to be made by, 1.46
duty of, 1.46
enquiries, 1.49
establishment of, 1.46
membership, 1.46
reports to Secretary of State, 1.47, 1.48
Health and Safety Executive,
enforcement of statutory provisions, 1.48, 12.6
enquiries, 1.49
membership, 1.48
powers, 1.48
Heath service. *See* NATIONAL HEALTH SERVICE
Holidays, 3.71–3.73
express term of contract, as, 3.9
Jewish, 5.2
Hours of work,
adult workers, 4.152
young persons, 4.151
House of Commons,
staff of, employment protection, 2.14

Ill-health,
dismissal because of, 8.115–8.129
effect on performance of contract of employment, 8.124–8.129
long-term sickness, 8.115–8.123
self certification, 5.86
short-term sickness, 8.124–8.129
statutory sick pay, 5.76–5.82
Implied resignation, 8.86
Implied terms,
agreement, of, 3.8, 3.17–3.24
basis for theory of, 3.22
collective agreement, incorporation in, 3.30–3.32A
vague or unpredictable terms, 3.18
Imprisonment,
sentence to, frustrating contract of employment, 8.87
Improvement notice,
appeal against, 12.10–12.16
form, appendix E
service of, 12.7
Independent contractor,
consultant surgeon as, 2.42
employer not vicariously liable for acts of, 2.42
'lump' contractors, 2.39–2.41
safety duties of employer not applicable to, 2.43
Industrial action. *See also* PICKETING: SECONDARY ACTION: STRIKE
affecting an individual, 15.93–15.94
ballot before. *See* BALLOT
dismissal in connection with, 13.63–13.77
notice to employers, 15.68
right to ballot before, 13.23–13.26
See also BALLOT
unofficial strikes, in support of, 15.70
Industrial injuries,
claims, 5.83
Industrial training boards,
constitution and functions, 1.40
levy on employers, 1.41
setting up of, 1.40
Industrial tribunal,
additional award, 9.51–9.52
appeal—
from decision of, 9.63–9.70
to Court of Appeal, 9.70
award—
interest on, 9.56A
Central Office, 1.20
claims to be heard before, 1.24
compensation awards, 9.36–9.40
compensatory awards, 9.41–9.50
complaint—
copies of, 9.9A
deductions, relating to, 5.141–5.143
must be in writing, 9.9
payments, relating to, 5.141–5.143
period within which to be laid, 9.1
settlement without hearing, 9.10

Industrial tribunal—*contd*
complaint—*contd*
submitting, 9.9–9.11
composition, 1.21
conciliation officer—
confidential nature of work, 9.10
duties of, 9.9A
constitutional basis, 1.20
costs, 1.23, 9.62
decision of, 9.26–9.28, 9.30
discovery of documents, 1.25
disparity of treatment, evaluation of reasons for, 7.29–7.29A
employer's reply, 9.12
employment, effective date of termination, 9.5–9.8
evidence and standard of proof, 9.21–9.25
extension of period for laying complaint, 9.1
failure to appear before, 9.29
forms, appendix D
hearing before, 9.15–9.30
High Court proceedings, effect of, 1.26
interest on award, 1.26A, 1.26B
jurisdiction, 1.21, 1.24, 1.24A
lay members, choice of, 1.21
misbehaviour at hearing, 9.29A
practice and procedure, 9.1 *et seq.*
pre-hearing assessment, 9.13
pre-hearing review, 9.14–9.14B
procedure, 1.22, 1.23, 9.15–9.30
reasons—
full, 9.32
summary, 9.31
regional offices, 1.20
reinstatement and re-engagement orders, 9.33–9.35B
remedies, 9.33–9.58
representation before, 1.23
review of decision by, 9.59–9.61
decision, where, 9.60A
special award, 9.53–9.56
time limit for claims before, 9.1–9.2
unemployment benefit, recoupment of, 9.57–9.58
witness, compelling attendance of, 1.25

Information,
disclosure of, 15.2–15.6
ex-employee's duty not to disclose, 11.5–11.8A
Information—*contd*
occupational pension scheme, 3.75–3.77

Injunction,
ex parte, in course of trade dispute, 15.88
strike, and, 15.90–15.91

Insolvency,
National Insurance Fund, payments from, 5.88–5.91
priority of debts, 5.87
rights in, 5.87

Instant dismissal. *See* DISMISSAL

Intimidation,
liability of trade union for, 15.34

Invention,
employee, by, 6.66–6.68

Investigation,
employer, by, in disciplinary matters, 7.17–7.23
precautionary suspension during, 7.23A–7.23D

Job description,
document detailing duties, 3.50

Judges,
position of, 2.11

Jury service,
time off for, 5.63

Lay-off,
meaning, 10.35
redundancy claim following, 10.35–10.38
whether remuneration payable during, 6.15

Listing,
trade unions, of, 14.7–14.8A

Local authorities,
race relations, duties relating to, 4.153–4.154, 4.155–4.158

Local government,
successive employment, 8.42

Lump,
position of workers claiming to be self-employed, 2.39–2.41

Management,
disciplinary powers—
appeal hearing, 7.15A
code of practice, 7.2, 7.23B
convicted employees, 7.61–7.62
deductions for negligent work, 7.38–7.40

Management—*contd*
disciplinary powers—*contd*
disparity of treatment, 7.29A
generally, 7.1–7.2
misconduct, suspension without pay for, 7.41–7.45
procedure—
absence of, 7.4
conduct must be fair, 7.14
contract of employment, incorporated into, 7.7
demotion, 7.57–7.58
disciplinary bodies, composition of, 7.11
drawing up of, 7.3
fair, 7.5
incorporation into contract, 3.47, 3.48
informant, 7.19A
investigations by employer, 7.17–7.23
misconduct, 7.3A
operation should be flexible, 7.12
precautionary suspension, 7.23B
reprimand, 7.56
shop steward, action against, 7.13
standards, 7.16A
trade union involvement, 7.3
transfer, 7.59
unfair, 7.4
warnings, 7.48–7.55
witnesses, 7.21A
disciplinary rules—
clear and understandable, must be, 7.25
clocking offences, 7.27
disparity of treatment, 7.29–7.29A
employee must have notice of, 7.1
failure to enforce, 7.30
general rules, 7.31, 7.32
generally, 7.24
inconsistencies in, 7.26
interpretation of, 7.36
must be brought to employee's attention, 7.24
notice board, posting on, 7.24
reasonableness, 7.28
special rules, 7.35–7.36
specific rules, 7.31, 7.33–7.34

March,
new rules, 15.123
Mass redundancies,
notification of, 10.63–10.65
Maternity,
ante-natal care, time off work for, 5.62
childbirth, dismissal on ground of, 5.30–5.34
deemed dismissal following, 8.79
leave, 5.13–5.29
pregnancy—
dismissal on ground of, 5.30–5.34
unfair dismissal for, 4.35
right to return to work, 5.19–5.29
statutory maternity pay—
amount, 5.45
disqualification, 5.42
introduction, 5.35
maternity allowance, application for, 5.44
period of, 5.41
qualifications for, 5.36–5.40
refusal to pay, 5.43
suspension from work, 5.9–5.10
suspension pay, 5.11–5.12
Medical grounds,
suspension from work on, 5.7–5.8
Medical reports,
access to, 5.71–5.75
Ministers of religion,
contracts of employment, 2.13
Minor,
contracts of employment entered into by, 4.2–4.3, 4.4, 4.4A
employment of children, 4.4, 4.4A
meaning, 4.2
part-time work by, 4.4, 4.4A
Misconduct,
fines for, 7.38–7.40
generally, 8.136, 8.142
minor breaches, 8.143
suspension without pay, 7.41–7.45
Moonlighting,
employee, by, 6.70–6.71, 8.151

Names and addresses,
Appendix F
National Health Service,
employment protection rights, 2.16
National Insurance Fund,
payments from—
insolvency, and, 5.88–5.91

National security,
certificate relating to employment, 2.64–2.65, 8.206
Negligence,
deductions from wages for negligent work, 7.38–7.40
defences to common law action—
contributory negligence, 6.48
denial of negligence, 6.43–6.44
generally, 6.42
injury sole fault of employee, 6.45–6.47
volenti non fit injuria, 6.46
limitation of actions, 6.49
summary dismissal for, 8.8
Notice,
dismissal—
counter-notice following, 10.9
subject to, 8.11–8.14
employee leaving before expiration of, 8.14
minimum period of, where given by employee, 8.13
period of, dismissal during, 10.39–10.40
Nuisance,
limitations of actions, 6.49

Occupational pension schemes,
disclosure of information, 3.75–3.77
Office holders,
earnings, 2.12
excluded from term 'workers', 2.3
privileges of, 2.11
Off-shore employment,
meaning, 2.62B
Off-shore installations,
workers on, 8.18
Overseas employment,
terms of, 2.60–2.62B
Overtime,
express term of contract, as, 3.9
negotiation of, 6.59
reduction of, 10.16
requirements must be reasonable, 3.21

Part-time employee,
exclusion from redundancy provisions, 10.41
position of, 2.49–2.52C
Partner,
junior, 2.10
Partner—*contd*
not employee for redundancy purposes, 10.4
position of, 2.10
salaried, 2.10
self-employed person, as, 2.10
Patent,
taken out by employee, 6.66–6.68
Pensions. *See* OCCUPATIONAL PENSION SCHEMES
Picketing,
code of practice, Appendix I
flying pickets, illegality of, 15.106
meaning, 15.100
no tort committed, where, 15.108
obstruction by, 15.104
peaceful, 15.100–15.108
vehicles, pickets have no power to stop, 15.105
Police,
dismissal, 2.17, 2.19
excluded from term 'worker', 2.3
rights of, 2.17–2.19, 15.117
Pollution,
control of, 12.37
Post,
notice of dismissal sent by, 8.18
Pregnancy. *See* MATERNITY
Probationary employees,
position of, 2.53–2.55
Procession,
new rules, 15.123
Prohibition notice. *See* HEALTH: SAFETY
Property,
employee, liability for, 3.13, 3.23
Protection,
employment, of. *See* EMPLOYMENT
Public assembly,
new rules, 15.123

Racial discrimination,
application of Act, 4.113
code of practice, Appendix I
Commission for Racial Equality, 4.118, 4.125, 4.125A
contract compliance, 4.155–4.158
contract workers, 4.112
direct discrimination, 4.100–4.102
discriminatory—
advertisements, 4.115
practices, 4.114
ethnic group, 4.106
generally, 4.110

Racial discrimination—*contd*
genuine occupational qualifications, 4.111
gypsies, 4.108
indirect discrimination, 4.103–4.103B
individuals, enforcement by, 4.122–4.124A
instructions to discriminate, 4.116
language requirements, 4.109
legislation, 4.98
local authorities, duty of, 4.153–4.154, 4.155–4.158
methods of discrimination—
direct, 4.100–4.102
indirect, 4.103–4.103B
victimisation, 4.104
nationality, 4.105
overseas employment, 2.62
police, 2.18
pressure to discriminate, 4.117–4.121
proof, burden of, 4.123
racial grounds, 4.105–4.109
religion not covered by legislation, 4.107
statutory immunity, 4.124B
vicarious liability of employer, 4.120
victimisation, 4.104
Welshmen, 4.109
Records,
trade union, of, 14.42
Redundancy,
amount of payment, determination of, 10.46
basic purpose of legislation, 10.1
'bumping', 10.20
cessation of business, 10.12
claims of payment, 10.42–10.46
company directors, 2.6
consideration of alternatives, 8.157–8.158
consultation, lack of, 8.159–8.161
continuity of employment, 10.43–10.44
dismissal, 8.154–8.171, 10.5–10.18
employees, application to, 10.3–10.4
excluded classes of employees, 10.41
fair dismissal due to, 8.158
generally, 10.1–10.2
illegal contract, effect of, 3.1B
Redundancy—*contd*
lay-off, 10.35–10.38
local government, 8.42
lump sum payment not redundancy payment, 10.46
mass redundancies, notification of, 10.63–10.65
maximum amount payable, 10.46
notice and counter-notice, 10.9
one-man business, director of, 2.6
oversea employment, 2.60–2.62A
pay, calculation of, 10.46, appendix B
persons not entitled to, 10.41
place of business moved, 10.13–10.14
points systems, 8.164
presumption of, 10.19
reorganisation of workforce, effect, 10.16
selection procedures, 8.162–8.171
sex discrimination, 4.31
short-time working, 10.35–10.36
suitable alternative employment, offer of, 10.21–10.24
surplus labour, 10.15–10.18
taxi-driver held self-employed, 2.22
time limit for claim, 9.1–9.2
trade union consultation. *See* TRADE UNION
trade union membership or non-membership, 8.168
transfer of undertakings, 10.28–10.31
transferred, 10.20
trial period in new employment, 10.32–10.34
unfair, 8.167
volunteers for, 10.6
Redundancy pay,
calculation table, Appendix B
Re-engagement,
discretion of tribunal, 9.34
order for, 9.33–9.35
orders unlikely to be made, 9.35
small businesses, 9.35
References,
defamatory or incorrect, 6.20
dismissal cases, 6.22
employer under no legal duty to provide, 6.20
unsatisfactory, 6.21
Rehabilitated persons,
generally, 4.130–4.136

Rehabilitated persons—*contd*
provision of jobs for, 4.130–4.136
rehabilitation periods, 4.134
Reinstatement,
order for, 9.33–9.35B
Remedies,
common law, 2.67
judicial review, 2.68–2.70
public law, 2.68–2.70
trade union, 14.39, 14.50–14.51
Remuneration,
payment where no work provided, 6.13–6.16
Reprimand,
employer, given by, 7.56
Resignation,
constructive, 8.84–8.85
employee, by, not dismissal unless constructive, 8.48
generally, 8.81–8.83
implied, 8.86
invited by employer, 8.50
without notice, effect, 8.76
Restraint of trade,
covenants in, 11.9–11.20
dismissal for refusal to sign covenant, 11.9
extent of—
legitimate interests only to be protected, 11.21
must not be too restrictive, 11.23–11.25
time and area, 11.22
interests entitling employer to protection—
competitors, working for,11.18–11.20
existing customers and connections, 11.14–11.17
trade secrets, 11.12–11.13
limitations on right to impose, 11.10
trade unions and doctrine of, 14.21
Retail employment,
deductions and payments, 5.137–5.140
Retainers,
contractual obligation, 2.63
Retiring age,
contract, not specified in, 8.18
contractual provision as to, 4.44
effect of reaching, 9.41
Retiring age—*contd*
employee having reached, excluded from unfair dismissal provisions, 8.18
redundancy legislation not applicable to persons of, 10.41
Review,
industrial tribunal decision, of, 9.59–9.61
Riot,
abolition of common law offence, 15.122
Rout,
abolition of common law offence, 15.122
Royal Commission on Civil Liability and Compensation for Personal Injuries,
appointment of, 6.50–6.52
Rules,
trade union, of, 14.21–14.21A
works. *See* WORKS RULES

Safety,
absolute and other duties, 12.24
belts, failure to use, 6.39
charge not to be made for safety equipment, 12.49
codes of practice to be issued, 12.23, 12.54–12.56
committee, 12.28–12.34
common law rules and statutory duties, 6.23
controllers of premises, duties of, 12.36
Crown Notices, 12.17
danger not known as foreseeable by employer, 6.25
defective equipment, 6.35, 6.36
duties, statutory, guiding rules as to, 12.23–12.26
duty of care owed to employees as individuals, 6.30
employees at work, duties of, 6.24, 12.47
employer, duties of, owed to employees, 6.23–6.27, 12.25–12.26
enforcement of statutory provisions—
generally, 12.6
powers of court, 12.19–12.20
failure to use safety precautions, 6.39–6.40

Safety—*contd*
foreigners unable to understand English, 6.31
former law, progressive repeal of, 12.1
Health and Safety Commission. *See* HEALTH AND SAFETY COMMISSION
Health and Safety Executive, 12.6
improvement notice—
appeal against, 12.10–12.16
form, Appendix E
service, 12.7
inexperienced employees, 6.30
insidious risks, 6.40
inspectors—
appointment of, 12.6
powers of, 12.6, 12.21–12.22
manufacturers, duty of, 12.38–12.46
new legislation, generally, 12.1 *et seq*.
non-employees, duty to, 12.35
obvious risks, 6.40
penalties for statutory offences, 12.57–12.61, Appendix A
personal nature of employer's duty, 6.29–6.32
pollution control, 12.37
prohibition notice—
appeal against, 12.10–12.16
contents, 12.9
form, Appendix E
service, 12.8
propositions illustrating needs for taking precautions, 6.40
protective clothing and safety equipment, provision of, 6.37, 6.38
provisions, duty not to interfere with, 12.48
regulations—
generally, 12.50–12.53
new, to supersede old, 12.23
relationship between employer and workman, 6.24
representatives—
responsibilities, 12.28–12.34E
safe plant and appliances, necessity for, 6.34–6.36
safe system of work, necessity for, 6.37–6.40
standard of care of employer, 6.24

Safety—*contd*
summary of steps to be taken by employer, 6.26
threefold nature of duty of care—
reasonably competent fellow-employees, 6.41
safe plant and appliances, 6.34–6.36
safe system of work 6.37–6.40
tools, defective, 6.35, 6.36
unborn child, duty to, 6.28
unfair contract terms, legislation relating to, 6.47
written policy, preparation and revision of, 12.27–12.27A

Salary,
equal pay, 4.68–4.71
equal value, 4.80–4.83A
express term of contract, as, 3.9
itemised pay statements, 3.69–3.70
like work, 4.72–4.77
pay structures, 4.94
payment where no work provided, 6.13–6.16
remedies under Act, 4.95–4.97A
work rated as being equivalent, 4.78–4.79

Search,
employees, of, works rules permitting, 3.46

Secondary action, 15.71–15.75
definition, 15.72
peaceful picketing, 15.75

Secondment,
employees, of, 2.45–2.46

Self certification,
illness, of, 5.86

Self-employed person,
attachment of earnings order not applicable to, 2.44
benefits not applicable to, 2.44
employee distinguished, 2.25–2.25A, 2.37–2.44
income tax payments by, 2.38
lecturer not treated as, 2.32, 2.34
lorry drivers, 2.29
'lump' contracting, 2.39–2.41
no claim for unfair dismissal, 2.33
partner as, 2.10
social security contributions, 2.38
tests to determine whether, 2.30–2.32
works under contract for services, 2.25

Servants,
redundancy provisions, 10.41
Service contract,
company and director, between, 2.6
Sex discrimination,
advertising, effects of, 4.19–4.20, 4.57–4.58
amendment of Act, 4.41–4.42
application forms, use of, 4.22
Barber decision, 4.45, 4.46
effect of, 4.47–4.53A
comparing 'like with like' 4.35–4.35D
different rates of pay, man and woman receiving, 4.90
dismissal on grounds of sex, 4.28–4.36
effect of 1975 Act, 4.8
employment, in, 4.18–4.36
employment outside Great Britain, 4.56A
enforcement of 1975 Act, 4.62–4.67
exceptions to 1975 Act, 4.43–4.46
interviews, questions asked at, 4.21
job opportunities must be available to all, 4.19
marital status, grounds of, 4.33–4.34
married person, 4.10A
objective test, 4.9
overseas employment, 2.62
permissible discrimination—
decency or privacy, preservation of, 4.55
employment abroad where customs differ, 4.55
essential nature of job, 4.55
generally, 4.54
health grounds, 4.53B
husband and wife, employment of, 4.55
legal discrimination, 4.55
non-separate sleeping accommodation, 4.55
personal services, provision of, 4.55
special care establishments, 4.55
police, 2.18
promotion opportunities, 4.27
reasonable needs of employer, 4.13A
redundancy situations, 4.31
Sex discrimination—*contd*
refusal or omission to offer employment, 4.25–4.26
sexual harassment, 4.37–4.40
short-time work, women only put on, 4.36
single persons, discrimination against, 4.8
terms, variation in, 4.23–4.24
unlawful acts—
direct discrimination, 4.10–4.11
employer, liability of, 4.61
generally, 4.59–4.60
indirect discrimination, 4.12–4.16
victimisation, 4.17
Sex Discrimination Act 1986, Appendix H
Shift,
refusal to work, 8.66
Shop steward,
disciplinary action against, 7.13
trade union liability for actions of, 15.31
Short-time working,
meaning, 10.35
redundancy claim following, 10.35–10.36
remuneration payable, 6.15
Sick pay,
leaver's statement, 5.82
statutory, 5.76–5.84
Sickness,
dismissal because of, 8.115–8.129
long-term, 8.115–8.123
payment of wages or salary during, 3.17
statutory sick pay, 5.76–5.84
Sit-in,
trade union immunity, 15.110
workers engaging in, 15.109
Staff,
effect of being employed as, 3.9
rules of employment, 3.42–3.46
Status,
employee, of, 2.20–2.21
Statutory rights,
enforcement, Appendix C
Strike,
ballot before. *See* BALLOT
breach of contract, as, 6.53, 8.9
continuity of employment not broken by, 8.32
criminal liabilities, 15.117–15.121

Strike—*contd*
injunctive relief, 15.90–15.92
legitimate, no conspiracy, 15.33
political reasons, called for, 15.43
unofficial—
industrial action in support of, 15.70
Suitable alternative employment,
redundancy, in place of, 10.21–10.24
Summary dismissal. *See* DISMISSAL
Suspension,
medical grounds, on, 5.7–5.8
misconduct, for, without pay, 7.41–7.45
precautionary, 7.23A–7.23D
right of, must be based on contractual power, 7.43
temporary termination of employment as result of, 7.44
wrongful—
employee's rights in case of, 7.44
resignation as result of, 7.45

Teacher,
part-time, additional hours worked at home, 2.51
unfair dismissal, 2.51, 3.10
Temporary workers,
agency workers, 2.47
position of, 2.48
Theft,
evidence of, 9.24
investigation into, 7.17
Time off,
agreement of employer, with 5.64
ante-natal care, for, 5.62
jury service, 5.63
public duties, for, 5.55–5.58
unauthorised, 5.64
work, to look for, 5.59
Tips,
not bribes or gifts but recognised method of payment, 6.62
Tools,
defective, 6.35, 6.36
Tort,
trade union, by, 15.35–15.36, 15.84–15.87
Trade dispute,
actions not in furtherance of, 15.47
circumstances in which existing, 15.40
conciliation, 1.5
Trade dispute—*contd*
'in contemplation of', 15.45
'in furtherance of', 15.46–15.48
injunction in course of, 15.88
meaning, 1.6, 15.38–15.44
teachers' workload, 15.41
Trade secrets,
protection of, 11.12–11.13
Trade union,
access to employment, and, 13.29–13.38
accounts, 14.42–14.47
annual statement, 14.43
power of Certification Officer, and, 14.47
Act of 1992, 14.1
action short of dismissal, 13.39–13.48
amalgamation, 14.62–14.63
amount of damages, 15.84–15.87
annual return, 14.42
ballots. *See also* BALLOTS
financial assistance for, 14.41
certification, 14.9–14.15A
check-off arrangements, 13.56–13.59
collective agreement, legal effect of, 15.95–15.99
collective bargaining by, 15.2–15.5
complaints by, 15.4
complaints of unjustified discipline, 13.12–13.17
conduct of union affairs, 14.23–14.23B
confederated organisation, 14.2
conspiracy, 15.32–15.33
consultations on redundancies, 15.6–15.24
consultation provisions, 15.9–15.16
definition of redundancy, 15.24
'establishment', 15.8
protective award, 15.17–15.23
recognised union, 15.7
contract, breach of, including or procuring, 15.30–15.31
criminal liabilities, 15.117–15.121
deductions for political fund, 13.60
derecognition, 13.44
disciplinary action by, 14.22–14.22F
disciplinary procedures, involvement in, 7.3

Trade union—*contd*
disclosure of information to, by employers, 15.2–15.5, Appendix I
dismissal due to industrial pressure, 13.78–13.79
dismissal in connection with industrial action, 13.63–13.77
exceptions in health and safety and maternity cases, 13.77
dismissal of unofficial strikes, 13.74–13.76
dismissal on ground of membership or activities, 13.61–13.62
dismissals in connection with lock-out, 13.63
dismissals in connection with official strike, 13.64, 13.65–13.73
dismissed trade unionists or non-unionists,
interim relief for, 13.82–13.88
election—
addresses, 14.30–14.31
candidates, 14.29
financial assistance for, 14.41
independent scrutineer, 14.32–14.38
remedies, 14.39
employment agencies, and, 13.34
executive committee, 14.24–14.28
immunity of, 15.54, 15.78–15.83
indemnifying unlawful conduct, 14.48–14.49
independent scrutineer, 14.32–14.38
individual rights, 13.1–13.88
injunctions against, 15.88–15.89
intimidation, liability for, 15.34
job advertisements, and, 13.32
legal—
advice provided by, 14.23
liabilities and proceedings, restrictions on, 15.29–15.36
position of, 14.3
protection, 15.37–15.48
listing of, 14.7–14.8
loss of immunities, 15.54
meaning, 14.2–14.4
membership, 14.20–14.20A
persons—
eligible to join, 14.20
not eligible for membership, 14.20

Trade union—*contd*
picketing, 15.100–15.107
political fund and political objects, 14.52–14.58
breaches of rules, 14.61
powers of, 14.3
pressure to impose recognition requirements, 15.76
professional organisations, 14.3
prohibition on union recognition requirements, 15.114–15.115
property of, 14.3
protected for legitimate objectives only, 15.37
provisions of TULR(C)A, s 219, 15.49–15.53
Public Order Act 1986, 15.122–15.123
quasi-legal personality, 14.4
recognition of, 15.114–15.115
records, 14.42
redundancy—
non-membership, for, 8.167
register of members, 14.17–14.17A
confidentiality, 14.18
remedies, 13.37, 13.38, 14.19, 14.50–14.51
remedies for wrongful exclusion or expulsion, 13.20
restraint of trade, doctrine of, 14.21
right not to be excluded from, 13.2–13.7
right not to be expelled from, 13.19
right not to be unjustifiably disciplined, 13.8–13.11
right of access to courts, 13.21–13.22
right to ballot before industrial action, 13.23–13.26
right to resign from, 13.18
rights vis-à-vis, 13.2 *et seq.*
rights vis-à-vis employer, 13.28–13.88
rules, 14.21–14.22F
copy of, 14.23C
disciplinary action, 14.22–14.22F
secret ballots before industrial action, 15.55–15.65
selection for dismissal on grounds of redundancy, 13.80
shop steward, liability for actions of, 15.31
sit-in, 15.109–15.110

Trade union—*contd*
statutory provisions, generally, 14.1
time off for activities, 13.54, 13.55
time off work for duties, 13.49–13.53
tort—
action against, 15.84–15.87
general liability in, 15.35–15.36
trade disputes, acts done in furtherance or contemplation of, 15.31–15.48
transfer of undertaking, consultation on, 15.25–15.28
transfers, 14.62–14.63
trustees, remedies against, 14.50–14.51
unfair practices, 13.33
unfair recruitment, and, exceptions, 13.35–13.36
union or non-union—
members only contracts, 15.111–15.113
unreasonable restriction of membership of, 14.20
see also COMMISSIONER FOR RIGHTS OF TRADE UNION MEMBERS
Trade Union Act 1984, Appendix H
Trade Union and Labour Relations (Consolidation) Act 1992, Appendix H
Trade Union Congress,
example of confederated organisation, as, 14.2
Trade Union Reform and Employment Rights Act 1993, Appendix H
Trainees,
position of, 2.56–2.57
Training agreements,
duty of employee, 11.27
Transfer,
employee, of, 7.59
Transfer of undertakings, 5.100–5.126
application of Regulations, 5.106–5.108
common law, 5.100
consultation on, 15.25–15.28
effect of transfer, 5.112–5.118
obligations transferred, 5.119–5.122
origin of Regulations, 5.104–5.105
Transfer of undertakings—*contd*
preservation of continuity, and, 8.44
redundancy, in case of, 10.28–10.31
transfer, meaning, 5.109–5.110
Tribunal. *See* EMPLOYMENT APPEAL TRIBUNAL; INDUSTRIAL TRIBUNAL
Trustees,
trade union, remedies against, 14.50–14.51

Unemployment benefit,
recoupment of, 9.57–9.58
Unfair dismissal,
case law, study of, 8.16
complaint to industrial tribunal as remedy for, 8.17
consultation, lack of, 8.116
continuous employment, computation of, 8.21–8.25
diplomatic immunity waiver, 8.18
employees in similar positions not dismissed, 8.167
evidence as to whether, 9.24–9.26
excluded employees, 8.18–8.19
fixed term contract, exclusion from provision, 8.18
incompetence not proved, 8.98, 8.106–8.114
law relating to, basic structure of, 8.15
maternity, 8.79
postponement of claim for, 1.26
pregnancy, 4.35
redundancy for non-membership of trade union, 8.167
re-engagement, offer of, 9.44
reference given to dismissed employee, effect, 6.22
remedies for—
additional award, 9.51–9.52
appeal from decision of tribunal, 9.63–9.70
compensation awards, 9.36–9.40
compensatory award, 9.41–9.50
generally, 9.1 *et seq.*
reinstatement and re-engagement orders, 9.33–9.35B
review of tribunal decision, 9.59–9.61
special award, 9.53–9.56

Unfair dismissal—*contd*
retiring age, effect of reaching, 9.41
statutory right against, creation of, 8.2
unfair selection for redundancy, 8.168
warning—
necessity for, 8.108
not given, 7.55
Unlawful assembly,
abolition of common law offence, 15.122

Vandalism,
dismissal for, 7.17
Variation,
contract of employment, of, 3.51–3.59, 10.5
Vicarious liability,
employer, of, 6.73–6.82
Victimisation,
employees, of, 4.17, 4.104
Volenti non fit injuria,
defence of, 6.46

Wages,
cashless pay, 5.127–5.128
deductions—
exceptions, 5.136
general restrictions, 5.129–5.130
retail employment, 5.137–5.140
equal pay. *See* EQUAL PAY
express term of contract, as, 3.9
industrial tribunal, complaints to, 5.141–5.143
itemised pay statements, 3.69–3.70
meaning, 5.131–5.135
non-payment, 5.133
payment where no work provided, 6.13–6.16
Wages Act 1986, Appendix H
Warning,
employer's power to issue, 7.48
failure to follow rules regarding, 7.54
formal, 7.53
general considerations, 7.49–7.51
how given, 7.11, 7.53
lapse of, 7.52
necessity for, before dismissal, 8.108, 8.124, 8.133
need to issue, before dismissal, 7.53
Warning—*contd*
part of good industrial relations practice, as, 7.55
qualified and educated employees, position of, 7.55
Welfare,
absolute and other duties, 12.24
codes of practice to be issued, 12.23, 12.54–12.56
employer, duties of, owed to employees, 12.25–12.26
former law, progressive repeal of, 12.1
interference with provisions relating to, 12.48
new legislation, 12.1–12.2
regulations—
generally, 12.50–12.53
new, to supersede old, 12.23
Women,
employment of, 4.148, 4.149, 4.150
maternity. *See* MATERNITY
Work,
duty to pay wages or remuneration where none provided, 6.13–6.17
employer not obliged to provide, 6.12
failure to provide, leading to loss of reputation, 6.12
safe system of, necessity for, 6.37–6.40
short-time working, payment in respect of, 6.15
skilled, whether duty to provide, 6.12
Work-to-rule,
breach of contract, as, 8.9
Worker,
every employee is, 2.3
meaning, 2.2, 2.3
Works rules,
breach of, dismissal for, 8.6
contents, 3.43
contract making express reference to, 3.45
generally, 3.42–3.46
non-negotiable instructions, as, 3.43
penalties for breach of, 3.43
suspension, stipulation of grounds for, 7.41
whether part of contractual terms, 3.42

Writer,
whether 'worker', 2.3
Wrongful dismissal,
action for, 8.17
Wrongful dismissal—*contd*
damages for, 7.9

Young persons,
hours of work, 4.151